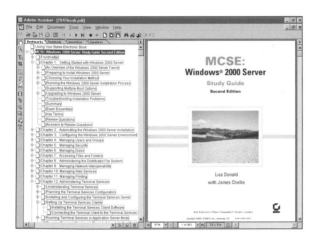

Search through the complete book in PDF.

✔ Access the entire *MCSE: Windows 2000 Server Study Guide*, complete with figures and tables, in electronic format.

✔ Search the *MCSE: Windows 2000 Server Study Guide* chapters to find information on any topic in seconds.

✔ Look up any networking term in the *Dictionary of Networking*.

Use the Electronic Flashcards for PCs or Palm devices to jog your memory and prep last-minute for the exam!

✔ Reinforce your understanding of key concepts with these hardcore flashcard-style questions.

✔ Download the Flashcards to your Palm device, and go on the road. Now you can study anywhere, any time.

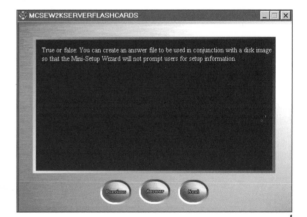

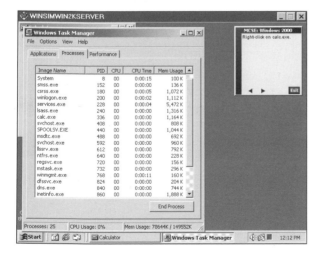

Prepare for Microsoft's tough simulation questions with the WinSim Windows 2000 Server program!

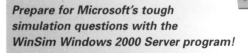

✔ Use the simulators to guide you through real-world tasks step-by-step, or watch the movies to see the "invisible hand" perform the tasks for you.

SYBEX

MCSE: Windows 2000 Server Study Guide

Exam 70-215

SYBEX

SYBEX

MCSE:
Windows 2000 Server

Study Guide

Second Edition

MCSE:
Windows® 2000 Server
Study Guide
Second Edition

Lisa Donald

with James Chellis

San Francisco • Paris • Düsseldorf • Soest • London

SYBEX®

Associate Publisher: Neil Edde
Contracts and Licensing Manager: Kristine O'Callaghan
Acquisitions and Developmental Editor: Jeff Kellum
Editors: Colleen Wheeler Strand, Linda Orlando
Production Editor: Jennifer Campbell
Technical Editors: Donald Fuller, Michelle A. Roudebush
Book Designer: Bill Gibson
Graphic Illustrator: Tony Jonick
Electronic Publishing Specialists: Jangshi Wang, Susie Hendrickson, Judy Fung, Sharon Page Ritchie
Proofreaders: Laurie O'Connell, Yariv Rabinovitch
Indexer: Ted Laux
CD Coordinator: Christine Harris
CD Technician: Kevin Ly
Cover Designer: Archer Design
Cover Photographer: The Image Bank

Library of Congress Card Number: 2001089812

ISBN: 0-7821-2947-1

SYBEX

To Our Valued Readers:

When Sybex published the first editions of the four core Windows® 2000 MCSE Study Guides, Windows® 2000 had been out for only six months, and the MCSE exams had just been released. In writing the Study Guides, the authors brought to the table their experience with Windows® 2000 as well as insights gained from years of classroom teaching. With the official Microsoft exam objectives as their guides, the authors set out to write comprehensive, yet ultimately clear, concise, and practical courseware. And we believe they succeeded.

Over the past year, however, our authors have learned many new things about how Windows® 2000 works and have received significant and useful feedback about how Microsoft is testing individuals on the vast array of topics encompassed by the four core exams. We at Sybex have also received a tremendous amount of invaluable feedback—both praise and criticism—regarding the four core Windows® 2000 Study Guides. The second edition that you hold in your hand is the product of the feedback that readers such as yourself have provided to us.

So what "new and improved" material will you find in this new edition? We have confidence in the core instructional material in the books, so the authors have made only minor modifications to this content. They have, however, made the chapter review questions and bonus exam questions more challenging, to better reflect the type of questions you'll encounter on the actual exams. We've also added Real World Scenarios throughout the book. This new feature allowed the authors to add critical context and perspective on Windows® 2000 technologies that wasn't available when Microsoft first released the products. Finally, we've added Exam Essentials to the end of each chapter. These re-emphasize those subject areas that are most important for success on the exams.

We believe you'll find this Study Guide to be an indispensable part of your exam prep program. As always, your feedback is important to us. Please send comments, questions, or suggestions to support@sybex.com. At Sybex we're continually striving to meet and exceed the needs of individuals preparing for IT certification exams. Readers like you are critical to these efforts.

Good luck in pursuit of your MCSE!

Neil Edde
Associate Publisher—Certification
Sybex, Inc.

SYBEX Inc. 1151 Marina Village Parkway, Alameda, CA 94501
Tel: 510/523-8233   Fax: 510/523-2373   HTTP://www.sybex.com

For Katie, you are my sunshine!

Acknowledgments

This book is the result of a great team, from both the first edition and the second edition. First, I'd like to thank Marilyn Smith from the first edition, who did a tremendous job of translating my writing into a form that is very readable. Marilyn put in countless hours and worked through my many revisions as the book evolved. From the second edition, I'd like to thank Colleen Strand and Linda Orlando, who did a great job of editing chapters at breakneck speeds usually only seen by Superman. Jennifer Campbell acted as the Production Editor, and did a fabulous job of keeping us on track.

I'd also like to thank the team that made this book possible: Thanks to James Chellis for allowing me to work on the MCSE series—James is a visionary and is my business idol; Neil Edde, the Associate Publisher for this series, has nurtured the MCSE Study Guides since the early days; Jangshi Wang and Sharon Page Ritchie handled the typesetting of the book; Tony Jonick and Jerry Williams! have provided all of the illustrations; Laurie O'Connell and Yariv Rabinovitch did the proofreading, and Ted Laux completed the index. I'd also like to thank my technical editors, Donald Fuller and Michelle Roudebush, for keeping me honest and minimizing the errors in the book. Jason Holt checked the CD, while Matthew Sheltz provided much of the CD content. Without the great work of the team, this book would not be possible.

On the local front, I'd like to thank my family who has lived with me through this entire project, and my best pals who have shown tremendous patience with me over the last few months. I'd also like to thank my friends and co-workers at my day job at CCC Network Systems who have supported this project, especially John Staples, Tom Scott, Dionne Werner, Bob Allen, Mike Warfield, and Curtis Quast. You guys are the best!

Contents at a Glance

Contents

Table of Exercises

Introduction

Microsoft's Microsoft Certified Systems Engineer (MCSE) track for Windows 2000 is the premier certification for computer industry professionals. Covering the core technologies around which Microsoft's future will be built, the MCSE Windows 2000 program is a powerful credential for career advancement.

This book has been developed to give you the critical skills and knowledge you need to prepare for one of the core requirements of the new MCSE certification program: Installing, Configuring, and Administering Microsoft Windows 2000 Server (Exam 70-215).

The Microsoft Certified Professional Program

Since the inception of its certification program, Microsoft has certified over one million people. As the computer network industry grows in both size and complexity, these numbers are sure to grow—and the need for *proven* ability will also increase. Companies rely on certifications to verify the skills of prospective employees and contractors.

Microsoft has developed its Microsoft Certified Professional (MCP) program to give you credentials that verify your ability to work with Microsoft products effectively and professionally. Obtaining your MCP certification requires that you pass any one Microsoft exam (excluding any of the MOUS exams). Other levels of certification are available based on specific suites of exams. Depending on your areas of interest or experience, you can obtain any of the following credentials:

Microsoft Certified System Engineer (MCSE)   This certification track is designed for network and systems administrators, network and systems analysts, and technical consultants who work with Microsoft Windows 2000 client and server software. You must take and pass seven exams to obtain your MCSE.

Since this book covers one of the Core MCSE exams, we will discuss the MCSE in detail in the following sections.

Microsoft Certified Solution Developer (MCSD) This track is designed for software engineers and developers and technical consultants who primarily use Microsoft development tools. Currently, you can take exams on Visual Basic, Visual C++, and Visual FoxPro. However, with Microsoft's pending release of Visual Studio 7, you can expect the requirements for this track to change by the end of the year. You must take and pass four exams to obtain your MCSD.

Microsoft Certified Database Administrator (MCDBA) This track is designed for database administrators, developers, and analysts who work with Microsoft SQL Server. As of this printing, you can take exams on either SQL Server 7 or SQL Server 2000, but Microsoft is expected to announce the retirement of SQL Server 7. You must take and pass four exams to achieve MCDBA status.

Microsoft Certified Trainer (MCT) The MCT track is designed for any IT professional who develops and teaches Microsoft-approved courses. To become an MCT, you must first obtain your MCSE, MCSD, or MCDBA; then you must take a class at one of the Certified Technical Training Centers. You will also be required to prove your instructional ability. You can do this in various ways: by taking a skills-building or train-the-trainer class; by achieving certification as a trainer from any of a number vendors; or by becoming a Certified Technical Trainer through the Chauncey Group (www.chauncey.com/ctt.html). Last of all, you will need to complete an MCT application.

As of March 1, 2001, Microsoft no longer offers MCSE NT 4 required exams. Those who are certified in NT 4 have until December 31, 2001, to upgrade their credentials to Windows 2000. Also, Microsoft has retired three other certification tracks: MCP+Internet, MCSE+Internet, and MCP+Site Builder. The topics and concepts that are tested in these certifications have been incorporated into the MCSE and MCSD exams.

How Do You Become an MCSE?

Attaining MCSE certification has always been a challenge. In the past, students have been able to acquire detailed exam information—even most of the exam questions—from online "brain dumps" and third-party "cram" books or software products. For the new MCSE exams, this is simply not the case.

Windows 2000

Over the next few years, companies around the world will deploy millions of copies of Windows 2000 as the central operating system for their mission-critical networks. This will generate an enormous need for qualified consultants and personnel to design, deploy, and support Windows 2000 networks.

Because Windows 2000 is such a vast product, its administrators must have a wealth of professional skills. As an example of Windows 2000's complexity, consider it has more than 35 million lines of code as compared to Windows NT 4's 12 million! Much of this code is needed to support the wide range of functionality that Windows 2000 offers.

The Windows 2000 line comprises several versions:

Windows 2000 Professional   This is the client edition of Windows 2000, which is comparable to Windows NT Workstation 4 but also includes the best features of Windows 98 as well as many new features.

Windows 2000 Server/Windows 2000 Advanced Server   A server edition of Windows 2000, this version is for small to mid-sized deployments. Advanced Server supports more memory and processors than Server does.

Windows 2000 Datacenter Server   This is a server edition of Windows 2000 for large, wide-scale deployments and computer clusters. Datacenter Server supports the most memory and processors of the three versions.

Companies implementing the expansive Windows 2000 operating system must be certain that you are the right person for the job being offered. The MCSE track is designed to help you prove that you are.

Microsoft has taken strong steps to protect the security and integrity of the new MCSE track. Now, prospective MSCEs must complete a course of study that develops detailed knowledge about a wide range of topics. It supplies them with the true skills needed, derived from working with Windows 2000 and related software products.

The new MCSE program is heavily weighted toward hands-on skills and experience. Microsoft has stated that, "Nearly half of the core required exams' content demands that the candidate have troubleshooting skills acquired through hands-on experience and working knowledge."

Fortunately, if you are willing to dedicate the time and effort to learn Windows 2000, you can prepare yourself well for the exams by using the proper tools. By working through this book, you can successfully meet the exam requirements.

This book is part of a complete series of Sybex MCSE Study Guides, published by Sybex, Inc., that together cover the core Windows 2000 requirements as well as the new Design exams needed to complete your MCSE track. Study Guide titles include the following:

- *MCSE: Windows 2000 Professional Study Guide,* Second Edition, by Lisa Donald with James Chellis (Sybex, 2001)

- *MCSE: Windows 2000 Server Study Guide,* Second Edition, by Lisa Donald with James Chellis (Sybex, 2001)

- *MCSE: Windows 2000 Network Infrastructure Administration Study Guide,* Second Edition, by Paul Robichaux with James Chellis (Sybex, 2001)

- *MCSE: Windows 2000 Directory Services Administration Study Guide,* Second Edition, by Anil Desai with James Chellis (Sybex, 2001)

- *MCSE: Windows 2000 Network Security Design Study Guide,* by Gary Govanus and Robert King (Sybex, 2000)

- *MCSE: Windows 2000 Network Infrastructure Design Study Guide,* by Bill Heldman (Sybex, 2000)

- *MCSE: Windows 2000 Directory Services Design Study Guide,* by Robert King and Gary Govanus (Sybex, 2000)

Exam Requirements

Candidates for MCSE certification in Windows 2000 must pass seven exams, including four core operating system exams, one design exam, and two electives, as described in the sections that follow.

Core Requirements

Windows 2000 Professional (70-210)

Windows 2000 Server (70-215)

Windows 2000 Network Infrastructure Administration (70-216)

Windows 2000 Directory Services Administration (70-217)

Plus one of the following

Design Requirement

Designing a Windows 2000 Directory Services Infrastructure (70-219)

Designing Security for Windows 2000 Network (70-220)

Designing a Windows 2000 Network Infrastructure (70-221)

Designing Web Solutions with Windows 2000 Server Technologies (70-226)

Plus two of the following

Electives

Any of the Design exams not taken for the Design requirement

Any current Elective exam. Topics include Exchange Server, SQL Server, and ISA Server

For a more detailed description of the Microsoft certification programs, including a list of current and future MCSE electives, check Microsoft's Training and Certification Web site at www.microsoft.com/trainingandservices.

The *Installing, Configuring, and Administering Microsoft Windows 2000 Server* Exam

The *Installing, Configuring, and Administering Microsoft Windows 2000 Server* exam covers concepts and skills required for the support of Windows 2000 Server computers. It emphasizes the following areas of Windows 2000 Server support:

- Installing Windows 2000 Server

- Implementing and managing access to resources

- Configuring and troubleshooting hardware and drivers

- Monitoring and optimizing system performance and reliability

- Configuring and managing disks and volumes

- Implementing, managing, and troubleshooting network protocols and services

- Implementing, monitoring, and troubleshooting security

This exam can be quite specific regarding Windows 2000 Server requirements and operational settings, and it can be particular about how administrative tasks are performed in the operating system. It also focuses on fundamental concepts relating to Windows 2000 Server's operation. Careful study of this book, along with hands-on experience, will help you prepare for this exam.

Microsoft provides exam objectives to give you a very general overview of possible areas of coverage on the Microsoft exams. For your convenience, this Study Guide includes objective listings positioned within the text at points where specific Microsoft exam objectives are discussed. Keep in mind, however, that exam objectives are subject to change at any time without prior notice and at Microsoft's sole discretion. Please visit Microsoft's Training and Certification Web site (www.microsoft.com/trainingandservices) for the most current exam objectives listing.

Types of Exam Questions

In an effort to both refine the testing process and protect the quality of its certifications, Microsoft has focused its Windows 2000 exams on real experience and hands-on proficiency. There is a higher emphasis on your past working environments and responsibilities, and less emphasis on how well you can memorize. In fact, Microsoft says an MCSE candidate should have at least one year of hands-on experience.

Microsoft will accomplish its goal of protecting the exams' integrity by regularly adding and removing exam questions, limiting the number of questions that any individual sees in a beta exam, limiting the number of questions delivered to an individual by using adaptive testing, and adding new exam elements.

Exam questions may be in a variety of formats: Depending on which exam you take, you'll see multiple-choice questions, as well as select-and-place and prioritize-a-list questions. Simulations and case study–based formats are included, as well. You may also find yourself taking what's called an *adaptive format exam*. Let's take a look at the types of exam questions and examine the adaptive testing technique, so that you'll be prepared for all of the possibilities.

With the release of Windows 2000, Microsoft has stopped providing a detailed score breakdown. This is mostly because of the various and complex question formats. Previously, each question focused on one objective. The Windows 2000 exams, however, contain questions that may be tied to one or more objectives from one or more objective sets. Therefore, grading by objective is almost impossible.

For more information on the various exam question types, go to www.microsoft.com/trainingandservices/default.asp?PageID= mcp&PageCall=tesinn&SubSite=examinfo.

Multiple-Choice Questions

Multiple-choice questions come in two main forms. One is a straightforward question followed by several possible answers, of which one or more is correct.

The other type of multiple-choice question is more complex and based on a specific scenario. The scenario may focus on a number of areas or objectives.

Select-and-Place Questions

Select-and-place exam questions involve graphical elements that you must manipulate in order to successfully answer the question. For example, you might see a diagram of a computer network, as shown in the following graphic taken from the select-and-place demo downloaded from Microsoft's Web site.

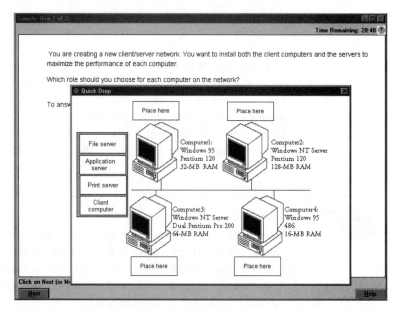

A typical diagram will show computers and other components next to boxes that contain the text "Place here." The labels for the boxes represent various computer roles on a network, such as a print server and a file server. Based on information given for each computer, you are asked to select each label and place it in the correct box. You need to place *all* of the labels correctly. No credit is given for the question if you correctly label only some of the boxes.

In another select-and-place problem you might be asked to put a series of steps in order, by dragging items from one column and placing them in the correct order in another column.

Another type of select-and-place question is building a hierarchy tree, which requires that you drag an item from one column and place it under an item in the other column.

Simulations

Simulations are the kinds of questions that most closely represent actual situations and test the skills you use while working with Microsoft software interfaces. These exam questions include a mock interface on which you are asked to perform certain actions according to a given scenario. The simulated interfaces look nearly identical to what you see in the actual product, as shown in this example:

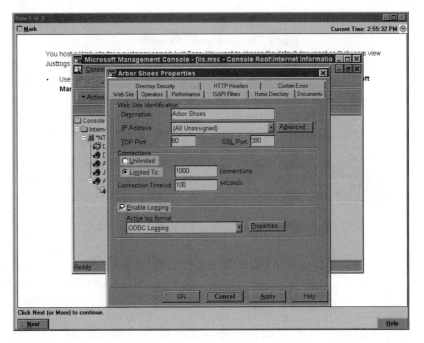

Because of the number of possible errors that can be made on simulations, you'll be wise to consider the following recommendations from Microsoft:

- Do not change any simulation settings that don't pertain to the solution directly.

- When related information has not been provided, assume that the default settings are used.

- Make sure that your entries are spelled correctly.

- Close all the simulation application windows after completing the set of tasks in the simulation.

The best way to prepare for simulation questions is to spend time working with the graphical interface of the product on which you will be tested.

We recommend that you study with the WinSim 2000 product, which is included on the CD that accompanies this study guide. By completing the exercises in this study guide and working with the WinSim 2000 software, you will greatly improve your level of preparation for simulation questions.

Case Study–Based Questions

Case study–based questions first appeared in the MCSD program. These questions present a scenario with a range of requirements. Based on the information provided, you answer a series of multiple-choice and select-and-place questions. The interface for case study–based questions has a number of tabs, each of which contains information about the scenario.

At present, this type of question appears only in most of the MCSE Design exams.

Adaptive Exam Format

Microsoft presents many of its exams in an *adaptive* format. This format is radically different from the conventional format previously used for Microsoft certification exams. Conventional tests are static, containing a fixed number of questions. Adaptive tests change depending on your answers to the questions presented.

The number of questions presented in your adaptive test will depend on how long it takes the exam to ascertain your level of ability (according to the statistical measurements on which exam questions are ranked). To determine a test-taker's level of ability, the exam presents questions in an increasing or decreasing order of difficulty.

Unlike the earlier test format, the adaptive test does *not* allow you to go back to see a question again. The exam only goes forward. Once you enter your answer, that's it—you cannot change it. Be very careful before entering your answers. There is no time limit for each individual question (only for the exam as a whole). Your exam may be shortened by correct answers (and lengthened by incorrect answers), so there is no advantage to rushing through questions.

Microsoft will regularly add and remove questions from the exams. This is called *item seeding*. It is part of the effort to make it more difficult for individuals to merely memorize exam questions that were passed along by previous test-takers.

Exam Question Development

Microsoft follows an exam-development process consisting of eight mandatory phases. The process takes an average of seven months and involves more than 150 specific steps. The MCP exam development consists of the following phases:

Phase 1: Job Analysis   Phase 1 is an analysis of all the tasks that make up a specific job function, based on tasks performed by people who are currently performing that job function. This phase also identifies the knowledge, skills, and abilities that relate specifically to the performance area being certified.

Phase 2: Objective Domain Definition   The results of the job analysis phase provide the framework used to develop objectives. Development of objectives involves translating the job-function tasks into a comprehensive package of specific and measurable knowledge, skills, and abilities. The resulting list of objectives—the *objective domain*—is the basis for the development of both the certification exams and the training materials.

Phase 3: Blueprint Survey The final objective domain is transformed into a blueprint survey in which contributors are asked to rate each objective. These contributors may be MCP candidates, appropriately skilled exam-development volunteers, or Microsoft employees. Based on the contributors' input, the objectives are prioritized and weighted. The actual exam items are written according to the prioritized objectives. Contributors are queried about how they spend their time on the job. If a contributor doesn't spend an adequate amount of time actually performing the specified job function, his or her data are eliminated from the analysis. The blueprint survey phase helps determine which objectives to measure, as well as the appropriate number and types of items to include on the exam.

Phase 4: Item Development A pool of items is developed to measure the blueprinted objective domain. The number and types of items to be written are based on the results of the blueprint survey.

Phase 5: Alpha Review and Item Revision During this phase, a panel of technical and job-function experts review each item for technical accuracy. The panel then answers each item and reaches a consensus on all technical issues. Once the items have been verified as being technically accurate, they are edited to ensure that they are expressed in the clearest language possible.

Phase 6: Beta Exam The reviewed and edited items are collected into beta exams. Based on the responses of all beta participants, Microsoft performs a statistical analysis to verify the validity of the exam items and to determine which items will be used in the certification exam. Once the analysis has been completed, the items are distributed into multiple parallel forms, or *versions*, of the final certification exam.

Phase 7: Item Selection and Cut-Score Setting The results of the beta exams are analyzed to determine which items will be included in the certification exam. This determination is based on many factors, including item difficulty and relevance. During this phase, a panel of job-function experts determine the *cut score* (minimum passing score) for the exams. The cut score differs from exam to exam because it is based on an item-by-item determination of the percentage of candidates who answered the item correctly and who would be expected to answer the item correctly.

Phase 8: Live Exam In the final phase, the exams are given to candidates. MCP exams are administered by Prometric and Virtual University Enterprises (VUE).

Tips for Taking the Windows 2000 Server Exam

Here are some general tips for achieving success on your certification exam:

- Arrive early at the exam center so that you can relax and review your study materials. During this final review, you can look over tables and lists of exam-related information.

- Read the questions carefully. Don't be tempted to jump to an early conclusion. Make sure you know *exactly* what the question is asking.

- Answer all questions. Remember that the adaptive format does *not* allow you to return to a question. Be very careful before entering your answer. Because your exam may be shortened by correct answers (and lengthened by incorrect answers), there is no advantage to rushing through questions.

- On simulations, do not change settings that are not directly related to the question. Also, assume default settings if the question does not specify or imply which settings are used.

- For questions you're not sure about, use a process of elimination to get rid of the obviously incorrect answers first. This improves your odds of selecting the correct answer when you need to make an educated guess.

Exam Registration

You may take the Microsoft exams at any of more than 1,000 Authorized Prometric Testing Centers (APTCs) and VUE Testing Centers around the world. For the location of a testing center near you, call Prometric at 800-755-EXAM (755-3926), or call VUE at 888-837-8616. Outside the United States and Canada, contact your local Prometric or VUE registration center.

Find out the number of the exam you want to take, and then register with the Prometric or VUE registration center nearest to you. At this point, you will be asked for advance payment for the exam. The exams are $100 each and you must take them within one year of payment. You can schedule exams up to six weeks in advance or as late as one working day prior to the date of the exam. You can cancel or reschedule your exam if you contact the center at least two working days prior to the exam. Same-day registration is available in some locations, subject to space availability. Where same-day registration is available, you must register a minimum of two hours before test time.

You may also register for your exams online at www.prometric.com or www.vue.com.

When you schedule the exam, you will be provided with instructions regarding appointment and cancellation procedures, ID requirements, and information about the testing center location. In addition, you will receive a registration and payment confirmation letter from Prometric or VUE.

Microsoft requires certification candidates to accept the terms of a non-disclosure agreement before taking certification exams.

Is This Book for You?

If you want to acquire a solid foundation in installing, configuring, and administering Windows 2000 Server, and your goal is to prepare for the exam by learning how to use and manage the new operating system, this book is for you. You'll find clear explanations of the fundamental concepts you need to grasp, and plenty of help to achieve the high level of professional competency you need to succeed in your chosen field.

If you want to become certified as an MCSE, this book is definitely for you. However, if you just want to attempt to pass the exam without really understanding Windows 2000, this Study Guide is *not* for you. It is written for people who want to acquire hands-on skills and in-depth knowledge of Windows 2000.

How to Use This Book

What makes a Sybex Study Guide the book of choice for over 100,000 MCSEs? We took into account not only what you need to know to pass the exam, but what you need to know to take what you've learned and apply it in the real world. Each book contains the following:

Objective-by-objective coverage of the topics you need to know Each chapter lists the objectives covered in that chapter, followed by detailed discussion of each objective.

Assessment Test Directly following this Introduction is an Assessment Test that you should take. It is designed to help you determine how much you already know about Windows 2000. Each question is tied to a topic discussed in the book. Using the results of the Assessment Test, you can figure out the areas where you need to focus your study. Of course, we do recommend you read the entire book.

Exam Essentials   To highlight what you learn, you'll find a list of Exam Essentials at the end of each chapter. The Exam Essentials section briefly highlights the topics that need your particular attention as you prepare for the exam.

Key Terms and Glossary   Throughout each chapter, you will be introduced to important terms and concepts that you will need to know for the exam. These terms appear in italic within the chapters, and a list of the Key Terms appears just after the Exam Essentials. At the end of the book, a detailed Glossary gives definitions for these terms, as well as other general terms you should know.

Review questions, complete with detailed explanations   Each chapter is followed by a set of Review Questions that test what you learned in the chapter. The questions are written with the exam in mind, meaning that they are designed to have the same look and feel of what you'll see on the exam. Question types are just like the exam, including multiple choice, exhibits, and select-and-place.

Hands-on exercises   In each chapter, you'll find exercises designed to give you the important hands-on experience that is critical for your exam preparation. The exercises support the topics of the chapter, and they walk you through the steps necessary to perform a particular function.

Real-World Scenarios   Because reading a book isn't enough to learn how to apply these topics in your every-day duties, we have provided Real World Scenarios in special sidebars. These explain when and why a particular solution would make sense, in a working environment you'd actually encounter.

Interactive CD   Every Sybex Study Guide comes with a CD complete with additional questions, flashcards for use with your PC or palm device, a Windows simulation program, and two complete electronic books. Details are in the following section.

The topics covered in this Study Guide map directly to Microsoft's official exam objectives. Each exam objective is covered completely.

What's On the CD?

With this new member of our best-selling MCSE Study Guide series, we are including quite an array of training resources. The CD offers numerous simulations, bonus exams, and flashcards to help you study for the exam. We have also included the complete contents of the Study Guide in electronic form. The CD's resources are described here:

The Sybex Ebook for Windows 2000 Server   Many people like the convenience of being able to carry their whole study guide on a CD. They also like being able to search the text via computer to find specific information quickly and easily. For these reasons, the entire contents of this Study Guide are supplied on the CD, in PDF format. We've also included Adobe Acrobat Reader, which provides the interface for the PDF contents as well as the search capabilities.

WinSim 2000   We developed the WinSim 2000 product to allow you to experience the multimedia and interactive operation of working with Windows 2000 Server. WinSim 2000 provides both audio/video files and hands-on experience with key features of the Windows 2000 tools you use to install, configure, and administer Windows 2000 Server. Built around the Study Guide's exercises, WinSim 2000 will help you attain the knowledge and hands-on skills that you must have in order to understand Windows 2000 (and pass the exam). Here is a sample screen from WinSim 2000:

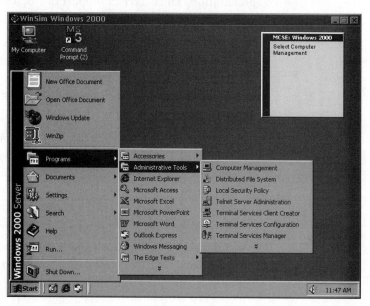

The Sybex MCSE EdgeTests   The EdgeTests are a collection of multiple-choice questions that will help you prepare for your exam. The questions are grouped into seven sets:

- The Assessment Test.

- Two bonus exams designed to simulate the actual live exam.

- All the questions from the Study Guide organized by chapter for your review.

- All the questions from the Study Guide, plus the two bonus exams, organized by objective area for your review.

- A random test generator that selects up to 75 questions from all of the questions listed above.

- An adaptive test simulator that will give the feel for how adaptive testing works.

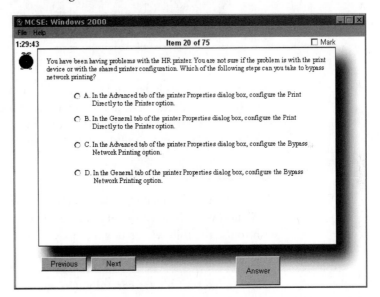

Sybex MCSE Flashcards for PCs and Palm Devices   The "flashcard" style of question offers an effective way to quickly and efficiently test your understanding of the fundamental concepts covered in the Windows 2000 Server exam. The Sybex MCSE Flashcards set consists of more than 150

questions presented in a special engine developed specifically for this study guide series. Here's what the Sybex MCSE Flashcards interface looks like:

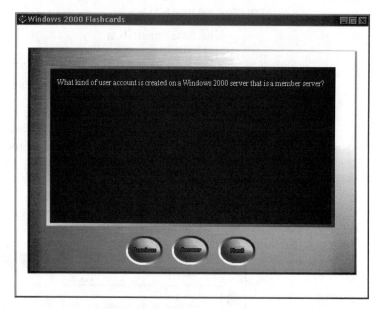

Because of the high demand for a product that will run on Palm devices, we have also developed, in conjunction with Land-J Technologies, a version of the flashcard questions that you can take with you on your Palm OS PDA (including the PalmPilot and Handspring's Visor).

How Do You Use This Book?

This book provides a solid foundation for the serious effort of preparing for the Windows 2000 Server exam. To best benefit from this book, you may wish to use the following study method:

1. Take the Assessment Test to identify your weak areas.

2. Study each chapter carefully. Do your best to fully understand the information.

3. Complete all the hands-on exercises in the chapter, referring back to the text as necessary so that you understand each step you take. If you don't have access to a lab environment in which you can complete the exercises, install and work with the exercises available in the WinSim 2000 software included with this study guide.

In order to complete the exercises in this book, your hardware should meet the minimum hardware requirements for Windows 2000. See Chapter 1, "Getting Started with Windows 2000 Server," for the minimum and recommended system requirements.

4. Read over the Real-World Scenarios, to improve your understanding of how to use what you learn in the book.

5. Study the Exam Essentials and Key Terms to make sure you are familiar with the areas you need to focus on.

6. Answer the review questions at the end of each chapter. If you prefer to answer the questions in a timed and graded format, install the Edge-Tests from the book's CD and answer the chapter questions there instead of in the book.

7. Take note of the questions you did not understand, and study the corresponding sections of the book again.

8. Go back over the Exam Essentials and Key Terms.

9. Go through the Study Guide's other training resources, which are included on the book's CD. These include WinSim 2000, electronic flashcards, the electronic version of the chapter review question (try taking them by objective), and the two bonus exams.

To learn all the material covered in this book, you will need to study regularly and with discipline. Try to set aside the same time every day to study, and select a comfortable and quiet place in which to do it. If you work hard, you will be surprised at how quickly you learn this material. Good luck!

Contacts and Resources

To find out more about Microsoft Education and Certification materials and programs, to register with Prometric or VUE, or to obtain other useful certification information and additional study resources, check the following resources:

Microsoft Training and Certification Home Page
www.microsoft.com/trainingandservices

This Web site provides information about the MCP program and exams. You can also order the latest Microsoft Roadmap to Education and Certification.

Microsoft TechNet Technical Information Network
www.microsoft.com/technet
800-344-2121

Use this Web site or phone number to contact support professionals and system administrators. Outside the United States and Canada, contact your local Microsoft subsidiary for information.

Palm Pilot Training Product Development: Land-J
www.land-j.com
407-359-2217

Land-J Technologies is a consulting and programming business currently specializing in application development for the 3Com PalmPilot Personal Digital Assistant. Land-J developed the Palm version of the EdgeTests, which is included on the CD that accompanies this Study Guide.

Prometric
www.prometric.com
800-755-3936

Contact Sylvan Prometric to register to take an MCP exam at any of more than 800 Prometric Testing Centers around the world.

Virtual University Enterprises (VUE)
www.vue.com
888-837-8616

Contact the VUE registration center to register to take an MCP exam at one of the VUE Testing Centers.

MCP Magazine Online
www.mcpmag.com

Microsoft Certified Professional Magazine is a well-respected publication that focues on Windows certification. This site hosts chats and discussion forums and tracks news related to the MCSE program. Some of the services cost a fee, but they are well worth it.

Windows 2000 Magazine
www.windows2000mag.com

You can subscribe to this magazine or read free articles at the Web site. The study resource provides general information on Windows 2000.

Cramsession on Brainbuzz.com
`cramsession.brainbuzz.com`

Cramsession is an online community focusing on all IT certification programs. In addition to discussion boards and job locators, you can download one of a number of free cramsessions, which are nice supplements to any study approach you take.

Assessment Test

1. When would you want to use the Dfs? Choose all that apply.

   A. If you are in a small workgroup where each user stores his or her files on the individual computer.

   B. If you are in a large domain where users need to access files that are scattered across many computers.

   C. If you are in a large domain where users only need to retrieve files from one server.

   D. If you are in a large domain where each user stores all of the files he or she needs on the workstation.

2. Which MMC mode allows users full access to Windows 2000 management commands, but prohibits users from adding or removing snap-ins?

   A. Author mode

   B. User mode-full access

   C. User mode-limited access

   D. Management mode

3. Which of the following application environments will offer the best performance with a Windows 2000 Terminal Services server?

   A. 8-bit

   B. 16-bit

   C. 32-bit

   D. 64-bit

4. You have several users who all need to access and update a single file simultaneously. How can you improve the performance of their access?

   A. Automatically replicate the file several times across several servers.

   B. Leave the file out of the Dfs system and have users store the file on their workstations.

   C. Provide several Dfs links to the file.

   D. Replicate the entire root across many servers.

5. Which remote access authentication method should you use if your clients connect via Shiva LAN Rovers?

   A. PAP

   B. SPAP

   C. MS-CHAP

   D. CHAP

6. Where would you configure whether or not Error, Warning, and Information events that relate to printing are logged to Event Viewer?

   A. In the General tab of the Print Server Properties dialog box

   B. In the Advanced tab of the Print Server Properties dialog box

   C. In the General tab of the printer Properties dialog box

   D. In the Advanced tab of the printer Properties dialog box

7. What is the minimum processor requirement for upgrading Windows NT Server 4 to Windows 2000 Server?

   A. Pentium 133MHz

   B. Pentium 166MHz

   C. Pentium 266MHz

   D. Pentium 333MHz

8. Which of the following services is not considered a part of Internet Information Services (IIS)?

A. SMTP

B. SNMP

C. NNTP

D. HTTP

9. Which driver signing option displays a warning message before installing an unsigned file and allows you to choose to continue with the installation or cancel it?

A. Ignore

B. Override

C. Warn

D. Notice

10. Which of the following disk configurations are supported as basic storage on Windows 2000 Server? Choose all that apply.

A. Primary partition

B. Extended partition

C. Mirrored volume

D. RAID-5 volume

11. You are creating a new user account that will not be used for two months. What option should you configure so that the account does not pose a security risk while it is unused?

A. Account Is Disabled

B. Account Must Use Password with Reversible Encryption

C. User Cannot Logon

D. Logon Is Disabled

12. Which command would you use in the Recovery Console if you wanted to fix the computer's boot sector?

A. FIXMBR

B. BOOTFIX

C. FIXBOOT

D. You can't fix the boot sector using the Recovery Console

13. Which of the following rights is not associated with the NTFS Write permission?

A. Change a folder's or file's attributes

B. Create new files and write data to the files

C. Create new folders and append data to files

D. Delete files

14. Julie wants to confirm that her RAS server is configured to use only outbound connections. Where in the Routing and Remote Access utility can this option be configured?

A. Through Routing Interface

B. Through Ports Properties

C. Through Remote Access Server Properties

D. Through Remote Access Logging

15. What commands can you use to start the Windows 2000 Server installation? Choose all that apply.

A. WIN2K

B. INSTALL

C. WINNT

D. WINNT32

16. How do you configure a printer pool?

    A. In the Ports tab of the printer Properties dialog box, select the Enable Printer Pooling check box, then check all of the ports that the print devices are attached to.

    B. Specify that you want to use a printer pool when you run the Add Printer Wizard. The Wizard will then allow you to configure multiple ports.

    C. In the Advanced tab of the printer Properties dialog box, select the Enable Printer Pooling check box, then check all of the ports that the print devices are attached to.

    D. In the Ports tab of the printer Properties dialog box, just select which ports the print devices are attached.

17. You are creating an answer file to be used with disk duplication. What is the name of the answer file that will be created automatically?

    A. sysprep.ini

    B. diskdup.ini

    C. sysprep.inf

    D. diskdup.inf

18. Your company is an ISP that hosts multiple Web sites on a single server. Which option should you configure if you want to limit the amount of processor utilization that can be used by each Web site?

    A. Processor bandwidth

    B. Processor utilization

    C. Process thunking

    D. Process throttling

19. If you had a striped volume set with five 10GB drives, how much space would be available to store data?

A. 40GB

B. 45GB

C. 48GB

D. 50GB

20. Which special character can you use to create a hidden share on a folder?

A. *

B. #

C. $

D. %

21. You are the XYZ Computer Corporation. You preinstall Windows 2000 Server on your computers before they are shipped out by using disk duplication. In conjunction with the disk duplication, you use answer files. Which of the following options in the Setup Manager utility will allow you to configure an optional background that displays your corporate logo?

A. OEM branding

B. OEM scorching

C. OEM duplicator

D. OEM manager

22. Which option is used as a tool to compare your desired security settings with your current security settings?

A. Security template

B. Security database

C. Security profile

D. Security analyst

23. What are the Microsoft recommendations for base RAM that will be required by a Windows 2000 Server computer running Terminal Services?

    A. 128MB

    B. 192MB

    C. 256MB

    D. 512MB

24. Milan is concerned that he will negatively impact system processing by running System Monitor. Which process in System Monitor will track the resources used by System Monitor?

    A. `sysmon.exe`

    B. `perfmon.exe`

    C. `mmc.exe`

    D. `monitor.exe`

25. Which of the following tasks can be completed through the Recovery Console? Choose all that apply.

    A. Copy a driver to the hard drive from a floppy.

    B. Copy important data from the hard drive to a floppy.

    C. Repair the Master Boot Record (MBR) for the computer.

    D. Create and format partitions on the drive.

26. Mike is installing the NWLink IPX/SPX/NetBIOS protocol. When would he need to configure the internal network number? Choose all that apply.

    A. When he will use CSNW

    B. When he will use GSNW

    C. When he will use File and Print Services for NetWare

    D. When he will use IPX routing

27. Bud wants to run the lala.exe program on his Windows 2000 Server computer. He wants minimize the impact of running the application on the server. Which of the following options should he used when he starts the lala.exe program?

    A. `start /min lala.exe`

    B. `run /min lala.exe`

    C. `start /low lala.exe`

    D. `run /low lala.exe`

28. When configuring a user account, which option is not configured on the Profile tab of the user Properties dialog box?

    A. User profile path

    B. Logon script

    C. Logon workstations

    D. Home folder

29. Which policy types are applied to the computer as opposed to users and groups?

    A. Password policies

    B. Account lockout policies

    C. User rights assignment policies

    D. Security options

30. Which of the following protocols is used with the PING command?

    A. ICMP

    B. UDP

    C. SNMP

    D. RCP

Answers to Assessment Test

1. B, C. The Dfs is useful for bringing files that are distributed across the network together in one central location. It also allows users to access files that would otherwise be unavailable if one of the domain member servers goes down. See Chapter 8 for more information.

2. B. The MMC user mode-full access allows users full access to Windows 2000 management commands, but does not allow users to add or remove snap-ins. See Chapter 3 for more information.

3. C. Windows 2000 Server is a 32-bit environment. In order to run 16-bit applications, Windows 2000 must employ a system called Windows on Windows (WOW), which consumes a lot of system resources. See Chapter 12 for more information.

4. A. If several users need to update one file simultaneously, it is usually a good idea to replicate the file several times across several servers to evenly distribute the load. If users copy the file to their workstations, then all of the changes will not be synchronized. Replicating the root is generally used for fault-tolerance purposes. See Chapter 8 for more information.

5. B. The Shiva Password Authentication Protocol (SPAP) is a form of authentication used by clients that connect to Shiva LAN Rovers. See Chapter 13 for more information.

6. B. You can manage whether or not Error, Warning, or Information events that relate to printing are sent to Event Viewer through the Advanced tab of the Print Server Properties dialog box. See Chapter 11 for more information.

7. A. The requirement for a Windows 2000 Server upgrade is the same as for a Windows 2000 Server clean install. You must have a Pentium 133MHz or better processor. See Chapter 1 for more information.

8. B. The Simple Network Management Protocol (SNMP) is not installed as a part of IIS. See Chapter 10 for more information.

9. C. If you configure driver signing with the Warn option, you can install unsigned drivers, but you will see a warning message before unsigned drivers are installed. See Chapter 3 for more information.

10. A, B. Mirrored volumes and RAID-5 volumes are supported disk configurations for Windows 2000 Server, but they are dynamic storage, not basic storage. See Chapter 6 for more information.

11. A. While the account is not in use, you should configure the Account Is Disabled option. See Chapter 4 for more information.

12. C. The FIXBOOT command is used to fix the boot sector with the Recovery Console. See Chapter 15 for more information.

13. D. The NTFS Write permission does not allow you to delete files. See Chapter 7 for more information.

14. B. You can configure whether the server will support inbound and outbound connections through the Ports Properties dialog box in the Routing and Remote Access utility. By default, RAS servers are configured to support only inbound connections. See Chapter 13 for more information.

15. C, D. The only programs you can use to start a Windows 2000 installation are WINNT and WINNT32. See Chapter 1 for more information.

16. A. A printer pool has one printer defined for multiple physical print devices. For each print device, you must configure the port that the print device will attach to. By default, you can only select one port per printer. To configure multiple ports, you access the Ports tab of the printer Properties dialog box, select the Enable Printer Pooling check box, and then check all of the ports that the print devices are attached to. See Chapter 11 for more information.

17. C. When Setup Manager creates an answer file that is to be used by Sysprep for disk duplication, the file is named sysprep.inf by default. See Chapter 2 for more information.

18. D. Process throttling is used to specify the percentage of CPU processing that can be used by each Web site. See Chapter 10 for more information.

19. D. Striped volume sets do not contain parity information and are not fault tolerant. You can use the entire striped volume set to store data. See Chapter 6 for more information.

20. C. Placing a $ at the end of a share name hides it from users when they are browsing network resources. See Chapter 7 for more information.

21. A. OEM branding is used to configure an optional logo or background that is configured through Setup Manager when you create an answer file to be used with a disk image for installing Windows 2000 Server. See Chapter 2 for more information.

22. A. Using the Security Configuration and Analysis Tool, you can compare the security settings defined in a security template with a specific computer's actual security settings. See Chapter 5 for more information.

23. A. A Terminal Services server requires at least a Pentium processor and 128MB RAM to perform adequately. You should also provide an additional 10MB to 20MB RAM per client connection, depending on the applications they will be running. See Chapter 12 for more information.

24. C. The Microsoft Management Console program, `mmc.exe`, is the process that can track resources used by MMC snap-ins such as System Monitor. See Chapter 14 for more information.

25. A, C, D. You can copy files to the hard drive, but you can't copy files from the hard drive. With the Recovery Console, you can repair the computer's MBR and create and format partitions on the drive. See Chapter 15 for more information.

26. C, D. The only time you need to configure the internal network number is when you use the NWLink IPX/SPX/NetBIOS protocol and you are using File and Print Services for NetWare or when you are using IPX routing. See Chapter 9 for more information.

27. C. You use the `start` command to start new applications. The `/low` switch is used to start applications in an idle priority class. See Chapter 14 for more information.

28. C. You cannot configure logon workstations from the Profile tab. On Windows 2000 domain controllers, you can configure logon workstations from the Account tab. See Chapter 4 for more information.

29. D. Security options apply to computers as opposed to users and groups. See Chapter 5 for more information.

30. A. The Internet Control Message Protocol (ICMP) is used with `PING` to send echo request and echo reply packets to test the communication path between two TCP/IP hosts. See Chapter 9 for more information.

Chapter

1

Getting Started with Windows 2000 Server

MICROSOFT EXAM OBJECTIVES COVERED IN THIS CHAPTER

✓ Perform an attended installation of Windows 2000 Server.

✓ Troubleshoot failed installations.

✓ Upgrade a server from Microsoft Windows NT 4.0.

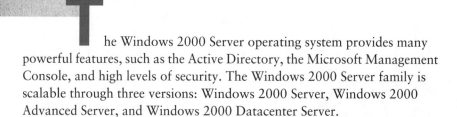

The Windows 2000 Server operating system provides many powerful features, such as the Active Directory, the Microsoft Management Console, and high levels of security. The Windows 2000 Server family is scalable through three versions: Windows 2000 Server, Windows 2000 Advanced Server, and Windows 2000 Datacenter Server.

Before you can do anything with Windows 2000 Server, you must first install the product. This process is actually fairly easy if you have prepared for the installation, know what the requirements are, and have met the pre-requisites for a successful installation.

You also need to decide if you want to perform a clean install or an upgrade. In order to upgrade, you must be running Windows NT Server 3.51 or 4. You should perform a clean install if your operating system does not support a Windows 2000 upgrade, if you want to dual-boot with your existing Windows NT system, or if you want to start from scratch. If your previous operating system can be upgraded to Windows 2000 Server and you want to retain your system settings, you should choose to perform an upgrade.

Once you've completed all of the planning, you are ready to install Windows 2000 Server. A clean install is a straightforward process that involves running a Setup program, running a Setup Wizard, and installing Windows 2000 Networking. If you are installing Windows 2000 as a domain controller, the final part of the process is to upgrade the server to a domain controller.

When you install Windows 2000 Server, you should also consider if the computer will be used for dual-boot or multi-boot purposes. Dual-booting or multi-booting allows you to have your computer boot with operating systems other than Windows 2000 Server.

If you have any problems with the installation, you will need to trouble-shoot them. Some problems that you might encounter are media defects or hardware that doesn't meet the minimum requirements.

In this chapter, you will learn how to install Windows 2000 Server. The first section of this chapter provides an overview of the Windows 2000 Server family. Next, you will learn how to prepare for a clean install of Windows 2000 Server, perform the installation, and set up for dual-booting. Then the upgrade process is covered. Finally, you will learn how to troubleshoot installation problems.

An Overview of the Windows 2000 Server Family

Windows 2000 Server is a powerful operating system with many features. The following are some of its main features:

- The Active Directory, which is based on Directory Services (the X.500 standard) and provides a scalable network architecture that can be used to support a single server with a few objects or thousands of servers with millions of objects

- An administrative console called the Microsoft Management Console (MMC), which can be customized by administrators to provide whatever administrative tools are required in a single logical framework

- Improved hardware support, including Plug-and-Play capabilities and hardware Wizards that facilitate new hardware installation

- File management services, which include features such as the Distributed file system (DFS), increased security through the Encrypting File System (EFS), and the ability to set disk quotas for users of volumes on a per volume basis

- High levels of security through utilities such as Security Configuration and Analysis, protocols such as Kerberos (for accessing resources in a Windows 2000 domain) and the IP Security Protocol (for authentication and data encryption), and the use of smart cards

Smart cards provide storage for protecting account numbers, passwords, and private keys.

- The ability to support remote operating system installations through services such as disk imaging

- Intellimirror services, which include features such as offline files and folders, automatic installation and repair of network applications, and the ability to control users' Desktops by specifying Desktop configurations

- Windows Terminal Services, which allow legacy Desktops to access the network using the server's processing power

- A high level of support for Internet connections through Internet Information Services (IIS)

- System recovery options available through Startup and Recovery Options when Windows 2000 Server is started

Windows 2000 Server is available in three different versions: Windows 2000 Server, Windows 2000 Advanced Server, and Windows 2000 Datacenter Server. You can choose the version that is best suited for your company's needs and budget. Windows 2000 Server is designed for use in small to medium-sized companies, and Windows 2000 Advanced Server and Windows 2000 Datacenter Server are designed for use by medium-sized to large companies or by Internet service providers (ISPs). The following sections describe the main features of the each of the three versions of Windows 2000 Server.

Windows 2000 Server

Windows 2000 Server contains all of the core features of the Windows 2000 Server family. Windows 2000 Server can serve as a file and print server, an applications server, a Web server, and a communications server. Some of the features that are supported by Windows 2000 Server include the following:

- Active Directory

- Internet and Web services

- High levels of security through Kerberos and a public key infrastructure

- Windows Terminal Services

- Support for up to 4GB of memory

- Support for up to four processors

Windows 2000 Advanced Server

Windows 2000 Advanced Server is a more powerful server designed for medium to large operations. It includes all of the features of Windows 2000 Server plus more, including the following:

- Network load balancing
- Cluster services for application fault tolerance
- Support for up to 8GB of memory
- Support for up to eight processors

Windows 2000 Datacenter Server

Windows 2000 Datacenter Server is the most powerful server in the Microsoft server family. This operating system is designed for large-scale enterprise networks. Windows 2000 Datacenter Server includes all of the features of Windows 2000 Advanced Server and adds the following features:

- More advanced clustering services
- Support for up to 64GB of memory
- Support for up to 16 processors (OEM versions can support up to 32 processors)

This book and the associated exam are based on Windows 2000 Server. All of the features of Windows 2000 Server are included in Windows 2000 Advanced Server and Windows 2000 Datacenter Server.

Preparing to Install Windows 2000 Server

Planning and preparation are key to making your Windows 2000 Server installation go smoothly. Before you begin the installation, you should know what is required for a successful installation and have all the pieces of information you'll need to supply during the installation process. In preparing for the installation, you should make sure you have the following information:

- What the hardware requirements are for Windows 2000 Server

- How to determine if your hardware is supported by Windows 2000 Server

- The difference between a clean installation and an upgrade

- What installation options are suitable for your system, such as which disk-partitioning scheme and file system you should select for Windows 2000 Server to use

Hardware Requirements

In order to install Windows 2000 Server successfully, your system must meet certain hardware requirements. Table 1.1 lists the minimum requirements as well as the more realistic recommended requirements.

The minimum hardware requirements for Windows 2000 Server and Windows 2000 Advanced Server are the same.

The minimum requirements specify the minimum hardware required before you should even consider installing Windows 2000 Server. These requirements assume that you are just installing the operating system and not running any special services or applications. For example, you may be able to get by with the minimum requirements if you are just installing the operating system in order to learn the basics of the software.

The recommended requirements are what Microsoft recommends for achieving what would be considered "acceptable performance" for the most common configurations. Since computer technology and the standard for acceptable performance are constantly changing, the recommendations are somewhat subjective. However, the recommended hardware requirements are based on the standards at the time that Windows 2000 Server was released.

The hardware requirements listed in Table 1.1 were those specified at the time this book was published. Check Microsoft's Web site at `www.microsoft.com/windows2000/guide/server/sysreq/default.asp` for the most current information.

TABLE 1.1   Hardware Requirements

Component	Minimum Requirement	Recommended Requirement
Processor	Pentium 133MHz or higher	Pentium 166MHz or higher
Memory	128MB	256MB
Disk space	2GB hard drive with 1GB of free disk space (more free space is required if you are installing Windows 2000 Server from over the network)	Depends on the applications and data you will store on your server
Network	None	Network card and any other hardware required by your network topology (if you want to connect to a network)
Display	Video adapter and monitor with VGA resolution	Video adapter and monitor with VGA resolution or higher

These requirements represent the operating system requirements. If you are running any processor- or memory-intensive tasks or applications, factor these requirements separately. When determining disk-space requirements for add-on software and data, a good rule of thumb is to plan what you need for the next 12 months, then double that number.

Depending on the installation method you choose, other devices may be required:

- If you are installing Windows 2000 Server from the CD, you should have at least a 12x CD-ROM drive.

- To start the installation locally and to create an Emergency Repair Disk, you need a high-density floppy drive.

- If you choose to install Windows 2000 Server from the network, you need a network connection and a server with the distribution files.

The Hardware Compatibility List (HCL)

Along with meeting the minimum requirements, your hardware should appear on the *Hardware Compatibility List (HCL)*. The HCL is an extensive list of computers and peripheral hardware that have been tested with the Windows 2000 Server operating system.

The Windows 2000 Server operating system requires control of the hardware for stability, efficiency, and security. The hardware and supported drivers on the HCL have been put through rigorous tests. Microsoft guarantees that the items on the list meet the requirements for Windows 2000 Server and do not have any incompatibilities that could affect the stability of the operating system.

If you call Microsoft for support, the first thing a Microsoft support engineer will ask about is your configuration. If you have any hardware that is not on the HCL, there is no guarantee of support.

To determine if your computer and peripherals are on the HCL, check the most up-to-date list at www.microsoft.com.

Clean Install or Upgrade?

Once you've determined that your hardware not only meets the minimum requirements but is also on the HCL, you need to decide whether you want to do a clean install or an upgrade.

If you already have Windows NT installed on your computer, you might want to upgrade that system to Windows 2000 Server. In an *upgrade*, you retain options such as the Desktop, users and groups, and program groups and items. During an upgrade, you point to a prior operating system, and the Windows 2000 Server files are loaded into the same folder that contained the former operating system. The upgrade process is covered in the "Upgrading to Windows 2000 Server" section later in this chapter.

The only operating systems that can be directly upgraded to Windows 2000 Server are Windows NT Server versions 3.51 and 4. Any other operating systems cannot be upgraded, but they may be able to coexist with Windows 2000 in a multi-boot environment. Multi-booting is covered in the "Supporting Multiple-Boot Options" section later in this chapter.

If you don't have Windows NT Server, you need to perform a clean install. A *clean install* puts the operating system into a new folder and uses its default settings the first time the operating system is loaded. You should perform a clean install if any of the following conditions are true:

- There is no operating system currently installed.

- You have an operating system installed that does not support an upgrade to Windows 2000 Server (such as DOS, Windows 3.*x*, Windows 9*x*, or Windows NT Workstation).

- You want to start from scratch, without keeping any existing preferences.

- You want to be able to dual-boot between Windows 2000 Server and your previous operating system.

The process for a clean installation is described in the "Running the Windows 2000 Server Installation Process" section later in this chapter.

Installation Options

There are many choices that you will need to make during the Windows 2000 Server installation process. The following are some of the options that you will configure:

- How your hard disk space will be partitioned

- The file system your partitions will use

- The licensing method the computer will use

- Whether the computer will be a part of a workgroup or a domain

- The language and locale for the computer's settings

Before you start the installation, you should know which choices you will select. The following sections describe the options and the considerations for picking the best ones for your installation.

Partitioning of Disk Space

Disk partitioning is the act of taking the physical hard drive and creating logical partitions. A *logical drive* is how space is allocated to the drive's primary and logical partitions. For example, if you have a 5GB hard drive, you might partition it into two logical drives: a C: drive, which might be 2GB, and a D: drive, which might be 3GB.

The following are some of the major considerations for disk partitioning:

- The amount of space required

- The location of the system and boot partition

- Any special disk configurations you will use

- The utility you will use to set up the partitions

These considerations are covered in detail in the following sections.

Size Matters

One important consideration in your disk-partitioning scheme is determining the partition size. You need to consider the amount of space taken up by your operating system, the applications that will be installed, and the amount of stored data. It is also important to consider the amount of space required in the future.

Just for Windows 2000 Server, Microsoft recommends that you allocate at least 1GB of disk space. This amount of space allows room for the operating system files and for future growth in terms of upgrades and installation files that are placed with the operating system files.

The System and Boot Partition

When you install Windows 2000, files will be stored in two locations: the system partition and the boot partition.

The *system partition* contains the files needed to boot the Windows 2000 Server operating system. The files stored on the system partition do not take any significant disk space. By default, the system partition uses the computer's active partition, which is usually the C: drive.

The *boot partition* contains the files that are the Windows operating system. By default, the Windows operating system files are located in a folder named WINNT. You can, however, specify the location of this folder during the installation process. Microsoft recommends that the boot partition be at least 1GB.

Special Disk Configurations

Windows 2000 Server supports several disk configurations. Options include simple, spanned, striped, mirrored, and RAID-5 volumes. These configuration options are covered in detail in Chapter 6, "Managing Disks."

Windows 2000 Professional does not support mirrored and RAID-5 volumes. It does support the dynamic volume types of simple, spanned, and striped.

Disk Partition Configuration Utilities

If you are partitioning your disk prior to installation, you can use several utilities, such as the DOS or Windows FDISK program or a third-party utility such as PowerQuest's Partition Magic. You might want to create only the first partition where Windows 2000 Server will be installed. You can then use the Disk Management utility in Windows 2000 to create any other partitions you need. The Windows 2000 Disk Management utility is covered in Chapter 6.

You can get more information about FDISK and other disk utilities from your DOS or Windows documentation. Also, basic DOS functions are covered in *MCSE 2000 JumpStart™ : Computer and Network Basics* by Lisa Donald (Sybex, 2000).

File System Selection

Another factor that determines your disk-partitioning scheme is the type of file system you use. Windows 2000 Server supports three file systems:

- File Allocation Table (FAT16)
- FAT32
- New Technology File System (NTFS)

FAT16

File Allocation Table (*FAT16*—originally just FAT) is the 16-bit file system widely used by DOS and Windows 3.*x*. FAT16 tracks where files are stored on a disk using a file allocation table and a directory-entry table. With FAT, the directory-entry table keeps track of the location of the file's first block, the filename and extension, the date and time stamps on the file, and any attributes associated with the file.

The disadvantages of FAT16 are that it only supports partitions up to 2GB and it does not offer the security features of NTFS.

The advantage of FAT is that it is backward compatible, which is important if the computer will be dual-booted with DOS or any other operating system. For example, DOS, Unix, Linux, OS/2, Windows 3.1, and Windows 9*x* are compatible with FAT16.

FAT32

FAT32 is the 32-bit version of FAT, which was first introduced in 1996 with Windows 95, OEM (original equipment manufacturer) Service Release 2 (OSR2).

FAT32's many advantages over FAT16 include the following:

- Disk partitions can be as large as 2TB (terabytes).

- More safeguards were added to provide fault tolerance in the event of disk failure.

- It improves disk-space usage by reducing cluster size.

The disadvantages of FAT32 are that it lacks several of the features offered by NTFS for a Windows 2000 system, such as local security, file encryption, disk quotas, and compression.

If you choose to use FAT, Windows 2000 will automatically format the partition with FAT16 if the partition is under 2GB. If the partition is over 2GB, it will be automatically partitioned as FAT32.

Windows NT 4 and earlier releases of NT do not support FAT32.

NTFS

New Technology File System (NTFS) is a file system designed to provide additional features for Windows NT and Windows 2000 computers. NTFS version 5 ships with Windows 2000. The following are some of the features of NTFS:

- The ability to set local security on files and folders.

- The option to compress data. This feature reduces disk-storage requirements.

- The flexibility to assign disk quotas. Disk quotas are used to limit the amount of disk space a user can use.

- The option to encrypt files. Encryption offers an additional level of security.

Unless you are planning on dual-booting your computer to an operating system other than Windows NT, Microsoft recommends using NTFS.

Licensing Mode

Licensing pays the good folks at Microsoft for all of the hard work they put into developing the Windows 2000 operating system. There are two main aspects to licensing: You pay for the local operating system, and you pay for client access. This means that if you are running Windows 2000 Server as your server and Windows 2000 Professional and Windows 98 for your clients, you must license the appropriate operating system for each individual computer. You also license the access of network servers.

When you install Windows 2000 Server, you are given the choice between Per Server or Per Seat licensing. *Per Server licensing* specifies the concurrent number of network connections that can be made to a server. *Per Seat licensing* specifies that each client will be licensed separately and that each client can access as many servers as it needs to.

You should choose Per Server licensing if your users access only one server at a time. For example, if you have ten users and one server, it will be less expensive to use Per Server than Per Seat licensing.

If your users access more than one server concurrently, you should use Per Seat licensing. For example, if you have ten users and two servers with Per Seat licensing, you will need to buy only ten client licenses, called *Client Access Licenses (CALs)*. If you used Per Server licensing, each server would need to be licensed for 10 connections.

Windows 2000 Professional only requires that you license the operating system.

Membership in a Domain or Workgroup

One Windows 2000 Server installation choice is whether your computer will be installed as a part of a *workgroup* or as part of a *domain*.

You should install as part of a workgroup if you are a part of a small, decentralized network or if you are running Windows 2000 Server on a nonnetworked computer. To join a workgroup, you simply choose that workgroup.

Domains are part of larger, centrally administered networks. You should install your computer as part of a domain if any Windows 2000 servers on your network are configured as domain controllers with the Active Directory installed. To join a domain, you must specify the name of a valid domain and provide the username and password of a user who has rights to add a computer to the domain. You can also pre-authorize a computer to join a domain through the Active Directory Users and Computers utility. A domain controller for the domain and a Domain Name System (DNS) server must be available to authenticate the request to join the domain.

Language and Locale

Language and locale settings are used to determine the language the computer will use. Windows 2000 supports many languages for the operating system interface and utilities.

Locale settings are used to configure the locality for items such as numbers, currencies, times, and dates. An example of a locality is that English for United States specifies a short date as *mm/dd/yyyy* (month/day/year), and English for South Africa specifies a short date as *yyyy/mm/dd* (year/month/day).

Choosing Your Installation Method

You can install Windows 2000 Server by using the distribution files on the Windows 2000 Server CD or by using files that have been copied to a network share point. The following sections describe each installation method.

Installing Windows 2000 from the CD

When you install Windows 2000 Server from the Windows 2000 Server CD, you have three options for starting the installation:

- You can boot to another operating system, access your CD-ROM drive, and run `WINNT.EXE` or `WINNT32.EXE`, depending on which operating system you are using.

- If your computer can boot to the CD, you can insert the Windows 2000 Server CD into its CD-ROM drive and restart your computer.

- If your computer has no operating system installed and does not support booting from the CD-ROM drive, you can use the Windows 2000 Server Setup Boot Disks.

Installing from Another Operating System

If your computer already has an operating system installed and you want to upgrade your operating system or dual-boot your computer, you boot your computer to the currently installed operating system, then start the Windows 2000 Server installation process.

Depending on which operating system you are running, you would use one of the following commands from the I386 folder to start the installation process:

- From Windows $9x$ or Windows NT, use `WINNT32.EXE`.

- From any other operating system, use `WINNT.EXE`.

Installing by Booting the Windows 2000 CD

If your computer can boot from the CD, then all you need to do to start the installation process is insert the Windows 2000 Professional CD and restart your computer. When the computer boots, the Windows 2000 Server installation process will launch automatically.

Installing from Setup Boot Disks

If your computer cannot boot from the CD-ROM drive, you can create floppy disks that boot to the Windows 2000 Server operating system. These disks are called the *Windows 2000 Server Setup Boot Disks*. Using these disks, you can install or reinstall the Windows 2000 Server.

The Windows 2000 Server Setup Boot Disks are not specific to a computer; they are general Windows 2000 Server disks that can be used on any computer running Windows 2000 Server.

To create the Windows 2000 Server Startup disks, you need four high-density floppy disks. They should be labeled Windows 2000 Server Setup Boot Disk, Windows 2000 Server Setup Disk #2, Windows 2000 Server Setup Disk #3, and Windows 2000 Server Setup Disk #4.

The command to create boot disks from Windows 2000 or Windows NT is MAKEBT32.EXE. The command to make boot disks from Windows 9x or a 16-bit operating system is MAKEBOOT.EXE. These utilities are located on the Windows 2000 Server CD in the BOOTDISK folder.

The Windows 2000 Server Setup Boot Disks are also used for the Recovery Console and the Emergency Repair Disk (disaster-recovery methods), which are covered in Chapter 15, "Performing System Recovery Functions." You will create Windows 2000 Server Setup Boot Disks in an exercise in Chapter 15.

Installing Windows 2000 over a Network Connection

If you are installing Windows 2000 Server over the network, you need a distribution server and a computer with a network connection. A *distribution server* is a server that has the Windows 2000 Server distribution files in a shared folder. To install Windows 2000 Server over the network, boot the target computer. Then, attach to the distribution server and access the share that has the WINNT folder shared. Next, launch WINNT.EXE or WINNT32.EXE (depending on the computer's current operating system). Finally, complete the Windows 2000 Server installation.

Running the Windows 2000 Server Installation Process

This section describes how to run the Windows 2000 Server installation process. As explained in the previous section, you can run the installation from a CD or over a network. The only difference in the installation procedure is the point where you start—from your CD-ROM drive or from a network share. The steps in the following sections assume that the disk drive is clean and that you are starting the installation using the Windows 2000 Server CD.

Microsoft ✓ *Exam Objective*

Perform an attended installation of Windows 2000 Server.

There are four main steps in the Windows 2000 Server installation process:

- Run the Setup program. If you boot from DOS or Windows 9*x*, the Setup program will be DOS-based. If you boot from Windows NT, the Setup program will be GUI-based.

- Run the Setup Wizard.

- Install Windows 2000 Networking.

- Upgrade the server to a domain controller (if this is a domain controller rather than a member server).

Each of these steps is covered in detail in the following sections.

The following sections give the details of the installation process to show how the process works. But you should not actually install Windows 2000 Server until you reach the "Setting Up Your Computer for Hands-on Exercises" section. In the exercises in that section, you'll set up a domain controller and a member server, which you'll use to complete the rest of the exercises in this book.

Running the Setup Program

The Setup program starts the Windows 2000 Server installation. In this stage of the installation, you start the installation program, choose the partition where Windows 2000 will be installed, and then copy files.

The following steps are involved in running the Setup program:

1. On an Intel computer, access your CD-ROM drive and open the I386 folder. This folder contains all of the installation files for an Intel-based computer.

2. Start the Setup program.

   - If you are installing Windows 2000 Server from an operating system other than Windows 9x or Windows NT, launch WINNT.EXE.

   - If you are installing Windows 2000 Server from 32-bit mode Windows 9x or Windows NT, launch WINNT32.EXE.

3. The Windows 2000 Setup dialog box appears. Your first choice is to specify the location of the distribution files. By default, this would be where you executed the WINNT program. Normally, you just accept the default path and press Enter.

4. The Setup files are copied to your disk. If the SMARTDRV program is not loaded on your computer, you will see a message recommending that you load SMARTDRV. This is a disk-caching program that speeds up the process of copying files. SMARTDRV ships with DOS and Windows.

With SMARTDRV, it usually takes a few minutes to copy the files. Without SMARTDRV, it can take more than an hour.

5. Once the files have been copied, you are prompted to remove any floppy disks and to restart the computer.

6. The opening Windows 2000 Setup dialog box appears. At this point, you can set up Windows by pressing Enter, repair a Windows 2000 installation by pressing R, or quit the setup process by pressing F3.

7. The Windows 2000 License Agreement dialog box appears. You can accept the License Agreement by pressing F8 or you can disagree by pressing Escape (or F3 if you are in DOS mode). If you press Escape, the installation program will terminate, and your name and address will be sent directly to Microsoft for further analysis (just kidding about that second part).

8. The next dialog box asks you which partition you want to use to set up Windows 2000. You can pick a partition that already exists, or you can choose free space and a partition will be created for you.

Whichever partition you choose must have at least 1GB of free space. The default folder name will be WINNT. At this point, you can create or delete partitions and the file systems the partitions will use.

After you indicate the partition that will be used as the Windows 2000 boot partition, the Windows installation files will be copied to the installation folders. Then the computer automatically reboots.

Running the Windows 2000 Setup Wizard

Once your computer finishes with the Setup program, the computer will restart, and the Windows 2000 Setup Wizard will start automatically. When the Setup Wizard starts, the first thing it will do is detect and install device drivers. This process will take several minutes, and during this process, your screen may flicker.

Then the Setup Wizard will gather information about your locale, name, product key, licensing mode, computer name, and password, using the following dialog boxes (you click Next after completing each dialog box):

Regional Settings   From this dialog box, you choose your locale and keyboard settings. Locale settings are used to configure international options for numbers, currencies, times, and dates. Keyboard settings allow you to configure your keyboard to support different local characters or keyboard layouts. For example, you can choose Danish or United States-Dvorak through this option.

Personalize Your Software   In this dialog box, you fill in the Name and Organization boxes. This information is used to personalize your operating system software and the applications that you install. If you install Windows 2000 Server in a workgroup, the Name entry here is used for the initial user.

Product Key   In the boxes at the bottom of this dialog box, you type in the 25-character product key, which can be found on the back of your Windows 2000 Server CD case.

Licensing Modes   You can choose from Per Server licensing or Per Seat licensing. (See the "Licensing Modes" section earlier in this chapter for details about these two choices.)

Computer Name and Administrator Password   Your computer name can be up to 15 characters. Here you specify a name that will uniquely identify your computer on the network. The Setup Wizard suggests a name, but you can change it to another name. In this dialog box, you also type and confirm the Administrator password. An account called Administrator will automatically be created as a part of the installation process.

Be sure that the computer name is a unique name within your network. If you are part of a corporate network, you should also verify that the computer name follows the naming convention specified by your Information Services (IS) department.

Modem Dialing Information   If you have a Plug-and-Play modem installed, you will see the Modem Dialing Information dialog box. Here, you specify your country/region, your area code (or city code), whether you dial a number to get an outside line, and whether the telephone system uses tone dialing or pulse dialing.

Date and Time Settings   In this dialog box, you set your date and time settings and the time zone in which your computer is located. You can also configure the computer to automatically adjust for daylight savings time.

Network Settings   This dialog box is used to specify how you want to connect to other computers, networks, and the Internet. You have two choices:

- Typical Settings installs network connections for Client for Microsoft Networks, as well as File and Print Sharing for Microsoft Networks. It also installs the TCP/IP protocol with an automatically assigned address.

- Custom Settings allows you to customize your network settings. You can choose whether or not you want to use Client for Microsoft Networks, File and Print Sharing for Microsoft Networks, and the TCP/IP protocol. You should use the custom settings if you need to specify particular network settings, such as a specific IP address and subnet mask (rather than using an automatically assigned address).

Workgroup or Computer Domain   In this dialog box, you specify whether your computer will be installed as a part of a local workgroup or as a part of a domain. (See the "Membership in Domain or Workgroup" section earlier in this chapter for details about these choices.)

The computer will perform some final tasks, including installing Start menu items, registering components, saving settings, and removing any temporary files. This will take several minutes. After the final tasks are complete, you will see the Completing the Windows 2000 Setup Wizard dialog box. Remove the CD from your computer, and click the Finish button to restart your computer.

Installing Windows 2000 Networking

Once your computer finishes with the Setup Wizard and the computer restarts, the Network Identification Wizard starts automatically. The Network Identification Wizard is responsible for the network component installation.

Depending on your server's configuration, you may see a dialog box that deals with how users will log on to the computer. This dialog box offers two choices:

- The Users Must Enter a User Name and Password to Use This Computer option does just what it says: Users must enter a username and password to log on to the computer.

- The Windows Always Assumes the Following User Has Logged On option sets up Windows 2000 so that the user does not need to enter a username or password to use the computer. If you are the only person using the computer in a secure, nonnetworked environment, you might choose this option. However, in a networked, business environment, you do not want to allow such a security risk.

Next, the Network Identification Wizard prompts you to finish the Wizard. If you chose the Users Must Enter a User Name and a Password option, you need to provide a valid Windows 2000 username and password in the Log On to Windows dialog box. At this point, the only users that are enabled are Administrator and the *initial user* (which is the username you entered for identification).

After the installation is complete, you are logged on and greeted with the Windows 2000 Server Getting Started Wizard. This Wizard helps new users navigate the operating system.

Upgrading a Member Server to a Domain Controller

Once a server has been installed with the Windows 2000 operating system, you can upgrade the server to a domain controller using the *DCPROMO* utility.

The Logical Organization of the Active Directory

The Windows 2000 *Active Directory* (*AD*) is designed to be a scalable network structure. The logical structure of the Active Directory consists of containers, domains, and organizational units (OUs).

A *container* is an Active Directory object that holds other Active Directory objects. Domains and OUs are examples of container objects.

A *domain* is the main logical unit of organization in the Active Directory. The objects in a domain share common security and account information. Each domain must have at least one domain controller. The *domain controller* is a Windows 2000 Server computer that stores the complete domain database.

Each domain can consist of multiple OUs, logically organized in a hierarchical structure. OUs may contain users, groups, security policies, computers, printers, file shares, and other Active Directory objects.

Domains are connected to one another through logical structure relationships. The relationships are implemented through domain trees and domain forests.

A *domain tree* is a hierarchical organization of domains in a single, contiguous namespace. In the Active Directory, a *tree* is a hierarchy of domains that are connected to each other through a series of trust relationships (logical links that combine two or more domains into a single administrative unit). The advantage of using trust relationships between domains is that they allow users in one domain to access resources in another domain, assuming the users have the proper access rights.

A *domain forest* is a set of trees that does not form a contiguous namespace. For example, you might have a forest if your company merged with another company. With a forest, you could each maintain a separate corporate identity through your namespace, but share information across the Active Directory.

You can specify that the server is the first domain controller in a new domain or add it to an existing domain. If you already have the Active Directory installed on your network, you can create a new child domain in the existing domain tree or install the domain tree as part of an existing forest. The steps in this section assume that you are creating the first domain controller in a new domain and that you are installing the Active Directory for the first time (this is our configuration for the exercises in the next section). These steps also assume that DNS is not yet configured on your network.

Configuring DNS and other networking services is covered in Chapter 9, "Managing Network Interoperability."

To upgrade a server to a domain controller, take the following steps:

1. Select Start ➢ Run, type **DCPROMO** in the Run dialog box, and click the OK button.

2. The Active Directory Installation Wizard starts. Click the Next button.

3. The Domain Controller Type dialog box appears, as shown in Figure 1.1. Select the Domain Controller for a New Domain option and click the Next button. (If you wanted to add the domain controller to an existing domain, you would select the Additional Domain Controller for an Existing Domain option.)

FIGURE 1.1   The Domain Controller Type dialog box

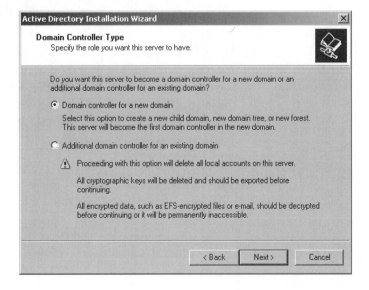

4. The Create Tree or Child Domain dialog box appears, as shown in Figure 1.2. To create a new domain tree, select the Create a New Domain Tree option and click the Next button. (If you already had the Active Directory installed on your network and you wanted to create a new child domain in the existing domain tree, you would select the Create a New Child Domain in an Existing Domain Tree option.)

FIGURE 1.2   The Create Tree or Child Domain dialog box

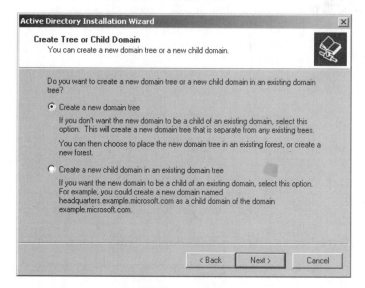

5. The Create or Join Forest dialog box appears, as shown in Figure 1.3. Select the Create a New Forest of Domain Trees option and click the Next button. (If you already had the Active Directory installed on your network and you wanted the domain tree to be installed as a part of an existing forest, you would select the Place This New Domain Tree in an Existing Forest option.)

FIGURE 1.3 The Create or Join Forest dialog box

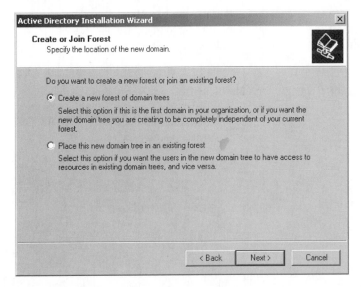

6. The New Domain Name dialog box appears, as shown in Figure 1.4. Specify the full DNS name for the new domain, such as `sampledomain .com`, and click the Next button to continue. (Usually, DNS is configured for the network before you create a domain controller.)

FIGURE 1.4 The New Domain Name dialog box

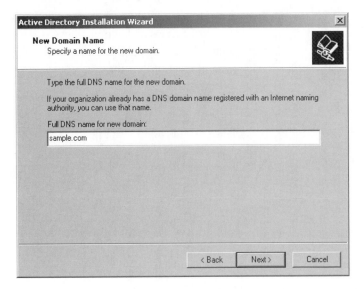

7. The NetBIOS Domain Name dialog box appears, as shown in Figure 1.5. NetBIOS domain names are used for compatibility with Windows NT clients. By default, the domain NetBIOS name is the same as the DNS name. You can change this to another name or accept the default. Click the Next button to continue.

FIGURE 1.5 The NetBIOS Domain Name dialog box

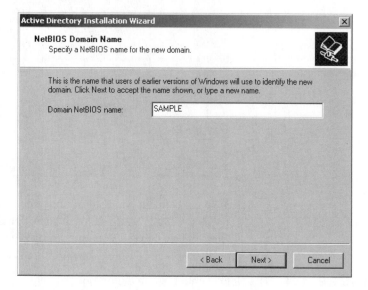

8. The Database and Log Locations dialog box appears, as shown in Figure 1.6. This dialog box allows you to specify the locations of the Active Directory database and the database log files. You can accept the default locations for these files or select other locations. Then click the Next button.

FIGURE 1.6 The Database and Log Locations dialog box

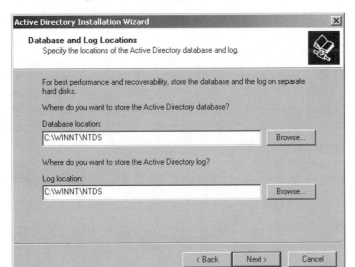

9. The Shared System Volume dialog box appears, as shown in Figure 1.7. This volume must be an NTFS 5 volume. You can accept the default folder location or select another location. Then click the Next button. (If the partition is not NTFS 5, you will see an error message indicating that the file system must be converted.)

FIGURE 1.7 The Shared System Volume dialog box

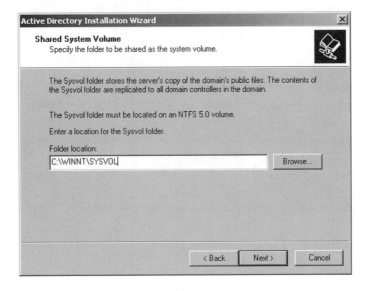

10. If DNS has not been configured, you will see an informational message stating that the DNS server can't be located. Click the OK button to continue.

11. The Configure DNS dialog box appears, as shown in Figure 1.8. To configure DNS, select the Yes, Install and Configure DNS on This Computer (Recommended) option. If you want to install DNS manually, select No, I Will Install and Configure DNS Myself. After you have made your selection, click the Next button to continue.

FIGURE 1.8   The Configure DNS dialog box

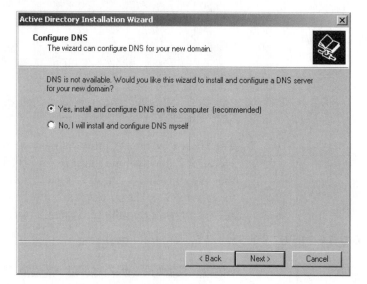

12. The Permissions dialog box appears, as shown in Figure 1.9. If you want to be able to use server programs on servers that run earlier versions of Windows or are in a domain operating under a previous version of Windows, select the Permissions Compatible with pre-Windows 2000 Servers option. Otherwise, select the Permissions Compatible only with Windows 2000 Servers option. After you have made your selection, click the Next button to continue.

FIGURE 1.9   The Permissions dialog box

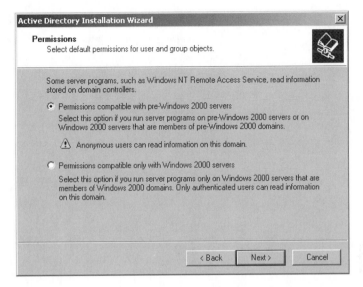

13. The Directory Services Restore Mode Administrator Password dialog box appears, as shown in Figure 1.10. This dialog box allows you to specify a password that can be used if the server needs to be restarted in the Directory Services Restore Mode. Enter and confirm this password, then click the Next button.

The Directory Services Restore Mode is an option on the Advanced Options menu, which is available at Windows 2000 startup. See Chapter 15 for details on this and other advanced startup options.

FIGURE 1.10 The Directory Services Restore Mode Administrator Password dialog box

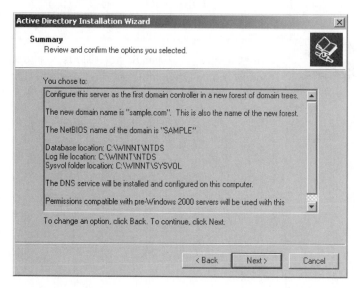

14. The Summary dialog box appears, as shown in Figure 1.11. This dialog box allows you to confirm all of the selections you have made. If this information is correct, click the Next button.

FIGURE 1.11 The Summary dialog box

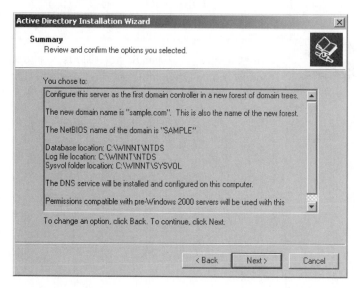

15. You see the Configuring Active Directory dialog box, which lets you know that the Wizard is configuring the Active Directory and that this process may take several minutes. Then you will be asked to insert your Windows 2000 Server CD so that additional files may be copied. Insert the CD and click the OK button.

16. The Configuring Active Directory dialog box reappears. When the process is complete, the Completing the Active Directory Installation Wizard dialog box appears. Click the Finish button.

17. You are prompted to restart Windows 2000 so that the changes will be in effect. Click the Restart Now button.

Once a server is upgraded to a domain controller, you can use the Active Directory. Creating domains, designing your DNS structure, and planning the Active Directory are covered in detail in *MCSE: Windows 2000 Directory Services Administration Study Guide*, 2nd. ed., by Anil Desai with James Chellis (Sybex, 2001).

Setting Up Your Computer for Hands-on Exercises

The exercises in this book assume that you have two computers configured in a specified manner. In the exercises in this chapter, you will install Windows 2000 Server on one computer as a domain controller and Windows 2000 Server on a second computer as a member server in the domain.

You should make a complete backup of your computer before doing any repartitioning or installation of new operating systems. All data will be lost during this process!

Installing Windows 2000 Server as a Domain Controller

For the exercises to work properly, you should make sure that the computer that will act as your server meets the list of requirements specified in Table 1.1. Your server should have a network card installed, and it should have at least a 3GB drive that is configured with the minimum space requirements and partitions. Other exercises in this book assume that your server is configured as follows:

- 2GB (about 2000MB) C: primary partition with the FAT or FAT32 file system

- 500MB D: extended partition with the FAT or FAT32 file system (this partition will be converted to NTFS in Chapter 6)

- 500MB of free space (you will create a new partition with this free space in Chapter 6)

Of course, you can allocate more space to your partitions if it is available. Exercise 1.1 assumes that you are not currently running Windows NT and that you are performing a clean install and not an upgrade. Your partitions should be created and formatted, and SMARTDRV should be loaded.

As noted earlier in this chapter, you can set up your partitions through the DOS or Windows FDISK utility or a third-party program. For example, if you have a Windows 98 computer, you can use it to create a Windows 98 boot disk. Set up the disk with FDISK, FORMAT, and SMARTDRV. The hard drive will then boot, providing a C: drive of 1.2MB, a D: drive of 400MB, unallocated disk space, and access to the E: drive, which is the CD-ROM drive.

Before you start, you should note what values you will use for the following options for the domain controller:

- Name and Organization

- Computer Name

- Workgroup Name

- Administrator Password (if one will be assigned)

- Domain Name

- Directory Services Restore Mode Administrator Password (if one will be assigned)

EXERCISE 1.1

Installing Windows 2000 Server as a Domain Controller

In this exercise, you will install Windows 2000 Server as a domain controller, which is a four-part process.

Running the Setup Program

1. Boot your computer and insert the Windows 2000 CD into your CD-ROM drive.

2. From the DOS prompt on your computer, access your CD-ROM drive. If you have configured your computer as we recommended, your CD-ROM drive should be E:.

3. From the CD-ROM drive prompt, change directories to I386 by typing **CD I386** and pressing Enter.

4. From the \I386> prompt, type **WINNT** and press Enter.

5. From the Windows 2000 Setup dialog box, press Enter to accept the default path location for the Windows 2000 distribution files. It will take a few minutes to copy the files.

6. Remove any floppy disks from the computer and press Enter to restart the computer.

7. The computer restarts, and the Welcome to Setup screen appears. Press Enter to set up Windows 2000.

8. The License Agreement dialog box appears. Scroll down to the bottom of the page. Press F8 to agree to the license terms if you wish to continue.

9. In the next dialog box, specify the C: partition as the one you want to use to set up Windows 2000. Then press Enter.

10. In the next dialog box, choose to convert the partition to NTFS. Then confirm the conversion by pressing C.

11. Setup now examines your disks. The Windows installation files will be automatically copied to the installation folder, which will take a few minutes. After the files are copied, the computer will automatically reboot. After the computer reboots, the Welcome to the Setup Wizard dialog box will appear. When prompted, click the Next button to continue. (If you do not make a selection within 10 seconds, the installation will continue automatically.)

Running the Windows 2000 Setup Wizard

After the computer reboots, the Windows 2000 Server Setup program will automatically detect and install drivers on your computer. This process will take a few minutes.

1. The Regional Settings dialog box appears. Click the Next button to accept the default settings and continue.

2. In the Personalize Your Software dialog box, type your name and organization. Click the Next button.

3. In the Product Key dialog box, type the 25-character product key (this key can be found on a sticker on the CD case). Click the Next button.

4. The Licensing Modes dialog box appears. Accept the default configuration of Per Server licensing and five concurrent connections. Click the Next button to continue.

5. The Computer Name and Administrator Password dialog box appears. Type in the computer name. You can also specify an Administrator password (since this computer will be used for practice, you can leave the Password field blank if you want to). Click the Next button.

6. If you have a Plug-and-Play modem installed, the Modem Dialing Information dialog box appears. Specify the settings for your environment and click the Next button.

7. The Date and Time Settings dialog box appears. Verify that all of the settings are correct and click the Next button.

8. After the Networking component files are copied (which takes a few minutes), the Network Settings dialog box appears. Click the Custom Settings button and then click the Next button.

9. In the Windows 2000 Server Setup dialog box, highlight Internet Protocol (TCP/IP) and click the Properties button.

10. In the Internet Protocol (TCP/IP) Properties dialog box, click the Use the Following IP Address radio button. In the IP Address text box, enter **131.200.2.1**. In the Subnet Mask text box, enter **255.255.0.0**. Click the OK button. (Installing and configuring TCP/IP is discussed in detail in Chapter 9, "Managing Network Interoperability.")

11. Click the Next button in the Windows 2000 Server Setup dialog box.

12. In the Workgroup and Computer Domain dialog box, confirm that the No, This Computer Is Not on a Network, or Is on a Network without a Domain option is selected to indicate that you don't want to put the computer in a domain (because no domain exists at this stage). In this dialog box, you can accept the default workgroup name, WORKGROUP, or specify a unique workgroup name. Because this computer is a practice one, the workgroup name is not important. Click the Next button. The Setup components are installed, which takes several minutes.

13. When the Completing the Windows 2000 Setup Wizard appears, remove the CD from the drive and click the Finish button. The computer will restart.

14. When the computer reboots, choose Microsoft Windows 2000 from the boot selection options screen by pressing Enter. (This is the default selection if no choice is made.)

Running the Network Identification Wizard

15. Windows 2000 Server starts and displays the Welcome to the Network Identification Wizard dialog box. Press Ctrl+Alt+Delete to begin. By default, the Administrator account is displayed. Click the OK button to continue.

16. The Windows 2000 Configure Your Server dialog box appears. Click the I Will Configure This Server Later radio button and click the Next button.

17. Uncheck the Show This Screen at Startup option. Then close the Windows 2000 Configure Your Server dialog box.

Upgrading the Server to a Domain Controller

18. Select Start ➢ Run, type DCPROMO in the Run dialog box, and click the OK button.

19. When the Active Directory Installation Wizard begins, click the Next button.

20. In the Domain Controller Type dialog box, select the Domain Controller for a New Domain option and click the Next button.

EXERCISE 1.1 *(continued)*

21. In the Create Tree or Child Domain dialog box, select the Create a New Domain Tree option and click the Next button.

22. In the Create or Join Forest dialog box, select the Create a New Forest of Domain Trees option and click the Next button.

23. In the New Domain Name dialog box, enter a domain name (such as **sampledomain.com**) for the full DNS name and click the Next button.

24. In the NetBIOS Domain Name dialog box, click the Next button to accept the default value and continue.

25. In the Database and Log Locations dialog box, click the Next button to accept the default values and continue.

26. In the Shared System Volume dialog box, click the Next button to accept the default value and continue.

27. When you see an informational message stating that the DNS server can't be located, click the OK button to continue.

28. In the Configure DNS dialog box, select the Yes, Install and Configure DNS on This Computer (Recommended) option. Click the Next button to continue.

29. In the Permissions dialog box, select either option (whether you have permissions that are compatible with pre–Windows 2000 servers or not doesn't matter for this test server). Click the Next button to continue.

30. In the Directory Services Restore Mode Administrator Password dialog box, you can specify a password or leave this dialog box blank (since this is a test server). Click the Next button to continue.

31. If the information in the Summary dialog box is correct, click the Next button.

32. The Configuring Active Directory dialog box appears. When you are prompted, insert your Windows 2000 Server CD so that additional files may be copied and click the OK button.

EXERCISE 1.1 *(continued)*

33. The Configuring Active Directory dialog box appears again as the Wizard is configuring the Active Directory. When the process is complete, click the Finish button in the Completing the Active Directory Installation Wizard dialog box.

34. When you are prompted to click the Restart Now button to restart Windows 2000 Server, remove the Windows 2000 Server CD, and then click the Restart Now button.

Installing Windows 2000 Server as a Member Server

In Exercise 1.2, you will install Windows 2000 Server as a member server of the domain you created in Exercise 1.1. This computer should be configured in the same manner as the computer in Exercise 1.1.

Before you start, you should note what values you will use for the following options for the member server:

- Name and Organization
- Computer Name

EXERCISE 1.2

Installing Windows 2000 Server as a Member Server

In this exercise, you will install Windows 2000 Server as a member server, which is a three-part process.

Running the Setup Program

1. Boot your computer and insert the Windows 2000 CD into your CD-ROM drive.

2. From the DOS prompt on your computer, access your CD-ROM drive. If you have configured your computer as we recommended, your CD-ROM drive should be E:.

3. From the CD-ROM drive prompt, change directories to I386 by typing **CD I386** and pressing Enter.

4. From the \I386> prompt, type **WINNT** and press Enter.

5. From the Windows 2000 Setup dialog box, press Enter to accept the default path location for the Windows 2000 distribution files. It will take a few minutes to copy the files.

6. Remove any floppy disks from the computer and press Enter to restart the computer.

7. The computer restarts, and the Welcome to Setup screen appears. Press Enter to set up Windows 2000.

8. The License Agreement dialog box appears. Scroll down to the bottom of the page. Press F8 to agree to the license terms if you wish to continue.

9. In the next dialog box, specify the C: partition as the one you want to use to set up Windows 2000. Then press Enter.

10. In the next dialog box, choose to convert the partition to NTFS. Then confirm the conversion by pressing C.

11. Setup now examines your disks. The Windows installation files will be automatically copied to the installation folder, which will take a few minutes. After the files are copied, the computer will automatically reboot.

Running the Windows 2000 Setup Wizard

After the computer reboots, the Windows 2000 Server Setup program will automatically detect and install drivers on your computer. This process will take a few minutes.

12. The Regional Settings dialog box appears. Click Next to accept the default settings and continue.

13. In the Personalize Your Software dialog box, type your name and organization. Click the Next button.

14. In the Product Key dialog box, type the 25-character product key. Click the Next button.

15. The Licensing Modes dialog box appears. Accept the default configuration of Per Server licensing and five concurrent connections. Click the Next button to continue.

16. The Computer Name and Administrator Password dialog box appears. Type in the computer name. Specify an Administrator password if desired. Click the Next button.

17. If you have a Plug-and-Play modem installed, the Modem Dialing Information dialog box appears. Specify the settings for your environment and click the Next button.

18. The Date and Time Settings dialog box appears. Verify that all of the settings are correct and click the Next button.

19. After the Networking component files are copied (which takes a few minutes), the Network Settings dialog box appears. Click the Custom Settings button and then click the Next button.

20. In the Windows 2000 Server Setup dialog box, highlight Internet Protocol (TCP/IP) and click the Properties button.

21. In the Internet Protocol (TCP/IP) Properties dialog box, click the Use the Following IP Address radio button. In the IP Address text box, enter **131.200.2.2**. In the Subnet Mask text box, enter **255.255.0.0**. Click the OK button.

22. Click the Next button in the Windows 2000 Server Setup dialog box.

23. In the Workgroup and Computer Domain dialog box, select the Yes, Make This Computer a Member of the Following Domain option. In the Workgroup or Computer Domain field, type the domain name you specified in Exercise 1.1. Click the Next button.

24. In the Join Computer to *domain* Domain dialog box, specify **Administrator** as the username and enter the password you used in Exercise 1.1. Then click the OK button. The Setup components are installed, which takes several minutes.

25. When the Completing the Windows 2000 Setup Wizard appears, remove the CD from the drive and click the Finish button. The computer will restart.

26. When the computer reboots, choose Microsoft Windows 2000 from the boot selection options screen by pressing Enter. (This is the default selection if no choice is made.)

Running the Network Identification Wizard

27. Windows 2000 Server starts and displays the Welcome to the Network Identification Wizard dialog box. Press Ctrl+Alt+Delete to begin. By default, the Administrator account is displayed. Click the OK button to continue.

28. The Windows 2000 Configure Your Server dialog box appears. Click the I Will Configure This Server Later radio button and click the Next button.

29. Uncheck the Show This Screen at Startup option. Then close the Windows 2000 Configure Your Server dialog box.

 Real World Scenario

Upgrading Your Network to Windows 2000

You are the network administrator of a Windows NT 4 network. You use the Windows NT domain model and have hundreds of NT Servers and Workstations. You want to upgrade to Windows 2000, but you're not sure how to proceed.

Upgrading a network from Windows NT 4.0 to Windows 2000 is not a trivial process and takes careful planning. The major steps that you should complete within the upgrade are as follows:

1. Create a deployment plan. This should include the goals and scope of the upgrade.

2. Build a test lab that can be used to test the upgrade in a nonproduction environment. Document all findings.

3. Prepare your network infrastructure for Windows 2000.

4. Determine the domain migration strategy. This will be used to migrate your Windows NT domains to the Windows 2000 Active Directory.

5. Plan the Windows 2000 security.

6. Upgrade or install your domain controllers.

7. Upgrade or install your member servers.

8. Ensure the availability of critical applications and services.

9. Test client computer's applications for compatibility.

10. Define the client requirements and configuration standards and upgrade client computers.

Microsoft provides documentation for Windows 2000 upgrade and deployment at www.microsoft.com/windows2000/library/resources/reskit/dpg/default.asp.

Supporting Multiple-Boot Options

You may want to install Windows 2000 Server but still be able to run other operating systems. *Dual-booting* or *multi-booting* allows your computer to boot multiple operating systems. Your computer will be automatically configured for dual-booting if there was a supported operating system on your computer prior to the Windows 2000 Server installation (and you didn't upgrade from that operating system).

One reason for dual-booting is to test various systems. If you have a limited number of computers in your test lab, and you want to be able to test multiple configurations, you dual-boot. For example, you might configure one computer to multiple-boot with Windows NT Workstation 4, Windows NT Server 4 configured as a primary domain controller (PDC), Windows 2000 Professional, and Windows 2000 Server.

Another reason to set up dual-booting is for software backward compatibility. For example, you may have an application that works with Windows 95 but not under Windows 2000 Server. If you want to use

Windows 2000 and still be able to access your legacy application, you can configure a dual-boot.

Here are the keys to successful dual-boot configurations:

- Make sure you have plenty of disk space. It's a good idea to put each operating system on a separate partition, although this is not required.

- Put the simplest operating systems on first. If you want to support dual-booting between DOS and Windows 2000 Server, DOS must be installed first. If you install Windows 2000 Server first, you cannot install DOS without ruining your Windows 2000 Server configuration. You would also install Windows 9x prior to installing Windows 2000 Server for the same reason.

- Never upgrade to Windows 2000 dynamic disks. Dynamic disks are seen only by Windows 2000 and are not recognized by any other operating system, including Windows NT.

- Do not convert your file system to NTFS if you are planning a dual-boot with any operating system other than Windows NT or Windows 2000. These operating systems are the only ones that recognize NTFS.

- If you will dual-boot with Windows NT 4, you must turn off disk compression, or Windows 2000 will not be able to read the drive properly.

If you are planning on dual-booting with Windows NT 4, you should upgrade it to NT 4 Service Pack 4 (or higher), which provides NTFS version 5 support.

Once you have installed each operating system, you can choose the operating system that you will boot to during the boot process. You will see a boot options screen that asks you to choose which operating system you want to boot.

Upgrading to Windows 2000 Server

An upgrade allows you to preserve existing settings. A clean install places Windows 2000 in a new folder. After a clean install, you need to reinstall all of your applications and reset your preferences.

Microsoft
Exam
Objective

Upgrade a server from Microsoft Windows NT 4.0.

You should perform an upgrade if the following conditions are true:

- You are running Windows NT Server 3.51 or 4.

- You want to keep your existing applications and preferences.

- You want to preserve any local users and groups you've created under Windows NT.

- You want to upgrade your current operating system with the Windows 2000 Server operating system.

The upgrade process for Windows 2000 Server and Professional is similar. The major differences involve the upgrade paths and hardware requirements.

Preparing to Upgrade to Windows 2000 Server

Before you run the upgrade process, you need to make sure that your system meets the operating system and hardware requirements. Then you should prepare your computer for the upgrade. These preparations are discussed in detail in the following sections.

Server Upgrade Paths and Requirements

The only operating systems that you can upgrade to Windows 2000 Server are Windows NT Server 3.51 and Windows NT Server 4. If you are running a version of Windows NT Server prior to 3.51, you first need to upgrade to Windows NT Server 3.51 or Windows NT Server 4 before you can upgrade to Windows 2000 Server.

There is no upgrade path from Windows NT Workstation to Windows 2000 Server.

The hardware requirements for upgrading are the same as those for a clean install:

- Pentium 133MHz or higher processor

- 128MB of RAM (256MB is better)

- 2GB hard drive with at least 1GB of free disk space

- VGA or better resolution monitor

Along with meeting these requirements, your hardware should be listed on the HCL, which was discussed earlier in this chapter.

The hardware requirements listed here were those specified at the time this book was published. Check Microsoft's Web site at www.microsoft.com/ windows2000/upgrade/ for the latest information about system requirements, upgrade issues, and hardware and software compatibility.

An Upgrade Checklist

Once you have made the decision to upgrade, you should develop a plan of attack. The following upgrade checklist will help you plan and implement a successful upgrade strategy.

- Back up all of your data and configuration files and verify that you can successfully restore your backup. Before you make any major changes to your computer's configuration, you should always back up your data and configuration files. Chances are if you have a valid backup, you won't have any problems. Chances are if you don't have a valid backup, you will have problems.

- Delete any unnecessary files or applications, and clean up any program groups or program items you don't use. Theoretically, you want to delete all of the junk on your computer before you upgrade. Think of this as the spring-cleaning step.

- Perform a disk scan, a current virus scan, and defragmentation. These are also similar to spring-cleaning chores. This step just prepares your drive for the upgrade. You should verify that there are no problems with your drive prior to the upgrade.

- Uncompress any partitions that have been compressed with DriveSpace or DoubleSpace. You cannot upgrade partitions that are currently compressed.

- Verify that your computer meets the requirements for an upgrade. Be sure that your computer meets the minimum hardware requirements for Windows 2000 Server and that all of your hardware is on the HCL.

- Take an inventory of your current configuration. This inventory should include documentation of your current network configuration, the applications that are installed, the hardware items and their configuration, the services that are running, and any profile and policy settings.

- Perform the upgrade. In this step, you upgrade from your previous operating system to Windows 2000 Server.

- Verify your configuration. After Windows 2000 Server has been installed, use your inventory to verify that the upgrade was successful.

Performing the Windows 2000 Server Upgrade

As you would expect, the process of upgrading to Windows 2000 is much simpler than performing a clean install. You pick the system from which you are upgrading, then follow the Setup Wizard's instructions to provide the information the Setup program needs. The final steps in the upgrade process are automatic.

If you are upgrading from a Windows NT domain controller, DCPROMO will be run automatically, as described in the "Upgrading a Member Server to a Domain Controller" section earlier in this chapter.

After the upgrade process is complete, verify that everything was upgraded properly. Using the inventory you made before upgrading (see the "Upgrade Checklist" section earlier in the chapter), check that your hardware and software have made it through the transition and are working properly.

Exercise 1.3 shows the steps for upgrading to Windows 2000 Server. To set up your computer for the exercises in this book, you installed

Windows 2000 Server from scratch in Exercises 1.1 and 1.2. You would follow the steps in Exercise 1.3 if you were upgrading from your current operating system, and you had not performed the clean install procedure outlined in the previous exercises.

For the purpose of studying for the MSCE exam with this book, it is recommended that you install Windows 2000 Server as outlined in Exercises 1.1 and 1.2. If you perform an upgrade instead, you may not be able to successfully complete some of the other exercises in this book.

EXERCISE 1.3

Upgrading to Windows 2000 Server

1. Insert the Windows 2000 Server CD into your CD-ROM drive. When the upgrade dialog box appears, click Yes to upgrade. (If necessary, from Windows NT 4, select Start ➢ Run and click the Browse button in the Run dialog box. Click My Computer and select your CD-ROM drive, then I386, then WINNT32. From Windows NT 3.51, open Program Manager, select File ➢ Run, and then click the Browse button in the Run dialog box. Select your CD-ROM drive, then I386, then WINNT32.)

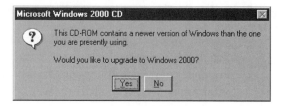

2. In the Welcome to the Windows 2000 Setup Wizard dialog box, click the Upgrade to Windows 2000 (Recommended) option. Click the Next button to continue.

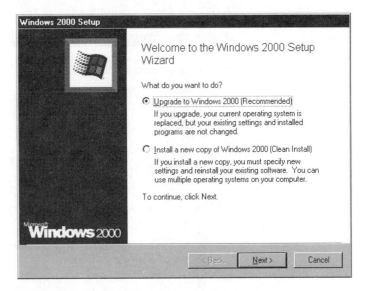

3. In the License Agreement dialog box, click the option to accept the agreement.

4. In the Product Key dialog box, type in your 25-character product key. Then click the Next button.

5. If your computer has FAT16 or FAT32 partitions, the Upgrading to the Windows 2000 NTFS File System dialog box appears. Select the No, Do Not Upgrade My Drive option. (You will upgrade to NTFS in an exercise in Chapter 6.) Then click the Next button.

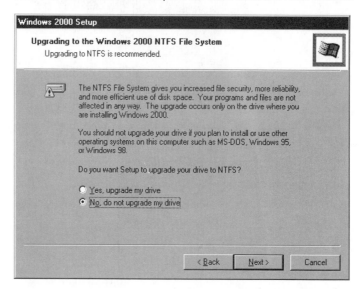

6. Wait while the computer copies files needed for installation and then automatically restarts. After the computer restarts, the Windows 2000 Server installation process automatically examines your disk and then begins copying more files. When the automated upgrade is complete, Windows 2000 Server will be installed on your computer.

7. Verify that everything was upgraded properly using the inventory you made before upgrading.

The computer will copy some files needed for installation and then will automatically restart. After the computer restarts, the Windows 2000 Server installation process automatically examines your disk and then begins copying files, which takes a few minutes. The installation will continue through several phases. When the automated upgrade is complete, Windows 2000 Server will be installed on your computer.

Troubleshooting Installation Problems

The Windows 2000 installation process is designed to be as simple as possible. The chances of installation errors are greatly minimized through the use of Wizards and the step-by-step process. However, it is possible that errors may occur.

Troubleshoot failed installations.

The following are some possible installation errors you might encounter:

Media errors	Media errors are caused by defective or damaged CDs. To check the CD, put it into another computer and see if you can read it. Also check your CD for scratches or dirt—it may just need to be cleaned.
Insufficient disk space	Windows 2000 needs at least 1GB of free space for the installation program to run properly. If the Setup program cannot verify that this space exists, the program will not let you continue.
Not enough memory	Make sure that your computer has the minimum amount of memory required by Windows 2000 Server (128MB). Not having enough memory may cause the installation to fail or blue-screen errors to occur after installation.
Not enough processing power	Make sure that your computer has the minimum processing power required by Windows 2000 Server (Pentium 133MHz). Not having enough processing power may cause the installation to fail or blue-screen errors to occur after installation.

Hardware that is not on the HCL	If your hardware is not on the HCL, Windows 2000 may not recognize the hardware, or the device may not work properly.
Hardware with no driver support	Windows 2000 will not recognize hardware without driver support.
Hardware that is not configured properly	If your hardware is Plug-and-Play compatible, Windows should configure it automatically. If your hardware is not Plug-and-Play compatible, you will need to manually configure the hardware per the manufacturer's instructions.
Incorrect CD key	Without a valid CD key, the installation will not go past the Product Key dialog box. Make sure that you have not typed in an incorrect key (check the back of your CD case for this key).
Failure to access TCP/IP network resources	If you install Windows 2000 with typical settings, the computer is configured as a DHCP client. If there is no DHCP server to provide IP configuration information, the client will be unable to access network resources through TCP/IP.
Failure to connect to a domain controller when joining a domain	Make sure that you have specified the correct domain name. If your domain name is correct, verify that your network settings have been set properly and that a domain controller and DNS server are available. If you still can't join a domain, install the computer in a workgroup, then join the domain after installation.

When you install Windows 2000 Server, several log files are created by the Setup program. You can view these logs to check for any problems during the installation process. Two log files are particularly useful for troubleshooting:

- The action log includes all of the actions that were performed during the setup process and a description of each action. These actions are listed in chronological order. The action log is stored as *Windir*\ `setupact.log`.

- The error log includes any errors that occurred during the installation. For each error, there is a description and an indication of the severity of the error. This error log is stored as *Windir\setuperr.log*.

In Exercise 1.4, you will view the Windows 2000 setup logs to determine if there were any problems with your Windows 2000 installation.

EXERCISE 1.4

Troubleshooting Failed Installations with Setup Logs

1. Select Start ➢ Programs ➢ Accessories ➢ Windows Explorer.

2. In Windows Explorer, double-click My Computer, double-click Local Disk (C:), and double-click WINNT (this is the default *Windir* folder, set up in Exercise 1.1).

3. Since this is the first time you have opened the WINNT folder, click the Show All Files option to display all the files that it contains.

4. In the WINNT folder, double-click the `setupact` file to view your action log in Notepad. When you are finished viewing this file, close Notepad.

5. Double-click the `setuperr` file to view your error file in Notepad. If no errors occurred during installation, this file will be empty. When you are finished viewing this file, close Notepad.

6. Close Windows Explorer.

Summary

In this chapter, you learned how to install Windows 2000 Server. We covered the following topics:

- The three Windows 2000 Server platforms and the features of the main Windows 2000 Server operating system. The three versions are Windows 2000 Server, Windows 2000 Advanced Server, and Windows 2000 Datacenter Server.

- Installation preparation, which includes making sure that your computer meets the minimum system requirements and that all of your hardware is on the Hardware Compatibility List (HCL). Then you need to decide whether you will perform a clean install or an upgrade. Only Windows NT Server computers can be upgraded to Windows 2000 Server. Finally, you should plan which options you will select during installation. Options include how to partition your disk space, how to select a file system, whether the computer will be installed as a part of a workgroup or a domain, your licensing method, and your language and locale settings. You also decide whether Windows 2000 Server will be installed from the CD-ROM or from a network connection.

- How to install Windows 2000 Server, which occurs in three main installation phases: running the Setup program, running the Setup Wizard, and installing Windows 2000 Networking. If you are installing Windows 2000 as a domain controller, there is a fourth phase, in which you upgrade the server to a domain controller. This section also includes exercises for setting up a domain controller and a member server for all of the hands-on exercises that are presented throughout this book.

- Guidelines for setting up for dual-booting or multi-booting. Dual-booting and multi-booting allow you to boot to a choice of two or more operating systems.

- How to upgrade to Windows 2000 Server. Client upgrade paths and requirements are used to determine if your operating system can be upgraded to Windows 2000 Server. In order to upgrade directly, you must be running Windows NT 3.51 or 4, and your hardware must meet the minimum requirements. Indirect upgrades from NT 3.1 or 3.5 are allowed by upgrading to NT 3.51 or 4.0 first.

- How to troubleshoot installation problems. Common errors are caused by media problems, lack of disk space or memory, and hardware problems.

Exam Essentials

Be able to install Windows 2000 Server.   Understand the requirements for installing Windows 2000 as well as the major steps required by the installation process.

Peform an upgrade to Windows 2000 Server.   Know the requirements for upgrading to Windows 2000 Server. Be able to list possible problems with an upgrade. List the steps required to upgrade to a Windows 2000 Server.

Be able to troubleshoot failed installations.   Know common installation problems and how to overcome them.

Key Terms

Before taking the exam, you should be familiar with the following terms:

Active Directory (AD)	FAT32
boot partition	File Allocation Table
clean install	Hardware Compatibility List (HCL)
Client Access Licenses (CALs)	logical drive
container	multi-booting
Disk partitioning	New Technology File System (NTFS)
distribution server	organizational unit (OUs)
domain	Per Seat licensing
domain controller	Per Server licensing
domain forest	system partition
domain tree	upgrade
dual-booting	Windows 2000 Server Setup Boot Disks
FAT16	workgroup

Review Questions

1. Tomas has just installed a Windows 2000 Server. The server needs to store the users, groups, and computers that compose the Active Directory. When Tomas installed the server he did not see any option to make the server a domain controller. What command should Tomas use to upgrade a Windows 2000 Server computer to a domain controller?

   A. UPGRADEDC

   B. DCUPGRADE

   C. PROMODC

   D. DCPROMO

2. Steve wants to multi-boot his computer with Windows 2000 Server and other operating systems. His other operating systems are Windows 95, OS/2, and Windows NT Server 4.0. His computer is currently configured as shown in the following exhibit. Which of the following file systems are supported by Windows 2000 Server and would be recognized when the Windows 2000 Server operating system was loaded? (Choose all that apply.)

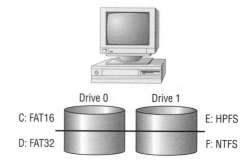

   A. FAT16

   B. FAT32

   C. HPFS

   D. NTFS

3. Ricki is installing Windows 2000 Server on 10 computers. The servers need to be a part of a domain, act as domain controllers, dual-boot with another operating system, and have specific networking components installed. Which of the following options can be specified during the installation of Windows 2000 Server? (Choose all that apply.)

    A. The workgroup or domain that the server will join

    B. Whether or not the server will be installed as a domain controller or member server

    C. What other operating systems should be presented in a dual-boot or multi-boot configuration

    D. The networking components that the server will use

4. You are in charge of a test lab that has servers installed in a variety of configurations. Many of the servers are configured for dual-booting so that you can test compatibility with a variety of operating systems. Which of the following operating systems could dual-boot with Windows 2000 Server if you converted your disks to dynamic disks?

    A. Windows 2000 Professional

    B. Windows NT Server 4

    C. Windows NT Workstation 4

    D. Windows 98

5. Oscar is in the process of designing his company's deployment guide for the rollout of Windows 2000. Part of the deployment guide contains guidelines on naming conventions. When new servers are installed, what is the maximum number of characters that each server's name can contain?

    A. 12

    B. 15

    C. 24

    D. 36

6. Tony has a server that is used as the company's external Web server. The hardware configuration that is required is that it support eight processors and 4GB of memory. What is the minimum version of Windows 2000 Server that he should install?

   A. Windows 2000 Server

   B. Windows 2000 Advanced Server

   C. Windows 2000 Datacenter Server

   D. Windows 2000 Application

7. Elena is installing a clean copy of Windows 2000 Server. Her computer offers multiprocessing support. How many processors can be recognized by Windows 2000 Server?

   A. 2

   B. 4

   C. 6

   D. 8

8. Jamila is trying to determine which version of Windows 2000 Server she should install on her computer. One of the criteria is the services that are available with each version. Which of the following services is not available with the standard version of Windows 2000 Server?

   A. Terminal services

   B. Cluster services

   C. DFS

   D. EFS

9. Brant is making the hardware recommendations for a new server that his company is purchasing. He knows that he will use Windows 2000 Server with several memory-intensive applications. What is the maximum amount of RAM that will be recognized by Windows 2000 Server?

   A. 256MB

   B. 512MB

   C. 4GB

   D. 8GB

10. Brett has just finished installing Windows 2000 Server. He used all of the default settings. What is the default name of the folder that holds the Windows 2000 operating system files?

   A. WINNT

   B. WIN2K

   C. WIN2000

   D. WINDOWS

11. You are configuring your Windows 2000 Server to dual-boot with Windows NT Server 4. Which of the following file systems will be recognized by both operating systems? (Choose all that apply.)

   A. FAT16

   B. FAT32

   C. HPFS

   D. NTFS

12. Your company has a variety of Windows computers including Windows 95/98 and various flavors of Windows NT. You want to upgrade as many computers as possible to Windows 2000 Workstation or Windows 2000 Server. Which of the following operating systems can you upgrade to Windows 2000 Server?

    A. Windows NT Server 3.5

    B. Windows NT Workstation 3.51

    C. Windows NT Server 4

    D. Windows 95

13. You are upgrading a Windows NT Server to Windows 2000. When you insert the Windows 2000 Server CD, nothing happens. What command do you use to start an upgrade to Windows 2000 Server from a Windows NT Server 4 computer that does not have auto-run enabled?

    A. WIN2K

    B. INSTALL

    C. WINNT

    D. WINNT32

14. Jessica wants to upgrade her Windows NT Server to a Windows 2000 Server. Which of the following configuration options would cause the upgrade to fail?

    A. Compressed drive

    B. Windows 98 application installed

    C. Network card not on HCL

    D. FAT16 partition

15. Dustin has just installed a Windows 2000 Server. He wants to view the error log to verify that no errors occurred during the setup process. Where should he look for this file?

A. *Windir*\error.log

B. *Windir*\logs\error.log

C. *Windir*\setuperr.log

D. *Windir*\logs\seterr.log

Answers to Review Questions

1. D. The DCPROMO command-line utility is used to upgrade a Windows 2000 Server computer to a domain controller.

2. A, B, D. The only file systems supported by Windows 2000 are FAT16, FAT32, and NTFS. HPFS is not supported by Windows 2000.

3. A, D. You can specify which workgroup or domain the server will join. You can't specify the server's role. If you want the server to be a domain controller, you upgrade the server through the DCPROMO utility. Your computer will be automatically configured for dual-boot or multi-boot if a supported operating system was on your computer prior to the Windows 2000 Server installation.

4. A. The only operating system that can recognize dynamic disks is Windows 2000.

5. B. Computer names are limited to a maximum of 15 characters.

6. B. Windows 2000 Advanced Server offers support for up to eight processors and up to 8GB of memory.

7. A. If you perform a clean installation of Windows 2000 Server, there is support for two processors. If you upgrade your server from Windows NT Server, there is support for up to four processors.

8. B. Cluster services are only available in Windows 2000 Advanced Server and Windows 2000 Datacenter Server.

9. C. Windows 2000 Server supports up to 4GB of memory. Windows 2000 Advanced Server supports up to 8GB of memory.

10. A. By default, the boot partition, which holds all of the operating system files, is called WINNT.

11. A, D. Windows NT 4 will not recognize FAT32 partitions. Windows 2000 and Windows NT 4 will not recognize HPFS partitions.

12. C. You can only upgrade to Windows 2000 Server from Windows NT Server 3.51 and Windows NT Server 4.

13. D. Windows 2000 Server does not use an INSTALL program for installations or upgrades. You use `WINNT32` to start an upgrade from NT Server 3.51 or Windows NT Server 4. There is no command called `WIN2K`.

14. A. You can't upgrade to Windows 2000 with compressed drives. Windows 98 applications may not work, but will not cause the installation to fail. A network card not on the HCL may also not work, but will not cause the installation to fail. Windows 2000 recognizes FAT16 partitions.

15. C. The error log includes any errors that occurred during the installation. For each error, there is a description and an indication of the severity of the error. This error log is stored as *Windir*\`setuperr.log`.

Chapter

2

Automating the Windows 2000 Server Installation

MICROSOFT EXAM OBJECTIVES COVERED IN THIS CHAPTER

✓ **Perform an unattended installation of Windows 2000 Server.**

- Create unattended answer files by using Setup Manager to automate the installation of Windows 2000 Server.

- Create and configure automated methods for installation of Windows 2000.

If you need to install Windows 2000 Server on multiple computers, you could manually install the operating system on each computer, as described in Chapter 1, "Getting Started with Windows 2000 Server." However, automated deployment will make your job easier, more efficient, and more cost effective.

You can automate the installation of Windows 2000 Server through the use of disk imaging or by using the unattended installation method. You can also use unattended answer files with automated installation to provide answers to the questions that are normally asked during the installation process. You can automate server installations for clean installations or for upgrades from Windows NT Server 3.51 or Windows NT 4.0 computers. This chapter details the use of disk images and unattended answer files, and briefly describes unattended installation.

Extracting the Windows 2000 Deployment Tools

The Windows 2000 Deployment Tools include two utilities that you can use to prepare for automated installations:

- The *System Preparation Tool (Sysprep)* utility is used for preparing disk images.

- The *Setup Manager (Setupmgr)* utility is used for creating unattended answer files.

The Deployment Tools are stored on the Windows 2000 Server CD, in the Support\Tools folder, in the Deploy.cab file. You can extract these tools by using the File ➢ Extract command in Windows Explorer.

In Exercise 2.1, you will extract the Windows 2000 Deployment Tools. This exercise should be completed from your member server.

EXERCISE 2.1

Extracting the Windows 2000 Deployment Tools

1. Log on to your Windows 2000 computer as Administrator.

2. Select Start ➤ Programs ➤ Accessories ➤ Windows Explorer.

3. In Windows Explorer, double-click My Computer, and then double-click Local Disk (C:).

4. Select File ➤ New ➤ Folder. Type in **Deployment Tools** for the folder name.

5. Insert the Windows 2000 Server CD. Using Windows Explorer, copy the Support\Tools\Deploy file (the .cab extension is hidden by default) to the C:\Deployment Tools folder.

6. Double-click the Deploy.cab file to display its contents.

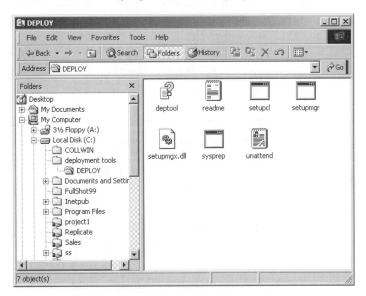

7. In Windows Explorer, select Edit ➤ Select All. Then select File ➤ Extract.

EXERCISE 2.1 *(continued)*

8. The Browse for Folder dialog box appears. Select Local Disk (C:) and then Deployment Tools. Click the OK button to extract the files to the specified folder.

9. Verify that the Deployment Tools were extracted to C:\Deployment Tools. There should be eight items (including the Deploy.cab file).

10. Close Windows Explorer.

Using Disk Images

*D*isk imaging, or *disk duplication*, is the process of creating a reference computer for the automated deployment. The reference, or source, computer has Windows 2000 Server installed and is configured with the settings and applications that should be installed on the target computers. Disk imaging is a good choice for automatic deployment when you have the hardware that supports disk imaging and you have a large number of computers with similar configuration requirements. For example, education centers that reinstall the same software every week might use this technology. Also, if a computer is having technical difficulties, you can use a disk image to quickly restore it to a baseline configuration.

Microsoft ✓ *Exam* *Objective*	**Perform an unattended installation of Windows 2000 Server.** • Create unattended answer files by using Setup Manager to automate the installation of Windows 2000 Server. • Create and configure automated methods for installation of Windows 2000.

Once you have your source computer configured with Windows 2000 Server and any applications that you wish to deploy, you use the System Preparation Tool utility to prepare the disk image. Then you remove the drive with the disk image and insert it into a special piece of hardware, called a disk duplicator, to copy the images. The copied disks are inserted into the target computers. After you add the hard drive that contains the disk image to the target computers, you can complete the installation from those computers. Figure 2.1 illustrates the disk-imaging process. You can also create and manage disk images through the use of third-party disk imaging software. This process uses an image boot disk and an image that is stored on a remote server. Then using the boot image disk, you are able to download the disk image to a remote computer.

FIGURE 2.1   Disk imaging uses a reference computer for configuring target computers.

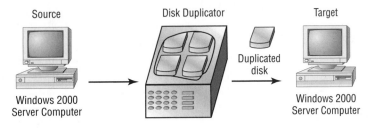

Preparing for Disk Duplication

In order to use a disk image, the source and target computers must meet the following requirements:

- The mass-storage controllers (SCSI or IDE) must be the same type on the source and destination computers.

- The HAL (Hardware Abstraction Layer) must be the same on the source and destination computers (this means that the processor type must be the same).

- The size of the destination computer's hard drive must be at least as large as the source computer's hard drive.

- Plug-and-Play devices on the source and destination computers do not need to match, as long as the drivers for the Plug-and-Play devices are available.

Using the System Preparation Tool

The System Preparation Tool (Sysprep) is included on the Windows 2000 Server CD in the Support\Tools folder, in the `Deploy.cab` file. After you extract this tool (see Exercise 2.1), you can run Sysprep on the source computer. Sysprep prepares the disk image, stripping out information from the master copy that must be unique for each computer, such as the security ID (SID).

After you install the copied image on the target computer, a Mini-Setup Wizard runs. This Wizard automatically creates a unique computer SID and then prompts the user for computer-specific information, such as the product ID, regional settings, and network configuration. The information that is required can also be supplied through an unattended answer file. Table 2.1 list some of the command switches that you can use to customize how Sysprep works.

TABLE 2.1 Sysprep Command Switches

Switch	Description
-quiet	Runs the installation with no user interaction
-pnp	Forces Setup to run Plug-and-Play detection of hardware
-reboot	Restarts the target computer
-nosidgen	Doesn't create a new SID on the destination computer (used with disk cloning)

After you run the System Preparation Tool on a computer, you need to run the Setup Manager Wizard to reconfigure all of the unique information for the computer. You should only run this utility on source reference computers that will be used for disk duplication purposes.

Creating a Disk Image

To run Sysprep and create a disk image, take the following steps:

1. Install Windows 2000 Server on a source computer. (See Chapter 1 for instructions on installing Windows 2000 Server.)

2. Log on to the source computer as Administrator, and if desired, install and configure any applications that also should be installed on the target computer.

3. Extract the Deploy.cab file from the Windows 2000 Server CD (see Exercise 2.1).

4. Select Start ➤ Run and click the Browse button in the Run dialog box. Select Local Drive (C:), then Deployment Tools. Double-click Sysprep and click the OK button.

5. The Windows 2000 System Preparation Tool dialog box appears. This dialog box warns you that the execution of this program will modify some of the security parameters of the computer. Click the OK button.

6. You will be prompted to turn off your computer.

In Exercise 2.2, you will use Sysprep to prepare the disk image. This exercise should be competed from your member server. In Exercise 2.3, you will complete the Windows 2000 Server installation on the target computer. This exercise assumes that you have completed Exercise 2.1.

EXERCISE 2.2

Using the System Preparation Tool

1. Log on to the source computer as Administrator, and if desired, install and configure any applications that also should be installed on the target computer.

2. Select Start ➤ Run and click the Browse button. Select Local Drive (C:), then Deployment Tools. Double-click Sysprep and click the OK button.

3. In the Windows 2000 System Preparation Tool dialog box, click the OK button.

4. When prompted, turn off your computer.

Copying and Installing from a Disk Image

After you've run Sysprep on the source computer, you can copy the image and then install it on the target computer.

If you are using special hardware (a disk duplicator) to duplicate the disk image, shut down the source computer and remove the disk. Copy the disk and install the copied disk into the target computer. If you are using special software, copy the disk image per the software vendor's instructions.

After the image is copied, turn on the destination computer. The Mini-Setup Wizard runs and prompts the user as follows (if you have not configured an answer file):

- Accept the End User License Agreement

- Specify regional settings

- Enter a name and organization

- Specify your product key

- Specify the licensing mode that will be used

- Specify the computer name and Administrator password

- Specify dialing information (if a modem is detected)

- Specify date and time settings

- Specify which networking protocols and services should be installed

- Join a workgroup or a domain

If you have created an answer file for use with disk images, as described in the next section, the installation will run without requiring any user input.

In Exercise 2.3, you will use the stripped image that you created in Exercise 2.2 to simulate the process of continuing an installation from a disk image. This exercise should be completed from your member server.

EXERCISE 2.3

Installing Windows 2000 Server from a Disk Image

1. Turn on your computer. The Windows 2000 Setup Wizard will start. Click the Next button to continue (this will happen automatically if you don't click the Next button after about 10 seconds).

2. In the License Agreement dialog box, click the I Accept This Agreement option and click the Next button.

3. In the Regional Settings dialog box, click Next to accept the default settings and continue.

4. In the Personalize Your Software dialog box, enter your name and organization. Then click the Next button.

5. In the Your Product Key dialog box, type the 25-character product key and click the Next button.

6. In the Licensing Mode dialog box, specify Per Server and click the Next button.

7. In the Computer Name and Administrator Password dialog box, specify the computer name and an Administrator password (if desired). Then click the Next button.

8. If you have a modem installed, the Modem Dialing Information dialog box appears. Specify your dialing configuration and click the Next button.

9. In the Date and Time Settings dialog box, specify the date, time, and time zone. Then click the Next button.

10. In the Network Settings dialog box, select Custom Settings and click the Next button.

11. In the Networking Components dialog box, select Internet Protocol (TCP/IP) and click the Properties button. The General tab of the Internet Protocol (TCP/IP) Properties dialog box appears. Select the Use the Following IP Address option and specify the IP address **131.200.2.2** with a subnet mask of **255.255.0.0**. Click the OK button to return to the Networking Components dialog box. Click the Next button.

12. In the Workgroup or Computer Domain dialog box, verify that the No, This Computer Is Not on a Network, or Is on a Network without a Domain Controller option is selected and click the Next button.

13. When the Completing the Windows 2000 Setup Wizard dialog box appears, click the Finish button.

14. When the computer restarts, start Windows 2000 Server.

Using Setup Manager to Create Answer Files

Answer files are automated installation scripts that are used to answer the questions that appear during a normal Windows 2000 Server installation. You can use answer files with Windows 2000 Server, Sysprep (disk image) installations or unattended installations. Setting up answer files allows you to easily deploy Windows 2000 Server to computers that may not be configured in the same manner, with little or no user intervention.

 Real World Scenario

Using Disk Duplication as an Easy Way to Recover Desktop Configurations

Your company has just purchased 10 computers to be used as servers for testing in the Help Desk area. These servers will have sample applications installed and tested, then they will need to be returned to the original configuration for future testing. Each computer will be configured identically as far as operating system, Service Packs, and hardware are concerned. Your job is to ensure that you have a quick and easy way to restore the computers after testing is completed.

You decide to use a disk imaging program in conjunction with the System Preparation Tool. In order to use this process, you should take the following steps:

1. Install Windows 2000 Server on a reference computer that has similar hardware to the target computers. When you build the reference computer, you should not join a domain or use an Administrator password.

2. Log on to the computer as the Administrator and install and configure the server with any Service Packs or applications that you want installed on the target computers.

3. Validate the image and remove any residual information such as audit and event logs.

4. Prepare the system for duplication and run the System Preparation Tool. At this point you should also use a third-party disk image program to create a disk image.

5. Duplicate the image on the target computers using the third-party disk image software. You can use the Sysprep.inf file as an answer file during the Mini-Setup process. You can place this file on the %systemdrive%\Sysprep folder or on a floppy disk.

Microsoft
✓ *Exam*
Objective

Perform an unattended installation of Windows 2000 Server.

- Create unattended answer files by using Setup Manager to auto-mate the installation of Windows 2000 Server.

- Create and configure automated methods for installation of Windows 2000.

You create answer files through the Setup Manager (Setupmgr) utility. There are several advantages to using Setup Manager to create answer files:

- You can easily create answer files through a graphical interface, which reduces syntax errors.

- The utility simplifies the addition of user-specific or computer-specific configuration information.

- With Setup Manager, you can include application setup scripts within the answer file.

- The utility creates the distribution folder that will be used for installation files.

The most common options that can be configured through Setup Manager are defined in Table 2.2.

TABLE 2.2   Common Options Configured through Setup Manager

Setup Manager Option	Description
Installation path	Specifies the target path on the Windows 2000 server where Windows 2000 will be installed.
Target computer name	Specifies the user name, organiza-tion name, and computer name that will be applied to the target com-puter.
Product ID	Specifies the Product ID (PID) that will be used by the target computer.

TABLE 2.2 Common Options Configured through Setup Manager *(continued)*

Setup Manager Option	Description
Workgroup or domain	Specifies the workgroup or domain that the target computer will be installed in. If you want the target computer to be a domain controller, you will have to run the DCPROMO utility after the automated installation is complete. This can be used with an answer file with the [DCInstall] section properly configured. This option would use the following command: `dcpromo /answer:answer_file_name`.
Time zone	Specifies the time zone that will be used by the target computer.
Network configuration information	Specifies the network adapter and configuration, as well as the network protocols that will be used by the target computer.

The Setup Manager utility is included on the Windows 2000 Server CD in the Support\Tools folder, in the `Deploy.cab` file. After you extract the Setup Manager utility (see Exercise 2.1), you can run it to create a new answer file, create an answer file that duplicates the current computer's configuration, or edit existing answer files.

The following steps describe how to create a new installation script. In this example, the instructions describe how to create an answer file for a Sysprep (disk image) installation that provides default answers, uses the default display configuration, configures typical network settings, and does not edit any additional options.

1. Select Start ➢ Run and click the Browse button in the Run dialog box. Double-click the Deployment Tools folder, double-click the Setupmgr program, and then click the OK button.

2. The Windows 2000 Setup Manager Wizard starts. Click the Next button.

3. The New or Existing Answer File dialog box appears, as shown in Figure 2.2. This dialog box provides choices for creating a new answer file, creating an answer file that duplicates this computer's configuration, or modifying an existing answer file. Select the Create a New Answer file option and click the Next button.

FIGURE 2.2 The New or Existing Answer File dialog box

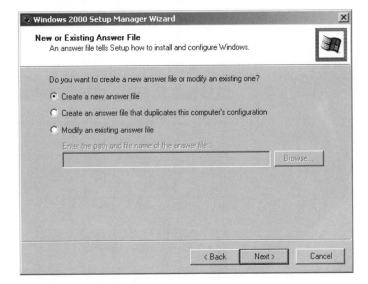

4. The Product to Install dialog box appears. You can select Windows 2000 Unattended installation, Sysprep Install, or Remote Installation Services. Select Sysprep Install and click the Next button.

With Remote Installation Services (RIS), the RIS server installs Windows 2000 on RIS clients. The RIS server must be configured with a CD-based image, which contains only the Windows 2000 operating system and optionally Remote Installation Preparation (RIPrep) images, which can contain the Windows 2000 operating system with applications. RIS is used for remote installation of Windows 2000 Professional.

5. The Platform dialog box appears. You can choose to create answer files for the Windows 2000 Professional platform or the

Windows 2000 Server platform. Select Windows 2000 Server and click the Next button.

6. The License Agreement dialog box appears, as shown in Figure 2.3. You can choose to accept the End User License Agreement (EULA), so that the installation is fully automated, or not to accept the EULA. If you do not accept the EULA, the end user will need to accept the license agreement, so the installation will not be fully automated. Select the Yes, Fully Automate the Installation option and click the Next button.

FIGURE 2.3 The License Agreement dialog box

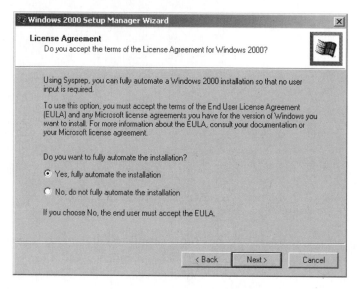

7. The Customize the Software dialog box appears, as shown in Figure 2.4. This dialog box allows you to specify the name and organization that will be used for licensing information. After you enter this information, click the Next button.

FIGURE 2.4   The Customize the Software dialog box

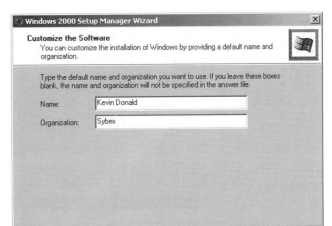

8. The Licensing Mode dialog box appears, as shown in Figure 2.5. In this dialog box, you specify whether you will license the server by concurrent connections (Per Server) or by seat (Per Seat). If you select Per Server, you can also set the number of concurrent connections allowed. (See Chapter 1 for more information about the Per Server and Per Seat licensing modes.) After you make your selection, click the Next button.

FIGURE 2.5   The Licensing Mode dialog box

9. The Computer Name dialog box appears. Type in the name of the destination computer and click the Next button.

10. The Administrator Password dialog box appears, as shown in Figure 2.6. In this dialog box, you can enter the Administrator password or specify that the user will be prompted for an Administrator password. You can also specify that when the computer starts, the Administrator will automatically be logged on for *x* number of times. Enter and confirm an Administrator password. Then click the Next button.

FIGURE 2.6 The Administrator Password dialog box

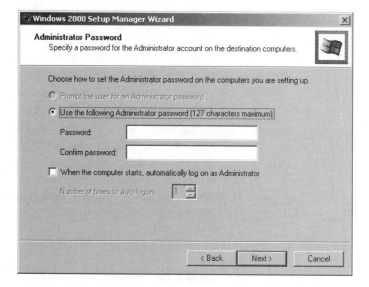

11. The Display Settings dialog box appears, as shown in Figure 2.7. From this dialog box, you can configure the following settings:

   - The Colors option allows you to set the display color to the Windows default, 16 colors, 256 colors, high color (16 bit), true color (24 bit), or true color (32 bit).

- The Screen Area option allows you to set the screen area to the Windows default, 640 × 480, 800 × 600, 1024 × 768, or 1280 × 1024, or 1600 × 1200.

- The Refresh Frequency option (the number of times the screen is updated) allows you to set the refresh frequency to the Windows default, 60Hz, 70Hz, 72Hz, 75Hz, or 85Hz.

- The Custom button displays a dialog box that allows you to further customize display settings for the color, screen area, and refresh frequency.

12. Click the Next button to accept the default configuration and continue.

FIGURE 2.7   The Display Settings dialog box

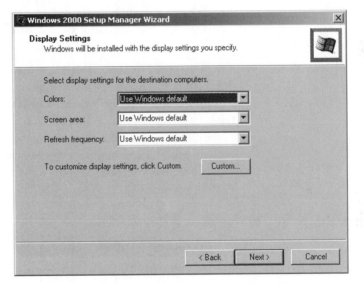

13. The Network Settings dialog box appears, as shown in Figure 2.8. You can choose Typical Settings (installs TCP/IP, enables DHCP, and installs Client for Microsoft Networks) or Custom Settings (allows you to customize the computer's network settings). Select the Typical Settings option and click the Next button.

FIGURE 2.8 The Network Settings dialog box

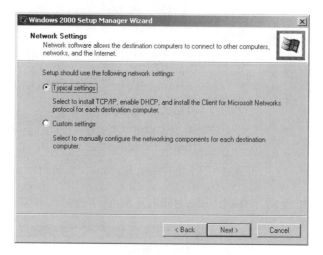

14. The Workgroup or Domain dialog box appears, as shown in Figure 2.9. Select the workgroup or Windows Server domain that the computer will be a part of and click the Next button. If you select a Domain, you must select Create a Computer Account in the Domain and provide the user name and password of a user who has rights to create a computer account within the domain for the Active Directory, or the computer must have an entry created through the Active Directory Users and Computers utility.

FIGURE 2.9 The Workgroup or Domain dialog box

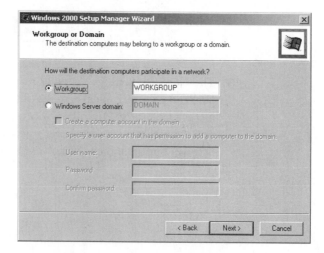

15. The Time Zone dialog box appears. Select your computer's time zone from the drop-down list and click the Next button.

16. The Additional Settings dialog box appears. If you select to edit additional settings, you can configure the following options:

- Telephony settings

- Regional settings

- Languages

- Install printers

- A command that will run once the first time a user logs on

17. Click the Next button to accept the default selection of No, Do Not Edit the Additional Settings.

18. The Sysprep Folder dialog box appears, as shown in Figure 2.10. This dialog box allows you to create a Sysprep folder that will be used during the Sysprep installation to customize the installation. As noted in the dialog box, you might use this option to supply additional language support or third-party device drivers. After you make your selection, click the Next button.

FIGURE 2.10 The Sysprep Folder dialog box

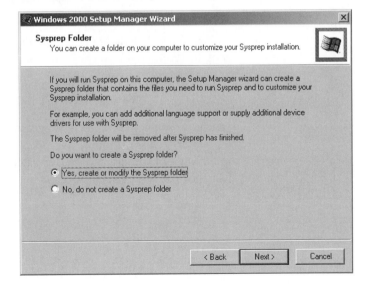

19. The Additional Commands dialog box appears, as shown in
   Figure 2.11. This dialog box allows you to run commands at the end
   of the automated installation. You can specify any command that
   does not require a user to be logged on, for example, CHKDSK. After
   you add any additional commands, click the Next button.

FIGURE 2.11 The Additional Commands dialog box

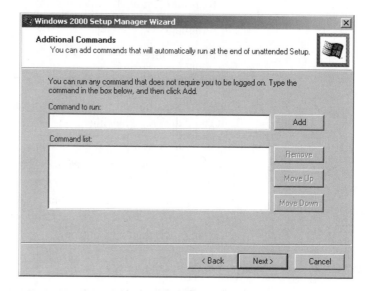

20. The OEM Branding dialog box appears, as shown in Figure 2.12. This
   dialog box allows you to configure an optional logo or background
   that can be used to display Original Equipment Manufacturer (OEM)
   information, called *OEM branding,* on the System Properties General
   page. If you want to use a logo and/or a background, specify the path
   to the appropriate files. The OEM agreement only allows a logo (must
   be 16 color format), a phone number to Tech Support, and a link to
   support info. No other info or advertisements of any kind are allowed.
   Then click the Next button.

FIGURE 2.12 The OEM Branding dialog box

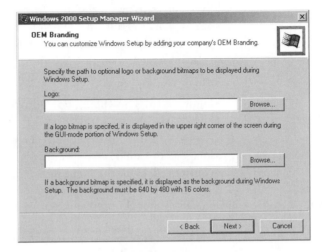

21. The Additional Files or Folders dialog box appears, as shown in Figure 2.13. This dialog box allows you to specify any additional files or folders that should automatically be copied on the destination computers. If you want to copy other files, select where you want the files to be stored on the destination computers, click the Add Files button, and choose the files to include. After this information is configured, click the Next button.

FIGURE 2.13 The Additional Files or Folders dialog box

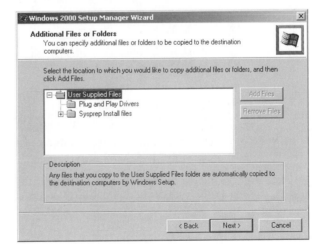

22. A message box appears, asking you to specify the location of the Sysprep.exe file. Click the OK button. The Open dialog box appears. By default, this dialog box should show the folder from which the Sysprep.exe command was run (in our example, C:\Deployment Tools). Click the Open button.

23. The OEM Duplicator String dialog box appears, as shown in Figure 2.14. This dialog box allows you to configure information about the Sysprep installation that will be included in the computer's Registry. This information can be used to determine which Sysprep image is installed on a specific computer. After this information is configured, click the Next button.

FIGURE 2.14   The OEM Duplicator String dialog box

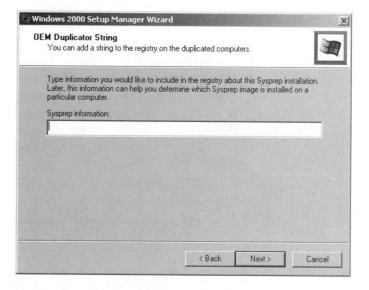

24. The Answer File Name dialog box appears, as shown in Figure 2.15. The Setup Manager Wizard will create a file in the folder that the Sysprep command was run from. This file is named sysprep.inf by default. You can edit the location and name of this file or accept the default settings. After this information is configured, click the Next button.

FIGURE 2.15   The Answer File Name dialog box

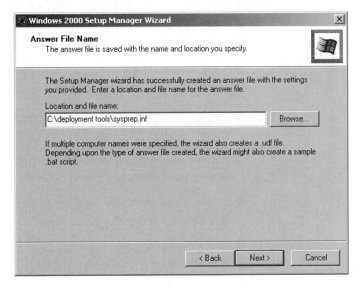

25. The Completing the Windows 2000 Setup Manager Wizard dialog box appears. Click the Finish button.

In Exercise 2.4, you will create an automated answer file that can be used with a Sysprep installation. This exercise should be completed from your member server.

EXERCISE 2.4

Creating an Unattended Answer File

1. Select Start ➢ Run and click the Browse button. Double-click the Deployment Tools folder, double-click the Setupmgr program, and then click the OK button.

2. When the Windows 2000 Setup Manager Wizard starts, click the Next button.

3. In the New or Existing Answer File dialog box, select the Create a New Answer file option and click the Next button.

4. In the Product to Install dialog box, select Sysprep Install and click the Next button.

5. In the Platform dialog box, select Windows 2000 Server and click the Next button.

6. In the License Agreement dialog box, select Yes, Fully Automate the Installation and click the Next button.

7. In the Customize the Software dialog box, enter your name and organization and click the Next button.

8. In the Licensing Mode dialog box, click the Next button to accept the default setting (Per Server) and continue.

9. In the Computer Name dialog box, type the name of the target computer and click the Next button.

10. In the Administrator Password dialog box, leave the Use the Following Administrator Password option selected, but do not enter a password (leave the Password box blank). Click the Next button.

11. In the Display Settings dialog box, click the Next button to accept the default settings and continue.

12. In the Network Settings dialog box, click the Next button to accept the default setting (Typical Settings) and continue.

13. In the Workgroup or Domain dialog box, click the Next button to accept the default setting (Workgroup) and continue.

14. In the Time Zone dialog box, select the target computer's time zone and click the Next button.

15. In the Additional Settings dialog box, click the Next button to accept the default setting (No, Do Not Edit the Additional Settings) and continue.

16. In the Sysprep Folder dialog box, accept the default setting of Yes, Create or Modify the Sysprep Folder and click the Next button.

17. In the Additional Commands dialog box, click the Next button to continue without specifying any additional commands.

18. In the OEM Branding dialog box, click the Next button to continue without specifying a logo or background file.

19. In the Additional Files or Folders dialog box, click the Next button to accept the default settings. A warning dialog box will appear prompting you to specify the location of sysprep.exe. Click the OK button. The Open dialog box will appear. Click sysprep and then click the Open button.

20. In the OEM Duplicator dialog box, click the Next button to continue without specifying any additional information.

21. In the Answer File Name dialog box, click the Next button to accept the default filename and location.

22. When the Completing the Windows 2000 Setup Manager Wizard dialog box appears, click the Finish button. Your answer file will be created.

WINNT Switches for Starting Unattended Installations

In order to start a remote installation, you must use the correct WINNT (or WINNT32 if you are performing an upgrade) command-line switches. The switches that can be used with WINNT or WINNT32 are defined in Table 2.3. The syntax that is associated with the WINNT command is as follows:

```
winnt [/s:sourcepath] [/t:tempdrive] [/u:answer file]
[/udf:id [,UDB_file]] [/r:folder][/rx:folder]
[/e:command][/a]
```

TABLE 2.3 WINNT Command Line Switches Defined

WINNT Switch	Description
/s:sourcepath	Specifies the source location of the Windows 2000 distribution files. The location must be a full path of the form x:\[*path*] or a Universal Naming Convention (UNC) path such as \\server\share[\path]. You can specify up to eight /s switches to point to multiple distribution servers.
/t:tempdrive	Directs the Setup program to place the temporary files on the specified drive and to install Windows 2000 on that drive. If you do not specify a location, the Setup program will attempt to locate a drive for you.
/u:answer file	Performs an unattended Setup using the specified answer file. The answer file provides answers to some or all of the prompts that would normally be responded to by the end user during Setup. This switch requires you to use the /s switch.
/udf:id [,UDB_file]	Indicates an identifier that the Setup program uses to specify how a Uniqueness Database (UDB) file modifies an answer file (see /u). The /udf parameter overrides values in the answer file, and the identifier determines which values in the UDB file are used. If no UDB file is specified, you will be prompted to insert a disk that contains the $Unique$.udb file.

TABLE 2.3   WINNT Command Line Switches Defined *(continued)*

WINNT Switch	Description
/r:folder	Specifies an optional folder to be installed. The folder will not be deleted when the Setup program is finished.
/rx:folder	Specifies an optional folder to be installed. The folder will be deleted when the Setup program is finished.
/e:command	Specifies a command to be executed at the end of GUI-mode Setup.
/a	Enables accessibility options.

Using Unattended Installation

*U*nattended installation is a practical method of automatic deployment when you have many servers to install and you do not want to use disk imaging. With an unattended installation, you use a distribution server to install Windows 2000 Server on a target computer.

The distribution server contains the Windows 2000 Server operating system files and possibly an answer file to respond to installation configuration queries. The target computer must be able to connect to the distribution server over the network. After the distribution server and target computers are connected, you can initiate the installation process. Figure 2.16 illustrates the unattended installation process.

FIGURE 2.16 Unattended installation uses a distribution server and a target computer.

Distribution Server

Stores:
Windows 2000 Server
operating system files
Answer files (optional)

Target

Requires enough software to
connect to the distribution server

The process for unattended installations is covered in *Mastering Windows 2000 Server*, by Mark Minasi (Sybex, 2000).

Summary

In this chapter, you learned how to install Windows 2000 Server through automated installation. We covered the following topics:

- How to extract the Deployment Tools from the `Deploy.cab` file, which is stored in the Support\Tools folder on the Windows 2000 Server CD

- How to create disk images for automated deployment by using the System Preparation Tool (Sysprep)

- How to use the Setup Manager utility to create unattended answer files, which provide automatic responses to Windows 2000 Server installation prompts

Exam Essentials

Know how to automate the installation of Windows 2000 Server using disk images.   List the requirements and steps that are used to install Windows 2000 servers through disk images.

Be able to use the Setup Manager to create answer files.   List the options that can be configured through the answer files. Know how to create and use answer files.

Key Terms

Before taking the exam, you should be familiar with the following terms:

answer	Setup Manager (Setupmgr)
disk imaging	System Preparation Tool (Sysprep)
OEM branding	unattended installation

Review Questions

1. You need to be able to install 25 Windows 2000 Servers and you would like to use an automated server installation. Which of the following automated deployment options can be used to install Windows 2000 Server?

   A. RIS

   B. Sysprep

   C. UAF

   D. RIPrep

2. You need to create an unattended installation answer file that can be used to support an unattended installation of Windows 2000 Server. You do not want to create the file with a text editor, because you want to use the easiest method to create the answer file. Which of the following utilities can you use to create unattended answer files to automate the installation of Windows 2000 Server?

   A. Sysprep

   B. UAM

   C. Setupmgr

   D. Deploy

3. Sam wants to access the Windows 2000 Deployment Tools so that he can use the Setupmgr utility. Where can he access these files on the Windows 2000 Server CD?

   A. Support\Tools\Deploy.cab

   B. Deployment\Deploy.cab

   C. Support\Support.cab

   D. Support\Tools\Support.cab

4. You want to install the Windows 2000 Deployment Tools and have accessed the appropriate `.cab` file. How do you uncompress the contents of the `.cab` file in Windows Explorer?

   A. Highlight the contents of the `.cab` file and select File ➢ Expand

   B. Highlight the contents of the `.cab` file, right-click, and select Unzip

   C. Highlight the contents of the `.cab` file and select File ➢ Extract

   D. Highlight the contents of the `.cab` file, right-click, and select Uncompress

5. Paula wants to install two Windows 2000 Servers that will be configured as domain controllers through automated installation. Which of the following commands should she use?

   A. WINNT /DC /Answer:*Answer_file_name*

   B. WINNT /DCPROMO /Answer:*Answer_file_name*

   C. DCPROMO /Answer:*Answer_file_name*

   D. There is no way to automate the process of upgrading a Windows 2000 Server to a domain controller.

6. You want to use Setup Manager to create all of the answer files for your automated installations across multiple Microsoft platforms. When you use Setup Manager to create Sysprep answer files, which of the following platforms are supported? (Choose all that apply.)

   A. Windows NT 4 Workstation

   B. Windows NT 4 Server

   C. Windows 2000 Professional

   D. Windows 2000 Server

7. You want to use the Sysprep utility to automate the installation of your Windows 2000 servers. Which of the following options is *not* associated with using disk images with the Sysprep utility?

   A. Disk imaging requires that you have third-party software or hardware to complete the disk-duplication process.

   B. The System Preparation Tool is used to strip out unique information about the computer.

    C. When the computer with the duplicated disk starts, a Mini-Setup Wizard is run to finish the computer's configuration.

    D. You can configure the computer through an RIPrep image.

8. You have decided to install your Windows 2000 servers through automated installation. The main goal of using automated installation is that you want the servers installed with as little user interaction as possible. Which Sysprep command-line switch supports this requirement?

    A. -nosid

    B. -nosidgen

    C. -skipsid

    D. -quiet

9. Bryan is using the Setup Manager utility to create an unattended answer file to be used to install Windows 2000 Server with the Sysprep utility. Which of the following options is *not* configured as a part of the answer file from Setup Manager?

    A. The product key that will be used

    B. Whether or not you agree to the EULA

    C. Whether the computer will be a part of a workgroup or a domain

    D. The Administrator password

10. Andrea is using the Setup Manager utility to create an answer file that will be used to install Windows 2000 Server with the Sysprep utility. Which of the following options *cannot* be specified by configuring settings in the Additional Settings dialog box?

    A. Regional settings

    B. Languages

    C. Install printers

    D. The configuration of the computer's page file

11. You are installing Windows 2000 Server through disk duplication. The problem is that your reference computer and your target computers do not use identical hardware. You want Sysprep to force Setup to run the Plug-and-Play detection of hardware. Which command-line option should you use?

A. -pnp

B. -usepnp

C. -forcepnp

D. -hardwaredetect

12. You are using Sysprep in conjunction with disk imaging to install your Windows 2000 servers. Each server has an application installed, which requires a server reboot before the application is properly configured and running. Which Sysprep command-line switch can you use to force the target computer to reboot after installation?

A. -restart

B. -reboot

C. -forceboot

D. -makeboot

13. You are using disk duplication to automate your server installations. You will manually complete the server installations, and you do not want new SIDs automatically generated on the destination computers. Which Sysprep command-line switch should you use if you do not want to create a SID on the destination computer?

A. -nosid

B. -nosidgen

C. -skipsid

D. -quiet

14. You want to use disk duplication as a way of automating the Windows 2000 server installations. You are trying to understand what the requirements are for the source and destination computers. Which of the following options is *not* a requirement for using disk duplication?

A. The HAL must be the same on the source and destination computer.

B. The Plug-and-Play devices must be the same on the source and destination computers.

C. The mass storage controllers (SCSI or IDE) must be the same type on the source and destination computers.

D. The size of the destination computer's hard drive must be at least as large as the hard drive on the source computer.

15. You have decided to use the System Preparation Tool in conjunction with unattended installations of Windows 2000 server using disk imaging. Which command-line utility would you use to access the System Preparation Tool?

A. Sysprep.exe

B. Systemprep.exe

C. Sprep.exe

D. Prep.exe

Answers to Review Questions

1. B. The only option that can be used to automate installations of Windows 2000 Server are disk images prepared through the Sysprep utility. Remote Installation Services (RIS) is used to install Windows 2000 Professional only.

2. C. The Setup Manager utility (Setupmgr) is used to create unattended answer files to be used in conjunction with partially or fully automated installations.

3. A. You can find the Windows 2000 Deployment Tools on the Windows 2000 Server CD in Support\Tools\`Deploy.cab`.

4. C. To access the contents of a `.cab` file, you use the Extract command on Windows Explorer's File menu.

5. C. If you want the target computer to be a domain controller, you will have to run the `DCPROMO` utility after the automated installation is complete. This can be used with an answer file with the [DCInstall] section properly configured. This option would use the following command:
DCPROMO /Answer:*answer_file_name.*

6. C, D. When you run Setup Manager to create Sysprep answer files, the only two options that you see in the Platform dialog box are Windows 2000 Professional and Windows 2000 Server.

7. D. RIPrep images are associated with an RIS server and are not used with disk duplication and the System Preparation Tool.

8. D. The `-quiet` switch is used to run the Sysprep installation with no user interaction.

9. A. You can configure options for the End User License Agreement (EULA), whether the computer will belong to a workgroup or domain, and the Administrator password. You cannot specify the product key that will be used through Setup Manager. The product key could be edited in manually to the answer file after the Wizard creates the file.

10. D. You can configure telephony settings, regional settings, languages, printer installation, and a command that will be run the first time a user logs on through Additional Settings dialog box.

11. A. The -pnp command switch is used to force Setup to run Plug-and-Play detection of hardware.

12. B. The -reboot command-line switch is used to force the target computer to reboot after installation.

13. B. The -nosidgen command-line switch is used to skip the creation of a new SID on the destination computer. This option is used with disk cloning.

14. B. Plug-and-Play devices on the source and destination computers do not need to match, as long as the drivers for the Plug-and-Play devices are on the HCL or are available from the vendor.

15. A. When you expand the Deployment Tools, you can access Sysprep.exe, which runs the System Preparation Tool.

Chapter

3

Configuring the Windows 2000 Server Environment

MICROSOFT EXAM OBJECTIVES COVERED IN THIS CHAPTER

- ✓ Configure hardware devices.
- ✓ Configure driver signing options.
- ✓ Update device drivers.
- ✓ Troubleshoot problems with hardware.

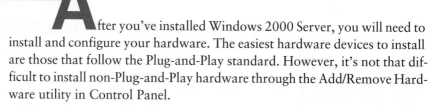

After you've installed Windows 2000 Server, you will need to install and configure your hardware. The easiest hardware devices to install are those that follow the Plug-and-Play standard. However, it's not that difficult to install non-Plug-and-Play hardware through the Add/Remove Hardware utility in Control Panel.

To configure your hardware, you generally use the Computer Management utility or Control Panel. You can also create custom administrative consoles through the Microsoft Management Console (MMC).

In this chapter, you will learn how to configure the Windows 2000 Server environment, beginning with an overview of the main configuration utilities. Then you will learn how to update drivers and manage driver signing. Finally, you will learn how to configure and manage Windows 2000 services.

The utilities and procedures for managing Windows 2000 Server devices and drivers are the same as those for managing Windows 2000 Professional devices and drivers.

Windows 2000 Management Utilities

Windows 2000 Server includes several utilities for managing various aspects of the operating system configuration:

- Control Panel allows you to configure a wide range of options, such as your display, mouse, and system properties.

- The Computer Management utility provides tools for managing common system functions, the computer's storage facilities, and the computer's services.

- The Microsoft Management Console (MMC) provides a common environment for administrative tools.

- The Registry Editor allows you to edit the Registry for advanced system configuration.

Each of these utilities is covered in detail in the following sections.

Control Panel

Control Panel is the main utility for configuring your computer's setup. You can access Control Panel by selecting Start ➤ Settings ➤ Control Panel or by opening My Computer and selecting Control Panel. The Control Panel window contains icons for its options, as shown in Figure 3.1. Table 3.1 provides brief descriptions of Control Panel options.

FIGURE 3.1   The Control Panel window

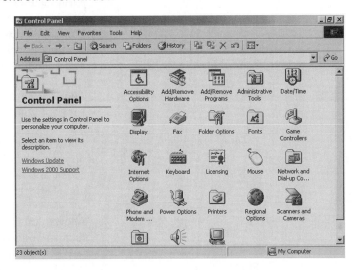

TABLE 3.1 Control Panel Options

Option	Description
Accessibility Options	Allows you to configure options that make Windows 2000 more accessible to users with limited sight, hearing, or mobility
Add/Remove Hardware	Allows you to install, remove, and trouble-shoot your hardware (primarily used for non-Plug-and-Play hardware)
Add/Remove Programs	Allows you to change or remove programs that are currently installed on your computer, add new programs, and add or remove Windows 2000 components
Administrative Tools	Provides access to Windows 2000 administrative utilities, including Component Services, Computer Management, Data Sources (ODBC), Event Viewer, Local Security Policy, Performance, Services, and Telnet Server Administration
Date/Time	Allows you to set the date, time, and time zone for your computer
Display	Allows you to configure your computer's display, including background, screen saver, appearance, Active Desktop, and visual effects
Fax	Allows you to configure fax send and receive options.
Folder Options	Allows you to configure folder options, such as general folder properties, file associations, and offline files and folders

TABLE 3.1 Control Panel Options *(continued)*

Option	Description
Fonts	Allows you to manage the fonts installed on your computer
Game Controllers	Allows you to add, remove, and configure game controllers, including joysticks and game pads
Internet Options	Allows you to configure Internet connection properties, including security, content settings, and Internet programs
Keyboard	Allows you to configure keyboard settings, including speed, input locales (language and keyboard layout), and the keyboard driver
Licensing	Allows you to specify how many licenses have been purchased and can be used by clients attaching to the server
Mouse	Allows you to configure mouse settings, including button configuration, mouse pointers, motion settings, and the mouse driver
Network and Dial-up Connections	Contains settings for network and dial-up connections and a Wizard to create new connections
Phone and Modem Options	Allows you to configure telephone dialing options and modem properties
Power Options	Allows you to configure power schemes, hibernation, APM, and UPS options
Printers	Allows you to install and manage printers

TABLE 3.1 Control Panel Options *(continued)*

Option	Description
Regional Options	Allows you to set regional options, including numbers, currency, time, date, and input locales
Scanners and Cameras	Allows you to configure cameras and scanners
Scheduled Tasks	Allows you to configure tasks to be run at specific times or intervals
Sounds and Multimedia	Allows you to configure sound devices and to assign sounds to system events
System	Allows you to configure system properties, including network identification, hardware, user profiles, and advanced settings
Users and Passwords	For Windows 2000 member servers, provides a simple tool for managing users and passwords (the Local Users and Groups utility is used for more advanced user management, as described in Chapter 4, "Managing Users and Groups")

Computer Management

Computer Management provides a single, consolidated tool for managing common management tasks. The interface is organized into three main areas:

- System Tools provides access to utilities for managing the computer, such as Event Viewer and System Information.

- Storage provides access to utilities for managing the computer's storage, such as Disk Management and Disk Defragmenter.

- Services and Applications provides access to utilities for managing the computer's services, such as Windows Management Instrumentation (WMI) Control and Indexing Service.

You can access Computer Management by right-clicking the My Computer icon on your Desktop and selecting Manage from the pop-up menu. The main Computer Management window is shown in Figure 3.2.

FIGURE 3.2 The Computer Management window

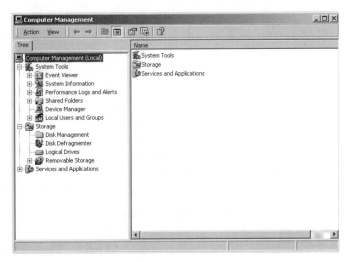

The following sections provide an overview of the utilities that can be accessed through Computer Management.

System Tools

System Tools includes six utilities that are used to manage common system functions.

Event Viewer   The *Event Viewer* utility tracks information about your hardware and software. You can also monitor Windows 2000–related security events. Event Viewer tracks information through three log files:

- The Application log includes events related to applications that are running on the computer, such as SQL Server or Outlook Express application errors.

- The Security log includes events related to security, such as the success or failure of actions monitored through auditing.

- The System log includes events related to the operating system, such as failure to load a device driver.

In addition, these logs are created on Windows 2000 domain controllers:

- The Directory Service log includes events related to directory services, such as directory database replication events.

- The DNS Server log includes events related to the DNS service, such as when the DNS server is started.

- The File Replication Service log includes events related to file replication, such as when connections have been established with other computers that will participate in file replication.

The Event Viewer utility is discussed in detail in Chapter 15, "Performing System Recovery Functions."

System Information   The *System Information* utility is used to collect and display information about the computer's current configuration. This information can be used to troubleshoot your computer's configuration. It can also be printed and kept for reference.

In System Information, the information is organized into five categories by default: System Summary, Hardware Resources, Components, Software Environment, and Internet Explorer 5.

Performance Logs and Alerts   Through the *Performance Logs and Alerts* utility, you can configure logs of performance-related data (called counter logs and trace logs) and generate alerts based on performance-related data. You can view the logs through the Windows 2000 System Monitor utility or through database or spreadsheet applications. The Performance Logs and Alerts utility is discussed in detail in Chapter 14, "Optimizing Windows 2000."

Shared Folders   Through the *Shared Folders* utility, you can create and manage shared folders on the computer. This utility displays the following information:

- All of the shares that have been created on the computer

- The user sessions that are open on each share

- The files that are currently open, listed by user

The Shared Folders utility is covered in more detail in Chapter 7, "Accessing Files and Folders."

Device Manager   The *Device Manager* utility provides information about all of the devices that your computer currently recognizes. For each device, Device Manager shows the following information:

- Whether or not the hardware on your computer is working properly
- Settings for the device
- Resources used by the device

From Device Manager, you can load, unload, and update *device drivers*. A device driver is software that allows a specific piece of hardware to communicate with the Windows 2000 operating system. You also can print a summary of all the device information for your computer. The Device Manager utility is discussed in more detail in the "Managing Hardware Devices through Device Manager" section later in this chapter.

Local Users and Groups   The *Local Users and Groups* utility is used to manage users and groups on a Windows 2000 Server running as a member server or standalone server. The Local Users and Groups utility is discussed in detail in Chapter 4, "Managing Users and Groups."

On Windows 2000 domain controllers, user accounts are managed through the Active Directory Users and Computers utility.

Storage

Storage contains four utilities that are used to manage the computer's storage facilities:

Disk Management   *Disk Management* is the Windows 2000 graphical interface for managing disks, volumes, partitions, logical drives, and dynamic volumes. The Disk Management utility is discussed in detail in Chapter 6, "Managing Disks."

Disk Defragmenter   The *Disk Defragmenter* utility is used to analyze and defragment your disk. The purpose of disk defragmentation is to optimize disk access by rearranging existing files so that they are stored contiguously. The Disk Defragmenter utility is discussed in detail in Chapter 6.

Logical Drives   The *Logical Drives* utility lists all of the logical drives that exist on your computer, so that you can manage the properties of each logical drive.

Removable Storage   The *Removable Storage* utility provides information about your computer's removable storage media. Removable storage media include CD-ROMs, DVDs, tapes, and jukeboxes containing optical discs.

Services and Applications

With the Services and Applications utility, you can manage all of the services installed on your computer. The services are grouped into three categories (you may see additional services, depending on your computer's configuration).

WMI Control   *WMI Control* provides an interface for monitoring and controlling system resources. Through WMI Control, you can view WMI status and manage Windows 2000 operations and configuration settings.

Services   *Services* lists all of the services on your computer. Through Services, you can manage general service properties, the logon account the service uses, and the computer's recovery response if the service fails. This utility also shows any dependencies that the service requires. The Services utility is covered in more detail in the "Managing Windows 2000 Services" section later in this chapter.

Indexing Service   The *Indexing Service* is used to create an index based on the contents and properties of files stored on your local hard drive. A user can then use the Windows 2000 Search function to search through or query the index for specific keywords. Figure 3.3 shows an example of an Indexing Service Query Form.

By default, the Indexing Service is not started on a Windows 2000 Server computer. This service is required for successful indexing and query support.

FIGURE 3.3 A query in the Indexing Service

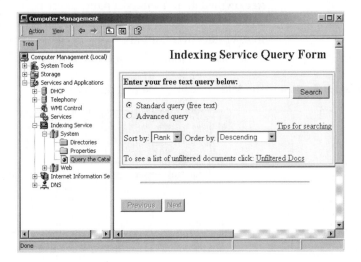

Microsoft Management Console

The *Microsoft Management Console (MMC)* is the console framework for management applications. The MMC provides a common environment for *snap-ins*, which are administrative tools developed by Microsoft or third-party vendors.

The MMC offers many benefits, including the following:

- The MMC is highly customizable—you add only the snap-ins you need.

- Snap-ins use a standard, intuitive interface, so they are easier to use than previous versions of administrative utilities.

- MMC consoles can be saved and shared with other administrators.

- You can configure permissions so that the MMC runs in authoring mode, which an administrator can manage, or in user mode, which limits what users can access.

- Most snap-ins can be used for remote computer management.

As shown in Figure 3.4, the MMC console contains two panes: a console tree on the left and a details pane on the right. The console tree lists the hierarchical structure of all of the snap-ins that have been loaded into the console. The details pane contains a list of properties or other items that are part of the snap-in that is highlighted in the console tree.

FIGURE 3.4 The MMC console tree and details pane

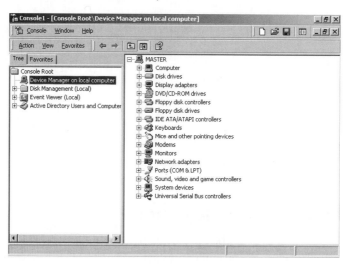

On a Windows 2000 Server computer, there is no item created for the MMC by default. To open the MMC, select Start ➢ Run and type **mmc** in the Run dialog box. When you first open the MMC, it contains only the Console Root folder. The MMC does not have any administrative functionality by default. It is simply a framework that is used to organize administrative tools through the addition of snap-in utilities.

Configuring MMC Modes

You can configure the MMC to run in author mode, for full access to the MMC functions, or in one of three user modes, which have more limited access to the MMC functions. To set a console mode, select Console ➢ Options to open the Options dialog box. In this dialog box, you can select from the console modes listed in Table 3.2.

TABLE 3.2 MMC Console Modes

Console Mode	Description
Author mode	Allows use of all the MMC functions
User mode–full access	Allows users full access to window management commands, but they cannot add or remove snap-ins
User mode–limited access, multiple window	Allows users to create new windows, but they can access only the areas of the console tree that were visible when the console was last saved
User mode–limited access, single window	Allows users to access only the areas of the console tree that were visible when the console was last saved, and they cannot create new windows

Adding Snap-Ins

To add snap-ins to MMC and save your console, take the following steps:

1. From the main console window, select Console ➤ Add/Remove Snap-in to open the Add/Remove Snap-in dialog box.

2. Click the Add button to open the Add Standalone Snap-in dialog box.

3. Highlight the snap-in you wish to add and click the Add button.

4. If prompted, specify whether the snap-in will be used to manage the local computer or a remote computer. Click the Close button, and then click the Finish button.

5. Repeat steps 3 and 4 to add each snap-in you want to include in your console.

6. When you are finished adding snap-ins, click the Close button.

7. Click the OK button to return to the main console screen.

8. After you have added snap-ins to create a console, you can save the console by selecting Console ➤ Save As and entering a name for your

console. You can save the console to a variety of locations, including in a program group or on the Desktop. By default, custom consoles have an .msc extension.

In exercises in later chapters, you will add MMC snap-ins to create different custom consoles and save them in various locations. This will give you an idea of the flexibility of the MMC and how you can set up custom consoles for your administrative tasks.

Registry Editor

The *Registry* is a database that the operating system uses to store configuration information. The Registry Editor program is used to edit the Registry. This utility is designed for advanced configuration of the system. Normally, when you make changes to your configuration, you use other utilities, such as Control Panel.

Only experienced administrators should use the Registry Editor. It is intended to be used to make configuration changes that can be made only directly through the Registry. For example, you might edit the Registry to specify an alternate location for a print spool folder. Improper changes to the Registry can cause the computer to fail to boot. You should use the Registry Editor with extreme caution.

Windows 2000 ships with two Registry Editor utilities:

- The *REGEDT32* program is the primary utility that you should use in Windows 2000. It supports full editing of the Registry. To use REGEDT32, select Start ➤ Run and type **REGEDT32** in the Run dialog box.

- The *REGEDIT* program is included with Windows 2000 because it has better search capabilities than REGEDT32. However, it lacks some of the options that are available with REGEDT32. For example, you can't set security for Registry keys through REGEDIT, and REGEDIT does not offer the option of using the utility in read-only mode. To use REGEDIT, select Start ➤ Run and type **REGEDIT** in the Run dialog box.

The Registry is organized in a hierarchical tree format of keys and subkeys that represent logical areas of computer configuration. By default, when you open the Registry Editor, you see five Registry key windows, as shown in Figure 3.5. The five Registry keys are described in Table 3.3.

FIGURE 3.5   The Registry key windows

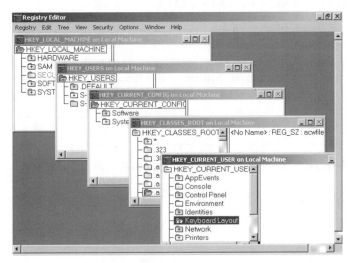

TABLE 3.3   Registry Keys

Registry Key	Description
HKEY_CURRENT_USER	Contains the configuration information for the user who is currently logged on to the computer. This key is a subkey of the HKEY_USERS key.
HKEY_USERS	Contains the configuration information for all users of the computer.
HKEY_LOCAL_MACHINE	Contains computer hardware configuration information. This computer configuration is used regardless of the user who is logged in.
HKEY_CLASSES_ROOT	Contains configuration information that is used by Windows Explorer to properly associate file types with applications.
HKEY_CURRENT_CONFIG	Contains the configuration of the hardware profile that is used during system startup.

Installing Hardware

If you buy new hardware, it will probably be *Plug-and-Play*, meaning it has a combination of hardware and software that allows the operating system to automatically recognize and configure new hardware without any user intervention. If you use older hardware, you will most likely need to configure the hardware to be properly recognized by the operating system.

Microsoft ✓ *Exam Objective*	**Configure hardware devices.**

Installing Plug-and-Play Devices

Windows 2000 Plug-and-Play support includes the following features:

- Automatic and dynamic recognition of hardware that is installed
- Automatic resource allocation (or reallocation, if necessary)
- Determination of the correct driver that must be loaded for hardware support
- Support for interaction with the Plug-and-Play system
- Support for power management features

To test Plug-and-Play device installation, I installed a second EIDE drive on my computer, upgraded my CD-ROM drive, and added a Zip drive. Each time I added a device, Windows 2000 Server automatically recognized it, and I did not need to set any configuration options.

Installing Non-Plug-and-Play Hardware

Legacy or older hardware is also supported by Windows 2000 Server. When you install this type of hardware, you need to configure it in the same manner you did before Plug-and-Play technology was introduced.

First, you need to configure the hardware device's resources manually on the device or through a software configuration program. Hardware resources include the interrupt request (IRQ), I/O port address, memory address, and Direct Memory Access (DMA) settings. Before you configure the resources for the new device, you should determine which resources are available. You can view a listing of the currently allocated resources in the Device Manager utility, as follows:

1. Right-click My Computer and select Manage. In the Computer Management window, select System Tools, and then select Device Manager.

2. Select View ≻ Resources by Connection.

3. Device Manager displays a list of the current resources. Click a resource to see all of the resources of that type that have been allocated. Figure 3.6 shows an example of an IRQ listing in Device Manager.

FIGURE 3.6   Viewing resource allocation in Device Manager

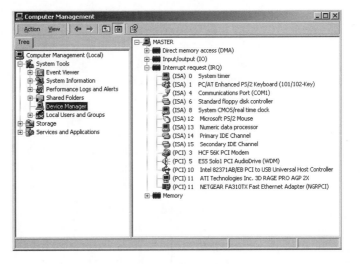

After you've configured the hardware resources, you can use the Add/Remove Hardware utility in Control Panel to add the new device to Windows 2000 Server and install the device driver. If the device is not listed, you will need to use a manufacturer-provided driver. Insert the disk that contains the driver and click the Have Disk button in Add/Remove Hardware.

Configuring Hardware Devices

You can manage hardware devices through the Device Manager utility and through Control Panel, depending on the device you wish to configure. Both utilities present Properties dialog boxes for the hardware connected to your computer.

Microsoft ✓ *Exam* *Objective*	**Configure hardware devices.**

Managing Hardware Devices through Device Manager

Along with displaying information about your hardware devices, the Device Manager utility provides some configuration options for these devices. It also offers help for troubleshooting problems with devices that are not working properly.

To manage a device through Device Manager, right-click My Computer and select Manage. In the Computer Management window, select System Tools, and then select Device Manager. In the right pane of the Device Manager window, double-click the category of the device you wish to manage to see a list of the devices of that type recognized by your computer. Then double-click the specific device you wish to manage. The device Properties dialog box that appears will have different tabs, depending on its type.

For example, to manage your CD-ROM drive, double-click DVD/CD-ROM Drives, and then double-click the CD-ROM. This brings up the device Properties dialog box, which has three tabs:

- The General tab, shown in Figure 3.7, lists the device type, manufacturer, and location. It also shows the device status, which indicates whether or not the device is working properly. If the device is not working properly, you can click the Troubleshooter button in the lower-right area of the dialog box to get some help with resolving the problem.

FIGURE 3.7   The General tab of a CD-ROM Properties dialog box

- The Properties tab, shown in Figure 3.8, allows you to set options such as volume and playback settings.

FIGURE 3.8   The Properties tab of a CD-ROM Properties dialog box

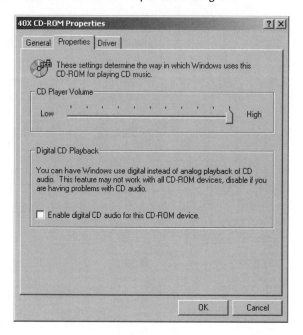

- The Driver tab, shown in Figure 3.9, shows information about the cur-rently loaded driver, as well as buttons that allow you to see driver details, uninstall the driver, or update the driver. (See the "Updating Drivers" section later in this chapter for details on updating a driver.)

FIGURE 3.9   The Driver tab of a CD-ROM Properties dialog box

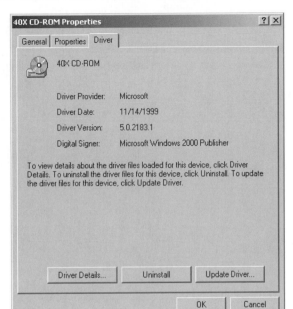

As another example, if your computer supports the Universal Serial Bus (USB), and USB is enabled in the BIOS, you will see Universal Serial Bus Controller listed in Device Manager. Double-click your USB controller to see the dialog box shown in Figure 3.10.

FIGURE 3.10   The USB controller Properties dialog box

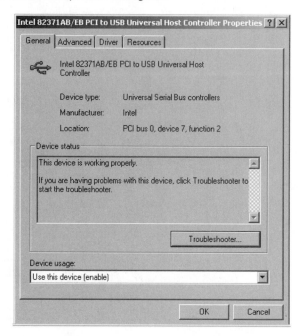

Universal Serial Bus (USB) is an external bus standard that allows you to connect USB devices through a USB port. USB supports transfer rates up to 12Mbps. A single USB port can support up to 127 devices. Examples of USB devices include modems, printers, and keyboards.

The USB controller Properties dialog box has four tabs with options and information for your USB adapter. The General and Driver tabs have the same type of information that is displayed for CD-ROM devices. The Advanced tab allows you to configure how much of the bandwidth each device that is connected to the USB adapter can use. The Resources tab shows all of the resources that are used by the USB adapter. After the USB adapter is configured, you can attach USB devices to the adapter in a daisy-chain configuration.

In Exercise 3.1, you will use Device Manager to manage a hardware device.

All of the exercises in this chapter can be performed from your domain controller or member server.

EXERCISE 3.1

Managing Hardware with Device Manager

1. From the Desktop, right-click My Computer and select Manage. In Computer Management, select System Tools, then Device Manager.

2. Double-click DVD/CD-ROM Drives, then double-click the DVD or CD-ROM device you wish to manage.

3. In the General tab of the device Properties dialog box, verify that your device is working properly. If the device is not working properly, click the Troubleshooter button. The Troubleshooter Wizard will ask you a series of questions and attempt to help you resolve the problem.

4. Click the Properties tab and configure the options to suit your personal preferences.

5. Click the Driver tab. Note the information about the currently loaded driver.

6. Click the OK button to save your settings and close the dialog box.

See Chapter 9, "Managing Network Interoperability," for details on installing and configuring network adapters.

Managing Hardware Devices through Control Panel

As noted earlier in the chapter, Control Panel is the main utility for configuring your computer. As examples of configuring your hardware through Control Panel, the following sections describe how to manage the video adapter, keyboard, and scanner or camera attached to your computer.

Configuring Video Adapters

The options for video adapters are on the Settings tab of the Display Properties dialog box, as shown in Figure 3.11. To access this dialog box, select the Display icon in Control Panel or right-click an empty area on your Desktop and select Properties from the pop-up menu.

The other tabs in the Display Properties dialog box allow you to customize the appearance of your Desktop.

FIGURE 3.11 The Settings tab of the Display Properties dialog box

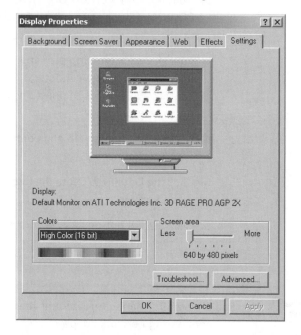

The Colors option in the Settings tab sets the color depth for your video adapter. The Screen Area option allows you to set the resolution for your video adapter.

To configure advanced settings for your video adapter, click the Advanced button in the lower-right corner of the Settings tab. This opens the monitor Properties dialog box, as shown in Figure 3.12. This dialog box has five tabs with options for your video adapter and monitor:

- The General tab allows you to configure the font size for the display. You can also specify what action Windows 2000 will take after you change your display settings.

- The Adapter tab allows you to view and configure the properties of your video adapter.

- The Monitor tab allows you to view and configure the properties of your monitor, including the refresh frequency (how often the screen is redrawn).

A lower refresh frequency setting can cause your screen to flicker. Setting the refresh frequency too high can damage some hardware.

- The Troubleshooting tab allows you to configure how Windows 2000 uses your graphics hardware. For example, you can configure hardware acceleration settings.

- The Color Management tab allows you to select color profiles (the colors that are displayed on your monitor).

FIGURE 3.12 The monitor Properties dialog box

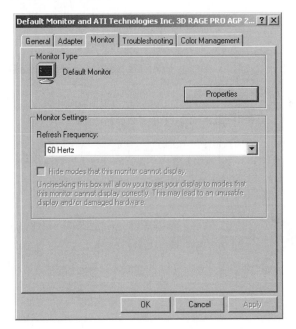

In Exercise 3.2, you will view the properties of your video adapter.

Usually, the video adapter is configured for typical use. Be careful if you change these settings, because improper settings may cause your display to be unreadable.

EXERCISE 3.2

Managing Your Video Adapter

1. Right-click an empty area on the Desktop, select Properties, and select the Settings tab.

2. Click the Advanced button at the bottom of the Settings tab. Note your current settings in the General tab.

3. Click the Adapter tab. Note your current settings.

4. Click the Monitor tab. Note your current settings.

5. Click the Troubleshooting tab. Note your current settings.

6. Click the OK button to close the monitor Properties dialog box.

7. Click the OK button to close the Display Properties dialog box.

Configuring the Keyboard

You can configure keyboard options through the Keyboard Properties dialog box, shown in Figure 3.13. To access this dialog box, select the Keyboard icon in Control Panel.

You must have a keyboard attached to your computer before you can install Windows 2000 Server.

FIGURE 3.13 The Keyboard Properties dialog box

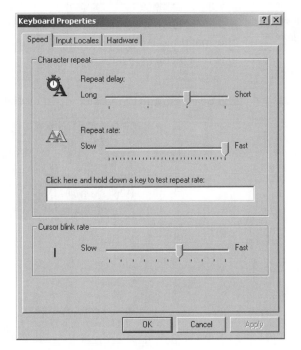

This dialog box has three tabs with options that control your keyboard's behavior:

- The Speed tab lets you configure how quickly characters are repeated when you hold down a key. You can also specify the cursor blink rate.

- The Input Locales tab allows you to specify the keyboard layout based on your input locale (for example, English United States or United States-Dvorak).

- The Hardware tab specifies the device settings for your keyboard.

Managing Imaging Devices

After you install a scanner or digital camera on a Windows 2000 Server computer, you can manage the device through the Scanners and Cameras Properties dialog box, shown in Figure 3.14. You access this dialog box by selecting the Cameras and Scanners icon in Control Panel.

A scanner is a device that can read text or graphics on paper and translate the information into digital data that the computer can understand. Digital cameras take pictures in a digital format that can be read by the computer.

FIGURE 3.14 The Scanners and Cameras Properties dialog box

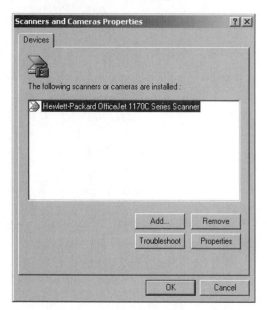

The Scanners and Cameras Properties dialog box lists the devices that are recognized by your computer. You can click the Add button to add a scanner or camera, the Remove button to remove the selected device, or the Troubleshoot button to run a Troubleshooter Wizard. Clicking the Properties button displays a dialog box with additional options, as shown in Figure 3.15.

FIGURE 3.15   A scanner Properties dialog box

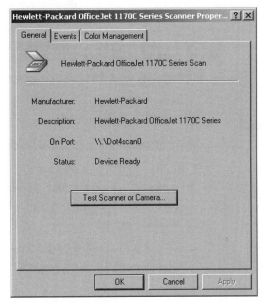

The scanner or camera Properties dialog box has three tabs with options and information about the device:

- The General tab lists the manufacturer, description, port, and status of the device. It also contains a button that you can click to test the scanner or camera.

- The Events tab allows you to associate an event with an application. For example, you can specify that when you scan a document, it should be automatically linked to the imaging program, and the imaging program will start and display the document you just scanned.

- The Color Management tab allows you to associate a color profile with the scanner or camera.

If you have a scanner or digital camera installed on your computer, you can complete the steps in Exercise 3.3 to view and configure its properties.

EXERCISE 3.3

Managing and Monitoring Imaging Devices

1. Select Start ➢ Settings ➢ Control Panel and double-click the Scanners and Camera icon.

2. In the Scanners and Cameras Properties dialog box, click the Properties button.

3. In the General tab of the scanner or camera Properties dialog box, click the Test Scanner or Camera button to make sure the device is working properly.

4. Click the Events tab. Set any associations based on your computer's configuration and your personal preferences.

5. Click the Color Management tab. If desired, associate a color profile with the scanner or camera.

6. Click the OK button to close the scanner or camera Properties dialog box.

7. Click the OK button to close the Scanner and Camera Properties dialog box.

8. Close Control Panel.

Managing Device Drivers

Most of the devices on the Microsoft Hardware Compatibility List (HCL) have device drivers that are included on the Windows 2000 Server distribution CD. Managing device drivers involves updating them when necessary and deciding how to handle drivers that may not have been properly tested.

Updating Drivers

Device manufacturers periodically update device drivers to add functionality or enhance driver performance. The updated drivers are typically posted on the device manufacturer's Web site.

Microsoft *Exam* *Objective*	**Update device drivers.**

You can update device drivers through the Device Manager utility, as follows:

1. From the Desktop, right-click My Computer and select Manage from the pop-up menu.

2. The Computer Management window opens. Select System Tools, then Device Manager.

3. The right side of the window lists all of the devices that are installed on your computer. Double-click the device whose driver you want to update.

4. The device Properties dialog box appears. Click the Driver tab.

5. The Driver tab appears. Click the Update Driver button in the lower-right corner.

6. The Upgrade Device Driver Wizard starts. Click the Next button.

7. The Install Hardware Device Drivers dialog box appears, as shown in Figure 3.16. You can choose to have the Wizard search for a suitable driver, which is recommended, or you can have the Wizard display a list of known drivers for the device so you can choose a specific driver. Make your selection and click the Next button.

FIGURE 3.16   The Install Hardware Device Drivers dialog box

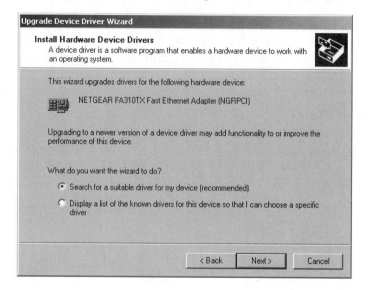

8. The Locate Driver Files dialog box appears, as shown in Figure 3.17. This dialog box allows you to specify the location of the driver files. You can have the Wizard look on your floppy disk or CD-ROM drive, specify a location, or use the Microsoft Windows Update utility. Once you make your selection, click the Next button.

The Microsoft Windows Update utility connects your computer to Microsoft's Web site and checks for driver and other updates. This utility is discussed in more detail in Chapter 14.

FIGURE 3.17   The Locate Driver Files dialog box

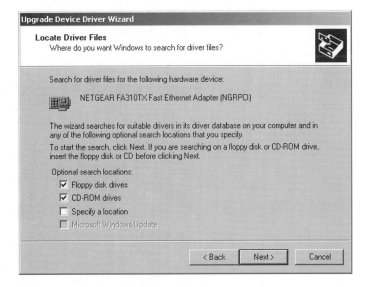

9. The Driver Files Search Results dialog box appears, as shown in
Figure 3.18. Select the driver you wish to install and click the Next button.

FIGURE 3.18   The Driver Files Search Results dialog box

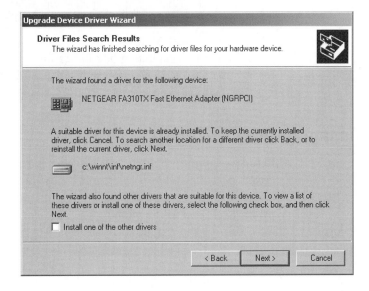

10. The files will be installed for your driver. Then you will see the Completing the Upgrade Device Driver Wizard dialog box, as shown in Figure 3.19. Click the Finish button to close this dialog box.

FIGURE 3.19 The Completing the Upgrade Device Driver Wizard dialog box

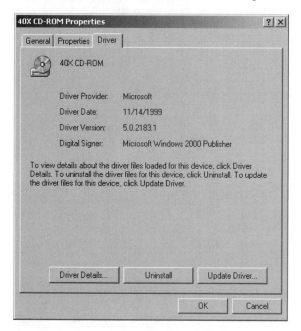

11. You may see a dialog box indicating that you must restart your computer before the change can be successfully implemented. If necessary, restart your computer.

Managing Driver Signing

In the past, poorly written device drivers have caused problems with Windows operating systems. Microsoft is now promoting a mechanism called *driver signing* as a way of ensuring that drivers are properly tested before they are released to the public.

Microsoft
✓ *Exam*
Objective

Configure driver signing options.

Configuring Driver Signing Options

You can specify how Windows 2000 Server will respond if you select to install an unsigned driver through the Driver Signing Options dialog box. To access this dialog box, right-click My Computer, select Properties from the pop-up menu, and click the Hardware tab in the System Properties dialog box. This tab has Hardware Wizard, Device Manager, and Hardware Profiles options, as shown in Figure 3.20. Clicking the Driver Signing button in the Device Manager section opens the Driver Signing Options dialog box, as shown in Figure 3.21.

FIGURE 3.20 The Hardware tab of the System Properties dialog box

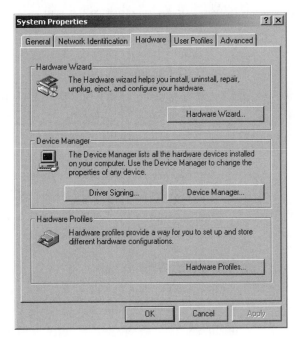

FIGURE 3.21 The Driver Signing Options dialog box

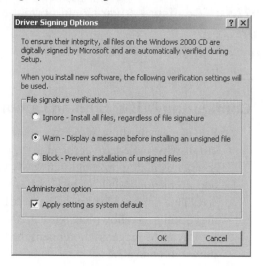

In the Driver Signing Options dialog box, you can select from three options for file system verification:

- The Ignore option has Windows 2000 install all of the files, whether or not they are signed. You will not see any type of message about driver signing.

- The Warn option has Windows 2000 display a warning message before installing an unsigned file. You can then choose to continue with the installation or cancel it. This is the default setting.

- The Block option has Windows 2000 prevent the installation of any unsigned file. You will see an error message when you attempt to install the unsigned driver, and you will not be able to continue.

If you check the Apply Setting As System Default option, the settings that you apply will be used by all users who log on to the computer.

Verifying File Signature

Windows 2000 includes a File Signature Verification utility that you can use to verify that system files have been digitally signed. The installation of unsigned drivers can cause random lockups of a server. To run this utility, you issue the `sigverif` command from the Command Prompt window. This starts the File Signature Verification utility, as shown in Figure 3.22.

FIGURE 3.22   The File Signature Verification utility

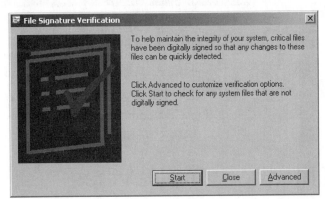

If you want to configure advanced verification options, such as advanced search options or logging options, click the Advanced button. When you are ready to check that your files have been digitally signed, click the Start button. The utility will scan all of your system files. When it's finished, it will display the signature verification results.

In Exercise 3.4, you will check the setting for driver signing and run the File Signature Verification utility.

EXERCISE 3.4

Managing Driver Signing

1. From the Desktop, right-click My Computer and select Properties.

2. In the System Properties dialog box, click the Hardware tab, and then click the Driver Signing button.

3. In the Driver Signing Options dialog box, verify that the Warn radio button is selected and the Apply Setting As System Default check box is checked.

4. Click the OK button to close the dialog box. Click the OK button within the System Properties dialog box.

5. Select Start ➢ Programs ➢ Accessories ➢ Command Prompt.

6. In the Command Prompt window, type **sigverif** and press Enter.

7. In the File Signature Verification window, click the Start button.

8. When the results of the signature verification appear, note if the utility detected any files that were not digitally signed. Click the Close button.

9. Close the Command Prompt window.

Troubleshooting Devices

If you are having a problem with a hardware device, you can check its properties through the Device Manager utility. If the source of the problem isn't obvious from the device's properties, or if the device isn't listed in Device Manager, you can use the Windows 2000 Troubleshooter Wizard to help you figure out what is wrong.

Microsoft ✓ *Exam Objective*	**Troubleshoot problems with hardware.**

Checking Device Properties

When Device Manager does not properly recognize a device, it reports the problem by displaying an exclamation point icon next to the device. To troubleshoot a device that is not working properly, double-click the device to open its Properties dialog box.

Figure 3.23 shows an example of the Properties dialog box for a device that does not have the proper driver loaded. In this case, you would make sure that you have the most up-to-date driver for the controller, and then click the Reinstall Driver button to correct the problem. Other device Properties dialog boxes contain a Troubleshoot button, which you can click to run the Troubleshooter Wizard, as described in the next section.

FIGURE 3.23   The device Properties dialog box reports that the device is not configured correctly.

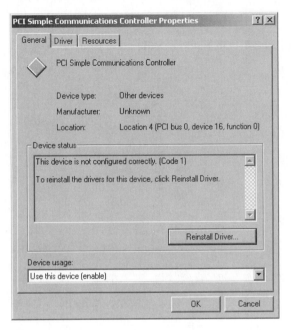

Running the Troubleshooter Wizard

If a device connected to your computer doesn't appear in Device Manager, you can get some hints on troubleshooting through the Troubleshooter Wizard. As an example, if your sound card is not working properly and is not listed in Device Manager, you can use the Troubleshooter Wizard as follows:

1. From the Desktop, right-click My Computer and select Manage. In Computer Management, select System Tools, then Device Manager.

2. In Device Manager, double-click Computer, and then double-click Standard PC.

3. The computer Properties dialog box appears. Click the Troubleshoot button.

4. The Windows 2000 Help window opens, with the Hardware Troubleshooter section displayed in the right pane, as shown in Figure 3.24.

You can select from a wide range of problems. In this example, select the My Sound Card Doesn't Work radio button and click the Next button.

FIGURE 3.24 Selecting a problem to troubleshoot

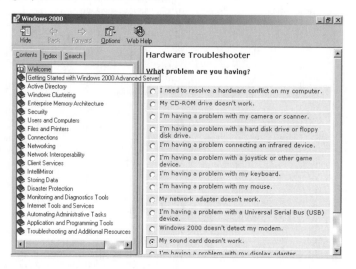

5. The Troubleshooter Wizard window for sound cards appears. Here, you specify whether or not you have a PCI sound card. In this example, select the Yes, I Have a PCI Sound Card option and click the Next button.

6. The Troubleshooter Wizard asks if your sound card is compatible with Windows 2000. If your sound card is not on the HCL, the Wizard directs you to the card manufacturer for assistance. In this example, select the Yes, Windows 2000 Supports My Sound Card option and click the Next button.

7. The Troubleshooter Wizard identifies a possible problem and solution. It suggests that your PCI card might be in a faulty slot. You are advised to move your PCI card to a different slot to see if this corrects the problem. (You may prefer to have this tested at a computer repair center.)

8. After you follow the suggested procedure, the Wizard asks if this fixed your problem. In this example, the problem is fixed. If your device still isn't working, the Troubleshooter Wizard will suggest other possible courses of action.

Managing Windows 2000 Services

A service is a program, routine, or process that performs a specific function within the Windows 2000 operating system. You manage services through the Services window, shown in Figure 3.25. You can access this window in a variety of ways, including through the Computer Management utility (right-click My Computer, select Manage, expand Services and Applications, and then expand Services), through Administrative Tools, or as an MMC snap-in.

FIGURE 3.25 The Services window

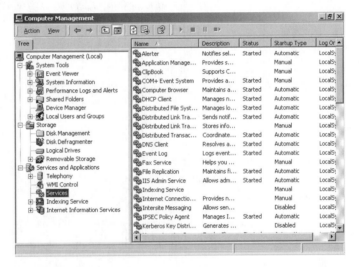

For each service, the Services window listing shows the name, a short description, the startup type, and the logon account that is used to start the service. To configure the properties of a service, double-click it to open its Properties dialog box. This dialog box contains four tabs of options for services, which are described in the following sections.

Configuring General Service Properties

The General tab of the service Properties dialog box (see Figure 3.26), allows you to view and configure the following options:

- The service display name
- A description of the service

- The path to the service executable

- The startup type, which can be automatic, manual, or disabled

- The current service status

- Startup parameters that can be applied when the service is started

The buttons across the lower part of the dialog box allow you to start, stop, pause, or resume the service.

FIGURE 3.26 The General tab of the service Properties dialog box

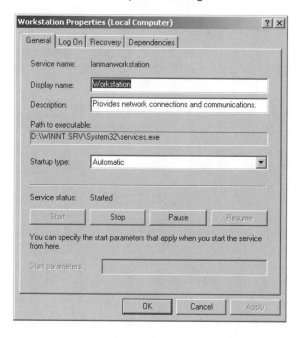

Configuring Service Log On Properties

The Log On tab of the service Properties dialog box, shown in Figure 3.27, allows you to configure the logon account that will be used to start the service. You can choose to use the local system account or specify another logon account.

FIGURE 3.27 The Log On tab of the service Properties dialog box

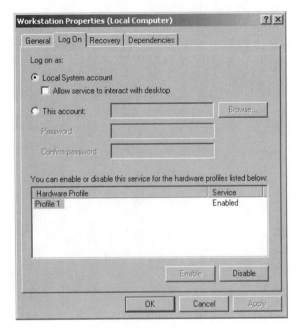

At the bottom of the Log On tab, you can select hardware profiles to associate the service with. For each hardware profile, you can set the service as enabled or disabled.

Configuring Service Recovery Properties

The Recovery tab of the service Properties dialog box, shown in Figure 3.28, allows you to configure what action will be taken if the service fails to load. For the first, second, and subsequent failures, you can select from the following actions:

- Take no action
- Restart the service
- Run a file
- Reboot the computer

FIGURE 3.28 The Recovery tab of the service Properties dialog box

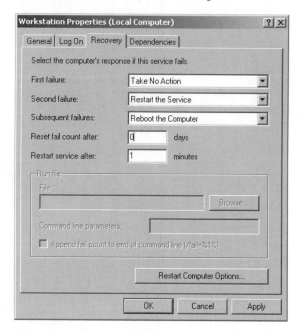

If you choose to run a file, you then specify the file and any command-line parameters. If you choose to reboot the computer, you can then configure a message that will be sent to users who are connected to the computer before it is restarted.

Checking Service Dependencies

The Dependencies tab of the service Properties dialog box, shown in Figure 3.29, lists any services that must be running in order for the specified service to start. If a service fails to start, you can use this information to determine what the dependencies are, then make sure that each dependency service is running.

FIGURE 3.29   The Dependencies tab of the service Properties dialog box

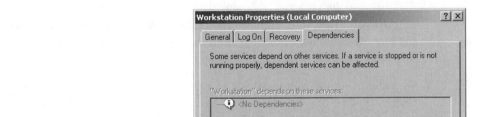

At the bottom of the Dependencies tab, you can see if any other services depend on this service. You should verify that there are no services that depend on a service that you are about to stop.

 **Real World Scenario**

Using Windows 2000 Services

Your company uses several applications that require a user to be logged on as a service. Some of the applications have specific instructions for setup, while other applications leave the specific configuration up to the administrator.

The problem with many of the applications is that they require the service to log on as a user with administrative rights. This could easily be a potential security violation, but there are steps you can take to manage your service accounts.

Consider using a naming convention so that you can easily identify the service accounts. For example, you could place a # sign in front of all service accounts. So if you have a virus scanner that uses a service account, you would create #VirScan as the user account that will be used to log on. Under user rights, you will typically assign this user account the Logon as a Service right. You should also make sure that the user account has a difficult password composed of alphanumeric and non-alphanumeric characters. If your domain uses password restrictions, you should configure the service accounts so that their passwords never expire.

Summary

In this chapter, you learned about configuring the Windows 2000 Server environment. We covered the following topics:

- Utilities used to manage configuration, which include Control Panel, Computer Management, the Microsoft Management Console (MMC), and the Registry Editor

- Installing hardware, including Plug-and-Play and non-Plug-and-Play devices

- Configuring hardware devices through Device Manager and Control Panel

- Managing device drivers, including how to update drivers and set options for driver signing

- Using the Windows 2000 Troubleshooter Wizard to troubleshoot problems with devices

- Managing Windows 2000 Server services

Exam Essentials

Be able to configure hardware devices for your server. Be aware of the different utilities that are used to install and configure hardware devices. Be able to successfully install Plug-and-Play hardware as well as non-Plug-and-Play hardware.

Successfully manage driver signing. Understand the purpose of driver signing and the levels of driver signing that are offered. Be able to configure driver signing based on the requirements of your organization.

Update device drivers. Understand the process of updating Win-dows 2000 device drivers. Know how to recover from failure due to updated drivers.

Be able to successfully troubleshoot hardware errors. Understand what causes hardware failure and be able to list common errors that cause hardware errors. Be able to successfully troubleshoot and correct hardware errors.

Key Terms

Before taking the exam, you should be familiar with the following terms:

Computer Management	Performance Logs and Alerts
Control Panel	Plug-and-Play
device driver	REGEDIT
Device Manager	REGEDT32
Disk Defragmenter	Registry
Disk Management	Removable Storage
driver signing	Services
Event Viewer	Shared Folders
Indexing Service	System Information
Local Users and Groups	System Tools
Logical Drives	Windows Management Instru-mentation (WMI) Control
Microsoft Management Console (MMC)	

Review Questions

1. Dan has four servers that are identically configured. One of the servers crashes and has to be completely reinstalled. He wants to document the configuration, including the drivers and versions that are loaded for each device. Which utility should he use to collect and display information about the reference computer's current configuration?

   A. System Information

   B. System Diagnostics

   C. Windows 2000 Diagnostics

   D. System Reports

2. Rena wants to edit her registry to add in a new subkey based on the setup and configuration instructions for a new application that she wants to install. How can she access the native 32-bit Windows Registry Editor?

   A. Through the Registry Editor program item in the Administrative Tools program group

   B. Through the Registry Editor icon in Control Panel

   C. Through the Registry Editor item in the Computer Management utility

   D. Through the command-line utility REGEDT32

3. Carlos has just upgraded the 10Mbps Ethernet card that was used by the Windows 2000 server to a 100Mbps Ethernet card. Which utility should he use to determine whether Windows 2000 properly recognized a newly installed network card?

   A. Device Manager

   B. Windows 2000 Diagnostics

   C. System Information

   D. Device Diagnostics

4. Kiesha's server uses a specialized video adapter. She recently received notification that there is an updated driver for the video adapter. Which utility should she use to update the device driver?

    A. Device Manager

    B. Windows 2000 Diagnostics

    C. System Information

    D. Device Diagnostics

5. Your company is a hardware manufacturer of printers. You are developing updated drivers for your most popular printers. During the development stage, none of the drivers are signed. You want to be able to install these drivers on your test Windows 2000 server without getting any messages in regard to driver signing. Which driver signing option allows Windows 2000 to install all files, whether or not they are signed, and does not display any type of message about driver signing?

    A. Ignore

    B. Override

    C. Install

    D. None

6. Your company IP policy requires that all drivers used by production servers be digitally signed. You are in charge of verifying that servers already in use comply with this policy. Which Windows 2000 command-line utility can be used to verify that system files have been digitally signed?

    A. `sigverify`

    B. `digsig`

    C. `digmanage`

    D. `sigverif`

7. Your Windows 2000 server is configured as a Global Catalog Master server. You want to make sure that no errors have been recorded through Event Viewer. Which of the following logs should you check to view events related to directory services?

    A. Application

    B. Security

    C. System

    D. Directory Service

8. The registered user of your server is currently listed as John Smith, who was the previous MIS manager. The server's registered user should be listed as the ABC Test Corporation. Which utility can you use to search the servers Registry for all references to John Smith?

    A. REGEDIT

    B. REGEDT32

    C. REGISTRY

    D. REGSEARCH

9. You have a Windows 2000 Server computer that is configured as a domain controller. You have configured auditing to track any changes a user makes to the server's configuration. Which of the following logs should you check to view any events that are related to auditing?

    A. Application

    B. Security

    C. System

    D. Directory Service

10. You back up your Windows 2000 Server each night. Each morning the network administrator removes the tape and inserts a new tape according to the tape rotation schedule. Which utility should the administrator use to manage the server's removable storage media, such as tapes and optical disks?

A. Removable Storage

B. Removable Media

C. Media Manager

D. Media Administrator

11. Jett is using File Replication Services. File Replication is not currently working. Which utility should he use to determine what the current status is of the File Replication Service?

A. Service Manager

B. Service Administrator

C. WMI Manager

D. Services

12. You are in charge of managing the Sales Windows 2000 server. You want to set up a customized MMC console screen. Which command-line utility should you use to start the Microsoft Management Console (MMC)?

A. mmconsole

B. adminconsole

C. mmc

D. managecon

13. When the Windows 2000 server was installed, 2GB of free space was left unassigned. Now you want to extend one of your volumes to include the free space. Which utility can you use to manage disks, volumes, partitions, logical drives, and dynamic volumes in Windows 2000?

A. Disk Manager

B. Disk Management

C. Disk Administrator

D. Local Disks and Volumes

14. You have a sound card that you want to install on your server that does not support Plug-and-Play. Which utility should you use to install the sound card?

A. Device Manager

B. System Information

C. Control Panel, Sound Cards

D. Control Panel, Add/Remove Hardware

15. Your Windows 2000 server has a generic video driver installed. You just updated the driver and now you want to set the display adapter's settings. Which utility should you use to set your display adapter's settings such as color and screen area?

A. Display Manager

B. Device Manager

C. Control Panel, Display

D. Control Panel, Video

Answers to Review Questions

1. A. The System Information utility is used to generate information about your computer's configuration.

2. D. She'll access the 32-bit Registry Editor through the command-line utility REGEDT32.

3. A. You can determine whether devices are working properly through the Device Manager utility.

4. A. You can update device drivers through the Device Manager utility.

5. A. If you configure driver signing with the Ignore option, drivers will be installed even if they are unsigned.

6. D. Windows 2000 includes the sigverif command-line utility, which verifies that system files have been digitally signed.

7. D. On Windows 2000 domain controllers, the Directory Service log in Event Viewer contains all of the events related to directory services.

8. A. The REGEDIT command is included with Windows 2000 because it provides better search capabilities than REDEDT32, which is the 32-bit Registry Editor intended to be used with Windows 2000.

9. B. The Security log in Event Viewer is used to monitor success and failure events that are related to auditing.

10. A. The Removable Storage utility provides information about your computer's removable storage media.

11. D. The Services utility lists all of the services on your computer. Through Services, you can manage general service properties, the logon account the service uses, and the computer's recovery response if the service fails. This utility also shows any dependencies that the service requires.

12. C. You can access the MMC through the mmc command-line utility.

13. B. Disk Management is the Windows 2000 graphical interface for managing disks, volumes, partitions, logical drives, and dynamic volumes. Windows NT used the Disk Administrator utility.

14. D. You use Control Panel, Add/Remove Hardware to add any hardware that does not support Plug-and-Play. Any device that you install should have a Windows 2000-compatible device driver.

15. C. Through Control Panel, Display you can set colors, screen area, and advanced options such as display font size.

Chapter

4

Managing Users and Groups

MICROSOFT EXAM OBJECTIVES COVERED IN THIS CHAPTER

✓ Implement, configure, manage, and troubleshoot local accounts.

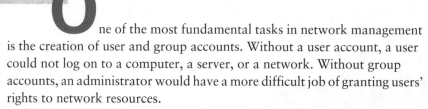

One of the most fundamental tasks in network management is the creation of user and group accounts. Without a user account, a user could not log on to a computer, a server, or a network. Without group accounts, an administrator would have a more difficult job of granting users' rights to network resources.

Windows 2000 Server supports local and Active Directory users and groups, so you can manage users from a local perspective as well as through the Active Directory.

This chapter begins with an overview of the types of Windows 2000 user and group accounts. Next, you will learn how to create and manage local and Active Directory user accounts. Finally, you will learn how to create and manage local and Active Directory groups.

Local and Active Directory User and Group Accounts

In Windows 2000, you can manage users and groups at the local level on Windows 2000 member servers and Windows 2000 Professional computers. On Windows 2000 domain controllers, you can manage users and groups using the Active Directory.

An Overview of User Accounts

A computer that is running Windows 2000 Professional or Windows 2000 Server (configured as a member server) has the ability to store its own user accounts database. The users that are stored at the local computer are known as *local users*.

The *Active Directory* is a directory service that is available with the Windows 2000 Server platform. It stores information in a central database that allows users to have a single user account for the network. The users and groups that are stored in the Active Directory's central database are called *Active Directory users* or *domain users*.

If you use local user accounts, they are required on each computer that the user needs access to within the network. For this reason, domain user accounts are commonly used to manage users on large networks.

On Windows 2000 Professional computers and Windows 2000 member servers, you create and manage local users through the *Local Users and Groups* utility. On Windows 2000 Server domain controllers, you manage users with the Microsoft *Active Directory Users and Computers* utility.

The Active Directory is covered in detail in *MCSE: Windows 2000 Directory Services Administration Study Guide*, 2nd ed., by Anil Desai with James Chellis (Sybex, 2000).

When you install Windows 2000 Server, there are several built-in user accounts that are created by default. The two most important accounts that are created are:

- The *Administrator* account, which is a special account that has full control over the computer. You provide a password for this account during Windows 2000 installation. The Administrator account can perform all tasks, such as creating users and groups, managing the file system, and setting up printing.

- The *Guest* account, which allows users to access the computer even if they do not have a unique username and password. Because of the inherent security risks associated with this type of user, this account is disabled by default. When this account is enabled, it is usually given very limited privileges.

By default, the name Administrator is given to the account with full control over the computer. You can increase the computer's security by renaming the Administrator account, and then creating an account named Administrator without any permissions. This way, even if a hacker is able to log on as Administrator, the intruder won't be able to access any system resources.

An Overview of Group Accounts

On a Windows 2000 member server, you can use only local groups. A *local group* resides on the Windows 2000 member server's local database.

On a Windows 2000 domain controller in the Active Directory, you can have security groups and distribution groups. A *security group* is a logical group of users who need to access specific resources. You use security groups to assign permissions to resources. A *distribution group* is a logical group of users who have common characteristics. Distribution groups can be used by applications and e-mail programs, for example Microsoft Exchange 2000.

Windows 2000 domain controllers also allow you to select group scope, which can be domain local, global, or universal. The scope types are used as follows:

- *Domain local groups* are used to assign permissions to resources. Local groups can contain user accounts, universal groups, and global groups from any domain in the tree or forest. A domain local group can also contain other domain local groups from its own local domain.

- *Global groups* are used to organize users who have similar network access requirements. Global groups can contain user and global groups from the local domain.

- *Universal groups* are used to logically organize users and appear in the global catalog (a special listing that contains limited information about every object in the Active Directory). Universal groups can contain users from anywhere in the domain tree or forest, other universal groups, and global groups.

On Windows 2000 Professional computers and Windows 2000 member servers, you create and manage local groups through the Local Users and Groups utility. On Windows 2000 Server domain controllers, you manage groups with the Microsoft Active Directory Users and Computers utility.

When you install Windows 2000 Server, there are several built-in group accounts that are created by default. Table 4.1 describes the built-in group accounts and indicates which environment (local, domain, or global) contains the built-in account.

TABLE 4.1 Built-in Group Accounts

Built-in Group	Description	Environment
Account Operators	Members of the Account Operators group can create domain user and group accounts, but can manage only the user and group accounts they create.	Domain
Administrators	The Administrators group has full rights and privileges. Its members can grant themselves any permissions they do not have by default to manage all of the objects on the computer. (Objects include the file system, printers, and account management.)	Local and domain

TABLE 4.1 Built-in Group Accounts *(continued)*

Built-in Group	Description	Environment
Backup Operators	The members of the Backup Operators group have rights to back up and restore the file system, even if the file system is NTFS and they have not been assigned permissions to the file system. However, the members of Backup Operators can access the file system only through the Backup utility. To be able to directly access the file system, they must have explicit permissions assigned. By default, there are no members of the Backup Operators local group.	Local and domain
Guests	The Guests group has limited access to the computer. This group is provided so that you can let people who are not regular users access specific network resources. As a general rule, most administrators do not allow Guest access because it poses a potential security risk. By default, the Guest user account is a member of the Guests local group.	Local and domain

TABLE 4.1 Built-in Group Accounts *(continued)*

Built-in Group	Description	Environment
Power Users	The Power Users group has fewer rights than the Administrators group, but more rights than the Users group. Power Users can create users and groups, but can manage only the users and groups they create. They can also create network shares and printers.	Local
Print Operator	The Print Operators group members can administer domain printers.	Domain
Replicator	The Replicator group is intended to support directory replication, which is a feature used by domain servers. Only domain users who will start the replication service should be assigned to this group. By default, there are no members of the Replicator local group.	Local and domain
Server Operators	The Server Operators group members can administer domain servers.	Domain

TABLE 4.1 Built-in Group Accounts *(continued)*

Built-in Group	Description	Environment
Users	The Users group is used by end users who should have very limited system access. If you have installed a fresh copy of Windows 2000 Server, the default settings for this group prohibit users from compromising the operating system or program files. By default, all users who have been created on the computer, except Guest, are members of the Users local group.	Local and domain
Cert Publishers	The Cert Publishers group members can manage enterprise certification and renewal agents.	Global
DHCP Administrators	The DHCP Administrators group has administrative rights to manage Dynamic Host Configuration Protocol (DHCP) servers.	Domain
DHCP Users	The DHCP Users group has the necessary rights to use DHCP services.	Domain
DnsAdmins	The DnsAdmins group has administrative rights to manage Domain Name System (DNS) servers.	Domain

TABLE 4.1 Built-in Group Accounts *(continued)*

Built-in Group	Description	Environment
DnsUpdateProxy	The DnsUpdateProxy group has permissions that allow DNS clients to perform dynamic updates on behalf of other clients, such as DHCP servers.	Global
Domain Admins	The Domain Admins group has complete administrative rights over the domain.	Global
Domain Computers	The Domain Computers group contains all of the workstations and servers that are a part of the domain.	Global
Domain Controllers	The Domain Controllers group contains all of the domain controllers in the domain.	Global
Domain Guests	The Domain Guests group has limited access to the domain. This group is provided so that you can let people who are not regular users access specific network resources.	Global
Domain Users	The Domain Users group contains all of the domain users. This group should have very limited system access.	Global

TABLE 4.1 Built-in Group Accounts *(continued)*

Built-in Group	Description	Environment
Enterprise Admins	The Enterprise Admins group has complete administrative rights over the enterprise. This group has the highest level of permissions of all groups.	Global
Group Policy Creator Owners	The Group Policy Creator Owners group has permissions to modify group policy for the domain.	Global
RAS and IAS Server Group	The RAS and IAS Server group contains the remote access service (RAS) and Internet Authentication Service (IAS) servers in the domain. Servers in this group can access remote access properties of users.	Domain
Schema Admins	The Schema Admins group has special permissions to modify the schema of the Active Directory.	Global
WINS Users	The WINS Users group has special permissions to view information on the Windows Internet Name Service (WINS) server.	Domain

On a Windows 2000 Server domain controller, groups are located in the Users folder and the Builtin folder.

Working with Local User Accounts

To set up and manage local users, you use the Local Users and Groups *utility*. With Local Users and Groups, you can create, delete, and rename user accounts, as well as change passwords.

Microsoft ✓ *Exam* *Objective*	**Implement, configure, manage, and troubleshoot local accounts.**

The procedures for many basic local user management tasks—such as creating, disabling, deleting, and renaming user accounts—are the same for both Windows 2000 Server and Professional.

Using the Local Users and Groups Utility

The first step to working with Windows 2000 Server local user accounts is to access the Local Users and Groups utility. There are two common methods for accessing this utility:

- You can load Local Users and Groups as a Microsoft Management Console (MMC) snap-in.

- You can access the Local Users and Groups utility through the Computer Management utility.

The following steps are used to add the Local Users and Groups snap-in to the MMC:

1. Select Start ➢ Run, type **mmc**, and press Enter to open the MMC window, as shown in Figure 4.1.

FIGURE 4.1 The MMC window

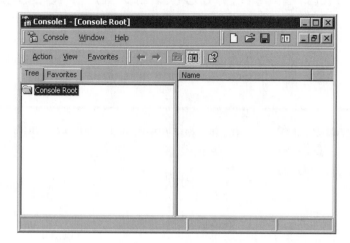

2. Select Console ➤ Add/Remove Snap-in to open the Add/Remove Snap-in dialog box.

3. Click the Add button to open the Add Standalone Snap-in dialog box.

4. Select Local Users and Groups and click the Add button.

5. The Choose Target Machine dialog box appears, with Local Computer selected. Click the Finish button. You return to the Add Standalone Snap-in dialog box.

6. Click the Close button. You return to the Add/Remove Snap-in dialog box.

7. Click the OK button. You will see that the Local Users and Groups snap-in has been added to the MMC.

8. Save the console by selecting Console ➤ Save. Specify the path and filename for your console. For easy access, you might want to save the console to your Desktop.

If your computer doesn't have the MMC configured, the quickest way to access the Local Users and Groups utility is through the Computer Management utility. Right-click My Computer and select Manage from the pop-up menu to open the Computer Management window. In the System Tools folder, you will see the Local Users and Groups folder. Expand that folder to access the Users and Groups folders in the utility, as shown in Figure 4.2.

FIGURE 4.2   The Local Users and Groups folder in Computer Management

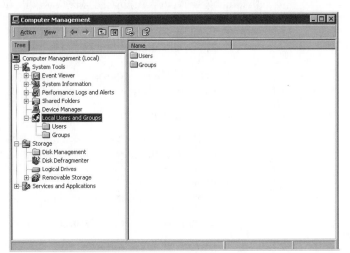

In Exercise 4.1, you will use both methods for accessing the Local Users and Groups utility. This exercise should be completed from your member server.

EXERCISE 4.1

Accessing the Local Users and Groups Utility

In this exercise, you will first add the Local Users and Groups snap-in to the MMC, so you can access it from the MMC. Next, you will add a shortcut to your Desktop that will take you to the MMC. Finally, you will use the other access technique of opening the Local Users and Groups utility from the Computer Management utility.

Adding the Local Users and Groups Snap-in to the MMC

1. Select Start ➤ Run. In the Run dialog box, type **mmc** and press Enter.

2. Select Console ➤ Add/Remove Snap-in.

3. In the Add/Remove Snap-in dialog box, click the Add button.

4. In the Add Standalone Snap-in dialog box, select Local Users and Groups and click the Add button.

5. In the Choose Target Machine dialog box, click the Finish button to accept the default selection of Local Computer.

6. Click the Close button in the Add Standalone Snap-in dialog box. Then click the OK button in the Add/Remove Snap-in dialog box.

7. In the MMC window, expand the Local Users and Groups folder to see the Users and Groups folders.

Adding the MMC to Your Desktop

1. Select Console ➢ Save. Click the folder with the up arrow icon until you are at the root of the computer.

2. Select the Desktop option and specify **Admin Console** as the filename. The default extension is .msc. Click the Save button.

Accessing Local Users and Groups through Computer Management

1. Right-click My Computer and select Manage.

2. In the Computer Management window, expand the System Tools folder, and then expand the Local Users and Groups folder.

Creating New Users

To create users on a Windows 2000 Server computer, you must be logged on as a user with permissions to create a new user, and you must be a member of the Administrators group or Power Users group.

Username Rules and Conventions

The only real requirement for creating a new user is that you must provide a valid username, meaning that the name must follow the Windows 2000 rules for usernames. However, it's also a good idea to have your own rules for usernames, which form your naming convention.

These are the Windows 2000 rules for usernames:

- A username must be between 1 and 20 characters.

- The username must be unique to the user, different from all other user and group names stored within the specified computer.

- The username cannot contain any of these characters:

  * / \ [ ] : ; | = , + * ? < > "

- A username cannot consist exclusively of periods or spaces or combinations of the two.

Keeping these rules in mind, you should choose a *naming convention*, which is a consistent naming format. For example, consider a user named Kate Donald. One naming convention might use the last name and first initial, for the username DonaldK. Another naming convention might use the first initial and last name, for the username KDonald. Other user-naming conventions are based on the naming convention defined for e-mail names, so that the logon name and e-mail name match. You should also provide a mechanism that would accommodate duplicate names. For example, if you had a user named Kate Donald and a user named Kevin Donald, you might use a middle initial, for the usernames KLDonald and KMDonald.

Naming conventions should also be applied to objects such as groups, printers, and computers.

Usernames and Security Identifiers

When you create a new user, a *security identifier (SID)* is automatically created on the computer for the user account. The username is a property of the SID. For example, a user SID might look like this:

S-1-5-21-823518204-746137067-120266-629-500

It's apparent that using SIDs would make administration a nightmare. Fortunately, for your administrative tasks, you see and use the username instead of the SID.

SIDs have several advantages. Because Windows 2000 uses the SID as the user object, you can easily rename a user while retaining all the properties of that user. SIDs also ensure that if you delete and recreate a user using the same username, the new user account will not have any of the properties of the old account, because it is based on a new, unique SID. Renaming and deleting user accounts are discussed later in this chapter.

Options for New User Accounts

To create a new user, you open the Local Users and Groups utility, highlight the Users folder, and select Action ≻ New User. This opens the New User dialog box, as shown in Figure 4.3.

FIGURE 4.3 The New User dialog box

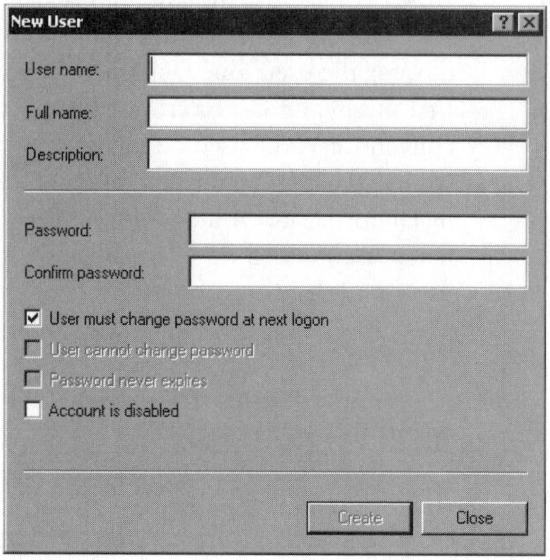

In this dialog box, you must fill in the User Name field. All of the other settings in the New User dialog box are optional. Here is a list of the text fields and check boxes in the New User dialog box:

User Name   Defines the username for the new account. Choose a name that is consistent with your naming convention (e.g., WSmith). This is the only required field. Usernames are not case-sensitive.

Full Name   Allows you to provide more detailed information about this user. This is typically the user's first and last name (e.g., Wendy Smith). By default, this field is the same as the entry in the User Name field.

Description   Allows you to provide additional information. This is typically used to specify a title and/or a location (e.g., Sales–Texas), but it can be used for any purpose.

Password   Assigns the initial password for the user. For security purposes, it is not advisable to use readily available information about the user. If your clients are not exclusively Windows 2000, passwords can be up to 14 characters and are case-sensitive. If you operate in a Windows 2000–only environment, passwords can be up to 127 characters.

Confirm Password   Confirms that you typed the password the same way two times, to verify that you entered the password correctly.

User Must Change Password at Next Logon   If selected, forces the user to change the password the first time that user logs on. This is done to increase security. By default, this option is selected.

User Cannot Change Password   If selected, prevents a user from changing the password. It is useful for accounts like Guest and those that are shared by more than one user. By default, this option is not selected.

Password Never Expires   If selected, specifies that the password will never expire, even if a password policy has been specified. For example, you might select this option if this is a service account and you do not want the administrative overhead of managing changing passwords. By default, this option is not selected.

Account Is Disabled   If selected, specifies that this account cannot be used for logon purposes. For example, you might select this option for template accounts or if an account is not currently being used. It helps keep inactive accounts from posing security threats. By default, this option is not selected.

Make sure that your users know that usernames are not case-sensitive, but passwords are.

In Exercise 4.2, you will create several new local user accounts. We will use these users for the subsequent exercises in this chapter. Before you start this exercise, make sure that you are logged on as user with permissions to create new users and have already added the Local Users and Groups snap-in to the MMC (see Exercise 4.1). This exercise must be completed from your member server.

EXERCISE 4.2

Creating New Local Users

1. Open the MMC and expand the Local Users and Groups snap-in.

2. Highlight the Users folder and select Action ≻ New User. The New User dialog box appears.

3. In the User Name field, type **Cam**.

4. In the Full Name field, type **Cam Presely**.

5. In the Description field, type **Sales Vice President**.

6. Click the Create button to add the user. (Leave the Password and Confirm Password fields empty and the defaults for the check boxes.)

7. Use the New User dialog box to create six more users. For each user, uncheck the User Must Change Password at Next Logon check box. Fill out the fields as follows:

   Name: **Dick**; Full Name: **Dick Jones**; Description: **Sales–Florida**; Password: (blank)

   Name: **Terry**; Full Name: **Terry Belle**; Description: **Marketing**; Password: (blank)

   Name: **Ron**; Full Name: **Ron Klein**; Description: **PR**; Password: **superman**

   Name: **Wendy**; Full Name: **Wendy Smith**; Description: **Sales–Texas**; Password: **supergirl**

   Name: **Emily**; Full Name: **Emily Buras**; Description: **President**; Password: **peach**

   Name: **Michael**; Full Name: **Michael Phillips**; Description: **Tech Support**; Password: **apple**

8. After you've finished creating all of the users, click the Close button to exit the New User dialog box.

Disabling User Accounts

When a user account is no longer needed, the account should be disabled or deleted. If you choose to disable an account, you can later enable that account to restore it with all of its associated user properties. An account that is deleted can never be recovered.

Real World Scenario

Creating Many Users at Once

You have just installed a new Windows 2000 network. You now need to populate your servers with users. You need to configure 1,500 user accounts. You do not want to use the Windows 2000 GUI utilities because the process will take forever.

Most of the tasks that you can do through GUI utilities in Windows 2000, you can also accomplish through command-line utilities. In this case, you could create a batch file using the NET USER command-line utility. You can get help for this command by typing NET USER /? at a command prompt window.

If you wanted to learn about all of the command-line utilities supported by Windows 2000, you would access Start ➢ Help, then click the Contents tab, select Reference, then MS-DOS commands. Each command is presented alphabetically with a description and example.

 User accounts that are not in use pose a security threat because an intruder could access your network though an inactive account. For example, after inheriting a network, I ran a network security diagnostic and noticed several accounts for users who no longer worked for the company. These accounts had Administrative rights, including dial-in permissions. This was not a good situation, and the accounts were deleted on the spot.

You might disable an account because a user will not be using it for a period of time, perhaps because that employee is going on vacation or taking a leave of absence. Another reason to disable an account is if you're planning on putting another user in that some function. For example, suppose that Rick, the engineering manager, quit. If you disable his account, when your company hires a new engineering manager, you can simply rename the user account (from Rick to the username for the new manager) and enable that account. This ensures that the user who takes over Rick's position will have all of the user properties and own all of the resources that original user Rick had.

Disabling accounts also provides a security mechanism for special situations. For example, if your company were laying off a group of people, a security measure would be to disable their accounts at the same time as these employees get their layoff notices. This prevents the users from inflicting any damage to the company's files on their way out. (Yes, this does seem cold-hearted, and the remaining employees are bound to fear for their jobs if they aren't able to log on later because the servers go down, but it does serve the purpose.)

You disable a user account by checking the Account Is Disabled check box in the user's Properties dialog box, shown in Figure 4.4.

FIGURE 4.4 A user Properties dialog box

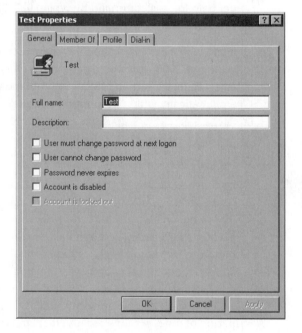

In Exercise 4.3, you will disable a user account. Before you follow this exercise, you should have already created the new users (see Exercise 4.2). This exercise must be completed from your member server.

EXERCISE 4.3

Disabling a User

1. Open the MMC and expand the Local Users and Groups snap-in.

2. Open the Users folder. Double-click user Dick to open his Properties dialog box.

3. In the General tab, check the Account Is Disabled box and click the OK button.

4. Log off as Administrator and attempt to log on as Dick. This should fail, since the account is now disabled.

5. Log on as Administrator.

You can also access a user's Properties dialog box by highlighting the user and right-clicking.

Deleting User Accounts

As noted in the previous section, you should delete a user account if you are sure that the account will never be needed again.

In Exercise 4.4, you will delete a user account. This exercise assumes that you have completed the previous exercises in this chapter. This exercise must be completed from your member server.

EXERCISE 4.4

Deleting a User

1. Open the MMC and expand the Local Users and Groups snap-in.

2. Open the Users folder and highlight user Dick.

EXERCISE 4.4

3. Select Action ➢ Delete.

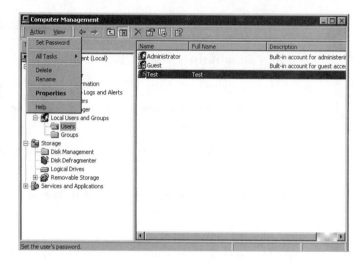

4. The dialog box for confirming user deletion appears. Click the Yes button.

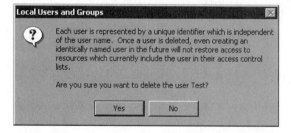

 The Administrator and Guest accounts cannot be deleted. The *initial user* account can be deleted.

Renaming Users

Once an account has been created, you can rename the account at any time. Renaming a user account allows the user to retain all of the associated user properties of the previous username. As noted earlier in the chapter, the name is a property of the SID.

You might want to rename a user account because the user's name has changed (for example, the user got married) or because the name was spelled incorrectly. Also, as explained in "Disabling User Accounts," earlier in this chapter, you can rename an existing user's account for a new user whom you want to have the same properties, such as someone hired to take an ex-employee's position.

In Exercise 4.5, you will rename a user account. This exercise assumes that you have completed all of the previous exercises in this chapter. This exercise must be completed from your member server.

EXERCISE 4.5

Renaming a User

1. Open the MMC and expand the Local Users and Groups snap-in.

2. Open the Users folder and highlight user Terry.

3. Select Action ➤ Rename.

4. Type in the username **Taralyn** and press Enter. Notice that the Full Name retained the original property of Terry in the Local Users and Groups utility.

Renaming a user does not change any "hard-coded" names, such as the user's home directory. If you want to change these names as well, you need to modify them manually.

Changing a User's Password

What do you do if user Terry forgot her password and can't log on? You can't just open a dialog box and see her old password. However, as the Administrator, you can change Terry's password, and then she can use the new one.

In Exercise 4.6, you will change a user's password. This exercise assumes that you have completed all of the previous exercises in this chapter. This exercise must be completed from your member server.

EXERCISE 4.6

Changing a User's Password

1. Open the MMC and expand the Local Users and Groups snap-in.

2. Open the Users folder and highlight user Ron.

3. Select Action ➤ Set Password. The Set Password dialog box appears.

4. Type in the new password **golf** and then confirm the password. Click the OK button.

Managing Local User Properties

For more control over user accounts, you can configure user properties. Through the user Properties dialog box, you can change the original password options, add the users to existing groups, and specify user profile information.

To open the user Properties dialog box, access the Local Users and Groups utility, open the Users folder, and double-click the user account. The user Properties dialog box has tabs for the four main categories of properties: General, Member Of, Profile, and Dial-in.

The General tab contains the information that you supplied when you set up the new user account, including any Full Name and Description information you entered, the password options you selected, and whether or not the account is disabled (see "Creating a New User," earlier in this chapter). If you want to modify any of these properties after you've created the user, simply open the user Properties dialog box and make the changes on the General tab.

The Member Of tab is used to manage the user's membership in groups. The Profile tab lets you set properties to customize the user's environment. These properties are discussed in detail in the following sections.

The Dial-in tab is used to define dial-in properties such as remote access permissions and callback options. These options are used in conjunction with remote access servers and virtual private network (VPN) servers, which are covered in Chapter 13, "Managing Remote Connections."

Managing Local User Group Membership

The Member Of tab displays all of the groups that the user belongs to, as shown in Figure 4.5. From this tab, you can add the user to an existing group or remove that user from a group. To add a user to a group, click the Add button and select the group that the user should belong to. If you want to remove the user from a group, highlight the group and click the Remove button.

FIGURE 4.5   The Member Of tab of the user Properties dialog box

The steps used to add a user to an existing group are shown in Exercise 4.7. This exercise assumes that you have completed all of the previous exercises in this chapter. This exercise must be completed from your member server.

EXERCISE 4.7

Adding a User to a Group

1. Open the MMC and expand the Local Users and Groups snap-in.

2. Open the Users folder and double-click user Wendy. The user Properties dialog box appears.

3. Select the Member Of tab and click the Add button. The Select Groups dialog box appears.

EXERCISE 4.7 *(continued)*

4. Highlight the Power Users group and click the Add button. Then click the OK button.

5. Click the OK button to close the user Properties dialog box.

Groups are covered in more detail later in "Working with Local and Active Directory Group Accounts," later in this chapter.

Setting Up the Local User Environment

The Profile tab, shown in Figure 4.6, allows you to customize the user's environment. Here, you can specify these items for the user:

- User profile path

- Logon script

- Home folder

The following sections describe how these properties work and when you might want to use them.

FIGURE 4.6   The Profile tab of the user Properties dialog box

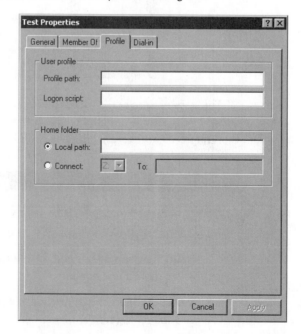

Setting a Profile Path

User profiles contain information about the Windows 2000 environment for a specific user. For example, profile settings include the Desktop arrangement, program groups, and screen colors that users see when they log on.

If the configuration option is a personal preference, it is most likely a part of the user profile. Configuration options that relate to the computer are not a part of the user profile. For example, the mouse driver is not a part of a user profile. However, the properties of the mouse configuration—such as the speed, pointer, and mouse button settings—reflect the user's personal preferences and are a part of a user profile.

By default, when a user logs on, a profile is opened for a user. The first time users log on, they receive a default user profile. A folder that matches the user's logon name is created for the user in the Documents and Settings folder. The user profile folder that is created holds a file called NTUSER.DAT, as well as subfolders that contain directory links to the user's Desktop items.

Any changes that the user makes to the Desktop are stored on the local computer when the user logs off. For example, suppose that user Rick logs on, picks his wallpaper, creates shortcuts, and customizes the Desktop to his personal preference. When he logs off, his profile is stored locally. If another user logs on at the same computer, that user's profile—not Rick's—is loaded.

The Profile Path option in the Profile tab is used to point to another location for profile files other than the default local location. This allows users to access profiles that have been stored on a shared network folder. This way, profiles can be used for an individual user or shared between a group of users. To specify a path, just type it in the Profile Path text box using Universal Naming Convention (UNC) format.

NOTE   User profiles are covered in more detail in *MCSE: Windows 2000 Professional Study Guide* 2nd ed., by Lisa Donald with James Chellis (Sybex, 2001).

In Exercise 4.8, you will create and manage user profiles. This exercise assumes that you have completed Exercise 4.2. This exercise must be completed from your member server.

Using User Profiles

1. Select Start ➤ Programs ➤ Accessories ➤ Windows Explorer, expand My Computer, then Local Disk (C:), then Documents and Settings. The folder will have subfolders for only those users who have logged in. Verify that no user profiles folders exist for the users Emily and Michael (since they haven't logged on yet).

2. Log off as Administrator and log on as Emily (with the password **peach**).

3. Right-click an open area on the Desktop and select Properties. In the Display Properties dialog box, click the Appearance tab. Select the color scheme Red, White, and Blue (VGA), click the Apply button, and then click the OK button.

4. Right-click an open area on the Desktop and select New ➤ Shortcut. In the Create Shortcut dialog box, type **CALC**. Accept the name CALC as the name for the shortcut and click the Finish button.

5. Log off as Emily and log on as Michael (with the password **apple**). Notice that user Michael sees the Desktop configuration stored in the default user profile.

6. Log off as Michael and log on as Emily. Notice that Emily sees the Desktop configuration you set up in steps 3, 4, and 5.

7. Log off as Emily and log on as Administrator. Select Start ➤ Programs ➤ Accessories ➤ Windows Explorer, expand My Computer, then Local Disk (C:), then Documents and Settings. Verify that user profile folders now exist for Emily and Michael.

Using Logon Scripts

Logon scripts are files that run every time a user logs on to the network. They are usually batch files, but they can be any type of executable file.

You might use logon scripts to set up drive mappings or to run a specific executable file each time a user logs on to the computer. For example, you could run an inventory management file that collects information about the computer's configuration and sends that data to a central management database. Logon scripts are also useful for compatibility with non–Windows 2000 clients who want to log on but still maintain consistent settings with their native operating system.

To run a logon script for a user, enter the script name in the Logon Script text box in the Profile tab of the user Properties dialog box.

Logon scripts are not commonly used in Windows 2000 networks. Windows 2000 automates much of the user's configuration. In older NetWare environments, for example, this isn't the case, and administrators use logon scripts to configure the users' environment.

Setting Up Home Folders

Users normally store their personal files and information in a private folder called a *home folder*. In the Profile tab of the user Properties dialog box, you can specify the location of a home folder as a local folder or a network folder.

To specify a local path folder, choose the Local Path option and type the path in the text box next to that option. To specify a network path for a folder, choose the Connect option and specify a network path using a UNC (Universal Naming Convention) path. In this case, a network folder should already be created and shared.

In Exercise 4.9, you will assign a home folder to a user. This exercise assumes that you have completed all of the previous exercises in this chapter. This exercise must be completed from your member server.

EXERCISE 4.9

Assigning a Home Folder to a User

1. Open the MMC and expand the Local Users and Groups snap-in.

2. Open the Users folder and double-click user Wendy. The user Properties dialog box appears.

3. Select the Profile tab and click the Local Path radio button to select it.

4. Specify the home folder path by typing **C:\Users\Wendy** in the text box for the Local Path option. Then click the OK button.

5. Use Windows Explorer to verify that this folder was created.

Working with Active Directory User Accounts

To create domain accounts for users, you use the Active Directory Users and Computers utility. With this utility, you can add accounts to a domain in the Active Directory. (The creation of Active Directory is discussed in Chapter 1.) The following sections describe how to create new domain users and manage domain user properties.

Creating Active Directory Users

The Active Directory Users and Computers utility, shown in Figure 4.7, is the main tool for managing the Active Directory users, groups, and computers. You access this utility through Administrative Tools.

FIGURE 4.7 The Active Directory Users and Computers window

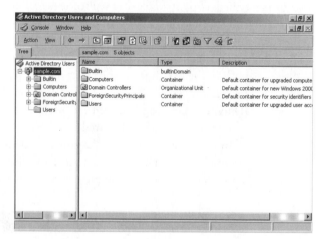

To create an Active Directory user, take the following steps:

1. Select Start ➢ Programs ➢ Administrative Tools ➢ Active Directory Users and Computers.

2. The Active Directory Users and Computers window appears. Right-click Users, select New from the pop-up menu, and select User.

3. The first New Object - User dialog box appears, as shown in Figure 4.8. Type in the user's first name, initials, last name, and logon name. The full name and pre–Windows 2000 logon name (for clients logging in from non–Windows 2000 operating systems) will be filled in

automatically when you enter the other information, but you can change them if desired. Click the Next button.

FIGURE 4.8   The New Object - User dialog box for username information

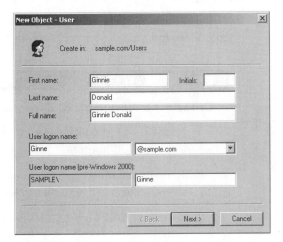

4. The second New Object - User dialog box appears, as shown in Figure 4.9. Type in and confirm the user's password. The check boxes in this dialog box allow you to specify that the user must change the password when the user logs on, the user cannot change the password, the password never expires, or the account is disabled. Click the Next button.

FIGURE 4.9   The New Object - User dialog box for password information

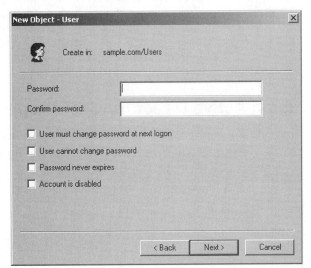

5. The final New Object - User dialog box appears. This dialog box shows the account you have configured. If all of the information is correct, click the Finish button.

In Exercise 4.10, you will create a new domain user. This exercise must be completed from your domain controller.

EXERCISE 4.10

Creating a New Active Directory User

1. Select Start ➢ Programs ➢ Administrative Tools ➢ Active Directory Users and Computers.

2. In the Active Directory Users and Computers window, right-click Users, select New, and then select User.

3. In the first New Object - User dialog box, enter the following information:

   In the First Name text box, type **Ginnie**.

   In the Initials text box, type **B**.

   In the Last Name text box, type **Donald**.

   In the User Logon Name, type **Ginnie**.

4. Click the Next button.

5. In the next New Object - User dialog box, type and confirm the password **cat**. Check the Password Never Expires check box. Then click the Next button.

6. In the final New Object - User dialog box, click the Finish button.

Managing Active Directory User Properties

For Active Directory users, you can configure a wide variety of properties. To access the Properties dialog box for an Active Directory user, open the Active Directory Users and Computers utility (by selecting Start ➢ Programs ➢ Administrative Tools ➢ Active Directory Users and Computers), open the

Users folder, and double-click the user account. The Active Directory user Properties dialog box has tabs for the 12 main categories of properties:

General	Member Of
Address	Dial-in
Account	Environment
Profile	Sessions
Telephones	Remote Control
Organization	Terminal Services Profile

Configuring General Active Directory User Properties

The General property tab, shown in Figure 4.10, contains the information that you supplied when you set up the new user account. You can add information in the Description and Office text boxes. You can also enter contact information for the user, including a telephone number, e-mail address, and Web page URL.

FIGURE 4.10   The General tab of the Active Directory user Properties dialog box

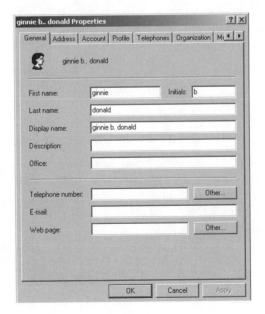

Adding Active Directory User Address Information

You can provide address information for the user on the Address tab, as shown in Figure 4.11. This tab has text boxes for the user's street address, post office box number, city, state or province, and zip code. You can also select a country or region identifier from the Country/Region drop-down list.

FIGURE 4.11 The Address tab of the Active User user Properties dialog box

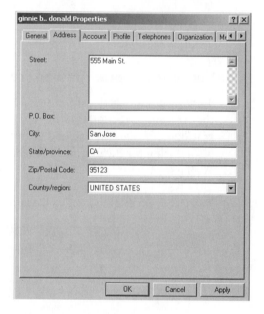

Controlling Active Directory Users' Accounts

Using the Account tab, shown in Figure 4.12, you can control the user's account. This tab shows the logon name information that you supplied when you set up the new user account and allows you to configure these settings:

- The logon hours for the user
- The computers that the user is allowed to log on from
- Account policies that apply to the user
- When the account expires

These settings are described in the following sections.

FIGURE 4.12   The Account tab of the Active Directory user Properties dialog box

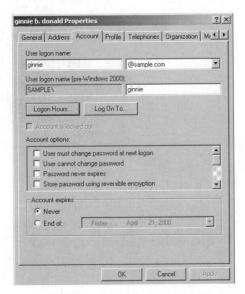

Controlling Logon Hours

When you click the Logon Hours button, you'll see the Logon Hours dialog box, as shown in Figure 4.13. By default, users are allowed to log on 24 hours a day, seven days a week. Logon hours are typically restricted during computer backups. You might also want to restrict logon hours for security reasons. A blue box indicates that logon is permitted. A white box indicates that logon is not permitted. You can change logon hours by selecting the hours you want to modify and clicking the Logon Permitted radio button or the Logon Denied radio button.

FIGURE 4.13 The Logon Hours dialog box

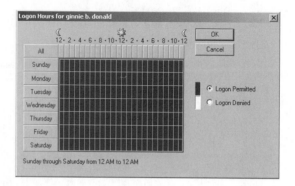

Controlling Computer Access

When you click the Log On To button, you'll see the Logon Workstations dialog box. This dialog box allows you to specify that the user can log on to all the computers in the network or limit the user to logging on to specific computers in the network. For example, if the Administrator works in a secure environment, you might limit the Administrator account to log on only from a specific computer. You configure the computers that the user can log on from based on the computer's name. You add the computers that are allowed by typing in the computer name and clicking the Add button.

Setting Account Options

The account options listed in the Account tab allow you to control password security for the user account. You can specify these account options:

- User must change password at next logon
- User cannot change password
- Password never expires
- Store password using reversible encryption

The account options are similar to the password policies that you can set for local user accounts. Password and other account policies are discussed in detail in Chapter 5, "Managing Security."

Setting Account Expiration

The End Of radio button at the bottom of the Account tab lets you set account expiration for a specific date. By default, accounts do not expire. You might want to set an expiration date if you have temporary employees and you want to disable their accounts on a specific date. This option is also useful in academic environments where students need user accounts, but their accounts should be disabled at the end of the academic period.

Setting Up the Active Directory User Environment

The Profile tab allows you to set up user profiles, logon scripts, and home folders. These options are configured in the same way as they are for local user accounts. See the "Setting Up the Local User Environment" section earlier in this chapter for details on using the options in the Profile tab.

Adding Active Directory User Telephone Information

The Telephones tab, shown in Figure 4.14, allows you to configure the user's telephone numbers for home, pager, mobile, fax, and IP phone. You can also add notes such as "Don't call home after 10:00 pm."

FIGURE 4.14   The Telephones tab of the Active Directory user Properties dialog box

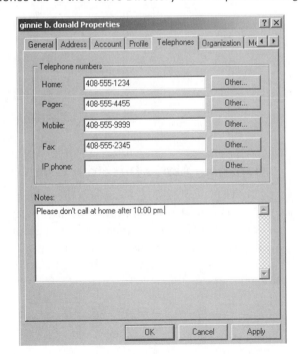

Adding Active Directory Organization Information

The Organization tab, shown in Figure 4.15, allows you to provide information about the user's role in your organization. You can enter the user's title, department, company, and manager. You can also specify to whom the user directly reports.

FIGURE 4.15 The Organization tab of the Active Directory user Properties dialog box

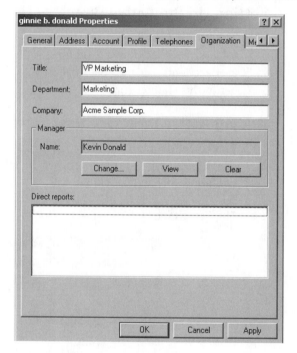

Managing Active Directory User Group Membership

The Member Of tab displays the groups that the user belongs to, as shown in Figure 4.16. You can add the user to an existing group by clicking the Add button. To remove the user from a group listed on this tab, highlight the group and click the Remove button.

FIGURE 4.16 The Member Of tab of the Active Directory user Properties dialog box

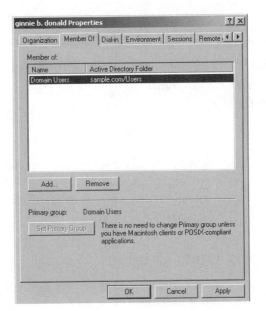

Configuring Dial-in Properties

Using the Dial-in tab, you configure the user's remote-access permissions for dial-in or VPN connections. Remote-access permissions are covered in Chapter 13 "Managing Remote Network Connections."

Configuring Terminal Services Properties

Four of the tabs in the Active Directory user Properties dialog box contain properties that relate to Terminal Services: Environment, Sessions, Remote Control, and Terminal Services Profile. Terminal Services is covered in Chapter 12, "Administering Terminal Services."

Working with Local and Active Directory Group Accounts

Groups are an important part of network management. Efficient administrators are able to accomplish the majority of their management tasks through the use of groups; they rarely assign permissions to individual users.

Microsoft ✓*Exam* *Objective*

Implement, configure, manage, and troubleshoot local accounts.

As explained earlier in the chapter, a Windows 2000 member server can have local groups. A Windows 2000 domain controller in the Active Directory can have security groups and distribution groups, and the groups can be assigned a scope of domain local, global, or universal.

Managing Local Groups

To set up and manage local groups, you use the Local Users and Groups utility. With Local Users and Groups, you can create, assign members to, rename, and delete groups.

Creating New Local Groups

In order to create a group, you must be logged on as a member of the Administrators group or the Power Users group. The Administrators group has full permissions to manage users and groups. The members of the Power Users group can manage only the groups that they create.

If possible, you should add users to the built-in local groups rather than creating new groups from scratch. This makes your job easier, because the built-in groups already have the appropriate permissions. All you need to do is add the users you want to be members of the group.

When you create a local group, you should use the following guidelines:

- The group name should be descriptive (for example, Accounting Data Users).

- The group name must be unique to the computer, different from all of the other group names and usernames that exist on that computer.

- Group names can be up to 256 characters. It is best to use alphanumeric characters for ease of administration. The backslash (\) character is not allowed.

As when you choose usernames, you should consider your naming conventions when assigning names to groups.

Creating groups is similar to creating users, and it is a fairly easy process. After you've added the Local Users and Groups snap-in to the MMC, you expand it to see the Users and Groups folders. Right-click the Groups folder and select New Group from the pop-up menu. This opens the New Group dialog box.

The only required entry in the New Group dialog box is the group name. Optionally, you can enter a description for the group and add (or remove) group members. When you're ready to create the new group, click the Create button.

In Exercise 4.11, you will create two new local groups. This exercise assumes that you have completed all of the exercises in the chapter. This exercise should be completed from your member server.

EXERCISE 4.11

Creating Local Groups

1. Open the MMC and expand the Local Users and Groups snap-in.

2. Right-click the Groups folder and select New Group.

3. In the New Group dialog box, type **Data Users** in the Group Name text box. Click the Create button.

4. In the New Group dialog box, type **Application Users** in the Group Name text box. Click the Create button. Click the Close button.

Managing Local Group Properties

After you've created a group, you can add members to it. A user can belong to multiple groups.

You can easily add and remove users through the group Properties dialog box, shown in Figure 4.17. To access this dialog box, from the Groups folder in the Local Users and Groups utility, double-click the group you want to manage.

FIGURE 4.17 The local group Properties dialog box

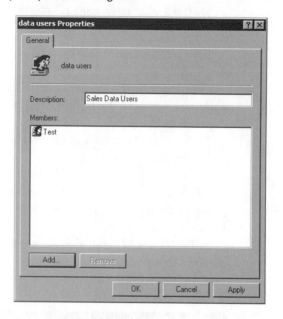

From the group Properties dialog box, you can change the group's description and add or remove group members. When you click the Add button to add members, the Select Users or Groups dialog box appears, as shown in Figure 4.18. In this dialog box, you select the user accounts you wish to add and click the Add button. Click the OK button to add the users to the group.

FIGURE 4.18 The Select Users or Groups dialog box

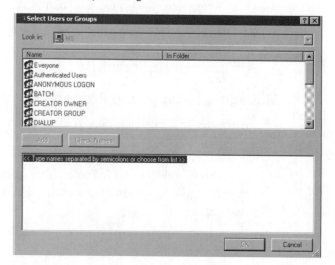

To remove a member from the group, select the member in the group Properties dialog box Members list and click the Remove button.

You can select multiple contiguous users to add to or remove from a group by Shift+clicking the first and last ones to add. To select multiple noncontiguous users to a group, Ctrl+click each one.

In Exercise 4.12, you will create new user accounts and then add these users to one of the groups you created in Exercise 4.11. This exercise must be completed from your member server.

EXERCISE 4.12

Adding Users to Local Groups

1. Open the MMC and expand the Local Users and Groups snap-in.

2. Create four new users: **Brent**, **Claire**, **Patrick**, and **Trina**. Deselect the User Must Change Password at Next Logon option for each user.

3. Expand the Groups folder.

4. Double-click the Data Users group (created in Exercise 4.11).

5. In the group Properties dialog box, click the Add button.

6. In the Select Users or Groups dialog box, select Brent, Claire, Patrick, and Trina (hold down the Ctrl key as you click each member).

7. Click the Add button. Then click the OK button.

8. In the group Properties dialog box, you will see that the users have all been added to the group. Click OK to close the group Properties dialog box.

Renaming Groups

Windows 2000 provides an easy-to-use mechanism for changing a group's name (a capability that was never offered in any versions of Windows NT). For example, you might want to rename a group because its current name does not conform to existing naming conventions.

As when you rename a user account, a renamed group keeps of all its properties, including its members and permissions.

In Exercise 4.13, you will rename one of the groups you created in Exercise 4.11. This exercise should be completed from your member server.

EXERCISE 4.13

Renaming a Local Group

1. Open the MMC and expand the Local Users and Groups snap-in.

2. Expand the Groups folder.

3. Right-click the Application Users group (created in Exercise 4.11) and select Rename.

4. Rename the group to **App Users** and press Enter.

Deleting Groups

If you are sure that you will never want to use a group again, you can delete it. Once a group is deleted, you lose all permissions assignments that have been specified for the group.

In Exercise 4.14, you will delete one of the groups that you created in Exercise 4.11 and renamed in Exercise 4.13. This exercise should be completed from your member server.

EXERCISE 4.14

Deleting a Local Group

1. Open the MMC and expand the Local Users and Groups snap-in.

2. Expand the Groups folder.

3. Right-click the App Users group and choose Delete.

4. In the dialog box that appears, click Yes to confirm that you want to delete the group.

If you delete a group and give another group the same name as the deleted group, it won't be created with the same properties as the deleted group.

Managing Active Directory Groups

You create and manage Active Directory groups through the Active Directory Users and Computers utility. When you create a new Active Directory group, you specify its scope and type, which were discussed in the "An Overview of Groups" section earlier in this chapter.

Creating New Active Directory Groups

To create a group on a domain controller, take these steps:

1. Select Start ➤ Programs ➤ Administrative Tools ➤ Active Directory Users and Computers to open the Active Directory Users and Computers utility.

2. Right-click the Users folder, select New from the pop-up menu, and then select Group.

3. The New Object - Group dialog box appears, as shown in Figure 4.19. Type in the group name for Windows 2000. The pre–Windows 2000 group name will be filled in automatically, but you can change it if desired.

FIGURE 4.19   The New Object - Group dialog box

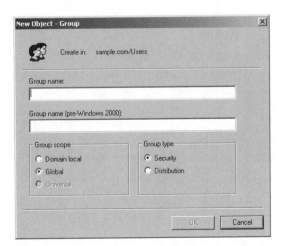

4. In the Group Scope section, select the scope for the group:

   - Choose the Domain Local option if you want to use the group to assign permissions to resources.

   - Choose the Global option if you want to use this group for users who require similar network access.

   - Choose the Universal option if you want to assign permissions related to resources in multiple domains.

5. In the Group Type section, select the type of group that you want to create:

   - Choose the Security option if this group is for users who need access to specific resources.

   - Choose the Distribution option if this group is for users who have common characteristics (for example, users who you may need to receive the same e-mail messages).

6. Click OK to close the dialog box and create the new group.

Managing Active Directory Group Properties

You can manage an Active Directory group through the group Properties dialog box, shown in Figure 4.20. To access this dialog box, right-click the group in the Active Directory Users and Computers utility and select Properties from the pop-up menu.

FIGURE 4.20 The Active Directory group Properties dialog box

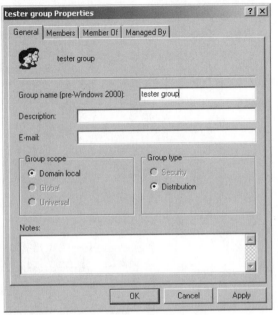

This dialog box has four tabs with options for managing the group:

- The General tab (see Figure 4.20) allows you to view and change the pre–Windows 2000 group name, description, and e-mail address. You can view the group scope and type but you can't change these entries. You can also add notes for the group.

- The Members tab, shown in Figure 4.21, allows you view and change group membership.

FIGURE 4.21   The Members tab of the Active Directory group Properties dialog box

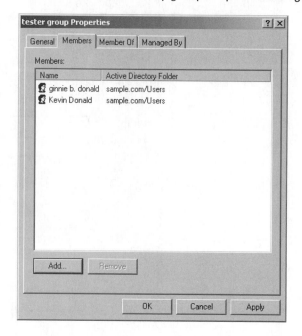

- The Member Of tab, shown in Figure 4.22, allows you to view, add groups to, or remove groups from other groups, if the group type allows group nesting (one group contained within another group).

FIGURE 4.22 The Members Of tab of the Active Directory group Properties dialog box

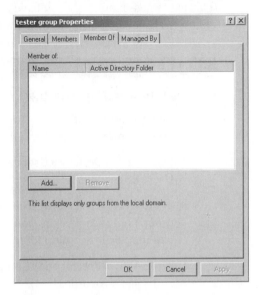

- The Managed By tab, shown in Figure 4.23, allows you to view and change the user who manages the group.

FIGURE 4.23 The Managed By tab of the Active Directory group Properties dialog box

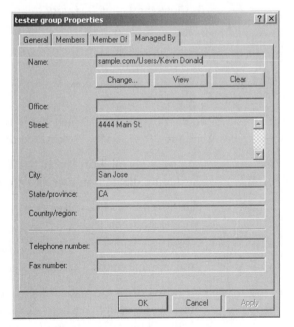

In Exercise 4.15, you will create and manage an Active Directory group. This exercise assumes that you have completed the other exercises in this chapter. This exercise should be completed from your domain controller.

EXERCISE 4.15

Creating and Managing an Active Directory Group

1. Select Start ➤ Programs ➤ Administrative Tools ➤ Active Directory Users and Computers.

2. In the Active Directory Users and Computers utility, right-click the Users folder, select New, and then select Group.

3. In the New Object - Group dialog box, enter **Test Group** as the group name. Choose the Domain Local option for the group scope and the Security option for the group type. Click the OK button.

4. In the Active Directory and Computers utility, right-click Test Group and select Properties.

5. In the Test Group Properties dialog box, click the Members tab and then click the Add button. Select user Ginnie B. Donald and click the Add button. Click the OK button. In the Test Group Properties dialog box, click the OK button.

6. Close the Active Directory Users and Computers utility.

Summary

In this chapter, you learned about user and group management features in Windows 2000 Server. We covered the following topics:

- An overview of local and Active Directory user and group accounts, including the built-in user and group accounts

- How to use the Local Users and Groups utility to create and manage local user accounts

- How to use the Active Directory Users and Computers utility to create and manage Active Directory user accounts

- How to create and manage local group accounts with the Local Users and Group utility and Active Directory group accounts with the Active Directory Users and Computers utility

Exam Essentials

Know how to create and manage users within local computers or within the Active Directory. Be able to create and manage local and domain user accounts. Know what the default user accounts are and the permissions associated with the default users.

Know how to create and manage groups within local computers or within the Active Directory. Be able to create and manage local and domain group accounts. Know what the default group accounts are and the permissions associated with the default groups.

Key Terms

Before you take the exam, be sure you're familiar with the following key terms:

Active Directory user	local group
Active Directory Users and Computers	local user
Administrator	Local Users and Groups
distribution group	logon script
domain local group	security group
global group	universal group
Guest	user profile
home folder	

Review Questions

1. You have created a user called ldonald on a Windows 2000 member server. This user has logged on to the server many times. When you check the user properties for this user, you see the following exhibit. Based on the exhibit, what type of profile will the user use?

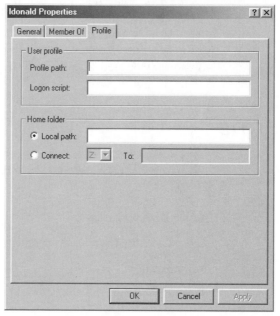

A. The user will use the default profile for the default_user that is stored on the domain controller.

B. The user will use the default profile for the default_user that is stored on the member server.

C. The user will use the ldonald user profile that is stored on the domain controller.

D. The user will use the ldonald user profile that is stored on the member server.

2. You are planning a Windows 2000 network. You want to use Active Directory and also want to centralize all of your account management to Windows 2000 domain controllers. Which utility would you use to create your domain user accounts?

   A. Domain Users and Groups

   B. Active Directory Users and Groups

   C. Domain Users and Computers

   D. Active Directory Users and Computers

3. Bella is the network administrator of a new network. She is in the process of defining the naming conventions that will be used for the network. Which of the following statements regarding Windows 2000 user accounts is *not* true?

   A. User account names are case-sensitive.

   B. User passwords are case-sensitive.

   C. A user account name can be up to 20 characters in length.

   D. A username cannot contain a : or = character.

4. You have just created a local user on a Windows 2000 member server. You want to specify that the user account can log on only during specified hours. Which user Properties dialog box tab should you use to configure logon hours?

   A. The General tab

   B. The Account tab

   C. The Profile tab

   D. You cannot restrict logon hours for a local user account

5. You have just created an Active Directory user on a Windows 2000 domain controller. You want to specify that the user account can log on only during specified hours. Which user Properties dialog box tab should you use to configure logon hours?

   A. The General tab

   B. The Account tab

   C. The Profile tab

   D. You cannot restrict logon hours for an Active Directory user account

6. Colin has installed Windows 2000 on a member server. He logged on to this server as a user named Test. He wants to verify that a local user profile was created for the Test user. Which folder is used to store user profiles by default?

   A. Boot partition:\WINNT\User Profiles

   B. Boot partition:\User Profiles

   C. Boot partition:\WINNT\Documents and Settings

   D. Boot partition:\Documents and Settings

7. You are creating groups within the Active Directory on a Windows 2000 server that is configured as a domain controller. Which one of the following options is not a valid group scope for Windows 2000 domain controllers?

   A. Domain local

   B. Global

   C. Distribution

   D. Universal

8. You have just created a new group on a Windows 2000 domain controller. Which of the following properties can be configured for an Active Directory group?

A. Logon hours

B. Logon computers

C. Logon scripts

D. Whom the group is managed by

9. One of your users has completely messed up his user profile. You have to delete the profile to restore the default user profile settings. Which of the following options would be stored within a user profile? (Choose all that apply.)

A. The mouse driver that the user will use

B. The mouse pointer that the user will use

C. The keyboard layout that the user will use

D. The screen saver that the user will use

10. You want to allow Jackie to back up and restore the file system, but you do not want her to be able to access the file system. To which of the following groups should you assign Jackie?

A. Server Operators

B. Backup Operators

C. Administrators

D. Replicator

11. You have just added Affie to the Power Users group on your Windows 2000 member server. Which of the following tasks will Affie not be able to complete based on this group membership?

A. Create any users and groups

B. Delete any users and groups

C. Create network shares

D. Create network printers

12. You are the network administrator of a small Windows 2000 network. One of your users has come to you because he can't remember the password he uses to log on to a Windows 2000 member server. Which utility should you use to change a user's password?

    A. Password Manager

    B. Password Administrator

    C. The Setpass utility

    D. Local Users and Groups

13. You are creating users through the Local Users and Groups utility on a Windows 2000 member server. The users that will connect to the server are a mixture of Windows 2000 clients and NT clients. Based on this configuration, what is the maximum password length that should be assigned to new users?

    A. 12

    B. 14

    C. 16

    D. 20

14. You have just installed a new Windows 2000 domain. You need to create 1,000 initial user accounts. You would like to create the accounts as quickly as possible and do not want to use the Windows GUI utilities. Which of the following command line utilities will allow you to automate the creation of users through scripting?

    A. NET USER

    B. NEW USER

    C. BAT USER

    D. USERMGR

15. Which default group is created on Windows 2000 domain controllers to allow members to administer domain controllers, but does not allow members to administer user and group accounts?

A. Domain Operators

B. Server Operators

C. Account Operators

D. Administrators

Answers to Review Questions

1. D. If no user profile is specified, the user will use the locally stored profile that is created the first time the user logs on by default.

2. D. On Windows 2000 domain controllers, you use the Active Directory Users and Computers utility to create Active Directory users and groups.

3. A. User account names are not case-sensitive. Passwords are case-sensitive.

4. D. There is no option to restrict logon hours for local user accounts.

5. B. If you create an Active Directory account, you can limit logon hours by clicking the Logon Hours button in the Account tab of the user Properties dialog box.

6. D. When a user logs on for the first time, a user profile folder is automatically created in the boot partition:\Documents and Settings folder.

7. C. Group scope can be domain local, global, or universal. Group types can be security or distribution.

8. D. Logon hours, logon computers, and logon scripts can be managed only on a per-user basis. You can configure who manages a group for an Active Directory group.

9. B, C, D. User profiles generally contain user preference items, which include mouse pointers, keyboard layout, and screen saver settings. User profiles do not contain computer configuration settings such as mouse drivers.

10. B. The members of the Backup Operators group have rights to back up and restore the file system, even if the file system is NTFS and they have not been assigned permissions to the file system. However, the members of Backup Operators can access the file system only through the Backup utility. To be able to directly access the file system, they must have explicit permissions assigned. By default, there are no members of the Backup Operators local group.

11. B. Members of the Power Users group can create users and groups; however, they can manage or delete only the users and groups that they have created.

12. D. To set up and manage local users, you use the Local Users and Groups utility. With Local Users and Groups, you can create, delete, and rename user accounts, as well as change passwords.

13. B. In a mixed environment, Windows 2000 passwords should be a maximum of 14 characters. The passwords are case-sensitive. If your environment only has Windows 2000 clients, then the passwords can be up to 127 characters.

14. A. Most of the tasks in Windows 2000 that can be completed through GUI utilities can also be completed through command-line utilities. The NET USER command is used to create users.

15. B. Members of the Server Operators group have special permissions to administer domain controllers.

Chapter

5

Managing Security

MICROSOFT EXAM OBJECTIVES COVERED IN THIS CHAPTER

✓ **Implement, configure, manage, and troubleshoot policies in a Windows 2000 environment.**

- Implement, configure, manage, and troubleshoot Local Policy in a Windows 2000 environment.
- Implement, configure, manage, and troubleshoot System Policy in a Windows 2000 environment.

✓ **Implement, configure, manage, and troubleshoot auditing.**

✓ **Implement, configure, manage, and troubleshoot Account Policy.**

✓ **Implement, configure, manage, and troubleshoot security by using the Security Configuration Tool Set.**

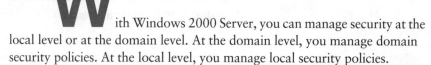

With Windows 2000 Server, you can manage security at the local level or at the domain level. At the domain level, you manage domain security policies. At the local level, you manage local security policies.

Security settings are configured through Group Policy. Account policies are used to control the logon process, such as password and account lockout configurations. Local policies are used to define security policies for the computer, such as auditing, user rights, and security options.

The Security and Analysis Configuration tool is a new Window 2000 Server utility that you can use to analyze your security configuration. Using a security template, this utility compares your actual security configuration to your desired configuration.

In this chapter, you will learn how to manage security in a Windows 2000 Server environment. You will first install an MMC console to manage security settings, and then learn how to configure account policies, local policies, and security policies. The final section of this chapter describes how to use the Security Analysis and Configuration utility to analyze your security configuration.

Managing Security Settings

Windows 2000 Server allows you to manage security settings at the local level, for a particular computer, or on a domain-wide level. Any domain security policies you define override the local policies of a computer.

You manage policies with Group Policy and the appropriate object:

- To manage *local policies*, you use Group Policy with the Local Computer Group Policy Objects (GPOs).

- To manage *domain policies*, you use Group Policy with the Domain Controller GPOs.

Group Policies within Active Directory

If Windows 2000 is installed as a part of Active Directory, group policies can be applied as Group Policy Objects (GPOs). Group policies contain configuration settings for the following options:

Software Software policies are used to configure system services, the appearance of the desktop, and application settings.

Scripts Scripts are special instructions that can be configured to run when the user logs on or off the computer, or when the computer is started or shut down.

Security Security policies define how security is configured and applied at the local computer or through Active Directory.

Application and File Deployment Application and file deployment policies are used to assign and publish applications, or to place files in the user's desktop, within a specific folder (for example, the Start menu), or within Favorites.

You create GPOs through the Active Directory Users and Computers MMC snap-in.

Quick Overview of Active Directory

Within Active Directory, you have several levels of hierarchical structure. A typical structure will consist of domains and organizational units. Other levels exist within Active Directory, but this section focuses on *domains* and *organizational units (OUs)* in the context of using GPOs.

The *domain* is the main unit of organization within Active Directory. Within a domain, there are many domain objects (including users, groups, and GPOs). Each domain object can have security applied that specifies who can access the object and the level of access they have.

Within a domain, you can further subdivide and organize domain objects through the use of organizational units. This is one of the key differences between Windows NT domains and Windows 2000 domains: the NT domains were not able to store information hierarchically. Windows 2000 domains, through the use of OUs, allow you to store objects hierarchically—typically based on function or geography.

For example, assume that your company is called ABCCORP. You have locations in New York, San Jose, and Belfast. You might create a domain called ABCCORP.COM with OUs called NY, SJ, and Belfast. In a very large corporation, you might also organize the OUs based on function. For example, the domain could be ABCCORP.COM and the OUs might be SALES, ACCT, and TECHSUPP. Based on the size and security needs of your organization, you might also have OUs nested within OUs. As a general rule, however, you will want to keep your Active Directory structure as simple as possible.

Group Policy Objects and Active Directory

GPOs are stored within Active Directory on all domain controllers in the \%SystemRoot%\Sysvol folder by default. Within each root folder, there is a policy file called gpt.ini that contains information about the group policy.

When GPOs are created within Active Directory there is a specific order of inheritance (meaning how the polices are applied within the hierarchical structure of Active Directory). When a user logs on to Active Directory, depending on where GPOs have been applied within the hierarchical structure of Active Directory, the order of application is as follows:

1. Local computer

2. Site (group of domains)

3. Domain

4. OU

If there are any conflicts between settings, the site policy overrides the local policy. Then the domain policies are defined. If the domain policy has any additional settings, they will be made. If there are any conflicts in settings, the domain policy overrides the site policy. Then the OU policies will be applied. Again, any additions to the settings will be made. If there are any conflicts in settings, the OU policy overrides the domain policy. If there are conflicts between computer and user policy settings, the user policy setting is applied.

The following options are available for overriding the default behavior of application of GPOs:

No Override   The No Override option is used to specify that child containers can't override the policy settings of higher-level GPOs. In this case, the order of precedence would be that site settings override domain settings, and domain settings override OU settings, assuming that No Override is set at both levels. You would use the No Override option if you wanted to set corporate-wide policies without allowing administrators of lower-level containers to override your settings. This option can be set on a per-container basis, as needed.

Block Inheritance   The Block Inheritance option is used to allow the child container to block GPO inheritance from parent containers. You would use this option if you did not want child containers to inherit GPO settings from parent containers and only wanted the GPO you had set for your container to be applied.

If there is a conflict between the No Override and the Block Inheritance settings, the No Override option would be applied.

Applying Policies to Different Network Clients

If your network consists of only Windows 2000 computers, you can use GPOs to manage your computer's configuration settings. If you want to manage configuration settings for NT 4 users within the domain, you would use NT System Policy files; these can be configured from the `Poledit` command, which calls the System Policy Editor utility.

By default the following administrative templates, which are used to apply group policy settings to the registry, are used by Windows 2000:

- System.adm
- Intres.adm
- Winnt.adm
- Windows.adm
- Common.adm

The function of each template is defined in Table 5.1.

TABLE 5.1 Administrative Templates Defined

Administrative Template	Description
System.adm	Template used by Windows 2000 clients.
Intres.adm	Template used to set Internet Explorer (IE) settings for Windows 2000 clients.
Winnt.adm	User interface options used by Windows NT clients. To configure options for Windows NT clients, use the System Policy Editor (Poledit.exe).
Windows.adm	User interface options used by Windows 95/98 clients. To configure options for Windows 95/98 clients, use the System Policy Editor (Poledit.exe).
Common.adm	User interface options that are common to both Windows NT 4.0 and Windows 95/98 clients.

Managing Local Computer Policy

You can manage local computer policies by adding the Group Policy snap-in to the MMC. Once you have added the snap-in, you will see an option called Local Computer Policy. When you expand the Group Policy snap-in, you'll see Computer Configuration, as shown in Figure 5.1. There are many options here that can be configured for local computer policies.

The options that can be set are shown in the following structure. As you can see, it is fairly easy to get lost within the levels when you are attempting to configure specific options. The most common options that you would configure for Local Computer Policy are defined in the following sections. You may want to refer back to this image to better understand where in the hierarchy particular policy settings can be found.

FIGURE 5.1   Local Computer Policies

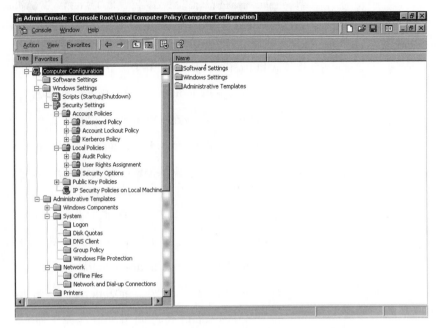

To manage your policy management tasks, you can add the Local Computer Policy and Domain Controller Security Policy snap-ins to the Microsoft Management Console (MMC). You can also access the domain policies and local policies by selecting Start ➢ Programs ➢ Administrative Tools ➢ Domain Security Policy or Local Security Policy.

In Exercise 5.1, you will add the Group Policy and Event Viewer snap-ins to your member server.

All of the exercises in this chapter, except Exercise 5.7, should be completed from the member server.

EXERCISE 5.1

Creating a Management Console for Security Settings

1. Select Start ➢ Run, type **MMC** in the Run dialog box, and click the OK button to open the MMC.

2. From the main menu, select Console ➢ Add/Remove Snap-in.

3. In the Add/Remove Snap-in dialog box, click the Add button.

4. Highlight the Group Policy option and click the Add button.

5. The Group Policy object specifies Local Computer by default. Click the Finish button.

6. In the Add/Remove Snap-in dialog box, click the OK button.

7. From the main menu, select Console ➢ Add/Remove Snap-in.

8. In the Add/Remove Snap-in dialog box, click the Add button.

9. Highlight the Event Viewer option and click the Add button.

10. The Select Computer dialog box appears with Local Computer selected by default. Click the Finish button. Then click the Close button.

11. In the Add/Remove Snap-in dialog box, click the OK button.

12. Select Console ➢ Save As. Save the console as **Security** in the Administrative Tools folder (which is the default location) and click the Save button.

You can now access this console by selecting Start ➢ Programs ➢ Administrative Tools ➢ Security.

You can also edit Local Computer Settings by using the command-line utility Gpedit.msc. To use this utility, select Start ➢ Run and at the Run dialog box, type **Gpedit.msc** and click the OK button.

Setting Computer Configuration Windows Settings

You configure security settings through Windows Settings\Security Settings. The three main options that can be configured for Windows Settings include:

- Account Policies
- Local Policies
- Public Key Policies

Using Account Policies

Account policies are used to specify the user account properties that relate to the logon process. They allow you to configure computer security settings for passwords, account lockout specifications, and Kerberos authentication within a domain.

Microsoft ✓ *Exam* *Objective*	**Implement, configure, manage, and troubleshoot Account Policy.**

After you have loaded the MMC snap-in for Group Policy, you will see an option for Local Computer Policy. To access the Account Policies folders, expand Local Computer Policy, Computer Configuration, Windows Settings, Security Settings, and Account Policies.

If you are on a Windows 2000 member server, you will see two folders: Password Policy and Account Lockout Policy. If you are on a Windows 2000 Server computer that is configured as a domain controller, you will see three folders: Password Policy, Account Lockout Policy, and Kerberos Policy. The account policies available for member servers and domain controllers are described in the following sections.

Setting Password Policies

Password policies ensure that security requirements are enforced on the computer. It is important to note that the password policy is set on a per-computer basis; it cannot be configured for specific users.

The password policies that are defined on Windows 2000 member servers are described in Table 5.2. On Windows 2000 domain controllers, all of these policies are configured as "not defined."

T A B L E 5.2 Password Policy Options

Policy	Description	Default	Minimum	Maximum
Enforce Password History	Keeps track of user's password history	Remember 0 passwords	Same as default	Remember 24 passwords
Maximum Password Age	Determines maximum number of days user can keep valid password	Keep password for 42 days	Keep password for 1 day	Keep password for 999 days
Minimum Password Age	Specifies how long password must be kept before it can be changed	0 days (password can be changed immediately)	Same as default	999 days
Minimum Password Length	Specifies minimum number of characters password must contain	0 characters (no password required)	Same as default	14 characters
Passwords Must Meet Complexity Requirements	Allows you to install password filter	Disabled	Same as default	Enabled

TABLE 5.2 Password Policy Options *(continued)*

Policy	Description	Default	Minimum	Maximum
Store Password Using Reversible Encryption for All Users in the Domain	Specifies higher level of encryption for stored user passwords	Disabled	Same as default	Enabled

The password policies are used as follows:

- The Enforce Password History option is used so that users cannot reuse the same password. Users must create a new password when their password expires or is changed.

- The Maximum Password Age option is used so that after the maximum number of days has passed, users are forced to change their password.

- The Minimum Password Age option is used to prevent users from changing their password several times in rapid succession in order to defeat the purpose of the Enforce Password History policy.

- The Minimum Password Length option is used to ensure that users create a password, as well as to specify that it meets the length requirement. If this option isn't set, users are not required to create a password at all.

- The Passwords Must Meet Complexity option is used to prevent users from using items found in a dictionary of common names as passwords.

- The Store Password Using Reversible Encryption for All Users in the Domain option is used to provide a higher level of security for user passwords.

In Exercise 5.2, you will configure password policies for your computer. This and the remaining exercises in this chapter assume that you have completed Exercise 5.1 to create the Security management console.

EXERCISE 5.2

Setting Password Policies

1. Select Start ≻ Programs ≻ Administrative Tools ≻ Security and expand the Local Computer Policy snap-in.

2. Expand the folders as follows: Computer Configuration, Windows Settings, Security Settings, Account Policies, Password Policy.

3. Open the Enforce Password History policy. In the Effective Policy Setting field, specify **5** passwords remembered. Click the OK button.

4. Open the Maximum Password Age policy. In the Local Policy Setting field, specify that the password expires in **60** days. Click the OK button.

5. Select Start ≻ Programs ≻ Accessories ≻ Command Prompt. At the command prompt, type `secedit /refreshpolicy machine_policy` and press Enter.

6. At the command prompt, type `exit` and press Enter.

 Real World Scenario

Updating Your Group Policies

You are the administrator of a large network. You have been making changes to your member server's local computer policies and notice that none of the options are being applied. You wait over 30 minutes and the changes are still not there. At this point you are beginning to think you edited something improperly.

If you edit your group policies and notice that your changes are not taking effect, it is because the group policies are only applied every 90 minutes to computers by default. You can force your policies to be updated by typing `secedit /refreshpolicy machine_policy` at a command prompt.

Setting Account Lockout Policies

The *account lockout policies* are used to specify how many invalid logon attempts should be tolerated. You configure the account lockout policies so that after *x* number of unsuccessful logon attempts within *y* number of minutes, the account will be locked for a specified amount of time or until the Administrator unlocks the account.

The account lockout policies are similar to how banks handle ATM access code security. You have a certain amount of chances to enter the correct access code. That way, if someone stole your card, they would not be able to keep guessing your access code until they got it right. Typically, after three unsuccessful attempts at your access code, the ATM machine takes the card. Then you need to request a new card from the bank.

The account lockout policies are described in Table 5.3.

TABLE 5.3   Account Lockout Policy Options

Policy	Description	Default	Minimum	Maximum	Suggested
Account Lockout Threshold	Specifies number of invalid attempts allowed before account is locked out	0 (disabled, account will not be locked out)	Same as default	999 attempts	5 attempts
Account Lockout Duration	Specifies how long account will remain locked if Account Lockout Threshold is exceeded	0; but if Account Lockout Threshold is enabled, 30 minutes	Same as default	99,999 minutes	5 minutes

TABLE 5.3 Account Lockout Policy Options *(continued)*

Policy	Description	Default	Minimum	Maximum	Suggested
Reset Account Lockout Counter After	Specifies how long counter will remember unsuccessful logon attempts	0, but if Account Lockout Threshold is enabled, 5 minutes	Same as default	99,999 minutes	5 minutes

In Exercise 5.3, you will configure account lockout policies and test their effects. This and the remaining exercises for configuring policies assume that you have already created user accounts, as described in Chapter 4 (see Exercise 4.2).

EXERCISE 5.3

Setting Account Lockout Policies

1. Select Start ➢ Programs ➢ Administrative Tools ➢ Security and expand the Local Computer Policy snap-in.

2. Expand the folders as follows: Computer Configuration, Windows Settings, Security Settings, Account Policies, Account Lockout Policy.

3. Open the Account Lockout Threshold policy. In the Local Policy Setting field, specify that the account will lock after **3** invalid logon attempts. Click the OK button.

4. The Suggested Value Changes dialog box will appear. Accept the default values for Account lockout duration and Reset account lockout counter by clicking the OK button.

5. Log off as Administrator. Try to log on as Emily with an incorrect password three times.

6. After you see the error message stating that account lockout has been enabled, log on as Administrator.

7. To unlock Emily's account, open the Local Users and Groups snap-in in the MMC, expand the Users folder, and double-click user Emily. In the General tab of Emily's Properties dialog box, click to remove the check from the Account Is Locked Out check box. Then click OK.

Setting Kerberos Policies

Kerberos version 5 is a security protocol that is used in Windows 2000 Server to authenticate users and network services. This is called dual verification, or *mutual authentication*.

When a Windows 2000 Server is installed as a domain controller, it automatically becomes a *key distribution center (KDC)*. The KDC is responsible for holding all of the client passwords and account information. Kerberos services are also installed on each Windows 2000 client and server.

The Kerberos authentication involves the following steps:

1. The client requests authentication from the KDC using a password or smart card.

2. The KDC issues the client a ticket-granting ticket (TGT). The client can use the TGT to access the ticket-granting service (TGS), which allows the user to authenticate to services within the domain. The TGS issues service tickets to the clients.

3. The client presents the service ticket to the requested network service. This service ticket authenticates the user to the service and the service to the user, for mutual authentication.

The *Kerberos policies* are described in Table 5.4.

TABLE 5.4 Kerberos Policy Options

Policy	Description	Default Local Setting	Effective Setting
Enforce User Logon Restrictions	Specifies that any logon restrictions will be enforced	Not defined	Enabled
Maximum Lifetime for Service Ticket	Specifies the maximum age of a service ticket before it must be renewed	Not defined	600 minutes
Maximum Lifetime for User Ticket	Specifies the maximum age for a user ticket before it must be renewed	Not defined	10 hours
Maximum Lifetime for User Ticket Renewal	Specifies how long a ticket may be renewed before it must be regenerated	Not defined	7 days
Maximum Tolerance for Computer Clock Synchronization	Specifies the maximum clock synchronization between the client and the KDC	Not defined	5 minutes

Using Local Policies

As you learned in the previous section, account policies are used to control logon procedures. When you want to control what a user can do after logging on, you use *local policies*. With local policies, you can implement auditing, specify user rights, and set security options.

Microsoft ✓ ***Exam*** ***Objective***

Implement, configure, manage, and troubleshoot policies in a Windows 2000 environment.

- Implement, configure, manage, and troubleshoot Local Policy in a Windows 2000 environment.

To use local policies, first add the Local Computer Policy snap-in to the MMC (see Exercise 5.1). Then, from the MMC, follow this path of folders to access the Local Policies folders: Local Computer Policy, Computer Configuration, Windows Settings, Security Settings, Local Policies.

There are three folders in Local Policies: Audit Policy, User Rights Assignment, and Security Options. These policies are covered in the following sections.

Setting Audit Policies

By implementing auditing, you can watch what your users are doing.

Microsoft ✓ ***Exam*** ***Objective***

Implement, configure, manage, and troubleshoot auditing.

You audit events that pertain to user management through the implementation of audit policies. By tracking certain events, you can create a history of specific tasks, such as user creation and successful or unsuccessful logon attempts. You can also identify security violations that arise when users attempt to access system management tasks that they do not have permission to access.

When you define an audit policy, you can choose to audit success or failure of specific events. The success of an event means that the task was successfully accomplished. The failure of an event means that the task was not successfully accomplished.

By default, auditing is not enabled, and it must be manually configured. Once auditing has been configured, you can see the results of the audit through the Event Viewer utility. (The Event Viewer utility is covered in Chapter 15, "Performing System Recovery Functions.")

WARNING Auditing too many events can degrade system performance due to the high processing requirements. Auditing can also use excessive disk space to store the audit log. You should use this utility judiciously.

The audit policies are described in Table 5.5.

TABLE 5.5 Audit Policy Options

Policy	Description
Audit Account Logon Events	Tracks when a user logs on, logs off, or makes a network connection
Audit Account Management	Tracks user and group account creation, deletion, and management actions
Audit Directory Service Access	Tracks directory service accesses
Audit Logon Events	Audits events related to logon, such as running a logon script or accessing a roaming profile
Audit Object Access	Audits access to files, folders, and printers
Audit Policy Change	Tracks any changes to the audit policy
Audit Privilege Use	Tracks any changes to who can or cannot define or see the results of auditing
Audit Process Tracking	Tracks events such as activating a program, accessing an object, and exiting a process
Audit System Events	Tracks system events such as shutting down or restarting the computer, as well as events that relate to the Security log within Event Viewer

In Exercise 5.4, you will configure audit policies and view their results.

EXERCISE 5.4

Setting Audit Policies

1. Select Start ➤ Programs ➤ Administrative Tools ➤ Security and expand the Local Computer Policy snap-in.

2. Expand the folders as follows: Computer Configuration, Windows Settings, Security Settings, Local Policies, Audit Policy.

3. Open the Audit Account Logon Events policy. In the Local Policy Setting field, specify Audit These Attempts. Check the boxes for Success and Failure. Click the OK button.

4. Open the Audit Account Management policy. In the Local Policy Setting field, specify Audit These Attempts. Check the boxes for Success and Failure. Click the OK button.

5. Log off as Administrator. Attempt to log on as KevinD. The logon should fail (because there is no user account with the username KevinD).

6. Log on as Administrator. Open the MMC and expand the Event Viewer snap-in (added in Exercise 5.1).

7. From Event Viewer, open the Security log. You should see the audited events listed in this log.

Assigning User Rights

The *user right* policies determine what rights a user or group has on the computer. User rights apply to the system. They are not the same as permissions, which apply to a specific object. (Permissions are covered in Chapter 7, "Accessing Files and Folders.")

An example of a user right is the Back Up Files and Directories right. This right allows a user to back up files and folders, even if the user does not have permissions through the file system. The other user rights are similar in that they deal with system access as opposed to resource access.

The user rights assignment policies are described in Table 5.6.

TABLE 5.6 User Rights Assignment Policy Options

Right	Description
Access This Computer from the Network	Allows a user to access the computer from the network
Act as Part of the Operating System	Allows low-level authentication services to authenticate as any user
Add Workstations to the Domain	Allows a user to create a computer account on the domain
Back Up Files and Directories	Allows a user to back up all files and directories, regardless of how the file and directory permissions have been set
Bypass Traverse Checking	Allows a user to pass through and traverse the directory structure, even if that user does not have permissions to list the contents of the directory
Change the System Time	Allows a user to change the internal time of the computer
Create a Pagefile	Allows a user to create or change the size of a page file
Create a Token Object	Allows a process to create a token if the process uses the NtCreate Token API
Create Permanent Shared Objects	Allows a process to create directory objects through the Windows 2000 Object Manager
Debug Programs	Allows a user to attach a debugging program to any process

TABLE 5.6 User Rights Assignment Policy Options *(continued)*

Right	Description
Deny Access to This Computer from the Network	Allows you to deny specific users or groups access to this computer from the network
Deny Logon as a Batch File	Allows you to prevent specific users or groups from logging on as a batch file
Deny Logon as a Service	Allows you to prevent specific users or groups from logging on as a service
Deny Logon Locally	Allows you to deny specific users or groups access to the computer locally
Enable Computer and User Accounts to Be Trusted by Delegation	Allows a user or group to set the Trusted for Delegation setting for a user or computer object
Force Shutdown from a Remote System	Allows the system to be shut down by a user at a remote location on the network
Generate Security Audits	Allows a user, group, or process to make entries in the Security log
Increase Quotas	Allows a user to manipulate how processes are served by manipulating the processor quota
Increase Scheduling Priority	Specifies that a process can increase or decrease the priority that is assigned to another process
Load and Unload Device Drivers	Allows a user to dynamically unload and load Plug-and-Play device drivers

TABLE 5.6 User Rights Assignment Policy Options *(continued)*

Right	Description
Lock Pages in Memory	This user right is no longer used in Windows 2000 (it was originally intended to force data to be kept in physical memory and not allow the data to be paged to the page file)
Log On as a Batch Job	Allows a process to log on to the system and run a file that contains one or more operating system commands
Log On as a Service	Allows a service to log on in order to run the specific service
Log On Locally	Allows a user to log on at the computer where the user account has been defined
Manage Auditing and Security Log	Allows a user to manage the Security log
Modify Firmware Environment Variables	Allows a user or process to modify the system environment variables
Profile Single Process	Allows a user to monitor nonsystem processes through tools such as the Performance Logs and Alerts utility
Profile System Performance	Allows a user to monitor system processes through tools such as the Performance Logs and Alerts utility
Remove Computer from Docking Station	Allows a user to undock a laptop through the Windows 2000 user interface

TABLE 5.6 User Rights Assignment Policy Options *(continued)*

Right	Description
Replace a Process Level Token	Allows a process to replace the default token that is created by the subprocess with the token that the process specifies
Restore Files and Directories	Allows a user to restore files and directories, regardless of file and directory permissions
Shut Down the System	Allows a user to shut down the local Windows 2000 computer
Synchronize Directory Service Data	Allows a user to synchronize data associated with a directory service
Take Ownership of Files or Other Objects	Allows a user to take ownership of system objects

In Exercise 5.5, you will apply a local user rights assignment policy.

EXERCISE 5.5

Setting Local User Rights

1. Select Start ➤ Programs ➤ Administrative Tools ➤ Security and expand the Local Computer Policy snap-in.

2. Expand folders as follows: Computer Configuration, Windows Settings, Security Settings, Local Policies, User Rights Assignment.

3. Open the Log On as a Service user right. The Local Security Policy Setting dialog box appears.

4. Click the Add button. The Select Users or Groups dialog box appears.

5. Select user Emily. Click the Add button. Then click the OK button.

Defining Security Options

Security options are used to configure security for the computer. Unlike user right policies, which are applied to a user or group, security option policies apply to the computer.

The security option policies are described in Table 5.7.

TABLE 5.7 Security Options

Option	Description	Default
Additional Restrictions for Anonymous Users	Allows you to impose additional restrictions on anonymous connections	None (rely on default permissions)
Allow Server Operators to Schedule Tasks (domain controllers only)	Allows server operators to schedule specific tasks to occur at specific times or intervals	Not defined
Allow System to Be Shut Down Without Having to Log On	Allows the user to shut down the system without logging on	Enabled (but the local policy settings are overridden if the domain-level policy settings are defined)
Allowed to Eject Removable NTFS Media	Allows removable NTFS media to be ejected	Administrators
Amount of Time Idle Before Disconnecting Session	Allows sessions to be disconnected when they are idle	15 minutes
Audit the Access of Global System Objects	Allows access of global system objects to be audited	Disabled
Audit Use of All User Rights including Backup and Restore Privilege	Allows all user rights, including backup and restore, to be audited	Disabled

TABLE 5.7   Security Options *(continued)*

Option	Description	Default
Automatically Log Off Users When Logon Time Expires	Automatically logs off users if they have limited logon hours and their logon time has expired	Enabled
Clear Virtual Memory Pagefile When System Shuts Down	Specifies that the page file should be cleared when the system is shut down	Disabled
Digitally Sign Client Communication (always)	Specifies that the server should always digitally sign client communication	Disabled
Digitally Sign Client Communication (when possible)	Specifies that the server should digitally sign client communication when possible	Enabled
Digitally Sign Server Communication (always)	Ensures that server communications will always be digitally signed	Disabled
Digitally Sign Server Communication (when possible)	Specifies that server communications should be signed when possible	Disabled
Disable CTRL+ALT+DEL Requirement for Logon	Allows the Ctrl+Alt+Delete requirement for logon to be disabled	Not defined

TABLE 5.7 Security Options *(continued)*

Option	Description	Default
Do Not Display Last User Name in Logon Screen	Prevents the last user-name in the logon screen from being displayed	Disabled
LAN Manager Authentication Level	Specifies the LAN Manager Authentication Level	Send LAN Manager and NTLM (NT LAN Manager) responses
Message Text for Users Attempting to Log On	Displays message text for users trying to log on	Text space is blank
Message Title for Users Attempting to Log On	Displays a message title for users trying to log on	Title space is blank
Number of Previous Logon Attempts to Cache (in case domain controller is not available)	Specifies the number of previous logon attempts stored in the cache	10
Prevent System Maintenance of Computer Account Password	Prevents the system maintenance of computer account passwords	Disabled
Prevent Users from Installing Print Drivers	Prevents users from installing print drivers	Disabled
Prompt User to Change Password Before Expiration	Prompts the user to change the password before expiration	14 days before password expiration

TABLE 5.7 Security Options *(continued)*

Option	Description	Default
Recovery Console: Allow Automatic Administrative Logon	Specifies that when the Recovery Console is loaded, Administrative logon should be automatic, as opposed to a manual process	Disabled
Recovery Console: Allow Floppy Copy and Access to All Drives and Folders	Allows you to copy files from all drives and folders when the Recovery Console is loaded	Disabled
Rename Administrator Account	Allows the Administrator account to be renamed	Not defined
Rename Guest Account	Allows the Guest account to be renamed	Not defined
Restrict CD-ROM Access to Locally Logged-On Users Only	Restricts CD-ROM access to users who are logged on locally	Disabled
Restrict Floppy Access to Locally Logged-On Users Only	Restricts floppy disk drive access to users who are logged on locally	Disabled
Secure Channel: Digitally Encrypt or Sign Secure Channel Data (always)	Specifies that secure channel data is always digitally encrypted or signed	Disabled
Secure Channel: Digitally Encrypt Secure Channel Data (when possible)	Specifies that secure channel data is digitally encrypted when possible	Disabled

TABLE 5.7   Security Options *(continued)*

Option	Description	Default
Secure Channel: Digitally Sign Secure Channel Data (when possible)	Specifies that secure channel data is digitally signed when possible	Enabled
Secure Channel: Require Strong (Windows 2000 or later) Session Key	Provides a secure channel and requires a strong (Windows 2000 or later) session key	Disabled
Send Unencrypted Passwords to Connect to Third-Party SMB Servers	Allows unencrypted passwords to connect to third-party SMB servers	Disabled
Shut Down System Immediately If Unable to Log Security Audits	Specifies that the system shuts down immediately if it is unable to log security audits	Disabled
Smart Card Removal Behavior	Changes the smart card removal behavior	No action
Strengthen Default Permissions of Global System Objects (e.g. Symbolic Links)	Strengthens the default permissions of global system objects	Enabled
Unsigned Driver Installation Behavior	Controls the behavior of the unsigned driver installation	Warn but allow installation
Unsigned Non-Driver Installation Behavior	Controls the behavior of the unsigned non-driver installation	Silently succeed

In Exercise 5.6, you will define some security option policies and see how they work. This exercise assumes that you have completed all of the previous exercises in this chapter.

EXERCISE 5.6

Defining Security Options

1. Select Start ➢ Programs ➢ Administrative Tools ➢ Security and expand the Local Computer Policy snap-in.

2. Expand folders as follows: Computer Configuration, Windows Settings, Security Settings, Local Policies, Security Options.

3. Open the policy Message Text for Users Attempting to Log On. In the Local Policy Setting field, type **Welcome to all authorized users**. Click the OK button.

4. Open the policy Prompt User to Change Password Before Expiration. In the Local Policy Setting field, specify **3** days. Click the OK button.

5. Select Start ➢ Programs ➢ Accessories ➢ Command Prompt. At the command prompt, type `secedit /refreshpolicy machine_policy` and press Enter.

6. At the command prompt, type `exit` and press Enter.

7. Log off as Administrator and log on as Michael (with the password **apple**).

8. Log off as Michael and log on as Administrator.

Using Public Key Policies

Using Public Key Policies allows you to set options so that computers can automatically submit requests to Certificate Authorities in order to install and access Public Keys—which are associated with cryptography.

You can also specify the Encrypted Data Recovery Agents that are used in conjunction with Encrypting File System (EFS). EFS is covered in greater detail in Chapter 6, "Managing Disks."

Using System Policies

System Policies are accessed from the Local Computer Policy MMC snap-in under Computer Configuration, Administrative Templates, System.

Through System Policies you can configure:

- Logon Policies
- Disk Quotas Policies
- DNS Client Policies
- Group Policy Policies
- Windows File Protection Policies

Microsoft ✓ Exam Objective

Implement, configure, manage, and troubleshoot policies in a Windows 2000 environment.

- Implement, configure, manage, and troubleshoot System Policy in a Windows 2000 environment.

Logon Policies

*L*ogon *policies* are used to specify how logon events, such as logon scripts and access of user profiles, are configured.

The logon option policies are described in Table 5.8.

TABLE 5.8 Logon Policy Options

Logon Policy	Description
Run Logon Scripts Synchronously	Specifies that the logon scripts should finish running before the Windows Explorer interface is run. Configuring this option can cause a delay in the Desktop appearing.
Run Startup Scripts Asynchronously	Allows the system to run startup scripts simultaneously. Otherwise, if you have multiple startup scripts, a startup script can't run until the previous script has finished running.

TABLE 5.8 Logon Policy Options *(continued)*

Logon Policy	Description
Run Startup Scripts Visible	Displays the startup script instructions as they are run.
Run Shutdown Scripts Visible	Displays the shutdown script instructions as they are run.
Maximum Wait Time for Group Policy Scripts	Specifies the maximum amount of time that the system will wait for scripts (logon, startup, and shutdown) to be applied before scripts stop processing and an error is recorded. This value is 600 seconds (10 minutes) by default.
Delete Cached Copies of Roaming Profiles	Specifies that a local copy of the roaming profile should not be saved to the local computer. Normally, you want to save a local copy of a roaming profile, because loading a copy locally is faster than loading from a network drive.
Do Not Detect Slow Network Connections	By default, the system will try to detect slow links and respond to slow links differently than it does to faster links. Setting this policy disables the detection of slow links.
Slow Network Connection Timeout for User Profiles	Allows you to specify what a slow network connection is.
Wait for Remote User Profile	Specifies that if a roaming profile is used, the roaming (network) copy of the profile should be used rather than a locally cached copy of the profile.
Prompt User When Slow Link Is Detected	Notifies users of a slow link and prompts users to select whether they will use a locally cached copy of a user profile or the roaming (network) copy.

TABLE 5.8 Logon Policy Options *(continued)*

Logon Policy	Description
Timeout for Dialog Boxes	Allows you to configure the default timeout value that will be used to display dialog boxes.
Log Users Off When Roaming Profile Fails	Specifies that if a roaming profile is not available, the user should be logged off. If you do not enable this option and a roaming profile fails to load, the user will use a locally cached copy or the default user profile.
Maximum Retries to Unload and Update User Profile	Determines the number of retries the system will take if it tries to update the portions of the Registry that store user profile information and the update is not successful.

Disk Quotas Policies

*D*isk quota policies are used to specify the how the computer will be used for disk quota configuration. Disk quotas are covered in greater detail in Chapter 6, "Managing Disks."

The disk quota policies are described in Table 5.9.

TABLE 5.9 Disk Quota Options

Disk Quota Policy	Description
Enable Disk Quotas	Forces the system to enable disk quota management on all NTFS volumes for the computer.
Enforce Disk Quota Limit	Specifies that if disk quotas are configured, they should be enforced.
Default Quota Limit and Warning Level	Allows you to configure the default quota limit for quota management and the threshold for disk use at which users see a warning message.

TABLE 5.9   Disk Quota Options *(continued)*

Disk Quota Policy	Description
Log Event when Quota Limit Exceeded	Specifies that if users reach their quota limit, an entry will be added to the Event Viewer Application log.
Log Event when Quota Warning Level Exceeded	Specifies that if users reach their warning limit, an entry will be added to the Event Viewer Application log.
Apply Policy to Removable Media	Extends the disk quota policies that are applied to fixed disks to removable media that are formatted as NTFS.

DNS Client Policies

Through *DNS client policies* you configure the Primary DNS Suffix. This Specifies the primary DNS suffix that will be used for DNS name registration and DNS name resolution.

Group Policy Policies

Group Policy policies are used to specify how group policies will be applied to the computer.

The group policy option policies are described in Table 5.10.

TABLE 5.10   Group Policy Options

Group Policy	Description
Disable Background Refresh of Group Policy	Prevents group policies from being updated if the computer is currently in use.

T A B L E 5 . 1 0   Group Policy Options *(continued)*

Group Policy	Description
Apply Group Policy for Computers Asynchronously during Startup	Specifies that the computer can display the logon dialog box before it finishes updating the computer's Group Policy.
Apply Group Policy for Users Asynchronously during Startup	Specifies that the computer can display the Windows Desktop before it finishes updating the computer's Group Policy.
Group Policy Refresh Intervals for Computers	Specifies the interval rate that will be used to update the computer's Group Policy. By default, this background operation occurs every 90 minutes, with a random offset of 0–30 minutes.
Group Policy Refresh Intervals for Domain Controllers	Specifies the interval rate that will be used to update the domain controller's Group Policy. By default, this background operation occurs every 5 minutes.
User Group Policy Loopback Processing Mode	Specifies how group policies are applied when a user logs on to a computer with this option configured. You can specify that the group policy is replaced or merged with other policy settings.
Group Policy Slow Link Detection	Defines what a slow link is for the purpose of applying and updating group policies.
Registry Policy Processing	Specifies how Registry policies are processed, such as whether Registry policies can be applied during periodic background processing.

TABLE 5.10 Group Policy Options *(continued)*

Group Policy	Description
Internet Explorer Maintenance Policy Processing	Determines when Internet Explorer Maintenance polices can be applied.
Software Installation Policy Processing	Determines how often software installation policies are updated. This option does not apply to local policies.
Folder Redirection Policy Processing	Specifies how folder redirection policies are updated.
Scripts Policy Processing	Specifies how shared script policies are updated.
Security Policy Processing	Specifies how security policies are updated.
IP Security Policy Processing	Specifies how IP security policies are updated.
EFS Recovery Policy Processing	Specifies how encryption policies are updated.
Disk Quota Policy Processing	Specifies how disk quota policies are updated.

Windows File Protection Policies

The *Windows File Protection policies* are used to specify how Windows file protection will be configured.

The Windows File Protection option policies are described in Table 5.11.

TABLE 5.11 Windows File Protection Options

Windows File Protection Policy	Description
Set Windows File Protection Scanning	Determines the frequency of Windows File Protection scans.
Hide the File Scan Progress Window	Suppresses the display of the File Scan Progress window.
Limit Windows File Protection Cache Size	Specifies the maximum amount of disk space that can be used by Windows File Protection.
Specify Windows File Protection Cache Location	Specifies an alternate location to be used by the Windows File Protection cache.

Using the Security Configuration and Analysis Tool

Windows 2000 Server includes a utility called *Security Configuration and Analysis*, which you can use to analyze and to help configure the computer's local security settings. This utility works by comparing your actual security configuration to a security template configured with your desired settings.

Microsoft ✓ *Exam Objective* **Implement, configure, manage, and troubleshoot security by using the Security Configuration Tool Set.**

The following steps are involved in the security analysis process:

1. Using the Security Configuration and Analysis utility, specify a working security database that will be used during the security analysis.

2. Import a security template that can be used as a basis for how you would like your security to be configured.

3. Perform the security analysis. This will compare your configuration against the template that you specified in step 2.

4. Review the results of the security analysis.

5. Resolve any discrepancies indicated through the security analysis results.

The Security Configuration and Analysis utility is an MMC snap-in. After you add this utility to the MMC, you can use it to run the security analysis process, as described in the following sections.

Specifying a Security Database

The security database is used to store the results of your security analysis. To specify a security database, take the following steps:

1. In the MMC, right-click the Security Configuration and Analysis snap-in and select the Open Database option from the pop-up menu, as shown in Figure 5.2.

FIGURE 5.2   Opening a security database

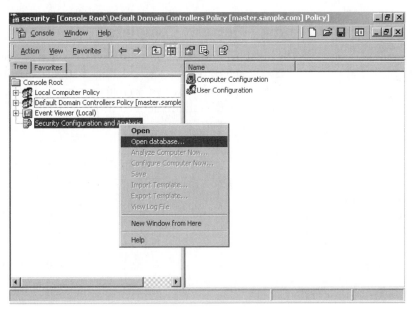

2. The Open Database dialog box appears. In the File Name text box, type the name of the database you will create. By default, this file will have a .sdb (for security database) extension. Then click the Open button.

3. The Import Template dialog box appears. Select the template that you want to import. You can select a predefined template through this dialog box. In the next section, you will learn how to create and use a customized template file. Make your selection and click the Open button.

Importing a Security Template

The next step in the security analysis process is to import a security template. The security template is used as a comparative tool. The Security and Configuration Analysis utility compares the security settings in the security template to your current security settings. You do not set security through the security template. Rather, the security template is where you organize all of your security attributes in a single location.

As an administrator, you can define a base security template on a single computer and then export the security template to all the servers in your network.

Creating a Security Template

By default, Windows 2000 ships with a variety of predefined security templates. Each of the templates defines a standard set of security values based on the requirements of your environment. The template groups that are included by default are defined in Table 5.12.

TABLE 5.12 Default Security Templates

Standard Security Template	Description	Default Templates
Basic (Basic*.inf)	Used to set security back to the default values, with the exception of user rights. User rights are modified by some applications so that the application will run properly. If user rights were also set back to default values, some of the applications that were installed on the computer might not function.	Basicdc, Basicsv, Basicwk
Compatible (Compat*.inf)	Used for backward-compatibility. This option relaxes the default security used by Windows 2000 so that applications that ran under Windows NT and are not certified for Windows 2000 will still run. This template is typically used on computers that have been upgraded, and are then having problems running applications.	Compatws
Secure (Secure*.inf)	Implements recommended security settings for Windows 2000 in all security areas except for files, folders, and registry keys.	Securedc, Securews

TABLE 5.12 Default Security Templates *(continued)*

Standard Security Template	Description	Default Templates
Highly secure (Hisec*.inf)	Defines highly secure network communications for Windows 2000 computers. If you apply this security template, Windows 2000 computers can only communicate with other Windows 2000 computers. In this case, the computers would not communicate with clients such as Windows 95/98 or even Windows NT 4 computers.	Hisecdc, Hisecws
Dedicated domain controller (dedica*.inf)	Provides a higher level of security for dedicated domain controllers. This option assumes that the domain controller will not run server-based applications, which would require a more lax security posture on the server.	Dedicadc

You create security templates through the Security Templates snap-in in the MMC. You can configure security templates with the items listed in Table 5.13.

TABLE 5.13 Security Template Configuration Options

Security Template Item	Description
Account Policies	Specifies configurations that should be used for password policies, account lockout policies, and Kerberos policies
Local Policies	Specifies configurations that should be used for audit policies, user rights assignments, and security options

TABLE 5.13 Security Template Configuration Options *(continued)*

Security Template Item	Description
Event Log	Allows you to set configuration settings that apply to Event Viewer log files
Restricted Groups	Allows you to administer local group memberships
Registry	Specifies security for local Registry keys
File System	Specifies security for the local file system
System Services	Sets security for system services and the startup mode that local system services will use

After you add the Security Templates snap-in to the MMC, you can open a sample security template and modify it, as follows:

1. In the MMC, expand the Security Templates snap-in and then expand the folder for \Windir\Security\Templates.

2. Double-click the sample template that you want to edit. There are several sample templates, including basicsv (for basic server) and basicdc (for basic domain controller).

3. Make any changes you want to the sample security template. Changes to the template are not applied to the local system by default. They are simply a specification for how you would like the system to be configured.

4. Once you have made all of the changes to the sample template, save the template by highlighting the sample template file, right-clicking, and selecting the Save As option from the pop-up menu. Specify a location and a filename for the new template. By default, the security template will be saved with an .inf extension in the \Windir\Security\Templates folder.

Opening a Security Template

Once you have configured a security template, you can import it for use with the Security Configuration and Analysis utility, assuming that a security database has already been configured. To import a security template, in the MMC, right-click the Security Configuration and Analysis utility and select the Import Template option from the pop-up menu. Then highlight the template file you wish to import and click the Open button.

Performing a Security Analysis

The next step is to perform a security analysis. To run the analysis, simply right-click the Security Configuration and Analysis utility and select the Analyze Computer Now option from the pop-up menu. You will see a Perform Analysis dialog box that allows you to specify the location and filename for the error log file path that will be created during the analysis. After this information is configured, click the OK button.

When the analysis is complete, you will be returned to the main MMC window. From there, you can review the results of the security analysis.

Reviewing the Security Analysis and Resolving Discrepancies

The results of the security analysis are stored in the Security Configuration and Analysis snap-in, under the configured security item (see Table 5.13). For example, to see the results for password policies, double-click the Security Configuration and Analysis snap-in, double-click Account Policies, and then double-click Password Policy. Figure 5.3 shows an example of security analysis results for password policies.

FIGURE 5.3   Viewing the results of a security analysis

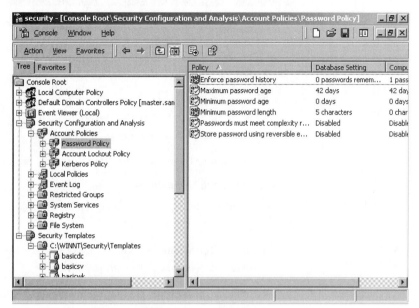

The policies that have been analyzed will have an × or a ✓ next to each policy, as shown in Figure 5.3. An × indicates that the template specification and the actual policy do not match. A ✓ indicates that the template specification and the policy do match. If any security discrepancies are indicated, you should use the Group Policy snap-in to resolve the security violation.

In Exercise 5.7, you will use the Security Configuration and Analysis utility to analyze your security configuration. This exercise assumes that you have completed all of the previous exercises in this chapter.

EXERCISE 5.7

Using the Security Configuration and Analysis Tool

In this exercise, you will add the Security and Configuration Analysis snap-in to the MMC, specify a security database, create a security template, import the template, perform an analysis, and review the results.

EXERCISE 5.7 *(continued)*

Adding the Security and Configuration Analysis Snap-in

1. Select Start ➤ Programs ➤ Administrative Tools ➤ Security.

2. Select Console ➤ Add/Remove Snap-in.

3. In the Add/Remove Snap-In dialog box, click the Add button. Highlight the Security Configuration and Analysis snap-in and click the Add button. Then click the Close button.

4. In the Add/Remove Snap-In dialog box, click the OK button.

Specifying the Security Database

5. In the MMC, right-click Security Configuration and Analysis and select Open Database.

6. In the Open Database dialog box, type **sampledb** in the File Name text box. Then click the Open button.

7. In the Import Template dialog box, select the template basicsv and click the Open button.

Creating the Security Template

8. In the MMC, select Console ➤ Add/Remove Snap-in.

9. In the Add/Remove Snap-In dialog box, click the Add button. Highlight the Security Templates snap-in and click the Add button. Then click the Close button.

10. In the Add/Remove Snap-In dialog box, click the OK button.

11. Expand the Security Templates snap-in, then expand the WINNT\Security\Templates folder.

12. Double-click the basicsv file.

13. Select Account Policies, then Password Policy.

14. Edit the password policies as follows:

Set the Enforce Password History option to **10** passwords remembered.

Enable the Passwords Must Meet Complexity Requirements option.

EXERCISE 5.7 *(continued)*

Set the Maximum Password Age option to **30** days.

15. Highlight the basicsv file, right-click, and select the Save As option.

16. In the Save As dialog box, place the file in the default folder and name the file **servertest**. Click the Save button.

Importing the Security Template

17. Highlight the Security Configuration and Analysis snap-in, right-click, and select the Import Template option.

18. In the Import Template dialog box, highlight the servertest file and click the Open button.

Performing and Reviewing the Security Analysis

19. Highlight the Security Configuration and Analysis snap-in, right-click, and select the Analyze Computer Now option.

20. In the Perform Analysis dialog box, accept the default error log file path and click the OK button.

21. When you return to the main MMC window, double-click the Security Configuration and Analysis snap-in.

22. Double-click Account Policies, and then double-click Password Policy. You will see the results of the analysis for each policy, indicated by an × or a ✓ next to the policy.

Summary

In this chapter, you learned about the security features of Windows 2000 Server. We covered the following topics:

- Security settings, which can be applied at the local or domain level. To manage local security policies, use Group Policy with the Local Computer Group Policy object. To manage domain security policies, use Group Policy with the Domain Controllers Group Policy object.

- Account policies, which control the logon process. The three types of account policies are password, account lockout, and Kerberos policies.

- Local policies, which control what a user can do at the computer. The three types of local policies are audit, user rights assignment, and security options policies.

- The Security and Analysis Configuration utility, which is used to analyze your security configuration. You run this utility to compare your existing security settings to a security template configured with your desired settings.

Exam Essentials

Understand the purpose and use of GPOs.   Know which options can be configured through GPOs. Understand how GPOs are applied through the Active Directory. Know how to override the default behavior of GPO execution.

Be able to define and configure Account Policies.   List the options that can be configured for Password Policy, Account Lockout Policy, and Kerberos Policy.

Be able to define and configure Local Policies.   List the options that can be configured for Audit Policy, User Rights Assignment, and Security Options.

Be able to define and configure System Policies.   List the options that can be configured for Logon Policy, Disk Quota Policy, DNS Client Policy, Group Policy, and Windows File Protection Policy.

Specify the purpose and use of the Security Configuration and Analysis Tool.   Be able to use the Security and Configuration and Analysis utility along with Security Templates to analyze the security of your Windows 2000 computers.

Key Terms

Before you take the exam, be sure you're familiar with the following key terms:

account lockout policies	local policies
account policies	logon policies
audit policies	mutual authentication
disk quota policies	password policies
DNS client policies	Security Configuration and Analysis tool
domain policies	security options
Group Policy policies	system policies
Kerberos	user rights
Kerberos policies	Windows File Protection policies
key distribution center (KDC)	

Review Questions

1. You recently made changes to the GPOs on your Windows 2000 domain controller. You notice that the changes are not being applied automatically when new users log on. Using the following exhibit, which option can you set so that new changes to the GPO are applied with 10 minutes for any computers that are logged onto the network?

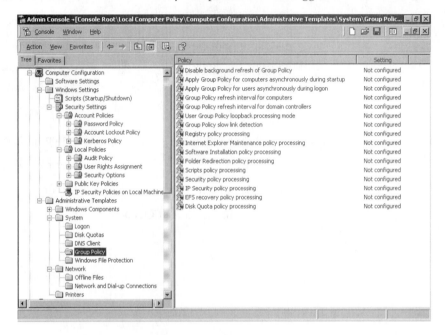

A. Enable and configure the Group Policy for Group Policy, Apply Group Policy for computers asynchronously during startup.

B. Enable and configure the Group Policy for Group Policy, Apply Group Policy for users asynchronously during startup.

C. Enable and configure the Group Policy for Group Policy, Group Policy Refresh Interval for Computers to 10 minutes.

D. Enable and configure the Group Policy for Group Policy, Group Policy Refresh Interval for Domain Controllers to 10 minutes.

2. You are the administrator of the TESTCORP.COM domain. You have configured Local Security Options for the Default Domain Policy object. You have delegated administrative control to the DENVER.TESTCORP.COM domain and the BELFAST.TESTCORP .COM domain to the respective local administrators. You want to make sure that the local administrators do not define any Group Policies that might conflict with the settings you have specified. What should you configure?

   A. Configure the No Override option on the TESTCORP.COM domain GPO.

   B. Configure the Block Inheritance option on the TESTCORP.COM domain GPO.

   C. Configure the Always Apply Root Level GPO option on the TESTCORP.COM domain GPO.

   D. Nothing, your options will override any local options by default.

3. You suspect that someone is attempting to log on to your domain using the Administrator account. You want to track anytime users log on successfully or unsuccessfully in the domain. Based on the following exhibit, which auditing event should you enable?

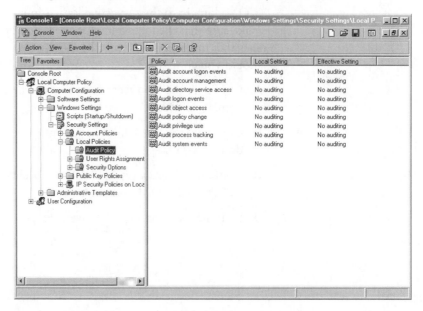

A. Audit Account Logon Events

B. Audit Account Management

C. Audit Logon Events

D. Audit Process Tracking

4. You are the administrator of a Windows 2000 network that uses Active Directory. Your network includes Windows 2000 domain controllers, Windows 2000 member servers, and Windows 2000 Professional computers. You are concerned that the security on your network is susceptible to network attacks. You want to use the Security Configuration and Analysis Tool snap-in to tighten the network's security. Which of the following options can be applied using this tool? (Choose all that apply.)

   A. Track changes to security options

   B. Create and apply group policies

   C. Set a working database of security options

   D. Import an existing security template

5. You are the system administrator of your network. You use two user accounts, one with administrative rights and one regular user account. When you attempt to log on to the domain controller with your regular user account, you receive an error message that you are not allowed to log on interactively. Which user right would allow a regular user to log on interactively at the domain controller?

   A. Log on Locally

   B. Log on Interactively

   C. Log on Natively

   D. Log on as a Local User

6. You need to quickly edit the Group Policy for a Windows 2000 member server. Which of the following command-line utilities could you use to access the Local Computer Policy utility?

   A. `EditGPO.exe`

   B. `GPOEdit.exe`

   C. `EditGPO.msc`

   D. `Gpedit.msc`

7. You are the administrator of the SF.ABCCORP.COM domain. You want to create a GPO that will be used by your domain. Which of the following utilities would you use?

    A. Security Configuration and Analysis snap-in

    B. Active Directory Users and Computers snap-in

    C. Group Policy Editor snap-in

    D. GPOEd command-line utility

8. Your network requires an extraordinary level of security. You want to configure the Windows 2000 domain controllers so that only Windows 2000 clients can communicate with them. Based on your requirements, which of the following security templates should you apply to your servers?

    A. securedc.inf

    B. hisecdc.inf

    C. dedicadc.inf

    D. w2kdc.inf

9. You are concerned about network security. You want to know as much as you can about the security protocols that are used in conjunction with Windows 2000. Which of the following security protocols is used with Windows 2000 Server to authenticate users and network services?

    A. Kerberos version 5

    B. C2\E2 Security

    C. KDS Security

    D. MS-CHAP

10. You are the administrator of the TESTCORP.COM domain. You have configured a GPO for your domain so that users have to change their passwords every 45 days. You want to ensure that users do not immediately reuse their old password. Which password policy specifies that users cannot reuse passwords until they have cycled through a specified number of unique passwords?

    A. Enforce Password History

    B. Use Unique Passwords

    C. Require C2/E2 Encryption Standards

    D. All Passwords Must Use High Level Standards

11. You suspect that one of your administrators is creating new users so that they can look at the Payroll folder, which has folder auditing enabled. Which audit policy should you enable to track when a user or group is created, deleted, or has management actions generated?

    A. Audit Object Access

    B. Audit Logon Events

    C. Audit Account Management

    D. Audit Process Tracking

12. Marco needs to monitor the system processes of three servers through the Performance Logs and Alerts utility. What user right should Marco be assigned so that he can accomplish this task?

    A. Profile System Performance

    B. Monitor System Performance

    C. Manage System Monitoring

    D. Monitor Performance Logs and Alerts

13. Scott's Windows 2000 Server computer also acts as an IIS server that allows anonymous access. He wants to minimize security risks as much as possible. Which of the following security options will allow him to specify additional restrictions for anonymous connections?

    A. Additional Restrictions for Anonymous Users

    B. Impose Additional Security for Anonymous Users

    C. Tight Security for Anonymous Users

    D. Audit Access of Anonymous Users

14. Serena has recently applied security options for her Windows 2000 Server computer. When she attempts to verify the security settings, they appear as if they have not been applied. What command-line utility can Serena use to force an update of the new security policies?

    A. secupdate

    B. secedit

    C. secrefresh

    D. secpol

15. You have configured group policies on your Windows 2000 domain controllers. Your Windows 2000 clients use the group policies, but the Windows NT 4 clients do not have the group policies applied. Which command-line utility is used to create and manage system policies for Windows NT 4 clients on Windows 2000 Servers?

    A. POLEDITOR

    B. SYSPOLED

    C. POLEDIT

    D. EDITPOL

Answers to Review Questions

1. C. The Group Policy Refresh Intervals for Computers specifies the interval rate that will be used to update the computer's Group Policy. By default, this background operation occurs every 90 minutes.

2. A. The No Override option is used to specify that child containers can't override the policy settings of higher-level GPOs. In this case, the order of precedence would be that site settings override domain settings, and domain settings override OU settings. The No Override option would be used if you wanted to set corporate-wide policies without allowing administrators of lower-level containers to override your settings. This option can be set on a per-container basis, as needed.

3. A. The Audit Account Logon Events policy is used to track events such as when a user logs on, logs off, or makes a network connection. The Audit Logon Events policy is used to track events such as running a logon script or accessing a roaming profile.

4. C, D. Through the Security Configuration and Analysis snap-in, you can analyze an existing template against your current configuration to identify any weakness in your security settings. This utility, Analyze Computer Now, does not configure any security options. The Configure Computer Now utility does change the security settings and should only be used with extreme caution.

5. A. In order to log on to the local computer, the user must have the Log on Locally user right.

6. D. You can edit Group Policies through the Group Policy MMC snap-on or by using the command-line utility `Gpedit.msc`. To use this utility, select Start ➢ Run and at the Run dialog box, type **Gpedit.msc** and click the OK button.

7. B. You create GPOs through the Active Directory Users and Computers. This administrative tool can be added to the MMC as a snap-in.

8. B. The hisecdc.inf security template defines highly secure network communications for Windows 2000 computers. If you apply this security template, Windows 2000 computers can only communicate with other Windows 2000 computers. In this case, the computers would not communicate with clients such as Windows 95/98 or even Windows NT 4 computers.

9. A. Windows 2000 uses the Kerberos version 5 security protocol to authenticate users and services through a mutual authentication process.

10. A. The Enforce Password History option is used so that users cannot reuse the same password. Users must create a new password when their password expires or is changed.

11. C. The Audit Account Management policy is used to track user and group creation, deletion, and management actions.

12. A. The Profile System Performance user right is used to monitor system processes through tools such as the Performance Logs and Alerts utility.

13. A. The Additional Restrictions for Anonymous Users security option allows you to impose additional restrictions, such as not allowing access without explicit anonymous permissions.

14. B. If you edit your security policy and notice that your changes are not taking effect, it may be because the group policies are only applied periodically. You can force your policies to be updated by issuing the command `secedit /refreshpolicy machine_policy` for computers and `secedit /refreshpolicy user_policy` for user settings.

15. C. In Windows 2000 Server, you access the System Policy Editor with the command-line utility `POLEDIT`. This utility is used to create and manage System Policies for Windows NT 4 clients.

Chapter

6

Managing Disks

MICROSOFT EXAM OBJECTIVES COVERED IN THIS CHAPTER:

- ✓ Monitor, configure, and troubleshoot disks and volumes.
- ✓ Configure data compression.
- ✓ Monitor and configure disk quotas.
- ✓ Recover from disk failures.
- ✓ Encrypt data on a hard disk by using Encrypting File System (EFS).

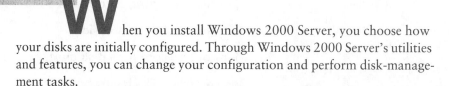

hen you install Windows 2000 Server, you choose how your disks are initially configured. Through Windows 2000 Server's utilities and features, you can change your configuration and perform disk-management tasks.

For your file system configuration, Windows 2000 supports the following filesystems: FAT, FAT32, or NTFS. You can convert a FAT16 or FAT32 partition to NTFS.

Another factor in disk management is choosing how your physical drives are configured. Windows 2000 Server supports basic storage and dynamic storage. When you install Windows 2000 or upgrade from Windows NT, the drives are configured as basic storage. Dynamic storage is new to Windows 2000 Server and allows you to create simple, spanned, striped, mirrored, and RAID-5 volumes. Once you decide how your disks should be configured, you implement the disk configurations through the Disk Management utility. This utility allows you to view and manage your physical disks and volumes. In this chapter, you will learn how to manage both types of storage and upgrade from basic storage to dynamic storage.

The other disk-management features covered in this chapter are data compression, disk quotas, data encryption, disk defragmentation, and disk cleanup.

The procedures for many disk-management tasks are the same for both Windows 2000 Server and Professional. The main difference is that Windows 2000 Professional does not support mirrored volumes or RAID-5 volumes.

Configuring File Systems

File systems are used to store and locate the files you save on your hard drive. As explained in Chapter 1, "Getting Started with Windows 2000

Server," Windows 2000 Server supports the *FAT16*, *FAT32*, and *NTFS* file systems. You should choose FAT16 or FAT32 if you want to dual-boot your computer, because these file systems are backward compatible with other operating systems. You should choose NTFS if you want to take advantage of features such as local security, file compression, disk quotas, and file encryption. Table 6.1 summarizes the capabilities of each file system.

TABLE 6.1 File System Capabilities

Feature	FAT16	FAT32	NTFS
Operating system support?	Most	Windows 95 OSR2, Windows 98, and Windows 2000	Windows NT and Windows 2000
Long filename support?	Yes	Yes	Yes
Efficient use of disk space?	No	Yes	Yes
Compression support?	No	No	Yes
Quota support?	No	No	Yes
Encryption support?	No	No	Yes
Local security support?	No	No	Yes
Network security support?	Yes	Yes	Yes
Maximum volume size	2GB	2TB	16EB

Windows 2000 Server also supports *CDFS* (*Compact Disk File System*). However, CDFS cannot be managed. It is only used to mount and read CDs.

Windows 2000 provides the *CONVERT* command-line utility for converting a FAT16 or FAT32 partition to NTFS. The syntax for the CONVERT command is:

```
CONVERT [drive:] /fs:ntfs
```

In Exercise 6.1, you will convert your D: drive from FAT16 to NTFS.

All of the exercises in this chapter can be done from either your Windows 2000 member server or domain controller.

EXERCISE 6.1

Converting a FAT16 Partition to NTFS

1. Copy some folders to the D: drive.

2. Select Start ➢ Programs ➢ Accessories ➢ Command Prompt.

3. In the Command Prompt dialog box, type **CONVERT D: /fs:ntfs** and press Enter.

4. After the conversion process is complete, close the Command Prompt dialog box. If the conversion doesn't occur immediately, specify that the conversion should take place the next time the computer is started.

5. Verify that the folders you copied in step 1 still exist on the partition.

Configuring Disk Storage

Windows 2000 Server supports two types of disk storage: basic storage and dynamic storage. Basic storage is backward compatible with other operating systems and can be configured to support up to four partitions. Dynamic storage is a new system that is configured as volumes. The following sections describe the basic storage and dynamic storage configurations.

You can convert a basic disk to a dynamic disk in Windows 2000 Server without losing any data, as described in the "Upgrading a Basic Disk to a Dynamic Disk" section later in this chapter. However, you cannot convert a dynamic disk to a basic disk without first deleting all of the volumes contained on the disk.

Basic Storage

Basic storage consists of primary and extended partitions. The first partition that is created on a hard drive is called a *primary partition*. The primary partition uses all of the space that is allocated to the partition. Each physical drive can have up to four partitions. You can have four primary partitions or three primary partitions and one extended partition. With *extended partitions* you can allocate the space however you like. For example, a 500MB extended partition could have a 250MB D: partition and a 250MB E: partition.

At the highest level of disk organization, you have a physical hard drive. You cannot use space on the physical drive until you have logically partitioned the physical drive. A *partition* is a logical definition of hard drive space.

An advantage of using a single partition on a single physical disk is that you can allocate the space however you want. For example, if you had a 1GB physical drive and you created a single primary partition, you could allocate the space on the drive as needed. On the other hand, if you created two 500MB partitions called C: and D:, and C: was full and D: had space left, you could not take space from the D: drive without deleting the partition first.

One of the advantages of using multiple partitions on a single physical hard drive is that each partition can have a different file system. For example, the C: drive might be FAT32 and the D: drive might be NTFS. Multiple partitions also make it easier to manage security requirements.

Laptop computers support only basic storage.

Dynamic Storage

Dynamic storage is a new Windows 2000 feature that consists of a *dynamic disk* divided into dynamic *volumes*. Dynamic volumes cannot contain partitions or logical drives, and they are only accessible through Windows 2000 systems.

Windows 2000 Server dynamic storage supports five dynamic volume types: simple volumes, spanned volumes, striped volumes, mirrored volumes, and RAID-5 volumes. These are similar to disk configurations that were used with Windows NT 4. When you install or upgrade to Windows 2000, you are using basic storage, and you can't add volume sets. Fortunately, you can upgrade from basic storage to dynamic storage, as explained in the "Upgrading a Basic Disk to a Dynamic Disk" section later in this chapter.

To set up dynamic storage, you create or upgrade a disk to a dynamic disk. Then you create dynamic volumes within the dynamic disk. You create dynamic storage with the Windows 2000 Disk Management utility, which is covered in the "Using the Disk Management Utility" section later in this chapter.

Simple Volumes

A *simple volume* contains space from a single dynamic drive. The space from the single drive can be contiguous or noncontiguous. Simple volumes are used when you have enough disk space on a single drive to hold your entire volume. Figure 6.1 illustrates two simple volumes on a physical disk.

FIGURE 6.1 Two simple volumes

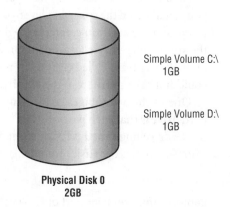

Simple Volume C:\
1GB

Simple Volume D:\
1GB

Physical Disk 0
2GB

Spanned Volumes

Spanned volumes consist of disk space on two or more dynamic drives; up to 32 dynamic drives can be used in a spanned volume configuration. Spanned volume sets are used to dynamically increase the size of a dynamic volume. When you create spanned volumes, the data is written sequentially, filling space on one physical drive before writing to space on the next physical drive in the spanned volume set. Typically, administrators use spanned volumes when they are running out of disk space on a volume and want to dynamically extend the volume with space from another hard drive.

You do not need to allocate the same amount of space to the volume set on each physical drive. This means that you could combine a 500MB partition on one physical drive with two 750MB partitions on other dynamic drives, as shown in Figure 6.2.

FIGURE 6.2 A spanned volume set

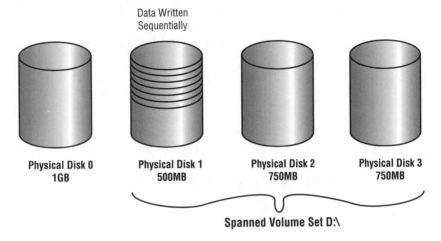

Because data is written sequentially, you do not see any performance enhancements with spanned volumes, as you do with striped volumes (discussed next). The main disadvantage of spanned volumes is that if any drive in the spanned volume set fails, you lose access to all of the data in the spanned set.

Striped Volumes

Striped volumes store data in equal stripes between two or more (up to 32) dynamic drives, as illustrated in Figure 6.3. Since the data is written sequentially in the stripes, you can take advantage of multiple I/O performance and increase the speed at which data reads and writes take place. Typically, administrators use striped volumes when they want to combine the space of several physical drives into a single logical volume and increase disk performance.

FIGURE 6.3 A striped volume set

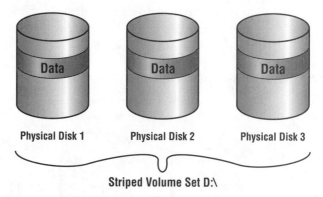

Physical Disk 1   Physical Disk 2   Physical Disk 3

Striped Volume Set D:\

The main disadvantage of striped volumes is that if any drive in the striped volume set fails, you lose access to all of the data in the striped set.

Mirrored Volumes

Mirrored volumes are copies of two simple volumes stored on two separate physical partitions, as illustrated in Figure 6.4. In a mirrored volume set, you have a primary drive and a secondary drive. The data written to the primary drive is mirrored to the secondary drive. Mirrored volumes provide fault tolerance—if one drive in the mirrored volume fails, the other drive still works without any interruption in service or loss of data.

Another advantage of mirrored volumes is enhanced disk-read performance, because the drive head closest to the sector being read is accessed for the operation. However, there is some reduction in disk-write performance, because one disk controller needs to write to two separate drives. To improve write performance and also increase your system's fault tolerance, you can use a variation of mirroring called *duplexing*. In duplexing, you add another disk controller, which is also illustrated in Figure 6.4. (Windows 2000 Server does not distinguish between mirroring and duplexing, essentially viewing both configurations as mirrored volumes.)

FIGURE 6.4   A mirrored volume set

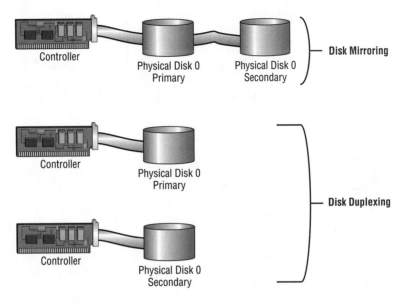

 The system and boot partition can exist on a mirrored volume set.

The main disadvantage of mirrored volumes is high overhead. All of your data is written to two locations. For example, if you mirrored a 4GB drive, you would need two 4GB disks (a total of 8GB of storage space), but you would not be able to store more than 4GB of data on your system.

RAID-5 Volumes

RAID-5 volumes are similar to striped volumes in that they stripe the data over multiple disk channels. In addition, RAID-5 volumes place a parity stripe across the volume. (*Parity* is a mathematical calculation performed on the data that provides information that can be used to rebuild data on failed drives.) If a single drive within the volume set fails, the parity information stored on the other drives can be used to rebuild the data on the failed drive. RAID-5 volumes require at least three physical drives (up to a maximum of 32 drives), using an equal size of free space on all of the drives, as illustrated in Figure 6.5.

FIGURE 6.5   A RAID-5 volume set

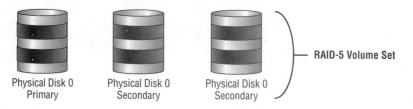

Physical Disk 0   Physical Disk 0   Physical Disk 0
     Primary   Secondary   Secondary

RAID-5 Volume Set

Unlike with mirrored volumes, the system and boot partition cannot exist on a RAID-5 volume.

The main advantages of RAID-5 volumes are that they are fault tolerant and provide good performance because this configuration uses multiple disk I/O channels. The other advantage of RAID-5 volumes is that they require less disk space for fault tolerance than mirrored volumes need. A mirrored volume set uses half of the volume set to store the mirror. A RAID-5 volume set requires only the storage space of one drive in the volume set to store the parity information. For example, if you have three 5GB drives in a RAID-5 volume set, 5GB of the volume set is used to store parity information, and the remaining 10GB can store data. If your volume set contained five 5GB drives, you could use 20GB for data and 5GB for storing parity information.

The main disadvantage of a RAID-5 volume is that once a drive fails, system performance suffers until you rebuild the RAID-5 volume. This is because the parity information must be recalculated through memory to reconstruct the missing drive. If more that one drive fails, the RAID-5 volume becomes inaccessible. At that point, you must restore your data from your backup media.

 Real World Scenario

Selecting Fault Tolerance for Mission Critical Servers

You are the network administrator of a large company. You need to install a Windows 2000 Server that will be used as a domain controller. This is a mission-critical server and must be as reliable as possible. One of your tasks is to plan the disk configuration.

In the real world, you would most likely use hardware RAID. Hardware RAID is more fault tolerant and is easier to recover from failure than the software RAID offered through Windows 2000. The difference between software RAID and hardware RAID is that software RAID is implemented solely through the software and requires no special hardware; hardware RAID uses special disk controllers and specific drives.

You decide to buy a high-end server that supports RAID with hot-swappable drives with an extra drive installed that can be used as an online spare. This allows you to have fault tolerance with a minimum of downtime in the event of failure.

Using the Disk Management Utility

The *Disk Management utility* is a graphical tool for managing disks and volumes within the Windows 2000 Server environment. In this section, you will learn how to access the Disk Management utility and use it to manage basic tasks, basic storage, and dynamic storage.

Microsoft
✓ *Exam*
Objective

Monitor, configure, and troubleshoot disks and volumes.

In order to have full permissions to use the Disk Management utility, you should be logged on with Administrative privileges. To access the utility, open the Control Panel, select Administrative Tools, then Computer Management. Expand the Storage folder to see the Disk Management utility. The Disk Management utility opening window is shown in Figure 6.6.

You can also access the Disk Management utility by right-clicking My Computer, selecting Manage, expanding Computer Management, expanding Storage, and finally expanding Disk Management. As an alternative, you can add Disk Management as an MMC snap-in. See Chapter 3, "Configuring the Windows 2000 Server Environment," for details on adding MMC snap-ins.

FIGURE 6.6   The Disk Management window

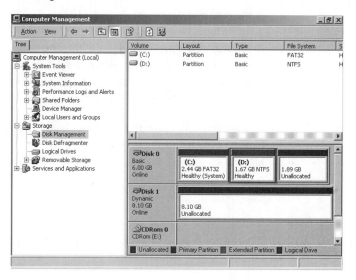

The main window shows the following information:

- The volumes that are recognized by the computer

- The type of partition, either basic or dynamic

- The type of file system used by each partition

- The status of the partition and whether or not the partition contains the system or boot partition

- The capacity, or amount of space, allocated to the partition

- The amount of free space remaining on the partition

- The amount of overhead associated with the partition

Managing Basic Tasks

With the Disk Management utility, you can perform a variety of basic tasks:

- View disk and volume properties

- Add a new disk

- Create partitions and volumes

- Upgrade a basic disk to a dynamic disk

- Change a drive letter and path
- Delete partitions and volumes

These tasks are covered in detail in the following sections.

Viewing Disk Properties

To view the properties of a disk, right-click the drive in the lower half of the Disk Management main window (see Figure 6.6) and choose Properties from the pop-up menu. This brings up the Disk Properties dialog box, as shown in Figure 6.7.

FIGURE 6.7   The Disk Properties dialog box

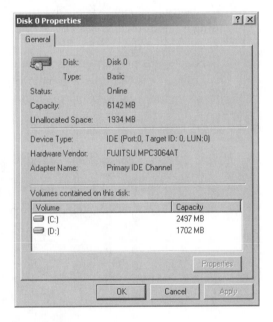

This dialog box displays the following disk properties:

- The disk number
- The type of disk (basic, dynamic, CD-ROM, removable, DVD, or unknown)
- The status of the disk (online or offline)
- The capacity of the disk

- The amount of unallocated space on the disk

- The hardware device type

- The hardware vendor who produced the drive

- The adapter name

- The logical volumes that have been defined on the physical drive

Viewing Volume and Local Disk Properties

On a dynamic disk, you manage volume properties. On a basic disk, you manage local disk properties. Volumes and local disks perform the same function, and the options discussed in the following sections apply to both. The examples are based on a dynamic disk using a simple volume. If you are using basic storage, you will view the local disk properties rather than the volume properties.

To view the properties of a volume, right-click the volume in the upper half of the Disk Management main window and choose Properties. This brings up the volume Properties dialog box, as shown in Figure 6.8.

FIGURE 6.8 The volume Properties dialog box

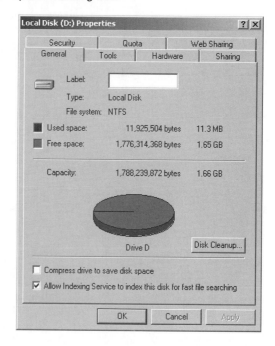

In the dialog box, the volume properties are organized on seven tabs (five for FAT volumes): General, Tools, Hardware, Sharing, Security, Quota, and Web Sharing. The Security and Quota tabs appear only for NTFS volumes. These tabs are covered in detail in the following sections.

Configuring General Properties

The information on the General tab of the volume Properties dialog box (see Figure 6.8) gives you a general idea of how the volume is configured. This dialog box shows the label, type, file system, used and free space, and capacity of the volume. The label is shown in an editable text box, and you can change it if desired. The space allocated to the volume is shown in a graphical representation as well as in text form.

The volume or local disk label is for informational purposes only. For example, depending on its use, you might give a volume a label like APPS or ACCTDB.

The Disk Cleanup button starts the Disk Cleanup utility, which allows you to delete unnecessary files and free disk space. This utility is covered in more detail later in this chapter in the "Using the Disk Cleanup Utility" section.

Accessing Tools

The Tools tab of the volume Properties dialog box, shown in Figure 6.9, provides access to three tools:

- Click the Check Now button to run the Check Disk utility. You would check the volume for errors if you were experiencing problems accessing the volume or if the volume had been open during a system restart that had not gone through a proper shutdown sequence. The Check Disk utility is covered later in this chapter in the "Troubleshooting Disk Devices and Volumes" section.

- Click the Backup Now button to run the Backup Wizard. This Wizard steps you through backing up the files on the volume. Backup procedures are covered in Chapter 15, "Performing System Recovery Functions."

- Click the Defragment Now button to run the Disk Defragmenter utility. This utility defragments files on the volume by storing files in a contiguous manner on the hard drive. Defragmentation is covered in detail later in this chapter in the "Defragmenting Disks" section.

FIGURE 6.9 The Tools tab of the volume Properties dialog box

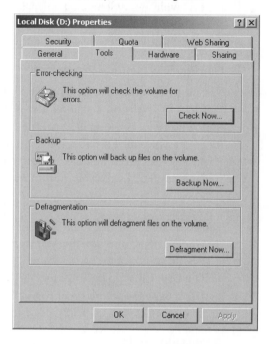

Viewing Hardware Information

The Hardware tab of the volume Properties dialog box, shown in Figure 6.10, lists the hardware associated with the disk drives that are recognized by the Windows 2000 operating system. The bottom half of the dialog box shows the properties of the device highlighted in the top half of the dialog box.

FIGURE 6.10   The Hardware tab of the volume Properties dialog box

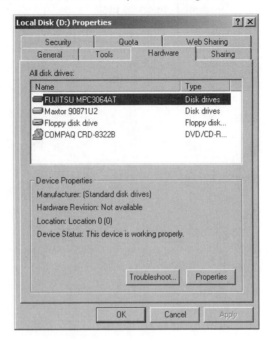

For more details about a hardware item, highlight it and click the Properties button in the lower-right corner of the dialog box. This brings up a Properties dialog box for the item. Figure 6.11 shows an example of the disk drive Properties dialog box. With luck, your device status will report that "This device is working properly." If the device is not working properly, you can click the Troubleshooter button to bring up a troubleshooting Wizard to help you discover what the problem is.

FIGURE 6.11 A disk drive Properties dialog box accessed through the Hardware tab of the volume Properties dialog box

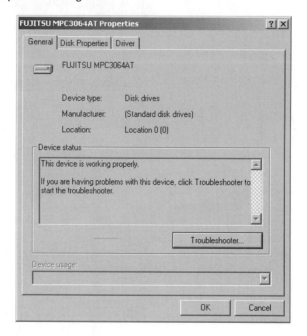

Sharing Volumes

The Sharing tab of the volume Properties dialog box, shown in Figure 6.12, allows you to specify whether or not the volume is shared. By default, all volumes are shared. The share name is the drive letter followed by a $ (dollar sign). The $ indicates that the share is hidden. From this dialog box, you can set the user limit, permissions, and caching for the share. Sharing is covered in Chapter 7, "Accessing Files and Folders."

FIGURE 6.12 The Sharing tab of the volume Properties dialog box

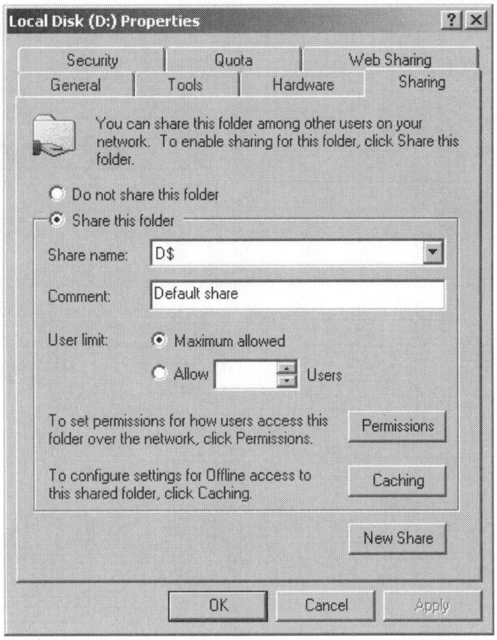

Configuring Security Options

The Security tab of the volume Properties dialog box, shown in Figure 6.13, appears only if the volume is NTFS. The Security tab is used to set the NTFS permissions for the volume. Notice that the default permissions allow the Everyone group Full Control permissions at the root of the volume. This could cause major security problems if any user decides to manipulate or delete the data within the volume. Managing file system security is covered in Chapter 7.

FIGURE 6.13 The Security tab of the volume Properties dialog box

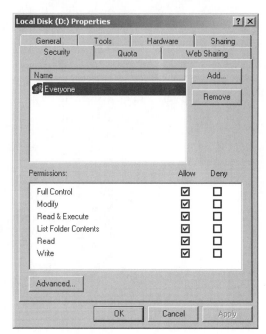

Setting Quotas

Like the Security tab, the Quota tab of the volume Properties dialog box appears only if the volume is NTFS. Through this tab, you can limit the amount of space users can use within the volume. Quotas are covered in detail later in this chapter in the "Setting Disk Quotas" section.

Configuring Web Sharing

By default, Internet Information Services (IIS) is installed and started on a Windows 2000 Server computer. If this service is running, you will see a tab for Web Sharing, The Web Sharing tab, shown in Figure 6.14, is used to configure folder sharing for IIS. IIS is covered in Chapter 10, "Managing Web Services."

Adding a New Disk

To increase the amount of disk storage you have, you can add a new disk. This is a fairly common task that you will need to perform as your application programs and files grow larger. How you add a disk depends on whether your computer supports hot swapping of drives. *Hot swapping* is the ability to add new hard drives while the computer is turned on. Most medium to high-end servers with hardware RAID support hot swapping.

FIGURE 6.14   The Web Sharing tab of the volume Properties dialog box

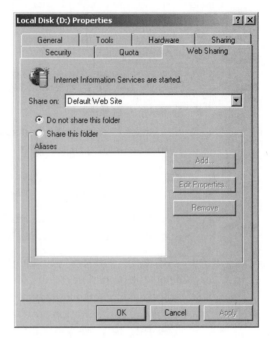

Computer Doesn't Support Hot Swap

If your computer does not support hot swapping, you need to shut down the computer before you add a new disk. Then add the drive according to the manufacturer's directions. When you're finished, restart the computer. The new drive should now be listed in the Disk Management utility. If it is not, open the Disk Management utility and select Action ➤ Rescan Disks. When you start the Disk Management utility, you will be prompted to write a signature to the disk so that it will be recognized by a Windows 2000 Server. By default, the new drive will be configured as a dynamic disk.

Computer Supports Hot Swap

If your computer does support hot swapping, you don't need to turn off your computer first. Just add the drive according to the manufacturer's directions. Then, open the Disk Management utility and select Action ➤ Rescan Disks. The new drive should appear in the Disk Management utility.

Creating Partitions and Volumes

If you have unallocated (free) space on a basic disk and you want to create a logical drive, you create a partition. If you have unallocated space on a dynamic disk and you want to create a logical drive, you create a volume. The processes for creating partitions and volumes are described in the following sections.

We will create a partition in Exercise 6.2.

EXERCISE 6.2

Creating a Partition

1. Right-click My Computer and select Manage. Expand Computer Management, then Storage, then Disk Management.

2. Right-click an area of free space and choose the Create Partition option from the pop-up menu.

3. The Welcome to the Create Partition Wizard dialog box appears. Click the Next button to continue.

4. The Select Partition Type dialog box appears. In this dialog box, select the type of partition you want to create: primary, extended, or logical drive. Only the options supported by your computer's hardware configuration are available. Click the radio button for the type, then click the Next button.

5. The Specify Partition Size dialog box appears. Here, you specify the maximum partition size, up to the amount of free disk space that is recognized. In this exercise, select 250MB and then click the Next button.

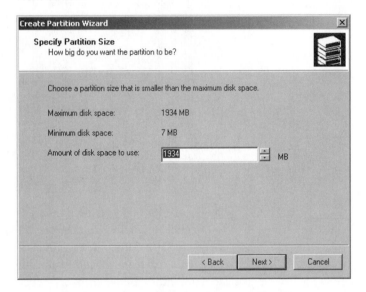

6. The Assign Drive Letter or Path dialog box appears. Through this dialog box, you can specify a drive letter, mount the partition as an empty folder, or choose not to assign a drive letter or drive path. If you choose to mount the volume as an empty folder, you can have an unlimited number of volumes, negating the drive-letter limitation. In this exercise, accept the default drive. Make your selections, then click the Next button.

EXERCISE 6.2 *(continued)*

Warning: If you choose not to assign a drive letter or path, users will not be able to access the partition.

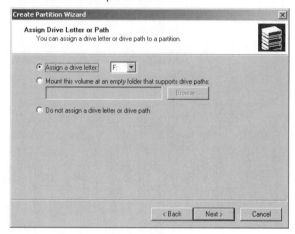

7. The Format Partition dialog box appears. This dialog box allows you to choose whether or not you will format the partition. If you choose to format the volume, you can format it as FAT, FAT32, or NTFS. You can also select the allocation unit size, enter a volume label (for informative purposes), specify a quick format, or choose to enable file and folder compression. Specifying a quick format is risky, because it will not scan the disk for bad sectors (which is done in a normal format operation). In this exercise, accept the default value to format as NTFS (leave the other settings as their defaults). After you've made your choices, click the Next button.

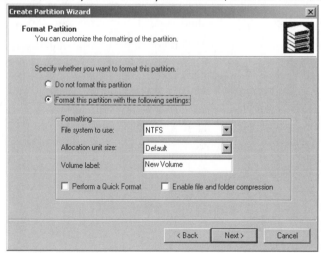

EXERCISE 6.2 *(continued)*

8. The Completing the Create Partition Wizard dialog box appears. Verify your selections. If you need to change any of them, click the Back button to reach the appropriate dialog box. Otherwise, click the Finish button.

When you right-click an area of free space on a dynamic disk and select the Create Volume option, the Create Volume Wizard starts. This Wizard displays a series of dialog boxes to guide you through the process of creating a partition:

- The Select Volume Type dialog box allows you to select the type of volume you want to create. Options include simple volume, spanned volume, striped volume, mirrored volume, or RAID-5 volume.

- The Select Disks dialog box allows you to select the disks and the size of the volume that is being created.

- The Assign Drive Letter or Path dialog box allows you to assign a drive letter or as a drive path. There is also an option to not assign a drive letter or path, but if you choose this option, users will not be able to access the volume.

- The Format Volume dialog box lets you specify whether or not you want to format the volume. If you choose to format the volume, you can select the file system, allocation unit size, and the volume label. You can also choose to perform a quick format and to enable drive compression.

Upgrading a Basic Disk to a Dynamic Disk

To take advantage of the features offered by Windows 2000 dynamic disks, you must upgrade your basic disks to dynamic disks.

Upgrading basic disks to dynamic disks without losing data is a one-way process. If you decide to revert to a basic disk, you must first delete all volumes associated with the drive. Also, this operation is potentially dangerous. Before you do this (or make any major change to your drives or volumes), create a new backup of the drive or volume and verify that you can successfully restore the backup.

The following steps are involved in the disk-upgrade process:

1. In the Disk Management utility, right-click the drive you want to convert and select the Upgrade to Dynamic Disk option, as shown in Figure 6.15.

FIGURE 6.15 Selecting the Upgrade to Dynamic Disk option

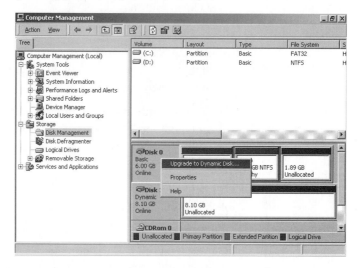

2. The Upgrade to Dynamic Disk dialog box appears, as shown in Figure 6.16. Select the disk that you want to upgrade and click the OK button.

FIGURE 6.16 The Upgrade to Dynamic Disk dialog box

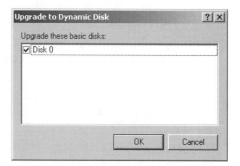

3. The Disks to Upgrade dialog box appears, as shown in Figure 6.17. Click the Upgrade button.

FIGURE 6.17   The Disks to Upgrade dialog box

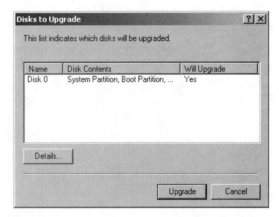

4. A confirmation dialog box warns you that you will no longer be able to boot previous versions of Windows from this disk. Click the Yes button to continue.

5. Another confirmation dialog box warns you that any file systems mounted on the disk will be dismounted. Click the Yes button to continue.

6. An information dialog box tells you that a reboot is required to complete the upgrade. Click the OK button. Your computer will restart, and the disk-upgrade process is complete.

Changing the Drive Letter and Path

Suppose that you have drive C: assigned as your first partition and drive D: assigned as your CD drive. You add a new drive and partition it as a new volume. By default, the new partition is assigned as drive E:. If you want your logical drives to appear before the CD drive, you can use the Disk Management utility's Change Drive Letter and Path option to rearrange your drive letters.

When you need to reassign drive letters, right-click the volume you want to change the drive letter on and choose the Change Drive Letter and Path option, as shown in Figure 6.18. This brings up the Change Drive Letter and

Paths for *drive* dialog box, as shown in Figure 6.19. Click the Edit button to access the Edit Drive Letter or Path dialog box. Use the drop-down list next to the Assign a Drive Letter option to select the drive letter you want to assign to the volume. Finally, confirm the change when prompted.

FIGURE 6.18   Selecting the Change Drive Letter and Path option

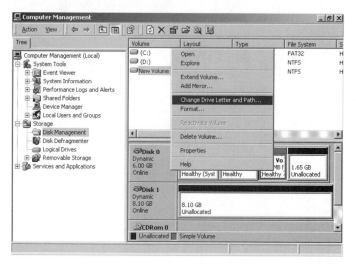

FIGURE 6.19   The Change Drive Letters and Paths dialog box

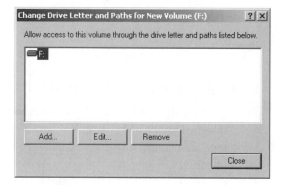

In Exercise 6.3, you will edit the drive letter of the partition you created in Exercise 6.2.

EXERCISE 6.3

Editing a Drive Letter

1. Right-click My Computer and select Manage. Expand Computer Management, then Storage, then Disk Management.

2. Right-click the drive you created in Exercise 6.2 and select Change Drive Letter and Path.

3. In the Change Drive Letter and Paths dialog box, click the Edit button.

4. In the Edit Drive Letter or Path dialog box, select a new drive letter and click the OK button.

5. In the confirmation dialog box, click the Yes button to confirm that you want to change the drive letter.

Deleting Partitions and Volumes

You would delete a partition or volume if you wanted to reorganize your disk or make sure that data would not be accessed. Once you delete a partition or volume, it is gone forever.

To delete a partition or volume, in the Disk Management window, right-click the partition or volume and choose the Delete Volume (or Delete Partition) option. You will see a dialog box warning you that all the data on the partition or volume will be lost, as shown in Figure 6.20. Click Yes to confirm that you want to delete the volume or partition.

FIGURE 6.20 Confirming volume deletion

Managing Basic Storage

The Disk Management utility offers limited support for managing basic storage. You can create, delete, and format partitions on basic drives. You also can delete volume sets and stripe sets that were created under Windows NT. Most other disk-management tasks require that you upgrade your drive to dynamic disks. (The upgrade process was described earlier in this chapter, in the "Upgrading a Basic Disk to a Dynamic Disk" section.)

Managing Dynamic Storage

As noted earlier in this chapter, a dynamic disk can contain simple, spanned, striped, mirrored, or RAID-5 volumes. Through the Disk Management utility, you can create volumes of each type. You can also create an extended volume, which is the process of adding disk space to a single simple volume. The following sections describe these disk-management tasks.

Creating Extended Volumes

When you create an extended volume, you are taking a single simple volume and adding more disk space to the volume from free space that exists on the same physical hard drive. When the volume is extended, it is seen as a single drive letter. In order to extend a volume, the simple volume must be formatted as NTFS. You cannot extend a system or boot partition. You also cannot extend volumes that were originally created as basic disk partitions, and then converted to dynamic disk.

An extended volume assumes that you are only using one physical drive. A spanned volume assumes that you are using two or more physical drives. The following steps are used to create an extended volume:

1. In the Disk Management utility, right-click the volume you want to extend and choose the Extend Volume option.

2. The Extend Volume Wizard starts. Click the Next button.

3. The Select Disks dialog box appears, as shown in Figure 6.21. Select the disk that you want to use for the extended volume and click the Next button.

FIGURE 6.21   The Select Disks dialog box

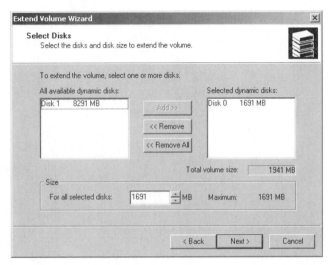

4. The Completing the Extend Volume Wizard dialog box appears. Click the Finish button.

Once a volume is extended, no portion of the volume can be deleted without losing data on the entire set.

Creating Spanned Volumes

When you create a spanned volume, you are forming a new volume from scratch that includes space from two or more physical drives, up to a maximum of 32 drives. You can create spanned volumes that are formatted as FAT, FAT32, or NTFS. In order to create a spanned volume, you must have at least two drives installed on your computer and each drive must contain unallocated space.

The following steps are used to create a spanned volume:

1. In the Disk Management utility, right-click an area of unallocated space on one of the drives that will be part of the spanned volume and select Create Volume from the pop-up menu.

2. The Create Volume Wizard starts. Click the Next button.

3. The Select Volume Type dialog box appears, as shown in Figure 6.22. Select the Spanned Volume radio button and click the Next button.

FIGURE 6.22 The Select Volume Type dialog box

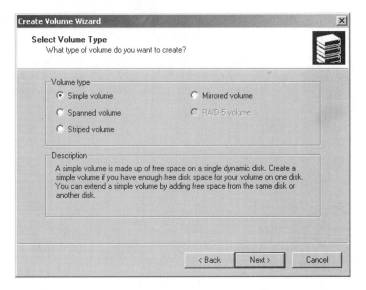

 Only the options that are supported by your computer's hardware will be available in the Select Volume Type dialog box.

4. The Select Disks dialog box appears. By default, the disk that you originally selected to create the spanned volume is selected. You need to select at least one other dynamic disk by highlighting the disk and clicking the Add button. The disks that you select appear in the Selected Dynamic Disks list box, as shown in Figure 6.23. When you have added all of the disks that will make up the spanned volume, click the Next button.

FIGURE 6.23 The Select Disks dialog box for spanned volumes

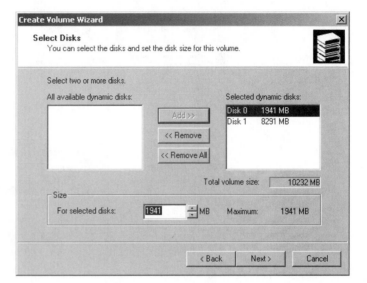

5. The Assign Drive Letter or Path dialog box appears. Specify a drive letter, mount the volume at an empty folder that supports drive paths, or choose not to assign a drive letter or drive path. Then click the Next button.

6. The Format Partition dialog box appears. You can choose whether or not you will format the partition, and if so, what file system will be used. After you've made your choices, click the Next button.

7. The Completing the Create Volume Wizard dialog box appears, offering you the opportunity to verify your selections. If you need to make changes, click the Back button. If the configuration is correct, click the Finish button. In the Disk Management window, you will see that the spanned volume consists of two or more drives that share a single drive letter, as in the example shown in Figure 6.24. Notice that in this example, the disks that make up the spanned volume are unequal in size.

FIGURE 6.24 A spanned volume shown in the Disk Management utility

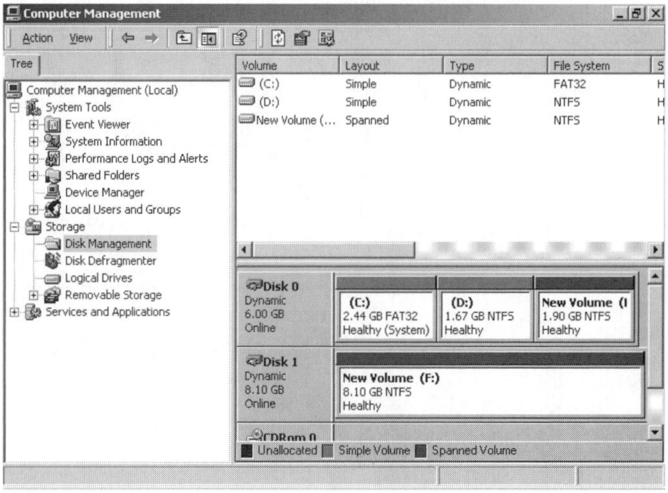

Once a spanned volume is created, no portion of the volume can be deleted without losing the data on the entire set.

Creating Striped Volumes

When you create a striped volume, you are forming a new volume that combines free space on 2 to 32 drives into a single logical partition. Data in the striped volume is written across all drives in 64KB stripes. (Data in spanned and extended volumes is written sequentially.) In order to create a striped volume, you must have at least two drives installed on your computer, and each drive must contain unallocated space. The free space on all drives must be equal in size.

The following steps are used to create a striped volume:

1. In the Disk Management utility, right-click an area of unallocated space on one of the drives that will be a part of the striped volume set and select Create Volume from the pop-up menu.

2. The Create Volume Wizard starts. Click the Next button.

3. The Select Volume Type dialog box appears. Select the Striped Volume radio button and click the Next button.

4. The Select Disks dialog box appears. By default, the disk that you originally selected to create the striped volume is selected. You need to select at least one other dynamic disk by highlighting the selected disk and clicking the Add button. The disks that you select appear in the Selected Dynamic Disks list box. When you have added all of the disks that will make up the striped volume, click the Next button.

5. The Assign Drive Letter or Path dialog box appears. Specify a drive letter, mount the volume at an empty folder that supports drive paths, or choose not to assign a drive letter or drive path. Then click the Next button.

6. The Format Partition dialog box appears. You can choose whether or not you will format the partition, and if so, what file system will be used. After you've made your choices, click the Next button.

7. The Completing the Create Volume Wizard dialog box appears, offering you the opportunity to verify your selections. If you need to make changes, click the Back button. If the configuration is correct, click the Finish button. In the Disk Management window, you will see that the striped volume consists of two or more drives that share a single drive letter, as in the example shown in Figure 6.25. Notice that the disks that make up the striped volume are equal in size.

FIGURE 6.25 A striped volume shown in the Disk Management utility

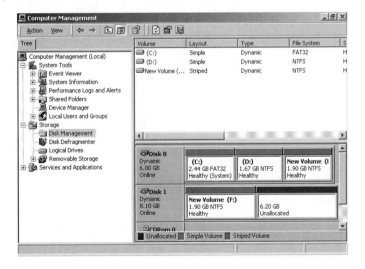

WARNING Once a striped volume is created, no portion of the volume can be deleted without losing the data on the entire set.

Creating Mirrored Volumes

When you create a mirrored volume, you are setting up two physical drives that contain volumes that mirror each other. You create mirrored volumes from areas of free space on the two drives. In order to create a mirrored volume, you must have at least two drives installed on your computer and each drive must contain unallocated space. Mirrored volumes require that the space on each drive used for the mirror set be equal in size.

In Exercise 6.4, you will create a mirrored volume. You can follow this exercise if you have at least two dynamic disks configured on your computer and they both contain unallocated space.

EXERCISE 6.4

Creating a Mirrored Volume

1. Right-click My Computer and select Manage. Expand Computer Management, then Storage, then Disk Management.

2. In the Disk Management utility, right-click an area of unallocated space on one of the drives that will be a part of the mirrored volume set and select Create Volume.

3. When the Create Volume Wizard starts, click the Next button.

4. In the Select Volume Type dialog box, select the Mirrored Volume radio button. Then click the Next button.

5. In the Select Disks dialog box, select the second dynamic disk to be part of the mirrored volume set and click the Add button. Then click the Next button.

6. In the Assign Drive Letter or Path dialog box, accept the default assignment of the next available drive letter and click the Next button.

7. In the Format Partition dialog box, you can choose whether or not you will format the partition, and if so, what file system will be used. For this exercise, select the Format This Volume As Follows radio button and format the file system to use NTFS. Then click the Next button.

8. In the Completing the Create Volume Wizard dialog box, verify that the configuration is correct and click the Finish button. You will now see the mirrored volume in the Disk Management window.

Creating RAID-5 Volumes

When you choose RAID-5 Volume, you are creating a new volume that combines free space on 3 to 32 physical drives. The volume will contain stripes of data and parity information for increased performance and fault tolerance. You must choose at least three disks (not including the system or boot volume) that will be part of the RAID-5 volume. The free space on all the drives must be equal in size.

The following steps are used to create a RAID-5 volume:

1. In the Disk Management utility, right-click an area of unallocated space on one of the drives that will be a part of the RAID-5 volume set and select Create Volume from the pop-up menu.

2. The Create Volume Wizard starts. Click the Next button.

3. The Select Volume Type dialog box appears. Select the RAID-5 Volume radio button and click the Next button.

4. The Select Disks dialog box appears. By default, the disk that you originally selected to create the RAID-5 volume is selected. Select at least two other dynamic disks by highlighting each disk and clicking the Add button. The disks that you select appear in the Selected Dynamic Disks list box. When you have finished adding the disks that will make up the RAID-5 volume, click the Next button.

5. The Assign Drive Letter or Path dialog box appears. Specify a drive letter, mount the volume at an empty folder that supports drive paths, or choose not to assign a drive letter or drive path. Then click the Next button.

6. The Format Partition dialog box appears. You can choose whether or not you will format the partition, and if so, what file system will be used. After you've made your choices, click the Next button.

7. The Completing the Create Volume Wizard dialog box appears. If you need to make changes, click the Back button. If the configuration is correct, click the Finish button. In the Disk Management window, you will see that the RAID-5 volume consists of three or more drives that share a single drive letter.

Recovering from Disk Failure

If your disk fails, you will need to implement a recovery process. If your failure occurred on a simple, extended, spanned, or striped volume, you will need to restore your data from your last backup. You use the Windows 2000 Backup utility to back up and restore data, as described in Chapter 15.

Microsoft
✓ *Exam*
Objective

Recover from disk failures.

When a disk in a mirrored or RAID-5 volume set fails, you can't miss it—you will see a system error and an error in Event Viewer. Also, in the Disk Management utility, the failed volume will be indicated by the description Failed Redundancy. If the disk that failed was part of a mirrored volume set, you need to remove and re-create the failed volume. If the disk was part of a RAID-5 volume set, you need to repair the volume. The following sections describe how to recover from mirrored and RAID-5 volume failures.

Recovering from a Mirrored Volume Failure

To recover from a mirrored volume failure, you need to remove the volume that failed and then re-create the volume. You can perform both of these tasks through the Disk Management utility.

Recovering from a Mirror Failure on Data Volume

If a drive fails in a mirrored volume set that contains only data (it does not contain your system or boot partition), take the following steps:

1. In the Disk Management utility, right-click the failed mirrored volume (marked as Failed Redundancy) and choose Remove Mirror from the pop-up menu.

2. The Remove Mirror dialog box appears. Select the disk that will be removed from the mirrored volume and click the Remove Mirror button.

3. You will see a dialog box asking you to confirm that you want to remove the mirror. Click the Yes button. The remaining drive will become a simple volume.

4. Remove the failed hard drive from the computer and replace the drive.

5. Use the Disk Management utility to re-create the mirrored volume, as described in the "Creating Mirrored Volumes" section earlier in this chapter.

Recovering from a Mirror Failure on Boot Partition

If a drive fails in a mirrored volume set that contains the boot partition, you must first determine if the failed drive is the primary drive (the one with the original data) or the secondary drive (the one with the mirrored data) in the set. If the secondary drive failed, you can remove the failed drive, replace it, and then re-create the mirrored volume, just as you do to recover from a failed mirrored volume set containing only data (described in the previous section).

If the primary drive fails and it contains the boot partition, then recovery becomes more complex, because the BOOT.INI file, which is used during the Windows 2000 boot process, contains the location of the boot partition. If this file points to the failed partition, Windows 2000 Server will not boot. To recover from this type of failure, you will need a Windows 2000 Server boot disk with a BOOT.INI file that points to the secondary drive in the mirrored set. (The BOOT.INI file and the process for creating a Windows 2000 Server boot disk are covered in Chapter 15.) Then you can follow the same steps as you would to recover from a failed data volume (described in the previous section).

If you have at least two dynamic disks configured on your computer and have created a mirrored volume, you can follow the steps in Exercise 6.5 to learn how to recover from a mirror failure:

EXERCISE 6.5

Recovering from a Mirrored Volume Failure

1. Power down your computer and remove the data cable from the second drive that you configured in the mirrored volume set.

2. Restart your server.

3. In the Disk Management utility, right-click the failed mirrored volume (marked as Failed Redundancy) and choose Remove Mirror.

4. In the Remove Mirror dialog box, select the disk that will be removed from the mirrored volume and click the Remove Mirror button.

5. In the next dialog box, click Yes to confirm that you want to remove the mirror.

6. Power down your computer and reconnect the data cable on your second drive. Restart and log on as Admininistrator.

7. Re-create the mirrored volume (discussed in Creating Mirrored Volumes above).

Recovering from a RAID-5 Volume Failure

If a drive in a RAID-5 volume set fails, you will still be able to access your volume set; however, your system performance will degrade significantly, and you will need to re-create the missing data through the parity information.

To recover from a RAID-5 volume failure, you would take the following steps:

1. Replace the failed hardware.

2. Open the Disk Management utility, right-click the failed RAID-5 volume set (marked as Failed Redundancy) and choose Repair Volume from the pop-up menu.

3. The Repair RAID-5 Volume dialog box appears. Choose the drive that you have replaced and click the OK button to regenerate the RAID-5 volume set.

Managing Data Compression

Data compression is the process of storing data in a form that takes less space than uncompressed data does. If you have ever "zipped" or "packed" a file, you have used data compression. With Windows 2000 Server, data compression is available only on NTFS partitions.

Microsoft ✔ *Exam* *Objective*	**Configure data compression.**

Both files and folders in the NTFS file system can be compressed or uncompressed. Files and folders are managed independently, which means that a compressed folder could contain uncompressed files, and an uncompressed folder could contain compressed files.

Access to compressed files by DOS or Windows applications is transparent. For example, if you access a compressed file through Microsoft Word, the file will be uncompressed automatically when it is opened, and then automatically compressed again when it is closed.

Data compression is only available on NTFS partitions. If you copy or move a compressed folder or file to a FAT partition (or a floppy disk), Windows 2000 will automatically uncompress the folder or file.

You cannot have a folder or file compressed and encrypted at the same time. Encryption is discussed in the "Managing Data Encryption with EFS" section later in this chapter.

You implement compression through the Windows Explorer utility. Compression is an advanced attribute of a folder's or file's properties.

You will compress folders and files in Exercise 6.6. This exercise assumes that you have completed Exercise 6.1.

EXERCISE 6.6

Compressing Folders and Files

1. Select Start ➤ Programs ➤ Accessories ➤ Windows Explorer.

2. In Windows Explorer, find and select a folder on the D: drive. The folder you select should contain files.

3. Right-click the folder and select Properties. In the General tab of the folder Properties dialog box, note the value listed for Size on Disk. Then click the Advanced button.

4. In the Advanced Attributes dialog box, check the Compress Contents to Save Disk Space option. Then click the OK button. In the folder Properties dialog box, click the OK button.

5. In the Confirm Attribute Changes dialog box, select Apply Changes to This Folder, Subfolder, and Files (if this dialog box does not appear, click the Apply button in the Properties dialog box to display it). Then click the OK button.

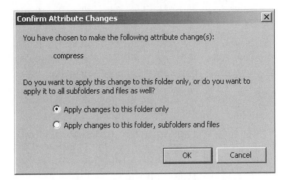

6. In the General tab of the folder Properties dialog box, note the value that now appears for Size on Disk. This size should have decreased because you compressed the folder.

You can specify that compressed files be displayed in a different color from the uncompressed files. To do so, in Windows Explorer, select Tools ➢ Folder Options ➢ Views. Under Files and Folders, check the Display Compressed Files and Folders with an Alternate Color option.

Setting Disk Quotas

Suppose that you have a server with an 18GB drive, which is mainly used for users' home folders, and you start getting "out of disk space" error messages. On closer inspection, you find that a single user has taken up 10GB of space by storing multimedia files that she has downloaded from the Internet. This type of problem can be avoided through the use of disk quotas.

Microsoft
✓ *Exam*
Objective

Monitor and configure disk quotas.

Disk quotas are used to specify how much disk space a user is allowed on specific NTFS volumes. You can specify disk quotas for all users, or you can limit disk space on a per-user basis.

Before you administer disk quotas, you should be aware of the following aspects of disk quotas:

- Disk quotas can be specified only for NTFS volumes.

- Disk quotas apply only at the volume level, even if the NTFS partitions reside on the same physical hard drive.

- Disk usage is calculated on file and folder ownership. When a user creates, copies, or takes ownership of a file, that user is the owner of the file.

- When a user installs an application, the free space that the application will see is based on the disk quota availability, not the actual amount of free space on the volume.

- Disk quota space used is based on actual file size. There is no mechanism to support or recognize file compression.

Disk quotas are not applied to the Administrator account or members of the Administrators group.

The following sections describe how to set up and monitor disk quotas.

Configuring Disk Quotas

You configure disk quotas through the NTFS volume Properties dialog box. This dialog box was discussed in detail earlier in the chapter in the "Managing Basic Tasks" section. You learned that you can access the volume Properties dialog box in the Disk Management utility by right-clicking the drive letter and selecting Properties from the pop-up menu. Another way to access this dialog box is from Windows Explorer—just right-click the drive letter in the listing and select Properties. In the volume Properties dialog box, click the Quota tab to see the dialog box shown in Figure 6.26. When you open the Quota tab, you will see that disk quotas are disabled by default.

FIGURE 6.26   The Quota tab of the volume Properties dialog box

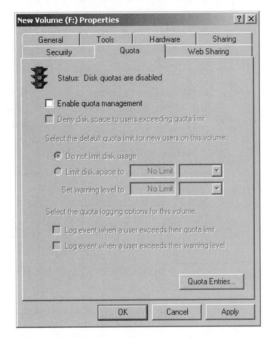

The options that can be configured through the Quota tab are described in Table 6.2.

TABLE 6.2   Disk Quota Configuration Options

Option	Description
Enable Quota Management	Specifies whether quota management is enabled for the volume.
Deny Disk Space to Users Exceeding the Quota Limit	Specifies that users who exceed their disk quota will not be able to override their disk allocation. Those users will receive "out of disk space" error messages.

TABLE 6.2 Disk Quota Configuration Options *(continued)*

Option	Description
Select the Default Quota Limit for New Users on This Volume	Allows you to define quota limits for new users. Options include not limiting disk space, limiting disk space, and specifying warning levels.
Select the Quota Logging Options for This Volume	Specifies whether log events that relate to quotas will be recorded. You can enable log events for users exceeding quota limits or users exceeding warning limits.

Notice the traffic light icon in the upper-left corner of the Quota tab. The traffic light indicates the status of disk quotas, as follows:

- A red light specifies that disk quotas are disabled.

- A yellow light specifies that Windows 2000 Server is rebuilding disk quota information.

- A green light specifies that the disk quota system is enabled and active.

The next sections describe how to set quotas for all new users as default quotas and how to set quotas for a specific user.

Setting Default Quotas

When you set default quota limits for new users on a volume, the quotas apply only to users who have not yet created files on that volume. This means that users who already own files or folders on the volume will be exempt from the quota policy. Users who have not created a file on the volume will be bound by the quota policy.

To set the default quota limit for new users, access the Quota tab of the volume Properties dialog box and check the Enable Quota Management box. Click the Limit Disk Space To radio button and enter a number in the first box next to the option. In the drop-down list in the second box, specify whether disk space is limited by KB (kilobytes), MB (megabytes), GB (gigabytes), TB (terabytes), PB (petabytes), or EB (exabytes). If you choose to limit disk space, you can also set a warning level, so that users will be warned if they come close to reaching their limit.

If you want to apply disk quotas for all users, you should apply the quota when the volume is first created. That way, no users can already have files on the volume and thus be exempt from the quota limit.

In Exercise 6.7, you will set a default quota limit on your D: drive. This exercise assumes that you have completed Exercise 6.1.

EXERCISE 6.7

Applying Default Quota Limits

1. Use the Local Users and Groups utility to create two new users: **Shannon** and **Dana**. (See Chapter 4, "Managing Users and Groups," for details on creating user accounts.) Deselect the User Must Change Password at Next Logon option for each user.

2. Log off as Administrator and log on as Shannon. Drop and drag some folders to drive D:.

3. Log on as Administrator. Select Start ➢ Programs ➢ Accessories ➢ Windows Explorer.

4. In Windows Explorer, expand My Computer. Right-click Local Disk (D:) and select Properties.

5. In the Local Disk Properties dialog box, select the Quota tab.

6. Check the Enable Quota Management check box and the Deny Disk Space to Users Exceeding Quota Limit check box.

7. Click the Limit Disk Space to radio button. Specify 5MB as the limit. Specify the Set Warning Level To value as 4MB.

8. Click the Apply button, then click the OK button.

9. If you currently have data stored on the volume, you will see a Disk Quota dialog box specifying that the volume will need to be rescanned. Click the OK button.

10. Log off as Administrator and log on as Dana. Drop and drag some folders to drive D:.

11. Log off as Dana and log on again as Administrator.

Setting an Individual Quota

You can also set quotas for individual users. There are several reasons for setting quotas this way:

- You can allow a user who routinely updates your applications to have unlimited disk space, while restricting other users.

- You can set warnings at lower levels for a user who routinely exceeds disk space.

- You can apply the quota to users who already had files on the volume before the quota was implemented and thus have been granted unlimited disk space.

To set an individual quota, click the Quota Entries button in the bottom-right corner of the Quota tab. This brings up the dialog box shown in Figure 6.27.

FIGURE 6.27 The Quota Entries for volume dialog box

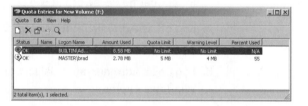

To modify a user's quota, double-click that user. This brings up a dialog box similar to the one shown in Figure 6.28. Here, you can specify whether or not the user disk space should be limited, the limit, and the warning level.

FIGURE 6.28 The Quota Settings for user dialog box

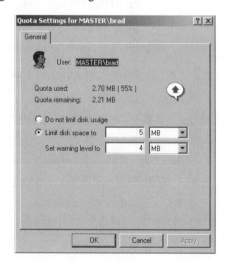

You can also modify the quotas of several users at once by Ctrl+clicking to highlight several users and selecting Quota ≻ Properties.

In Exercise 6.8, you will configure the quotas for individual users. This exercise assumes that you have completed Exercise 6.7.

EXERCISE 6.8

Applying Individual Quota Limits

1. Select Start ≻ Programs ≻ Accessories ≻ Windows Explorer.

2. In Windows Explorer, expand My Computer. Right-click Local Disk (D:) and select Properties.

3. In the Local Disk Properties dialog box, select the Quota tab. Then click the Quota Entries button.

4. Double-click user Dana to bring up his Quota Settings dialog box. Notice that Dana has limited disk space (because he first created files on the volume after disk quotas were applied). Click the Do Not Limit Disk Usage radio button. Click the Apply button and then click the OK button.

5. Double-click user Shannon to bring up his Quota Settings dialog box. Notice that Shannon does not have his disk space limited (because he created files on the volume before disk quotas were applied). Click the Limit Disk Space To radio button and specify the limit as 100MB. Set the warning level to 95MB. Click the Apply button and then click the OK button.

Monitoring Disk Quotas

If you implement disk quotas, you will want to monitor disk quotas on a regular basis. Monitoring allows you to check the disk usage by all the users who own files on the volume with the quotas applied.

It is especially important to monitor quotas if you have specified that disk space should be denied to users who exceeded their quota limit. Otherwise, some users may not be able to get their work done. For example, suppose that you have set a limit for all users on a specific volume. Your boss tries to save a file she has been working on all afternoon, but she gets an "out of disk space" error message because she has exceeded her disk quota. While your intentions of setting up and using disk quotas were good, the boss is still cranky.

You monitor disk quotas through the Quota Entries dialog box that appears when you click the Quota Entries button in the Quota tab of the volume Properties dialog box as shown in Figure 6.26.

The dialog box shows the following information:

- The status of the user's disk quota. Status icons include:

  - A green arrow in a dialog bubble indicates the status is OK.

  - An exclamation point in a yellow triangle indicates the warning threshold has been exceeded.

  - An exclamation point in a red circle indicates the user threshold has been exceeded.

- The name and logon name of the user who has stored files on the volume

- The amount of disk space the user has used on the volume

- The user's quota limit

- The user's warning level

- The percent of disk space the user has used in relation to their disk quota

Managing Data Encryption with EFS

*D*ata encryption is a way to increase data security. Encryption is the process of translating data into code that is not easily accessible. Once data has been encrypted, you must have a password or key to decrypt the data. Unencrypted data is known as plain text, and encrypted data is known as *cipher text*.

Microsoft Exam Objective

Encrypt data on a hard disk by using Encrypting File System (EFS).

The *Encrypting File System* (*EFS*) is the Windows 2000 technology that is used to store encrypted files on NTFS partitions. Encrypted files add an extra layer of security to your file system. A user with the proper key can transparently access encrypted files. A user without the proper key is denied access. There is a recovery agent that can be used by the Administrator if the owner is unavailable to provide the proper key to decrypt folders or files.

You can encrypt and decrypt files through the volume Properties dialog box or by using the CIPHER utility, as explained in the following sections.

Encrypting and Decrypting Folders and Files

To use EFS, a user specifies that a folder or file on an NTFS partition should be encrypted. The encryption is transparent to the user, who has access to the file. However, when other users try to access the file, they will not be able to unencrypt the file—even if those users have Full Control NTFS permissions. Instead, they will receive an error message.

To encrypt a folder or a file, take the following steps.

1. Open Windows Explorer by selecting Start ➢ Programs ➢ Accessories ➢ Windows Explorer.

2. In Windows Explorer, find and select the folder or file you wish to encrypt.

3. Right-click the folder or file and select Properties from the pop-up menu.

4. In the General tab of the folder or file Properties dialog box, click the Advanced button.

5. The Advanced Attributes dialog box appears (as shown in the Exercise 6.6 box). Check the Encrypt Contents to Secure Data check box. Then click the OK button.

6. The Confirm Attribute Changes dialog box appears. Specify whether you want to apply encryption to only this folder (Apply Changes to This Folder Only) or if you want to apply encryption to the subfolders and files within the folder as well (Apply Changes to This Folder, Subfolder, and Files). Then click the OK button.

To decrypt folders and files, repeat the steps above, but uncheck the Encrypt Contents to Secure Data option in the Advanced Attributes dialog box.

By default, the Administrator has rights to access the properties of another user's encrypted folder or file and decrypt it. This means that if the user who encrypted a file is unavailable to decrypt the file (for example, because that user left the company), the Administrator can recover it.

In Exercise 6.9, you will use EFS to encrypt a folder. This exercise assumes that you have completed Exercise 6.1.

EXERCISE 6.9

Using EFS to Manage Data Encryption

1. Use the Local Users and Groups utility to create the new user **Lauren**. (See Chapter 4 for details on creating user accounts.) Deselect the User Must Change Password at Next Logon option for this user.

2. Select Start ➢ Programs ➢ Accessories ➢ Windows Explorer.

3. In Windows Explorer, find and select a folder on the D: drive. The folder you select should contain files. Right-click the folder and select Properties.

4. In the General tab of the folder Properties dialog box, click the Advanced button.

5. In the Advanced Attributes dialog box, check the Encrypt Contents to Secure Data option. Then click the OK button.

6. In the Confirm Attribute Changes dialog box (if this dialog box does not appear, click the Apply button in the Properties dialog box to display it), select Apply Changes to This Folder, Subfolder, and Files. Then click the OK button.

7. Log off as Administrator and log on as Lauren.

8. Open Windows Explorer and attempt to access one of the files in the folder you encrypted. You should receive an error message stating that the file is not accessible.

9. Log off as Lauren and log on as Administrator.

NOTE

To decrypt folders and files, repeat the steps above but uncheck the Encrypt Contents to Secure Data option in the Advanced Attributes dialog box.

Using the *CIPHER* Utility

CIPHER is a command-line utility that can be used to encrypt files on NTFS volumes. The syntax for the CIPHER command is:

CIPHER /[*command parameter*] [*filename*]

Table 6.3 lists the command parameters associated with the CIPHER command.

TABLE 6.3 CIPHER Command Parameters

Parameter	Description
/e	Specifies that files or folders should be encrypted.
/d	Specifies that files or folders should be decrypted.
/s:*dir*	Specifies that subfolders of the target folder should also be encrypted or decrypted based on the option specified.
/I	Causes any errors that occur to be ignored. By default, the CIPHER utility stops whenever an error occurs.
/f	Forces all files and folders to be encrypted or decrypted, regardless of their current state. Normally, if a file is already in the specified state, it is skipped.
/q	Runs in a quiet mode and displays only the most important information.

In Exercise 6.10, you will use the CIPHER utility to encrypt and decrypt files. This exercise assumes that you have completed Exercise 6.9.

EXERCISE 6.10

Using the CIPHER Utility to Manage Data Encryption

1. Select Start ➤ Programs ➤ Accessories ➤ Command Prompt.

2. In the Command Prompt dialog box, type **D:** and press Enter to access the D: drive.

3. From the D:\> prompt, type **cipher**. You will see a list of folders and files and the state of encryption. The folder you encrypted in Exercise 6.9 should be indicated by an E.

4. Type **MD TEST** and press Enter to create a new folder named Test.

5. Type **cipher /e test** and press Enter. You will see a message verifying that the folder was encrypted.

Recovering Encrypted Files

If the user who encrypted the folders or files is unavailable to decrypt the folders or files, you can use the recovery agent to access the encrypted files. On Windows 2000 Server computers that are not a part of a domain, the default recovery agent is the Administrator. (However, a user who is a member of the Administrators group is not considered a Recovery Agent and would not have default recovery privileges.) You can specify which users are recovery agents through Group Policies.

The following steps are used to recover decrypted files:

1. Back up the encrypted files using the Windows Backup utility. (Backing up and restoring files are covered in Chapter 15.)

2. Restore the backup of the encrypted files on the computer where the recovery agent is located. This partition must be formatted with NTFS.

3. In Windows Explorer, access the folder or file Properties dialog box. In the General tab, click the Advanced button.

4. In the Advanced tab, clear the Encrypt Contents to Secure Data check box.

Because this procedure decrypts the backup copy of the folder or file, the original folder or file should remain encrypted.

Because this procedure decrypts the backup copy of the folder or file, the original folder or file remains encrypted. If you don't want to keep the original file encrypted, you could simply decrypt the file with the Recovery Agent without using the Backup and Restore procedure.

Using the Disk Defragmenter Utility

Data is normally stored sequentially on the disk as space is available. Fragmentation naturally occurs as users create, delete, and modify files. The access of noncontiguous data is transparent to the user. However, when data is stored in this manner, the operating system must search through the disk drive to access all of the pieces of a file. This slows down data access.

Microsoft ✓ *Exam* *Objective*

Monitor, configure, and troubleshoot disks and volumes.

Disk defragmentation rearranges the existing files so that they are stored contiguously, which optimizes access to those files. In Windows 2000 Server, you use the *Disk Defragmenter utility* to defragment your disk.

To access the Disk Defragmenter utility, select Start ➤ Programs ➤ Accessories ➤ System Tools ➤ Disk Defragmenter. The main Disk Defragmenter window, shown in Figure 6.29, lists each volume, the file system used, capacity, free space, and the percent of free space.

FIGURE 6.29 The main Disk Defragmenter window

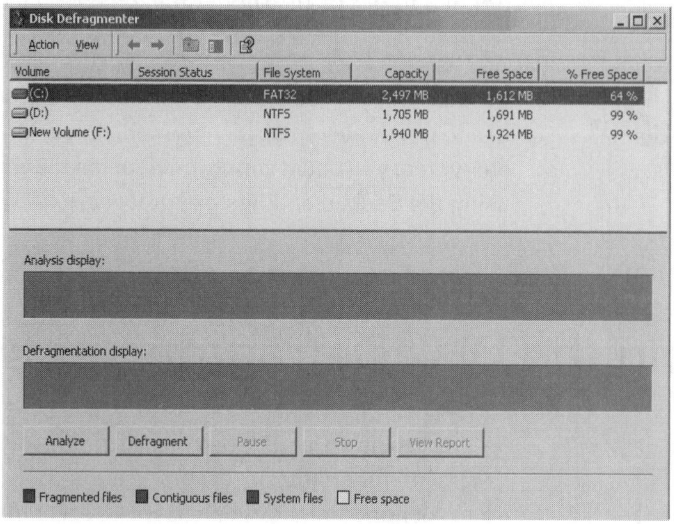

Along with defragmenting disks, this utility can analyze your disk and report on the current file arrangement. Analyzing and defragmenting disks are covered in the following sections.

Analyzing Disks

To analyze a disk, open the Disk Defragmenter utility, select the drive to be analyzed, and click the Analyze button on the bottom-left side of the window. When you analyze a disk, the Disk Defragmenter utility checks for fragmented files, contiguous files, system files, and free space. The results of the analysis are shown in the Analysis display bar that is color-coded as follows:

Fragmented file	Red
Contiguous files	Blue
System files	Green
Free space	White

Even though you can't see the colors, you can get an idea of what this Analysis bar looks like in Figure 6.30.

FIGURE 6.30   The Disk Defragmenter Analysis bar

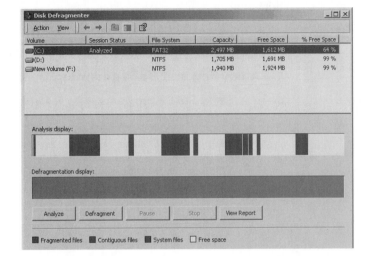

The disk analysis also produces a report, which is displayed when you click the View Report button. The report contains the following information:

- Whether or not the volume needs defragmenting

- Volume information that includes general volume statistics, volume fragmentation, file fragmentation, page file fragmentation, directory fragmentation, and master file table (MTF) fragmentation

- A list of the most fragmented files

Defragmenting Disks

To defragment a disk, open the Disk Defragmenter utility, select the drive to be defragmented, and click the Defragment button (to the right of the Analyze button at the bottom of the window). Defragmenting causes all files to be stored more efficiently in contiguous space. When defragmentation is complete, you can view a report of the defragmentation process.

You will use the Disk Defragmenter utility in Exercise 6.11 to analyze and defragment a disk.

EXERCISE 6.11

Analyzing and Defragmenting Disks

1. Select Start ➤ Programs ➤ Accessories ➤ System Tools ➤ Disk Defragmenter.

2. Highlight the C: drive and click the Analyze button.

3. When analysis is complete, click the View Report button to see the analysis report. Record the following information:

   Volume size: _____

   Cluster size: _____

   Used space: _____

   Free space: _____

   Volume fragmentation-Total fragmentation: _____

   Most fragmented file: _____

4. Click the Defragment button.

5. When defragmentation is complete, click the Close button.

Using the Disk Cleanup Utility

The *Disk Cleanup utility* identifies areas of disk space that can be deleted to free hard disk space. Disk Cleanup works by identifying temporary files, Internet cache files, and unnecessary program files.

Microsoft ✓ *Exam Objective*

Monitor, configure, and troubleshoot disks and volumes.

In Exercise 6.12, you will run the Disk Cleanup utility.

EXERCISE 6.12

Using the Disk Cleanup Utility

1. Select Start ➢ Programs ➢ Accessories ➢ System Tools ➢ Disk Cleanup. The Disk Cleanup Select Drive dialog box asks you to select the drive you want to clean up. In this exercise, select the C drive and click OK.

2. The Disk Cleanup utility will run and calculate the amount of disk space you can free. After the analysis is complete, the Disk Cleanup dialog box appears, as shown in below. This dialog box lists files that are suggested for deletion and shows how much space will be gained by deleting those files. In this exercise, leave all the boxes checked and click OK.

3. You will be asked to confirm the deletions. Click Yes. The Disk Cleanup utility will delete the files and automatically close the Disk Cleanup dialog box.

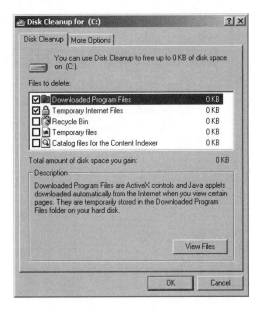

Troubleshooting Disk Devices and Volumes

If you are having trouble with your disk devices or volumes, you can use the Windows 2000 *Check Disk utility*. This utility detects bad sectors, attempts to fix file system errors, and scans for and attempts to recover bad sectors.

<table>
<tr>
<td>

Microsoft
Exam
Objective

</td>
<td>

Monitor, configure, and troubleshoot disks and volumes.

</td>
</tr>
</table>

File system errors can be caused from a corrupt file system or from hardware errors. There is no way to fix hardware errors through software. If you have software errors, the Check Disk utility may help you find them. You can choose the Automatically Fix File System Errors and Scan for and Attempt Recovery of Bad Sectors options. If you have excessive hardware errors, you should replace your disk drive.

In Exercise 6.13, you will run the Check Disk utility.

EXERCISE 6.13

Using the Check Disk Utility

1. Select Start ➢ Settings ➢ Control Panel ➢ Administrative Tools. Expand Computer Management, then Storage, then Disk Management.

2. Right-click the D: drive and choose Properties.

3. Click the Tools tab, then click the Check Now button.

EXERCISE 6.13 *(continued)*

4. In the Check Disk dialog box, check both of the disk options check boxes. Then click the Start button.

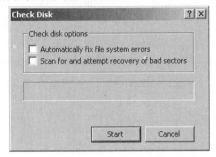

5. When you see the Disk Check Complete dialog box, click the OK button and close any open dialog boxes.

 If the system cannot gain exclusive access to the partition, the check will be executed the next time the system is restarted. You cannot gain exclusive access to partitions or volumes that contain the system or boot partition.

Summary

In this chapter, you learned about managing disks with Windows 2000 Server. We covered the following topics:

- File system options, which can be FAT16, FAT32, or NTFS

- Disk storage configuration, which can be basic storage or dynamic storage

- The Disk Management utility, which is used to manage routine tasks, basic storage, and dynamic storage

- Data compression, which is used to store files in a compressed format that uses less disk space

- Disk quotas, which are used to limit the amount of disk space that users can have on an NTFS partition

- Data encryption, which is implemented through Encrypting File System (EFS) and provides increased security for files and folders

- Disk defragmentation, which is accomplished through the Disk Defragmenter utility and allows you to store files contiguously on your hard drive for improved access speeds

- The Disk Cleanup utility, which is used to free disk space by removing unnecessary files

- The Check Disk utility, which can be used to troubleshoot disk errors

Exam Essentials

Understand the disk configurations that are used by Windows 2000. Define the differences between Basic and Dynamic disks. Be able to configure options such as simple, spanned, striped, mirrored, and RAID-5 volumes. Be able to define the characteristics of each volume configuration.

Be able to recover from disk failure. List the steps that would be used to recover from failure for disks that are spanned, striped, mirrored, or configured as RAID-5.

Define and Set data compression. Define the requirements for disk compression and be able to configure data compression.

Set and manage disk quotas. Be able to specify the purpose of disk quotas, and successfully set disk quotas.

Protect data by using EFS. Be able to encrypt data with EFS and also recover data that is encrypted in the event that the user who encrypted the data is unavailable.

Key Terms

Before you take the exam, be sure you're familiar with the following key terms:

basic storage	Encrypting File System (EFS)
CDFS (Compact Disk File System)	extended partition
Check Disk utility	FAT16
CIPHER	FAT32
cipher text	hot swapping
CONVERT	mirrored volume
data compression	NTFS
data encryption	partition
Disk Cleanup utility	primary partition
disk defragmentation	RAID-5 volume
Disk Defragmenter utility	simple volume
Disk Management utility	spanned volume
disk quotas	striped volume
dynamic disk	volume
dynamic storag	

Review Questions

1. You are the network administrator for a small company. One of your engineers stores large CAD files on a server called ENGINEERING in a folder called C:\DRAWINGS. The C:\ drive is running out of space, and you want to maximize space as much as possible until you can add another hard drive to the server. The C: partition is on a Basic Disk, which uses the NTFS file system. You would like to use disk compression. What process would you use to compress the folder?

   A. Within Disk Management, Volume Properties, click the Advanced tab, check the box Compress Contents to Save Disk Space

   B. Within Disk Management, Folder Properties, Select C:\DRAWINGS, click the Advanced tab, check the box Compress Contents to Save Disk Space

   C. Right-click on C:\DRAWINGS, select Properties, click the Advanced tab, check the box Compress Contents to Save Disk Space

   D. You can't compress data that is stored on Basic Disks, so the disk must be converted to a Dynamic Disk before you can compress the files.

2. You are the network administrator for a large network. There is an accounting server called ACCOUNTING. On the ACCOUNTING server there is a folder called C:\PAYROLL. This folder is located on an NTFS partition, but the Accounting manager would like to set up additional security. He thinks that he has properly configured EFS, but wants you to verify that EFS is working. Which of the following command-line utilities can you use to display the current encryption state of the files in the C:\PAYROLL folder?

   A. Cipher

   B. EFSStatus

   C. DIR /EFS

   D. DIR /encryption

3. You are the network administrator for a large network. There is an accounting server called ACCOUNTING. On the ACCOUNTING server there is a folder called C:\PAYROLL. This folder is located on an NTFS partition, but the Accounting manager would like to set up additional security. What step should he take to enable file encryption?

   A. Within Disk Management, Volume Properties, click the Advanced tab, check the box Encrypt Contents to Secure Data

   B. Within Disk Management, Folder Properties, Select C:\PAY-ROLL, click the Advanced tab, check the box Encrypt Contents to Secure Data

   C. Right-click on C:\PAYROLL, select Properties, click the Advanced tab, check the box Encrypt Contents to Secure Data

   D. From the Command Prompt, when you are in the C:\PAYROLL folder execute the command `CIPHER /d*.*`

4. You are the manager of a large network. Your Engineering department uses a server called ENGINEERING. The server has a 40GB hard drive that stores all of the company's engineering data. You want to add additional fault tolerance to the drive in case of failure and add a second drive so that you can use disk mirroring. When you right-click the new free space within Disk Management, you do not see any option to create a new volume or a mirrored volume. What action should you take to create a mirrored volume on both of the drives?

   A. Make sure that the drive that you want to convert is formatted as NTFS 4.0

   B. Make sure that the drive that you want to convert is formatted as NTFS 5.0

   C. Convert both drives to Enhanced Disks

   D. Convert both drives to Dynamic Disks

5. Your Windows 2000 Server hosts the company's data files on a 20GB hard drive. Users are complaining that access to the files has slowed down over the past six months. You verify that the average access, size, and number of files has remained fairly constant. What should you do to improve access speeds?

   A. Defragment the disk

   B. Configure the volume with EFS

   C. Upgrade the disk to a Dynamic Disk

   D. Compress the data files

6. You are preparing to install a Windows 2000 Server that will act as a domain controller. You are trying to determine what disk configuration will be used by the server. Which of the following disk configurations could you use to store the system or boot partition? Choose all that apply.

   A. Simple volume

   B. Striped volume

   C. Mirrored volume

   D. RAID-5 volume

7. Brad is the Accounting manager and has encrypted the C:\PAYROLL folder on his computer. His appendix bursts, and he is not able to process the company's payroll. His assistant, Carrie, can process the payroll if she can access the C:\PAYROLL files. What process should you use to decrypt the files?

   A. While logged in as Administrator, access the folder and use the command-line utility CIPHER /d *.*

   B. While logged in as Administrator, access the folder and use the command-line utility CIPHER /u *.*

   C. While logged in as Administrator, access the Disk Management utility and for the volume, clear the Encrypt Contents to Secure Data check box

   D. Backup the encrypted folder using Windows Backup, restore the folder on a computer where you are logged in as the Administrator, access the folder's Properties dialog box, within the Advanced tab clear the Encrypt Contents to Secure Data check box.

8. When would you need to use a Windows 2000 Server boot disk with an edited BOOT.INI file in the event of a drive failure in a mirrored volume?

   A. If the primary drive in a data mirror volume fails

   B. If the secondary drive in a data mirror volume fails

   C. If the primary drive that contains the boot partition in a mirror volume fails

   D. If the secondary drive that contains the boot partition in a mirror volume fails

9. You are having a problem with users storing large files on the Windows 2000 Server computer and want to impose disk quotas. When you try and impose the quotas, you realize that the volume that stores users' files is FAT32. In order to use quotas, you must have an NTFS partition. Which command or utility can you use to change the partition to NTFS without losing any data?

   A. NTFSCONV

   B. CONVERT

   C. Disk Administrator

   D. Disk Manager

10. You are installing Windows 2000 Server on a computer with the configuration shown in the following exhibit. You want to make sure that you use the maximum amount of disk space with the fastest access. What configuration should you use?

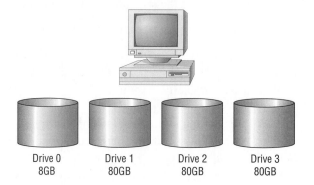

| Drive 0 | Drive 1 | Drive 2 | Drive 3 |
| 8GB | 80GB | 80GB | 80GB |

A. Install Windows 2000 Server on the 8GB drive. Create a spanned volume set with the three remaining drives.

B. Install Windows 2000 Server on the 8GB drive. Create a striped volume set with the three remaining drives.

C. Install Windows 2000 Server on the 8GB drive. Create a RAID-3 volume set with the three remaining drives.

D. Install Windows 2000 Server on the 8GB drive. Create a RAID-5 volume set with the three remaining drives.

11. You have a server that contains a single 36GB hard drive. The server stores a database that must be accessed as a single drive letter. You are starting to receive messages that the disk is almost out of space. The server supports hot swapping and there is a hot-swappable drive bay on your server. You purchase an identical 36GB drive and want to add it to your server. You back up the data on your hard drive. Which of the following options will allow you to overcome your disk space shortage with the least amount of downtime?

   A. Shut down the server and add the disk to the computer. Restart the computer and create a striped volume set.

   B. Shut down the server and add the disk to the computer. Restart the computer and create a spanned volume set.

   C. Add the disk to the computer, rescan the disks, and create a striped volume set.

   D. Add the disk to the computer, rescan the disks, and create a spanned volume set.

12. You have a mirrored volume set on your Windows 2000 Server computer. You open Disk Management and realize that the secondary drive in the mirror set has failed. You make a full backup at the end of each day. Which of the following courses of action should you take?

   A. Remove the mirror, replace the failed drive, and recreate the mirrored set.

   B. Replace the failed drive, right-click the mirrored set, and choose to regenerate the mirrored set.

   C. Replace the failed drive, right-click the mirror set, and choose to repair the volume. On the drive you replaced, select to regenerate mirrored set.

   D. Replace the failed drive, rescan the disks, and restore the volume set from tape backup.

13. You have a RAID-5 volume set on your Windows 2000 Server computer. You open Disk Management and realize one of the drives in the RAID-5 set has failed. Which of the following courses of action should you take?

    A. Remove the RAID-5 volume set, replace the failed drive, and re-create the RAID-5 volume set.

    B. Replace the failed drive, right-click the RAID-5 volume set, and choose to reactivate the mirrored set.

    C. Replace the failed drive, right-click the RAID-5 volume set, and choose to repair the volume. On the drive you replaced, select to regenerate the RAID-5 set.

    D. Replace the failed drive and select to rescan the disks.

14. You have a striped volume set on your Windows 2000 Server. One of the drives in the striped volume set fails. You create a full backup of your server each night. Which of the following courses of action should you take?

    A. Remove the striped set, replace the failed drive, and re-create the striped set.

    B. Replace the failed drive, right-click the striped set, and choose to regenerate the striped set.

    C. Replace the failed drive, right-click the striped set, and choose to repair the volume. On the drive you replaced, select to regenerate the striped set.

    D. Replace the failed drive, re-create and format the stripe set, and restore the volume set from tape backup.

15. You have a server that supports hot-swappable drives and you have open drive bays. You add two new disks to your computer that are identical to your existing drives, but when you open Disk Management, you see the dialog screen shown in the following exhibit. What additional step should you take that will allow your computer to recognize the disk with the least amount of downtime?

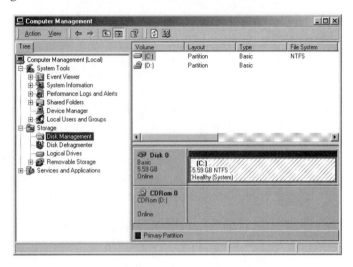

A. Install the driver for the new drives

B. Restart your computer

C. In Disk Management, rescan the disks

D. In Disk Management, select to commit the changes now

Answers to Review Questions

1. C. As long as the partition is NTFS you can set compression for the folder, through the Advanced tab of the folders properties by checking the box Compress Contents to Save Disk Space.

2. A. The CIPHER command is used to display the current status of file encryption.

3. C. As long as the partition is NTFS, you can set EFS for the folder through the Advanced tab of the folder's properties by checking the box Encrypt Contents to Secure Data. You could use the CIPHER command-line utility, but it would require the /e option for encryption.

4. D. When you mirror a volume, the drive can contain FAT or NTFS partitions, but the drive must be defined as a Dynamic Disk as opposed to a Basic Disk.

5. A. If the files have become fragmented, you can improve disk access by defragmenting the drive.

6. A, C. You cannot put the system or boot partition on a striped or RAID-5 volume. Simple volumes and mirrored volumes can contain the system or boot partition.

7. D. If the user who encrypted the data is not available, you must backup and restore the data using Windows Backup on a computer where you are logged in as Administrator (since this user is the default Recovery Agent). After you restore the files you can then uncheck the Encrypt Contents to Secure Data check box. The original files will then remain intact for Brad's return.

8. C. You only need to use an edited BOOT.INI file when the primary drive that contains the boot partition in a mirror set fails. If any drive in a mirror set fails, the BOOT.INI file will still point to the correct location of the Windows 2000 Server operating system files.

9. B. You can't upgrade a partition to NTFS through any of the GUI utilities. You must use the CONVERT command-line utility.

10. B. You should create a striped volume set if you want to maximize the amount of storage and increase performance. A spanned volume set will not increase performance, and a RAID-5 volume set will not maximize space. Windows 2000 Server does not support RAID-3.

11. D. Since the computer supports hot swapping and you have a hot-swappable drive bay, you can add the disk to the computer and rescan the disk without shutting down the computer. You can then create a spanned volume set. Striped volume sets can only be created from new space and can't be created with existing data.

12. A. If a mirrored set fails, you right-click the mirrored volume in Disk Management and remove the mirror. Then you select the disk that has failed. The remaining disk will become a simple volume. Replace the failed drive, and then use Disk Management to recreate the mirrored volume. If you restore the set from backup, you will lose any of the data that had been created or edited since the last backup.

13. C. If a drive in a RAID-5 volume set fails, you should take the following steps to re-create the data through the parity on your other drives: Replace the failed hardware. Open the Disk Management utility, right-click the failed RAID-5 volume set (marked as failed redundancy), and choose Repair Volume from the pop-up menu. In the Repair RAID-5 Volume dialog box, choose the drive that has been replaced and click OK to regenerate the RAID-5 volume set.

14. D. Since a striped set is not fault tolerant, if any drives in the set fail, you will need to re-create the striped set and restore your data from your backups.

15. C. After you add new disks to a computer that supports hot-swappable drives, you need to select Action ≻ Rescan Disks so that the new disks can be accessed.

Chapter

7

Accessing Files and Folders

MICROSOFT EXAM OBJECTIVES COVERED IN THIS CHAPTER

✓ **Monitor, configure, troubleshoot, and control access to files, folders, and shared folders.**

  - Monitor, configure, troubleshoot, and control local security on files and folders.

  - Monitor, configure, troubleshoot, and control access to files and folders in a shared folder.

✓ **Install, configure, and troubleshoot shared access.**

*L*ocal access defines what access a user has to local resources. You can limit local access by applying NTFS permissions to files and folders.

A powerful feature of networking is the ability to allow network access to local folders. In Windows 2000 Server, it is very easy to share folders. You can also apply security to shared folders in a manner that is similar to applying NTFS permissions. Once you share a folder, users with appropriate access rights can access the folders through a variety of methods.

To effectively manage both local and network resource access and troubleshoot related problems, you should understand the resource-access process. Windows 2000 Server uses access tokens, access control lists, and access control entries to handle resource access.

In this chapter, you will learn how to manage local and network access to resources, including how to configure NTFS permissions and network share permissions.

The procedures for managing access to files and folders are the same for Windows 2000 member servers, Windows 2000 domain controllers, and Windows 2000 Professional computers.

Managing Local Access

The two common types of file systems used by local partitions are FAT (which includes FAT16 and FAT32) and NTFS. FAT partitions do not support local security; NTFS partitions do support local security. This means that if the file system on the partition that users access is configured as a FAT partition, you cannot specify any security for the file system once a user has logged on. However, if the partition is NTFS, you can specify the access each user has to specific folders on the partition, based on the user's logon name and group associations.

Microsoft
✓ ***Exam***
Objective

Monitor, configure, troubleshoot, and control access to files, folders, and shared folders.

• Monitor, configure, troubleshoot, and control local security on files and folders.

This chapter covers information about managing local and network access to files and folders for the "Monitor, configure, troubleshoot, and control access to files, folders, and shared folders" objective. The subobjectives for this objective related to managing the Distributed file system (Dfs) are covered in Chapter 8, "Administering the Distributed File System." The subobjective related to managing access to files and folders through Web services is covered in Chapter 10, "Managing Web Services."

NTFS permissions control access to NTFS folders and files. You configure access by allowing or denying NTFS permissions to users and groups. NTFS permissions are usually cumulative, based on group memberships if the user has been allowed access. However, if the user has been denied access through user or group memberships, those permissions override allowed permissions.

Windows 2000 Server offers five levels of NTFS permissions:

- The Full Control permission allows these rights:
    - Traverse folders and execute files (programs) in the folders
    - List the contents of a folder and read the data in a folder's files
    - See a folder's or file's attributes
    - Change a folder's or file's attributes
    - Create new files and write data to the files
    - Create new folders and append data to files
    - Delete subfolders and files
    - Delete files

- Change permissions for files and folders
- Take ownership of files and folders

- The Modify permission allows these rights:

  - Traverse folders and execute files in the folders
  - List the contents of a folder and read the data in a folder's files
  - See a folder's or file's attributes
  - Change a folder's or file's attributes
  - Create new files and write data to the files
  - Create new folders and append data to files
  - Delete files

- The Read & Execute permission allows the following rights:

  - Traverse folders and execute files in the folders
  - List the contents of a folder and read the data in a folder's files
  - See a folder's or file's attributes

- The List Folder Contents permission allows the following rights:

  - Traverse folders
  - List the contents of a folder
  - See a folder's or file's attributes

- The Read permission allows the following rights:

  - List the contents of a folder and read the data in a folder's files
  - See a folder's or file's attributes

- The Write permission allows the following rights:

  - Change a folder's or file's attributes
  - Create new files and write data to the files
  - Create new folders and append data to files

Any user with Full Control access can manage the security of a folder. By default, the Everyone group has Full Control permission for the entire NTFS partition. However, in order to access folders, a user must have physical access to the computer as well as a valid logon name and password. By default, regular users can't access folders over the network unless the folders have been shared. Sharing folders is covered in the "Managing Network Access" section later in this chapter.

In Exercise 7.1, you will create a directory structure that will be used throughout the exercises in this chapter. This exercise should be completed from your member server.

EXERCISE 7.1

Creating a Directory and File Structure

1. Select Start ➤ Programs ➤ Accessories ➤ Windows Explorer.

2. In Windows Explorer, expand My Computer, then Local Disk (D:). Select File ➤ New ➤ Folder and name the new folder **DATA**.

3. Double-click the DATA folder to open the folder. Select File ➤ New ➤ Folder and name the new folder **WP DOCS**.

4. Double-click the Data folder, select File ➤ New ➤ Folder, and name the new folder **SS DOCS** folder.

5. Confirm that you are still in the DATA folder. Select File ➤ New ➤ Text Document. Name the file **DOC1.TXT**.

6. Double-click the WP DOCS folder. Select File ➤ New ➤ Text Document. Name the file **DOC2.TXT**.

7. Double-click the SS DOCS folder. Select File ➤ New ➤ Text Document. Name the file **DOC3.TXT**. Your structure should look like the one shown below.

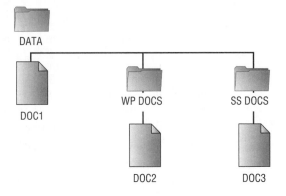

Applying NTFS Permissions

You apply NTFS permissions through Windows Explorer. Right-click the file or folder that you want to control access to and select Properties from the pop-up menu. This brings up the folder or file Properties dialog box. Figure 7.1 shows a folder Properties dialog box.

> The process for configuring NTFS permissions for folders and files is the same. The examples in this chapter use a folder, because NTFS permissions are most commonly applied at the folder level.

FIGURE 7.1   The folder Properties dialog box

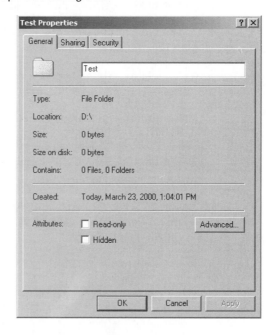

The tabs in the file or folder Properties dialog box depend on the options that have been configured for your computer. For files and folders on NTFS partitions, the dialog box will contain a Security tab, which is where you configure NTFS permissions. (The Security tab is not present in the Properties dialog box for files or folders on FAT partitions, because FAT partitions do not support local security.) The Security tab lists the users and groups that have been assigned permissions to the folder (or file). When you click a user or group in the top half of the dialog box, you see the permissions that have been allowed or denied for that user or group in the lower half of the dialog box, as shown in Figure 7.2.

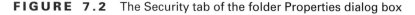

FIGURE 7.2   The Security tab of the folder Properties dialog box

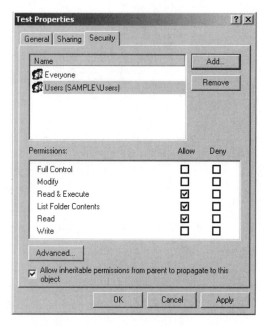

To apply NTFS permissions, take the following steps:

1. In Windows Explorer, right-click the file or folder that you want to control access to, select Properties from the pop-up menu, and click the Security tab of the Properties dialog box.

2. Click the Add button to open the Select Users, Computers, or Groups dialog box, shown in Figure 7.3. You can select users in the computer's local database or your domain (or trusted domains) from the list box at the top of the dialog box. The list box at the bottom of the dialog box lists all of the groups and users for the location that was specified in the top list box.

FIGURE 7.3 The Select Users, Computers, or Groups dialog box

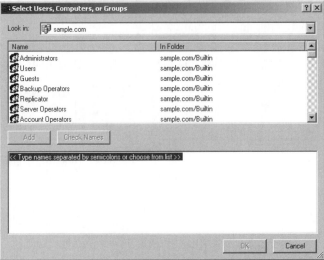

3. Click the user, computer, or group that you wish to add and click the Add button. The user, computer, or group appears in the bottom list box. Use Ctrl+click to select noncontiguous users, computers, or groups or use Shift+click to select contiguous users, computers, or groups.

4. You return to the Security tab of the folder Properties dialog box. Highlight each user, computer, or group in the top list box individually and specify the NTFS permissions that should be applied. When you are finished, click the OK button.

Through the Advanced button of the Security tab, you can configure more granular NTFS permissions, such as Traverse Folder/Execute File and Read Attributes permissions.

To remove the NTFS permissions for a user, computer, or group, highlight the user, computer, or group you wish to remove in the Security tab and click the Remove button. Note that if the permissions are being inherited, you must first uncheck the Allow Inheritable Permissions from Parent to Propagate to This Object check box before removing the permissions.

Be careful when you remove NTFS permissions. Unlike when you delete most other types of items in Windows 2000 Server, you won't be asked to confirm the removal of NTFS permissions.

Controlling Permission Inheritance

Normally, the directory structure is organized in a hierarchical manner. This means that you are likely to have subfolders in the folders that you apply permissions to. In Windows 2000 Server, by default, parent folder permissions are applied to any files or subfolders in that folder. These are called *inherited permissions*.

In Windows NT 4, by default, files in a folder inherited permissions from the parent folder, but subfolders did not inherit parent permissions. In Windows 2000 Server, the default is for the permissions to be inherited by subfolders.

You can specify that permissions should not be inherited by subfolders and files through the Security tab of the folder Properties dialog box. If you deselect the Allow Inheritable Permissions from Parent to Propagate to This Object check box at the bottom of the dialog box, you have disabled inherited permissions at this folder level. You are then given a choice of either copying the permissions or removing the permissions from the parent folder.

If an Allow or a Deny check box in the Permission list in the Security tab has a shaded check mark, this indicates that the permission was inherited from an upper-level folder. If the check mark is not shaded, it indicates that the permission was applied at the selected folder. This is known as an explicitly assigned permission. It is useful to see inherited permissions so that you can more easily troubleshoot permissions.

Determining Effective Permissions

To determine a user's *effective rights* (the rights the user actually has to a file or folder), add all of the permissions that have been allowed through the user's assignments based on that user's username and group associations. After you determine what the user is allowed, you subtract any permissions that have been denied the user through the username or group associations.

As an example, suppose that user Marilyn is a member of the Accounting and Execs groups. The following assignments have been made:

Accounting Group Permissions

Permission	Allow	Deny
Full Control		
Modify	✓	
Read & Execute	✓	
List Folder Contents		
Read		
Write		

Execs Group Permissions

Permission	Allow	Deny
Full Control		
Modify		
Read & Execute		
List Folder Contents		
Read	✓	
Write		

To determine Marilyn's effective rights, you combine the permissions that have been assigned. The result is that Marilyn's effective rights are Modify, Read & Execute, and Read.

As another example, suppose that user Dan is a member of the Sales and Temps groups. The following assignments have been made:

Sales Group Permissions

Permission	Allow	Deny
Full Control		
Modify		✓
Read & Execute		

List Folder Contents

Read

Write   ✓

Temps Group Permissions

Permission	Allow	Deny
Full Control		
Modify	✓	
Read & Execute	✓	
List Folder Contents	✓	
Read	✓	
Write	✓	

To determine Dan's effective rights, you start by seeing what Dan has been allowed: Modify, Read & Execute, List Folder Contents, Read, and Write permissions. You then remove anything that he is denied: Modify and Write permissions. In this case, Dan's effective rights are Read & Execute, List Folder Contents, and Read.

In Exercise 7.2, you will configure NTFS permissions based on the preceding examples. This exercise should be completed from your member server.

EXERCISE 7.2

Configuring NTFS Permissions

1. Using the Local Users and Groups utility, create two users: **Marilyn** and **Dan**. (See Chapter 4, "Managing Users and Groups," for details on using the Local Users and Groups utility.) Deselect the User Must Change Password at Next Logon option.

2. Using the Local Users and Groups utility, create four groups: **Accounting**, **Execs**, **Sales**, and **Temps**. Add Marilyn to the Accounting and Execs groups, and add Dan to the Sales and Temps groups.

3. Select Start ➢ Programs ➢ Accessories ➢ Windows Explorer. Expand the D:\DATA folder you created in Exercise 7.1.

4. Right-click DATA, select Properties, and click the Security tab.

5. In the Security tab of the folder Properties dialog box, highlight the Everyone group and click the Remove button. You see a dialog box telling you that you cannot remove Everyone because this group is inheriting permissions from a higher level. Click the OK button.

6. In the Security tab, deselect the Allow Inheritable Permissions from Parent to Propagate to This Object. In the dialog box that appears, click the Remove button.

7. Configure NTFS permissions for the Accounting group by clicking the Add button. In the Select Users, Computers, or Groups dialog box, highlight the Accounting group and click the Add button. Shift+click to select the Execs, Sales, and Temps groups and click the Add button. Then click OK.

8. In the Security tab, highlight each group and check the Allow or Deny check boxes to add permissions as follows:

   For Accounting, allow Read & Execute (List Folder Contents and Read will automatically be allowed) and Write.

   For Execs, allow Read.

   For Sales, allow Modify (Read & Execute, List Folder Contents, Read, and Write will automatically be allowed).

   For Temps, deny Write.

9. Click the OK button to close the folder Properties dialog box.

10. You will see a Security dialog box cautioning you about the deny entry. Click the Yes button to continue.

11. Log off as Administrator and log on as Marilyn. Access the D:\DATA\DOC1 file, make changes, and then save the changes. Marilyn's permissions should allow these actions.

12. Log off as Marilyn and log on as Dan. Access the D:\DATA\DOC1 file, make changes, and then save the changes. Dan's permissions should allow you to open the file but not to save any changes.

13. Log off as Dan and log on as Administrator.

You may want to remove permissions from the Everyone group to test how the permissions of other groups combine. If you decide to do this, adding the Administrators group with Full Control permission will make it easier to troubleshoot any problems that arise.

Determining NTFS Permissions for Copied or Moved Files

When you copy or move NTFS files, the permissions that have been set for those files might change. The following guidelines can be used to predict what will happen:

- If you move a file from one folder to another folder on the same volume, the file will retain the original NTFS permissions.

- If you move a file from one folder to another folder between different NTFS volumes, the file is treated as a copy and will have the same permissions as the destination folder.

- If you copy a file from one folder to another folder (on the same volume or on a different volume), the file will have the same permissions as the destination folder.

- If you copy or move a folder or file to a FAT partition, it will not retain any NTFS permissions.

Using Folder and File Auditing

If you have configured a partition or volume as NTFS you can take advantage of an additional security feature called *auditing*. Auditing allows you to track the success or failure of folder and file access. In order to use auditing, two options must be configured:

- Configure the computer to enable auditing for object access

- Configure the events that you want to audit on the specific NTFS folder or file

After you configure auditing, you view the results through the Event Viewer utility.

Setting Audit Policy

To enable folder and file auditing, you must first enable auditing for object access. This setting is either enabled or disabled for the entire computer. You enable object access from Local Security Settings, Local Policy, Audit Policy, Audit Object Access, and then configure success and/or failure, as shown is Figure 7.4. By default, object access is not active.

FIGURE 7.4 Local Security Policy Setting—Audit object access

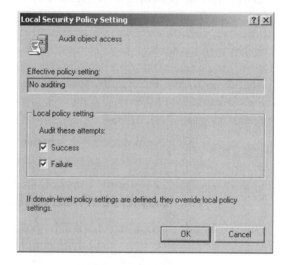

Configuring NTFS Auditing

You can configure only folder and file auditing on NTFS partitions. When you configure auditing, you must specify which users and groups are being tracked through auditing, which folders and/or files are being audited, and what types of events you want to audit for success or failure. To enable folder or file auditing, take the following steps:

1. Within the NTFS partition, right-click the folder or file you want to configure.

2. Select Properties, and then click the Security tab.

3. Within the Security tab, click the Advanced button.

4. Click the Auditing tab, and then click the Add button.

5. Select the group or user that you want to audit and click the OK button.

6. Specify the events that will be audited. You can select Success or Failure for the following events:

- Traverse folder/Execute file
- List folder/Read data
- Read attributes
- Read extended attributes
- Create files/Write data
- Create folders/Append data
- Write attributes
- Write extended attributes
- Delete subfolders and files
- Delete
- Read permissions
- Change permissions
- Take ownership

Click the OK button.

Viewing the Results of Folder and File Auditing

Once you have enabled auditing, you can view the results of auditing through Event Viewer. To view the results of auditing, access Event Viewer through Control Panel, Administrative Tools, Event Viewer, or Security Log. A key icon indicates that a successful event occurred, while a lock icon indicates that a failed event occurred.

 Real World Scenario

Tracking Folder and File Access

Suppose you are the network administrator of a server called HR. Several managers have access to a folder called C:\REPORTS with Full Control access. There has recently been a problem where reports that are copied to the network share are disappearing. You want to track who is accessing the files and when.

In order to track folder and file access you would enable auditing for the Everyone group on the C:\REPORTS folder. Select Successful and Failed events for Delete subfolders and files and Delete. If you want to track Read access, select List folder/Read data for the Everyone group.

Then, if files or folders are manipulated in a malicious way, you can track exactly what access occurred in the Security log stored within Event Viewer. The drawback to auditing is that, depending on the amount of data you are tracking, auditing can be very processor intensive. If there is frequent access, log files can also become cumbersome very quickly.

By being able to audit folders and files you, as a network administrator, can track any access to a folder or file on any NTFS partition or volume.

Managing Network Access

Sharing is the process of allowing network users to access a folder, called a *shared folder*, located on a Windows 2000 Server computer. A network share provides a single location to manage shared data used by many users. Sharing also allows an administrator to install an application once, as opposed to installing it locally at each computer, and to manage the application from a single location.

Microsoft ✓ *Exam Objective*

Monitor, configure, troubleshoot, and control access to files, folders, and shared folders.

- Monitor, configure, troubleshoot, and control access to files and folders in a shared folder.

Install, configure, and troubleshoot shared access.

Creating Shared Folders

To share a folder on a Windows 2000 member server, you must be logged on as a member of the Administrators or Power Users group. To share a folder on a Windows 2000 domain controller, you must be logged on as a member of the Administrators or Server Operators group. You enable and configure sharing through the Sharing tab of the folder Properties dialog box, as shown in Figure 7.5.

FIGURE 7.5   The Sharing tab of the folder Properties dialog box

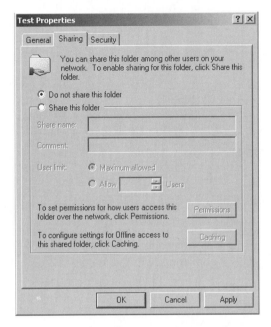

When you share a folder, you can configure the options listed in Table 7.1.

TABLE 7.1   Shared Folder Options

Option	Description
Do Not Share This Folder	Specifies that the folder is available only through local access
Share This Folder	Specifies that the folder is available through local access and network access
Share Name	Specifies a descriptive name by which users will access the folder.
Comment	Allows you to enter more descriptive information about the share (optional)

TABLE 7.1   Shared Folder Options *(continued)*

Option	Description
User Limit	Allows you to specify the maximum number of connections to the share at any one time
Permissions	Allows you to configure how users will access the folder over the network
Caching	Specifies how folders are cached when the folder is offline

If you share a folder and then decide that you do not want to share it, just select the Do Not Share This Folder radio button in the Sharing tab of the folder Properties dialog box.

In Windows Explorer, you can easily tell that a folder has been shared by the hand icon under the folder.

In Exercise 7.3, you will create a shared folder.

EXERCISE 7.3

Creating a Shared Folder

1. Select Start ➤ Programs ➤ Accessories ➤ Windows Explorer. Expand My Computer, and then expand Local Disk (D:).

2. Select File ➤ New ➤ Folder and name the new folder **Share Me**.

3. Right-click the Share Me folder, select Properties, and click the Sharing tab.

4. In the Sharing tab of the folder Properties dialog box, click the Share This Folder radio button.

5. Type **Test Shared Folder** in the Share Name text box.

6. Type **This is a comment for a shared folder** in the Comment text box.

7. Under User Limit, click the Allow radio button and specify 5 Users.

8. Click the OK button to close the dialog box.

Configuring Share Permissions

You can control users' access to shared folders by assigning *share permissions*. Share permissions are less complex than NTFS permissions and can be applied only to folders (unlike NTFS permissions, which can be applied to folders and files).

To assign share permissions, click the Permissions button in the Sharing tab of the folder Properties dialog box. This opens the Share Permissions dialog box, as shown in Figure 7.6.

FIGURE 7.6   The Share Permissions dialog box

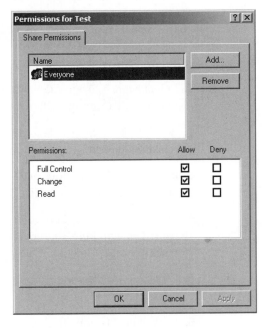

You can assign three types of share permissions:

- The Full Control share permission allows full access to the shared folder.

- The Change share permission allows users to change data in a file or to delete files.

- The Read share permission allows a user to view and execute files in the shared folder.

Full Control is the default permission on shared folders for the Everyone group. When the Full Control permission is assigned, the Change and Read permissions are checked as well.

Shared folders do not use the same concept of inheritance as NTFS folders. If you share a folder, there is no way to block access to lower-level resources through share permissions.

In Exercise 7.4, you will apply share permissions to a folder. This exercise assumes that you have completed the other exercises in this chapter.

EXERCISE 7.4

Applying Share Permissions

1. Select Start ≻ Programs ≻ Accessories ≻ Windows Explorer. Expand My Computer, then expand Local Disk (D:).

2. Right-click the Share Me folder, select Sharing, and click the Permissions button.

3. In the Share Permissions dialog box, highlight the Everyone group and click the Remove button. Then click the Add button.

4. In the Select Users, Computers, and Groups dialog box, select users Dan and Marilyn, click the Add button, and then click the OK button.

5. Click user Marilyn and check the Allow box for the Full Control permission.

6. Click user Dan and check the Allow box for the Read permission.

7. Click the OK button to close the dialog box.

Managing Shares with the Shared Folders Utility

Shared Folders is a Computer Management utility for creating and managing shared folders on the computer. The Shared Folders window displays all of the shares that have been created on the computer, the user sessions that are open on each share, and the files that are currently open, listed by user.

To access Shared Folders, right-click My Computer on the Desktop and select Manage from the pop-up menu. In Computer Management, expand System Tools and then expand Shared Folders.

You can add the Shared Folders utility as an MMC snap-in. See Chapter 3, "Configuring the Windows 2000 Server Environment," for information about adding snap-ins to the MMC.

Viewing Shares

When you select Shares in the Shared Folders utility, you see all of the shares that have been configured on the computer. Figure 7.7 shows an example of a Shares listing.

FIGURE   7.7   The Shares listing in the Shared Folders window

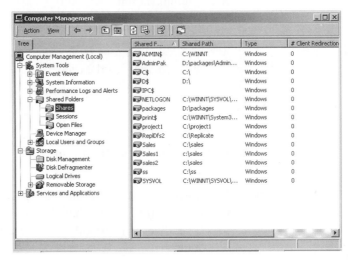

Along with the shares that you have specifically configured, you will also see the Windows 2000 special shares, which are shares created by the system automatically to facilitate system administration. A share that is followed by a dollar sign ($) indicates that the share is hidden from view when users access utilities such as My Network Places and browse network resources. The following special shares may appear on your Windows 2000 Server computer, depending on how the computer is configured:

- The *drive_letter*$ share is the share for the root of the drive. By default, the root of every drive is shared. For example, the C: drive is shared as C$.

On Windows 2000 member servers and Windows Professional computers, only members of the Administrators and Backup Operators group can access the *drive_letter*$ share. On Windows 2000 domain controllers, members of the Administrators, Backup Operators, and Server Operators group can access this share.

- The ADMIN$ share points to the Windows 2000 system root (for example, C:\WINNT).

- The IPC$ share allows remote administration of a computer and is used to view a computer's shared resources. (IPC stands for interprocess communication.)

- The PRINT$ share is used for remote printer administration.

- The FAX$ share is used by fax clients to cache fax cover sheets and documents that are in the process of being faxed.

Creating New Shares

In Shared Folders, you can create new shares through the following steps:

1. Right-click the Shares folder and select New File Share from the pop-up menu.

2. The Create Shared Folder Wizard starts, as shown in Figure 7.8. Specify the folder that will be shared (you can use the Browse button to select the folder) and provide a share name and description. Click the Next button.

FIGURE 7.8   The Create Shared Folder Wizard dialog box

3. The Create Shared Folder Wizard dialog box for assigning share permissions appears, as shown in Figure 7.9. You can select from one of
the predefined permissions assignments or customize the share permissions. After you specify the permissions that will be assigned, click
the Finish button.

FIGURE 7.9   Assigning share permissions

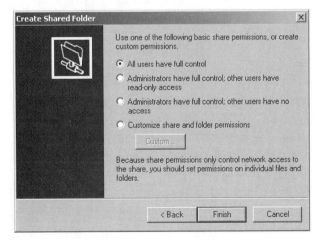

4. The Create Shared Folder dialog box appears. This dialog box verifies that the folder has been shared successfully. Click the Yes button to create another shared folder or the No button if you are finished creating shared folders.

You can stop sharing a folder by right-clicking the share and selecting Stop Sharing from the pop-up menu. You will be asked to confirm that you want to stop sharing the folder.

Viewing Share Sessions

When you select Sessions in the Shared Folders utility, you see all of the users who are currently accessing shared folders on the computer. Figure 7.10 shows an example of a Sessions listing in Shared Folders.

FIGURE 7.10 The Sessions listing in the Shared Folders window

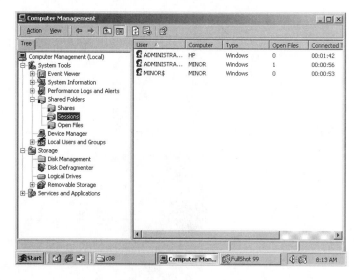

The Sessions listing includes the following information:

- The username that has connected to the share
- The computer name that the user has connected from
- The client operating system that is used by the connecting computer
- The number of files that the user has open
- The amount of time that the user has been connected

- The amount of idle time for the connection
- Whether or not the user has connected through Guest access

Viewing Open Files in Shared Folders

When you select Open Files in the Shared Folders utility, you see a list of all the files that are currently open from shared folders. Figure 7.11 shows an example of an Open Files listing in Shared Folders.

FIGURE 7.11 The Open Files listing in the Shared Folders window

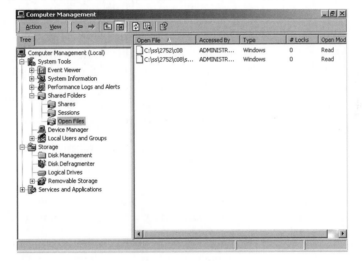

The Open Files listing shows:

- The path and files that are currently open
- The username that is accessing the file
- The operating system used by the user who is accessing the file
- Whether or not any file locks have been applied (file locks are used to prevent two users from opening the same file and editing it at the same time)
- The open mode that is being used (such as read or write)

Providing Access to Shared Resources

There are many ways that a user can access a shared resource. Here, we will look at three common methods:

- Through My Network Places

- By mapping a network drive in Windows Explorer

- Through the NET USE command-line utility

Accessing a Shared Resource through My Network Places

The advantage of mapping a network location through *My Network Places* is that you do not use a drive letter. This is useful if you have already exceeded the limit of 26 drive letters.

To access a shared resource through My Network Places

1. Double-click the My Network Places icon on the Desktop.

2. Double-click Add Network Place.

3. The Add Network Place Wizard starts. Type in the location of the Network Place. This can be a UNC path to a shared network folder, an HTTP path to a Web folder, or an FTP path to an FTP site. If you are unsure of the path, you can use the Browse button to search for your path. After specifying the path, click the Next button.

4. Enter the name that you want to use for the network location. This name will appear in the computer's My Network Places listing.

Mapping a Network Drive through Windows Explorer

Through Windows Explorer, you can map a network drive to a drive letter that appears to the user as a local connection on their computer. Once you create a *mapped drive*, it can be accessed through a drive letter using My Computer.

To map a network drive

1. Select Start ➢ Programs ➢ Accessories ➢ Windows Explorer to open Windows Explorer.

2. Select Tools ➢ Map Network Drive.

3. The Map Network Drive dialog box appears, as shown in Figure 7.12. Choose the drive letter that will be associated with the network drive.

FIGURE 7.12   The Map Network Drive dialog box

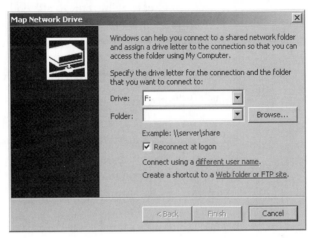

  4. Choose the shared network folder that you will map the drive to from
     the Folder drop-down list.

  5. If you want this connection to be persistent (you want to save the con-
     nection and use it every time you log on), make sure that the Recon-
     nect at Logon check box is checked.

  6. If you will connect to the share using a different username, click the
     underlined part of Connect Using a Different User Name. This opens
     the Connect As dialog box, shown in Figure 7.13. Fill in the User
     Name and Password text boxes, then click OK.

FIGURE 7.13   The Connect As dialog box

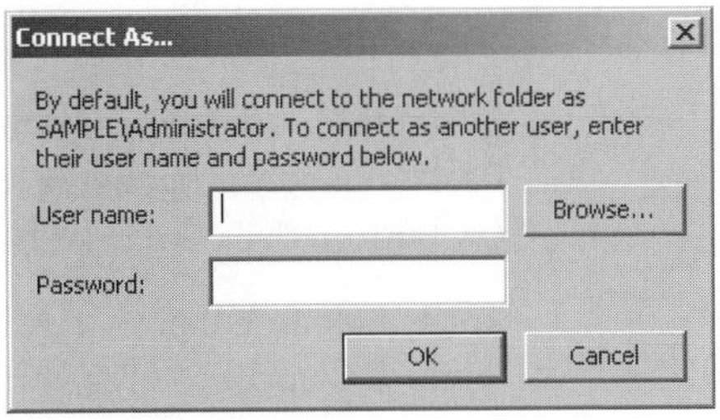

7. If you want to create a shortcut to a Web folder, click the underlined part of Create a Shortcut to a Web Folder or FTP Site. This starts the Add Network Place Wizard, which was described in the previous section.

Using the NET USE Command-Line Utility

The *NET USE* command-line utility provides a quick and easy way to map a network drive. This command has the following syntax:

NET USE *x*: *computername**sharename*

For example, the following command maps drive G to a share called App-Data on a computer named AppServer:

NET USE G: \\AppServer\AppData

You can get more information about the NET USE command by typing **NET USE** /? from a command prompt.

In Exercise 7.5, you will access shared resources through My Network Places and map a drive in Windows Explorer. This exercise assumes that you have completed Exercise 7.4.

EXERCISE 7.5

Accessing Network Resources

1. Log on as user Marilyn. Double-click the My Network Places icon on the Desktop.

2. Double-click Add Network Place. When the Add Network Place Wizard starts, click the Browse button.

3. Select the workgroup or domain that your computer is installed in. Click your computer name. Select Test Shared Folder and click the OK button. Click the Next button.

4. Enter the name that you want to use for the network location. This name will appear in the computer's My Network Places listing.

5. Accept the default name for the Network Place and click the Finish button.

6. The folder opens automatically. Close the folder. You will see the new folder in My Network Places.

7. Log off as Marilyn and log on as Dan.

8. Double-click My Network Places. You will not see the Network Place that you created as user Marilyn.

9. Open Windows Explorer and select Tools ➢ Map Network Drive.

10. In the Map Network Drives dialog box, accept the default drive letter and click the Browse button to select the folder. Select the workgroup or domain that your computer is installed in. Click your computer name. Select Test Shared Folder and click the Finish button.

11. Log off as Dan and log on as Administrator.

Reviewing the Flow of Resource Access

Understanding the resource-flow process will help you to troubleshoot access problems. As you've learned, a user account must have the appropriate permissions to access a resource. Resource access is determined through the following steps:

1. At logon, an *access token* is created for the logon account.

2. When a resource is accessed, Windows 2000 Server checks the *access control list (ACL)* to see if the user should be granted access.

3. If the user is on the list, the ACL checks the *access control entries (ACEs)* to see what type of access the user should be given.

Access tokens, ACLs, and ACEs are covered in the following sections.

Access Token Creation

Each time a user account logs on, an access token is created. The access token contains the security identifier (SID) of the currently logged-on user. It also contains the SIDs for any groups the user is associated with. Once an access token is created, it is not updated until the next logon.

Let's assume that user Kevin needs to access the Sales database and that SALESDB is the name of the shared folder that contains the database. Kevin logs on, but he is not able to access the database. You do some detective work and find that Kevin has not been added to the Sales group, which is necessary in order for him to have proper access to SALESDB. You add Kevin to the Sales group and let him know that everything is working. Kevin tries to access SALESDB, but he is still unable to do so. Kevin logs out and logs back on, and now he can access the database. This is because Kevin's access token was not updated to reflect his new group membership until he logged off and logged back on. When he logged back on, a new access token was created, identifying Kevin as a member of the Sales group.

Access tokens are updated only during the logon sequence. They are not updated in real time. This means that if you add a user to a group, that user needs to log off and log on for their access token to be updated.

ACLs and ACEs

Each object in Windows 2000 Server has an ACL. An object is defined as a set of data that can be used by the system or as a set of actions that can be used to manipulate system data. Examples of objects include folders, files, network shares, and printers. The ACL is a list of user accounts and groups that are allowed to access the resource. Figure 7.14 shows how ACLs are associated with each object.

FIGURE 7.14 Access control lists (ACLs) for network shares

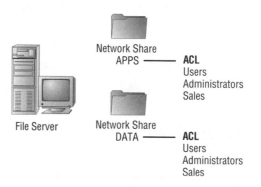

For each ACL, there is an ACE that defines what a user or a group can actually do at the resource. Deny permissions are always listed first. This

means that if users have Deny permissions through user or group membership, they will not be allowed to access the object, even if they have explicit Allow permissions through other user or group permissions. Figure 7.15 illustrates the interaction between the ACL and the ACE.

FIGURE 7.15   Access control entries (ACEs) associated with an ACL

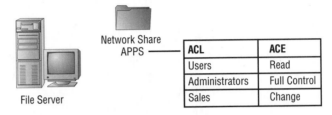

ACL	ACE
Users	Read
Administrators	Full Control
Sales	Change

Local and Network Resource Access

Local and network security work together. The most restrictive access will determine what a user can do. For example, if the local folder is NTFS and the default permissions have not been changed, the Everyone group has the Full Control permission. On the other hand, if that local folder is shared and the permissions are set so that only the Sales group had been assigned the Read permission, then only the Sales group can access that shared folder.

Conversely, if the local NTFS permissions allow only the Managers group the Read permission to a local folder, and that folder has been shared with default permissions allowing the Everyone group Full Control permission, only the Managers group can access the folder with Read permissions, because Read is the more restrictive permission.

For example, suppose that you have set up the NTFS and share permissions for the DATA folder as shown in Figure 7.16, and Jose is a member of the Sales group and wants to access the DATA folder. If he accesses the folder locally, he will be governed by only the NTFS security, so he will have the Modify permission. However, if Jose accesses the folder from another workstation through the network share, he also will be governed by the more restrictive share permission, Read.

FIGURE 7.16 Local and network security govern access.

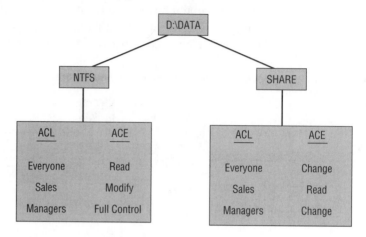

As another example, suppose that Chandler is a member of the Everyone group. He wants to access the DATA folder. If he accesses the folder locally, he will have Read permission. If he accesses the folder remotely via the network share, he will still have Read permission. Even though the share permission allows the Everyone group the Change permission to the folder, the more restrictive permission (in this case, the NTFS permission Read) will be applied.

Summary

In this chapter, you learned about managing access to files and folders. We covered the following topics:

- Local access management, which involves assigning NTFS permissions
- Network access management, which includes creating shared folders, assigning share permissions, and accessing network resources
- How resources are accessed when local NTFS permissions and network share permissions have been applied
- The flow of resource access, which includes access token creation and accessing objects by checking the ACL and ACEs

Exam Essentials

Be able to define local NTFS security options and be able to configure local security.   Be able to list NTFS permissions and understand how they work together when combined (especially No Access). Know who can manage NTFS permissions and how they are applied.

Create network shares and apply share permissions.   Know what group memberships can create network shares and be able to apply share permissions.

Understand how NTFS and share permission interact with each other. Be able to specify how NTFS permissions and share permissions interact and determine what the effective permissions are based on user and group memberships.

Key Terms

Before you take the exam, be sure you're familiar with the following key terms:

access control entry (ACE)	My Network Places
access control list (ACL)	NTFS permissions
access token	NET USE
effective rights	share permissions
inherited permissions	shared folders
mapped drive	

Review Questions

1. You are currently logged in to the SALES server as an Administrator. You want to add additional security to the D:\DATA folder. When you attempt to set permissions, the folder's Property dialog box does not display a Security tab. What is the most likely error?

   A. The partition is not configured as NTFS.

   B. Your account has been assigned No Access rights through the user account or through group membership.

   C. You need to be logged on as a member of the Server Operators group.

   D. The folder has already been encrypted with EFS.

2. Your company has a server called ACCT, which contains a folder called C:\REVIEWS. You want to verify that only authorized users view the data within this folder. You configure the folder's Properties for Auditing Success and Failure for Read access for the Everyone group. When you check the Event Viewer Security log after a week, no events are logged even through you know that users have accessed files with the folder. What is the most likely error?

   A. You have not started the Auditing service.

   B. You did not enable audit for Object Access through the computers Local Policy.

   C. Auditing can only occur on Dynamic Disks, and the disk is configured as a Basic Disk.

   D. You did not restart the server after configuring auditing.

3. You want Kim to be able to manage the permissions on the C:\DATA folder that is located on your SALES server. You want to assign Kim the lowest possible rights to manage the folder. By default, what is the lowest user or group level that can change the permissions of an NTFS folder?

    A. Administrator

    B. Domain Admins

    C. Power Users

    D. Everyone

4. You have just created a folder called C:\DATA on the TECHSUP-PORT server. The server has subfolders called C:\DATA\CALLS and C:\DATA\COMP. What is the default permission that will be applied to subfolders when you apply NTFS permissions to parent folders?

    A. Full Control

    B. Read

    C. Whatever permissions are applied to the parent folder

    D. You are prompted to specify what permissions should be applied

5. Your TEST server has C:, D:, and E: volumes. You want to see what shares have been created on the server for all volumes. Which utility can be used to quickly view all of the folders that have been shared on a Windows 2000 computer?

    A. Shared Folders

    B. File Manager

    C. Windows Explorer

    D. Share Manager

6. Your computer runs Windows 2000 Professional and is named WS1. You have administrative rights to a server called DATA. You need to remotely administer the DATA server from your local computer. Which special share allows remote administration of a computer and is used to view a computer's shared resources?

   A. ADMIN$

   B. WINNT$

   C. IPC$

   D. NET$

7. Elisa is a member of the Sales and Sales Temps group. The following NTFS permissions have been applied to the C:\Sales folder:

Sales Group Permissions

Permission	Allow	Deny
Full Control	✓	
Modify	✓	
Read & Execute	✓	
List Folder Contents		
Read		
Write		

Sales Temps Group Permissions

Permission	Allow	Deny
Full Control		✓
Modify		
Read & Execute		
List Folder Contents		
Read	✓	
Write		

What will Elisa's effective permission be to the C:\Sales folder?

A. Full Control

B. Modify

C. Read & Execute

D. Read

8. Rashid is assigning NTFS permissions to the D:\DATA folder for the Managers group. He wants the Managers group to be able to list the contents of the folder and read the data in the folder's files. He does not want anyone from the group to change or delete any of the data. Which NTFS permission should he apply?

A. Full Control

B. Modify

C. Read

D. Write

9. Marcus has assigned the NTFS Read permission to the Managers group for the D:\DATA folder. What will be the default right assigned to the Managers group for the D:\DATA\1999 subfolder?

A. Full Control

B. Modify

C. Read

D. Write

10. Marty is planning on copying the Test.txt file from the D:\DATA folder to the D:\TEST folder. The D: drive is NTFS. The Test.txt file currently has Modify permission applied for the Users group. The D:\TEST folder has the Write permission applied for the Users group. What permission will the Test.txt file have after it has been copied?

A. Full Control

B. Modify

C. Read

D. Write

11. Lynne is planning on moving the `Test.txt` file from the D:\DATA folder to the D:\TEST folder. The D: drive is NTFS. The `Test.txt` file currently has Modify permission applied for the Users group. The D:\TEST folder has the Write permission applied for Users. What permission will the `Test.txt` file have after it has been moved?

    A. Full Control

    B. Modify

    C. Read

    D. Write

12. Dustin is planning on moving the `Test.txt` file from the D:\DATA folder to the E:\TEST folder. The D: and E: drives are NTFS. The `Test.txt` file currently has Modify permission applied for the Users group. The E:\TEST folder has the Write permission applied for Users. What permission will the `Test.txt` file have after it has been moved?

    A. Full Control

    B. Modify

    C. Read

    D. Write

13. You have two user accounts. When you log on to the MIS member server and try to create a share with your regular user account, there is no Sharing tab available through the folder's Property tab. You want to be able to create shares on the server. Which of the following groups could you add your user account to so that you would have permissions to create network shares? (Choose all that apply.)

    A. Power Users

    B. Power Operators

    C. Server Operators

    D. Administrators

14. Maria needs to disconnect all users that are connected to the APPS share. Which of the following utilities can she use to see which users are currently connected to the share?

   A. Shared Folders

   B. File Manager

   C. Windows Explorer

   D. Server Manager

15. Which command-line utility can be used to access a shared network folder?

   A. NET SHARE

   B. NET USE

   C. NET ACCESS

   D. NET MANAGE

Answers to Review Questions

1. A. If you are logged in as Administrator and do not see a Security tab on the folders Property page, then the most likely problem is that the partition is not formatted as NTFS.

2. B. In order to support folder, file, and print auditing, you must be on an NTFS partition, or the option to configure Security and Auditing will not even appear. In order to support auditing you must enable auditing for Object Access through the computers Local Policy. Then you enable auditing through the folder or files Properties.

3. D. By default, the Everyone group is assigned Full Control permission for NTFS volumes, so the Everyone group is able to change the permissions of an NTFS folder.

4. C. When you apply NTFS permissions to a folder with subfolders, the default is to allow inheritable permissions to propagate from the parent to this object. This means that whatever permissions have been applied to the parent folder will be automatically applied to subfolders.

5. A. The Shared Folders utility displays all of the folders that have been shared. You can see shared folders through Windows Explorer, but the process is more time-consuming.

6. C. The IPC$ (Interprocess Communication) special share is used for remote administration of a computer and to view a computer's shared resources.

7. B. Elisa's effective permission will be Modify, since Modify includes the Read & Execute and the Read permissions. She will not have Full Control access, because this was explicitly denied for the Sales Temp group.

8. C. The Managers group should be assigned the most restrictive permission that will still allow the members to read the data in the D:\DATA folder, which is the NTFS Read permission.

9. C. In Windows 2000 Server, a parent folder's permissions are applied to any files or subfolders in that folder by default. That means that by default, the D:\DATA\1999 subfolder will inherit the parent folder's NTFS permissions, and the Managers group will inherit the Read permission.

10. D. If you copy a file from one folder to another folder (on the same volume or on a different volume), the file will have the same permissions as the destination folder.

11. B. If you move a file from one folder to another folder on the same volume, the file will retain the original NTFS permissions.

12. D. If you move a file from one folder to another folder between different NTFS volumes, the file is treated as a copy and will have the same permissions as the destination folder.

13. A, D. To share a folder on a Windows 2000 member server, you must be logged on as a member of the Administrators or Power Users group.

14. A. When you select Sessions in the Shared Folders utility, you see all of the users who are currently accessing shared folders on the computer.

15. B. The three common methods for accessing shared folders are through My Network Places, by mapping a network drive in Windows Explorer, and through the NET USE command-line utility.

Chapter

8

Administering the Distributed File System

MICROSOFT EXAM OBJECTIVES COVERED IN THIS CHAPTER

✓ **Monitor, configure, troubleshoot, and control access to files, folders, and shared folders.**

- Configure, manage, and troubleshoot a stand-alone Distributed file system (Dfs).
- Configure, manage, and troubleshoot a domain-based Distributed file system (Dfs).

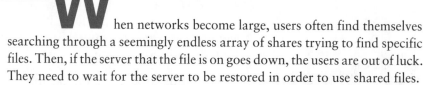

When networks become large, users often find themselves searching through a seemingly endless array of shares trying to find specific files. Then, if the server that the file is on goes down, the users are out of luck. They need to wait for the server to be restored in order to use shared files.

Administrators can use the Windows 2000's *Distributed file system (Dfs)* to create a central database of links that point to shares across the network. This makes it much easier for users to quickly find the files they need. If your network has domains, the Dfs is particularly useful because you can replicate this central database across multiple domain member servers. Even if one server goes down, users will still have access to their files.

In this chapter, you will learn how the Dfs works and how to configure and manage the Dfs.

Understanding the Dfs

The Dfs gives users a central location to access files and folders that are physically distributed across a network. For example, if users in your sales department need to access files that are stored on several computers in the Sales domain, you can use the Dfs to make it appear as though all of the files reside in the same network share. When you use the Dfs, users won't need to search through multiple computers to find the files or folders they need. Figure 8.1 illustrates how the Dfs works.

FIGURE   8.1   The Dfs provides a central location for network files and folders.

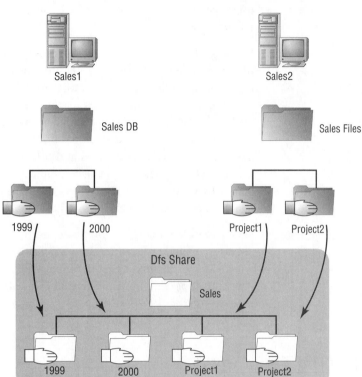

Before you set up and manage the Dfs, you should understand how it is implemented. The Dfs uses a simple topology similar to that used by the Windows file system. The following sections describe the main benefits of the Dfs, its topology, and its architecture.

Benefits of the Dfs

The Dfs offers three main benefits for network users:

Easier file access   The Dfs makes it easy for users to access files. Users need to know about only one location on the network to access files that might actually be distributed across several physical computers. Even if you change the physical location of a folder that is part of the Dfs, the users will not be affected. The folder will still appear to be in the central Dfs location.

Increased file availability   The Dfs increases the availability of network files and folders. Windows 2000 automatically publishes all of the Dfs information to the Active Directory, thus ensuring that users on every server in the domain have access to the files in the Dfs. Administrators can also replicate the contents of the Dfs to multiple servers across the domain. If one of your servers goes down or needs to be taken offline for maintenance purposes, the files and folders contained in the Dfs can be accessed from other member servers in the domain. This process is transparent to the user, who always sees the same files and folders, regardless of where they are physically stored.

Server load balancing   Sometimes multiple users in a domain need access to a single file simultaneously. This can present a significant network load to the server that contains the file. The Dfs helps to ease this load by supporting multiple shared folders that are physically distributed across the network. Again, to users, the file appears to reside in only one network location.

The Dfs Topology

A Dfs topology consists of three main components: a *Dfs root*, one or more *Dfs links*, and one or more *Dfs shared folders*, or *replicas*. Each Dfs link points to one shared folder and all of its replicas. You can replicate the Dfs root by creating *root shares* on other member servers in the domain.

When you create a Dfs root, you can specify whether it is a stand-alone Dfs root or a domain-based Dfs root.

Stand-Alone Dfs Roots

A *stand-alone Dfs root* offers no replication or backup capabilities, so it is not fault tolerant. These rules apply to a stand-alone Dfs root:

- It cannot use the Active Directory.

- It cannot have root-level Dfs shared folders.

- It can have only a single level of Dfs links in its hierarchy.

Domain-Based Dfs Roots

A *domain-based Dfs root* automatically publishes its Dfs topology to the Active Directory. These rules apply to a domain-based Dfs root:

- It can be hosted only on a domain member server.

- It can have root-level Dfs shared folders.

- It can have multiple levels of Dfs links in its hierarchy.

- It must have fault-tolerant roots located on NTFS version 5 (or higher) partitions

The domain server that contains the Dfs root is known as the *host server*. The host server automatically publishes the Dfs topology to the Active Directory and provides synchronization of the topology across the domain member servers.

You can replicate the Dfs root by creating root shares on other member servers in the domain. To administrators, the Dfs topology appears as a single DNS namespace. The DNS names for the Dfs root shares resolve to the host servers for the Dfs root.

The Dfs Architecture

The Dfs consists of a server-based component, administered through the Distributed File System utility, and a client-based component. Table 8.1 summarizes the Dfs clients and servers available for the various Windows platforms.

TABLE 8.1   Dfs Client and Server Platforms

Platform	Dfs Client	Dfs Server
DOS, Windows 3.*x*, Windows for Workgroups, NetWare servers	No	No
Windows 95	Client version 4.*x* and 5.0 available for download	No

TABLE 8.1 Dfs Client and Server Platforms *(continued)*

Platform	Dfs Client	Dfs Server
Windows 98	Client version 4.*x* and 5.0 (stand-alone) included; client version 5.0 (domain-based) available for download	No
Windows NT 4	Client version 4.*x* and 5.0 (stand-alone) included	Stand-alone server on server version only
Windows 2000	Client version 5.0 included	Stand-alone and domain-based server on server version only

In order to integrate Dfs with Windows 95, Windows 98, and Windows NT Workstation clients, you need to add the DFS Services for Microsoft Network Client service to the client. This client software can be downloaded from www.microsoft.com.

 Real World Scenario

Managing Distributed Data

Your network is fairly extensive and is spread over three primary locations: San Jose, Belfast, and New York. Each office has a training department that creates and manages training documents. Users in each office want to store their data locally, but want to access any training documentation from a single network access point.

Dfs provides a mechanism for managing data stored in different locations within a LAN or over a WAN. With Dfs you can logically structure your data within a single structure, regardless of where the data is physically stored.

The main benefit of using Dfs is that it allows users within the corporation to have a single access point for retrieving data instead of mapping drives to each local training share and trying to figure out where specific documents are within a decentralized structure.

Configuring and Managing the Dfs

You use the *Distributed File System utility* to configure and manage the Dfs for your network. This utility allows you to create a Dfs root, add a root share, add a Dfs link, configure replication, and check the status of Dfs shared folders.

Microsoft Exam Objective

Monitor, configure, troubleshoot, and control access to files, folders, and shared folders.

- Configure, manage, and troubleshoot a stand-alone Distributed file system (Dfs).
- Configure, manage, and troubleshoot a domain-based Distributed file system (Dfs).

This chapter covers information about managing the Dfs for the "Monitor, configure, troubleshoot, and control access to files, folders, and shared folders" objective. The subobjectives for this objective related to managing shared folders and local security for files and folders are covered in Chapter 7, "Accessing Files and Folders." The subobjective related to managing access to files and folders through Web services is covered in Chapter 10, "Managing Web Services."

To access the Distributed File System utility (the Dfs console), select Start ➢ Programs ➢ Administrative Tools ➢ Distributed File System. This utility's opening window is shown in Figure 8.2.

You can also add the Distributed File System utility snap-in to the MMC. See Chapter 3, "Configuring the Windows 2000 Server Environment." for more information about adding snap-ins to the MMC.

FIGURE 8.2 The opening Distributed File System window

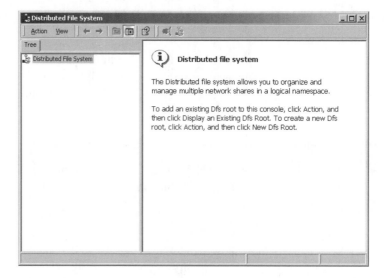

Creating a Dfs Root

There can be only one Dfs root per server, although there can be unlimited Dfs roots per domain. You should create the Dfs root on an NTFS partition. Automatic replication is available only on the NTFS file system. You can also take advantage of the security features offered by NTFS to control access to Dfs shared folders.

To create a Dfs root, take the following steps:

1. Select Start ➢ Programs ➢ Administrative Tools ➢ Distributed File System.

2. The Dfs console opens (see Figure 8.2). Highlight Distributed File System and select Action ➢ New Dfs Root from the menu bar.

3. The New Dfs Root Wizard starts. Click the Next button.

4. The Select the Dfs Root Type dialog box appears. In this dialog box, you choose whether to create a domain Dfs root or a stand-alone Dfs root. As explained earlier in the chapter, if you are in a domain environment, you can create a domain Dfs root, which uses the Active Directory and supports automatic replication. If you are in a workgroup environment, you can create only a stand-alone Dfs root, which does not use the Active Directory or support automatic replication. In this example, you will create a domain Dfs root. Click the Next button.

5. The Select the Host Domain for the Dfs Root dialog box appears, as shown in Figure 8.3. Specify the host domain that will be used and click the Next button.

FIGURE 8.3 The Select the Host Domain for the Dfs Root dialog box

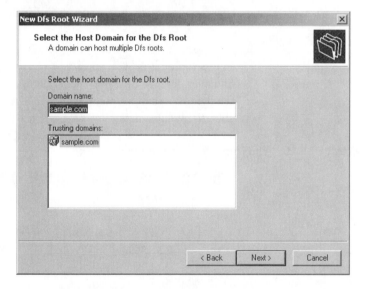

6. The Specify the Host Server for the Dfs Root dialog box appears. Specify the name of the host server and click the Next button.

7. The Specify the Dfs Root Share dialog box appears, as shown in Figure 8.4. In this dialog box, you choose whether your DFS root share will use an existing share or you will create a new share. Make your selection and click the Next button. If you choose to create a new share, you will be prompted to confirm the creation of the new folder.

FIGURE 8.4 The Specify the Dfs Root Share dialog box

8. The Name the Dfs Root dialog box appears, as shown in Figure 8.5. In this dialog box, you specify the Dfs root name (which is the share name by default) and provide a comment (optional). You can accept the default name or enter another one and enter comment text. Then click the Next button.

FIGURE 8.5 The Name the Dfs Root dialog box

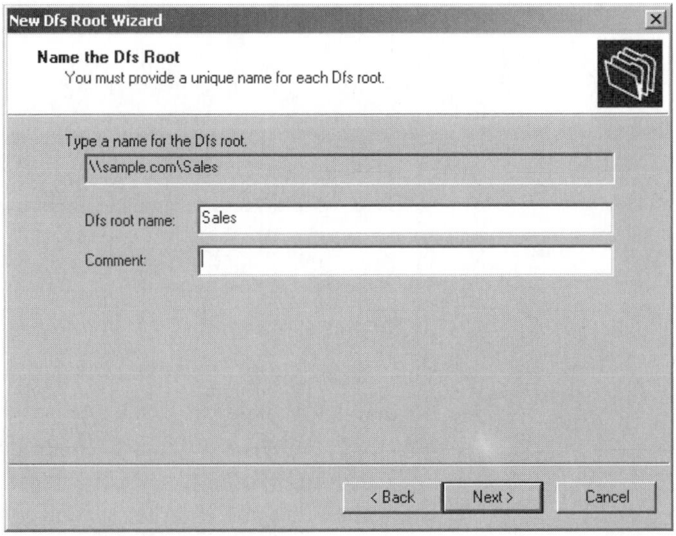

9. The Completing the New Dfs Root Wizard dialog box appears. This dialog box shows the settings you have specified. If the information is correct, click the Finish button.

In Exercise 8.1, you will create a new Dfs root. This exercise should be completed from your domain controller.

Creating a New Dfs Root

1. From your Windows 2000 domain controller, use Windows Explorer to create the C:\Sales folder.

2. Select Start ➢ Programs ➢ Administrative Tools ➢ Distributed File System.

3. In the Dfs console, highlight Distributed File System and select Action ➢ New Dfs Root.

4. When the New Dfs Root Wizard starts, click the Next button.

5. In the Select Dfs Root Type dialog box, verify that the Create a Domain Dfs Root option is selected and click the Next button.

6. In the Select the Host Domain for the Dfs Root dialog box, confirm that your domain is shown in the Domain Name text box and click the Next button.

7. In the Specify the Host Server for the Dfs Root dialog box, verify that your server's name is selected and click the Next button.

8. In the Specify the Dfs Root Share dialog box, click the Create a New Share radio button. In the Path to Share text box, type **C:\Sales**. In the Share Name text box, type **Sales**. Click the Next button.

9. In the Name the Dfs Root dialog box, leave the default Dfs root name and add the comment **This is a test Dfs root**. Click the Next button.

10. When the Completing the New Dfs Root Wizard dialog box appears, click the Finish button.

Adding a Dfs Link

A Dfs link is a link from the Dfs root to one or more shared folders. Dfs links are added at the root of the Dfs topology. You can have up to 1,000 Dfs links assigned to a Dfs root.

To create a Dfs link, right-click the Dfs root and select New Dfs Link from the pop-up menu. The Create a New Dfs Link dialog box appears, as shown in Figure 8.6. In this dialog box, you specify the link name, the path to the shared folder that will be used as the Dfs link, and an optional comment to provide additional information about the Dfs link. The Dfs path can be up to 260 characters.

You can also set a value for how long clients cache the referral. The client cache option allows you to specify the number of seconds that client systems will store information regarding the location of the requested Dfs shared folder.

FIGURE 8.6 The Create a New Dfs Link dialog box

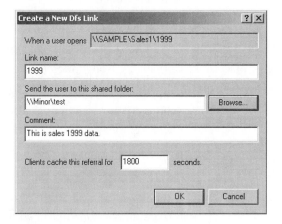

After you supply the Dfs link information and close the Create a New Dfs Link dialog box, you will see the new Dfs link listed under the Dfs root in the Dfs console window.

In Exercise 8.2, you will create two Dfs links that point to a shared folder on your Windows 2000 member server. This exercise assumes that you have completed Exercise 8.1.

EXERCISE 8.2

Creating Dfs Links

1. On your Windows 2000 domain controller, create a folder called C:\Project1. Share this folder as **Project1**.

2. On your Windows 2000 member server, create a folder called C:\1999. Share this folder as **1999**.

3. On your Windows 2000 domain controller, select Start ➢ Programs ➢ Administrative Tools ➢ Distributed File System.

4. In the Dfs console, right-click your Dfs root and select New Dfs Link.

5. In the Create a New Dfs Link dialog box, type **Project1** in the Link Name text box. In the Send the User to This Shared Folder text box, specify the UNC path to the Project1 folder you created in step 1 (**computername***Project1*). In the Comment text box, type **Data for Sales Project1**. Click the OK button.

6. In the Dfs console window, right-click your Dfs root and select New Dfs Link.

7. In the Create a New Dfs Link dialog box, type **1999** in the Link Name text box. In the Send the User to This Shared Folder text box, specify the UNC path to the 1999 folder you created in step 2 (**computername***1999*). In the Comment text box, type **Sales data for 1999**. Click the OK button.

After you have created the Dfs structure, with a Dfs root and links, users can access the Dfs root in the same manner that they would access a regular share.

Configuring Replication

Replication ensures that if the host server goes down, the files and folders that are part of the Dfs will be available. Automatic replication can be used only in conjunction with NTFS volumes. If you do not specify automatic replication, you must replicate your Dfs shared folders manually.

You can enable the Dfs to automatically replicate the contents of one or more shared folders using the *File Replication Service (FRS)*. When changes are made to one shared folder, FRS updates the other shared folders to reflect the changes (by default, this happens every 15 minutes). You should specify that all of the shared folders in a Dfs link are replicated automatically, if possible. This ensures that all of the shared folders in a Dfs link are synchronized properly. You must select one of your shared folders to be the initial master, which replicates its contents to the other shared folders in the Dfs link the first time the replication policy is set. After the Initial Master is set, the Set Master button will disappear. If the Initial Master goes down, the button will reappear. Also, the Initial Master should be the share with write access. The Initial Master is the folder that is replicated (in a single master design); the replica folders require only read access.

WARNING You should not mix and match manual replication with automatic replication. If you do, all of your shared folders may not be synchronized correctly.

To configure shared folder replication, take the following steps:

1. Create and share the folder that will be used to hold the replicated folder.

2. Select Start ≻ Programs ≻ Administrative Tools ≻ Distributed File System to open the Dfs console.

3. In the Dfs console window, right-click the Dfs link you will replicate and select New Replica from the pop-up menu.

4. The Add a New Replica dialog box appears, as shown in Figure 8.7. In the Send the User to This Shared Folder text box, specify the shared folder that will hold the replica. In the Replication Policy section, choose Manual Replication or Automatic Replication. Then click the OK button.

5. Repeat steps 3 and 4 to add additional replicas.

6. To configure the replication policy, right-click the Dfs link that you added the replica to and select Replication Policy from the pop-up menu.

FIGURE 8.7 The Add a New Replica dialog box

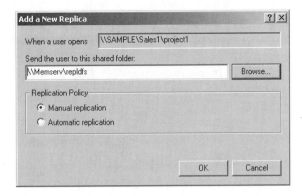

7. The Replication Policy dialog box appears, as shown in Figure 8.8. Highlight the master Dfs link and click the Set Master button. Select the shared folder that will be used for replication and click the Enable button. Then click the OK button.

FIGURE 8.8 The Replication Policy dialog box

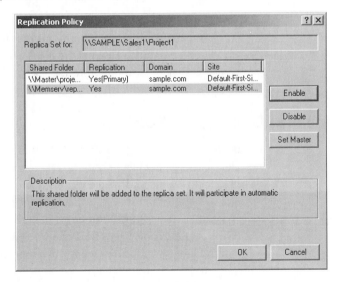

In Exercise 8.3, you will configure manual Dfs replication. This exercise assumes that you have completed the previous exercises in this chapter

---

EXERCISE 8.3

Implementing Dfs Replication

1. On your member server, create a folder called C:\Replicate and share the folder as **ReplDfs**.

2. On your Windows 2000 domain controller, select Start ➤ Programs ➤ Administrative Tools ➤ Distributed File System.

3. In the Dfs console, right-click the Dfs link Project1 (created in Exercise 8.2) and select New Replica.

4. In the Add a New Replica dialog box, specify the share you created in step 1 (**computername**\ReplDfs) in the Send the User to This Shared Folder text box. For Replication Policy, select the Manual Replication option. Then click the OK button.

5. Right-click the Dfs link and select Replication Policy.

6. In the Replication Policy dialog box, select the Dfs shared folder Project1 as the master folder for the first replication and click the Set Master button. Select the *computername**ReplDfs* shared folder and click the Enable button. Click the OK button.

Checking Dfs Shared Folder Status

You can check to see if your Dfs shared folders are being referenced properly by right-clicking any element in the Dfs topology and selecting Check Status from the pop-up menu. If you check the status of a Dfs link, the Dfs will verify the status of all of the shared folders in that link. If you check the status of a Dfs root, the Dfs will verify the status of every shared folder in every Dfs link.

A link that is properly configured will appear with a green check mark, as shown in Figure 8.9. A link that is not properly configured will appear with a red × mark.

FIGURE 8.9   Checking Dfs shared folder status

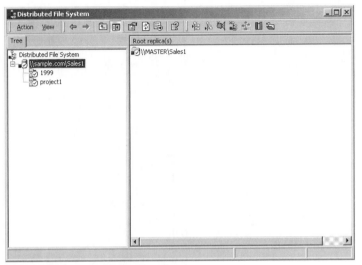

Configuring Dfs Security

Permissions that apply to folders and files are not lost in the Dfs. If a user
has access to a specific shared folder, that user will also have access to that
folder when using the appropriate Dfs share. If users have access to one Dfs
shared folder, they will also be able to see all of the other Dfs shared
folders, but they won't be able to use them unless they have the appropriate
permissions.

To manage Dfs security, right-click the Dfs root in the Dfs console
and select Properties from the pop-up menu. This opens the Dfs root
Properties dialog box. Click the Security tab to access the properties shown
in Figure 8.10.

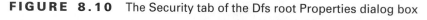

FIGURE 8.10 The Security tab of the Dfs root Properties dialog box

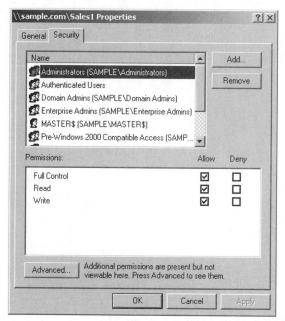

In the Security tab, you can specify who has access to the Dfs object and what access has been allowed or denied. Permissions include Full Control, Read, and Write. By default, the Administrators group is allowed Full Control, Read, and Write permissions. The Authenticated Users group is allowed Read permission by default.

Troubleshooting Dfs

If you are unable to access a Dfs shared folder, you should check the following:

- Make sure that the server that hosts the Dfs root is available.

- Make sure that the users have appropriate permissions on the NTFS folder that they are trying to access through Dfs.

- Make sure that the users have appropriate permissions assigned from the Distributed File System utility for the resource they are trying to access.

- Use the Distributed File System utility to check the status of your Dfs shared folders.

Summary

In this chapter, you learned about the Dfs and how to implement its features. Specifically, we covered these topics:

- Reasons for using the Dfs, which include easy access to files, increased availability, and server load balancing

- The Dfs topology, which consists of the Dfs root, Dfs links, and Dfs shared folders

- The Dfs architecture, which includes the server-based components and client-based components

- How to use the Dfs, including how to create a Dfs root, a Dfs root share, a Dfs link, and a Dfs shared folder

- How to implement Dfs replication, which can be automatic or manual

- Some tips for troubleshooting Dfs access problems

Exam Essentials

Understand the key features of Dfs.   Know the benefits of Dfs and the differences between stand-alone Dfs and domain-based Dfs. Know which clients can be Dfs clients and which servers can act as Dfs servers.

Be able to configure and manage Dfs.   Be able to install Dfs roots and Dfs links. Be able to configure replication, verify Dfs shared folder status, and set Dfs security.

Know how to troubleshoot Dfs.   If users are unable to access Dfs resources, understand what steps should be taken to resolve access issues.

Key Terms

Before you take the exam, be sure you're familiar with the following key terms:

Dfs link	domain-based Dfs root
Dfs replication	File Replication Service (FRS)
Dfs root	host server
Dfs shared folder	replica
Distributed file system (Dfs)	root share
Distributed File System utility	stand-alone Dfs root

Review Questions

1. You are looking for a way to logically organize your network's data. You are considering using Dfs. What are the main advantages of the Dfs? (Choose all that apply.)

   A. Provides a centralized location for network files and folders

   B. Increases availability of network files and folders

   C. Helps ease network congestion

   D. Helps ease loads on the server

2. Your NT 4.0 network used stand-alone Dfs. You have now upgraded your network to Windows 2000 with Active Directory. You want to use domain-based Dfs. Which of the following features can you use if you switch to domain-based Dfs? (Choose all that apply.)

   A. Automatic replication

   B. Automatic publication of topology to the Active Directory

   C. Hosted on any computer in the domain

   D. Does not require administration

3. You have configured domain-based Dfs for the Sales department's data structure, so that users can easily use and track sales data. The sales users all use a variety of client operating systems. Based on the following exhibit, drag and drop onto the network those clients that are able to use the features of Dfs.

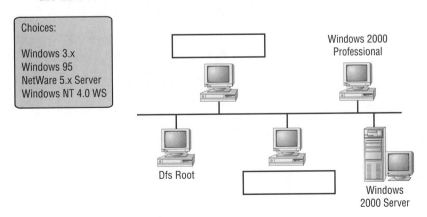

Choices:

Windows 3.x
Windows 95
NetWare 5.x Server
Windows NT 4.0 WS

Windows 2000 Professional

Dfs Root

Windows 2000 Server

4. You have configured Dfs for a data structure used by the Accounting department. One of the new accounting users reports that she is not able to access the Dfs structure. Which of the following permissions should you verify that she has, so that she can access the Dfs structure?

   A. She must have permission to access a link before she can access the shared folders in the link.

   B. She must have permission to access the Dfs root before she can access any shared folders in the Dfs root.

   C. She must have permission to access only the network shares that the Dfs links point to. No additional permissions are required.

   D. She must have Dfs permissions enabled.

5. You have defined a Dfs structure for the Human Resources department. The Dfs structure contains important corporate documentation that you want to ensure is always available. You decide to use Dfs replication to provide fault tolerance. Which of the following requirements must be met in order to support replication?

   A. You must configure Directory Replication through Server Manager

   B. The file system that the Dfs structure is on must be NTFS

   C. You must configure Directory Replication through the Backup utility

   D. Use the DfsRepl command-line utility to configure replication

6. You are trying to decide whether you should use stand-alone Dfs or domain-based Dfs on your network. Which of the following options are available if you use stand-alone Dfs?

   A. Can be hosted on a Windows 2000 member server that is not a part of a domain

   B. Supports root-level Dfs shared folders

   C. Supports multiple levels of Dfs links in a hierarchical structure

   D. Supports automatic replication

7. You have configured a domain-based Dfs root. You want to create links to folders located on servers spread throughout your organization. How many Dfs links are supported by a single Dfs root?

   A. 100

   B. 250

   C. 500

   D. 1,000

8. You are using domain-based Dfs. You are trying to configure replication, but are having problems getting replication to work properly. Which of the following services should you verify is running properly?

   A. File Replication Service

   B. Directory Replication Service

   C. Dfs Replication Service

   D. NTFS Replication Service

9. Which Dfs link option allows you to specify how long the client computer will store information regarding the location of the requested Dfs shared folder?

   A. Clients Cache the Referral for x Seconds

   B. Maximum Cache Time

   C. Save Dfs Referrals for x Seconds

   D. Remember Dfs Referrals for x Seconds

10. The previous administrator of your network installed and configured Dfs. You now want to make changes to the Dfs configuration. Which of the following options can you use to configure the Dfs? Choose two answers.

   A. Access the Distributed File System utility through Administrative Tools

   B. Double-click the Dfs icon in Control Panel

   C. Double-click the Dfs tab in Windows Explorer

   D. Add the Distributed File System utility as an MMC snap-in

11. Your network has Windows 95 and Windows 98 clients that need to access Dfs structures that you have created. These users report that they can't access the Dfs folders. What service needs to be installed on these clients so that they can access Dfs services?

    A. Dfs Services for Microsoft Network Client

    B. Windows Dfs

    C. Dfs Client Services

    D. Dfs Client Kit

12. You are creating a Dfs structure that will be used by your Tech Support group. You are concerned because some of the paths within the Dfs structure are fairly long. What is the maximum number of characters that are allowed in a Dfs path?

    A. 64

    B. 128

    C. 260

    D. 512

13. You want to create several Dfs structures through your corporate network to support easier file access for the different corporate departments. Which of the following operating systems can be used as Dfs Servers? (Choose all that apply.)

    A. Windows 95

    B. Windows 98

    C. Windows NT 4 Server

    D. Windows 2000 Server

14. You are considering implementing Dfs within your company. You are trying to determine what the key components of Dfs are. Which of the following items is not a component of the Dfs topology?

A. Dfs root

B. Dfs link

C. Dfs shared folders

D. Dfs shared files

15. You have installed Dfs on a Windows 2000 member server called Test that is part of the ABCCORP.COM domain. How many Dfs roots can exist on the Test server?

A. One

B. Two

C. Four

D. Eight

Answers to Review Questions

1. A, B, D. The Dfs provides a central database of links that point to files and folders that are distributed throughout the network. It also provides replication so that if one server goes down, the files on that server will still be available. Another benefit of replication is that a single file can be accessed from more than one server, which reduces the load on any one server.

2. A, B. Domain-based Dfs roots automatically publish their topology to the Active Directory and can be automatically replicated. They can be hosted only on domain member servers and they require administrators to perform certain setup tasks.

3. The Dfs client runs on Windows 95, Windows 98, Windows NT 4, and Windows 2000. By default, Windows 95 and Windows 98 clients do not ship with the Dfs client software. Windows NT 4 clients with Service Pack 3 or higher and Windows 2000 clients have the Dfs client software included with the operating system files by default.

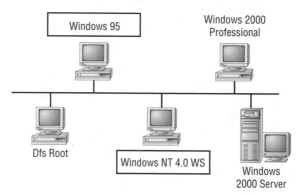

4. C. Permissions that apply to folders and files also apply when you are using the Dfs. If users have access to a particular shared folder, they will also have access to that folder when they open the appropriate Dfs share.

5. B. Automatic replication can be used only on NTFS volumes.

6. A. Stand-alone Dfs roots are fairly limited. They don't use Active Directory, have no support for root-level Dfs shared folders, can have only a single level of Dfs within the Dfs hierarchy, and offer no support for automatic replication. You would typically use this option only if you had a Windows 2000 member server that was not a part of a domain and you still wanted to use Dfs.

7. D. A domain-based Dfs root can support up to 1,000 Dfs links.

8. A. When you enable file replication services in Dfs, you use the File Replication Service (FRS).

9. A. The Clients Cache the Referral for *x* Seconds option allows you to specify how long the client computer will store information regarding the location of the requested Dfs shared folder.

10. A, D. You can access the Distributed File System utility through Administrative Tools or as an MMC snap-in.

11. A. In order to integrate Dfs with Windows 95, Windows 98, and Windows NT Workstation clients (unless they are Windows NT 4 with Service Pack 3 or higher applied), you need to add the DFS Services for Microsoft Network Client service to the client.

12. C. A limitation of Dfs is that there can be only 260 characters in a Dfs path.

13. C, D. Dfs is hosted on Windows NT Server 4 or Windows 2000 Server computers. Dfs Server cannot be hosted on client operating systems. Clients can access the Dfs topology if the appropriate software is installed on their computers.

14. D. A Dfs topology consists of three main components: a Dfs root, one or more Dfs links, and one or more Dfs shared folders, or replicas. Each Dfs link points to one shared folder and all of its replicas. You can replicate the Dfs root by creating root shares on the other member servers in the domain.

15. A. There can be only one Dfs root per server, although there can be unlimited Dfs roots per domain.

Chapter

9

Managing Network Interoperability

MICROSOFT EXAM OBJECTIVES COVERED IN THIS CHAPTER

- ✓ Install and configure network services for interoperability.
- ✓ Install, configure, and troubleshoot network protocols.
- ✓ Install and configure network services.
- ✓ Install, configure, and troubleshoot network adapters and drivers.

Before you can connect computers over a network, you need to install and configure network adapters on the computers. You also need drivers for the network adapters installed on the computers.

Network connections require the proper network protocols. The three primary protocols that are used by Windows 2000 Server are TCP/IP, NWLink IPX/SPX/NetBIOS, and NetBEUI.

Network services provide IP address management and address resolution functions. The main services used for Windows 2000 network interoperability are Dynamic Host Configuration Protocol (DHCP), Domain Name System (DNS), and Windows Internet Name Service (WINS).

In this chapter, you will learn how to install and configure network adapters, manage network protocols, and install and configure networking services.

Installing and Configuring Network Adapters

Network adapters are hardware used to connect computers (or other devices) to the network. Network adapters are responsible for providing the physical connection to the network and the physical address of the computer. Like all other hardware devices, network adapters need a *driver* in order to communicate with the Windows 2000 operating system.

Microsoft ✓ *Exam* *Objective*	**Install, configure, and troubleshoot network adapters and drivers.**

In the following sections, you will learn how to install and configure network adapters, as well as how to troubleshoot network adapters that are not working properly.

Installing a Network Adapter

Before you physically install your network adapter, you should read the instructions that came with your hardware. If your network adapter is new, it should be self-configuring, with Plug-and-Play capabilities. After you install a network adapter that supports Plug-and-Play, it should work the next time you start up the computer.

New devices will auto-detect settings and be self-configuring. Older devices rely on hardware setup programs to configure hardware. Really old devices require you to manually configure the adapter through switches or jumpers.

If the network adapter is not Plug-and-Play, after you install it, the operating system should detect that you have a new piece of hardware and start a wizard that leads you through the process of loading the adapter's driver. If the Add New Hardware Wizard does not start automatically, you can add the network adapter through the Add/Remove Hardware icon in Control Panel.

Configuring a Network Adapter

After you have installed a network adapter, you can configure it through its Properties dialog box. To access this dialog box, select Start ➢ Settings ➢ Control Panel and double-click the Network and Dial-up Connections icon. Then double-click the Local Area Connection option and click the Configure button in the Local Area Connections Properties dialog box. Alternatively, right-click My Network Places and choose Properties, then right-click Local Area Connection and choose Properties, and then click the Configure button.

In the network adapter Properties dialog box, the properties are grouped on four tabs: General, Advanced, Driver, and Resources. The properties on these tabs are covered in the following sections.

General Network Adapter Properties

The General tab of the network adapter Properties dialog box, shown in Figure 9.1, shows the name of the adapter, the device type, the manufacturer, and the location. The Device Status box reports whether or not the device is working properly. If the device is not working properly, you can click the Troubleshooter button to have Windows 2000 display some general troubleshooting tips. You can also enable or disable the device through the Device Usage drop-down list options.

FIGURE 9.1 The General tab of the network adapter Properties dialog box

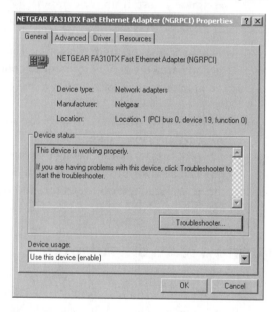

Advanced Network Adapter Properties

The contents of the Advanced tab of the network adapter Properties dialog box will vary depending on the network adapter and driver that you are using. Figure 9.2 shows an example of the Advanced tab for a Fast Ethernet adapter. To configure options in this dialog box, choose the property you want to modify in the Property list box on the left and specify the value for the property in the Value box on the right.

FIGURE 9.2 The Advanced tab of the network adapter Properties dialog box

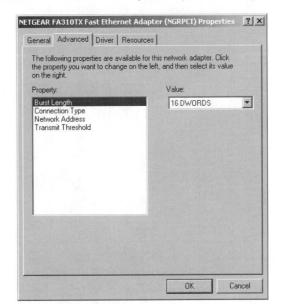

 You should not need to change the settings on the Advanced tab of the network adapter Properties dialog box unless you have been instructed to do so by the manufacturer.

Driver Properties

The Driver tab of the network adapter Properties dialog box, shown in Figure 9.3, provides the following information about your driver:

- The driver provider, which is usually Microsoft or the network adapter manufacturer

- The date that the driver was released

- The driver version, which is useful in determining if you have the latest driver installed

- The digital signer, which is the company that provides the digital signature for driver signing (driver signing is covered in Chapter 3, "Configuring the Windows 2000 Server Environment")

FIGURE 9.3   The Driver tab of the network adapter Properties dialog box

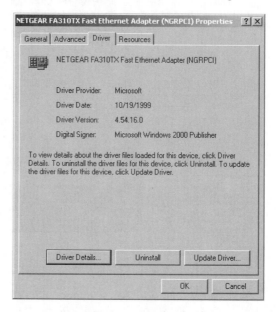

Clicking the Driver Details button at the bottom of the Driver tab brings up the Driver File Details dialog box. This dialog box lists the following details about the driver:

- The location of the driver file, which is useful for troubleshooting

- The original provider of the driver, which is usually the manufacturer

- The file version, which is useful for troubleshooting

- Copyright information about the driver

The Uninstall button at the bottom of the Driver tab removes the driver from your computer. You would uninstall the driver if you were going to replace the driver with a completely new driver. Normally, you update the driver rather than uninstalling it.

To update a driver, click the Update Driver button at the bottom of the Driver tab. This starts the Upgrade Device Driver Wizard, which steps you through upgrading the driver for an existing device.

If you cannot find the driver for your network card or the configuration instructions, check the vendor's Web site. Usually, you will be able to find the latest drivers. You also should be able to locate a list of Frequently Asked Questions (FAQs) about your hardware.

Resource Properties

Each device installed on a computer uses that computer's resources. Resources include interrupt request (IRQ), memory, and I/O (input/output) settings. The Resources tab of the network adapter Properties dialog box lists the resource settings for your network adapter, as shown in Figure 9.4. This information is important for troubleshooting, because if other devices are trying to use the same resource settings, your devices will not work properly. The Conflicting Device List box at the bottom of the Resources tab shows if any conflicts exist.

FIGURE 9.4   The Resources tab of the network adapter Properties dialog box

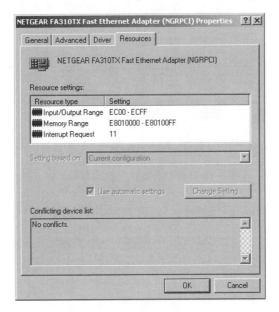

In Exercise 9.1, you will view the properties of your network adapter. This exercise assumes that you have a network adapter installed in your computer.

EXERCISE 9.1

Viewing Network Adapter Properties

1. Select Start ➤ Settings ➤ Control Panel and double-click the Network and Dial-up Connections icon. Double-click the Local Area Connection option. In the Local Area Connection Properties dialog box, click the Configure button.

2. In the General tab of the connection Properties dialog box, click the Configure button under Connect Using.

3. In the General tab of the network adapter Properties dialog box, verify that the Device Status box shows "This device is working properly."

4. Click the Advanced tab. Note the properties that are available for your driver.

5. Click the Driver tab. Note the driver date and version information. Click the Driver Details button to see the location of your network adapter's driver file. Click OK to close the Driver File Details dialog box.

6. Click the Resources tab. Note the resources that are being used by your network adapter. Verify that the Conflicting Device List box shows "No conflicts."

Troubleshooting Network Adapters

If your network adapter is not working, the problem may be with the hardware, the driver software, or the network protocols. The following are some common causes for network adapter problems:

Network adapter not on the HCL — If the device is not on the HCL, you should contact the adapter vendor for advice.

Outdated driver — Make sure that you have the most up-to-date driver for your adapter. You can check for the latest driver on your hardware vendor's Web site.

Network adapter not recognized by Windows 2000	Check Device Manager to see if Windows 2000 recognizes your device. If you do not see your adapter, you will need to manually install it (through the Add/Remove Hardware icon in Control Panel). You should also verify that the adapter's resource settings do not conflict with the resource settings of other devices (check the Resources tab of the network adapter Properties dialog box).
Hardware that is not working properly	Verify that your hardware is working properly. Run any diagnostics that came with the adapter. If everything seems to work properly, make sure that the cable is good and that all of the applicable network hardware is installed properly and is working. This is where it pays off to have spare hardware (such as cables and extra network adapters) that you know works properly.
Improperly configured network protocols	Make sure that your network protocols have been configured properly. Network protocols are covered in detail in the next section of this chapter.

 Check Event Viewer to see if there any messages that give you a hint about what is causing a network adapter error. See Chapter 15, "Performing System Recovery Functions," for details on using Event Viewer.

Installing and Configuring Network Protocols

Network protocols function at the Network and Transport layers of the OSI model. They are responsible for transporting data across an internetwork. You can mix and match the network protocols you use with Windows 2000 Server.

Microsoft ✓ **Exam** **Objective**	**Install, configure, and troubleshoot network protocols.**

Windows 2000 Server supports the following protocols:

- TCP/IP, which is the most commonly used protocol and is installed on Windows 2000 Server computers by default

- NWLink IPX/SPX/NetBIOS, which is used to connect to Novell NetWare networks

- NetBEUI, which is a nonroutable protocol, useful for small networks

- AppleTalk, which is used to support Apple Macintosh computers and is a fully functional, routable protocol

- DLC (Data Link Control), which is primarily used for printers and connections to IBM environments

The following sections describe how to install and configure TCP/IP, NWLink IPX/SPX/NetBIOS, and NetBEUI, which are the primary protocols used with Windows 2000 Server. You will also learn how to manage network bindings.

Using TCP/IP

TCP/IP *(Transmission Control Protocol/Internet Protocol)* is one of the most commonly used network protocols. TCP/IP was originally developed in the 1970s for the Department of Defense (DoD) as a way of connecting dissimilar networks. Since then, TCP/IP has become an industry standard.

On a clean installation of Windows 2000 Server, TCP/IP is installed by default. TCP/IP has the following benefits:

- It is the most commonly used protocol and is supported by almost all network operating systems. It is the required protocol for Internet access.

- TCP/IP is scalable for use in small and large networks. In large networks, TCP/IP provides routing services.

- TCP/IP is designed to be fault tolerant and is able to dynamically reroute packets if network links become unavailable (assuming alternate paths exist).

- Protocol companions like Dynamic Host Configuration Protocol (DHCP) and Domain Name System (DNS) offer advanced functionality.

In the next sections, you will learn how to configure and test TCP/IP.

TCP/IP Protocol Architecture

While the TCP and IP protocols are the most commonly used protocols within the TCP/IP protocol suite, TCP/IP is actually a suite made up of hundreds of protocols. The core protocols that are used by the TCP/IP protocol suite within the framework of the Open Systems Interconnection (OSI) model are shown in Figure 9.5 and defined in Table 9.1.

FIGURE 9.5 TCP/IP Protocol Architecture

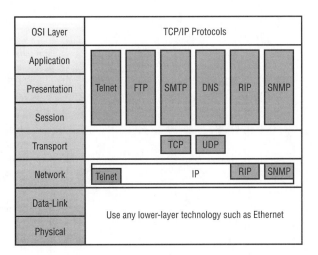

TABLE 9.1 TCP/IP Protocol Descriptions

TCP/IP Protocol	Description
Telnet	Used to provide remote terminal service, or terminal emulation.
FTP	File Transfer Protocol is one of the most widely used TCP/IP protocols. FTP uses TCP to provide connection-oriented file transfer capabilities.
SMTP	Simple Mail Transfer Protocol provides underlying mail transfer capabilities over TCP/IP.
DNS	Domain Name System is used to resolve domain names (host names) to IP addresses.
RIP	Routing Information Protocol is used to provide routing services for TCP/IP networks.
SNMP	Simple Network Management Protocol is a network management protocol that allows SNMP managers to collect information from SNMP agents that run on SNMP clients.
TCP	TCP is used for connection-oriented, reliable services.
UDP	User Datagram Protocol is used for connectionless services. There is no built-in reliability associated with UDP, but because it does not have the overhead associated with connection-oriented services, it transfers data more quickly than TCP.

TABLE 9.1   TCP/IP Protocol Descriptions *(continued)*

TCP/IP Protocol	Description
IP	IP is used to route packets across an internetwork by using network addresses.
ARP	Address Resolution Protocol maps IP addresses to the Media Access Control (MAC) address. The MAC is a hardware address associated with network interface cards.
IGMP	Internet Group Management Protocol is used to manage IP multicast groups.
ICMP	Internet Control Message Protocol is used to detect errors associated with IP transmissions. ICMP is used by the PING utility.

Configuring TCP/IP

TCP/IP requires an IP address and a subnet mask. You can also configure many other optional parameters, such as DNS and Windows Internet Name Service (WINS) settings. Depending on your network setup, TCP/IP configuration is done either manually or dynamically.

Some of the guidelines for TCP/IP configuration include the following:

- The network (IP) address used by a host must be unique to all other network addresses on the network. If you connect directly to the Internet, your IP address must be unique to the Internet.

- The network address can't start with 127. This is a special address range used to test the loopback capability of the local host.

- You can't have a network address of 255 (all 1s). The 255 address is reserved for broadcast transmissions.

- You can't have a network address of 0 (all 0s). The 0 address is reserved to specify that no routing is required for the network packet.

IP Address

The *IP address* uniquely identifies your computer on the network. The IP address is a four-field, 32-bit address, separated by periods. Part of the address is used to identify your network address, and part of the address is used to identify the host (or local) computer's address.

If you use the Internet, then you should register your IP addresses with one of the Internet registration sites. There are three main classes of IP addresses. Depending on the class you use, different parts of the address show the network portion of the address and the host address, as illustrated in Figure 9.6.

FIGURE 9.6   IP class network and host addresses

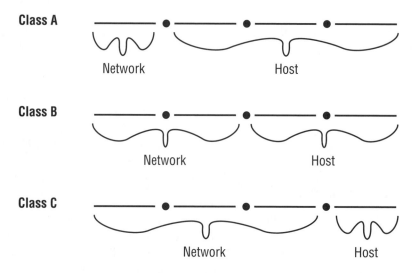

You can find more information about Internet registration at InterNIC's Web site, www.internic.net.

Table 9.2 shows the three classes of network addresses and the number of networks and hosts that are available for each network class.

TABLE 9.2   IP Class Assignments

Network Class	Address Range of First Field	Number of Networks Available	Number of Host Nodes Supported
A	1–126	126	16,777,214

TABLE 9.2 IP Class Assignments *(continued)*

Network Class	Address Range of First Field	Number of Networks Available	Number of Host Nodes Supported
B	128–191	16,384	65,534
C	192–223	2,097,152	254

Subnet Mask

The *subnet mask* is used to specify which part of the IP address is the network address and which part of the address is the host address. By default, the following subnet masks are applied:

Address Class	Subnet Mask	Bits Used by Subnet
Class A	255.0.0.0	11111111 00000000 00000000 00000000
Class B	255.255.0.0	11111111 11111111 00000000 00000000
Class C	255.255.255.0	11111111 11111111 11111111 00000000

By using 255, you are selecting the octet or octets (or in some cases, a piece of an octet) used to identify the network address. For example, in the class B network address 191.200.2.1, if the subnet mask is 255.255.0.0, then 191.200 is the network address and 2.1 is the host address.

The network portion of the network address must always use contiguous bits. Because of this requirement, the network ID is sometimes denoted by using a prefix notation—/<*number of bits*>—to specify the network address. This is also known as Classless Interdomain Routing (CIDR) notation.

The following prefix notations are used by the default network addresses:

- Class A networks would use /8 to represent the number of bits used by the network address.

- Class B networks would use /16 to represent the number of bits used by the network address.

- Class C networks would use /24 to represent the number of bits used by the network address.

Planning Your Subnet Masks

Subnet masks are fairly easy to apply when you use the default subnet masks associated with Class A, B, and C networks. However, life is not always that easy, and you should know how subnets can be further configured to offer greater flexibility in IP address management.

When plan your subnet structure, there are three main steps:

1. Determine the number of network addresses and hosts required by your network. This will be used to determine the number of bits within the IP address that will be used for the network and host addresses.

2. Determine the subnet mask that you will use based on the network class address you are using and the number of network addresses and host addresses you require.

3. Determine the IP address that you will allocate based on the subnet mask you are using.

Subnet masking is covered in greater detail in *MCSE: Windows 2000 Network Infrastructure Administration Study Guide*, 2nd ed., by Paul Robichaux with James Chellis (Sybex, 2001).

Default Gateway

You configure a *default gateway* if the network contains routers. A router is a device that connects two or more network segments together. Routers function at the Network layer of the OSI model.

You can configure a Windows 2000 server to act as a router by installing two or more network cards in the server, attaching each network card to a different network segment, and then configuring each network card for the segment that it will attach to. You can also use third-party routers, which typically offer more features than Windows 2000 servers configured as routers.

As an example, suppose that your network is configured as shown in Figure 9.7. Network A uses the IP network address 131.1.0.0. Network B uses the IP network address 131.2.0.0. In this case, each network card in the router should be configured with an IP address from the segment that the network card is addressed to.

FIGURE 9.7   Configuring default gateways

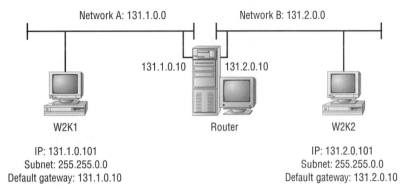

Network A: 131.1.0.0   Network B: 131.2.0.0

131.1.0.10   131.2.0.10

W2K1   Router   W2K2

IP: 131.1.0.101   IP: 131.2.0.101
Subnet: 255.255.0.0   Subnet: 255.255.0.0
Default gateway: 131.1.0.10   Default gateway: 131.2.0.10

You configure the computers on each segment to point to the IP address of the network card on the router that is attached to their network segment. For example, in Figure 9.7, the computer W2K1 is attached to Network A. The default gateway that would be configured for this computer is 131.1.0.10. The computer W2K2 is attached to Network B. The default gateway that would be configured for this computer is 131.2.0.10.

DNS Servers

DNS servers are used to resolve host names to IP addresses. This makes it easier for people to access domain hosts.

Do you know what the IP address is for the White House? It's 198.137.240.91. Do you know the host name of the White House? It's `www.whitehouse.gov`. You can understand why many people might not know the IP address but would know the host name.

When you access the Internet and type in `www.whitehouse.gov`, there are DNS servers that resolve the host name to the proper IP address. If you do not have access to a properly configured DNS server, you can configure a *HOSTS file* for your computer. A HOSTS file contains the mappings of IP addresses to the domain hosts that you need to access. DNS servers are covered in greater detail in the "Using DNS" section later in this chapter.

WINS Servers

WINS servers are used to resolve *Network Basic Input/Output System (NetBIOS)* names to IP addresses. Windows 2000 uses NetBIOS names in addition to host names to identify network computers. This is mainly for backward-compatibility with Windows NT 4, which used this addressing scheme extensively. When you attempt to access a computer using the Net-BIOS name, the system must be able to resolve the NetBIOS name to an IP address. This address resolution can be accomplished by using one of the following methods:

- Through a broadcast (if the computer you are trying to reach is on the same network segment)

- Through a WINS server

- Through an *LMHOSTS file*, which is a static mapping of IP addresses to NetBIOS computer names

WINS servers are covered in greater detail in the "Using DNS" section later in this chapter.

Manual IP Configuration

You can manually configure IP if you know your IP address and subnet mask. If you are using optional components such as a default gateway or a DNS server, you need to know the IP addresses of the computers that host these services as well.

To manually configure IP, take the following steps:

1. From the Desktop, right-click My Network Places and choose Properties.

2. Right-click Local Area Connection and choose Properties.

3. In the Local Area Connection Properties dialog box, highlight Internet Protocol (TCP/IP) and click the Properties button.

4. The Internet Protocol (TCP/IP) Properties dialog box appears, as shown in Figure 9.8. Choose the Use the Following IP Address radio button.

5. In the appropriate text boxes, specify the IP address, subnet mask, and default gateway (optional) that you want to use.

6. Optionally, select the Use the Following DNS Server Addresses radio button and specify a preferred and alternate DNS server in the corresponding text boxes.

7. Click the OK button to save your settings and close the dialog box.

FIGURE 9.8   The Internet Protocol (TCP/IP) Properties dialog box

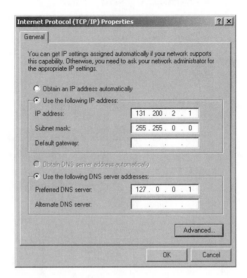

Advanced Configuration

Clicking the Advanced button in the Internet Protocol (TCP/IP) dialog box (see Figure 9.8) opens the Advanced TCP/IP Settings dialog box, shown in Figure 9.9. From this dialog box, you can configure advanced DNS and WINS settings.

FIGURE 9.9   The Advanced TCP/IP Setting dialog box

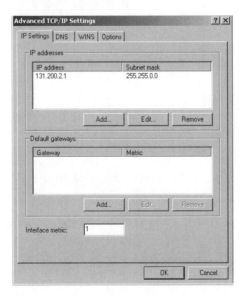

ADVANCED DNS SETTINGS

You can configure additional DNS servers that can be used for name resolution and other advanced DNS settings through the DNS tab of the Advanced TCP/IP Settings dialog box, shown in Figure 9.10. The options in this dialog box are described in Table 9.3.

FIGURE 9.10   The DNS tab of the Advanced TCP/IP Settings dialog box

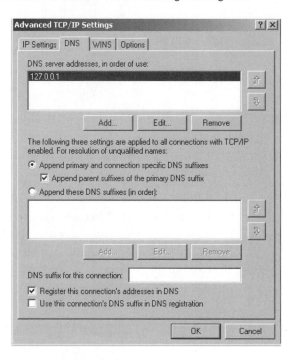

TABLE 9.3   Advanced DNS TCP/IP Settings Options

Option	Description
DNS Server Addresses, in Order of Use	Specifies the DNS servers that are used to resolve DNS queries. You can use the arrow buttons on the right side of the list box to move the servers up or down in the list.

TABLE 9.3   Advanced DNS TCP/IP Settings Options *(continued)*

Option	Description
Append Primary and Connection Specific DNS Suffixes	Specifies how unqualified domain names are resolved by DNS. For example, if your primary DNS suffix is TestCorp.com and you type ping lala, DNS will try to resolve the host name as lala.TestCorp.com.
Append Parent Suffixes of the Primary DNS Suffix	Specifies whether name resolution includes the parent suffix for the primary domain DNS suffix, up to the second level of the domain name. For example, if your primary DNS suffix is SanJose.TestCorp.com and you type ping lala, DNS will try to resolve the host name as lala.SanJose.TestCorp.com. If this doesn't work, DNS will try to resolve the host name as lala.TestCorp.com.
Append These DNS Suffixes (in order)	Specifies the DNS suffixes that will be used to attempt to resolve unqualified name resolution. For example, if your primary DNS suffix is TestCorp.com and you type ping lala, DNS will try to resolve the host name as lala.TestCorp.com. If you append the additional DNS suffix MyCorp.com and type ping lala, DNS will try to resolve the host name as lala.TestCorp.com and lala.MyCorp.com.
DNS Suffix for This Connection	Specifies the DNS suffix for the connection. If this value is configured by a DHCP server and you specify a DNS suffix, it will override the value set by DHCP.

TABLE 9.3 Advanced DNS TCP/IP Settings Options *(continued)*

Option	Description
Register This Connection's Address in DNS	Specifies that the computer will try to register its address dynamically using the computer name that was specified through the Network Identification tab of the System Properties dialog box (accessed through the System icon in Control Panel).
Use This Connection's DNS Suffix in DNS Registration	Specifies that when the computer registers automatically with the DNS server, it should use the combination of the computer name and the DNS suffix.

ADVANCED WINS SETTINGS

You can configure advanced WINS options through the WINS tab in the Advanced TCP/IP Settings dialog box, shown in Figure 9.11. The options in this dialog box are described in Table 9.4.

FIGURE 9.11 The WINS tab of the Advanced TCP/IP Settings dialog box

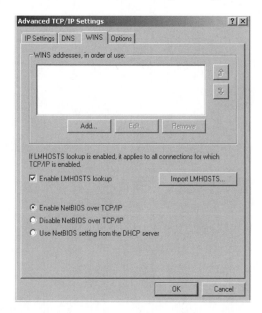

TABLE 9.4   Advanced WINS TCP/IP Settings Options

Option	Description
WINS Addresses, in Order of Use	Specifies the WINS servers that are used to resolve WINS queries. You can use the arrow buttons on the right side of the list box to move the servers up or down in the list.
Enable LMHOSTS Lookup	Specifies whether an LMHOSTS file can be used for name resolution. If you configure this option, you can use the Import LMHOSTS button to import an LMHOSTS file to the computer.
Enable NetBIOS over TCP/IP	Allows you to use statically config-ured IP addresses so that the com-puter is able to communicate with pre–Windows 2000 computers.
Disable NetBIOS over TCP/IP	Allows you to disable NetBIOS over TCP/IP. Use this option only if your network includes only Windows 2000 clients or DNS-enabled clients.
Use NetBIOS Settings from the DHCP Server	Specifies that the computer should obtain its NetBIOS-over-TCP/IP and WINS settings from the DHCP server.

Dynamic IP Configuration

Dynamic IP configuration assumes that you have a *DHCP server* on your network. DHCP servers are configured to provide DHCP clients with all of their IP configuration information automatically. DHCP servers are covered in greater detail in the "Using DHCP" section later in this chapter.

By default, when TCP/IP is installed on a Windows 2000 Server com-puter, the computer is configured for dynamic IP configuration. If your computer is configured for manual IP configuration and you want to use dynamic IP configuration, take the following steps:

  1. From the Desktop, right-click My Network Places and choose Properties.

2. Right-click Local Area Connection and choose Properties.

3. In the Local Area Connection Properties dialog box, highlight Internet Protocol (TCP/IP) and click the Properties button.

4. The Internet Protocol (TCP/IP) Properties dialog box appears (see Figure 9.8). Choose the Obtain an IP Address Automatically radio button. Then click the OK button.

Testing IP Configuration

After you have configured IP, you can test the IP configuration by using the IPCONFIG and PING commands.

The *IPCONFIG* Command

The *IPCONFIG* command displays your IP configuration. Table 9.5 lists some of the command switches that can be used with IPCONFIG command.

TABLE 9.5 IPCONFIG Switches

Switch	Description
/all	Shows verbose information about your IP configuration, including your computer's physical address, the DNS server you are using, and whether you are using DHCP
/release	Releases an address that has been assigned through DHCP
/renew	Renews an address through DHCP
/flushdns	Purges the local DNS resolver cache
/registerdns	Refreshes all DHCP leases and re-registers the computer name and IP address with the DNS server
/displaydns	Displays the contents of the local DNS resolver cache
/showclassid	Displays all of the DHCP class IDs that the adapter can use
/setclassid	Allows you to modify the DHCP class ID

In Exercise 9.2, you will verify your configuration with the IPCONFIG command.

EXERCISE 9.2

Using the IPCONFIG Command

1. Select Start ➢ Programs ➢ Accessories ➢ Command Prompt.

2. In the Command Prompt dialog box, type **IPCONFIG** and press Enter. Note the IP address, which should be the address that you configured when the computer was installed.

3. In the Command Prompt dialog box, type **IPCONFIG /all** and press Enter. You now see more information.

4. Type **exit** and press Enter.

The *PING* Command

The *PING* command is used to send an Internet Control Message Protocol (ICMP) echo request and echo reply to verify if the remote computer is available. The PING command has the following syntax:

```
PING IP address
```

For example, if your IP address is 131.200.2.30, type the following command:

```
PING 131.200.2.30
```

PING is useful for verifying connectivity between two hosts. For example, if you were having trouble connecting to a host on another network, you would use PING to verify that a valid communication path existed by pinging the following addresses:

- The loopback address, 127.0.0.1

- The local computer's IP address (you can verify this with IPCONFIG)

- The local router's (default gateway's) IP address

- The remote computer's IP address

If PING failed to get a reply from any of these addresses, you would have a starting point for troubleshooting the connection error.

Using NWLink IPX/SPX/NetBIOS

NWLink IPX/SPX/NetBIOS Compatible Transport is Microsoft's implementation of the Novell Internetwork Packet Exchange/Sequenced Packet Exchange (IPX/SPX) protocol stack. The Windows 2000 implementation of the IPX/SPX protocol stack adds NetBIOS support.

The main function of NWLink is to act as a transport protocol to route packets through internetworks. By itself, the NWLink protocol does not allow you to access NetWare File and Print Services. However, it does provide a method of transporting the data across the network. If you want to access NetWare File and Print Services, you need to install NWLink and Client Services for NetWare (CSNW) on your Windows 2000 client or Gateway Services for NetWare (GSNW) on your Windows 2000 Server computer. CSNW and GSNW are software packages that work at the upper layers of the OSI model to allow access to NetWare File and Print Services.

One advantage of using NWLink is that it is easy to install and configure. The following sections describe how to install and configure this protocol.

Installing NWLink IPX/SPX/NetBIOS

To install NWLink, take the following steps:

1. From the Desktop, right-click My Network Places and choose Properties.

2. Right-click Local Area Connection and choose Properties.

3. In the Local Area Connection Properties dialog box, click the Install button.

4. The Select Network Component Type dialog box appears. Highlight Protocol and click the Add button.

5. The Select Network Protocol dialog box appears. Select NWLink IPX/SPX/NetBIOS Compatible Transport Protocol from the list. Then click the OK button.

In Exercise 9.3, you will install the NWLink IPX/SPX protocol. This exercise assumes that you have a network adapter installed in your computer.

Installing the NWLink IPX/SPX Protocol

1. From the Desktop, right-click My Network Places and choose Properties.

2. Right-click Local Area Connection and choose Properties.

3. In the Local Area Connection Properties dialog box, click the Install button.

4. In the Select Network Component Type dialog box, highlight Protocol and click the Add button.

5. In the Select Network Protocol dialog box, select NWLink IPX/SPX/ NetBIOS Compatible Transport Protocol and click the OK button.

Configuring NWLink IPX/SPX

The only options that you need to configure for NWLink are the *internal network number* and the *frame type*. Normally, you leave both settings at their default values.

The internal network number is usually used to identify NetWare file servers. It is also used if you are running File and Print Services for NetWare or are using IPX routing.

The frame type specifies how the data is packaged for transmission over the network. If the computers that are using NWLink use different frame types, they are not able to communicate with each other. By default, the frame type is set to Auto Detect, which will attempt to automatically choose a compatible frame type for your network. If you are using NetWare 3.12 or higher, the default frame type used by the NetWare server is Ethernet 802.2. If you select Auto Detect, and Ethernet 802.2 is detected on the network, then this is the frame type that will be used by your computer. If you need to connect to NetWare servers using different frame types, you will have to manually configure all of the frame types in use through the NWLink Properties dialog box.

To configure NWLink IPX/SPX, take the following steps:

1. From the Desktop, right-click My Network Places and select Properties.

2. Right-click Local Area Connection and select Properties.

3. In the Local Area Connection Properties dialog box, highlight NWLink IPX/SPX/NetBIOS Compatible Transport Protocol and click the Properties button.

4. The NWLink IPX/SPX/NetBIOS Compatible Transport Protocol Properties dialog box appears, as shown in Figure 9.12. In this dialog box, you can configure your internal network number and frame type.

FIGURE 9.12 The NWLink IPX/SPX/NetBIOS Compatible Transport Protocol Properties dialog box

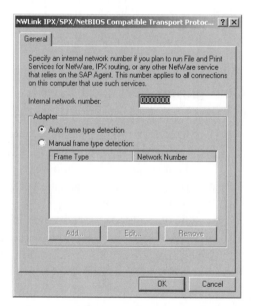

Using NetBEUI

NetBEUI stands for NetBIOS Extended User Interface. It was developed in the mid-1980s to connect workgroups that were running the OS/2 and LAN Manager operating systems.

The NetBEUI protocol offers the following advantages:

- It is easy to install.
- There are no configuration requirements.
- NetBEUI has self-tuning capabilities.
- NetBEUI has less overhead than TCP/IP and IPX/SPX and thus offers better performance.
- NetBEUI uses less memory than TCP/IP and IPX/SPX.

The main disadvantage of the NetBEUI protocol is that it is not routable, so you cannot use it in networks that have more than one network segment. Also, NetBEUI is not as commonly accepted as the TCP/IP protocol.

To install NetBEUI, take the following steps:

1. From the Desktop, right-click My Network Places and select Properties.

2. Right-click Local Area Connection and select Properties.

3. In the Local Area Connection Properties dialog box, click the Install button.

4. In the Select Network Component Type dialog box, highlight Protocol and click the Add button.

5. In the Select Network Protocol dialog box, select NetBEUI Protocol from the list and click the OK button.

Managing Network Bindings

Bindings are used to enable communication between your network adapter and the network protocols that are installed. If you have multiple network protocols installed on your computer, you can improve performance by binding the most commonly used protocols higher in the binding order.

To configure network bindings, access the Network and Dial-up Connections window and then select Advanced ➢ Advanced Settings from the main menu bar. The Adapters and Binding tab of the Advanced Settings dialog box appears, as shown in Figure 9.13. For each local area connection, if there are multiple protocols listed, you can use the arrow buttons on the right side of the dialog box to move the protocols to the top or bottom of the binding order.

FIGURE 9.13 The Adapters and Bindings tab of the Advanced Settings dialog box

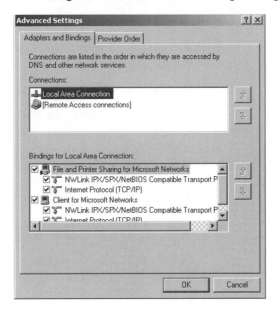

Installing and Configuring Network Services

T he main services that are used for network interoperability are DHCP, DNS, and WINS. In Windows 2000 networks, only Windows 2000 Server computers can act as DHCP, WINS, and DNS servers. A single computer can have all three services loaded on it.

Microsoft ✓ *Exam* *Objective*

Install and configure network services for interoperability.

Install and configure network services.

The following operating systems are supported as clients:

- Windows 2000 Professional or Server
- Windows NT 3.51 or later, Workstation or Server
- Windows 95 or Windows 98
- Windows for Workgroups 3.11 (with TCP/IP-32)
- Microsoft Network Client version 3.0 for Microsoft MS-DOS with the real-mode TCP/IP driver
- Microsoft LAN Manager version 2.2c (OS/2 version not supported)

Installing Network Services

You install the DHCP, WINS, and DNS services through the Add/Remove Programs icon in Control Panel. The following steps are used to install a network service on a Windows 2000 Server computer:

1. Confirm that the server is configured with a static IP address by checking the TCP/IP properties.

2. Select Start ➢ Settings ➢ Control Panel. Double-click the Add/Remove Programs icon.

3. The Add/Remove Programs window appears. Click the Add/Remove Windows Components option.

4. The Windows Components Wizard starts, as shown in Figure 9.14. Select Networking Services and click the Details button.

FIGURE 9.14 The Windows Components Wizard dialog box

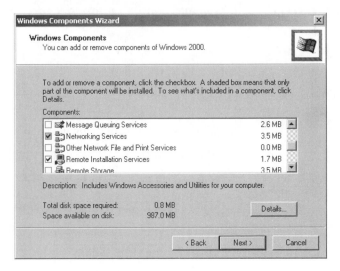

5. The Networking Services dialog box appears, as shown in Figure 9.15. Check the check box for the service you want to install: Dynamic Host Configuration Protocol (DHCP), Windows Internet Name Service (WINS), or Domain Name System (DNS). Then click the OK button.

FIGURE 9.15 The Networking Services dialog box

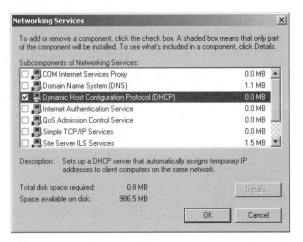

6. You return to the Windows Components dialog box. Click the Next button.

7. The Completing the Windows Components Wizard dialog box appears. Click the Finish button.

8. You return to the Add/Remove Programs window. Click the Close button. Close Control Panel.

After you've installed the appropriate networking service, you can configure the DHCP, WINS, or DNS server. For each networking service installed, you will see a corresponding item in the Administrative Tools group.

You can also add the DHCP, WINS, and DNS snap-ins to the MMC. See Chapter 3, "Configuring the Windows 2000 Server Environment," for more information about snap-ins to the MMC.

In Exercise 9.4, you will install DHCP, WINS, and DNS on your member server.

EXERCISE 9.4

Installing DHCP, WINS, and DNS

1. From the Desktop, right-click My Network Places, choose Properties, right-click Local Area Connection, and choose Properties. In the Local Area Connection Properties dialog box, highlight Internet Protocol (TCP/IP) and click the Properties button. Confirm that the Windows 2000 Server computer is configured with a static IP address. Close all open dialog boxes.

2. Select Start ➢ Settings ➢ Control Panel and double-click the Add/ Remove Programs icon.

3. In the Add/Remove Programs window, click the Add/Remove Windows Components option.

4. In the Windows Components Wizard dialog box, select Networking Services and click the Details button.

5. In the Networking Services dialog box, check the Dynamic Host Configuration Protocol (DHCP), the Windows Internet Name Service (WINS), and the Domain Name System (DNS) check boxes and click the OK button.

6. In the Windows Components dialog box, click the Next button.

7. In the Completing the Windows Components Wizard dialog box, click the Finish button.

8. In the Add/Remove Programs dialog box, click the Close button. Then close Control Panel.

Using DHCP

Each device that will use TCP/IP on your network must have a valid, unique IP address. In order to help alleviate the problem of tracking and assigning valid IP addresses, the Internet Engineering Task Force (IETF) has worked with industry leaders to develop DHCP. As with all development on the Internet, this protocol has been discussed in a series of Requests for Comments (RFCs), which are available at numerous Internet sites.

The RFCs that pertain to DHCP are 1533, 1534, 1541, and 1542. These RFCs can be found at www.ietf.org/rfc.html.

In order to act as a DHCP server, the Windows 2000 Server computer must meet the following requirements:

- Have the DHCP networking service installed

- Have a static IP address configured

- Have a valid range of IP addresses that can be assigned to DHCP clients

All of the Microsoft operating systems listed earlier are supported as DHCP clients, as well as non-Microsoft operating systems such as Unix and Macintosh.

Understanding DHCP Implementation

DHCP is implemented as a client/server service, as illustrated in Figure 9.16. DHCP works in the following manner:

1. When the client computer starts up, it sends a broadcast DHCPDIS-COVER message, requesting a DHCP server. The request includes the hardware address of the client computer.

2. Any DHCP server receiving the broadcast that has available IP addresses will send a DHCPOFFER message to the client, offering an IP address for a set period of time (called a *lease*), a subnet mask, and a server identifier (the IP address of the DHCP server). The address that is offered by the server is marked as unavailable and will not be offered to any other clients during the DHCP negotiation period.

3. The client selects one of the offers and broadcasts a DHCPREQUEST message, indicating its selection. This allows any DHCP offers that were not accepted to be returned to the pool of available IP addresses.

4. The DHCP server that was selected sends back a DHCPACK message as acknowledgment, indicating the IP address, subnet mask, and the duration of the lease that the client computer will use. It may also send additional configuration information, such as the address of the default gateway or the DNS server address.

FIGURE 9.16 The DHCP lease-generation process

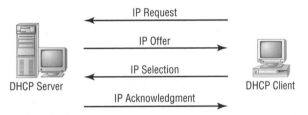

DHCP Server   DHCP Client

 TIP

A mnemonic device for remembering the four steps in the DHCP lease-generation process is ROSA: IP lease **R**equest, IP lease **O**ffer, IP lease **S**election, IP lease **A**cknowledgment.

 Real World Scenario

The Need for DHCP

You have inherited a network that has been using static IP addresses. Whenever an IP address needs to be assigned you must check a database that lists all of the available IP addresses. This is a time consuming task as you have many users who travel between your company's four offices.

Many problems have been encountered as a result of static IP management. Unfortunately, the methods used to manage IP addresses manually are only as good as their last update. If an administrator forgets to note that an address is already assigned, the same address could be assigned twice. This would be equivalent to the phone company assigning two customers the same phone number. It's also possible for administrators to mistype IP addresses, which can lead to duplicate addresses or completely wrong addresses. Sometimes, users unwittingly contribute to the problem by copying configuration information from a co-worker's computer or by trying to guess an IP address when the system administrator is not available.

Microsoft TCP/IP tries to minimize the problems of duplicate IP addresses by sending out an Address Resolution Protocol (ARP) broadcast when a computer initializes the TCP/IP protocol stack. If another computer replies to the ARP broadcast, that means that the IP address that is being requested is already in use, and TCP/IP will not be initialized on the new computer. Both computers will receive a warning message that an IP address has been duplicated.

Computers being moved from one subnet to another without reconfiguring the IP address cause another common problem. If a computer moves from one subnet to another, the IP address must be modified to reflect the new network and subnet address. If the IP address isn't updated after such a move, TCP/IP will initialize, but the computer will not be able to communicate with other computers on the network, because it will think that local traffic is remote and remote traffic is local.

By deciding to implement DHCP, you can eliminate the problems associated with static IP management. You can create a pool of IP addresses that can be dynamically allocated to users as needed. As users attach to the network as DHCP clients, the DHCP server will automatically offer the appropriate IP configuration for the network the client attaches to. This will also greatly simplify network management for users who travel between offices.

Configuring a DHCP Server

After the DHCP service is installed (see Exercise 9.4), you will see the DHCP program item in Administrative Tools.

To configure your DHCP server, take the following steps:

1. Select Start ➢ Programs ➢ Administrative Tools ➢ DHCP.

2. The DHCP window appears, as shown in Figure 9.17. Right-click your server and select New Scope from the pop-up menu.

FIGURE 9.17 The DHCP window

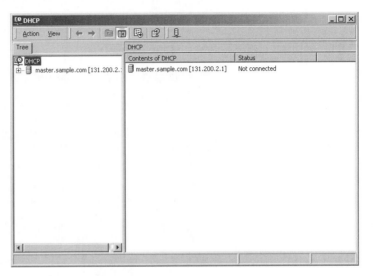

3. The New Scope Wizard starts. Click the Next button.

4. The Scope Name dialog box appears, as shown in Figure 9.18. Type in a name and comment that will be used to identify the scope. Click the Next button.

FIGURE 9.18 The Scope Name dialog box

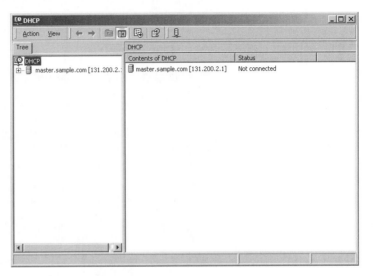

5. The IP Address Range dialog box appears, as shown in Figure 9.19. Type the starting and ending IP addresses in the corresponding text boxes to define the address range for the DHCP scope. Specify the subnet mask that will be used by the DHCP scope, either by selecting a length or by entering an IP address, and click the Next button.

FIGURE 9.19 The IP Address Range dialog box

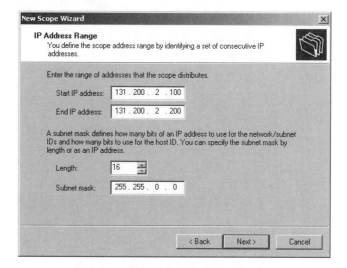

6. The Add Exclusions dialog box appears, as shown in Figure 9.20. In this dialog box, you can identify any addresses to exclude within the specified DHCP scope. Exclusions are used to reserve IP addresses that are already in use or are static. To exclude a single address, type the address in the Start IP Address text box and click the Add button. To exclude a range of contiguous IP addresses, type the starting and ending IP addresses in the respective text boxes and click the Add button. The Remove button is used to remove excluded addresses. When you have configured any address exclusions, click the Next button.

FIGURE 9.20 The Add Exclusions dialog box

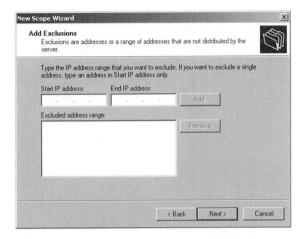

7. The Lease Duration dialog box appears, as shown in Figure 9.21. In this dialog box, you specify how long the client will be able to use the IP address before the IP address is returned to the DHCP scope. By default, a DHCP client will attempt to renew its IP address when half of the lease period has expired. The default lease period is eight days. You might want to shorten the lease period if you have a limited number of IP addresses in your scope compared to the number of clients who require IP addresses. After you configure your scope, click the Next button.

FIGURE 9.21 The Lease Duration dialog box

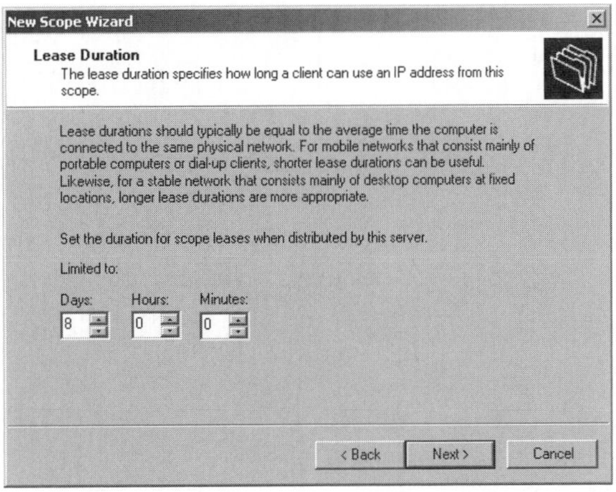

8. The Configure DHCP Options dialog box appears. You can choose to configure the most common IP configuration options from this dialog box. The alternative is to select No, I Will Configure These Options Later, and assign default gateways, DNS servers, and WINS servers at another time (but before clients use any of the IP addresses in the DHCP scope). In this example, the Yes, I Want to Configure These Options Now option is selected to configure additional DHCP settings. Click the Next button to continue.

9. The Router (Default Gateway) dialog box appears, as shown in Figure 9.22. Specify the IP address of the default gateway that will be used by your DHCP clients and click the Add button. Click the Next button.

FIGURE 9.22 The Router (Default Gateway) dialog box

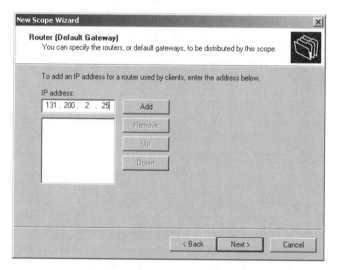

10. The Domain Name and DNS Servers dialog box appears, as shown in Figure 9.23. This dialog box allows you to configure the parent domain that your DHCP clients will use for DNS name resolution. You can also configure the server name and IP addresses of DNS servers that will be used for DNS name resolution. After you specify this information, click the Next button.

FIGURE 9.23   The Domain Name and DNS Servers dialog box

11. The WINS Servers dialog box appears, as shown in Figure 9.24. This dialog box allows you to configure the primary and secondary WINS servers that are used to resolve NetBIOS computer names to IP addresses. Specify the WINS server information and click the Next button.

FIGURE 9.24   The WINS Servers dialog box

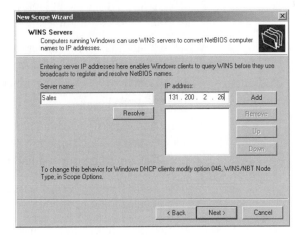

12. The Activate Scope dialog box appears. This dialog box allows you to specify whether or not you will activate the DHCP scope. DHCP clients can only use the services of active DHCP scopes. You can choose to activate this scope now or to activate it later. After you specify whether or not to activate the scope, click the Finish button.

13. The Completing the New Scope Wizard dialog box appears. Click the Finish button.

14. In order to protect the network against rogue DHCP servers, you must also authorize the DHCP server. To do this, right-click the DHCP server in the main DHCP window and select Authorize from the pop-up menu.

In Exercise 9.5, you will configure the DHCP server that you installed in Exercise 9.4.

EXERCISE 9.5

Configuring a DHCP Server

1. Select Start ➤ Programs ➤ Administrative Tools ➤ DHCP.

2. In the DHCP window, right-click your server and select New Scope.

3. When the New Scope Wizard starts, click the Next button.

4. In the Scope Name dialog box, type **Practice** in the Name text box and leave the Comment box blank. Click the Next button.

5. In the IP Address Range dialog box, type **131.200.2.100** in the Start IP Address text box, and type **131.200.2.200** in the End IP Address Range text box. In the Subnet Mask text box, type **255.255.0.0**. Click the Next button.

6. In the Add Exclusions dialog box, type **131.200.2.150** in the Start IP Address text box, and type **131.200.2.159** in the End IP Address text box. Click the Add button, and then click the Next button.

7. In the Lease Duration dialog box, click the Next button to accept the default values and continue.

8. In the Configure DHCP Options dialog box, select the No, I Will Configure These Options Later option and click the Next button. You can configure these options later by clicking Server Options in the DHCP utility.

EXERCISE 9.5 *(continued)*

9. In the Completing the New Scope Wizard dialog box, click the Finish button.

10. In the DHCP window, right-click your scope and select Activate.

If the DHCP server and DHCP clients are on different network subnets, the DHCP server will not serve the DHCP clients by default since DHCP clients rely on broadcasts to contact the DHCP server and most routers do not forward broadcasts. To overcome this problem, you can either use the Microsoft DHCP Relay Agent or use an RFC 2131 (supercedes RFC 1542) compliant router which contains a DHCP Relay Agent. You will also need to configure a scope on the DHCP server for the remote subnet. On a Windows 2000 Server, the DHCP Relay Agent is configured in the Routing and Remote Access utility.

Using WINS

Prior to Windows 2000, Windows clients such as Windows 9*x* and Windows NT 4 clients used NetBIOS names to communicate with other computers on the network. WINS servers are used to resolve NetBIOS computer names to IP addresses.

When a client attempts to communicate with another computer using a NetBIOS name in a WINS environment, the following steps are used to resolve the NetBIOS name to an IP address:

1. The client will check its local NetBIOS name cache to see if it contains a NetBIOS-to-IP address mapping.

2. If the request is not resolved, the client will send a name query to the primary WINS server.

3. If the primary WINS server is not available after three attempts, the client will send a name query to the secondary WINS server.

4. If no WINS server can resolve the name, a network broadcast is initiated to attempt to locate the remote computer.

Once a WINS server is installed and the WINS clients are configured, WINS name registration will occur automatically. When the WINS client starts, it will automatically send its IP address and NetBIOS name to the designated WINS server. It queries the WINS server to verify that the NetBIOS name that the client is using is not already in use. This process also occurs if the IP address information changes (for example, the computer moves to another subnet or DHCP assigns new configuration information). Name registration is temporary, so the WINS client must renew its name registration on a periodic basis.

You can install a WINS server as described in the "Installing Network Services" section earlier in this chapter. In order to act as a WINS server, the Windows 2000 Server computer must meet the following requirements:

- Have the WINS service installed

- Have a static IP address, subnet mask, and default gateway (if routing is used) configured

After WINS is installed, you will see the WINS program item in the Administrative Tools group. You can view WINS database entries and configure the WINS server through this utility.

Using DNS

DNS is used with the Internet and with private networks to resolve host (computer) names to IP addresses. The host name does not need to be the same as the Windows 2000 computer name, but this is the default setting.

DNS is a hierarchical structure that is used to logically organize domain names. The top of the hierarchical structure is represented by a period. Examples of top-level domains include .com, .edu, .gov, and extensions for geographical locations. Companies, organizations, and individuals register second-level domains.

In order to access a host, you use a fully qualified domain name (FQDN). DNS then uses the FQDN to resolve the host name to a specific IP address.

To act as a DNS server, the Windows 2000 Server computer must be configured with the TCP/IP protocol using a static IP address. DNS can only be installed on Windows 2000 Server computers.

Understanding Name Resolution

The following process is used when DNS clients query DNS servers for name resolution:

1. The DNS client queries the DNS server that it is configured to use for name resolution.

2. If the DNS server can resolve the query, it returns a response to the DNS client. This is called an iterative query.

3. If the DNS server cannot resolve the query, the DNS server contacts other DNS servers on behalf of the DNS client to attempt to resolve the query. This is called a recursive query.

When you query a DNS server, you can make two types of queries:

- Forward lookup queries are requests to map an FQDN to an IP address.

- Reverse lookup queries are requests to map an IP address to a FQDN.

Windows 2000 supports dynamic DNS. This means that if you use DHCP to assign IP addresses, the name-to-IP mapping will be automatically registered with DNS servers when the DHCP configuration information is registered with the DHCP configuration.

Configuring a DNS Server

After DNS is installed (see Exercise 9.4), you will see the DNS program item in the Administrative Tools group.

The following steps are used to configure a DNS server:

1. Select Start ➤ Programs ➤ Administrative Tools ➤ DNS.

2. The DNS window appears, as shown in Figure 9.25. Right-click your DNS server and select Configure the Server from the pop-up menu.

FIGURE 9.25 The DNS window

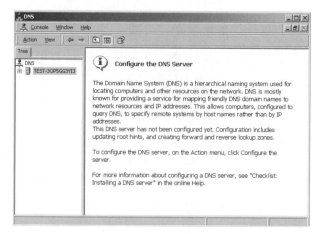

3. The Configure DNS Server Wizard starts. Click the Next button.

4. The Root Server dialog box appears, as shown in Figure 9.26. In this dialog box, you indicate whether this is the first DNS server on your network or if your network already has a DNS server. If you choose the This Is the First DNS Server on This Network option, this computer becomes the root server. If you are configuring DNS on a server in a network that is using the Active Directory, a DNS server will already be running. In this example, the One or More DNS Servers Are Running on This Network option is selected. Click the Next button.

FIGURE 9.26 The Root Server dialog box

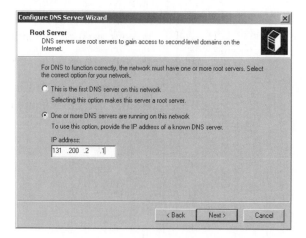

5. The Forward Lookup Zone dialog box appears. Forward lookup zones are database files that contain the DNS domain name-to-IP address mappings. Choose whether or not this file is created. In this example, the Yes, Create a Forward Lookup Zone option is selected. Click the Next button.

6. The Zone Type dialog box appears, as shown in Figure 9.27. In this dialog box, you specify the type of zone that is created. There are three types of zones that can be configured:

   - Active Directory-integrated, which is used with the Active Directory to store and replicate zone files. Zone database files are replicated when Active Directory replication occurs. This option is only available on a Domain Controller.

   - Standard primary, which is a master copy of a new zone and stores the zone database file as a text file.

   - Standard secondary, which is a copy (replica) of an existing zone file. This option is used for redundancy and load balancing.

   After you make your selection, click the Next button.

FIGURE 9.27 The Zone Type dialog box

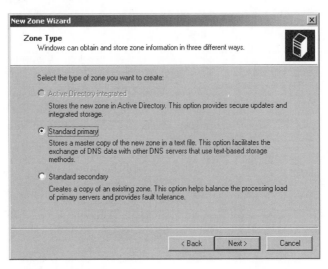

7. If you chose to create a standard primary zone in the previous step, the Zone Name dialog box appears. This dialog box allows you to specify

the name of the zone. The zone name should be your registered domain name. Enter a name and click the Next button.

8. The Zone File dialog box appears, as shown in Figure 9.28. This dialog box allows you to create a new file for the zone or to use an existing file that may have been copied from another computer. After you make your selection, click the Next button.

FIGURE 9.28 The Zone File dialog box

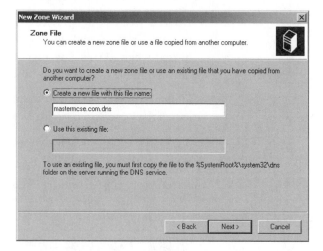

9. The Reverse Lookup Zone dialog box appears. A reverse lookup zone file is used to translate IP addresses to DNS names. If you want people to access your DNS server via an IP address select yes, otherwise select No. In this example, the No, Do Not Create a Reverse Lookup Zone option is selected. Click the Next button.

10. The Completing the Configure the DNS Server Wizard dialog box appears. If all of the information is correct, click the Finish button.

In Exercise 9.6, you will configure the DNS server you created in Exercise 9.4.

EXERCISE 9.6

Configuring a DNS Server

1. Select Start ➤ Programs ➤ Administrative Tools ➤ DNS.

2. In the DNS window, right-click your DNS server and select Configure the Server.

3. When the Configure DNS Server Wizard starts, click the Next button.

4. In the Root Server dialog box, click the This Is the First DNS Server on the Network radio button, and then click the Next button.

5. In the Forward Lookup Zone dialog box, select the Yes, Create a Forward Lookup Zone option and click the Next button.

6. In the Zone Type dialog box, select the Standard Primary option and click the Next button.

7. In the Zone Name dialog box, type `mastermcse.com` and click the Next button.

8. In the Zone File dialog box, select the Create a New File with This File Name option and accept the default filename. Click the Next button.

9. In the Reverse Lookup Zone dialog box, select the No, Do Not Create a Reverse Lookup Zone and click the Next button.

10. In the Completing the Configure the DNS Server Wizard dialog box, click the Finish button.

Summary

The chapter described how to manage network connections. We covered the following topics:

- How to install, configure, and troubleshoot network adapters. You install adapters that are not Plug-and-Play through the Add/Remove

Hardware Wizard. You configure a network adapter through its Properties dialog box.

- How to install, configure, and test network protocols. The default protocol installed with Windows 2000 Server is TCP/IP. You can also install the NWLink IPX/SPX/NetBIOS, NetBEUI, AppleTalk, and DLC protocols.

- How to install and configure network services. Network services include DHCP, WINS, and DNS.

Exam Essentials

Be able to install and configure network adapters. Know how to install and configure Plug-and-Play or non–Plug-and-Play network adapters. Know which options can be configured for network adapters and how configuration is managed. Be able to troubleshoot network adapters that are not working properly.

Know how to install and configure network protocols. Be able to list the network protocols and those features of each protocol that are supported by Windows 2000. Know which options need to be configured for each protocol type, especially the TCP/IP protocol. Know how to troubleshoot IP protocol problems.

Be able to install and configure network services. Know how to install and configure DHCP, WINS, and DNS. Understand the options that must be configured for each service.

Key Terms

Before you take the exam, be sure you're familiar with the following key terms:

binding	IPCONFIG
default gateway	LMHOSTS file
DHCP server	NetBEUI
DNS (Domain Name System) server	network adapter
driver	Network Basic Input/Output System (NetBIOS) names
Dynamic Host Configuration Protocol (DHCP)	NWLink IPX/SPX/NetBIOS Compatible Transport
frame type	PING
HOSTS file	subnet mask
internal network number	TCP/IP (Transmission Control Protocol/Internet Protocol)
IP address	WINS (Windows Internet Name Service) server

Review Questions

1. You have a domain called ABCCorp.com. Within the domain, you have a Windows 2000 domain controller and a database server called SalesDB. Both of the servers use static IP addresses. The domain controller acts as a DNS server. You take the domain controller offline in order to perform maintenance. When you bring the server back up, some clients can no longer connect to SalesDB. When you check the DNS entries, you don't see an entry for the SalesDB server. What command can you issue on the SalesDB server to recreate its dynamic DNS entry?

   A. `IPCONFIG /dnsupdate`

   B. `IPCONFIG /registerdns`

   C. `DNSUPDATE`

   D. `REGDNS`

2. You have just installed a DHCP server and have configured your network clients to use TCP/IP with automatic configuration. Based on the following exhibit, select and place in order, the process that the DHCP server and DHCP clients will use to interact with each other.

   Choices:

   IP Acknowledgements
   IP Request
   IP Selection
   IP Offer

   DHCP Server

   DHCP Client

3. Your network is configured as shown in the following exhibit. Clients on Subnet A are able to dynamically allocate IP addresses, but clients on Subnet B are not getting automatic IP configuration. Which of the following options would resolve this problem? (Choose all that apply.)

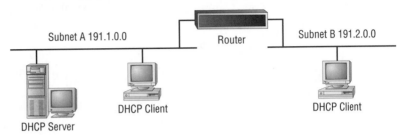

    A. Configure a DHCP Relay Agent.

    B. Configure the DHCP Forwarder service.

    C. Use a RFC 2131 Compliant router between Subnet A and Subnet B.

    D. Use a RFC 3546 Compliant router between Subnet A and Subnet B.

4. You have been assigned an IP address of 193.5.78.122. By default, based on the address class this address uses, what will the default subnet mask be?

    A. 255.255.255.255

    B. 255.255.255.0

    C. 255.255.0.0

    D. 255.0.0.0

5. You are trying to connect to Sales.ABCCorp.com. When you try to attach to the server using the host name, you can't attach to the server. When you use the server's IP address, you can attach to server. Which of the following services should you check for proper configuration?

    A. DHCP

    B. DNS

    C. WINS

    D. RIS

6. Your network uses a mixture of Windows 2000 and Windows NT computers. You are trying to attach to a Windows NT server called SALESDB. When you try and attach to the server by using the computer's NetBIOS name, you are unable to connect. You try and PING the server's IP address and the PING is successful. Which type of server should be configured to resolve NetBIOS computer names to IP addresses ?

   A. DHCP

   B. DNS

   C. WINS

   D. RIS

7. You are unable to connect to the network and suspect that you may have been unable to access your DHCP server. Which of the following commands should you use to determine the configuration of your IP settings?

   A. CONFIG

   B. PING

   C. IPCONFIG

   D. IPPING

8. You are designing a new Windows 2000 network. You are trying to decide which protocol you will use. The network will consist of multiple network segments, so you must be able to route packets between different subnets. Which of the following protocols does *not* offer routing capabilities?

   A. NetBEUI

   B. NWLink IPX/SPX/NetBIOS

   C. TCP/IP

   D. AppleTalk

9. Judy is trying to determine which network protocols she should install on her Windows 2000 Server computer. When would she use the DLC protocol? (Choose all that apply.)

    A. If she had Macintosh computers on her network

    B. If she wanted to connect to a printer using the DLC protocol

    C. If she needed to connect to an IBM environment using the DLC protocol

    D. If she wanted to connect to a NetWare network using the DLC protocol

10. Allie has installed her Windows 2000 Server computer in a workgroup. Her workgroup does not have a DNS server installed. What file can Allie install on Windows 2000 Server to facilitate the resolution of IP addresses to host names?

    A. DNS.txt

    B. DNS.cfg

    C. HOSTS

    D. LMHOSTS

11. Ian has installed his Windows 2000 Server computer in a workgroup of Windows NT clients and Windows 2000 clients. His workgroup does not have a WINS server installed. What file can Ian install on his Windows 2000 Server to facilitate the resolution of the computers' NetBIOS names to IP addresses ?

    A. WINS.txt

    B. WINS.cfg

    C. HOSTS

    D. LMHOSTS

12. Kaitlin wants her Windows 2000 Server computer to be automatically registered with the DNS server on her network when her computer is started. Which of the following advanced DNS settings should she configure?

    A. Register This Connection's Address in DNS

    B. Append This Computer's Address to the DNS Server

    C. Primary DNS Server

    D. This cannot be automatically configured

13. Maddie wants her Windows 2000 Server computer to be automatically registered with the WINS server on her network when her computer is started. Which of the following advanced WINS settings should she configure?

    A. Register This Connection's Address in WINS

    B. Append This Computer's Address to the WINS Server

    C. Add a WINS server for the server

    D. This cannot be automatically configured

14. Bob wants to access a NetWare 4 server's file and print resources. What software needs to be installed on the Windows 2000 Server computer? (Choose all that apply.)

    A. NWLink IPX/SPX/NetBIOS

    B. CSNW

    C. GSNW

    D. File and Print Services for NetWare

15. Elisa is configuring her Windows 2000 Server computer to communicate with a NetWare server that is on the same network. She is not sure which frame type is being used by the NetWare server. How should she configure the frame type for NWLink IPX/SPX/NetBIOS on the Windows 2000 Server computer?

    A. Use the 802.2 frame type.

    B. Use the 802.3 frame type.

    C. Use the Auto Detect frame type.

    D. Use the Discover frame type.

Answers to Review Questions

1. B. The `IPCONFIG /registerdns` command is used to refresh all DHCP leases and re-registers the computer's name and IP address in the DNS server's zone.

2. The proper order for DHCP negotiation is "ROSA": IP lease **R**equest, IP lease **O**ffer, IP lease **S**election, IP lease **A**cknowledgment.

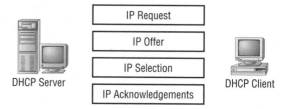

3. A, C. If your DHCP clients are on a different subnet than the DHCP server, your DHCP broadcast requests will not be forwarded by default. You can forward DHCP requests through the DHCP Relay Agent or by using an RFC 2131 compliant router.

4. B. If the first field of the IP address starts between 192 and 223, the IP address is a class C address. Class C addresses use a subnet mask of 255.255.255.0 by default.

5. B. Domain Name System (DNS) servers are used to resolve host names to IP addresses.

6. C. Windows Internet Name Service (WINS) servers are used to resolve computer's NetBIOS names to IP addresses. Prior to Windows 2000, Windows clients used NetBIOS names to communicate with each other.

7. C. The `IPCONFIG` command is used to display your current IP configuration settings.

8. A. NWLink IPX/SPX/NetBIOS, TCP/IP, and AppleTalk all support routing. The only protocol listed that does not support routing is NetBEUI.

9. B, C. The only environments that use the DLC protocol are some network printers and some IBM networks.

10. C. The HOSTS file is used to map host names to IP addresses. This file can be used in place of a DNS server.

11. D. The LMHOSTS file is used to map computers' NetBIOS names to IP addresses. This file can be used in place of a WINS server.

12. A. You can automatically register your computer with a DNS server through the Register This Connection's Address in DNS option. This is the default setting.

13. C. When you configure the TCP/IP WINS properties with a primary WINS server, the computer will register with the WINS server when the computer is started.

14. A, C. In order for a Windows 2000 Server computer to support Windows client access to a NetWare server's file and print resources, the server must use the NWLink IPX/SPX/NetBIOS protocol and have the Gateway Services for NetWare (GSNW) service installed. The client software that allows you to access NetWare file and print resources is Client Services for NetWare (CSNW). If NWLink is not installed and you add CSNW or GSNW, NWLink will be automatically installed.

15. C. By default, NWLink IPX/SPX/NetBIOS will use Auto Detect for the frame type. Auto Detect will attempt to automatically choose a compatible frame type for your network.

Chapter

10

Managing Web Services

MICROSOFT EXAM OBJECTIVES COVERED IN THIS CHAPTER

✓ **Monitor, configure, troubleshoot, and control access to files, folders, and shared folders.**

  ▪ Monitor, configure, troubleshoot, and control access to files and folders via Web services.

✓ **Monitor, configure, troubleshoot, and control access to Web sites.**

Windows 2000 Server comes with Internet Information Services, which allows you to create and manage Web sites. This software provides a wide range of options for configuring the content, performance, and access controls for your Web sites.

In this chapter, you will learn how to learn to install Internet Information Services (if it was not installed during the original Windows 2000 Server installation) and how to configure and manage Web site properties. You will also learn how to create a new Web site. The final section of the chapter includes tips for troubleshooting problems with Web site access.

Installing Internet Information Services

Windows 2000 Server uses *Internet Information Services (IIS)* to publish resources on the Internet or a private intranet. IIS is a full-featured Web server, designed to support heavy Internet usage. The IIS software is installed on Windows 2000 Server computers by default.

If you chose not to install IIS as a part of the Windows 2000 Server installation process, or you upgraded to Windows 2000 Server from a computer that was not running IIS, you can install IIS through the following steps:

1. Select Start ➢ Settings ➢ Control Panel and double-click the Add/ Remove Programs icon.

2. The Add/Remove Programs window appears. Click the Add/Remove Windows Components option.

3. The Windows Components Wizard starts. Check the Internet Information Services (IIS) box and click the Next button.

4. When prompted, insert the Windows 2000 Server CD and click the OK button. If you see the Files Needed dialog box, you will need to

specify the location of your CD-ROM drive (you can use the Browse button) and the I386 folder. Click the OK button.

5. After all of the files have been copied, you will see the Completing the Windows Components Wizard. Click the Finish button.

6. Close the Add/Remove Programs window.

Configuring and Managing Internet Information Services

When IIS is installed, you see the Internet Services Manager program item in Administrative Tools. This is the primary utility used to manage IIS.

Microsoft ✓ Exam Objective	Monitor, configure, troubleshoot, and control access to Web sites.

The following services are installed as a part of IIS:

- *File Transfer Protocol (FTP)*, which is used to transfer files between two computers using the TCP/IP protocol

- *Hypertext Transfer Protocol (HTTP)*, which is used to create content for Web sites as well as to navigate Web sites

- *Simple Mail Transfer Protocol (SMTP)*, which is used to transfer mail between two SMTP mail systems

- *Network News Transfer Protocol (NNTP)*, which is used to provide newsgroup services between NNTP servers and NNTP clients

Managing a Web Site

To access Internet Services Manager, select Start ➤ Programs ➤ Administrative Tools ➤ Internet Services Manager. When you start Internet Services Manager, you will see that five items are defined by default: Default FTP Site, Default Web Site, Administration Web Site, Default SMTP Virtual

Server, and a Default NNTP Virtual Server. These default sites and virtual servers are provided to help you get IIS up and running as quickly as possible.

Through Internet Services Manager, you can configure many options for your Web site, such as the number of connections allowed, performance settings, and access controls. To access a Web site's properties, right-click the Web site you want to manage in the Internet Information Services window and select Properties from the pop-up menu. This brings up the Web site Properties dialog box, as shown in Figure 10.1.

FIGURE 10.1   The Default Web Site Properties dialog box

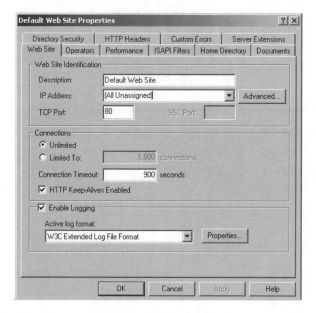

The Web site Properties dialog box has 10 tabs with options for configuring and managing your Web site. The options on these tabs are described briefly in Table 10.1 and in more detail in the following sections.

TABLE 10.1   The Web Site Properties Dialog Box Tabs

Tab	Description
Web Site	Allows you to configure Web site identification, connections, and logging
Operators	Allows you to configure which users and groups can manage the Web site

TABLE 10.1 The Web Site Properties Dialog Box Tabs *(continued)*

Tab	Description
Performance	Allows you to configure performance tuning, bandwidth throttling, and process throttling.
ISAPI Filters	Allows you to set ISAPI (Internet Server Application Programming Interface) filters
Home Directory	Allows you to configure the content location, access permissions, content control, and application settings
Documents	Allows you to specify the default document users will see if they access your Web site without specifying a specific document
Directory Security	Allows you to configure anonymous access and authentication control, IP address and domain name restrictions, and secure communications
HTTP Headers	Allows you to configure values that will be returned to Web browsers in the Hypertext Markup Language (HTML) headers of the Web pages
Custom Errors	Allows you to present a customized error message that will appear when there is a Web browser error
Server Extensions	Allows you to configure publishing controls for FrontPage options

Setting Web Site Properties

The Web Site tab (see Figure 10.1) includes options for identifying the Web site, controlling connections, and enabling logging.

Web Site Identification

The description of the Web site appears in the Internet Information Services window. By default, the Web site description is the same as the name of the Web site. You can enter another description in the Description text box.

You also configure the IP address that is associated with the site. The IP address must already be configured for the computer. If you leave the IP address at the default setting of All Unassigned, all of the IP addresses that are assigned to the computer and that have not been assigned to other Web sites will be used.

The TCP port specifies the port that will be used to respond to HTTP requests by default. The default TCP port that is used is TCP port 80. If you change this value, clients attempting to connect to the Web site must specify the correct port value. This option can be used for additional security.

Common ports that are used by IIS and can be modified for additional security include FTP on port 21, Telnet on port 23, and HTTP on port 80.

Connections

You can allow unlimited connections to the Web site, or you can control the number of connections. To specify a connection limit, select the Limited To option and enter the maximum number of connections allowed.

The Connection Timeout is used to specify how long an inactive user can remain connected to the Web site before the connection is automatically terminated.

If you select the HTTP Keep-Alives Enabled option, the client will maintain an open connection with the server, as opposed to opening a new connection for each client request. This enhances client performance, but may degrade server performance.

Logging

Logging is used to enable logging features, which record details of Web site access. If logging is enabled, you can select from several log formats that collect information in a specified format. If you want to log user access to the Web site, the Log Visits check box on the Home Directory tab must also be checked (which is the default setting).

Specifying Operators

You can configure which users and groups are able to manage the Web site through the Operators tab, as shown in Figure 10.2. By default, the Administrators group is assigned operator priviliges. You can add or remove operators from this list.

FIGURE 10.2 The Operators tab of the Web site Properties dialog box

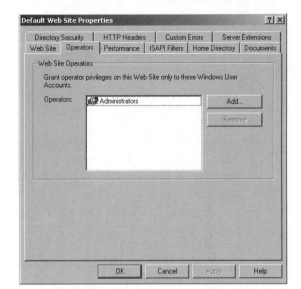

Setting Performance Options

The Performance tab, shown in Figure 10.3, allows you to configure performance tuning, enable bandwidth throttling, and enable process throttling.

FIGURE 10.3 The Performance tab of the Web site Properties dialog box

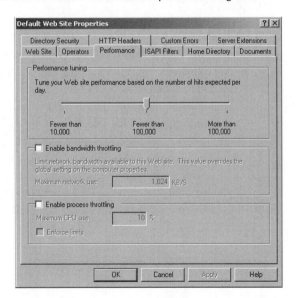

Performance Tuning

Performance tuning allows you to tune your Web site based on the number of hits your Web site is expected to receive each day. Based on the number you specify, server memory is allocated to the Web site to maximize user access. Tuning options allow you to configure hits per day at fewer than 10,000, fewer than 100,000 (the default setting), or more than 100,000.

Bandwidth Throttling

Bandwidth is defined as the total capacity of your transmission media. This can be expressed as bits per second (bps) or as Hertz (frequency). IIS allows you to specify how much bandwidth can be used in terms of kilobytes per second (KB/S).

If the server is used to host other Web sites or is used for other purposes, such as hosting an e-mail server, you might want to limit the maximum amount of bandwidth that can be used by your Web server. This is called *bandwidth throttling*. If bandwidth throttling is not enabled, your Web server can use the maximum amount of bandwidth that is available.

Process Throttling

When you enable *process throttling*, you can specify the percentage of CPU processing that can be used by the Web site. If you select the Enforce Limits option, whatever value is set for process throttling will be enforced. If this option is not selected, the Web site will be able to exceed the process throttling settings, and an event will be written to the event log.

Setting ISAPI Filters

Internet Server Application Programming Interface (ISAPI) filters direct Web browser requests for specific URLs to specific ISAPI applications, which are then run. ISAPI filters are commonly used to manage customized logon authentication. These filters work by monitoring HTTP requests and responding to specific events that are defined through the filter. The filters are loaded into the Web site's memory.

Through the ISAPI Filters tab, shown in Figure 10.4, you can add ISAPI filters for your Web site. The filters are applied in the order they are listed in the list box. You can use the up and down arrow buttons to the left of the list box to change the order of the filters.

FIGURE 10.4 The ISAPI Filters tab of the Web site Properties dialog box

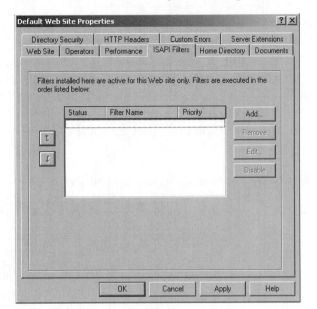

Configuring Home Directory Options

The Home Directory tab, shown in Figure 10.5, includes options for the content location, access permissions, content control, and application settings.

Microsoft ✓ *Exam Objective*

Monitor, configure, troubleshoot, and control access to files, folders, and shared folders.

- Monitor, configure, troubleshoot, and control access to files and folders via Web services.

This chapter covers material related to managing access to Web site resources for the "Monitor, configure, troubleshoot, and control access to files, folders, and shared folders" objective. Controlling local security and controlling access to shared folders, two other subobjectives for this objective, are covered in Chapter 7, "Accessing Files and Folders." The subobjectives related to the Distributed file system (Dfs) are covered in Chapter 8, "Administering the Distributed File System."

FIGURE 10.5 The Home Directory tab of the Web site Properties dialog box

Content Location

The home directory is used to provide Web content. The default directory is called inetpub\wwwroot. You have three choices for the location of the home directory:

- A directory on the local computer

- A share on another computer (stored on the local network and identified by a UNC name)

- A redirection to a resource using a URL

Access Permissions and Content Control

Access permissions define what access users have to the Web site. Content control specifies whether logging and indexing are enabled. By default, users have only Read access, and logging and indexing are enabled. The access permissions and content control options are described in Table 10.2.

TABLE 10.2   Access Permissions and Content Control Options

Option	Description
Script Source Access	Allows users to access source code for scripts, such as ASP (Active Server Pages) applications, if the user has either Read or Write permissions.
Read	Allows users to read or download files located in your home folder. This is used if your folder contains HTML files. If your home folder contains CGI applications or ISAPI applications, you should uncheck this option so that users can't download your application files.
Write	Allows users to modify or add to your Web content. This access should be granted with extreme caution.
Directory Browsing	Allows users to view Web site directories. This option is not commonly used because it exposes your directory structure to users who access your Web site without specifying a specific HTML file.
Log Visits	Allows you to log access to your Web site. In order to log access, the Enable Logging box in the Web Site tab of the Properties dialog box also must be checked.
Index This Resource	Allows you to index your home folder for use with the Microsoft Indexing Service.

Web service access permissions and NTFS permissions work together. The more restrictive of the two permissions will be the effective permission.

Application Settings

Application, in this context, is defined as the starting point of a specific folder (and its subfolder and files) that has been defined as an application. For example, if you specify that your home folder is an application, every folder in your content location can participate in the application.

The Execute Permissions setting specifies how applications can be accessed within this folder. If you select None, no applications or scripts can be executed from this folder. The Scripts Only setting allows you to run script engines, even if no execute permissions have been set. This permission is used for folders that contain ASP scripts. The other option is Scripts and Executables, which allows all file types (including binary files with .EXE and .DLL extensions) to be executed.

The Application Protection setting specifies how applications will be run. There are three choices:

- Low (IIS Process) means that the application runs in the same process as the Web service.

- Medium (Pooled) means that the application is run in an isolated pooled process with other applications.

- High (Isolated) means that each application runs as a separate isolated application.

Setting a Default Document

The Documents tab, shown in Figure 10.6, allows you to specify the default document users will see if they access your Web site without specifying a specific document. You normally set your default document as your Web site's home page.

FIGURE 10.6   The Documents tab of the Web site Properties dialog box

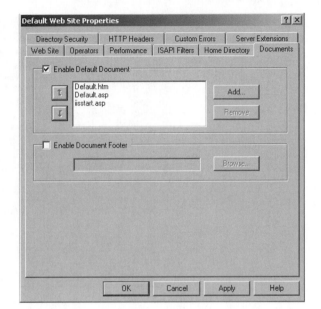

You can specify multiple documents in the order you prefer. This way, if a document is unavailable, the Web server will access the next default document that has been defined.

You can also specify document footers. A document footer is an HTML document that will appear at the bottom of each Web page that is sent to Web clients.

Setting Directory Security

The Directory Security tab, shown in Figure 10.7, includes options for anonymous access and authentication control, IP address and domain name restrictions, and secure communications.

FIGURE 10.7 The Directory Security tab of the Web site Properties dialog box

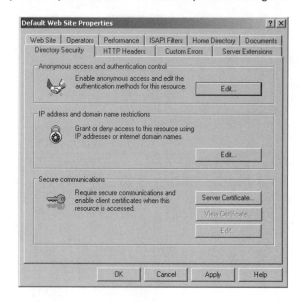

Anonymous Access and Authentication Control

To enable anonymous access and specify authentication control methods, click the Edit button in the Anonymous Access and Authentication Control section of the dialog box. This brings up the Authentication Methods dialog box, as shown in Figure 10.8.

FIGURE 10.8 The Authentication Methods dialog box

If your Web site is available for public use, you will most likely allow *anonymous access*. If you enable anonymous access, by default, your computer will use the IUSR_*computername* user account. You can limit the access the Anonymous user account has by applying NTFS permissions to your Web content.

There are three choices in the Authenticated Access section of the Authentication Methods dialog box:

- The Basic Authentication option requires a Windows 2000 user account. If anonymous access is disabled or the anonymous account tries to access data that the account does not have permission to access, the system will prompt the user for a valid Windows 2000 user account. With this method, all passwords are sent as clear text. You should use this option with caution since it poses a security risk.

- The Digest Authentication for Windows Domain Servers option works only for Windows 2000 domain accounts. This method requires accounts to store passwords as encrypted clear text.

- The Integrated Windows Authentication option uses secure authentication to transmit the Windows 2000 username and password.

IP Address and Domain Name Restrictions

To control access to the Web site based on IP addresses or domain names, click the Edit button in the IP Address and Domain Name Restrictions section of the dialog box. This brings up the dialog box shown in Figure 10.9.

FIGURE 10.9   The IP Address and Domain Name Restrictions dialog box

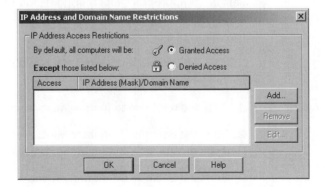

In the IP Address and Domain Name Restrictions dialog box, you can specify that all computers will be granted or denied access and then specify exceptions. The exceptions can be based on their IP address, IP network address and subnet mask, or domain name (this requires DNS reverse lookup capabilities, which are described in Chapter 9, "Managing Network Interoperability").

Secure Communications

You can increase the security of your Web site by using secure communications. With secure communications, you are able to create and manage key requests and key certificates. These options are used in conjunction with Certificate Server. This allows you to specify that you will require secure channel services (using certificates) when accessing your Web site.

Real World Scenario

Setting Security for IIS

You are installing IIS on a Windows 2000 server that will be used by internal employees to access corporate documents. You are very concerned about security since this resource will be accessible to anyone with an Internet connection. Your task is to set security so that the server is accessible from the intranet and impenetrable from the Internet.

Remember back in Chapter 5, when you learned about security templates? Microsoft provides a template called highsecweb.inf, a baseline security template that is appropriate for securing Windows 2000 IIS servers. The template is available at download.microsoft.com/download/win2000srv/scm/1.0/nt5/en-us/hisecweb.exe.

Once you download and extract the template, take the following steps to use the template:

1. Copy the template to the %windir%\security\templates directory.

2. Open the Security Templates MMC snap-in and review the settings for this template, to ensure that they are appropriate for your environment.

3. Open the Security Configuration and Analysis tool and load the high-secweb template as a database.

4. Right-click the Security Configuration and Analysis tool and select Analyze Computer Now.

5. Review the results of the analysis and update the template for any changes you wish to make.

6. Once you have the appropriate configuration for the template, right-click the Security Configuration and Analysis tool and select Configure Computer Now. The settings from the template file will be applied to the server.

Configuring HTTP Headers

The HTTP Headers tab, shown in Figure 10.10, allows you to configure values that will be returned to Web browsers in the HTML headers of the Web pages.

FIGURE 10.10   The HTTP Headers tab of the Web site Properties dialog box

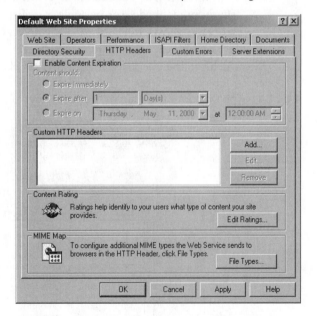

You can configure four options:

- If your Web site contains information that is time-sensitive, you can specify that you want to use content expiration. You can set content to expire immediately, after a specified number of minutes, or on a specific date. This helps the Web browser determine whether it should use a cached copy of a requested page or it should request an updated copy of the Web page from the Web site.

- Custom HTTP headers are used to send customized HTTP headers from your Web server to the client browser. For example, you may want to specify a custom HTTP header to send instructions that may not be supported by the HTML specification that is currently in use.

- Content ratings allow you to specify appropriate restrictions if a site contains violence, sex, nudity, or adult language. Most Web browsers can then be configured to block objectionable material based on how the content rating has been defined.

- MIME (Multipurpose Internet Mail Extensions) maps are used to configure Web browsers so that they can view files that have been configured with different formats.

Specifying Custom Error Messages

If the Web browser encounters an error, it will display an error message. By default, predefined error messages are displayed. Through the Custom Errors tab, shown in Figure 10.11, you can customize the error message that the user will see. To generate a custom error message, you create an .HTM file, which can then be mapped to a specific HTML error.

FIGURE 10.11 The Custom Errors tab of the Web server Properties dialog box

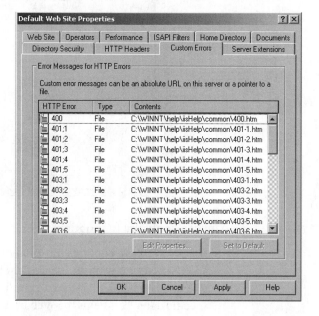

Setting Server Extensions

The Server Extensions tab, shown in Figure 10.12, allows you to configure publishing controls for FrontPage options. FrontPage is used to create and edit HTML pages for your Web site through a What You See Is What You Get (WYSIWYG) editor.

FIGURE 10.12   The Server Extensions tab of the Web site Properties dialog box

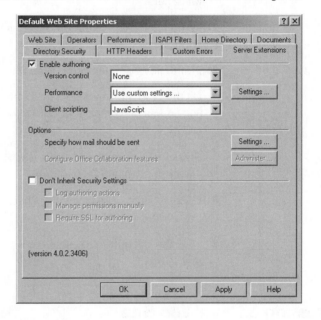

This tab includes the following options:

- The Enable Authoring option specifies whether authors can modify the content of the Web site. If this option is selected, you can specify version control, performance based on how many pages the Web site hosts, and the client scripting method that will be used.

- The Options section includes Settings and Administer buttons, which allow you to specify how mail should be sent and Office Collaboration features (this option is enabled only if Office is configured).

- The Don't Inherit Security Settings option overrides the global security settings for the Web site.

In Exercise 10.1, you will configure and manage the properties of the default Web site.

Configuring and Managing the Default Web Site

1. Select Start ➤ Programs ➤ Administration Tools ➤ Internet Services Manager.

2. In the Internet Information Services window, double-click your computer.

3. Right-click Administration Web Site and select Properties.

4. On the Web Site tab, select the Limited To radio button and specify **500** connections. For the Connection Timeout option, specify **1200** seconds.

5. Click the Performance tab. Set the Performance Tuning slider for Fewer than 10,000 Connections.

6. Click the Home Directory tab. Check the Directory Browsing check box for the Local Path.

7. Click the OK button to close the Default Web Site Properties dialog box.

Creating a New Web Site

IIS allows you to host multiple Web sites on a single computer. To create a new Web site, take the following steps:

1. Select Start ➤ Programs ➤ Administration Tools ➤ Internet Services Manager.

2. In the Internet Information Services window, right-click the computer that is running IIS and select New ➤ Web Site from the pop-up menu.

3. The Welcome to the Web Site Creation Wizard starts. Click the Next button.

4. The Web Site Description dialog box appears. Type in a descriptive name for your site and click the Next button.

5. The IP Address and Port Settings dialog box appears, as shown in Figure 10.13. You can specify the IP address, TCP port, and host header for the Web site. Host headers are used to route requests to the proper Web site (when a computer hosts multiple Web sites). After this information is configured, click the Next button.

FIGURE 10.13   The IP Address and Port Settings dialog box

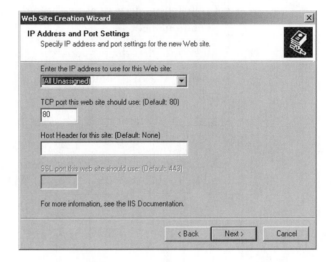

6. The Web Site Home Directory dialog box appears. Enter the path that will be used for the home directory. You can also specify if anonymous access will be allowed for the Web site. After this information is configured, click the Next button.

7. The Web Site Access Permissions dialog box appears. Select the check boxes for the access you want to allow, and then click the Next button.

After you create your new Web site, you can configure and manage it as described in the previous sections.

Troubleshooting Web Site Access

If users are unable to access your Web site, the problem may be caused by improper access permissions, an improperly configured home folder or default document, or use of the wrong TCP port. Here are some tips for troubleshooting Web site access problems:

- Determine if anonymous access is allowed. If so, verify that the user-name and password that have been configured through Internet Services Manager match the name of the user account and password that are in the Windows 2000 user database.

- Confirm that access has not been denied based on the IP address or domain name.

- Make sure that the proper access permissions have been configured.

- Confirm that the home folder is properly configured and that the default document has been properly configured.

- Make sure that the TCP port is set to port 80 or that you are accessing the Web site using the proper TCP port number.

- Make sure that the NTFS permissions have not been set on the home folder so that they deny access to Web site users.

Summary

In this chapter, you learned how to manage Web services. We covered the following topics:

- How to install IIS. If IIS was not installed during Windows 2000 Server installation, you can add it through the Add/Remove Programs icon in Control Panel.

- How to manage and configure IIS. The Web site Properties dialog box contains 10 tabs full of options for your Web site.

- How to create a new Web site. A single computer can host multiple Web sites.

- How to troubleshoot Web site access problems. If users can't access your Web site, you should check the access permissions, the home folder and default document configuration, and the TCP port settings.

Exam Essentials

Be able to install and configure a Web server.   Know how to install and configure IIS. Know which protocols are used to support different services. Be able to configure IIS security.

Troubleshoot Web access problems.   Be able to list the common problems that would cause user access problems and be able to correct access problems.

Key Terms

Before taking the exam, you should be familiar with the following terms:

anonymous access	Internet Server Application Programming Interface (ISAPI) filters
bandwidth throttling	Internet Services Manager
File Transfer Protocol (FTP)	Network News Transfer Protocol (NNTP)
Hypertext Transfer Protocol (HTTP)	process throttling
Internet Information Services (IIS)	Simple Mail Transfer Protocol (SMTP)

Review Questions

1. You are installing IIS to act as an internal intranet resource. Which of the following IIS services would you use to create content for Web sites as well as to navigate Web sites?

   A. SNMP

   B. NNTP

   C. FTP

   D. HTTP

2. You want to set up a corporate intranet that provides a common location for users within your company to download corporate documents. You decide to use IIS. Which of the following IIS services is used to transfer files between two computers using the TCP/IP protocol?

   A. SNMP

   B. NNTP

   C. FTP

   D. HTTP

3. You have installed IIS on your corporate network. Your company has remote offices in ten locations across the U. S. You want to configure newsgroup services to propagate corporate information. Which of the following IIS services is used to provide newsgroup services?

   A. SNMP

   B. NNTP

   C. FTP

   D. HTTP

4. Kate has a Windows 2000 Server computer that was upgraded from a Windows NT Server 4 computer that did not have IIS installed. What option can she use to install IIS on her Windows 2000 Server computer?

A. From Control Panel, Network, add the IIS service

B. From Control Panel, Service, add the IIS service

C. From Control Panel, Internetworking, add the IIS service

D. From Control Panel, Add/Remove Programs, use Add/Remove Windows Components

5. You are setting up an IIS server that needs to be as secure as possible. You want to change the default port that is used to service HTTP requests. What is the default TCP port that is used by this service on IIS Web sites?

A. Port 60

B. Port 80

C. Port 82

D. Port 120

6. You have a corporate intranet that uses IIS services. You want to allow users the fastest access possible to the server. Which Web site option should you configure if you want users to maintain open connections with the server for faster access?

A. HTTP Keep-Alives

B. HTTP Connections Open

C. HTTP Heartbeat

D. HTTP Keep-Aways

7. You have an IIS server that hosts two external Web sites, ABC-CORP.com and XYZCORP.com. You want to ensure that neither site is able to use too much of the available bandwidth. Which Web site performance option is used to specify how much network bandwidth will be available to the Web site?

   A. Bandwidth management

   B. Bandwidth allocation

   C. Bandwidth pipeline

   D. Bandwidth throttling

8. Linda is in charge of her company's internal Web site. She decides to use the default Web site. What is the default home directory that is used by the default Web site?

   A. \inetpub\wwwroot

   B. \iis\wwwroot

   C. \inetpub\www

   D. \iis\www

9. The AcmeToyStore Corporation is configuring a Web site using IIS. This Web site will allow the public to access the company's online toy catalog. Which of the following directory security options should be configured?

   A. Anonymous access

   B. Basic access

   C. Remote access

   D. Public access

10. You have a corporate Web site that will be used by local and remote users. You want to ensure that security is maintained and you want users to log on to the Web site with their Windows 2000 user accounts and passwords. Which of the following Web site authentication methods require the user to present a valid Windows 2000 user account and password? (Choose all that apply.)

    A. Basic authentication

    B. Digest authentication for Windows domain servers

    C. Integrated Windows authentication

    D. Anonymous access

11. Chuck has specified that his Web site will use anonymous access. Users are not able to access his Web site. Which user account should he confirm is properly configured?

    A. IUSR_*computername*

    B. IUSR_IIS

    C. IUSR_Anonymous

    D. IIS_Anonymous

12. Your Web site's home page lists a special offer that expires at the end of the month. Which option should you configure to specify that clients' Web browsers should request an updated copy of the Web page from your Web server when the offer expires?

    A. HTTP Keep-Alives

    B. Content Expiration

    C. Content is Soured

    D. HTTP Expiration

13. Faith manages her company's internal Web site. She wants users to contact her directly if they receive error 404: Not found. She creates a custom error file with the message "Error: Contact Faith at (408) 555-1234." Which extension should be applied to the custom error message?

    A. .ERR

    B. .MSG

    C. .HTM

    D. .TXT

14. When Kyle accesses his company's internal network, he does not see a list of the documents in the Web site's home folder. Since this is an internal site, the managers decide that users should be able to access a directory list. Which option should be configured?

    A. Directory Browsing

    B. File Lists

    C. Display Contents of Folder

    D. DOS-style Directory Listing

15. Your server hosts two Web sites, MASTERMCSE.COM and YOMCSE.COM. Wendy needs to manage the MASTERMCSE.COM site but does not need to manage the YOMCSE.COM site. What action should you take?

    A. Make Wendy a member of the Administrators group

    B. Make Wendy a member of the Server Operators group

    C. Give Wendy the Manage right for the MASTERMCSE.COM object

    D. Make Wendy an operator for MASTERMCSE.COM through the Operator tab of the Web site Properties dialog box

Answers to Review Questions

1. D. The Hypertext Transfer Protocol (HTTP) is used to create content for Web sites as well as to navigate Web sites.

2. C. The File Transfer Protocol (FTP) is used to transfer files between two TCP/IP hosts using the TCP protocol.

3. B. The Network News Transfer Protocol (NNTP) is used to provide newsgroup services between NNTP servers and NNTP clients.

4. D. You can install IIS on a Windows 2000 Server computer through the Add/Remove Programs icon in Control Panel. Select Add/Remove Windows Components, and then check the Internet Information Services (IIS) check box.

5. B. By default, TCP port 80 is used by IIS Web sites. If you change this value, the Web browser clients must know which port you are using in order to access the Web site.

6. A. HTTP Keep-Alives are used to maintain open connections between the server and Web clients. If this option is not selected, a new connection is opened for each client request. This option speeds up client requests, but it can degrade server performance.

7. D. Bandwidth throttling is used to specify the maximum kilobytes per second (KB/S) that the Web site can consume.

8. A. The home directory is used to provide Web content for the Web server. The default Web site's home directory is \inetpub\wwwroot.

9. A. If the public will access your Web site, you should configure anonymous access.

10. A, B, C. If you configure your Web site to use basic authentication, digest authentication for Windows domain servers, or integrated Windows authentication, the user will be prompted for a Windows 2000 username and password.

11. A. If your Web site is available for public use, you will most likely use anonymous access. If you allow anonymous access, by default, your computer will use the IUSR_*computername* user account. You can limit the access the Anonymous user account has by applying NTFS permissions to your Web content.

12. B. If your Web site contains information that is time-sensitive, you can specify that you want to use content expiration. You can set the content to expire immediately, after a specified number of minutes, or on a specific date. The Web browser determines if it should use a cached copy of a requested page or if it should request an updated copy of the Web page from the Web site.

13. C. To create a custom error message, you create an .HTM file, which can then be mapped to a specific HTML error.

14. A. The Directory Browsing option exposes your directory structure to users who access your Web site without specifying a specific HTML file.

15. D. You can configure which users and groups are able to manage a Web site through the Operators tab of the Web site Properties dialog box.

Chapter

11

Managing Printing

MICROSOFT EXAM OBJECTIVES COVERED IN THIS CHAPTER

✓ Monitor, configure, troubleshoot, and control access to printers.

The process of creating, managing, and deleting printers is fairly easy. When you create printers, you use a Wizard, which leads you through each step of the configuration. Anything that is not configured through the Add Printer Wizard can be configured through the printer's properties. You can also manage printing options such as pausing and deleting print jobs for the entire printer or for specific print documents.

In this chapter, you will learn the basics of Windows 2000 Server printing, how to set up and configure printers, how to support non-Windows print clients, how to manage printers and print jobs, and how to manage print servers.

The printing processes used by Windows 2000 Server and Windows 2000 Professional are the same.

Setting Up Printers

Before you can access your physical *print device* under Windows 2000 Server, you must first create a *logical printer*. After you create printers, you may need to delete or rename printers. These tasks are covered in the following sections.

Microsoft ✓ *Exam* *Objective*

Monitor, configure, troubleshoot, and control access to printers.

To create a printer, you use the Add Printer Wizard, which guides you through all of the steps. In order to create a new printer in Windows 2000 Server, you must be logged on as a member of the Administrators or Power Users group.

The computer on which you run the Add Printer Wizard and create the printer automatically becomes the *print server* for that printer. As the print server, the computer must have enough processing power to support incoming print jobs and enough disk space to hold all of the print jobs that will be queued.

To create a new *local printer* or *network printer*, take the following steps:

1. Select Start ➤ Settings ➤ Printers to open the Printers folder, as shown in Figure 11.1. Then double-click the Add Printer icon.

FIGURE 11.1 The Printers folder with the Add Printer icon

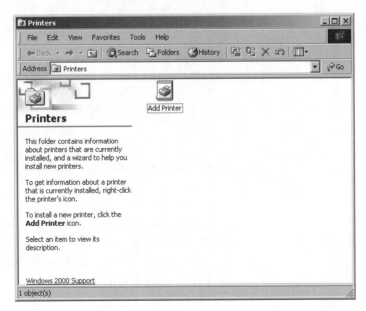

2. The Add Printer Wizard starts. Click the Next button to continue.

3. The Local or Network Printer dialog box appears. Choose Local Printer if you have a printer directly attached to computer, or choose Network Printer if you have a printer attached to a network. Then click the Next button. If you have a Plug-and-Play print device attached to your computer, it should be automatically detected, and you can skip to step 6. If your print device is not attached or recognized, deselect the Automatically Detect and Install My Plug and Play Printer option and continue with the following steps to manually specify the print device configuration.

4. If you chose to manually configure a print device, the Select the Printer Port dialog box appears, as shown in Figure 11.2. Specify the port the print device will use and then click the Next button.

FIGURE 11.2 The Select the Printer Port dialog box

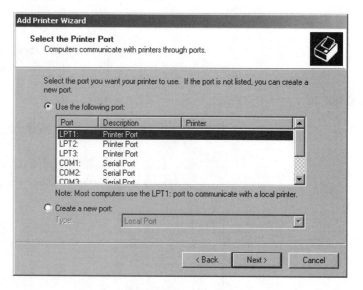

5. A dialog box that lists printer manufacturers and models appears, as shown in Figure 11.3. Specify the print device manufacturer and model and then click the Next button. If the print device is not listed, click the Have Disk button and insert the disk that contains the driver that came with your print device.

FIGURE 11.3 Selecting the printer manufacturer and model

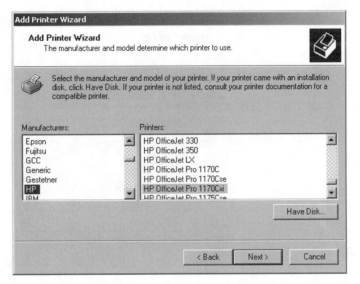

 If you have already installed this driver on your computer, the dialog box that lists the printer manufacturers and models will also include a Windows Update button next to the Have Disk button.

6. The Name Your Printer dialog box appears. Accept the default name or enter another name for your printer and click the Next button.

7. The Printer Sharing dialog box appears. You can choose to not share the printer or to share the printer. If you choose to share the printer, specify a share name to be used by the printer. Then click the Next button.

8. If you chose to share the printer, the Location and Comment dialog box appears, as shown in Figure 11.4. In this dialog box, specify location information and a comment. Network users can use this information to search for a description of the printer's location, configuration, and capabilities. Click the Next button.

FIGURE 11.4 The Location and Comment dialog box

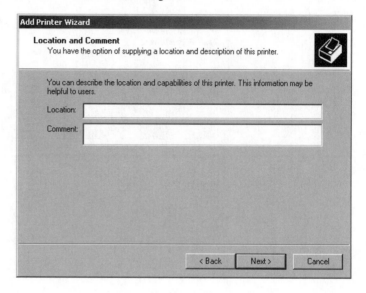

9. The Print Test Page dialog box appears. If the print device is attached to your computer, you should print a test page to verify that everything is configured properly. Otherwise, you should skip this step. Click the Next button to continue.

10. The Completing the Add Printer Wizard dialog box appears. This gives you a chance to verify that all of the printer settings have been set correctly. If there are any problems, click the Back button to make corrections. If everything is configured properly, click the Finish button.

To complete the setup process, the Add Printer Wizard will copy files (if necessary) and create your printer. An icon for your new printer will appear in the Printers folder, as shown in Figure 11.5.

FIGURE 11.5   An icon for a printer in the Printers folder

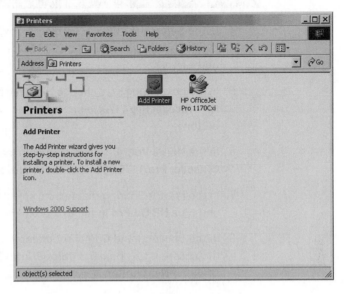

In Exercise 11.1, you will create printers using the Add Printer Wizard.

EXERCISE 11.1

Creating Printers

In this exercise, you will create two local printers—one to share and one that will not be shared. You will manually specify their print device configuration.

Adding the First Printer

1. Select Start ➢ Settings ➢ Printers to open the Printers folder. Then double-click the Add Printer icon.

2. The Add Printer Wizard starts. Click the Next button to continue.

3. In the Local or Network Printer dialog box, select the Local Printer radio button. Make sure that the Automatically Detect and Install My Plug and Play Printer box check box is not checked (unless you have a print device attached to your computer) and click the Next button.

EXERCISE 11.1 *(continued)*

4. In the Select the Printer Port dialog box, select the Use the Following Port radio button, select LPT1 in the list box, and click the Next button.

5. In the next dialog box, choose HP in the Manufacturers list box and HP OfficeJet Pro 1170cxi in the Printers list box. Then click the Next button.

6. In the Name Your Printer dialog box, leave the default name of HP OfficeJet Pro 1170cxi and click the Next button.

7. In the Printer Sharing dialog box, select the Share As radio button and type **HP OJ Pro** in the text box. Then click the Next button.

8. In the Location and Comment dialog box, type **Training Room** in the Location text box and **Color Printer** in the Comment text box. Click the Next button.

9. In the next dialog box, select the No radio button to skip printing a test page and click the Next button.

10. In the Completing the Add Printer Wizard dialog box, click the Finish button.

Adding the Second Printer

11. In the Printers folder, double-click the Add Printer icon.

12. When the Add Printer Wizard starts, click the Next button to continue.

13. In the Local or Network Printer dialog box, select the Local Printer radio button. Make sure that Automatically Detect and Install My Plug and Play Printer is not checked (unless you have a print device attached to your computer) and click the Next button.

14. In the Select the Printer Port dialog box, select the Use the Following Port radio button, select LPT2 in the list box, and click the Next button.

EXERCISE 11.1 *(continued)*

15. In the dialog box that appears, choose HP in the Manufacturers list box and HP LaserJet 4Si in the Printers list box. Then click the Next button.

16. In the Name Your Printer dialog box, leave the default name of HP LaserJet 4Si and click the Next button.

17. In the Printer Sharing dialog box, select the Do Not Share This Printer radio button and click the Next button.

18. In the Print Test Page dialog box, select No to skip printing a test page and click the Next button.

19. In the Completing the Add Printer Wizard dialog box, click the Finish button.

Managing Printer Properties

Printer properties allow you to configure options such as the printer name, whether or not the printer is shared, and printer security. To access the printer Properties dialog box, open the Printers folder, right-click the printer you want to manage, and choose Properties from the pop-up menu.

Microsoft
✓ *Exam*
Objective

Monitor, configure, troubleshoot, and control access to printers.

The printer Properties dialog box has six tabs: General, Sharing, Ports, Advanced, Security, and Device Settings. The following sections describe the properties on these tabs.

The Properties dialog boxes for some printers will contain additional tabs to allow advanced configuration of the printer. For example, if you install an HP DeskJet 970Cse printer, its Properties dialog box will have additional tabs for Color Management and Services.

Configuring General Properties

The General tab of the printer Properties dialog box, shown in Figure 11.6, contains information about the printer. It also lets you set printing preferences and print test pages.

FIGURE 11.6 The General tab of the printer Properties dialog box

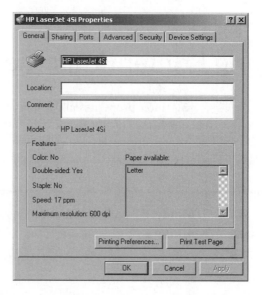

The name of the printer, the location of the printer, and comments about the printer shown here reflect your entries when you set up the printer (as described in the previous section). You can add or change this information in the text boxes.

Beneath the Comment box, you see the model of the printer. The items listed in the Features section of the dialog box depend on the model and driver you are using. The following are some examples of printer features:

- Color printing support

- Double-sided printing support

- Stapling support

- The maximum number of pages that can be printed per minute (ppm)

- The maximum resolution for the printer, in dots per inch (dpi)

At the bottom of the dialog box, you see the Printing Preferences and Print Test Page buttons. Their functions are described in the following sections.

Setting Printing Preferences

Clicking the Printing Preferences button opens the Printing Preferences dialog box, which allows you to specify the layout of the paper, page order, and paper source. This dialog box has Layout and Paper Quality tabs, as well as an Advanced button that allows you to configure more printer options.

Layout Settings

The Layout tab of the Printing Preferences dialog box, shown in Figure 11.7, allows you to specify the orientation and page order. Your choices for the Orientation setting are Portrait (vertical) or Landscape (horizontal).

FIGURE 11.7 The Layout tab of the Printing Preferences dialog box

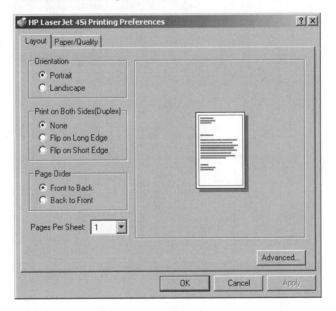

The Page Order setting is new to Windows 2000. It specifies whether you want page 1 of the document to be on the top of the stack (Front to Back) or on the bottom of the stack (Back to Front).

In Windows NT 4, your documents always printed back to front, meaning that page 1 printed first. At the end of the print job, you needed to reorder your pages.

The Pages Per Sheet setting determines how many pages should be printed on a single page. You might use this feature if you were printing a book and wanted two pages to be printed side by side on a single page.

Paper/Quality Settings

The Paper/Quality tab of the Printing Preferences dialog box allows you to configure properties that relate to the paper and quality of a print job. The options that are available depend on the features of your printer. For example, a printer may have only one option, such as Paper Source. For an HP DeskJet 970Cxi printer, you can configure Paper Source, Media, Quality Settings, and Color options, as shown in Figure 11.8.

FIGURE 11.8 The Paper/Quality tab of the Printing Preferences dialog box

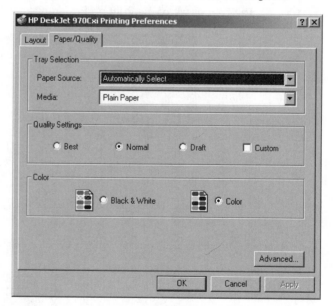

Advanced Settings

Clicking the Advanced button in the lower-right corner of the Printing Preferences dialog box opens the Advanced Options dialog box, as shown in

Figure 11.9. Here, you can configure printer options such as Paper/Output, Graphic, Document Options, and Printer Features. The availability of these options depends on the specific *print driver* you are using.

FIGURE 11.9 The Advanced Options dialog box

Printing a Test Page

The Print Test Page button at the bottom of the General tab of the printer Properties tab allows you to print a test page. This option is especially useful in troubleshooting printing problems. For example, you might use the Print Test Page option in a situation where no print driver is available for a print device and you want to try to use a compatible print driver. If the print job doesn't print or doesn't print correctly (it might print just one character per page, for example), you will know that the print driver isn't compatible.

Configuring Sharing Properties

The Sharing tab of the printer Properties dialog box, shown in Figure 11.10, allows you to specify whether the printer will be configured as a local printer or as a shared network printer. If you choose to share the printer, you also need to specify a share name, which will be seen by the network users.

FIGURE 11.10 The Sharing tab of the printer Properties dialog box

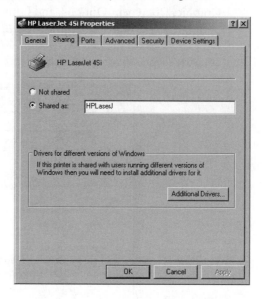

The other option that can be configured through the Sharing tab is driver support for print clients other than Windows 2000 clients. This is a significant feature of Windows 2000 Server print support, because it allows you to specify print drivers for other clients to automatically download. By default, the only driver that is loaded is the Intel driver for Windows 2000. To provide the additional drivers for the clients, click the Additional Drivers button at the bottom of the Sharing tab. This opens the Additional Drivers dialog box, as shown in Figure 11.11.

FIGURE 11.11 The Additional Drivers dialog box

Windows 2000 Server supports adding print drivers for the following platforms:

- Windows 95 or Windows 98 Intel
- Windows NT 3.1 Alpha, Intel, and MIPS
- Windows NT 3.5 or 3.51 Alpha, Intel, MIPS, and PowerPC
- Windows NT 4 Alpha, Intel, MIPS, and PowerPC

In Exercise 11.2, you will share an existing printer. This exercise assumes that you have completed Exercise 11.1.

EXERCISE 11.2

Sharing an Existing Printer

1. Select Start ➤ Settings ➤ Printers to open the Printers folder.

2. Right-click HP LaserJet 4Si, choose Properties, and click the Sharing tab.

3. Click the Shared As radio button. Accept the default value, HPLaserJ, and click the OK button.

4. Click the Apply button, then click the OK button to close the dialog box.

Once a printer has been shared, users with the Print permission can connect to the network printer through their network connection. To connect to a network printer, from the Desktop, open My Network Places, expand Entire Network, and click View Entire Contents. Expand Microsoft Window Network, then Workgroup, then *computername*. Finally, double-click the printer to connect to it.

Configuring Port Properties

A *port* is defined as the interface that allows the computer to communicate with the print device.

Windows 2000 Server supports *local ports* (or *physical ports*) and standard *TCP/IP ports* (or *logical ports*). Local ports are used when the printer attaches directly to the computer. In the case where you are running Windows 2000 Server in a small workgroup, you would likely run printers attached to the local port LPT1.

Standard TCP/IP ports are used when the printer is attached to the network by installing a network card in the printer. The advantage of network printers is that they are faster than local printers and can be located anywhere on the network. When you specify a TCP/IP port, you must know the IP address of the network printer.

The Ports tab, shown in Figure 11.12, allows you to configure all of the ports that have been defined for printer use. Along with deleting and configuring existing ports, you can also set up printer pooling and redirect print jobs to another printer, as described in the next sections.

The Enable Bidirectional Support option on the Ports tab will be available if your printer supports this feature. It allows the printer to communicate with the computer. For example, your printer may be able to send more informative printer errors.

FIGURE 11.12 The Ports tab of the printer Properties dialog box

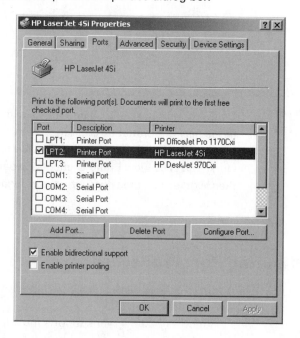

Printer Pooling

Printer pools are used to associate multiple physical print devices with a single logical printer, as illustrated in Figure 11.13. You would use a printer pool if you had multiple physical printers in the same location that were the same type and could use a single print driver. The advantage of using a printer pool is that the first available print device will print your job. This is useful in situations where there is a group of print devices shared by a group of users, such as a secretarial pool.

FIGURE 11.13   Printer pooling

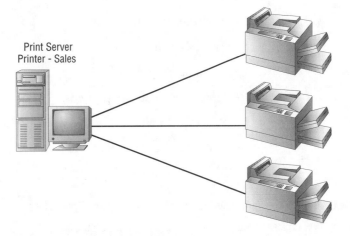

To configure a printer pool, click the Enable Printer Pooling check box at the bottom of the Ports tab and then check all of the ports that the print devices in the printer pool will attach to. If you do not select the Enable Printer Pooling option, you can select only one port per printer.

All of the print devices within a printer pool must be able to use the same print driver.

Redirecting Print Jobs to Another Printer

If your print device fails, you can redirect all of the jobs that are scheduled to be printed to that print device to another print device that has been configured as a printer. For this redirection to work, the new print device must be able to use the same print driver as the old print device.

To redirect print jobs, click the Add Port button in the Ports tab, highlight New Port, and choose New Port Type. In the Port Name dialog box, type the UNC name of the printer that you want to redirect the jobs to, in the format *computername**printer.*

Configuring Advanced Properties

The Advanced tab of the printer Properties dialog box, shown in Figure 11.14, allows you to control many characteristics of the printer. You can configure the following options:

- The availability of the printer
- The priority of the printer
- The driver the printer will use
- Spooling properties
- How documents are printed
- Printing defaults
- The print processor that will be used
- The separator page

FIGURE 11.14 The Advanced tab of the printer Properties dialog box

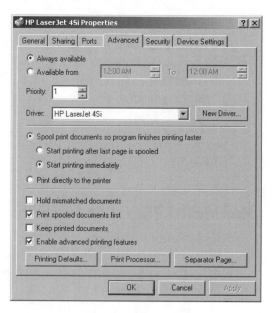

These options are covered in the following sections.

In Windows NT 4, the options that are in the Windows 2000 Server Advanced tab of the printer Properties dialog box were located in the General tab and the Scheduling tab of the printer Properties dialog box.

Printer Availability

Availability, or scheduling, specifies when a printer will service jobs. Usually, you control availability when you have multiple printers that use a single print device. By default, the Always Available radio button in the Advanced tab is selected, so that users can use the printer 24 hours a day. To limit the printer's availability, select the Available From radio button and specify the range of time when the printer should be available.

 Real World Scenario

Using Printer Availability to Manage Printing

You have a printer defined for the Accounting department. Typically users send small jobs to the printer, but during the month-end closing, there are several reports generated for archival purposes that are several hundred pages in length. Users who send short jobs to the printer complain about long waits while the archival reports are being printed.

Printer availability can be used to manage this situation. For example, you could schedule the large jobs to print only during a specified time, say between 10:00 P.M. and 4:00 A.M. To set this up, you would create two printers on the same port, such as printers named ACCT and REPORTS on the LPT1 port. (Both printers are on the same port since the same physical print device services them.) Configure ACCT to always be available. Configure REPORTS to be available only from 10:00 P.M. to 4:00 A.M. You would then instruct your users to send short jobs to ACCT and long jobs to REPORTS, with the understanding that print jobs sent to REPORTS print only during the specified hours. Since the long jobs are for archival purposes only, the delay should not matter.

Printer Priority

Priority is another option that you might configure if you have multiple printers that use a single print device. When you set priority, you specify how jobs are directed to the print device. For example, you might use this option when two groups share a printer and you need to control the priority in which print jobs are serviced by the print device. In the Advanced tab of the printer Properties dialog box, you can set the Priority value to a number from 1 to 99, with 1 as the lowest priority and 99 as the highest priority.

As an example, suppose that a single print device is used by the accounting department. The managers in the accounting department always want their print jobs to print before the jobs created by the other workers in the accounting department. To configure this arrangement, you could create a printer called MANAGERS on port LPT1 with a priority of 99. You would then create a printer on port LPT1 called WORKERS with a priority of 1. Through the Security tab of the printer Properties dialog box, you would allow only managers to use the MANAGERS printer and allow the other accounting users to use the WORKERS printer (Security tab options are covered later in this chapter). When the print manager (which is responsible for polling the print queue for print jobs and directing the print jobs to the correct port) polled for print jobs, it would always poll the higher-priority printer for print jobs before the lower-priority printer.

Print Driver

The Driver setting in the Advanced tab shows which driver is associated with your printer. If you have configured multiple printers on the computer, you can select to use any of the installed drivers. Clicking the New Driver button starts the Add Printer Driver Wizard, which allows you to update or add new print drivers.

Spooling

When you configure spooling options, you specify whether print jobs are spooled or sent directly to the printer. Spooling means that print jobs are saved to disk in a queue before they are sent to the printer. Consider spooling as the traffic controller of printing—it keeps all of the print jobs from trying to print at the same time.

By default, spooling is enabled, with printing beginning immediately. Your other option is to wait until the last page is spooled before printing. An analogy for these choices is the actions you can take in a grocery store cashier line. Let's say you have an entire cart full of groceries and the guy behind you has only a few things. Even if you've started loading your groceries onto the belt, as long as the cashier hasn't started with your items, you can choose to let the person with fewer items go before you, or you can make him wait. If the cashier has already started totaling your groceries, then you don't have that choice. Windows 2000 Server spooling options allow you to configure your print environment for similar situations.

In the Advanced tab, you can leave the Start Printing Immediately option selected, or you can choose the Start Printing After Last Page Is Spooled option. If you choose the latter option, a smaller print job that finishes spooling first will print before your print job, even if your job started spooling before it did. If you specify Start Printing Immediately, the smaller job will need to wait until your print job is complete.

The other main option is to Print Directly to the Printer, which bypasses spooling altogether. This option doesn't work well in a multi-user environment, where multiple print jobs are sent to the same device. However, it is useful in troubleshooting printer problems. If you can print to a print device directly, but you can't print through the spooler, then you know that your spooler is corrupt or has other problems. You also use the Print Directly to the Printer option to print from DOS.

Print Options

The Advanced tab contains check boxes for four print options:

- The Hold Mismatched Documents option is useful when you're using multiple forms with a printer. By default, this feature is disabled, and jobs are printed on a *first-in-first-out* (FIFO) basis. For example, you might enable this option if you need to print on both plain paper and certificate forms. Then all the jobs with the same form will print first. Forms are discussed in more detail later in this chapter in the "Managing Print Servers" section.

- The Print Spooled Documents First option specifies that the spooler print jobs that have completed spooling before large jobs that are still spooling, even if the large print job that is still spooling has a higher priority. By default, this option is enabled, which increases printer efficiency.

- The Keep Printed Documents option specifies that print jobs should not be deleted from the *print spooler* (queue) when they are finished printing. You normally want to delete the print jobs as they print, because saving print jobs can take up a lot of disk space. By default, this option is disabled.

- The Enable Advanced Printing Features option specifies that any advanced features that your printer supports, such as Page Order and Pages Per Sheet, should be enabled. By default, this option is enabled. You would disable these features if there were compatibility problems. For example, if you are using the driver for a similar print device that does not support all of the features of the print device that the driver was written for, you should disable the advanced printing features.

Enabling the Keep Printed Documents option can be useful if you need to identify the source or other attributes of a finished print job. For example, this option helped track down a person who had been sending nasty notes to a co-worker. The workers knew that the notes were being printed on the company laser printer. Since the print queue was on an NTFS volume, the administrator enabled the Keep Printed Documents option and was able to identify the offender through the owner attribute of the file.

Printing Defaults

The Printing Defaults button in the lower-left corner of the Advanced tab calls up the Printing Preferences dialog box (see Figure 11.7, earlier in this chapter). This is the same dialog box that appears when you click the Printing Preferences button in the General tab of the printer Properties dialog box, and its options were covered in the "Configuring General Properties" section earlier in this chapter.

Print Processor

Print processors are used to specify whether Windows 2000 Server needs to do additional processing to print jobs. The five print processors supported by Windows 2000 Server are listed in Table 11.1.

T A B L E   1 1 . 1   Print Processors Supported by Windows 2000

Print Processor	Description
RAW	Makes no changes to the print document
RAW (FF appended)	Makes no changes to the print document except to always add a form-feed character

TABLE 11.1 Print Processors Supported by Windows 2000 *(continued)*

Print Processor	Description
RAW (FF Auto)	Makes no changes to the print document except to try to detect if a form-feed character needs to be added
NT EMF	Generally spools documents that are sent from other Windows 2000 clients
TEXT	Interprets all of the data as plain text, and the printer will print the data using standard text commands

To modify your Print Processor settings, click the Print Processor button at the bottom of the Advanced tab to open the Print Processor dialog box, shown in Figure 11.15. You would generally leave the default settings in this dialog box, unless otherwise directed by the print device manufacturer.

FIGURE 11.15 The Print Processor dialog box

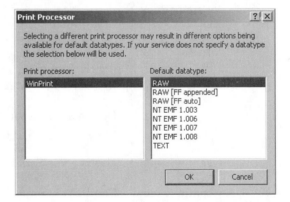

Separator Pages

Separator pages are used at the beginning of each document to identify the user who submitted the print job. If your printer is not shared, a separator page is generally a waste of paper. If the printer is shared by many users, the separator page can be useful for distributing finished print jobs.

To add a separator page, click the Separator Page button in the lower-right corner of the Advanced tab of the printer Properties dialog box. This opens the Separator Page dialog box, shown in Figure 11.16. Click the Browse button to locate and select the separator page file that you want to use. Windows 2000 Server supplies the separator files listed in Table 11.2, which are stored in *Windir*\System32.

FIGURE 11.16 The Separator Page dialog box

TABLE 11.2 Separator Page Files

Separator Page File	Description
Pcl.sep	Used to send a separator page on a dual-language HP printer after switching the printer to PCL (Printer Control Language), which is a common printing standard
pscript.sep	Does not send a separator page, but switches the computer to PostScript printing mode
sysprint.sep	Used by PostScript printers to send a separator page
sysprintj.sep	Same as sysprint.sep, but with support for Japanese characters

You can also create custom separator pages. For more information about creating separator pages, refer to the Windows 2000 Resource Kit.

In Exercise 11.3, you will configure some advanced printer properties. This exercise assumes you have completed Exercise 11.2.

EXERCISE 11.3

Managing Advanced Printer Properties

1. Select Start ➢ Settings ➢ Printers to open the Printers folder.

2. Right-click HP LaserJet 4Si, choose Properties, and click the Advanced tab.

3. Click the Available From radio button and specify that the printer is available from 12:00 A.M. to 6:00 A.M.

4. Click the Start Printing After Last Page Is Spooled radio button.

5. Click the Separator Page button. In the Separator Page dialog box, click the Browse button and choose the sysprint.sep file. Click the Open button, then click the OK button in the Separator Page dialog box.

6. Click the OK button to close the printer Properties dialog box.

Security Properties

You can control which users and groups can access Windows 2000 printers by configuring the print permissions. In Windows 2000 Server, you can allow or deny access to a printer. If you deny access, the user or group will not be able to use the printer, even if their user or group permissions allow such access.

You assign print permissions to users and groups through the Security tab of the printer Properties dialog box, as shown in Figure 11.17. The print permissions that can be assigned are defined in Table 11.3.

FIGURE 11.17 The Security tab of the printer Properties dialog box

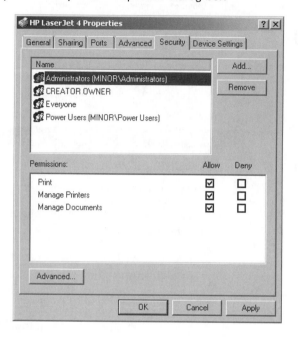

TABLE 11.3 Print Permissions

Print Permission	Description
Print	Allows a user or group connect to a printer and can send print jobs to the printer.
Manage Printers	Allows administrative control of the printer. With this permission, a user or group can pause and restart the printer, change the spooler settings, share or unshare a printer, change print permissions, and manage printer properties.
Manage Documents	Allows users to manage documents by pausing, restarting, resuming, and deleting queued documents. Users cannot control the status of the printer.

By default, whenever a printer is created, default print permissions are assigned. The default permissions are normally appropriate for most network environments. Table 11.4 shows the default print permissions that are assigned.

TABLE 11.4   Default Print Permissions

Group	Print	Manage Printers	Manage Documents
Administrators	✓	✓	✓
Power Users	✓	✓	✓
Creator Owner			✓
Everyone	✓		

Print Permission Assignment

Usually, you can accept the default print permissions, but you might need to modify them for special situations. For example, if your company bought an expensive color laser printer for the marketing department, you probably wouldn't want to allow general access to that printer. In this case, you would deselect the Allow check box for the Everyone group, add the Marketing group to the Security tab list, and then allow the Marketing group the Print permission.

To add print permissions, take the following steps:

1. In the Security tab of the printer Properties dialog box, click the Add button.

2. The Select Users, Computers, or Groups dialog box appears. Click the user, computer, or group that you want to assign print permissions to and click the Add button. After you specify all of the users you want to assign permissions to, click the OK button.

3. Highlight the user, computer, or group and select Allow or Deny access for the Print, Manage Printers, and Manage Documents permissions. Click the OK button when you are finished assigning permissions.

To remove an existing group from the permissions list, highlight the group and click the Remove button. That group will no longer be listed in the Security tab and cannot be assigned permissions.

In Exercise 11.4, you will assign print permissions. This exercise assumes that you have completed Exercise 11.1.

Assigning Print Permissions

1. Using the Local Users and Groups utility, create two users: **Kim** and **Jennifer**. (See Chapter 4, "Managing Users and Groups," for details on creating user accounts.) Deselect the User Must Change Password at Next Logon option.

2. Using the Local Users and Groups utility, verify that you have a group named **Execs**. (See Chapter 4 for details on creating groups.) Place Kim in the Execs group.

3. Select Start ➢ Settings ➢ Printers to open the Printers folder.

4. Right-click HP LaserJet 4Si, select Properties, and click the Security tab. Click the Add button.

5. In the Select Users, Computers, or Groups dialog box, click Execs and click the Add button. Click the OK button to continue.

6. In the Security tab, highlight the Execs group. By default, the Allow check box should be selected for the Print permission. Leave the default setting. Highlight the Everyone group and click the Remove button.

7. Log off as Administrator and log on as Kim.

8. Open the Printers folder and select HP LaserJet 4Si. Kim should be able to connect to this printer based on her membership in the Execs group.

9. Log off as Kim and log on as Jennifer.

10. Open the Printers folder and select HP LaserJet 4Si. At the top of the dialog box, you should see the message "HP LaserJet 4Si Access denied, unable to connect."

11. Log off as Jennifer and log on as Administrator.

Advanced Settings

The advanced settings accessed from the Security tab allow you to configure permissions, auditing, and owner properties. Clicking the Advanced button in the lower-left corner of the Security tab opens the Access Control Settings dialog box, shown in Figure 11.18. This dialog box has three tabs that you can use to add, remove, or edit print permissions:

- The Permissions tab lists all of the users, computers, and groups that have been given permission to the printer, the permission that has been granted, and whether the permission applies to documents or to the printer.

- The Auditing tab allows you to keep track of who is using the printer and what type of access is being used. You can track the success or failure of the six events: Print, Manage Printers, Manage Documents, Read Permissions, Change Permissions, and Take Ownership.

- The Owner tab shows the owner of the printer (the user or group who created the printer), which you can change if you have the proper permissions. For example, if the print permissions excluded the Administrator from using or managing the printer, and the print permissions needed to be reassigned, an Administrator could take ownership of the printer and then reapply print permissions.

FIGURE 11.18   The Access Control Settings dialog box

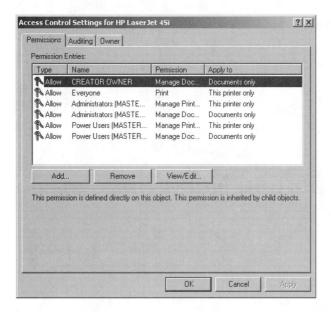

Device Settings Properties

The properties that you see on the Device Settings tab of the printer Properties dialog box depend on the printer and print driver that you have installed. You might configure these properties if you want to manage which forms are associated with tray assignments. For example, you could configure the upper tray to use letterhead and the lower tray to use regular paper. An example of the Device Settings tab for an HP LaserJet 4Si printer is shown in Figure 11.19.

FIGURE 11.19 The Device Settings tab of the printer Properties dialog box

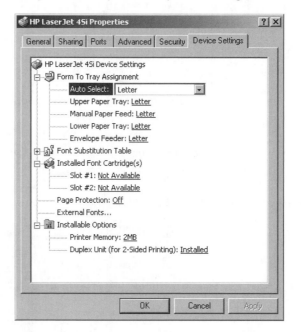

Supporting Non-Windows Print Clients

The Windows 2000 print environment allows you to support Unix, NetWare, and Macintosh clients that want to print to Windows 2000 print devices. The requirements for configuring these options are defined in the following sections.

Support for Unix Clients

Unix clients send print jobs to printers via the *Line Printer Remote (LPR)* utility. This utility is installed on Unix clients and allows them to print files to computers that are running the *Line Printer Daemon (LPD)* service. Windows 2000 allows a Unix client to send print jobs to Windows 2000 printers if these options have been configured:

1. The appropriate print driver must be available to the Unix client for the print device that the client will attach to. This is loaded at the client, as Windows 2000 print servers do not store Unix print drivers.

2. Verify that the Windows 2000 print server is using TCP/IP. The Unix client should automatically be using the TCP/IP protocol.

3. Verify that the Unix client is using a *Request for Comment (RFC)* compliant version of LPR. Some versions of Unix do not use an RFC compliant LPR. If this is the case, the client will not be able to print to Windows 2000.

4. Install Print Services for Unix on the Windows 2000 Server or Professional client. Verify that the service is started and is configured to start automatically through Services.

5. From the Unix client, connect to the Windows 2000 printer using the LPR utility. The syntax used with LPR is dependent on the version of Unix you are using. This command is typical of how the LPR syntax is used:

```
lpr -Sserver_name -Pqueue_name file_name
```

If you want to send a document from a Windows 2000 Professional client to a Unix host that is using LPD, then the Windows 2000 Professional computer must have Print Services for Unix installed.

Support for NetWare Clients

If you want NetWare clients to be able to print to Windows 2000 print devices, you must install a separate product called *File and Print Services for NetWare* (NWLink IPX/SPX is required to support File and Print Services for NetWare) on the Windows 2000 print server. When this product is installed, the Windows 2000 server emulates a NetWare server. This software does not require any changes to the NetWare client's configuration.

Windows 2000 Server ships with *GSNW (Gateway Services for NetWare)*. While File and Print Services for NetWare allows NetWare clients to access Windows 2000 resources, GSNW is used to allow Windows 2000 clients to access NetWare resources.

Support for Macintosh Clients

In order to allow Macintosh clients to print to a Windows 2000 printer, you must install Print Services for Macintosh on the Windows 2000 print server. In Control Panel, select Add/Remove Programs and then Add/Remove Windows components. Next, select Other Network File and Print Services and click on the Details button. Lastly, select Print Services for Macintosh. This software allows the Windows 2000 server to emulate an AppleTalk device. No other configuration changes are required for the Macintosh client.

Managing Printers and Print Documents

Administrators or users with the Manage Printers permission can manage how the printer services print jobs and the print documents in a *print queue*. When you manage a printer, you manage all of the documents in a queue. When you manage print documents, you manage specific documents.

Microsoft ✓ Exam Objective

Monitor, configure, troubleshoot, and control access to printers.

As you would expect, you manage printers and print documents from the Printers folder (select Start ➤ Settings ➤ Printers). The following sections describe the printer management and print document management options.

Managing Printers

To manage a printer, right-click the printer you want to manage. From the pop-up menu, shown in Figure 11.20, select the appropriate option for the area you want to manage. Table 11.5 describes these options.

FIGURE 11.20   The printer management options

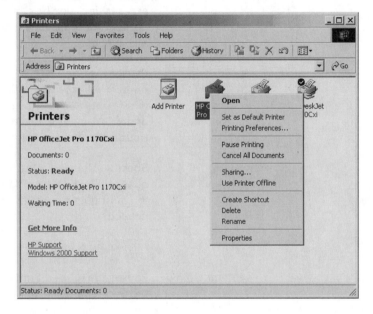

TABLE 11.5   Printer Management Options

Option	Description
Set as Default Printer	Allows you to specify the default printer that will be used when the user does not send a job to an explicit printer (if the computer is configured to access multiple printers).

TABLE 11.5 Printer Management Options *(continued)*

Option	Description
Printing Preferences	Opens the Printing Preferences dialog box (see Figure 11.7), which allows you to configure printer settings for page layout and paper quality. You can also access this dialog box through the General tab of the printer Properties dialog box, as described earlier in this chapter.
Pause Printing	Pauses the printer. Print jobs can be submitted to the printer, but they will not be forwarded to the print device until you resume printing (by unchecking this option). You might use this option if you need to troubleshoot the printer or maintain the print device.
Cancel All Documents	Specifies that any jobs that are currently in the queue will be deleted. You might use this option if the print queue contains jobs that are no longer needed.
Sharing	Allows the printer to be shared or unshared.
Use Printer Offline	Pauses the printer. Print documents will remain in the print queue, even if you restart the computer.
Delete	Removes the printer. You might use this option if you no longer need the printer, if you want to move the printer to another print server, or if you suspect the printer is corrupt and you want to delete and recreate it.
Rename	Allows you to rename the printer. You might use this option to give a printer a more descriptive name or a name that follows naming conventions.

Managing Print Documents

As an Administrator or a user with the Manage Printers or Manage Documents permission, you can manage print documents within a print queue. For example, if a user has sent the same job multiple times, you might need to delete the duplicate print jobs.

To manage print documents, in the Printers folder double-click the printer that contains the documents to open a dialog box with information about the documents in its print queue. Select Document from the menu bar to access the pull-down menu of options that you can use to manage documents, as shown in Figure 11.21. These menu options are described in Table 11.6.

FIGURE 11.21 The Document menu options

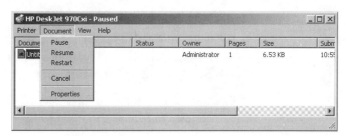

TABLE 11.6 Document Management Options

Option	Description
Pause	Places the printing of this document on hold
Resume	Allows the document to print normally (after it has been paused)
Restart	Resends the job from the beginning, even if it has already partially printed
Cancel	Deletes the job from the print spooler
Properties	Opens the document Properties dialog box, which allows you to set options such as user notification when a print job is complete, document priority, document printing time, page layout, and paper quality

In Exercise 11.5, you will manage printers and print documents.

EXERCISE 11.5

Managing Printers and Print Documents

1. Select Start ➢ Settings ➢ Printers to open the Printers folder.

EXERCISE 11.5 *(continued)*

2. Right-click HP LaserJet 4Si and select Pause Printing.

3. Select Start ➤ Programs ➤ Accessories ➤ Notepad.

4. Create a new text file and then select File ➤ Save As. In the Save As dialog box, save the file in the default location, My Documents, as `PrintMe.txt`. Click the Save button.

5. While still in Notepad, select File ➤ Print. Select HP LaserJet 4Si and click the Print button. Repeat this step two more times so that you have sent a total of three print jobs. Close Notepad.

6. In the Printers folder, double-click HP LaserJet 4Si. At the top of the window, you will see that the status of the printer is Paused.

7. Right-click one of the print jobs in the print queue and select Cancel. The print job will be deleted.

8. Right-click one of the print jobs in the print queue and select Properties. The print job Properties dialog box appears. Change Notify from Administrator to Emily. Set the Priority from 1 to 99. For Schedule, select Only from 12:00 AM to 4:00 AM. Then click the OK button.

9. Close all of the dialog boxes.

Managing Print Servers

A print server is the computer on which printers have been defined. When you send a job to a network printer, you are actually sending it to the print server first.

Microsoft ✓ *Exam* *Objective*	**Monitor, configure, troubleshoot, and control access to printers.**

You can manage print servers by configuring their properties. To access the Print Server Properties dialog box, open the Printers folder and select File ➤ Server Properties. The Print Server Properties dialog box contains Forms, Ports, Drivers, and Advanced tabs. The properties on each of these tabs are discussed in the following sections.

Configuring Form Properties

If your printer has support for multiple trays and you use a different kind of paper in each tray, you will want to configure forms and assign them to specific trays. The Forms tab of the Printer Server Properties dialog box, shown in Figure 11.22, allows you to create and manage forms for a printer. Forms can be given any description and are configured primarily based on size.

FIGURE 11.22   The Forms tab of the Print Server Properties dialog box

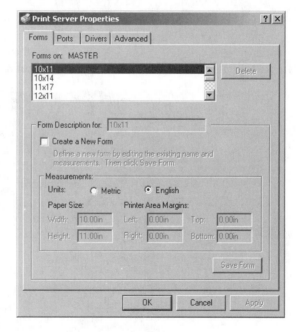

To add a new form, take the following steps:

1. In the Forms tab, select the Create a New Form option.

2. Type the form name in the Form Description For text box.

3. Specify the form measurements in the Measurements section of the dialog box.

   4. Click the Save Form button.

   You associate a form with a specific printer tray through the printer Properties dialog box, rather than through the Printer Server Properties dialog box. In the Device Settings tab of the printer Properties dialog box (see Figure 11.19 earlier in the chapter), under Form To Tray Assignment, select the paper tray that you will associate with the form. Then choose the form that will be used with the paper tray from the drop-down list.

Configuring Print Server Port Properties

   The Ports tab of the Printer Server Properties dialog box, shown in Figure 11.29, is very similar to the Ports tab of the printer Properties dialog box. The properties you can configure for ports were described in the "Configuring Port Properties" section earlier in this chapter. The difference between the two Ports tabs is that the one in the Print Server Properties dialog box is used to manage all of the ports for the print server, rather than the ports for a particular print device.

FIGURE 11.23   The Ports tab of the Print Server Properties dialog box

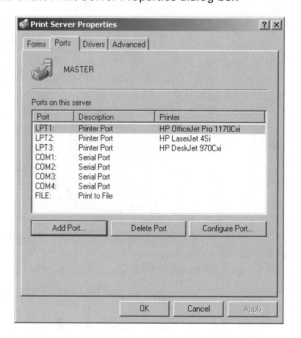

Configuring Driver Properties

The Drivers tab of the Print Server Properties dialog box, shown in Figure 11.24, allows you to manage the print drivers installed on the print server. For each print driver, the tab shows the name, the environment that the driver was written for (for example, Intel or Alpha), and the operating system platform that the driver supports.

FIGURE 11.24 The Drivers tab of the Print Server Properties dialog box

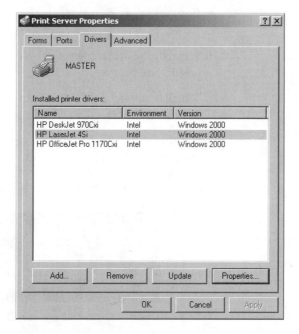

Using the options on the Drivers tab, you can add, remove, and update print drivers. To see a print driver's properties, select the driver and click the Properties button. A print driver's properties include:

- Name
- Version
- Environment
- Language monitor
- Default data type
- Driver path

Configuring Print Server Advanced Properties

The Advanced tab of the Print Server Properties dialog box, shown in Figure 11.25, allows you to configure the spool file, spooler event logging, and notifications about remote documents. You can set these:

- The spool file or hard disk location where the print files wait until they can be serviced by the print device (by default, the print spool folder is located in the *\Windir*\System32\Spool\Printers folder)

- Whether Error, Warning, and Information events are logged in Event Viewer

- Whether the print server will beep if there are errors when remote documents are printed

- Whether notification should be sent to the print server when remote documents are printed

- Whether the computer, as opposed to the user, should be notified when remote documents are printed

FIGURE 11.25 The Advanced tab of the Print Server Properties dialog box

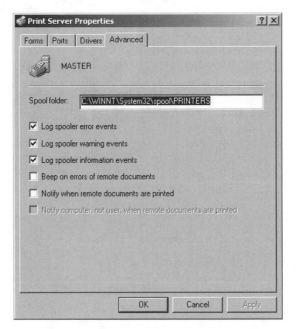

Summary

This chapter explained how to manage printing with Windows 2000 Server. We covered the following topics:

- How to create local and network printers

- Printer properties, which include general properties, sharing properties, port properties, advanced properties, security properties, and device settings

- Print management tasks, such as setting default printers and canceling all print documents

- Document management tasks, such as pausing, resuming, and canceling print documents

- How to manage print server properties, which include form, port, driver, and advanced properties

Exam Essentials

Be able to setup and manage printers   Know how to install and configure Windows 2000 printers for general properties, sharing properties, port properties, advanced properties, and security properties.

Know how to support non-Windows clients   Support Unix, NetWare, and Macintosh clients so that they can submit print jobs to Windows 2000 printers.

Manage printers and print documents   Know how to manage printers and print documents and be able to troubleshoot print problems.

Manage print servers   Know the options that are used to configure print servers as opposed to individual printers and when it is appropriate to configure each option.

Key Terms

Before taking the exam, you should be familiar with the following terms:

local printer	print processor
logical port	print queue
logical printer	print server
network printer	print spooler
physical port	printer pool
print device	separator page
print driver	TCP/IP port

Review Questions

1. Your company uses Windows 2000 with Active Directory. Within the network, there are a variety of clients, including Unix clients. One of the Windows 2000 servers on your network is configured as a print server with a printer called ColorLaser. You have a Unix client that wants to submit jobs to the printer. The Unix client has obtained the proper Unix print driver for the print device. Which of the following options must be configured on the Windows 2000 print server to support printing from the Unix client?

   A. Install the DLC protocol.

   B. Install File and Print Sharing for Unix clients.

   C. Install Print Services for Unix.

   D. If TCP/IP is already installed, no further configuration is required.

2. You have a Unix client who is trying to print a document to a Windows 2000 printer, but is unsuccessful. You verify that the Windows 2000 print server is properly configured to support Unix printing. You also verify that other Unix clients are able to send print jobs to the Windows 2000 printer. What option should you check on the Unix client's computer that is unable to print?

   A. Verify that the Unix client is using a RFC compliant version of LPR.

   B. Verify that the Unix client is using a RFC compliant version of LPD.

   C. Verify that the Unix client has File and Print Services for Microsoft Networks installed.

   D. Verify that the Unix client has File and Print Services for Unix clients installed.

3. Your network uses both Windows 2000 and NetWare. You have
    several Windows 2000 printers configured that the NetWare clients
    would like to access. Which of the following options must be installed
    in order for the NetWare clients to send print jobs to Windows 2000
    printers?

    A. Install GSNW on the Windows 2000 print servers.

    B. Install GSNW on the NetWare clients.

    C. Install File and Print Services for NetWare on the Windows 2000
    print servers.

    D. Install File and Print Services for NetWare on the NetWare clients.

4. Your company has an HP LaserJet 4050. You have created a printer
    called HP LaserJet 4050 Series PCL for use with the print device. Your
    users print documents on letter size paper and legal size paper. You
    configure the paper trays as shown in the first exhibit. You also con-
    figure the Advanced printer properties for the printer as shown in the
    second exhibit. The users' computers are configured to send print jobs
    to the appropriate print tray based on the document type they are
    printing. You have left the printer's security settings at the default val-
    ues. What is the result of your configuration?

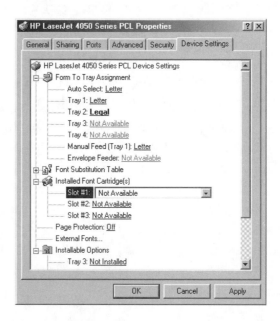

A. Letter-sized jobs will always print first.

B. Legal-sized jobs will always print first.

C. You need to configure print permissions before this scenario will work.

D. Everything is set up properly, and jobs will be printed in the order that they are spooled, regardless of the form you use.

5. Your print server has Windows 2000 server installed on the C: drive, which is 2GB in size. Your users send very large jobs to the Windows 2000 printers and you are getting errors when sending print jobs because the spool file has run out of disk space. You have a D: drive that has 10GB of free disk space. You want to specify the D: drive as an alternate spool file location. Where do you configure this?

A. In the Advanced tab of the Print Server Properties dialog box.

B. In the Advanced tab of the printer Properties dialog box.

C. In the Device Settings tab of the Print Server Properties dialog box.

D. You can't change the location of the spool file without moving the printer to another print server.

6. Your network has a print device that is used by 20 people in the accounting department. Most of the print jobs are between one and 10 pages. However, at the end of the month, several print jobs that average 300 pages are sent to the print device. When these large print jobs are generated, you receive complaints about how long people are waiting for their shorter print jobs. What is the best solution to this problem?

   A. Specify two groups, Accountants and Reports. Create two printers that will point to the same print device called AcctPrinter and ReportPrinter. Assign the AcctPrinter priority 99 and the Report-Printer priority 1. Specify that print jobs that are more than 50 pages be sent to the ReportPrinter printer.

   B. Create two printers that will point to the same print device called AcctPrinter and ReportPrinter. Configure the AcctPrinter so that it is available 24 hours a day and the ReportPrinter so that it is only available during off-peak hours. Instruct users to send the long print jobs to the ReportPrinter.

   C. Specify that users should submit long print jobs only when they are ready to leave for the day, so that their print jobs will print during off-peak hours.

   D. Specify that long print jobs be submitted, then place them on hold until you leave for the day, at which time they can be released.

7. Your network has a network print device that is used by 20 people in the accounting department. The accounting department has two managers, and the rest of the department is staff level. The managers have complained that sometimes they have a long wait before their print jobs are printed. They want their print jobs to always go to the top of the print queue. What is the best solution to this problem?

   A. Specify two groups, Managers and Accountants. Create two printers that will point to the same print device called ManagerPrinter and AcctPrinter. Assign the ManagerPrinter priority 99 and the AcctPrinter priority 1. Tell the regular accounting staff to send their print jobs to the AcctPrinter and the managers to send their print jobs to the ManagerPrinter.

B. Specify two groups, Managers and Accountants. Create two printers that will point to the same print device called ManagerPrinter and AcctPrinter. Assign Print permission to the Managers group with a priority of 99. Assign Print permission to the Accountants group with a priority of 1.

C. Specify two groups, Managers and Accountants. Create two printers that will point to the same print device called ManagerPrinter and AcctPrinter. Assign the ManagerPrinter priority 99 and the AcctPrinter priority 1. Remove the Print permission from the Everyone group on the ManagerPrinter and assign the Managers group Print permission. Tell the regular accounting staff to send their print jobs to the AcctPrinter and the managers to send their print jobs to the ManagerPrinter.

D. Specify two groups, Managers and Accountants. Create one printer called AcctPrinter. Assign the Manage Documents permission to the Managers group and leave the Everyone group with Print permission. Instruct the managers to send their jobs to the AcctPrinter and through their Manage Documents permission, place their print jobs at the top of the print queue.

8. You have users who need to print documents on letter-sized paper, legal-sized paper, and envelopes. Your print device has three paper trays and you have loaded each tray with the three types of paper that will be used. Where within the printer properties do you configure each type of paper to be associated with a different form?

   A. In the Forms tab of the Print Server Properties dialog box

   B. In the Advanced tab of the Print Server Properties dialog box

   C. In the Forms tab of the printer Properties dialog box

   D. In the Advanced tab of the printer Properties dialog box

9. You have a print device that has failed. The print device services a printer called AcctLaser1 that is located on Server1. You want to redirect the print jobs that would normally be sent to the AcctLaser1 printer to a printer called AcctLaser2 that is located on Server2. You do not want the users to need to change any of their configuration settings. What should you do?

   A. In the AcctLaser1 port properties, create a new port that is redirected to \\Server1\AcctLaser1. Specify that AcctLaser1 will use this port.

   B. In the AcctLaser1 port properties, create a new port that is redirected to \\Server2\AcctLaser2. Specify that AcctLaser1 will use this port.

   C. In the AcctLaser2 port properties, create a new port that is redirected to \\Server1\AcctLaser1. Specify that AcctLaser1 will use this port.

   D. In the AcctLaser2 port properties, create a new port that is redirected to \\Server2\AcctLaser2. Specify that AcctLaser1 will use this port.

10. You have installed a Windows 2000 member server. This server will support 10 printers that need to be created. You have assigned George the task of creating the printers. Right now George is configured as a regular user. Which of the following group memberships would allow George to create a printer? (Choose all that apply.)

    A. Administrators

    B. Server Operators

    C. Power Users

    D. Print Operators

11. Bart sits near the network printers and is competent to manage network printing. You have decided to grant Bart the Manage Printers print permission for theAcctLaser printer. Which of the following tasks will Bart be able to accomplish? (Choose all that apply.)

    A. Pause or restart the printer

    B. Change spooler settings

    C. Create a new printer

    D. Share or unshare the printer

12. Your company uses a color laser printer. This printer uses very expensive consumables. You suspect that the printer is being heavily used for non-business purposes. You want to track anytime a user sends a print job to this printer. Which feature should you configure to track these events?

    A. Configure auditing for Print events on the printer

    B. Configure auditing for Access events on the printer

    C. Configure object access for Print events on the printer

    D. Configure object access for Access events on the printer

13. You are having trouble with the SalesLaser printer and are trying to determine if the problem is with the physical print device or with the logical printer and spool file. Which of the following options will allow you to bypass the print spooler and print directly to the printer?

    A. In the General tab of the printer Properties dialog box, select Bypass Network Printing

    B. In the Advanced tab of the printer Properties dialog box, select Bypass Network Printing

    C. In the General tab of the printer Properties dialog box, select Print Directly to the Printer

    D. In the Advanced tab of the printer Properties dialog box, select Print Directly to the Printer

14. You have a new print device that attaches to the network through a network card that is installed in the print device. Which port should you specify for this device when you create the printer?

    A. Printer port

    B. Serial port

    C. Network port

    D. Standard TCP/IP port

15. You are trying to troubleshoot a printing problem and want to track print jobs as they are being sent to the print spooler folder. What is the default location of the print server's spool folder?

    A. *Windir*\\Spool

    B. *Windir*\\System32\\Spool

    C. *Windir*\\System32\\Spool\\Printers

    D. *Windir*\\System32\\Spool\\Print Server

Answers to Review Questions

1. C. In order to support Unix print clients, you must Install Print Services for Unix on the Windows 2000 server or Professional client. You should also verify that the service is started and is configured to start automatically through Services.

2. A. Verify that the Unix client is using an RFC (Request for Comments) compliant version of LPR. Some versions of Unix do not use an RFC compliant LPR. If this is the case, the client will not be able to print to Windows 2000.

3. C. If you want NetWare clients to be able to print to Windows 2000 print devices, you must install a separate product called File and Print Services for NetWare (NWLink IPX/SPX is required to support File and Print Services for NetWare) on the Windows 2000 print server. When this product is installed, the Windows 2000 server emulates a NetWare server. This software does not require any changes to the NetWare client's configuration.

4. D. Because you have multiple paper trays, and everything is configured properly, jobs will be printed as they are spooled, regardless of the form you are using.

5. A. You can change the location of the print server's spool file through the Advanced tab of the Print Server Properties dialog box.

6. B. You want users to be able to easily submit jobs and have those jobs automatically print at the correct time. This can be accomplished by creating two printers that are configured with different availability. You can then instruct users to send long print jobs to the printer that has availability configured for off-peak business hours.

7. C. Option A is a possible answer, but this does not prevent members of the Accountants group from sending their print jobs to the ManagerPrinter. In option C, you manage the print permissions so that only members of the Managers group can send jobs to the Manager-Printer. Since this printer is configured with a higher priority, its print jobs will always be serviced before jobs from the AcctPrinter.

8. A. You create new forms through the Print Server Properties dialog box. After you create the forms, you associate them with the printer through the Device Settings tab of the printer Properties dialog box.

9. B. In this case, you are redirecting the jobs from AcctLaser1 to AcctLaser2. You must modify the port properties on AcctLaser1 to point to AcctLaser2, which is \\Server2\AcctLaser2.

10. A, C. The only groups that have the permissions necessary to create new printers on Windows 2000 member server computers are Administrators and Power Users.

11. A, B, D. A user with the Manage Printers permission has administrative control of the printer. With this permission, a user or group can pause and restart the printer, change the spooler settings, share or unshare a printer, change print permissions, and manage printer properties.

12. A. When you access advanced security properties, you'll see the Auditing tab, which allows you to keep track of who is using the printer and what type of access is being used. You can track the success or failure of six events: Print, Manage Printers, Manage Documents, Read Permissions, Change Permissions, and Take Ownership.

13. D. In the Advanced tab of the printer Properties dialog box, you can specify how you will spool print documents or if you will print directly to the printer.

14. D. For a network printer, you create a standard TCP/IP port based on the TCP/IP address of the network device.

15. C. When you access the Advanced tab of the Print Server Properties dialog box, you will see that the default location of the spool folder is *Windir*\System32\Spool\Printers.

Chapter

12

Administering Terminal Services

MICROSOFT EXAM OBJECTIVES IN THIS CHAPTER

✓ **Install, configure, monitor, and troubleshoot Terminal Services.**

- Remotely administer servers by using Terminal Services.
- Configure Terminal Services for application sharing.
- Configure applications for use with Terminal Services.

Windows 2000 requires significantly more computing power than any other Windows-based operating system to date. Administrators can spend countless hours upgrading machines and deploying Windows 2000. An alternative is to deliver many of the features of Windows 2000 to users through Terminal Services.

Rather than installing the full operating system on each machine in the network, you can upgrade one machine to Windows 2000 Server and install the Terminal Services client on every other computer. The client can be run on just about any Windows-based computer or terminal, eliminating the need for costly hardware upgrades. The server then handles the entire computing load for every Terminal Services client.

Another use of Terminal Services is for remote administration. Through Terminal Services, administrators can perform all types of administration tasks from virtually any client.

Terminal Services does require a certain amount of planning. You should make sure that the computer you use as the Terminal Services server is powerful enough to handle all of the users who will be connected to it and that your clients are able to run the client software. You also need to purchase and configure all of the proper licenses that are required to run Terminal Services.

After you have planned your Terminal Services configuration, you can begin deploying the server and client software. Terminal Services includes a configuration utility, a management utility, and a client creator tool for managing the server and clients.

In this chapter, you will learn how Terminal Services works and how to install, configure, and manage Terminal Services servers and clients.

Understanding Terminal Services

The main function of Terminal Services is to enable all client application execution, data processing, and data storage to occur on the Windows 2000 server. Clients use terminal emulation software to access the server desktop. Many clients can access the server through terminal emulation software, including personal computers, Windows CE–based Handheld PCs (H/PC), or traditional terminal clients. The term *Windows-based Terminal (WBT)* broadly describes a class of thin-client terminal devices that can gain access to servers running a multi-user Windows operating system, such as Terminal Services.

The main purpose of terminal emulation software is to send keystrokes and mouse movements to the server. The Terminal Services server processes all information locally and sends the data response back to the Terminal Services client. This approach allows remote control of servers and centralized application management, minimizing network bandwidth requirements between the server and client.

Clients can access Terminal Services through TCP/IP from a local connection or a WAN connection (for example, through a *Virtual Private Network (VPN)* connection). VPNs are covered in greater detail in Chapter 13, "Managing Remote Network Connections."

Some of the clients that can act as Terminal Services clients include:

- MS-DOS-based clients

- Windows for Workgroups clients, version 3.11 or later

- Windows-based terminals (Windows CE devices)

- UNIX terminals

- Macintosh clients

Terminal Services Modes

You can run *Terminal Services* in either of two modes:

- In *remote administration mode*, administrators can perform administrative tasks from virtually any client on the network.

- In *application server mode,* users have remote access to applications running on the server. Using this mode, Terminal Services delivers the Windows 2000 Desktop environment to computers that might not otherwise be able to run Windows 2000 because of hardware or other limitations.

Remote Administration Mode

Remote Administration gives system administrators the ability to remotely administer any Windows 2000 server over any TCP/IP connection. Some of the tasks that can be administered include administration of file and print sharing, making changes to the registry, or performing any of the tasks that you would normally be able to perform on the remote computer

When you install Terminal Services in Remote Administration mode, only the remote access components of Terminal Services are installed. None of the application sharing components are installed. This option places very little overhead on the server where Terminal Services is installed that uses Remote Administration capabilities. Terminal Services allows a maximum of two concurrent Remote Administration connections. With this option, no additional licensing is required and you do not need a license server.

Application Server Mode

In application server mode, applications can be deployed and managed from the Terminal Services server. The server's graphical user interface is transmitted to the remote client, and the client sends keyboard and mouse signals to the server. The client computers are called *thin clients.* Users log on through any client on the network and can see only their individual *session.* Terminal Services manages unique client sessions transparently. Many different types of hardware devices can run the thin client software, including Windows-based terminals and computers.

You can deploy applications by installing them directly on the server or you could use Group Policy and Active Directory to publish Windows Installer application packages to a Terminal Services server or a group of Terminal Services servers. Applications can be installed by an Administrator only on a per server basis, and only if the appropriate Group Policy setting is enabled.

With application server mode, you must use a license server and each client computer that will connect to the Terminal Services server must have a Terminal Services Client Access License and a Windows 2000 Client Access License. Terminal server licensing is covered in detail in the section "Determining Proper Licensing Requirements," later in this chapter.

Benefits of Terminal Services

Terminal Services offers many benefits that could make it the most advantageous solution for your network:

Wider deployment of Windows 2000   Rather than installing a full version of Windows 2000 on every desktop, you can deploy Terminal Services instead. Computers whose hardware might not be supported by the full version of Windows 2000 can still take advantage of many of Windows 2000's features.

Simultaneous operation of both the thin client software and a stand-alone operating system   With Terminal Services, network users can continue to use their existing computer systems, but they can also enjoy the benefits of the Windows 2000 Desktop environment.

Simplified application deployment   Instead of installing and updating applications on every machine in the network, the administrator can install and update one copy on the Terminal Services server. This ensures that every user has access to the latest version of the application.

Remote administration of the server   Terminal Services allows you to administer the server remotely. This is useful if the administrator needs to be away from the server at any time.

Terminal Services includes many features that make it easy to use and manage. These features are described in Table 12.1.

TABLE 12.1   Terminal Services Features

Feature	Description
Multiple logon support	Users can log on multiple times simultaneously, either from many clients or from one client, and can log on to multiple servers as well. This allows users to perform several tasks at the same time.
Roaming disconnect support	A user can disconnect from a session without logging off. The session remains active while disconnected, allowing the user to reconnect at another time or from another client.
Performance enhancements	Enhanced use of caching improves performance significantly.

TABLE 12.1 Terminal Services Features *(continued)*

Feature	Description
Clipboard redirection	Users can cut and paste between applications on the local computer and applications on the Terminal Services server.
Automated local printer support	Printers attached to clients are automatically added and reconnected.
Security	The logon process is encrypted, and administrators can specify the number of logon attempts and the connection time of individual users. Data transmitted between the server and client can be encrypted at three levels (low, medium, or high) depending on your security needs.
Session remote control	Two users can view the same session concurrently. This helps support personnel diagnose problems or train users.
Network load balancing	Terminal Services can evenly distribute client connections across a group of servers, thus alleviating the load on any one server.
Windows-based terminals	Windows-based terminals that run on a modified version of Windows CE and Remote Desktop Protocol are available.
Client Connection Manager	This utility creates an icon on the Desktop that allows quick connectivity to servers for either single program or full Desktop access.
Terminal Services Licensing	This tool helps administrators track clients and their licenses.
Dfs support	Users can connect to a Dfs share. Administrators can host a Distributed file system (Dfs) share from a Terminal Services server. (See Chapter 8, "Administering the Distributed File System," for details on using Dfs.)
Terminal Services Manager	This tool is used by administrators to query and manage sessions, users, and processes.

TABLE 12.1   Terminal Services Features *(continued)*

Feature	Description
Terminal Services Configuration	This tool is used to create, modify, and delete sessions.
Integration with local users and groups and the Active Directory	Administrators can create Terminal Services accounts in much the same way as they create regular user accounts.
Integration with System Monitor	System performance characteristics of Terminal Services can be tracked by System Monitor.
Messaging support	Administrators can send messages to clients.
Remote administration	Users with appropriate permissions can remotely manage all aspects of a Terminal Services server.
Configurable session timeout	Administrators can configure how long a session can remain either active or idle before disconnecting it.

Terminal Services Components

Terminal Services consists of three components: the Terminal Services server, the Remote Desktop Protocol, and the Terminal Services client. The Terminal Services server communicates with the Terminal Services client using the Remote Desktop Protocol.

The Terminal Services Server

Most Terminal Services operations take place on the *Terminal Services server* (or *Terminal server*). When Terminal Services is in application server mode, all of the applications are run on the server. The Terminal Services server sends only screen information to the client and receives only mouse and keyboard input. The server must keep track of the active sessions.

The Remote Desktop Protocol

When you install Terminal Services, the *Remote Desktop Protocol (RDP)* is automatically installed. RDP is the only connection that needs to be configured in order for clients to connect to the Terminal Services server. You can configure only one RDP connection per network adapter.

You use the Terminal Services Configuration tool to configure the properties of the RDP connection. You can set encryption settings and permissions, and limit the amount of time client sessions can remain active.

The Terminal Services Client

The *Terminal Services client* (or *Terminal client*) uses thin-client technology to deliver the Windows 2000 Server Desktop to the user. The client needs only to establish a connection with the server and display the graphical user interface information that the server sends. This process requires very little overhead on the client's part, and it can be run on older machines that would not otherwise be able to use Windows 2000.

Planning the Terminal Services Configuration

Before you can use Terminal Services, you need to determine which applications will be shared and what kind of hardware you will be using. The requirements for running a Terminal Services server are more substantial than those for running a normal Windows 2000 server, especially if you are using application server mode.

You must also consider the extent and cost of licensing a Terminal Services configuration. Each client that will connect to the Terminal Services server must have a special Terminal Services client license.

Determining Client Applications

Applications used with Terminal Services are installed on a per-computer basis, rather than a per-user basis. They must be available to every user who accesses the Terminal Services server. Administrators can install applications on the Terminal Services server directly or from a remote session.

Terminal Services tends to require extra system resources to manage all of the client traffic. You should be aware of certain program characteristics that might inordinately tax the server. Intel-based programs running on Alpha machines, video-intensive applications, MS-DOS applications, and continuously running bits of code (such as automatic spell checkers) can drain system resources. You should limit access to these types of programs to only those users who really need them, and turn off any optional application features that might burden the server unnecessarily.

Windows 2000 Server is a 32-bit environment. In order to run 16-bit applications, Windows 2000 must employ a system called Windows on Windows (WOW), which consumes a lot of system resources. Using 16-bit applications can reduce the number of users that a single processor can handle by 40 percent and can increase the amount of memory required for each user by 50 percent. Obviously, it's best to use 32-bit applications whenever possible.

Determining Hardware Requirements

You will need a computer that can handle the Terminal Services loads for your Terminal Services server. The requirements for Terminal Services clients are minimal.

Terminal Services Server Requirements

The hardware requirements for a Terminal Services server depend on how many clients will be connecting at a time and the usage requirements of the clients. The following are some guidelines:

- A Terminal Services server requires at least a Pentium processor and 128MB RAM to perform adequately. You should also provide an additional 10MB to 20MB RAM per client connection, depending on the applications the clients will be using. A Terminal Services server shares executable resources among users, so memory requirements for additional users running the same application are less than the requirements for the first user to load the program.

- You should use a high-performance bus architecture such as EISA, MCA, or PCI. The ISA (AT) bus cannot move enough data to support the kind of traffic that is generated by a typical Terminal Services installation.

- You should consider using a SCSI disk drive, preferably one that is compatible with Fast SCSI , Ultra2 SCSI-2, or Ultra160 SCSI. For the best performance, you should use a SCSI disk with RAID, which significantly increases disk-access time by placing data on multiple disks.

- Because many users will be accessing the Terminal Services server simultaneously, you should use a high-performance network adapter. The best solution would be to install two adapters in your machine and dedicate one to RDP traffic only.

Terminal Services Client Requirements

The Terminal Services client runs well on a variety of machines, including older computers and terminals that would not otherwise be able to run Windows 2000. The client software runs on the following machines:

- Windows-based terminal devices (embedded)

- Intel and Alpha-based computers running Windows for Workgroups 3.11, Windows 95, Windows 98, Windows NT 3.1, 3.5, and 3.51, Windows NT 4, and Windows 2000

- Macintosh and Unix-based computers (with additional third-party software)

Determining Proper Licensing Requirements

Terminal Services uses its own licensing method. A Terminal client must receive a valid license from a Terminal Services *license server* before logging on to a Terminal Services server. This applies only to the application server mode. When remote administration mode is being used, two concurrent client sessions are allowed automatically; you do not need to receive a license from a license server.

You can enable Terminal Services Licensing when you install Windows 2000 Server or later, through the Add/Remove Programs icon in Control Panel. When you enable Terminal Services Licensing, you can select between two types of license servers:

- An enterprise license server can serve Terminal Services servers on any Windows 2000 domain, but cannot serve workgroups or Windows NT 4 domains.

- A domain license server can serve only Terminal Services servers that are in the same domain. In Windows 2000 domains, domain license servers must be installed on domain controllers. In workgroups or Windows NT 4 domains, domain license servers can be installed on any member server.

In order to deploy Terminal Services, you will be required to obtain server and client licenses. The licenses you may need are described in Table 12.2.

TABLE 12.2 Terminal Services Licenses

License	Description
Windows 2000 Server license	This server license is included when you purchase Windows 2000 Server.
Windows 2000 Server Client Access license	This license is required for all computers or Terminal Services clients that connect to a Windows 2000 server. This license is required by all connecting computers to use file, print, and other network services, regardless of whether they are using Terminal Services.
Windows 2000 Terminal Services Client Access license or Windows 2000 Professional license	Every Terminal Services client needs to have a Windows 2000 Terminal Services Client Access license in addition to a Windows 2000 Server Client Access license. This license provides each Terminal Services client the right to connect to a Terminal Services server and run applications on the server. Windows 2000 Professional machines that are used as Terminal Services clients are automatically licensed to connect to Terminal Services.
Windows 2000 Terminal Services Internet Connector license	This license can be purchased and used separately from the client access licenses described above. This license allows up to 200 clients to connect anonymously from the Internet. This is useful for providing Windows-based applications to the public without porting them to a Web-based format.

TABLE 12.2 Terminal Services Licenses *(continued)*

License	Description
Work at Home Windows 2000 Terminal Services Client Access license	This license is required for users who want to use Terminal Services to access the Windows 2000 Desktop and applications from home. You can purchase a Work at Home Windows 2000 Terminal Services Client Access license for each Terminal Services Client Access license owned. The Work at Home license includes a Windows 2000 Server Client Access license, but does not include application licenses, which must be purchased separately.

Installing and Configuring the Terminal Services Server

The Terminal Services server controls all of the Terminal clients that are connected to it. All Terminal Services operations actually take place on the Terminal Services server. The clients are nothing more than dummy windows that display information sent from the server and send mouse and keyboard information to the server.

Microsoft ✓ *Exam Objective*

Install, configure, monitor, and troubleshoot Terminal Services.

- Remotely administer servers by using Terminal Services.
- Configure Terminal Services for application sharing.

After you install Terminal Services, you can configure many settings that control how users and sessions are handled by the Terminal Services server through the Terminal Services server Configuration utility. You can use the Terminal Services Manager utility to view every server and session on the network and manually perform actions such as immediately disconnecting from or sending messages to sessions.

Installing the Terminal Services Server

You install Terminal Services through the Add/Remove Programs icon in Control Panel. Terminal Services can only be configured to support one mode at a time, either remote administration mode or application server mode. In the following sections, you will learn how to install both Terminal Services modes.

Installing Terminal Services in Remote Administration Mode

You should install Terminal Services in remote administration mode if you want to be able to perform administrative tasks from any client on the network, rather than needing to work from the server console. To install Terminal Services in remote administration mode:

1. Select Start ➢ Settings ➢ Control Panel. Double-click the Add/Remove Programs icon.

2. The Add/Remove Programs window appears. Click the Add/Remove Windows Components option.

3. The Windows Components Wizard starts. Check the Terminal Services box and click the Next button.

4. The Terminal Services Setup dialog box appears, as shown in Figure 12.1. Confirm that the Remote Administration Mode radio button is selected and click the Next button.

FIGURE 12.1 Selecting the Terminal Services mode

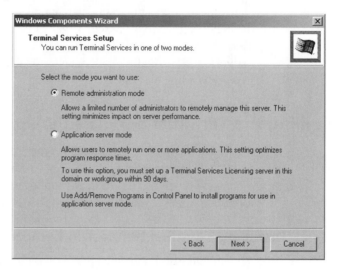

5. The Configuring Components dialog box appears. If the Windows 2000 Server CD is not already in your CD-ROM drive, you will be prompted to insert the Windows 2000 Server CD. Files will be copied, and the Terminal Services components will be configured. This may take a few minutes.

6. The Completing the Windows Components Wizard dialog box appears. Click the Finish button.

7. You will be prompted to restart the computer for the changes to be effective. Click the Yes button to restart your computer.

Installing Terminal Services in Application Server Mode

If you want to give users remote access to applications running on the server, you should install Terminal Services in application server mode. Take the following steps to install Terminal Services in application server mode (this assumes that remote administration mode is not installed):

1. Select Start ➢ Settings ➢ Control Panel. Double-click the Add/Remove Programs icon.

2. The Add/Remove Programs window appears. Click the Add/Remove Windows Components option.

3. The Windows Components Wizard starts. Check the Terminal Services box and click the Next button.

4. The first Terminal Services Setup dialog box appears (see Figure 12.1). Select the Application Server Mode radio button and click the Next button.

5. The second Terminal Services Setup dialog box appears, as shown in Figure 12.2. In this dialog box, you select the default permissions for application compatibility. The Permissions Compatible with Windows 2000 Users option provides the highest level of security. The Permissions Compatible with Terminal Services 4.0 Users option provides the highest compatibility for legacy applications. Make your selection and click the Next button.

FIGURE 12.2   Selecting Terminal Services application permissions compatibility

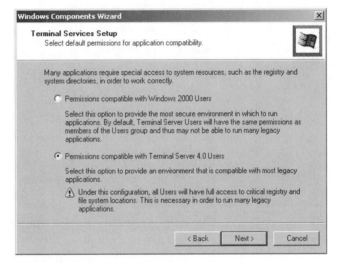

6. You might be notified that certain applications may not work properly after installing Terminal Services in application server mode. You should reinstall these applications after Terminal Services Setup is complete. If the application does not support network access, it will not work with Terminal Services. Click the Next button.

7. The Configuring Components dialog box appears. If the Windows 2000 Server CD is not already in your CD-ROM drive, you will be prompted to insert the Windows 2000 Server CD. Files will be copied, and the Terminal Services components will be configured. This may take a few minutes.

8. The Completing the Windows Components Wizard dialog box appears. Click the Finish button.

9. You will be prompted to restart the computer for the changes to be effective. Click the Yes button to restart your computer.

In Exercise 12.1, you will install Terminal Services in application server mode on your domain controller.

EXERCISE 12.1

Installing Terminal Services on a Server

1. Select Start ➤ Settings ➤ Control Panel and double-click the Add/Remove Programs icon.

2. In the Add/Remove Programs window, click Add/Remove Windows Components.

3. When the Windows Components Wizard begins, check the Terminal Services check box and click the Next button.

4. In the first Terminal Services Setup dialog box, click the Application Server Mode radio button and click the Next button.

5. In the next Terminal Services Setup dialog box, select the Permissions Compatible with Windows 2000 Users radio button and click the Next button.

6. If you are notified that certain applications may not work properly after installing Terminal Services in application server mode, click the Next button. (You should reinstall these applications after you've installed Terminal Services.)

7. The appropriate files will be copied from the Windows 2000 Server CD. Reboot when prompted by clicking the Yes button.

After you install Terminal Services, three new items are added to the Administrative Tools program group: Terminal Services Client Creator, Terminal Services Configuration, and Terminal Services Manager. The Terminal Services Client Creator is used to create 32-bit and 16-bit client software diskettes for use with client machines, as explained in the "Installing and Configuring Terminal Services Clients" section later in the chapter. The following sections describe how to configure and manage Terminal Services with the Terminal Services Configuration and Terminal Services Manager utilities.

Configuring the Terminal Services Server

With the *Terminal Services Configuration* utility, you can change the properties of the RDP-Tcp (Remote Desktop Protocol-Transmission Control Protocol) connection that is created when you install Terminal Services. You can also add new connections with this utility. To open Terminal Services Configuration, select Start ➢ Programs ➢ Administrative Tools ➢ Terminal Services Configuration. The main Terminal Services Configuration window is shown in Figure 12.3.

FIGURE   12.3   The Terminal Services Configuration window

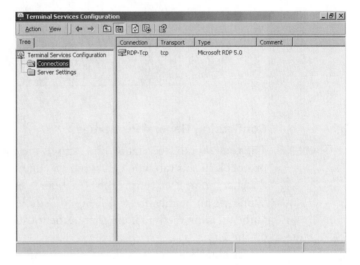

Managing Connections

To configure the properties for a specific connection, select the Connections folder, right-click the connection in the Terminal Services Configuration window, and select Properties from the pop-up menu. This opens the RDP-Tcp Properties dialog box, as shown in Figure 12.4. This dialog box has eight tabs: General, Logon Settings, Sessions, Environment, Remote Control, Client Settings, Network Adapter, and Permissions. The options on these tabs are described in the following sections.

FIGURE 12.4 The General tab of the RDP-Tcp Properties dialog box

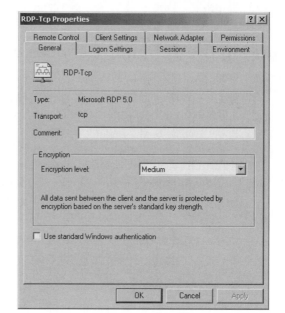

Configuring General Properties

The General tab (see Figure 12.4) shows the connection type and transport protocol. In this tab, you can specify a comment for the connection, select the encryption level that will be used, and choose whether or not standard Windows authentication will be used. You will see an option for another authentication method if another authentication package has been installed on the server.

Terminal Services uses the standard RSA RC4 encryption method when transferring data between the server and clients. You can change the level of encryption depending on your needs. The Encryption Level drop-down list has three choices:

- The Low setting secures all data sent from the client to the server, but not from the server to the client. Windows 2000-based clients use a 56-bit key. Earlier versions of the client use a 40-bit key.

- The Medium setting secures data traveling in both directions. This encryption level uses the same keys as the Low setting.

▪ The High setting secures data traveling in both directions. This encryption level uses a 128-bit key.

Configuring Logon Settings

The Logon Settings tab, shown in Figure 12.5, allows you to specify whether the client will provide logon information or whether the logon information will be pre-configured. You can also specify whether the user will always be prompted for a password.

FIGURE 12.5   The Logon Settings tab of the RDP-Tcp Properties dialog box

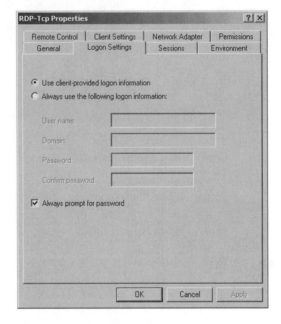

Configuring Sessions Settings

The Sessions tab, shown in Figure 12.6, allows you to configure session time-out and reconnection settings. You can limit the amount of time that active, idle, and disconnected sessions remain running on the server. You also can set whether the session should end or be disconnected when the time limit is reached. A disconnected session is saved on the server, and the disconnected user can reconnect from any client without losing any data. Ending a session closes all of the user's applications immediately, usually resulting in lost data.

FIGURE 12.6 The Sessions tab of the RDP-Tcp Properties dialog box

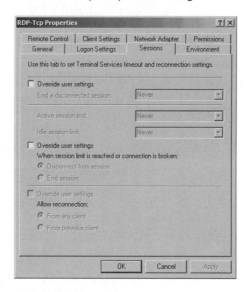

Configuring Environment Settings

The Environment tab, shown in Figure 12.7, allows you to override the settings that are created in Client Connection Manager Wizard or the user profile and start a specific program when the user logs on. You can also specify that no wallpaper will be displayed on the client, which speeds up screen redrawing.

FIGURE 12.7 The Environment tab of the RDP-Tcp Properties dialog box

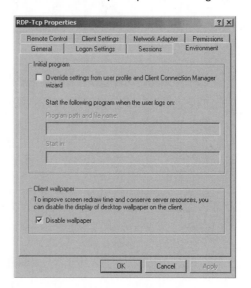

Configuring Remote Control Options

Remote control allows you to view or control a user's session from another session. You cannot control a session from the Terminal Services server console. The Remote Control tab, shown in Figure 12.8, allows you to enable or disable remote control and set whether the user needs to give permission for remote control.

FIGURE 12.8 The Remote Control tab of the RDP-Tcp Properties dialog box

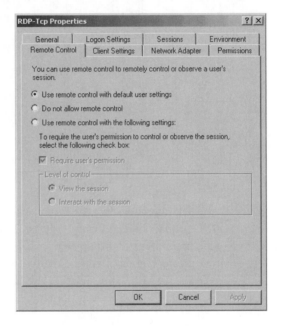

You can access a session for remote control management through the Terminal Services Manager utility, as described in "Managing Terminal Services," later in this chapter.

Configuring Client Settings

The Client Settings tab, shown in Figure 12.9, allows you to configure connection settings and specify which options are disabled.

FIGURE 12.9 The Client Settings tab of the RDP-Tcp Properties dialog box

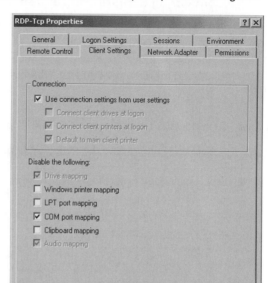

By default, mappings that a user sets in a session are lost when the user logs off. Terminal Services Configuration allows you to automatically restore the user's mappings every time he or she logs on. Users can map drives and Windows printers, and can set the main client printer as the default.

You can also specify whether the following options are disabled:

- Drive mapping

- Windows printer mapping

- LPT port mapping

- COM port mapping

- Clipboard mapping

- Audio mapping

Configuring the Network Adapter

The Network Adapter tab, shown in Figure 12.10, allows you to specify the network adapter that will service Terminal Services clients. You can also allow unlimited connections or set the maximum number of connections that can be made. You might choose to limit connections to conserve your server's resources and improve its ability to service clients.

FIGURE 12.10   The Network Adapter tab of the RDP-Tcp Properties dialog box

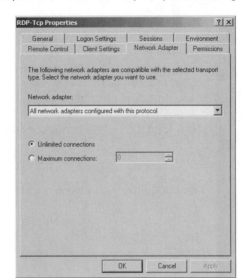

Configuring Connection Permissions

The Permissions tab, shown in Figure 12.11, allows you to configure permissions that allow or deny Terminal Services server access to users and groups. The specific permissions you can set are described in Table 12.3.

FIGURE 12.11   The Permissions tab of the RDP-Tcp Properties dialog box

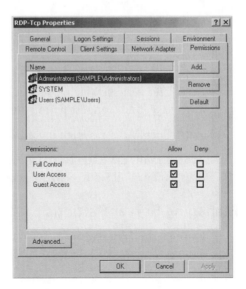

TABLE 12.3 Terminal Services Connection Permissions

Permission	Description
Query Information	Query sessions and servers for information
Set Information	Configure connection properties
Reset	End a session
Remote Control	View or control another session
Logon	Log on to a Terminal Services session
Logoff	Log off another user from a session
Message	Send a message to another session
Connect	Connect to another session
Disconnect	Disconnect another session
Virtual Channels	Use virtual channels, which provide access from a server program to client devices

Permission lists make permissions easier to administer. There are three lists that are available for connection permissions:

- Full Control, which includes all of the permissions listed in Table 12.3
- User Access, which is limited to the Query Information, Logon, Message, and Connect permissions
- Guest Access, which includes the Logon permission

By default, the RDP-Tcp connection that is installed with Terminal Services assigns Full Control to Administrators and User Access to Users.

Managing Server Settings

Through the Terminal Services Configuration utility, you can also configure settings that apply to the server. Select the Server Settings folder in the

Terminal Services Configuration window to see the settings available. These settings are described in Table 12.4.

TABLE 12.4 Terminal Services Server Settings

Setting	Value	Description
Active Desktop	Enable/Disable	Turns on or off the Active Desktop.
Delete Temporary Folders on Exit	Yes/No	Specifies whether or not temporary folders are deleted after a session ends
Internet Connector Licensing	Enable/Disable	Allows anonymous users to open sessions across the Internet (this license must be purchased separately)
Permission Compatibility	Windows 2000/Terminal Services 4.0	Specifies permission compatibility
Terminal Server Mode	Application Server/Remote Administration	Specifies the Terminal Server mode
Use Temporary Folders per Session	Yes/No	Specifies whether or not temporary folders should be created for each session

In Exercise 12.2, you will use the Terminal Services Configuration utility to configure the Terminal Services server you installed in Exercise 12.1.

EXERCISE 12.2

Configuring a Terminal Services Server

1. Select Start ➢ Programs ➢ Administrative Tools ➢ Terminal Services Configuration.

2. In the Terminal Services Configuration window, right-click the RDP-Tcp connection and select Properties.

3. In the General tab of the RDP-Tcp Properties dialog box, select Medium from the Encryption Level drop-down list.

4. Click the Sessions tab. Check the first Override User Settings check box and specify 15 minutes for the Idle Session Limit option.

5. Click the Remote Control tab. Click the Use Remote Control with the Following Settings radio button and select the Interact with Session radio button.

6. Click OK to close the RDP-Tcp Properties dialog box.

Managing Terminal Services Users

You can also configure properties that apply to users on a per-user basis. When you install Terminal Services, new tabs that are specific to Terminal Services are added to the user and group Properties dialog boxes. From these tabs, you can set properties such as connect-time limits. If you want these properties to apply to all of the users on a connection, use Terminal Services Configuration to override the individual user settings.

To set Terminal Services properties for an Active Directory user, open the Active Directory Users and Computers utility (by selecting Start ➢ Programs ➢ Administrative Tools ➢ Active Directory Users and Computers), open the Users folder, and double-click the user account. Four of the tabs in the Active Directory user Properties dialog box contain properties that relate to Terminal Services:

- The Environment tab, shown in Figure 12.12, contains options for configuring the user's Terminal Services startup environment. This allows you to specify programs that should be started at logon and any devices that the client should connect to at logon.

FIGURE 12.12 The Environment tab of the Active Directory user Properties dialog box

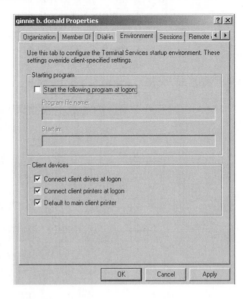

- The Sessions tab, shown in Figure 12.13, allows you to configure Terminal Services timeout and reconnection settings.

FIGURE 12.13 The Sessions tab of the Active Directory user Properties dialog box

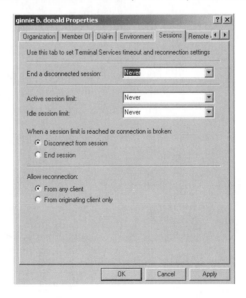

- The Remote Control tab, shown in Figure 12.14, allows you to configure Terminal Services remote control settings. You can configure if remote control will be enabled and whether remote control access requires the user's permission.

FIGURE 12.14   The Remote Control tab of the Active Directory user Properties dialog box

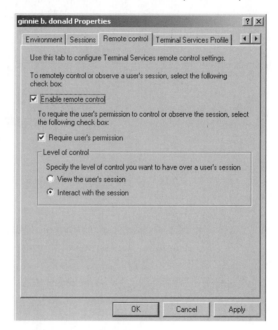

- The Terminal Services Profile tab, shown in Figure 12.15, allows you to set up a Terminal Services user profile. You can also specify the location of the Terminal Services home directory that will be used by the user.

FIGURE 12.15   The Terminal Services Profile tab of the Active Directory user Properties dialog box

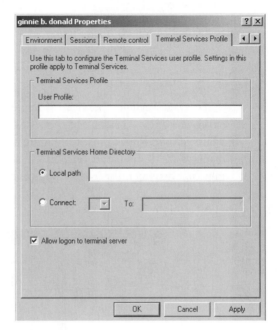

Managing Terminal Services

The *Terminal Services Manager* utility allows you to manage and monitor users, sessions, and processes that are connected to or running on any Terminal Services server on the network. With this utility, you can perform the following tasks:

- Display information about servers, sessions, users, and processes
- Connect to and disconnect from sessions

- Monitor sessions

- Reset sessions

- Send messages to users

- Log off users

- Terminate processes

To open Terminal Services Manager, select Start ➤ Programs ➤ Administrative Tools ➤ Terminal Services Manager. The main Terminal Services Manager window is shown in Figure 12.16. The navigation pane on the left displays the domains, servers, and sessions. The details pane on the right has tabs that display information about the selected item in the navigation pane.

FIGURE 12.16 The Terminal Services Manager window

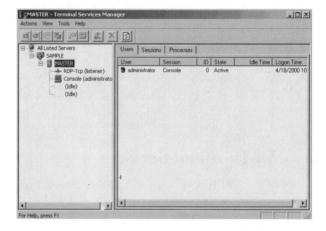

The options on the Actions menu allow you to perform several actions on sessions and processes. Most of these actions require special permissions. The Actions menu options are described in Table 12.5.

TABLE 12.5 Terminal Services Manager Actions Menu Options

Action	Description	Permission Required
Connect	Allows a user to connect to a session from another session. This option can be used only from a session; it cannot be used from the console.	Full Control or User Access

TABLE 12.5   Terminal Services Manager Actions Menu Options *(continued)*

Action	Description	Permission Required
Disconnect	Disconnects a user from a session. The session is saved, and all running applications continue to run.	Full Control
Send Message	Allows a user to send a message to any or all sessions.	Full Control or User Access
Remote Control	Allows a user to use the session to view or control another user's session. Sessions cannot be controlled from the console.	Full Control
Reset	Immediately ends a session. Any unsaved data will be lost.	Full Control
Status	Displays information about a session, such as bytes sent and received.	Full Control or User Access
Log Off	Logs off a user from a session.	Full Control
End Process	Ends a process on a session. This is useful if a program has crashed and is no longer responding.	Full Control

Configuring Terminal Services Licensing

The first time a client attempts to log on to the Terminal Services server in application server mode, the server will recognize that the client has not been issued a license and will locate a license server to issue a license to the client. This license is a digitally signed certificate that will remain with the client forever and cannot be used by any other client.

Before you can begin using a license server, you must activate it through the Microsoft Clearinghouse using the Terminal Services Licensing tool.

You can configure Terminal Services Licensing through the following steps:

1. Select Start ➢ Settings ➢ Control Panel and double-click the Add/Remove Programs icon.

2. The Add/Remove Programs window appears. Click the Add/Remove Windows Components option.

3. The Windows Components Wizard starts. Check the Terminal Services Licensing check box and click the Next button.

4. The Terminal Services Setup dialog box appears. Specify the mode that Terminal Services will use (this is used to verify that Terminal Services is running in application server mode) and click the Next button.

5. The Terminal Services Licensing Setup dialog box appears. Specify if the license server will be available for your enterprise or for your domain or workgroup. Click the Next button.

6. If your Windows 2000 Server CD is not already in the CD-ROM drive, you will be prompted to insert the Windows 2000 Server CD so that the necessary files can be copied.

7. The Completing the Windows Components Wizard dialog box appears. Click the Finish button. Close the Add/Remove Windows Components window, and then close Control Panel.

8. Select Start ➢ Programs ➢ Administrative Tools ➢ Terminal Services Licensing.

9. The Terminal Services Licensing utility starts, as shown in Figure 12.17. Right-click your license server and select Activate Server from the pop-up menu.

FIGURE 12.17 The Terminal Services Licensing window

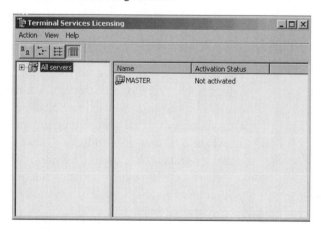

10. The Licensing Wizard starts. Click the Next button.

11. The Connection Method dialog box appears, as shown in Figure 12.18. You can select to connect to the Microsoft Clearinghouse via the Internet, the World Wide Web, telephone, or fax. In this example, we will connect by telephone. Select the Telephone option and click the Next button.

FIGURE 12.18   The Connection Method dialog box

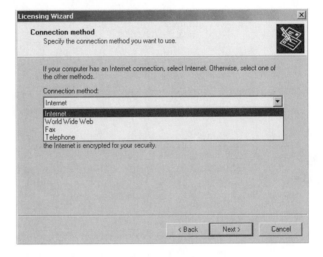

12. The Country/Region Selection dialog box appears. Select your country or region and click the Next button.

13. The License Server Activation dialog box appears, as shown in Figure 12.19. Type in the license number provided by Microsoft (or leave this blank and provide a valid number within 90 days). Click the Next button.

FIGURE 12.19 The License Server Activation dialog box

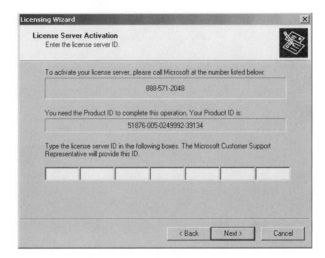

 While you are waiting for the registration process to complete, you can issue temporary 90-day licenses to clients who need to use Terminal Services immediately.

After a license server is activated, you can begin installing *client license key packs*. The key packs are sets of client licenses that the license server distributes to your clients. You install key packs either at the end of the license server activation process or by right-clicking a license server in the Terminal Services Licensing tool and selecting Install Licenses from the pop-up menu. Terminal Services Licensing will contact Microsoft in any of the four ways mentioned earlier (in step 11) and request the number of keys that you specify. Microsoft will send the keys to the license server, and the keys will be available for use immediately after they are received by the license server.

Setting Up Terminal Services Clients

The Terminal Services client software is a relatively small package that allows a wide range of machines to connect to a Windows 2000 Terminal Services server. The client installer should be distributed to every machine on the network that needs to use Terminal Services. There is a 16-bit version of the client for older machines, and there is a 32-bit version for newer machines.

Microsoft
✓ ***Exam***
Objective

Install, configure, monitor, and troubleshoot Terminal Services.

- Remotely administer servers by using Terminal Services.
- Configure Terminal Services for application sharing.

Installing the Terminal Services Client Software

You can install the Terminal Services client software through a network share. The client installation files are located in *Windir*\\System32\\ Clients\\Tsclient\\Net. Alternatively, you can create client installation disks through the Terminal Services Client Creator utility. The following sections describe both methods.

Installing the Terminal Client through a Network Share

You can install the client software over the network by connecting to a share that has been created on the Terminal Services server that points to the *Windir*\\System32\\Clients\\Tsclient\\Net folder and accessing the appropriate subfolder (Win16 or Win32). Take the following steps to install the Terminal Services client software on the computer that will connect to a share on the Terminal Services server:

1. Run the Setup.exe program in the *Windir*\\System32\\Clients\\ Tsclient\\Net\\Win32 folder to install the client on the Terminal Services server.

2. The Terminal Services Client Setup window opens. Click the Continue button.

3. The Name and Organization Information dialog box appears, as shown in Figure 12.20. Type in your name and organization and click the OK button.

FIGURE 12.20 The Name and Organization Information dialog box

4. The Confirm Name and Organization Information dialog box appears. If the information is correct, click the OK button.

5. The License Agreement dialog box appears. Click the I Agree button to agree to the license agreement.

6. The Terminal Services Client Setup dialog box appears, as shown in Figure 12.21. This dialog box allows you to specify the location where the Terminal Services client will be installed. Click the large button (to the left of the description, "Setup will install all of the Terminal Services client components in the specified destination folder.") to continue.

FIGURE 12.21 The Terminal Services Client Setup dialog box

7. The next dialog box asks if you want all of the users of this computer to have the same initial settings, as shown in Figure 12.22. You can click the Yes button to install the client software for all users, or click the No button to install the software for only the current user.

FIGURE 12.22   Choosing to install the Terminal Services client software for all users or just the current user

8. When the installation is complete, you will see a message indicating that Terminal Services Client Setup has completed successfully. Click the OK button.

In Exercise 12.3, you will install the Terminal Services client software on your member server using a network connection to the client software.

EXERCISE 12.3

Creating and Installing a Terminal Services Client

1. From your Terminal Services server (your domain controller), share the C:\WINNT\System32\Clients\Tsclient folder as **Tsclient**.

2. From your Terminal client (your member server), attach to the Tsclient share on your Terminal Services server and open the Net\Win32 folder.

3. Double-click the Setup icon.

4. In the Terminal Services Client Setup window, click the Continue button.

5. In the Name and Organization Information dialog box, enter your name and organization and click the OK button.

6. In the Confirm Name and Organization Information dialog box, click the OK button.

7. In the License Agreement dialog box, click the I Agree button.

8. In the Terminal Services Client Setup dialog box, click the large button to accept the default settings and continue.

EXERCISE 12.3 *(continued)*

9. In the next Terminal Services Client Setup dialog box, click the Yes button.

10. When you see the message confirming that Terminal Services Client Setup has completed successfully, click the OK button.

Creating Terminal Services Client Installation Disks

If you cannot access a network share that contains the Terminal Services client software, you can create installation disks through the *Terminal Services Client Creator* utility. Open this utility on the Terminal Services server by selecting Start ➤ Programs ➤ Administrative Tools ➤ Terminal Services Client Creator. The Create Installation Disk(s) dialog box appears, as shown in Figure 12.23.

FIGURE 12.23 The Create Installation Disk(s) dialog box

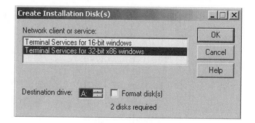

You can specify that you will create installation disks for Terminal Services 16-bit or 32-bit clients. After you make your selection, click the OK button, and then insert the floppy disks as prompted to create the Terminal Services client disks.

Connecting the Terminal Client to the Terminal Services Server

After you install the Terminal Services client software on a Terminal client, you see a new program group called Terminal Services Client, which contains these two items:

- The Client Connection Manager utility is used to create predefined connections that can be used to connect to a Terminal Services server.

- The Terminal Services Client utility is used to create a Terminal Services connection manually.

To create a connection with the Client Connection Manager utility:

1. Select Start ➢ Programs ➢ Terminal Services Client ➢ Client Connection Manager.

2. The Client Connection Manager window opens. Select File ➢ New Connection.

3. The Client Connection Manager Wizard starts. Click the Next button.

4. The Create a Connection dialog box appears, as shown in Figure 12.24. In this dialog box, you specify the connection name and the name or IP address of the Terminal Services server. Enter the information and click the Next button.

FIGURE 12.24   The Create a Connection dialog box

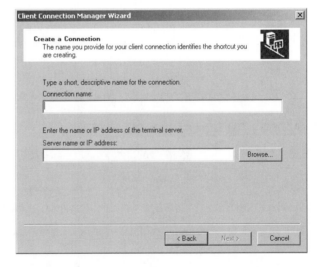

5. The Automatic Logon dialog box appears, as shown in Figure 12.25. In this dialog box, you can specify that the user will log on automatically. If you choose to allow automatic logon, you must specify a username and password. This option should be used with caution because it poses a potential security risk. After you make your selection, click the Next button.

FIGURE 12.25 The Automatic Logon dialog box

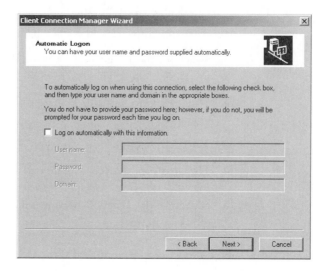

6. The Screen Options dialog box appears, as shown in Figure 12.26. This dialog box allows you to configure the screen area for the client window. Only the options that are valid for your configuration will be available. You can also specify if the connection should be displayed in full-screen mode. After you make your selection, click the Next button.

FIGURE 12.26 The Screen Options dialog box

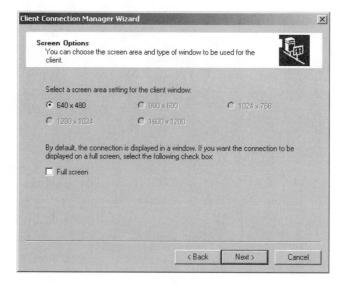

7. The Connection Properties dialog box appears, as shown in Figure 12.27. This dialog box allows you to enable data compression (which is used if you will connect by modem or through a slow network connection) and select whether you want to cache bitmaps. After you make your selections, click the Next button.

FIGURE 12.27   The Connection Properties dialog box

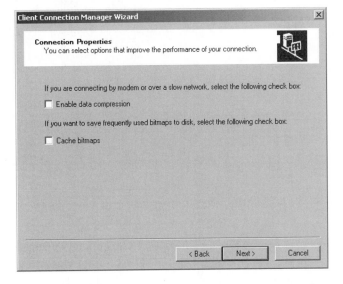

8. The Starting a Program dialog box appears. This dialog box allows you to specify whether a program should be started automatically when a Terminal Services connection is opened. Make your selection and click the Next button.

9. The Icon and Program Group dialog box appears, as shown in Figure 12.28. This dialog box allows you to change the icon and program group that will be used for the Terminal client. Make your selections and click the Next button.

FIGURE 12.28 The Icon and Program Group dialog box

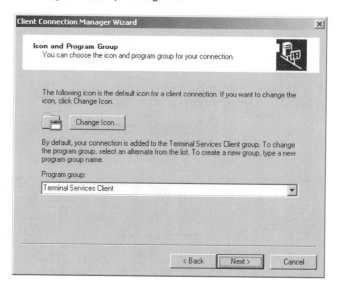

10. The Completing the Client Connection Manager Wizard dialog box appears. Click the Finish button.

11. The connection you created appears in the Client Connection Manager window. Double-click this connection to access the Terminal Services server.

12. If you did not configure automatic logon, you will see the Log On to Windows dialog box. Type in a valid username and password and click the OK button.

13. You are attached to the Terminal Services server as a Terminal client and see the Terminal Services Client Desktop, as shown in Figure 12.29. When you are finished with your Terminal Services session, close the Terminal Services Client Desktop to access the Disconnect Windows Session dialog box. Choose to disconnect.

FIGURE 12.29 Terminal Services Client Desktop

 You can change the configuration of your connection by right-clicking the connection that you created through Client Connection Manager and selecting Properties.

In Exercise 12.4, you will create a terminal session from the Terminal client that you created in Exercise 12.3.

EXERCISE 12.4

Creating a Terminal Session

1. Select Start ➢ Programs ➢ Terminal Services Client ➢ Client Connection Manager.

2. In the Client Connection Manager window, select File ➢ New Connection.

3. When the Client Connection Manager Wizard starts, click the Next button.

4. In the Create a Connection dialog box, specify the connection name of **Test** and the computer name of your Terminal Services server. Click the Next button.

5. In the Automatic Logon dialog box, click the Next button to accept the default setting and continue.

6. In the Screen Options dialog box, click the Next button to accept the default settings.

7. In the Connection Properties dialog box, click the Next button to accept the default settings.

8. In the Starting a Program dialog box, click the Next button to accept the default setting.

9. In the Icon and Program Group dialog box, click the Next button to accept the default settings.

10. When the Completing the Client Connection Manager Wizard dialog box appears, click the Finish button.

11. In the Client Connection Manager window, double-click the connection you created.

12. In the Log On to Windows dialog box, enter **Administrator** in the User Name field and the Administrator's password in the Password field. Click the OK button.

13. You are attached to the Terminal Services server and see the Terminal Services Client Desktop. Close the Desktop. In the Disconnect Windows Session dialog box, choose to close the Terminal Services session.

Running Terminal Services in Application Server Mode

When you have configured Terminal Services in application server mode, the Terminal clients you have installed will be able to access the applications running on the Terminal Services server. The following sections describe how to install applications on your Terminal Services server and configure applications for multi-session use.

Installing Applications

The Registry and .ini file mapping support that is built into Terminal Services allows programs to run correctly in Terminal Services, even if they were not designed to run in a multi-user environment. Terminal Services automatically replicates the .ini files and Registry settings from the system to each user if the application is installed properly. It places the .ini files in the user's home folder, or if no home folder is specified, in *Windir*\Documents and Settings*Username*. Registry settings are moved from HKEY_LOCAL_MACHINE\SOFTWARE \Microsoft\WindowsNT\CurrentVersion\Terminal Server\Install \Software to HKEY_CURRENT_USER \Software.

To install applications on a Terminal Services server, use the Add/Remove Programs icon in Control Panel. Add/Remove Programs automatically runs the change user command, which ensures that the .ini files and Registry entries are replicated and the program you install will work properly for all Terminal Services clients. You should install the applications on an NTFS partition, so that you can set permissions for your programs.

If you need to install applications after your Terminal Services server is up and running, you should make sure that all of the users have ended their sessions (because applications often require a reboot after they have been installed). You can send a message to every session notifying them of the impending shutdown so that users have a chance to save their work.

Always remember to test your application from at least two clients before allowing users access to the Terminal Services server. This gives you the chance to test your programs before users can access them, reducing the amount of errors that might occur. Some programs need to be fine-tuned before they can be run in multi-session mode. This is explained in more detail in the next section.

Configuring Application Sharing

Terminal Services allows several users to simultaneously run the same program at once. Because of this, applications that are run with Terminal Services must be configured for multi-session use. Most of the time, you will not need to perform any extra steps for a program to run correctly with Terminal Services server. However, you might need to configure certain applications for multi-session use.

Compatibility Scripts

Most well-known applications have been tested for use with Terminal Services. Some of these applications require *compatibility scripts* that should be run after the program is installed to achieve the best performance on a Terminal Services server. These scripts can be found in *\Windir*Application Compatibility Scripts\Install. The compatibility scripts may include notes on specific script capabilities and instructions on modifying them for custom installations. You can edit compatibility scripts in Notepad.

Table 12.6 lists the compatibility scripts and which program they are used with.

TABLE 12.6 Application Compatibility Scripts

Script	Application
Coffice7.cmd	Corel Perfect Office 7.0 32-bit
Coffice8.cmd	Corel Perfect Office 8.0 32-bit
Diskpr20.cmd	DiskKeeper 2.0
Eudora4.cmd	Eudora 4.0
Msexcl97.cmd	Microsoft Excel 97
Msproj95.cmd	Microsoft Project 95
Msproj98.cmd	Microsoft Project 98
Mssna30.cmd	Microsoft SNA Server 3.0
Msvs6.cmd	Microsoft Visual Studio 6.0
Msword97.cmd	Microsoft Word 97

TABLE 12.6 Application Compatibility Scripts *(continued)*

Script	Application
Netcom40.cmd	Netscape Communicator 4.0
Netnav30.cmd	Netscape Navigator 3.0
Office43.cmd	Microsoft Office 4.3
Office95.cmd	Microsoft Office 95
Office97.cmd	Microsoft Office 97
Outlk98.cmd	Microsoft Outlook 98
Pchtree6.cmd	Peachtree 2000
Pwrbldr6.cmd	PowerBuilder 6.0
Sna40cli.cmd	Microsoft SNA Client 4.0
Sna40srv.cmd	Microsoft SNA Server 4.0
Ssuite9.cmd	Lotus SmartSuite 9.0
Ssuite97.cmd	Lotus SmartSuite 97 32-bit
Visio5.cmd	Visio 5.0
Winmsg.cmd	Microsoft Exchange Client 5.5

Per-User Data

Each user is given an HKEY_CURRENT_USER Registry key, which stores user-specific data. There is also a Registry key called HKEY_LOCAL_MACHINE, which stores information that is shared among users. Unfortunately, applications that assume one computer equals one user also assume that they can store user-specific data in HKEY_LOCAL_MACHINE. They also assume that they can store any file-based information, such as user preferences, in the System folder or the program directory. You should always make sure that any per-user data is stored in HKEY_CURRENT_USER, in the user's home folder, or in a user-specified folder. Any global data should always be stored in either

HKEY_LOCAL_MACHINE or in a specific location on the disk that is write-protected, such as the System folder.

Problems can arise when programs need to store user-specific data in either the Registry or in a file. This data could consist of path information, such as to a mailbox, or per-user preference settings, such as enabling background spell checking. If all of this data is stored in one location, the users will need to either use the same settings or readjust their settings every time they log on. If one user updates the settings, the changes will affect every other user.

Another problem is that programs sometimes update files in the *Windir* folder. Administrators have write access to the *Windir* folder, but most users do not. You will know that write access to this folder is necessary if a program executes properly for an Administrator but not for other users. You can audit all write operations and see which ones fail in order to detect and remedy the problem.

 Real World Scenario

Maximizing Terminal Services in Application Server Mode

You have installed Terminal Services in application server mode. Your users are complaining that performance is much slower than expected. Before you resort to a hardware upgrade on the Terminal Services server, consider the following options that can improve the performance between a Terminal Services server and a Terminal Services client. These options would be configured on the Terminal Services server.

- Minimize the use of animated graphics. This includes animated graphics and the animated Microsoft Office Assistant.

- When configuring the desktop appearance, do not use bitmap files for wallpaper and set wallpaper to none. Select a single color for the display appearance. Do not use screen savers.

- Disable the smooth scrolling option.

- Do not use Active Desktop.

Avoid the use of DOS or Windows 16-bit applications. Use Windows 32-bit applications, if possible.

Running Terminal Services in Remote Administration Mode

If you install Terminal Services in remote administration mode, you will be able to perform every administrative function from a client, just as if you were actually at the console. For example, you can set up file sharing, manage users and groups, and edit the Registry.

Microsoft ✓ *Exam* *Objective*

Install, configure, monitor, and troubleshoot Terminal Services.

- Remotely administer servers by using Terminal Services.

Remote administration mode allows only two concurrent connections to the Terminal Services server, but you do not need additional Terminal Services client licenses to use this mode. It does not install any application-sharing features, which significantly decreases the overhead associated with running Terminal Services. This is important when the server you are administering is mission-critical and can't be burdened with extraneous processes.

If you already have Terminal Services installed in application server mode, you can switch to remote administration mode through the Add/Remove Programs icon in Control Panel.

In Exercise 12.5, you will switch to remote administration mode, and then remotely administer a server using Terminal Services.

EXERCISE 12.5

Remotely Administering a Server using Terminal Services

1. From the Terminal Services server, make sure that all terminal connections have ended, and then select Start ➢ Settings ➢ Control Panel. Double-click the Add/Remove Programs icon.

2. In the Add/Remove Programs window, select Add/Remove Windows Components.

3. When the Windows Components Wizard begins, the Terminal Services check box should already be checked (from Exercise 12.1). Click the Next button.

4. In the Terminal Services Setup dialog box, click the Remote Administration Mode radio button and click the Next button.

5. Setup configures components and displays a dialog box when it's finished. Click the Finish button.

6. In the System Settings Change dialog box, click the Yes button to restart your computer so that the changes will take effect.

7. After the Terminal Services server has finished rebooting, from the Terminal client, select Start ➢ Programs ➢ Terminal Services Client ➢ Client Connection Manager. Double-click the connection you created in Exercise 12.4.

8. In the Log On to Windows dialog box, enter **Administrator** in the User Name field and the Administrator's password in the Password field. Click the OK button.

9. The Terminal Services server's Desktop appears in the client window. To create a folder on the Terminal Services server from the Terminal client, open My Computer and select drive C:. Select File ➢ New ➢ Folder, and name the folder **Test**.

10. Right-click Test and select Properties.

11. In the folder Properties dialog box, select the Security tab and click the Add button.

12. In the Select Users, Computers, or Groups dialog box, select the Users group and click Add. Click the OK button.

13. Deselect every check box except Allow for the Read permission. Click the OK button.

14. Close the Desktop. In the Disconnect Windows Session dialog box, choose to close the Terminal Services session.

Troubleshooting Terminal Services

When you are running Terminal Services in application server mode, you might find that installed applications do not work properly on Terminal clients. You may encounter this problem if the application was installed before Terminal Services was installed. To fix this problem, uninstall the application, and then reinstall it using the Add/Remove Programs icon in Control Panel.

Another problem that may occur is that the automatic logon connections do not work from Windows NT 4 Terminal clients. To fix this problem, run the Client Connection Manager utility. Choose automatic logon and specify the username, password, and domain.

If you install Terminal Services on a domain controller, and discover that the Administrator can log on to the Terminal Services server but regular users can't, you should verify that users have the Log on Locally user right.

Summary

In this chapter, you learned about Terminal Services. We covered these topics:

- The features and benefits of Terminal Services, including rapid deployment, application sharing, and remote administration.

- Planning for Terminal Services deployment, including hardware requirements, licensing requirements, and client application requirements

- Installing a Terminal Services server

- Managing Terminal Services with the Terminal Services Configuration and Terminal Services Manager utilities

- Installing Terminal Services clients and creating connections to the Terminal Services server

- Installing applications and configuring application sharing on a Terminal Services server

- Remotely administering a server through Terminal Services

Exam Essentials

Understand the primary purpose of Terminal Services. Know what terminal emulation is and how it can be used to support a wide variety of client types. Describe the two types of Terminal Services modes.

List and describe the components of Terminal Services. Know the function and requirements for the Terminal Services server and the Terminal Services clients. Understand the function of the Remote Desktop Protocol.

Be able to install and configure Terminal Services for application server mode. List the utilities and options that are used to install and configure Terminal Services in application server mode. Be able to configure applications for use with Terminal Services.

Know how to install and configure Terminal Services client software. Know where the client software can be accessed and the options for deploying client software to different Terminal Services clients.

Be able to manage servers remotely through Terminal Services. Configure Terminal Services for remote administration. Know what options can be remotely managed.

Know how to troubleshoot Terminal Services. Know the common causes of Terminal Services errors and how they can be corrected.

Key Terms

Before you take the exam, be sure you're familiar with these key terms:

application server mode	Terminal Services
compatibility script	Terminal Services client
client license key packs	Terminal Services server
license server	Terminal Services Client Creator
remote administration mode	Terminal Services Configuration
remote control	Terminal Services Manager
Remote Desktop Protocol (RDP)	thin client
session	

Review Questions

1. Your company uses a specialized application that is constantly changing. Instead of managing the application on the users' local computers, you decide to deploy the application through Terminal Services in application server mode. You want members of the IT group to be able to remotely manage and troubleshoot any application problems that the users may have. What needs to be configured so that the IT department can manage and troubleshoot the users' sessions?

   A. Grant the IT group Read permission to the RDP-Tcp protocol

   B. Grant the IT group Full Control permission to the RDP-Tcp protocol

   C. Add the IT group to the built-in TS-Operators group

   D. Add the IT group to the built-in TS-Admins group

2. Greta is planning on using Terminal Services to host 20 Windows for Workgroups computers. She will be using a Windows 2000 member server as the Terminal Services server. When planning the amount of RAM she will need for the server, how much extra RAM should Greta plan to allow for each Terminal Services client?

   A. 10MB to 20MB

   B. 1MB to 2MB

   C. 64MB to 128MB

   D. 100MB to 200MB

3. Your network is configured with the clients shown in the following diagram. Based on your network, which of the clients will run as Terminal Services clients without having to install third-party software? (Choose all that apply.)

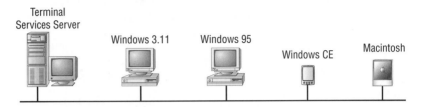

A. Windows 3.11 clients

B. Windows CE devices

C. Windows 95 clients

D. Macintosh computers

4. Darryl wants to use Terminal Services to remotely administer 25 servers within his organization. He wants to ensure that he meets all of the proper licensing agreements for Terminal Services. Which license does he need in order to run Terminal Services in remote administration mode?

A. Windows 2000 Terminal Services Client Access license

B. Windows 2000 Terminal Services Internet Connector license

C. Windows 2000 Server license

D. Windows 2000 Professional license

5. You are using Terminal Services in application server mode. You will have 100 various clients accessing the Terminal Services server. You want to ensure that you meet the licensing requirements for all of the Terminal Services clients. Who must you contact in order to activate a license server?

A. A system administrator

B. The Microsoft Clearinghouse

C. A Microsoft License Center

D. The Terminal Services clients

6. You have installed Terminal Services server on a Windows 2000 domain controller. You are using Terminal Services in application server mode. You then installed a Terminal Services client and tested the configuration as Administrator. When you tried to log on to Terminal Services as a regular user, you received an error message that reported that you could not log on interactively. What is the most likely cause of this problem?

    A. You need to grant the users Read permission to the Tcp-RDP protocol

    B. You need to grant the users Full Control permission to the Tcp-RDP protocol

    C. You need to grant the users the User Right Log On Locally

    D. You need to grant the users the User Right Allow Interactive Logon

7. You have a user who is connected to the Terminal Services application server. The session seems to have hung and you want to manually disconnect the user. Which utility should you use?

    A. Terminal Services Client Creator

    B. Terminal Services Configuration

    C. Terminal Services Manager

    D. Terminal Services Licensing

8. You want to use Terminal Services to allow your Windows 3.11 clients to run Windows 32-bit applications. The clients are not able to access the Terminal Services server to download the software that they need to connect to the Terminal Services server. You want to create client disks that these clients can use to install the Terminal Services client software. Which tool can you use to create Terminal Services client disks?

    A. Terminal Services Client Creator

    B. Terminal Services Configuration

    C. Terminal Services Manager

    D. Terminal Services Licensing

9. You are using Terminal Services in application server mode. Clients are complaining that they are not able to access the Terminal Services server. You want to verify that the service required by the Terminal Services server is running properly. Which of the following services is required for use with Terminal Services?

   A. RDP-TCP

   B. NetBEUI

   C. TS-TCP

   D. RTS-TCP

10. Scott is the system administrator for a Windows 2000 Server computer that is running as a Terminal Services server. Which of the following utilities can he use to view all of the users that are currently connected to the Terminal Services server?

   A. Terminal Services Client Manager

   B. Terminal Services Configuration

   C. Terminal Services Manager

   D. Terminal Services Administration

11. Martina has a Windows 2000 Server computer with Terminal Services installed. She wants to be able to interact with the clients that are connecting to her Terminal Services server. Which of the following utilities should she use to specify that she wants to be able to interact with users' sessions, with the users' permission?

   A. Terminal Services Client Manager

   B. Terminal Services Configuration

   C. Terminal Services Manager

   D. Terminal Services Administration

12. You have installed a Terminal Services license server. You are trying to determine how many licenses you will need to purchase. Which of the following Terminal Services server modes requires you to use a Terminal Services license server?

    A. Remote administration mode

    B. Application server mode

    C. Remote control mode

    D. Resource management mode

13. Malka wants to create a share on her Terminal Services server so that clients can access the share and install the Terminal Services client software. What folder does Malka need to share?

    A. \Clients\TS\Net

    B. *Windir*\Services\Clients\TS

    C. *Windir*\Clients\Tsclients

    D. *Windir*\System32\Clients\Tsclient\Net

14. You are running an application on a Terminal Services server from a Terminal Services client. The application is not saving user preferences properly. What is most likely the problem?

    A. The application was installed by running `Setup.exe`, and therefore is not properly configured.

    B. There is a bug in the program that is affecting only the saving of user preferences.

    C. You have not activated the license server.

    D. The application was not installed using Control Panel, Add/Remove Programs, and therefore did not replicate the `.ini` files and Registry entries for each user.

15. One of your Terminal Services users complains that the application he is using has stopped responding. What should you do?

A. In Terminal Services Manager, click the session that is having the problem. In the Processes tab, end the process that has stopped responding.

B. In Terminal Services Manager, disconnect the session that is having the problem.

C. In Terminal Services Manager, reset the session that is having the problem.

D. Run the application compatibility script for the program.

Answers to Review Questions

1. B. If you grant the IT group the Full Control permission to the RDP-Tcp protocol, they can manage the users' Terminal Services sessions. You configure Terminal Services permissions through the Terminal Services Configuration utility.

2. A. Depending on usage requirements, each client session will probably require between 10MB and 20MB of RAM on the server, in addition to the 128MB needed to run the Terminal Services server.

3. A, B, C. Terminal Services can run on Macintosh-based computers, but this requires third-party software. Windows-based computers can use the client software provided with Windows 2000 Terminal Services.

4. C. You do not need any special Terminal Services licenses in order to run Terminal Services in remote administration mode.

5. B. You need to contact the Microsoft Clearinghouse by telephone, fax, the Internet, or the World Wide Web in order to activate your license server.

6. C. If you install Terminal Services on a Windows 2000 member server, the default user rights allow Domain Users to log on interactively. If you install Terminal Services on a domain controller, you will have to grant regular users the User Right Log on Locally. Otherwise users will receive an error message that they cannot log on interactively.

7. C. You manage sessions and servers with the Terminal Services Manager utility.

8. A. The Terminal Services Client Creator utility is used to create floppy disks containing the client software.

9. A. The Remote Desktop Protocol-Transmission Control Protocol (RDP-TCP) service is used by all Terminal Services connections.

10. C. You can manage and access Terminal Services sessions through the Terminal Services Manager utility.

11. B. Through the Remote Control tab of Terminal Services Configuration, you can configure the connection property to allow you to interact with user sessions.

12. B. The first time a client attempts to log on to the Terminal Services server in application server mode, the server will recognize that the client has not been issued a license and will locate a license server to issue a license to the client.

13. D. You can install the Terminal Services client software by connecting to a share that has been created on the Terminal Services server that points to the *Windir*\System32\Clients\Tsclient\Net folder.

14. D. You should always use the Add/Remove Programs icon in Control Panel to install applications on a Terminal Services server. This ensures that your applications will be properly configured to work correctly for all users.

15. A. You can end processes on a per-session basis in Terminal Services Manager. Disconnecting the session would not end any of the processes associated with the session, and ending the session could result in data loss if the session was running any other applications. Application compatibility scripts would not help in this instance.

Chapter
13

Managing Remote Network Connections

MICROSOFT EXAM OBJECTIVES IN THIS CHAPTER

✓ Install, configure, and troubleshoot a virtual private network (VPN).

✓ Configure, monitor, and troubleshoot remote access.

  ▪ Configure inbound connections.

  ▪ Create a remote access policy.

  ▪ Configure a remote access profile.

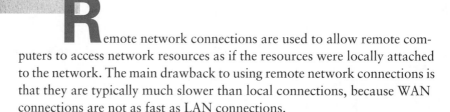

emote network connections are used to allow remote computers to access network resources as if the resources were locally attached to the network. The main drawback to using remote network connections is that they are typically much slower than local connections, because WAN connections are not as fast as LAN connections.

In Windows 2000, you can configure your server to support remote network connections through the use of Remote Access Service (RAS) servers and virtual private network (VPN) servers. RAS servers allow users to connect directly to the server through a modem, an ISDN adapter, or a null-modem cable. VPN servers allow users to connect to your network through a private network or an Internet connection.

This chapter describes how to configure the server side of remote networking. The client side of remote networking is covered In *MSCE: Windows 2000 Professional Study Guide*, 2nd ed., by Lisa Donald with James Chellis (Sybex, 2001).

Installing and Configuring a Remote Access Service Server

*R*emote Access Service (RAS) servers connect mobile users to the network through the *Routing and Remote Access service*. A Windows 2000 Server computer that is running the Routing and Remote Access service can authenticate and service requests from remote clients. This allows users to access resources remotely in the same manner as they would access the resources if they were locally connected to the network.

Microsoft ✓ *Exam* *Objective*

Configure, monitor, and troubleshoot remote access.

- Configure inbound connections.

In the following sections, you will learn how to install a RAS server, configure inbound and outbound connections, manage the RAS server's properties, and assign dial-in permissions to users.

Installing a RAS Server

You can install and configure your RAS server through the Routing and Remote Access utility. The following steps are used to install a RAS server:

1. Select Start ➢ Programs ➢ Administrative Tools ➢ Routing and Remote Access.

2. The Routing and Remote Access utility starts, as shown in Figure 13.1. In the left pane of the Routing and Remote Access window, right-click your server and select Configure and Enable Routing and Remote Access from the pop-up menu.

FIGURE 13.1 The Routing and Remote Access window

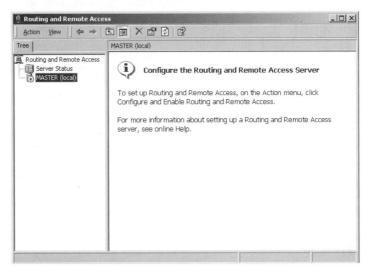

3. The Routing and Remote Access Server Setup Wizard starts. Click the Next button to continue.

4. The Common Configurations dialog box appears, as shown in Figure 13.2. Select the Remote Access Server option and click the Next button.

FIGURE 13.2   The Common Configurations dialog box

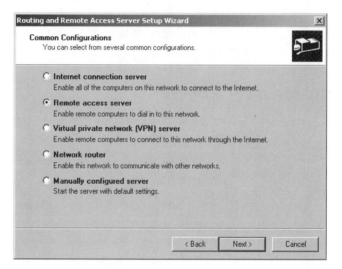

5. The Remote Client Protocols dialog box appears. This dialog box lists the protocols that are installed on your computer. If you wish to add other protocols to service remote clients, select the No, I Need to Add Protocols option. Otherwise, accept the default selection, Yes, All of the Required Protocols Are on This List and click the Next button.

6. If you specified that the RAS server should use the TCP/IP protocol, the IP Address Assignment dialog box appears. You can choose to assign IP addresses automatically or assign them from a specified range of IP addresses. If you choose the Automatically option, the IP addresses are assigned through a DHCP server or by the server automatically generating the addresses. In this example, the Automatically option is selected. Click the Next button to continue.

See Chapter 9, "Managing Network Interoperability" for information about adding network protocols and networking services.

7. The Managing Multiple Remote Access Servers dialog box appears, as shown in Figure 13.3. This dialog box allows you to specify whether you will use a *Remote Authentication Dial-In User Service (RADIUS) server*. If you have multiple RAS servers, you can set up a RADIUS server, which stores a central authentication database and allows you to manage the RAS servers from a single location. A RADIUS system requires a RADIUS server and RADIUS client. RADIUS is equipment-to-equipment authentication. Once the two pieces of equipment authenticate with each other, user authentication begins. In this example, a RADIUS server is not installed. Click the Next button.

FIGURE 13.3   The Managing Multiple Remote Access Servers dialog box

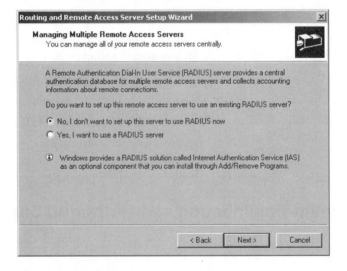

8. The Completing the Routing and Remote Access Server Setup Wizard dialog box appears. If you want to see Help information after you close the Wizard, select the check box in the dialog box. Make your selection and click the Finish button.

In Exercise 13.1, you will install a RAS server on your domain controller.

Installing a RAS Server

1. Select Start ➢ Programs ➢ Administrative Tools ➢ Routing and Remote Access.

2. In the Routing and Remote Access window, right-click your server and select Configure and Enable Routing and Remote Access.

3. When the Routing and Remote Access Server Setup Wizard starts, click the Next button to continue.

4. In the Common Configurations dialog box, select the Remote Access Server option and click the Next button.

5. In the Remote Client Protocols dialog box, click the Next button to accept the default selection (Yes, All of the Required Protocols Are on This List).

6. In the IP Address Assignment dialog box, select the Automatically option and click the Next button.

7. In the Managing Multiple Remote Access Servers dialog box, click the Next button to accept the default option (No, I Don't Want to Set Up This Server to Use RADIUS Now).

8. In the Completing the Routing and Remote Access Server Setup Wizard dialog box, click the Finish button.

Configuring Inbound and Outbound Connections

Inbound connections allow incoming access to the RAS server. *Outbound connections* allow users to dial out to external resources through a RAS server. Users can connect to the RAS server through a modem, ISDN connection, or direct connection (through a null-modem cable).

You configure inbound and outbound connections through the Ports Properties dialog box in the Routing and Remote Access utility, as shown in Figure 13.4. To access this dialog box, expand your computer in the Routing and Remote Access window, right-click Ports, and select Properties from the pop-up menu.

FIGURE 13.4 The Ports Properties dialog box

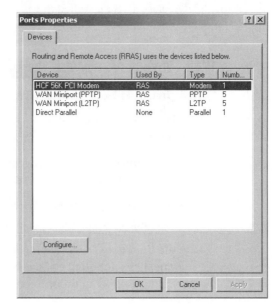

In the Ports Properties dialog box, highlight the RAS connection device you want to configure (typically the modem) and click the Configure button. This brings up the Configure Device dialog box, as shown in Figure 13.5. This dialog box allows you to specify if the computer will be used for inbound connections (the default setting) or for *demand-dial routing connections*, which support both inbound and outbound connections. In addition, you can configure the telephone number that will be used for the device.

FIGURE 13.5 The Configure Device dialog box

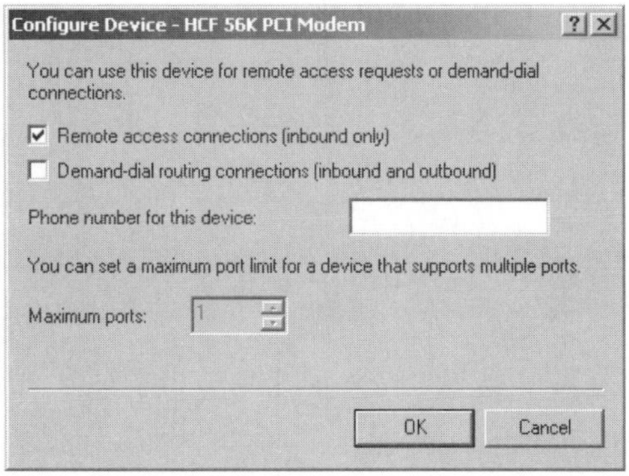

In Exercise 13.2, you will configure inbound and outbound connections for the RAS server you installed in Exercise 13.1. This exercise assumes that you have a modem or null-modem cable installed on your server.

EXERCISE 13.2

Configuring Inbound and Outbound Connections

1. Select Start ➢ Programs ➢ Administrative Tools ➢ Routing and Remote Access.

2. In the Routing and Remote Access window, expand your computer, right-click Ports, and select Properties.

3. In the Ports Properties dialog box, highlight the RAS connection device you want to configure and click the Configure button.

4. In the Configure Device dialog box, select: Demand-dial Routing Connections (Inbound and Outbound). Specify the telephone number to be used for outbound connections. Then click the OK button.

5. In the Ports Properties dialog box, click the OK button.

Managing RAS Server Properties

To configure the properties of a RAS server, right-click your server in the Routing and Remote Access utility and select Properties from the pop-up menu. This brings up the RAS server Properties dialog box, as shown in Figure 13.6. This dialog box contains General, Security, and Event Logging tabs, as well as tabs for each protocol you've installed for remote access connections. The options on these tabs are covered in the following sections.

FIGURE 13.6 The General tab of the RAS server Properties dialog box

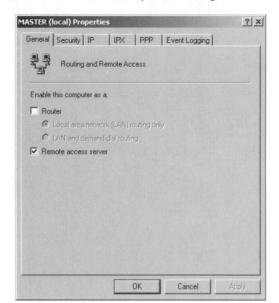

Configuring General Properties

The General tab (see Figure 13.6) allows you to enable the computer as a router or as a RAS server. If you enable your computer as a router, you can specify whether the computer will route packets between two or more network segments.

Setting Security Options

The Security tab, shown in Figure 13.7, allows you to select and configure an authentication provider and select an accounting provider.

FIGURE 13.7 The Security tab of the RAS server Properties dialog box

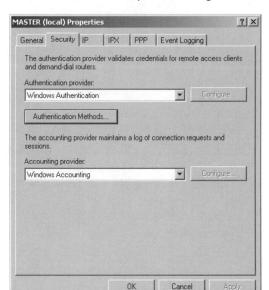

Authentication Provider and Authentication Methods

The authentication provider is the server that will provide authentication services for remote access or demand-dial users. You can choose from two types of authentication providers:

- Windows authentication uses a Windows 2000 local server, Windows 2000 domain controller, or Windows NT 4 domain controller to authenticate remote access requests.

- RADIUS authentication uses a RADIUS server to authenticate remote access requests.

To configure authentication methods, click the Authentication Methods button in the Security tab. This brings up the Authentication Methods dialog box, as shown in Figure 13.8. Table 13.1 describes the options in this dialog box.

FIGURE 13.8 The Authentication Methods dialog box

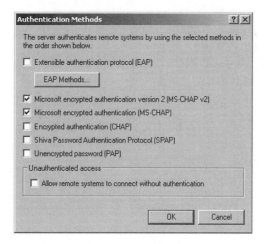

TABLE 13.1 Remote Access Authentication Methods

Authentication Method	Description
Extensible Authentication Protocol (EAP)	A protocol that allows the RAS server and the remote access client to negotiate an authentication scheme. Some of the authentication schemes that can be selected are Generic Token Card, MD5-Challenge, Transport Level Security (used with smart cards), and S/Key. This protocol is also designed to support emerging authentication technologies.
Microsoft Encrypted Authentication Version 2 (MS-CHAP v2)	An enhanced version of MS-CHAP that uses a higher level of security than MS-CHAP. This version is only supported in Windows 2000.

TABLE 13.1 Remote Access Authentication Methods *(continued)*

Authentication Method	Description
Microsoft Encrypted Authentication (MS-CHAP)	A nonreversible authentication protocol that uses an encrypted password authentication process.
Encrypted Authentication (CHAP)	A challenge-response authentication protocol used by non-Microsoft clients to provide challenge-response authentication using the Message Digest 5 (MD5) hashing scheme to encrypt the response that is sent from the RAS client to the RAS server. MD5 is the default authentication method used in IP v6.
Shiva Password Authentication Protocol (SPAP)	A form of authentication used by clients that connect to Shiva LAN Rovers.
Unencrypted Password (PAP)	A protocol that uses plain text passwords. This is the least secure authentication method.
Unauthenticated Access	An option that allows the remote computers to connect to your network without any authentication. This option should be enabled with extreme caution.

Click the EAP Methods button in the Authentication Methods dialog box to configure options for MD5-Challenge, Smart Card, or other Certificate EAP protocols. You can add other EAP methods through remote access policies. Remote access policies are covered in the "Configuring Remote Access Policies and Profiles" section later in this chapter.

Accounting Provider

The accounting provider is the server that will provide accounting services for remote access or demand-dial connections. RADIUS accounting is used to charge customers for their connection time. You can specify that you will use Windows accounting, RADIUS accounting, or no accounting provider (None).

Configuring IP Options

The IP tab, shown in Figure 13.9, has options for enabling IP routing and allowing IP-based remote access and demand-dial connections.

FIGURE 13.9 IP tab of the RAS server Properties dialog box

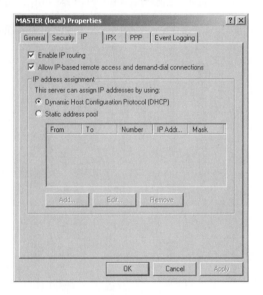

You can also configure IP address assignment through the IP tab. You can specify that remote clients will get their IP addresses from a DHCP server or from a static IP address pool. If you choose to use a static address pool, you configure the IP addresses in this dialog box.

Configuring IPX Options

If you have specified that the IPX protocol will be used for remote access connections, the RAS server Properties dialog box will include an IPX tab, as shown in Figure 13.10. Through this tab, you can allow IPX-based remote access and demand-dial connections, and enable network access for those connections.

You can also configure IPX network number assignment through the IPX tab. You can choose automatic IPX address assignment or specify an address range. You can specify that the same network number should be used for all IPX clients, and you can allow remote clients to request an IPX node number. Normally, you specify that IPX addresses should be assigned automatically and leave these settings at default values. However, you may need to adjust the IPX settings if you will be using File and Print Services for NetWare or your computer is functioning as an IPX router.

FIGURE 13.10 The IPX tab of the RAS server Properties dialog box

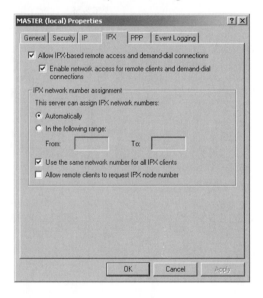

Configuring PPP Options

The PPP tab, shown in Figure 13.11, allows you to configure several *Point-to-Point Protocol (PPP)* options:

- *Multilink* connections are used to allow several physical connections to be combined into a single logical connection. If you use multilink connections, you can specify if the amount of bandwidth should be controlled using the *Bandwidth Allocation Protocol (BAP)* or the Bandwidth Allocation Control Protocol (BACP). BAP sets two thresholds on an output buffer. For example, if the output buffer hits 70 percent full, the second line kicks in. When the output buffer hits 40 percent full, it will drop the second line. You set the percentages. This system provides additional bandwidth for high traffic communications and minimizes phone line charges.

- Link Control Protocol (LCP) extensions are used to specify that LCP should send Time-Remaining and Identification packets as well as request callback during an LCP negotiation.

- Software compression is used to specify that the Microsoft Point-to-Point Compression Protocol (MPPC) should be used to compress any data that is sent over the remote access or demand-dial connection. This setting reduces traffic and is commonly enabled.

FIGURE 13.11 The PPP tab of the RAS server Properties dialog box

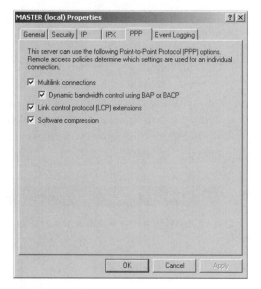

Setting Event Logging Options

The Event Logging tab, shown in Figure 13.12, allows you to configure how RAS server events are logged. You can choose to log errors only, log errors and warnings, log the maximum amount of information, or disable event logging.

FIGURE 13.12 The Event Logging tab of the remote access Properties dialog box

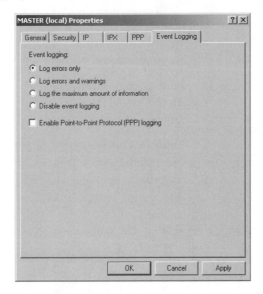

You can also specify whether PPP logging is enabled. If you enable PPP logging, all of the events related to the PPP connection process will be written to the *Windir*\Tracing\ppp.log file. This log file should be enabled only for troubleshooting remote access problems.

In Exercise 13.3, you will configure the properties for the RAS server you installed in Exercise 13.1.

EXERCISE 13.3

Configuring RAS server Properties

1. Select Start ➢ Programs ➢ Administrative Tools ➢ Routing and Remote Access.

2. In the Routing and Remote Access window, right-click your server and select Properties.

3. Click the Security tab and click the Authentication Methods button.

4. In the Authentication Methods dialog box, select Encrypted Authentication (CHAP). Click the OK button.

5. Click the Event Logging tab. Select the Log the Maximum Amount of Information option and the Enable Point-to-Point Protocol (PPP) Logging option. Click the OK button.

6. When you see the dialog box warning you that your changes to the router configuration require the router to be restarted, click the Yes button to restart the router.

Assigning Dial-in Permissions to Users

You assign permissions to users who can access a RAS server through the user Properties dialog box, in the Local Users and Groups utility on a member server or in the Active Directory Users and Computers utility on a Windows 2000 domain controller. To open the user Properties dialog box, access the appropriate utility, open the Users folder, and double-click the user account. Click the Dial-in tab to see the dialog box shown in Figure 13.13.

FIGURE 13.13   The Dial-in tab of the user Properties dialog box

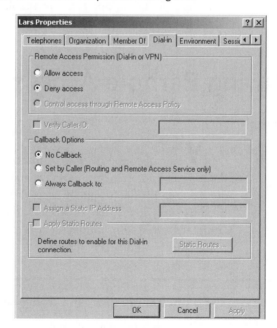

See Chapter 4, "Managing Users and Groups" for details on creating and configuring local and Active Directory users and groups.

The options on the Dial-in tab allow you to configure the following dial-in properties:

- Whether to allow or deny the user remote access permission, and whether a remote access policy will be used. The Control Access through Remote Access radio button will only be enabled if the domain is in Native Mode. Once enabled, the Remote Access policy is based on three criteria: Conditions, Permissions and Profile. All three criteria must be met to allow remote access. (remote access policies are covered in the next section)

- Which callback options are desired: No callback, callback set by the caller, or to always use callback to a specified telephone number

- Whether static IP address or static routes should be applied to the user's connection

If a Dial-in tab option is not available, that means that your computer is not configured to support that option.

Configuring Remote Access Policies and Profiles

You can configure who is authorized to access your RAS server by defining a *remote access policy*. Through a remote access policy, you can create a dial-in profile to specify access based on Windows 2000 group membership, time of day, day of week, and type of connection. You can also configure settings for options such as maximum session time, authentication requirements, and BAP policies.

**Microsoft
Exam
Objective**

Configure, monitor, and troubleshoot remote access.

- Create a remote access policy.

- Configure a remote access profile.

You set up your remote access policy through the Routing and Remote Access utility. Expand your computer, and then expand Remote Access Policies.

Modifying an Existing Remote Access Policy

By default, there is a remote access policy called Allow Access If Dial-in Permission Is Enabled. You can access this policy by double-clicking Remote Access Policies in the Routing and Remote Access window. To manage the properties of this policy, right-click it and select Properties from the pop-up menu. The Settings tab of the policy Properties dialog box will appear, as shown in Figure 13.14.

You control who can access the remote access policy by clicking the Add button in the Settings tab and selecting the Windows-Groups attribute from the Select Attribute dialog box. After you add the Windows groups that the policy will apply to, you can specify if the group is granted remote access permission or denied remote access permissions.

FIGURE 13.14   The Settings tab of the remote access policy Properties dialog box

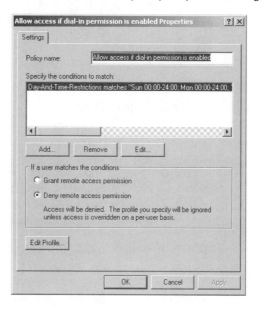

Click the Edit Profile button at the bottom of the Settings tab to display the Edit Dial-in Profile dialog box, as shown in Figure 13.15. This dialog box

has six tabs with dial-in options that you can configure, as described in Table 13.2.

FIGURE 13.15 The Edit Dial-in Profile dialog box

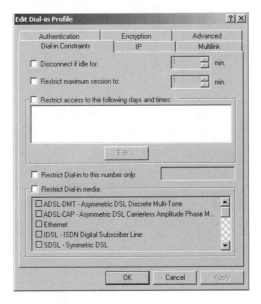

TABLE 13.2 Edit Dial-in Profile Options

Tab	Description
Dial-in Constraints	Allows you to specify when a connection is disconnected based on idle time, maximum session time, and day and time restrictions. You can also restrict dial-in access to a specific number and restrict dial-in media.
IP	Allows you to restrict IP address assignment and configure IP packet filters for the connection.
Multilink	Allows you to configure multilink settings and BAP settings.
Authentication	Allows you to configure which authentication methods will be allowed for the connection (see Table 13.1).

TABLE 13.2 Edit Dial-in Profile Options *(continued)*

Tab	Description
Encryption	Allows you to specify which encryption settings will be used by the Routing and Remote Access Service connections.
Advanced	Allows you to specify which connection attributes will be used by the RAS server.

In Exercise 13.4, you will edit the existing remote access policy and profile.

EXERCISE 13.4

Managing Remote Access Policies and Profiles

1. Select Start ➤ Programs ➤ Administrative Tools ➤ Routing and Remote Access.

2. In the Routing and Remote Access window, expand your computer, then expand Remote Access Policies. Right-click Allow Access If Dial-in Permission Is Enabled and select Properties.

3. In the Settings tab of the remote access policy Properties dialog box, click the Add button.

4. In the Select Attribute dialog box, select the Windows-Groups attribute and click the Add button.

5. In the Groups dialog box, click the Add button.

6. In the Select Groups dialog box, click the Domain Users group and click the Add button. Click the OK button.

7. In the Groups dialog box, click the OK button.

8. In the If a User Matches the Conditions section of the Settings tab, click the Grant Remote Access Permission radio button. Then click the Edit Profile button.

9. In the Dial-in Constraints tab of the Edit Dial-in Profile dialog box, select the Disconnect If Idle option and set it for 10 minutes. Select the Restrict Maximum Session To option and set it to 60 minutes.

EXERCISE 13.4 *(continued)*

10. Click the IP tab. Configure IP address assignment so that the server must supply an IP address.

11. Click the Multilink tab. Select the Allow Multilink option and limit the maximum ports to two ports. Leave the Bandwidth Allocation Protocol (BAP) settings at the default values.

12. Click the Authentication tab. Deselect the default protocols and select Encrypted Authentication (CHAP).

13. Click the Encryption tab and note the default settings.

14. Click the Advanced tab and note the default settings.

15. Click the OK button to close the Edit Dial-in Profile dialog box.

16. In the Settings tab, click the OK button.

Creating a New Remote Access Policy

You can also create new remote access policies. When you define your policy, you can select from a list of attributes as conditions to match. Table 13.3 shows the options for remote access policies.

TABLE 13.3 Remote Access Policy Options

Remote Access Policy Option	Description
Called-Station-ID	Specifies the telephone number that the remote user is dialing into.
Calling-Station-ID	Specifies the telephone number that the remote dialing user is dialing from.
Client-Friendly-Name	For RADIUS servers, specifies the friendly name of the RADIUS client.
Client-IP-Address	For RADIUS servers, specifies the IP address of the RADIUS client.

TABLE 13.3 Remote Access Policy Options *(continued)*

Remote Access Policy Option	Description
Client-Vendor	For RADIUS servers, specifies the manufacturer of the RADIUS proxy or network access server (NAS).
Day-and-TimeRestrictions	Specifies time periods when the remote user is allowed or denied access to the RAS server.
Framed-Protocol	Specifies which protocols can be used for remote access.
NAS-Identifier	For RADIUS servers, specifies a string that identifies the NAS that originated the request.
NAS-IP-Address	For RADIUS servers, specifies the IP address of the NAS that originated the request.
NAS-Port-Type	For RADIUS servers, specifies the physical port of the NAS that originated the request.
Service-Type	Specifies the type of service that the user has requested.
Tunnel-Type	Specifies what type of tunneling protocols can be used.
Windows-Groups	Specifies which Windows groups can access the RAS server.

To create a remote access policy, take the following steps:

1. Start the Routing and Remote Access utility, make sure your computer is expanded, and right-click Remote Access Policies. From the pop-up menu, select New, and then select Remote Access Policy.

2. The Add Remote Access Policy dialog box appears, as shown in Figure 13.16. Enter a name for this policy. In this example, the name **Group Restrictions** is used. Click the Next button.

FIGURE 13.16 The Add Remote Access Policy dialog box

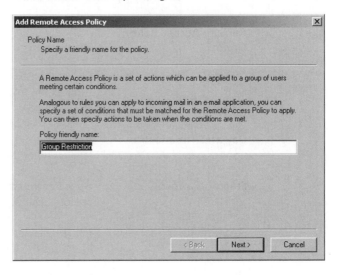

3. The Conditions dialog box appears. Click the Add button.

4. The Select Attribute dialog box appears, as shown in Figure 13.17. You can select from the attributes listed in Table 13.3. In this example, Windows-Groups is selected. Click the Add button.

FIGURE 13.17 The Select Attribute dialog box

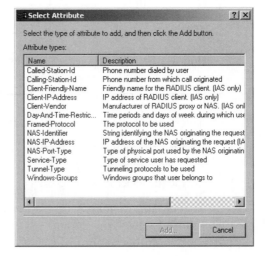

5. The Groups dialog box appears. Click the Add button.

6. The Select Groups dialog box appears, as shown in Figure 13.18. Select the groups you want to have access permission and click the Add button. Click the OK button.

FIGURE 13.18   The Select Groups dialog box

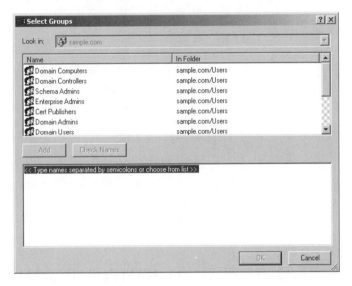

7. You return to the Groups dialog box. Click the OK button. In the Conditions dialog box, click the Next button.

8. The Permissions dialog box appears. You can specify whether the groups you have selected will be granted remote access permission or denied remote access permission. In this example, remote access permission is granted. Click the Next button.

9. The User Profile dialog box appears. This dialog box allows you to specify additional user profile settings for the remote access policy. If you want to configure the profile for users who match the policy's conditions, click the Edit Profile button. This brings up the Edit Dial-in Profile dialog box (see Figure 13.15), which includes the options listed in Table 13.2. After you have configured your remote access policy, click the Finish button.

Once a RAS policy is used, the last three of these steps *must* be followed to allow access.

 Real World Scenario

Taking Advantage of Existing Internet Connectivity

Your company allows employees the option to telecommute one day a week. You install a RAS server to provide remote access to the server. Many of the employees live within an hour of the office and connect to the RAS server for hours at a time. After the first month, users are submitting expenses for outrageous phone bills associated with dialing into the network.

This is a perfect case for using a VPN. With VPN connections, a user simply has to access an Internet connection. Since most users already have local Internet access, this allows you to avoid large phone bills.

Installing and Configuring a Virtual Private Network

Virtual private networks (VPNs) are used to allow VPN clients to access VPN servers through a private network or through the Internet.

Microsoft *Exam* *Objective*	**Install, configure, and troubleshoot a virtual private network (VPN).**

Like a RAS server, a VPN server is installed and configured through the Routing and Remote Access utility. In fact, you will notice that the process is similar to installing a RAS server.

The following steps are used to install a VPN server:

1. Select Start ➤ Programs ➤ Administrative Tools ➤ Routing and Remote Access.

2. The Routing and Remote Access utility starts. In the Routing and Remote Access window, right-click your server and select Configure and Enable Routing and Remote Access from the pop-up menu.

3. The Routing and Remote Access Server Wizard starts . Click the Next button to continue.

4. The Common Configurations dialog box appears. Select the Virtual Private Network (VPN) Server option and click the Next button.

5. The Remote Client Protocols dialog box appears. You can select the No, I Need to Add Protocols option and specify other protocols. Alternatively, accept the default selection (Yes, All of the Required Protocols Are on This List) and click the Next button.

6. The Internet Connection dialog box appears, as shown in Figure 13.19. Select the Internet connection (typically the modem) that will be used by the VPN server and click the Next button.

FIGURE 13.19 The Internet Connection dialog box

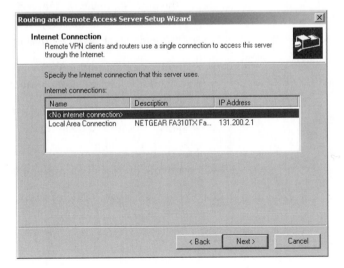

7. The IP Address Assignment dialog box appears. You can specify that IP addresses will be automatically assigned or that IP addresses will be assigned from a specified range of addresses. In this example, IP addresses will be assigned automatically. Click the Next button.

8. The Managing Multiple Remote Access Servers dialog box appears. This dialog box allows you to specify whether you will install a RADIUS server that will be used to manage remote access servers centrally. In this example, a RADIUS server is not installed. Click the Next button.

9. The Completing the Routing and Remote Access Server Setup Wizard dialog box appears. Click the Finish button.

In Exercise 13.5, you will install and configure a VPN server.

EXERCISE 13.5

Installing and Configuring a VPN Server

1. Select Start ➢ Programs ➢ Administrative Tools ➢ Routing and Remote Access.

2. The Routing and Remote Access utility starts. If you have completed the other exercises in this chapter, you need to disable your RAS server before configuring the VPN server. Right-click your computer and select Disable Routing and Remote Access.

3. In the Routing and Remote Access window, right-click your server and select Configure and Enable Routing and Remote Access.

4. When the Routing and Remote Access Server Setup Wizard starts, click the Next button to continue.

5. In the Common Configurations dialog box, select the Virtual Private Network (VPN) Server option and click the Next button.

6. In the Remote Client Protocols dialog box, click the Next button to accept the default values and continue.

EXERCISE 13.5 *(continued)*

7. In the Internet Connection dialog box, select the Internet connection that will be used by the VPN server (if you have no Internet connection, select the No Internet Connection option) and click the Next button.

8. In the IP Address Assignment dialog box, specify that IP addresses will be automatically assigned and click the Next button.

9. In the Managing Multiple Remote Access Servers dialog box, select the No, I Don't Want to Set Up This Server to Use RADIUS Now option and click the Next button.

10. When the Completing the Routing and Remote Access Server Setup Wizard dialog box appears, click the Finish button.

11. A message box appears, stating that in order to support the relaying of DHCP messages from remote access clients, you must configure the properties of the DHCP Relay Agent with the IP address of your DHCP server. Click the OK button.

Summary

In this chapter, you learned how to install and manage remote network connections. We covered the following topics:

- How to install and configure a RAS server by using the Routing and Remote Access utility, as well as how to configure inbound and outbound connections and manage a RAS server's properties

- How to configure remote access policies which consist of conditions, permissions, and profiles

- How to install and configure a virtual private network (VPN) server for remote access

Exam Essentials

Be able to install and configure a RAS server. Know the requirements and steps for installing RAS servers. Be able to configure inbound and outbound connections. Be able to manage RAS server properties, especially security options.

Be able to configure remote access policies and profiles. Know which options can be configured through remote access policies and profiles and how they are applied.

Know how to install and configure a virtual private network. Know what the advantage of using a VPN is and how to install and configure a VPN.

Key Terms

Before taking the exam, you should be familiar with the following terms:

Bandwidth Allocation Protocol (BAP)	remote access policy
demand-dial routing connections (DDR)	Remote Access Service (RAS) server
inbound connections	Remote Authentication Dial-in User Service (RADIUS) server
multilink	Routing and Remote Access service
outbound connections	virtual private network (VPN)
Point-to-Point Protocol (PPP)	

Review Questions

1. Your company has a user who works from home two days a week. The user uses offline files, so most of the files he needs are already on his laptop. However, occasionally the user requires access to the most up-to-date files on the server. You decide to configure a RAS server that will allow the user dial-in access. Which of the following connection types is *not* supported by RAS servers in Windows 2000 Server?

   A. Modem

   B. ISDN

   C. Null-modem

   D. PPTP

2. Your company has several salespeople that travel quite a bit. These users need to be able to access local network resources. You want to allow this access through a RAS server. Which utility do you use to install RAS servers in Windows 2000 Server?

   A. Routing and Remote Access

   B. Control Panel, Networking

   C. Control Panel, Network and Dial-up Connections

   D. Control Panel, Add/Remove Programs

3. You have installed a RAS server for your network. You are very concerned that this will open your network up to potential security risks. Which service can be used with RAS servers and VPN servers to provide a central authentication database for remote connections?

   A. Authentication server

   B. Certificate server

   C. RADIUS server

   D. SECIP server

4. Juana is configuring her RAS server. She wants to ensure that she provides as much client compatibility for authentication requests as possible. Which of the following authentication providers can be used to authenticate remote access requests? (Choose all that apply.)

   A. Windows authentication

   B. Hybrid authentication

   C. Shiva authentication

   D. RADIUS authentication

5. Due to the security risks associated with allowing remote access, you have decided to require your remote access clients to use smart cards as an additional layer of security. Based on the following exhibit, which remote access authentication method should you use if you want the RAS server and the remote access client to negotiate an authentication scheme or use an authentication scheme that clients with smart cards can use?

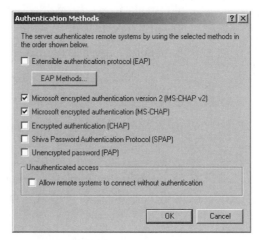

   A. EAP

   B. MS-CHAP v2

   C. CHAP

   D. PAP

6. Your company has decided to use RAS as a way to allow users remote access to your network. The data that they will access is not sensitive and does not need excessive security applied. Which remote access authentication method should you use if you have no idea which client software will be used and you want to support plain text passwords?

    A. EAP

    B. MS-CHAP v2

    C. CHAP

    D. PAP

7. Which remote access authentication method should you use if you need to support non-Microsoft clients using the Message Digest 5 hashing scheme to encrypt the response that is sent from the RAS client to the RAS server?

    A. EAP

    B. MS-CHAP v2

    C. CHAP

    D. PAP

8. Your company does not have access to any high-speed remote access connections. You do have three medium-speed access lines and want to combine the bandwidth of all three connections. Which technology is used to allow several physical connections to be combined into a single logical connection for remote network access?

    A. MPPC

    B. BAP

    C. LCP

    D. Multilink

9. You have installed a VPN server to allow remote access to your network. On the pipeline coming in, you notice that a user's transferring of large graphics files is saturating the bandwidth. Which of the following protocols is used with remote access to specify how much bandwidth should be allocated to a specific connection?

   A. MPPC

   B. BAP

   C. LCP

   D. Multilink

10. You have installed a RAS server for accessing the corporate network. You want to ensure that the network bandwidth is used as efficiently as possible. Which of the following protocols is used to specify that any data that is sent over the remote access or demand-dial connection should be compressed?

    A. MPPC

    B. BAP

    C. LCP

    D. Multilink

11. A user is having difficulty connecting to the RAS server. You decide to enable PPP logging to attempt to troubleshoot the problem. After logging is enabled, where can you find the log file?

    A. *Windir*\Logs\ppp.log

    B. *Windir*\Ras\ppp.log

    C. *Windir*\Tracing\ppp.log

    D. *Windir*\System32\ppp.log

12. Your company has decided to use a VPN to allow remote access to the local network. You need to define as much security as possible. You decide to use remote access profiles for your RAS server in order to configure as secure an environment as possible. Which of the following options is *not* set as a part of the remote access profile?

A. Dial-in constraints, which are used to configure restrictions such as maximum session time and the dial-in access telephone number

B. IP settings, which restrict IP address assignment and allow you to configure IP packet filters for the connection

C. Port settings, which define whether users have dial-in or dial-out access

D. Multilink settings, which are used to configure multilink settings and BAP settings

13. Your network uses a RAS server to allow for remote access. You have 10 users who should be allowed to access the network remotely. The rest of the users should have no remote access. Which of the following utilities is used to configure dial-in permissions for a specific user on a Windows 2000 domain controller?

A. Routing and Remote Access

B. Dial-in Administrator

C. Active Directory Users and Computers

D. Routing and Remote Access Security

14. You want your remote users to be able to connect to your Windows 2000 Server computer through the Internet. Which of the following routing and remote access configurations should you configure?

A. Internet connection server

B. RAS server

C. Virtual private network (VPN) server

D. Internet private network (IPN) server

15. You installed a RAS server using all of the default options. Some of the RAS clients can access the RAS server, and other clients are unable to connect. You suspect that the problem may be due to protocol mismatches. Which of the following remote client protocols are installed on a RAS server by default?

A. TCP/IP

B. IPX

C. NetBEUI

D. Whatever protocols are installed on the server

Answers to Review Questions

1. D. The Point-to-Point Tunneling Protocol (PPTP) is not a connection mechanism.

2. A. You can create server-side connections through Administrative Tools ➢ Routing and Remote Access. Client-side connections are created through Control Panel, Network and Dial-up Connections, Make New Connection.

3. C. When you install RAS or VPN servers, you have the option of installing a Remote Authentication Dial-in User Service (RADIUS) server, which is used to manage RAS servers by providing a central authentication database. The database contains either computer names or IP addresses used for equipment to equipment verification.

4. A, D. The only authentication services that are provided by a RAS server are Windows authentication and RADIUS authentication. RADIUS authentication requires a RADIUS server and a RADIUS client.

5. A. Extensible Authentication Protocol (EAP) is an authentication protocol that allows the RAS server and the remote access client to negotiate an authentication scheme, such as Generic Token Card, MD5-Challenge, Transport Level Security (used with smart cards), and S/Key.

6. D. The PAP protocol uses plain text passwords and is the least secure authentication protocol.

7. C. CHAP is a challenge-response authentication protocol. It is used by non-Microsoft clients to provide challenge-response authentication using the Message Digest 5 (MD5) hashing scheme to encrypt the response that is sent from the RAS client to the RAS server.

8. D. Multilink connections are used to allow several physical connections to be combined into a single logical connection. This allows you to combine several slow-speed lines into a single logical higher-speed line.

9. B. The Bandwidth Allocation Protocol (BAP) or the Bandwidth Allocation Control Protocol (BACP) can be used to control how much bandwidth will be allocated to a specific connection.

10. A. The Microsoft Point-to-Point Compression Protocol (MPPC) is used to compress any data that is sent over the remote access or demand-dial connection.

11. C. In the Event Logging tab of the RAS server Properties dialog box, you can specify whether Point-to-Point (PPP) logging is enabled. If you enable PPP logging, all of the events related to the PPP connection process will be written to the *Windir*\Tracing\ppp.log file.

12. C. Port settings are not configured as a part of the remote access profile.

13. C. On a domain controller, you assign permissions to users who can access a RAS server through the Dial-in tab of the user Properties dialog box in the Active Directory Users and Computers utility.

14. C. VPN servers allow remote computers to connect to the network through the Internet.

15. D. When you install a RAS server, by default, it will try to install whatever network protocols you have installed on your server as the remote client protocols.

Chapter 14

Optimizing Windows 2000

MICROSOFT EXAM OBJECTIVES COVERED IN THIS CHAPTER

✓ Deploy service packs.

✓ Monitor and optimize usage of system resources.

✓ Manage processes.

  ▪ Set priorities and start and stop processes.

✓ Optimize disk performance.

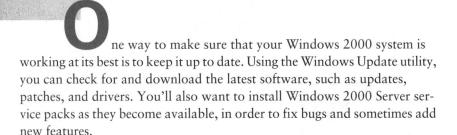

One way to make sure that your Windows 2000 system is working at its best is to keep it up to date. Using the Windows Update utility, you can check for and download the latest software, such as updates, patches, and drivers. You'll also want to install Windows 2000 Server service packs as they become available, in order to fix bugs and sometimes add new features.

To have an optimized system, you must monitor its performance. The tools for monitoring Windows 2000 Server are System Monitor, Performance Logs and Alerts, and Task Manager. With these tools, you can track memory, processor activity, the disk subsystem, the network subsystem, and other computer subsystems.

This chapter begins with discussions of the Windows Update utility and service packs. Then you will learn how to monitor and optimize Windows 2000 Server using the System Monitor, Performance Logs and Alerts, and Task Manager utilities. You will also learn how to manage processes.

The procedures for monitoring and optimizing Windows 2000 are the same for both Windows 2000 Server and Windows 2000 Professional.

Keeping Windows 2000 Up to Date

An optimal operating system is one that is running the most up-to-date software and has had the most recent service pack installed. Microsoft provides the Windows Update utility to help you obtain updated Windows 2000 software. Microsoft issues service packs as necessary to update the operating system with bug fixes and new features.

Using the Windows Update Utility

The *Windows Update* utility connects your computer to Microsoft's Web site and checks your files to make sure that you have all of the latest and greatest updates.

To use Windows Update, you must first have a valid Internet connection. Then simply choose Start ➤ Windows Update to go to the correct URL for updates.

For product updates, click the Product Updates option on the home page and follow the directions to choose which files you want to update. The files in the update section are arranged by the following categories:

- Critical updates

- Picks of the month

- Recommended updates

- Additional Windows features

- Device drivers

Within each category, you will see the available updates, along with a description, file size, and download time estimate for each update. Just check the files you want to update and click the Download icon to download your selections.

Using Windows Service Packs

Service packs are used to update the Windows operating system—to increase operating system reliability, increase application compatibility, facilitate Windows setup, and address security issues. Windows 2000 offers a new technology for service packs called *slipstream*. With slipstream technology, service packs are applied once, and they are not overwritten as new services are added to the computer. This means that you should not need to reapply service packs after new services are added, which was sometimes required when Windows NT 4 service packs were applied.

Microsoft
✓ *Exam*
Objective

Deploy service packs.

You can determine if any service packs have been installed on your computer by using the WINVER command, as shown in Figure 14.1. To issue this command, select Start ➢ Programs ➢ Accessories ➢ Command Prompt. In the Command Prompt dialog box, type **WINVER** and press Enter. You will see a dialog box that shows which service packs are currently installed.

FIGURE 14.1 Response to the WINVER command

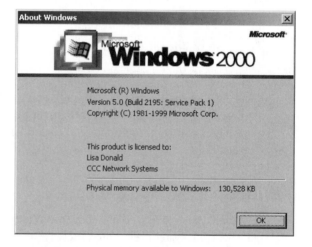

Windows 2000 Service Packs come in two versions:

- Standard, which uses 56-bit encryption.

- High, which uses 128-bit encryption.

The version you install is based on the encryption that is set on your computer. You can determine the level of encryption that is set on your computer through the command-line utility WINMSD, then expand Internet Explorer 5,

Summary. As shown in Figure 14.2, the Cipher Strength field will display the level of encryption that is installed on your computer.

FIGURE 14.2   Using WINMSD to determine encryption level

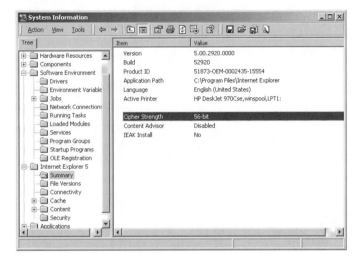

You can find out what the current available service pack is from Microsoft's Web site—www.microsoft.com. The current service pack can be downloaded from the Web site at no cost or ordered on CD for a minimal charge.

Once you download the proper version of service pack (based on your computer's encryption), click the file to begin the installation process. You will have to accept the license agreement, and you will have the option to create an Uninstall folder. Then, the files will be installed on your computer. If you choose to create an Uninstall folder, it will require about 215–315MB of disk space. This Uninstall folder is stored in *winder*\$NT ServicePackUninstall$.

Using System Monitoring Tools

Before you can optimize the performance of Windows 2000 Server, you must monitor critical subsystems to determine how your system is currently performing and what (if anything) is causing system bottlenecks. Windows 2000 Server ships with two tools that you can use to track and monitor system performance: the System Monitor utility and the Performance Logs and Alerts utility.

Microsoft Exam Objectives

Monitor and optimize usage of system resources.

Optimize disk performance.

You can access the monitoring tools by adding the System Monitor snap-in and the Performance Logs and Alerts snap-in to the MMC. The System Monitor snap-in is added as an ActiveX control.

In Exercise 14.1, you will create a management console for monitoring system performance.

> **NOTE** All of the exercises in this chapter can be performed from either your Windows 2000 member server or domain controller.

EXERCISE 14.1

Creating a Management Console for Monitoring System Performance

1. Select Start ➢ Run, type **MMC** in the Run dialog box, and click the OK button.

2. Select Console ➢ Add/Remove Snap-in.

3. In the Add/Remove Snap-in dialog box, click the Add button. In the Add Standalone Snap-in dialog box, select ActiveX Control and click the Add button.

4. In the Insert ActiveX Control dialog box, click the Next button.

5. In the Insert ActiveX Control dialog box, select System Monitor Control and click the Next button. Click the Finish button.

6. In the Add Standalone Snap-in dialog box, select Performance Logs and Alerts and click the Add button, then click the Close button.

7. In the Add/Remove Snap-in dialog box, click the OK button.

EXERCISE 14.1 *(continued)*

8. Select Console ➢ Save As.

9. In the Save As dialog box, select Save in Administrative Tools (the default selection) and save the file as **Monitor**.

You can now access this console by selecting Start ➢ Programs ➢ Administrative Tools ➢ Monitor.

In Windows NT 4, the functions of the System Monitor utility and the Performance Logs and Alerts utility were implemented in the Performance Monitor utility.

Now that you've added the monitoring tools to the MMC, you can use them to monitor and optimize Windows 2000. The following sections describe how to evaluate your system's current performance; how to use System Monitor and Performance Logs and Alerts; and how to monitor and optimize the system memory, processor, disk subsystem, and network subsystem.

Determining System Performance

The monitoring tools allow you to assess your server's current health and determine what it requires to improve its present condition. With System Monitor and Performance Logs and Alerts, you can perform the following tasks:

- Create baselines
- Identify system bottlenecks
- Determine trends
- Create alert thresholds

Each of these tasks is discussed in the following sections.

Creating Baselines

A *baseline* is a snapshot of how your system is currently performing. Suppose that your computer's hardware has not changed over the last six months, but the computer seems to be performing more slowly now than it did six months ago. If you have been using the Performance Logs and Alerts utility and taking baseline logs, as well as noting the changes in your workload, you can more easily determine what resources are causing the system to slow down.

You should create baselines at the following times:

- When the system is first configured without any load

- At regular intervals of typical usage

- Whenever any changes are made to the system's hardware or software configuration

Baselines are particularly useful for determining the effect of changes that you make to your computer. For example, if you are adding more memory to your computer, you should take baselines before and after you install the memory to determine the effect of the change. Along with hardware changes, system configuration modifications also can affect your computer's performance, so you should create baselines before and after you make any changes to your Windows 2000 Server configuration.

For the most part, Windows 2000 Server is a self-tuning operating system. If you decide to tweak the operating system, you should take baselines before and after each change. If you do not notice a performance gain after the tweak, you should consider returning the computer to its original configuration, because some tweaks may cause more problems than they solve.

You create baselines by using the Performance Logs and Alerts utility to create a baseline counters log file. This process is described in the "Creating Baseline Reports" section later in this chapter.

Identifying System Bottlenecks

A *bottleneck* is a system resource that is inefficient compared with the rest of the computer system as a whole. The bottleneck can cause the rest of the system to run slowly.

You need to pinpoint the cause of a bottleneck in order to correct it. Consider a system that has a Pentium 166 processor with 128MB of RAM. If your applications are memory-intensive, and lack of memory is your bottleneck, then upgrading your processor will not eliminate the bottleneck.

By using System Monitor, you can measure the performance of the various parts of your system, which allows you to identify system bottlenecks in a scientific manner. You will learn how to set counters to monitor your network and spot bottlenecks in the "Using System Monitor" section later in this chapter.

Determining Trends

Many of us tend to manage situations reactively instead of proactively. With reactive management, you focus on a problem when it occurs. With proactive management, you take steps to avoid the problem before it happens. In a perfect world, all management would be proactive.

System Monitor and Performance Logs and Alerts are great tools for proactive network management. If you are creating baselines on a regular basis, you can identify system trends. For example, if you notice average CPU utilization increasing 15 percent every month, you can assume that within the next six to twelve months, you're going to have a problem. Before performance becomes so slow that your system is not responding, you can upgrade the hardware.

Using Alerts for Problem Notification

The Performance Logs and Alerts utility provides another tool for proactive management in the form of *alerts*. Through Performance Logs and Alerts, you can specify alert thresholds (when a counter reaches a specified value) and have the utility notify you when these thresholds are reached.

For example, you could specify that if your logical disk has less than 10 percent of free space, you want to be notified. Once alerted, you can add more disk space or delete unneeded files before you run out of disk space. You will learn how to create alerts in the "Using Performance Logs and Alerts" section later in this chapter.

Using System Monitor

Through *System Monitor*, you can view current data or data from a log file. When you view current activity, you are monitoring real-time activity. When you view data from a log file, you are importing a log file from a previous session.

After you've added the System Monitor snap-in to the MMC (see Exercise 14.1), you can open it by selecting Select Start ➢ Programs ➢

Administrative Tools ➢ Monitor. Figure 14.3 shows the main System Monitor window when you first open it.

FIGURE 14.3 The main System Monitor window

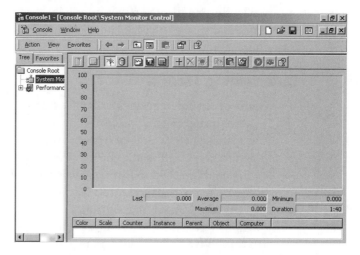

The System Monitor toolbar, shown below, provides access to all of the System Monitor functions.

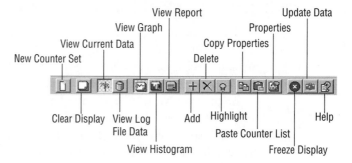

When you first start System Monitor, you will notice that nothing is tracked by default. In order for System Monitor to be useful, you must configure it to track some type of system activity, which is done by adding counters, as described shortly. After you've added counters, they will be listed at the bottom of the System Monitor window. The fields just above the counter list will contain data, based on the counter that is highlighted in the list, as follows:

- The Last field displays the most current data.

- The Average field shows the average of the counter.

- The Minimum field shows the lowest value that has been recorded for the counter.

- The Maximum field shows the highest value that has been recorded for the counter.

- The Duration field shows how long the counter has been tracking data.

The following sections describe the three System Monitor views, how to add counters to track data, and how to configure System Monitor properties.

Selecting the Appropriate View

By clicking the appropriate button in the System Monitor toolbar, you can see your data in three views:

Chart view   The chart view, shown in Figure 14.4, is the default view used with System Monitor. This view is useful for viewing a small number of counters in a graphical format. The main advantage of chart view is that you can see how the data has been tracked during the defined time period. When you start to track a large number of counters, it can be difficult to view the data in chart form.

Histogram view   The histogram view, shown in Figure 14.5, shows System Monitor data in bar graph form. This view is useful for viewing large amounts of data. However, it only shows performance for the current period. You do not see a record of performance over time, as you do with the chart view.

Report view   The report view, shown in Figure 14.6, is used to list all of the counters that are being tracked through System Monitor in a logical report. The data that is displayed is for the current session. Watching these numbers in real-time is like watching someone on a pogo stick, because the numbers are constantly jumping up and down. The advantage of this view is that it allows you to easily track large numbers of counters in a real-time manner.

FIGURE 14.4 The chart view in System Monitor

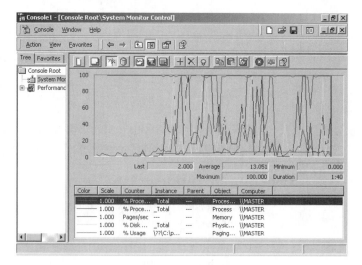

FIGURE 14.5 The histogram view in System Monitor

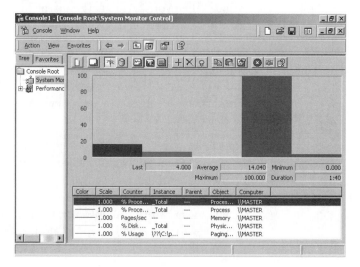

FIGURE 14.6 The report view in System Monitor

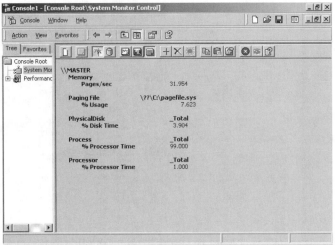

Adding Counters

To use System Monitor, you must add *counters*. To add counters, use the following steps:

1. In System Monitor, click the Add button on the toolbar. This brings up the Add Counters dialog box, as shown in Figure 14.7.

To see information about a specific counter, select it and click the Explain button in the upper-right corner of the Add Counters dialog box. System Monitor will display text regarding the highlighted counter.

FIGURE 14.7 The Add Counters dialog box

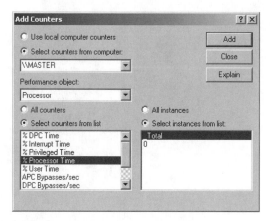

2. In the Add Counters dialog box, select the Use Local Computer Counters radio button to monitor the local computer. Alternatively, select the Select Counters from Computer radio button and choose a computer from the drop-down list to select counters from a specific computer. You can monitor remote computers if you have Administrative permissions on that computer. This option is useful when you do not want the overhead of System Monitor running on the computer you are trying to monitor.

3. Select the performance object from the drop-down list. All Windows 2000 system resources are tracked as performance objects, such as Cache, Memory, Paging File, Process, and Processor. The sum of all objects represents your total system. Some performance objects exist on all Windows 2000 computers; other objects appear only if specific processes or services are running. For example, if you want to track how busy the physical disk is, choose the PhysicalDisk performance object.

4. Select the All Counters radio button to track all the associated counters, or select the Select Counters from List radio button and choose specific counters from the list box below. Each performance object has an associated set of counters. Counters are used to track specific information regarding a performance object. For example, for the PhysicalDisk performance object, there is a %Disk Time counter, which will tell you how busy a disk has been servicing read and write requests. PhysicalDisk also has %Disk Read Time and %Disk Write

Time counters, which will show you what percentage of disk requests are read requests and what percentage of disk requests are write requests, respectively.

 You can select multiple counters of the same performance object by Shift+clicking contiguous counters or Ctrl+clicking noncontiguous counters.

5. Select the All Instances radio button to track all the associated instances, or select the Select Instances from List radio button and choose specific instances from the list box below. An instance is a mechanism that allows you to track how a specific object is performing if you have more than one item associated with a specific performance object. For example, suppose that your computer has two physical drives. When you track the PhysicalDisk performance object, you can track both of your drives, or you could track drive 0 and drive 1 separately.

6. Click the Add button to add the counters for the performance object.

7. Repeat steps 2 through 6 to specify any additional counters you want to track. When you are finished, click the Close button.

After you've added counters, you can select a specific counter by highlighting it in System Monitor. To highlight a counter, click it and then click the Highlight button on the System Monitor toolbar. Alternatively, you can highlight a counter by selecting it and pressing Ctrl+H.

To remove a counter, highlight the counter in System Monitor and click the Delete button on the System Monitor toolbar.

Managing System Monitor Properties

To configure the System Monitor properties, click the Properties button on the System Monitor toolbar. This brings up the System Monitor Properties dialog box, as shown in Figure 14.8. This dialog box has six tabs: General, Source, Data, Graph, Colors, and Fonts. The properties you can configure on each of these tabs are described in the following sections.

FIGURE 14.8 The General tab of the System Monitor Properties dialog box

General Properties

The General tab of the System Monitor Properties dialog box (see Figure 14.8) contains the following options:

- The view that will be displayed: graph, histogram, or report

- The display elements that will be used: legend, value bar, and/or toolbar

- The data that will be displayed: default (for reports or histograms this is current data; for logs, this is average data), current, average, minimum, or maximum

- The appearance, either flat or 3D

- The border, either none or fixed single

- How often the data is updated, in seconds

- Whether duplicate counter instances are allowed

Source Properties

The Source tab, shown in Figure 14.9, allows you to specify the data source. This can be current activity, or it can be data that has been collected in a log file. If you import data from a log file, you can specify the time range that you wish to view.

FIGURE 14.9 The Source tab of the System Monitor Properties dialog box

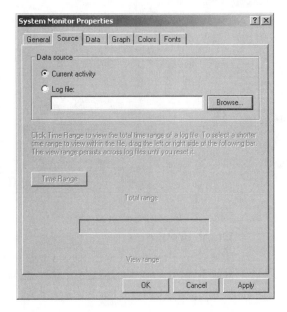

Data Properties

The Data tab, shown in Figure 14.10, lets you specify the counters that you wish to track. You can add and remove counters by clicking the Add and Remove buttons. You can also select a specific counter and define the color, scale, width, and size that is used to represent the counter in the graph.

FIGURE 14.10 The Data tab of the System Monitor Properties dialog box

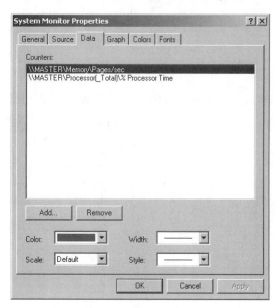

Graph Properties

The Graph tab, shown in Figure 14.11, contains the following options, which can be applied to the chart or histogram view:

- A title

- A vertical axis label

- Whether you will show a vertical grid, a horizontal grid, and/or vertical scale numbers

- The minimum and maximum numbers for the vertical scale

Color and Font Properties

The Colors and Fonts tabs of the System Monitor Properties dialog box have options for customizing the appearance of the System Monitor display. In the Colors tab, you can choose the colors that will be used by System Monitor. In the Fonts tab, you can choose the fonts that System Monitor will use.

FIGURE 14.11   The Graph tab of the System Monitor Properties dialog box

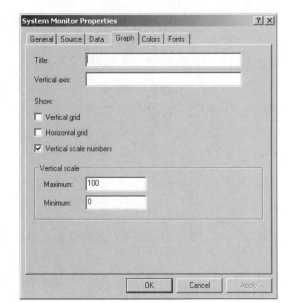

Using Performance Logs and Alerts

Through *Performance Logs and Alerts*, you can create counter logs and trace logs, and you can define alerts. After you've created logs, you can view log files with the System Monitor, as described in the previous section.

After you've added the Performance Logs and Alerts snap-in to the MMC (see Exercise 14.1), you can open it by selecting Start ➤ Programs ➤ Administrative Tools ➤ Monitor and clicking Performance Logs and Alerts. Figure 14.12 shows the expanded Performance Logs and Alerts snap-in. From here, you can define new counter logs, trace logs, and alerts, as described in the following sections.

FIGURE 14.12 The expanded Performance Logs and Alerts snap-in

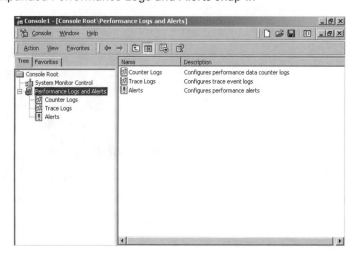

Creating a Counter Log

Counter logs record data about hardware usage and the activity of system services. You can configure logging to occur manually or on a predefined schedule.

To create a counter log, take the following steps:

1. Expand Performance Logs and Alerts, right-click Counter Logs, and select New Log Settings from the pop-up menu.

2. The New Log Settings dialog box appears, as shown in Figure 14.13. Type in a name for the log file. For example, you might give the log a name that indicates its type and the date (Counter*mmddyy*). Then click the OK button.

FIGURE 14.13 The New Log Settings dialog box

3. The counter log file Properties dialog box appears. You can configure counter log properties as follows.

- In the General tab, shown in Figure 14.14, you can specify the counters you want to track in the log and the interval for sampling data. Click the Add button to add counters.

FIGURE 14.14 The General tab of the counter log file Properties dialog box

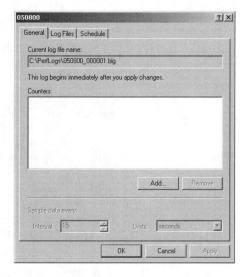

- In the Log Files tab, shown in Figure 14.15, you can configure the location of the log file, the filename, the log file type, and the log file size.

FIGURE 14.15 The Log Files tab of the counter log Properties dialog box

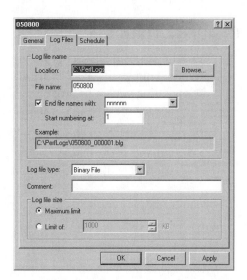

■ In the Schedule tab, shown in Figure 14.16, you can specify when the log file will start, when the log file will stop, and what action should be taken, if any, when the log file is closed.

FIGURE 14.16 The Schedule tab of the counter log Properties dialog box

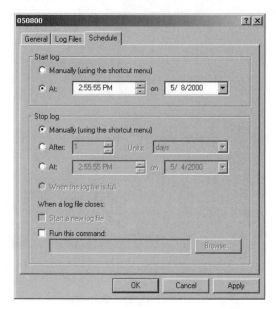

4. When you are finished configuring the counter log file properties, click the OK button. The log will be created and will record the activity for the counters you specified.

Creating a Trace Log

Trace logs measure data continuously as opposed to measuring data through periodic samples. Trace logs are also used to track data that is collected by the operating system or programs. For example, you could specify that you want to trace the creation or deletion of processes or threads.

To create a trace log, take the following steps:

1. Expand Performance Logs and Alerts, right-click Trace Logs, and select New Log Settings from the pop-up menu.

2. The New Log Settings dialog box appears. Type in a name for the log file, such as the type of log and the date (Trace*mmddyy*), and click the OK button.

3. The trace log file Properties dialog box appears. You can configure trace log properties as follows:

   - In the General tab, shown in Figure 14.17, you can select which system events you want to track. For example, you can check the Process Creations/Deletions and Thread Creations/Deletions check boxes. You can also specify which system providers you want to track.

FIGURE 14.17   The General tab of the trace log file Properties dialog box

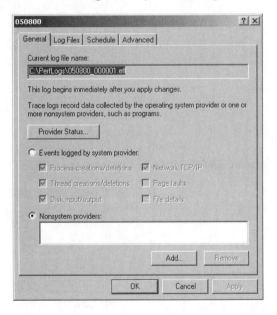

   - In the Log Files tab, shown in Figure 14.18, you can configure the location, filename, log file type, and log file size.

FIGURE 14.18 The Log Files tab of the trace log file Properties dialog box

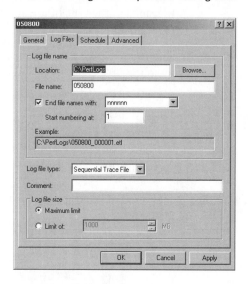

- In the Schedule tab, shown in Figure 14.19, you can configure when the log file will start, when the log file will stop, and what action should be taken, if any, when the log file is closed.

FIGURE 14.19 The Schedule tab of the trace log file Properties dialog box

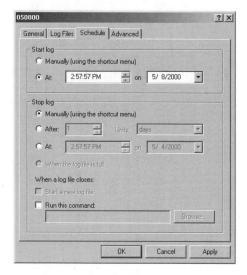

- In the Advanced tab, shown in Figure 14.20, you can configure the buffer settings for the log file. By default, the log service will save the trace file to memory and then transfer the data to the log file.

FIGURE 14.20   The Advanced tab of the trace log file Properties dialog box

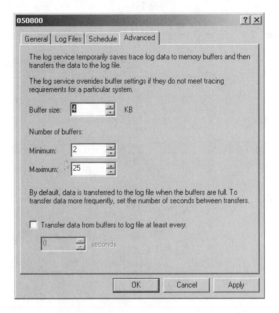

4. When you are finished configuring the trace file properties, click the OK button. The log will be created and will record the activity for the system events you specified.

Creating an Alert

Alerts can be generated when a specific counter exceeds or falls below a specified value. You can configure alerts so that a message is sent, a program is run, or a more detailed log file is generated.

To create an alert, take the following steps:

1. Expand Performance Logs and Alerts, right-click Alerts, and select New Alert Settings from the pop-up menu.

2. The New Alert Settings dialog box appears. Type in a name for the alert file and click the OK button.

3. The alert file Properties dialog box appears. You can configure alert properties as follows:

- In the General tab, shown in Figure 14.21, you can select which counters you want to track. When you add a counter, you must specify that the alert be generated when the counter is under or over a certain value. You can also set the interval for sampling data.

FIGURE 14.21 The General tab of the alert Properties dialog box

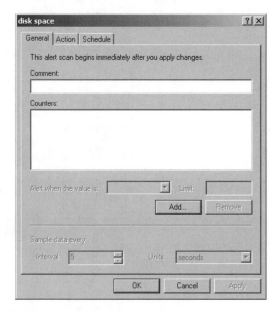

- In the Action tab, shown in Figure 14.22, specify what action should be taken if an alert is triggered. You can select to log an entry in the application event log, send a network message, start another performance data log, and/or run a specific program.

FIGURE 14.22 The Action tab of the alert Properties dialog box

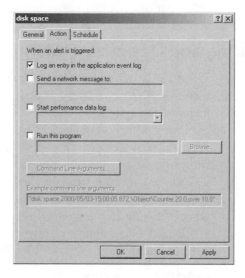

- In the Schedule tab, shown in Figure 14.23, you can configure when scans of the counters you have defined will start and stop.

FIGURE 14.23 The Schedule tab of the alert Properties dialog box

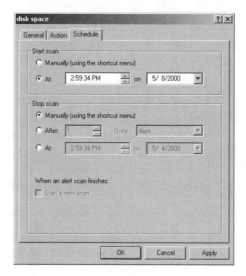

4. When you are finished configuring the alert properties, click the OK button.

Monitoring and Optimizing Memory

When a program or process is required by the operating system, the first place it looks is physical memory. If the program or process is not in physical memory, the system will look in logical memory (the page file). If the program or process is not in logical memory, the system will need to retrieve the program or process from the hard disk. It has been estimated that it can take from 100,000 to 1,000,000 times longer to access information from the hard disk than to access it from physical RAM.

Memory is the most likely cause of system bottlenecks. If you have no idea what is causing a system bottleneck, memory is usually a good place to start checking. To determine how memory is being used, there are two areas you need to examine:

- Physical memory, which is the physical RAM you have installed on your computer. You can't have too much memory. It's actually a good idea to have more memory than you think you will need just to be on the safe side. As you've probably noticed, each time you add or upgrade applications, you require more system memory.

- The *page file*, which is logical memory that exists on the hard drive. If you are using excessive paging (swapping between the page file and physical RAM), it's a clear sign that you need to add more memory.

For example, suppose that the accounting department has just started using a new accounting application that runs on the accounting manager's local computer. The accounting manager complains that this application is slow, and he says that he needs a new computer. You decide to use System Monitor to determine why the computer is responding so slowly. You see that the processor utilization is low, and that the system is using excessive paging. Based on this information, you determine that the account manager's computer will work with the application, but it needs a memory upgrade.

In this book, we use the format *performance object > counter*. For example, Memory > Available MBytes denotes the Memory performance object and the Available MBytes counter.

The following are the three most important counters for monitoring memory:

- Memory > Available MBytes measures the amount of physical memory that is available to run processes on the computer. If this number is less than 4MB, you should consider adding more memory.

- Memory > Pages/Sec shows the number of times that the requested information was not in memory and the request had to be retrieved from disk. This counter's value should be below 20. For optimal performance, this counter's value should be 4 to 5.

- Paging File > %Usage indicates how much of the allocated page file is currently in use. If this number is consistently over 99 percent, you may need to add more memory.

These counters work together to show what is happening on your system, so you should use the Paging File > % Usage counter value in conjunction with the Memory > Available Bytes and Memory > Pages/Sec counters to determine how much paging is occurring on your computer.

In Exercise 14.2, you will monitor your computer's memory subsystem. This exercise assumes that you have completed Exercise 14.1.

EXERCISE 14.2

Monitoring System Memory

1. Select Start ➢ Programs ➢ Administrative Tools ➢ Monitor. Click System Monitor Control to open the System Monitor window.

2. In the System Monitor window, click the Add button on the toolbar.

3. In the Add Counters dialog box, select the following performance objects and counters:

   Select Memory from the performance object drop-down list, select Available MBytes in the counter list box, and click the Add button.

   Select Memory from the performance object drop-down list, select Pages/Sec in the counter list box, and click the Add button.

   Select Paging File from the performance object drop-down list, select %Usage in the counter list box, and click the Add button.

---

4. Click the Close button. You should see a chart showing how your computer's memory is being used.

5. To generate some activity, select Start ➢ Help. Close Help. Open Help again and then close Help. You should have seen that the first time you opened Help, your Memory > Pages/Sec counter spiked, and the second time you accessed Help, the spike was much lower. This is because the first time you accessed the program, it needed to be retrieved from disk; the second time you accessed this program, it was already in memory.

6. Note the Paging > %Usage counter. If this counter is below 99 percent, you are not using excessive paging.

7. Note the Memory > Available MBytes counter. If this counter is above 4MB, you should have sufficient RAM.

Leave System Monitor open, because you will use this utility again in Exercise 14.3.

Monitoring and Optimizing Processors

Although processors are usually not the source of bottlenecks, you should still monitor this subsystem to make sure that processor utilization is at an efficient level. If your Windows 2000 Server computer has multiple processors, you can monitor them through System Monitor and configure them through Task Manager.

Monitoring the System Processor

The following are the two most important counters for monitoring the system processor:

- Processor > %Processor Time measures the time that the processor spends responding to system requests. If this value is consistently above an average of 80 percent, you may have a processor bottleneck.

- Processor > Interrupts/Sec shows the average number of hardware interrupts the processor receives each second. If this value is more than

3,500 on a Pentium class computer, you might have a problem with a program or hardware that is generating spurious interrupts.

If you suspect that you have a processor bottleneck, you can try the following solutions:

- Use less processor-intensive applications.

- Upgrade your processor.

- If your computer supports multiple processors, add a processor. Windows 2000 Server can support up to four processors, which will help if you use multithreaded applications.

Beware of running 3-D screen savers on your computer. As you will see in Exercise 14.3, they can use quite a bit of the processor's time.

In Exercise 14.3, you will monitor your computer's processor. This exercise assumes that you have completed the other exercises in this chapter.

EXERCISE 14.3

Monitoring the System Processor

1. If System Monitor is not already open, select Start ➢ Programs ➢ Administrative Tools ➢ Monitor.

2. In the System Monitor window, click the Add button on the toolbar.

3. In the Add Counters dialog box, select the following performance objects and counters:

    Select Processor from the performance object drop-down list, select %Processor Time in the counter list box, and click the Add button.

    Select Processor from the performance object drop-down list, select Interrupts/Sec in the counter list box, and click the Add button.

4. Click the Close button. You should see these counters added to your chart.

EXERCISE 14.3 *(continued)*

5. To generate some activity, select Start ➢ Settings ➢ Control Panel ➢ Display. Click the Screen Saver tab. Select 3D FlowerBox (OpenGL) and click the Preview button. Let this process run for about five seconds. Close all of the dialog boxes you opened in this step. You should see that the %Processor Time counter spiked during this process.

6. Note the Processor > %Processor Time counter. If this counter's average is below 80 percent, you do not have a processor bottleneck.

7. Note the Processor > Interrupts/Sec counter. If this counter is below 3,500 on a Pentium computer, you do not have any processes or hardware that are generating excessive interrupts.

Leave System Monitor open, because you will use this utility again in Exercise 14.5

Using Multiple Processors

Windows 2000 Server can support up to four processors. Windows 2000 Advanced Server can support up to eight processors. If your computer is capable of supporting multiple processors, you should follow the computer manufacturer's instructions for installing the additional processors. This usually involves updating the processor's driver to a driver that supports multiple processors through the Upgrade Device Driver Wizard.

Once you install your second processor, you can monitor the processors through the System Monitor utility, as described in the previous section. You can verify that multiple processors are recognized by the operating system, as well as configure multiple processors, through the Task Manager utility.

To configure multiple processors, you can associate each processor with specific processes that are running on the computer. This is called *processor affinity*. Once you have two or more processors installed on your computer, you can set processor affinity. We will do this in Exercise 14.4.

EXERCISE 14.4

Configuring Multiple Processors

1. Press Ctrl+Alt+Delete to access the Windows Security dialog box. Click the Task Manager button.

2. The Task Manager dialog box opens. Click the Processes tab to see a list of all the processes that are currently running on your computer.

3. Right-click the process you want to associate with a specific processor and select Processor Affinity from the pop-up menu.

4. The Processor Affinity dialog box appears. Specify the specific processor that the process will use and click the OK button.

5. Close the Task Manager utility.

Task Manager is covered in greater detail in the "Using Task Manager" section later in this chapter.

Monitoring and Optimizing Processes

If you suspect that an application or process is consuming a large share of resources, you can monitor specific processes through the Process performance object. For example, suppose that you are running an application called abc.exe and you want to track how much of the processor time is spent servicing this application and how many bytes of the page file are allocated to this application. To collect this information, you should add the following counters to System Monitor (for a chart) or Performance Logs and Alerts (for a log):

- Process > %Processor Time, abc.exe instance

- Process > Page File Bytes, abc.exe instance

By default, all DOS and Windows 16-bit applications run in a process called ntvdm.exe, which stands for NT Virtual DOS Machine. By default DOS applications will run in separate ntvdm sessions. If you run 16-bit Windows applications, they will run in a single ntvdm session. Within System Monitor, you will see the DOS and Windows 16-bit applications listed as ntvdm.

Monitoring and Optimizing the Disk Subsystem

Disk access is the amount of time it takes your disk subsystem to retrieve data that is requested by the operating system. The two factors that determine how quickly your disk subsystem will respond to system requests are the average disk access time on your hard drive and the speed of your disk controller. On writes, the OS only writes to the controller. Therefore, high-speed writes mandate a very fast controller. On reads, the data is accessed from the disk to the controller. Therefore, on reads the disk access speed is critical. Using high-speed disk controllers and drives in a stripe set, you can attain a disk access time of approximately 5.1 milliseconds.

Microsoft
✓ *Exam*
Objective

Optimize disk performance.

You can monitor the PhysicalDisk object, which is the sum of all logical drives on a single physical drive, or you can monitor the LogicalDisk object, which represents a specific logical disk. The following are the most important counters for monitoring the disk subsystem:

- PhysicalDisk > %Disk Time shows the amount of time the physical disk is busy because it is servicing read or write requests. If the disk is busy more than 90 percent of the time, you will improve performance by adding another disk channel and splitting the disk I/O requests between the channels.

- PhysicalDisk > Current Disk Queue Length indicates the number of outstanding disk requests that are waiting to be processed. This value should be less than 2. A value greater than 2 indicates a disk bottleneck.

These counters can be tracked for both the PhysicalDisk object and the LogicalDisk object.

If you suspect that you have a disk subsystem bottleneck, the first thing you should check is your memory subsystem. If you do not have enough physical memory, it can cause excessive paging, which in turn affects the disk subsystem. If you do not have a memory problem, you can try the following solutions to improve disk performance:

- Use faster disks and controllers.

- Use disk striping to take advantage of multiple I/O channels.

- Balance heavily used files on multiple I/O channels.

- Add another disk controller for load balancing.

In Windows NT 4, you enabled all disk counters through the DISKPERF -Y command. Physical disk counters are automatically enabled in Windows 2000 Server. However, you must enable DISKPERF in order to track logical disk counters.

In Exercise 14.5, you will monitor your disk subsystem. This exercise assumes that you have completed the other exercises in this chapter.

EXERCISE 14.5

Monitoring the Disk Subsystem

1. If System Monitor is not already open, select Start ➤ Programs ➤ Administrative Tools ➤Monitor.

2. In the System Monitor window, click the Add button on the toolbar.

3. Notice that there is a Performance object for PhysicalDisk, but not LogicalDisk.

4. Select Start ➤ Programs ➤ Accessories ➤ Command Prompt.

5. At the command prompt, type **DISKPERF** -Y and press Enter. You see a message indicating that both logical and physical disk performance counters are set to start when the computer boots. Close the Command Prompt dialog box and restart your computer.

6. Select Start ➤ Programs ➤ Administrative Tools ➤ Monitor.

7. In the System Monitor window, click the Add button on the toolbar.

8. In the Add Counters dialog box, select the following performance objects and counters:

   Select PhysicalDisk from the performance object drop-down list, select %Disk Time from the counter list box, and click the Add button.

Select PhysicalDisk from the performance object drop-down list, select Current Disk Queue Length from the counter list box, and click the Add button.

Select LogicalDisk from the performance object drop-down list, select %Idle Time from the counter list box, and click the Add button.

9. Click the Close button. You should see these counters added to your chart.

10. To generate some activity, open and close some applications and copy some files between your domain controller and the member server.

11. Note the PhysicalDisk > %Disk Time counter. If this counter's average is below 90 percent, you are not generating excessive requests to this disk.

12. Note the PhysicalDisk > Current Disk Queue Length counter. If this counter's average is below 2, you are not generating excessive requests to this disk.

Leave System Monitor open, because you will use this utility again in Exercise 14.6.

You can monitor your logical disk's amount of free disk space through the LogicalDisk > %Free Space counter. This counter can also be used as an alert. For example, you might set an alert to notify you when the LogicalDisk > %Free Space counter on your C: drive is under 10 percent.

Monitoring and Optimizing the Network Subsystem

Windows 2000 Server does not have a built-in mechanism for monitoring the entire network. However, you can monitor and optimize the traffic that is generated on the specific Windows 2000 computer. You can monitor the network interface (your network card), and you can monitor the network protocols that have been installed on your computer.

The following are two of the counters that are useful for monitoring the network subsystem:

- Network Interface > Bytes Total/Sec measures the total number of bytes that are sent or received from the network interface and includes all network protocols.

- TCP > Segments/Sec measures the number of bytes that are sent or received from the network interface and includes only the TCP protocol.

Normally, you monitor and optimize the network subsystem from a network perspective rather than from a single computer. For example, you can use a network protocol analyzer to monitor all of the traffic on the network to determine if the network bandwidth is acceptable for your requirements or if the network bandwidth is saturated.

The following suggestions can help to optimize and minimize network traffic:

- Use only the network protocols you need. For example, use TCP/IP and don't use NWLink and NetBEUI.

- If you need to use multiple network protocols, place the most commonly used protocols higher in the binding order.

- Use network cards that take full advantage of your bus width. For example, use 32-bit cards instead of 16-bit cards.

- Use faster network cards. For example, use 100Mbps Ethernet instead of 10Mbps Ethernet.

In Exercise 14.6, you will monitor your network subsystem. This exercise assumes that you have completed the other exercises in this chapter.

EXERCISE 14.6

Monitoring the Network Subsystem

1. If System Monitor is not already open, select Start ➢ Programs ➢ Administrative Tools ➢ Monitor.

2. In the System Monitor window, click the Add button on the toolbar.

3. In the Add Counters dialog box, select the following performance objects and counters:

   Select Network Interface from the performance object drop-down list, select Bytes Total/Sec in the counter list box, and click the Add button.

   Select TCP from the performance object drop-down list, select Segments/Sec from the counter list box, and click the Add button.

4. Click the Close button. You should see these counters added to your chart.

5. To generate some activity, copy some files between your domain controller and the member server.

6. Note the Network Interface > Bytes Total/Sec and TCP > Segments/Sec counters. These numbers are cumulative. Use them in your baselines to determine network activity.

7. Leave your Monitor console open, because you will use it again in Exercise 14.7.

Creating Baseline Reports

As explained earlier in this chapter, baselines show how your server is performing at a certain time. By taking baselines at regular intervals and also whenever you make any changes to the system's configuration, you can monitor your server's performance over time.

You can create baselines by setting up a counter log file in the Performance Logs and Alerts utility. After you've created the baseline log file, you can view it in System Monitor, as shown in Figure 14.24.

FIGURE 14.24   Viewing a baseline in System Monitor

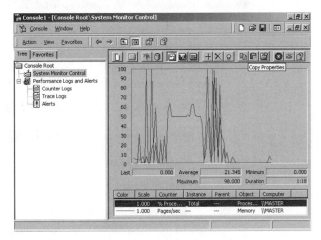

In Exercise 14.7, you will create a baseline report for your computer.

EXERCISE 14.7

Creating a Baseline Report

1. If the Monitor console is not already open, select Start ≻ Programs ≻ Administrative Tools ≻ Monitor.

2. Double-click Performance Logs and Alerts.

3. Right-click Counter Logs and select New Log Settings.

4. In the New Log Settings dialog box, type **Counter***mmddyy* (replace *mmddyy* with the current month, date, and year) as the log name. The log file should be stored in the C:\PerfLogs folder by default. Click the OK button.

5. In the General tab of the counter log Properties dialog box, click the Add button and add the following counters:

    Memory > Available MBytes

    Memory > Pages/Sec

    Paging File > %Usage

Processor > %Processor Time

Processor > Interrupts/Sec

PhysicalDisk > %Disk Time

PhysicalDisk > Current Disk Queue Length

Network Interface > Bytes Total/Sec

TCP > Segments/Sec

6. Set the interval for sampling data to five seconds.

7. Click the Log Files tab. Uncheck the End File Names With check box. This will prevent the filename from being appended with *mmddhh* (month/day/hour). Click the OK button to close the Properties dialog box and start the log file.

8. To generate system activity, start and stop some applications, copy a few files, and run a screen saver for one to two minutes.

9. To view your log file, open System Monitor. Click the View Log File Data button on the toolbar.

10. In the open file dialog box, select C:\PerfLogs\ Counter*mmddyy* and click the Open button.

11. Add the counters from the log file you created to see the data that was collected in your log.

Using Task Manager

The *Task Manager* utility shows the applications and processes that are currently running on your computer, as well as CPU and memory usage information. You can use Task Manager to manage application, process, and performance tasks.

Microsoft
✓ **Exam**
Objective

Manage processes.

- Set priorities and start and stop processes.

To access Task Manager, press Ctrl+Alt+Delete and click the Task Manager button. Alternatively, right-click an empty area in the Taskbar and select Task Manager from the pop-up menu.

Managing Application Tasks

The Applications tab of the Task Manager dialog box, shown in Figure 14.25, lists all of the applications that are currently running on the computer. For each task, you will see the name of the task and the current status (running, not responding, or stopped).

FIGURE 14.25   The Applications tab of the Task Manager dialog box

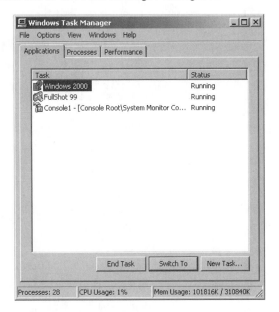

From the application tab, you can manage application tasks as follows:

- To close an application, select it and click the End Task button at the bottom of the dialog box. This option is especially useful for closing applications that have stopped responding.

- To make the application window active, select it and click the Switch To button.

- To start an application, click the New Task button to bring up the Create New Task dialog box. Type in the name of the program or click the Browse button to select the program you wish to start and click the OK button.

Managing Process Tasks

The Processes tab of the Task Manager dialog box, shown in Figure 14.26, lists all of the processes that are currently running on the computer. This is a convenient way to get a quick look at how your system is performing. Unlike using System Monitor, you don't need to first configure the collection of this data; it's gathered automatically.

FIGURE 14.26 The Processes tab of the Task Manager dialog box

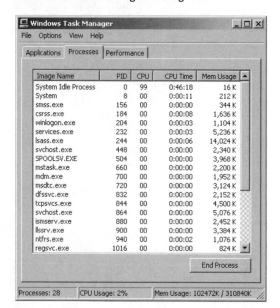

For each process, you will see a unique process ID (PID) that changes each time a process is started, the amount of CPU utilization that the process is using, and the amount of time the processor spent running the process.

From the Processes tab, you can organize the listing and control processes as follows:

- To organize the processes based on usage, click the column headings. For example, if you click the CPU column, the listing will start with the processes that use the most CPU resources. If you click the CPU column a second time, the listing will be reversed.

- To manage a process, right-click it and choose an option from the pop-up menu. You can choose to end the process, end the process tree, or set the priority of the process, as described in the following sections. If your computer has multiple processors installed, you can also set processor affinity, as described in the "Using Multiple Processors" section earlier in the chapter.

- To customize the counters that are listed, select View ➤ Select Columns. This brings up the Select Columns dialog box, shown in Figure 14.27, where you can select the information that you want to see listed on the Processes tab.

FIGURE 14.27   The Select Columns dialog box

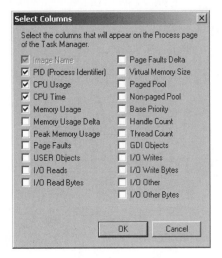

The counters that can be tracked through the Process page of the Task Manger are listed in Table 14.1.

TABLE 14.1 Task Manager Process Counters

Counter	Description
Image Name	The name of the process, as displayed through Task Manager.
PID (Process Identifier)	Unique numerical identifier used to identify a process through Task Manager.
CPU Usage	The percent of time used by the process since the last update.
CPU Time	Time in seconds, used by the process since it was started.
Memory Usage	Number of kilobytes currently in use by the current working set of a process.
Memory Usage Delta	Change in memory (in kilobytes) used since the last update.
Peak Memory Usage	Peak amount of memory used since the process was started.
Page Faults	Number of times the software tried to read from memory and had to get the requested information from disk.
User Objects	Number of user objects currently used by a process. User objects include windows, menus, cursors, icons, and other internal objects.
I/O Reads	The number of read input/output (I/O) events that have been generated by the process.

TABLE 14.1   Task Manager Process Counters *(continued)*

Counter	Description
I/O Read Bytes	The number of bytes that have been generated by I/O read events.
Page Faults Delta	Number of page faults since the last update.
Virtual Memory Size	Amount of virtual memory that has been allocated to a process.
Paged Pool	Amount of virtual memory that is being served by physical memory.
Non-Paged Pool	Amount of virtual RAM that is being processed from disk.
Base Priority	Order in which the threads of a process are scheduled for the processor.
Handle Count	Number of object handles used by a specific process.
Thread Count	Number of threads generated for the current process.
GDI Objects	Number of objects that have been generated by the process from the Graphics Driver Interface (GDI) library of application programming interfaces (APIs).
I/O Writes	Number of write I/O events that have been generated by the process.
I/O Write Bytes	Number of bytes that have been generated by I/O write events.
I/O Other	Number of I/O operations that are not read or write events. For example, network or other device I/O.

TABLE 14.1 Task Manager Process Counters *(continued)*

Counter	Description
I/O Other Bytes	Number of bytes that have been generated by I/O other events.

 Real World Scenario

Using Task Manager to Monitor Processes

Your Windows 2000 Server is primarily used as an applications server running an application called ABC.EXE. Users are complaining that when they access this application, it is slow to respond. You check the processor utilization through Task Manager and see that it is averaging 95 percent.

Your server has an empty slot for an extra processor. However, before you add the second processor, you want to verify that the ABC.EXE application is multithreaded. If the application uses a single thread, then it will only be processed on a single processor. If the application is multithreaded, then it can take advantage of multiple processors.

To verify how many threads are being used by a process, run Task Manager while the process is running. Click on the Processes tab and from View, choose Select Columns. Verify that Thread Count is selected. When you click OK, you can see the number of threads that have been generated by the process.

Stopping Processes

You may need to stop a process that isn't executing properly. To stop a specific process, select the process you want to stop in the Task Manager's Processes tab and click the End Process button. Task Manager displays a Warning dialog box. Click the Yes button to terminate the process.

If you right-click a process, you can end the specific process or you can use the option End Process Tree. The End Process Tree option ends all processes that have been created either directly or indirectly by the process.

Some of the common processes that can be managed through Task Manager are listed in Table 14.2.

TABLE 14.2 Common Processes

Process	Description
System Idle Process	A process that runs when the processor is not executing any other threads
smss.exe	Session Manager subsystem
csrss.exe	Client-server runtime server service
mmc.exe	Microsoft Management Console program (used to track resources used by MMC snap-ins such as System Monitor)
explorer.exe	Windows 2000 Explorer interface
ntvdm.exe	MS-DOS and Windows 16-bit application support

Managing Process Priority

You can manage process priority through the Task Manager utility or through the start command-line utility.

To change the priority of a process that is already running, use the Processes tab of Task Manager. Right-click the process you want to manage and select Set Priority from the pop-up menu. You can select from Realtime, High, Abovenormal, Normal, Belownormal, and Low priorities.

To start applications and set their priority at the same time, use the start command. The options that can be used with the start command are listed in Table 14.3.

TABLE 14.3 Options for the start Command-Line Utility

Option	Description
/low	Starts an application in the idle priority class.
/normal	Starts an application in the normal priority class.
/high	Starts an application in the high priority class.

TABLE 14.3   Options for the start Command-Line Utility *(continued)*

Option	Description
/realtime	Starts an application in the real-time priority class.
/abovenormal	Starts an application in the abovenormal priority class.
/belownormal	Starts an application in the belownormal priority class.
/min	Starts the application in a minimized window.
/max	Starts the application in a maximized window.
/separate	Starts a DOS or Windows 16-bit application in a separate memory space.
/shared	Starts a DOS or Windows 16-bit application in a shared memory space.

Running a process-intensive application in the real-time priority class can significantly impact Windows 2000 performance.

In Exercise 14.8, you will manage your computer's processes.

EXERCISE 14.8

Managing Computer Processes

1. Right-click an empty space on your taskbar and select Task Manager from the pop-up menu.

2. In the Applications tab, click the New Task button.

3. In the Create a New Task dialog box, type **CALC** and click the OK button.

4. Click the Processes tab. Right-click calc.exe and select Set Priority, then Low. In the Task Manager Warning dialog box, click the Yes button to continue.

5. Right-click calc.exe and select End Process. In the Task Manager Warning dialog box, click the Yes button.

Managing Performance Tasks

The Performance tab of the Task Manager dialog box, shown in Figure 14.29, provides an overview of your computer's CPU and memory usage. This is similar to the information that System Monitor tracks, and you don't need to configure it first as you do with System Monitor.

FIGURE 14.28   The Performance tab of the Task Manager dialog box

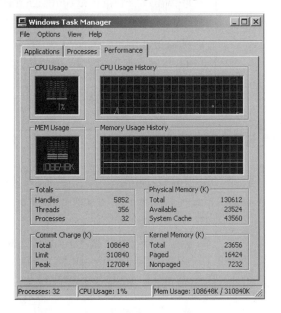

The Performance tab shows the following information:

- CPU usage, real-time and history graph
- Memory usage, real-time and history graph
- Totals for handles, threads, and processes

- Physical memory statistics
- Commit change memory statistics
- Kernel memory statistics

Summary

In this chapter, you learned about Windows 2000 Server optimization and reliability. We covered the following topics:

- How to keep your operating system up to date by using the Windows Update utility and applying Windows 2000 service packs

- How to use the System Monitor utility and the Performance Logs and Alerts utility to track and monitor your system's performance

- How to monitor and optimize memory, the processor, the disk subsystem, and the network subsystem, and how to create a system baseline

- How to use the Task Manager utility to view and manage running applications and processes, and to get an overview of CPU and memory usage

Exam Essentials

Be able to deploy service packs. Understand the purpose of service packs. Know how to successfully deploy them and how to verify that they are installed correctly.

Be able to monitor and troubleshoot Windows 2000 performance. Know which utilities can be used to track Windows 2000 performance events and issues. Know how to track and identify performance problems related to memory, the processor, the disk subsystem, and the network subsystem. Be able to correct system bottlenecks when they are identified.

Be able to manage processes. Know how to manage processes including identifying which resources are used by a process, how to stop and start processes, and how to assign priorities to processes.

Key Terms

Before taking the exam, you should be familiar with the following terms:

alert	processor affinity
baseline	service pack
bottleneck	slipstream technology
counter	System Monitor
page file	Task Manager
Performance Logs and Alerts	Windows Update

Review Questions

1. Your server has been running for several months with no problems. Yesterday you installed a new application called ABC. Today your users are complaining that the access to the other applications on the server is very slow. You use Task Manager to end the ABC application, but the processor utilization is still very high. You restart the ABC application. Which of the following actions should you take?

   A. Right-click the ABC process through Task Manager and select End Process Tree

   B. Use Service Manager to stop the ABC process

   C. Right-click the ABC process through Application Manager and select End All Child Processes

   D. Use Control Panel, Applications to end the ABC process

2. Peter has just installed a service pack on his Windows 2000 Server. After he installed the service pack, he added the DHCP service. What action should Peter take?

   A. He should reapply the service pack since some files may have been overwritten.

   B. He should run the `chcksp` command-line utility to make sure that the service pack has been properly applied.

   C. He should run the `verifysp` command-line utility to make sure that the service pack has been properly applied.

   D. He doesn't need to take any action.

3. Dave has called Microsoft with a problem he is experiencing with his Windows 2000 Server computer. The technician he is speaking with asks him which service pack is installed on his server. Which command-line utility can Dave use to verify whether a service pack has been loaded, and if so, what version is being used?

A. `verifysp`

B. `spver`

C. `winver`

D. `windiag`

4. Tomisa is using the ABC application on her Windows 2000 Server. After she added the application, she noticed that the processor utilization was very high. Tomisa knew that the application was processor intensive, so she installed it on a computer that supports dual-processors. Tomisa wants to install a second processor on her server, but wants to verify that the application is multithreaded before she performs the upgrade. Based on the following exhibit, which of the following columns should she enable for monitoring process-related events?

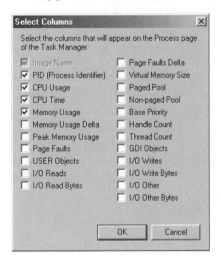

A. User Objects

B. Base Priority

C. Thread Count

D. GDI Objects

5. Vadim wants to monitor all of the processes that are running on his computer to determine if any one process is using excessive processing. He wants to create a report that will sample the system every five minutes. Which of the following utilities should he use?

   A. Performance Monitor

   B. System Monitor

   C. Performance Logs and Alerts

   D. Report Manager

6. Brad wants to track what effect running a new application will have on his server. He comes into his lab to run tests on the weekend. He has already started System Monitor with counters added for each major subsystem. Next, he will start the application and run a program, which will simulate usage of the application. Which of the following views in System Monitor will allow Brad to watch the counters over a period of time so that he can see the effect that the application has on the server's performance?

   A. Chart

   B. Histogram

   C. History

   D. Report

7. Jeff starts the abc.exe program and immediately notices that his server has slowed down. He suspects that the application is improperly allocating memory. He wants to quit the application as quickly as possible in order to restore the server to its normal operating environment. Which of the following options can he use to stop the abc.exe program?

   A. Performance Logs and Alerts

   B. System Monitor

   C. Performance Monitor

   D. Task Manager

8. Marta is running the `xyz.exe` application, which is a 16-bit Windows application. She wants to track the processor usage for this application in System Monitor. When she checks System Monitor, she sees no listing for `xyz.exe`. Which process should she track?

   A. `xyz.exe`

   B. `ntvdm`

   C. `win16`

   D. `wow`

9. You have used System Monitor to determine that you have a disk subsystem bottleneck on your Windows 2000 Server. Which of the following options *cannot* be used to optimize disk performance to help alleviate the bottleneck?

   A. Use faster disks and controllers

   B. Balance heavily used files on multiple I/O channels

   C. Use disk striping

   D. Use online volume growth

10. You run several Windows 16-bit applications on your Windows 2000 server. When you try to track resource usage for the applications, they are all listed as a single `ntvdm` session. You want to run the `1234.exe` program in its own memory space so that you can track resource usage for this specific application. Which of the following command-line options could be used to start the DOS `1234.exe` program in its own memory space?

   A. `start /separate 1234.exe`

   B. `run /separate 1234.exe`

   C. `start /min 1234.exe`

   D. `run /min 1234.exe`

11. Kelly wants to run the `lala.exe` program on Windows 2000 Server. She notices that when this program is run at the server, the server slows down significantly. Which of the following utilities can she use to set the priority of the `lala.exe` program to low?

    A. Performance Monitor

    B. System Monitor

    C. Task Manager

    D. Service Manager

12. Which process is used in Task Manager to indicate that a process is running when the processor is not executing any other threads?

    A. System Idle Process

    B. Processor Free Time

    C. Processor Idle Time

    D. Processor Available

13. You have noticed that your server is performing sluggishly. You have been steadily adding users and applications to the server over the last six months. You suspect that you may have a memory bottleneck and want to determine how much of the paging file is currently in use. Which of the following System Monitor counters should you use if you want to determine how much of the allocated page file is currently in use?

    A. Memory > %Paging File

    B. Memory > Pages/Sec

    C. Paging File > %Usage

    D. Paging File > Pages/Sec

14. Dave has two processors in his Windows 2000 Server. The server primarily acts as an applications server. One of the applications that is run is called 1234.exe. Dave wants to configure the application so that it always runs on the second processor. Which of the following utilities can be used to set processor affinity for the 1234.exe application?

A. Performance Monitor

B. System Monitor

C. Task Manager

D. Service Manager

15. You are an applications developer and you want to perform testing on the application you have written to work with Windows 2000 Server. You want to verify what priority your application is using. Based on the following exhibit, which of the following columns should you enable for monitoring which priority processes are being used?

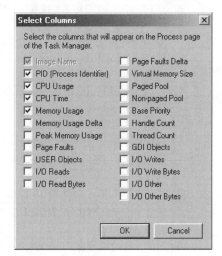

A. PID

B. CPU Time

C. Base Priority

D. GDI Objects

Answers to Review Questions

1. A. Through Task Manager, when you right-click a process you can end the specific process or you can use the option End Process Tree. The End Process Tree option ends all processes that have been created either directly or indirectly by the process. Sometimes the child processes are actually creating the processor or memory bottleneck.

2. D. Windows 2000 service packs use the slipstream technology. With slipstream technology, when a service pack is installed, the service pack files are written to the Windows 2000 distribution files. If you add a new service, the correct files with the service pack are applied, and there is no need to reapply service packs (as was necessary with previous versions of Windows NT).

3. C. You can determine if any service packs have been installed on your computer by using the winver command. To issue this command, select Start ➢ Programs ➢ Accessories ➢ Command Prompt. In the Command Prompt dialog box, type **winver** and press Enter. You will see a dialog box that shows which service packs are currently installed.

4. C. Thread Count is used to display how many threads are associated with the application.

5. C. The Performance Logs and Alerts utility is used to create reports, which can then be viewed with the System Monitor utility.

6. A. The only System Monitor view that allows you to see how the data is being tracked over time is the chart view.

7. D. Task Manager can be used to stop applications or processes that are currently running on the computer.

8. B. When you are running DOS or Windows 16-bit applications, they are automatically run in a shared memory space called ntvdm, which stands for NT Virtual DOS Machine.

9. D. You can improve disk performance by using faster disks and controllers, by using disk striping to take advantage of multiple I/O channels, by balancing heavily used files in multiple I/O channels, and by adding another disk controller for load balancing.

10. A. You use the `start` command to start new applications. The `/separate` switch is used to start Windows 16-bit applications in their own memory space.

11. C. The Processes tab of Task Manager can be used to manage process priorities. To change the priority of a process that is already running, right-click the process you want to manage and select Set Priority. You can select from realtime, high, abovenormal, normal, belownormal, and low priorities.

12. A. The System Idle Process is used to specify that the processor is not executing any other threads.

13. C. The Paging File > %Usage counter indicates how much of the allocated page file is currently in use. If this number is consistently over 99 percent, you may need to add more memory.

14. C. The Processes tab of Task Manager can be used to set processor affinity for processes on a server with more than one processor. Right-click the process you want to associate with a specific processor and select Processor Affinity.

15. C. The Base Priority option is used to display the priority that the current process is using.

Chapter 15

Performing System Recovery Functions

MICROSOFT EXAM OBJECTIVES COVERED IN THIS CHAPTER

✓ **Recover System State and user data.**

- Recover System State data and user data by using Windows Backup.
- Troubleshoot system restoration by starting in safe mode.
- Recover System State data and user data by using the Recovery Console.

✓ **Manage and optimize availability of System State data and user data.**

System recovery is the process of making your computer work again in the event of failure. The benefit of having a disaster recovery plan is that when you expect the worst to happen and you are prepared for it, you can easily recover from most system failures.

One utility that you can use to diagnose system problems is Event Viewer. Through the Event Viewer utility, you can see logs that list events related to your operating system and applications.

If your computer will not boot, an understanding of the Window 2000 boot process will help you identify the area of failure and correct the problem. You should know the steps in each stage of the boot process, the function of each boot file, and how to edit the BOOT.INI file.

When you have problems starting Windows 2000, you can press F8 when prompted during the boot sequence. This calls up the Windows 2000 Advanced Options menu, which is new to Windows 2000. This menu includes several special boot options, such as Safe Mode and Last Known Good Configuration, which are useful for getting your system started so you can track down and correct problems.

Startup and Recovery options are used to specify how the operating system will react in the event of system failure. For example, you can specify whether or not the system should automatically reboot and whether or not administrative alerts should be sent.

If you cannot boot the operating system and your CD-ROM is not accessible, you can recover by using the Windows 2000 Server Setup Boot Disks. After you've created these setup disks, you can use them to reinstall Windows 2000, start the Recovery Console, or access your Emergency Repair Disk.

Backups are the best protection you can have against system failure. You can create backups through the Windows Backup utility. The Windows Backup utility offers options to run the Backup Wizard, run the Restore Wizard, and create an Emergency Repair Disk.

Another option that experienced administrators can use to recover from a system failure is the Recovery Console. The Recovery Console boots your computer so that you have limited access to FAT16, FAT32, and NTFS volumes.

In this chapter, you will learn how to use the Windows 2000 Server system recovery functions. We'll begin with an overview of the techniques you can use to protect your computer and recover from disasters.

The procedures for system recovery are the same for both Windows 2000 Server and Windows 2000 Professional.

Safeguarding Your Computer and Recovering from Disaster

One of the worst events you will experience is a computer that won't boot. An even worse experience is discovering that there is no recent backup for that computer.

The first step in preparing for disaster recovery is to expect that a disaster will occur at some point and take proactive steps before the failure to plan your recovery. The following are some of the preparations you can make:

- Perform regular system backups.

- Use virus-scanning software.

- Perform regular administrative functions, such as monitoring the logs in the Event Viewer utility.

In the event that the dreaded day arrives and your system fails, there are several processes you can analyze and Windows 2000 utilities that you can use to help you get up and running. These options are summarized in Table 15.1.

TABLE 15.1 Windows 2000 Server Recovery Techniques

Recovery Technique	When to Use
Event Viewer	If the Windows 2000 operating system can be loaded through normal or Safe Mode, one of the first places to look for hints about the problem is Event Viewer. Event Viewer displays System, Security, and Application logs.
Safe Mode	This is generally your starting point for system recovery. Safe Mode loads the absolute minimum of services and drivers that are needed to boot Windows 2000. If you can load Safe Mode, you may be able to troubleshoot devices or services that keep Windows 2000 from loading normally.
Last Known Good Configuration	You can use this option if you made changes to your computer and are now having problems. Last Known Good Configuration is an Advanced Options menu item that you can select during startup. It loads the configuration that was used the last time the computer booted successfully. This option will not help if you have hardware errors.
Windows 2000 Server Setup Boot Disks	You can use this option if you suspect that Windows 2000 is not loading due to missing or corrupt boot files. This option allows you to load all the Windows 2000 boot files. If you can boot from a boot disk, you can restore the necessary files from the Emergency Repair Disk.

TABLE 15.1   Windows 2000 Server Recovery Techniques *(continued)*

Recovery Technique	When to Use
Emergency Repair Disk (ERD)	You can use this option if you need to correct configuration errors or to repair system files. The ERD can be used to repair problems that prevent your computer from starting. The ERD stores portions of the Registry, the system files, a copy of your partition boot sector, and information that relates to the startup environment.
Windows Backup	You should use this utility to safeguard your computer. Through the Backup utility, you can create an ERD, back up the system or parts of the system, and restore data from backups that you have made.
Recovery Console	You can use this option if none of the other options or utilities works. The Recovery Console starts Windows 2000 without the graphical interface and allows the administrator limited capabilities, such as adding or replacing files and starting and stopping services.

All of these Windows 2000 Server recovery techniques are covered in detail in this chapter.

Using Event Viewer

You can use the *Event Viewer* utility to track information about your computer's hardware and software, as well as to monitor security events. The information that is tracked is stored in three types of log files:

- The *System log* tracks events that are related to the Windows 2000 operating system.

- The *Security log* tracks events that are related to Windows 2000 auditing.

- The *Application log* tracks events that are related to applications that are running on your computer.

On Windows 2000 domain controllers, Event Viewer also includes Directory Service, DNS Server, and File Replication Service logs. Depending on how your server is configured, you may also have other Event Viewer logs.

You can access Event Viewer by selecting Start ➤ Programs ➤ Administrative Tools ➤ Event Viewer. Alternatively, right-click My Computer, select Manage from the pop-up menu, and access Event Viewer under System Tools. From Event Viewer, select the log you want to view. Figure 15.1 shows Event Viewer with the System log displayed.

FIGURE 15.1 A System log in Event Viewer

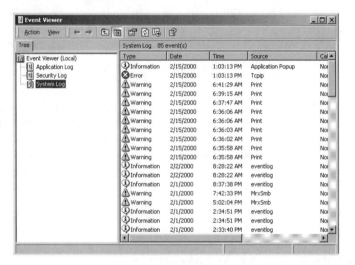

In the log file, you will see all of the events that have been recorded. By default, you see the oldest events at the bottom of the screen and the newest events at the top of the screen. This can be misleading in troubleshooting, since one error can precipitate other errors. You should always resolve the oldest errors first. To change the default listing order, click one of the three logs and select View ➤ Oldest First.

The following sections describe how to view events and manage logs.

Reviewing Event Types

The Event Viewer logs display five event types, denoted by their icons. Table 15.2 describes each event type.

TABLE 15.2 Event Viewer Log Events

Event Type	Icon	Description
Information	White dialog bubble with blue *I*	Informs you of the occurrence of a specific action, such as a system shutting down or starting. *Information events* are logged for informative purposes.
Warning	Yellow triangle with black exclamation point	Indicates that you should be concerned with the event. *Warning events* may not be critical in nature but may be indicative of future errors.
Error	Red circle with white *X*	Indicates the occurrence of an error, such as a driver failing to load. You should be very concerned with *Error events*.
Success Audit	Yellow key	Indicates the occurrence of an event that has been audited for success. For example, a *Success Audit event* is a successful logon when system logons are being audited.
Failure Audit	Yellow lock	Indicates the occurrence of an event that has been audited for failure. For example, a *Failure Audit event* is a failed logon due to an invalid username and/or password when system logons are being audited.

Getting Event Details

Clicking an event in an Event Viewer log file brings up the Event Properties dialog box, which shows details about the event. An example of the Event Properties dialog box for an Error event is shown in Figure 15.2. Table 15.3 describes the information that appears in this dialog box.

FIGURE 15.2 The Event Properties dialog box

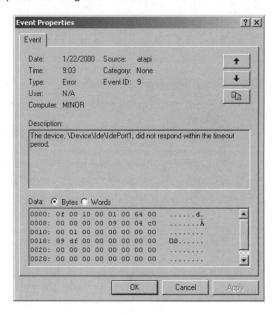

TABLE 15.3 Event Properties Dialog Box Items

Item	Description
Date	The date that the event was generated
Time	The time that the event was generated
Type	The type of event that was generated: Information, Warning, Error, Success Audit, or Failure Audit
User	The name of the user that the event is attributed to, if applicable (not all events are attributed to a user)
Computer	The name of the computer on which the event occurred
Source	The software that generated the event (e.g., operating system components or drivers)

TABLE 15.3   Event Properties Dialog Box Items *(continued)*

Item	Description
Category	The source that logged the event (this field will say None until this feature has been fully implemented in Windows 2000)
Event ID	The event number specific to the type of event that was generated (e.g., a print error event has the event ID 45)
Description	A detailed description of the event
Data	The binary data generated by the event (if any; some events do not generate binary data) in hexadecimal bytes or DWORD format (programmers can use this information to interpret the event)

Managing Log Files

Over time, your log files will grow, and you will need to decide how to manage them. You can clear a log file for a fresh start. You may want to save the existing log file before you clear it, to keep that log file available for future reference or further analysis.

To clear all log file events, right-click the log you wish to clear and choose Clear All Events from the pop-up menu. Then specify whether or not you want to save the log before it is cleared.

If you just want to save as existing log file, right-click that log and choose Save Log File As. Then specify the location and name of the file.

To open an existing log file, right-click the log you wish to open and choose Open Log File. Then specify the name and location of the log file and click the Open button.

Setting Log File Properties

Each Event Viewer log has two sets of properties associated with it:

- General properties control items such as the log filename, its maximum size, and the action to take when the log file reaches its maximum size.

- Filter properties specify which events are displayed.

To access the log Properties dialog box, right-click the log you want to manage and select Properties from the pop-up menu. The following sections describe the properties available on the General and Filter tabs of this dialog box.

General Properties

The General tab of the log Properties dialog box, shown in Figure 15.3, displays information about the log file and includes options to control its size. Table 15.4 lists the properties on the General tab.

FIGURE 15.3 The General tab of the System Log Properties dialog box

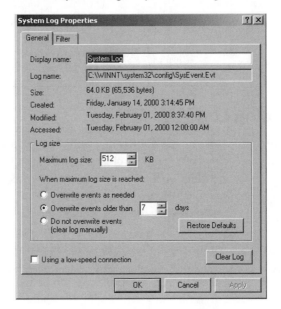

TABLE 15.4 General Log Properties

Property	Description
Display Name	Allows you to change the name of the log file. For example, if you are managing multiple computers and want to distinguish the logs for each computer, you can make the names more descriptive (e.g., DATA-Application and ROVER-Application).

TABLE 15.4   General Log Properties *(continued)*

Property	Description
Log Name	Displays the path and filename of the log file.
Size	Displays the current size of the log file.
Created	Specifies the date and time that the log file was created.
Modified	Specifies the date and time that the log file was last modified.
Accessed	Specifies the date and time that the log file was last accessed.
Maximum Log Size	Allows you to specify the maximum size that the log file can grow to. You can use this option to prevent the log file from taking up excessive disk space.
When Maximum Log Size Is Reached	Allows you to specify what action will be taken when the log file reaches the maximum size (if a maximum size is specified). You can choose to overwrite events as needed (on a first-in-first-out basis), overwrite events that are over a certain age, or specify that events should not be overwritten (which means that you would need to clear log events manually).
Using a Low-Speed Connection	Specifies that you are monitoring the log file of a remote computer and that you connect to that computer through a low-speed connection.

The Clear Log button in the General tab of the log Properties dialog box clears all log events.

Filter Properties

The Filter tab of the log Properties dialog box, shown in Figure 15.4, allows you to control which events are listed in the log. For example, if your system generates a large number of log events, you might want to set the Filter properties so that you can track specific events. You can filter log events based on the event type, source, category, ID, users, computer, or specific time period. Table 15.5 lists the properties on the Filter tab.

FIGURE 15.4 The Filter tab of the log Properties dialog box

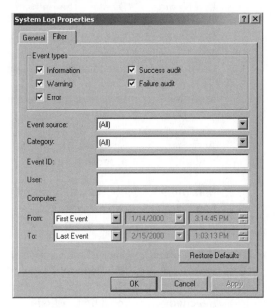

TABLE 15.5 Filter Properties for Logs

Property	Description
Event Type	Allows you to list only the specified event types (Warning, Error, Success Audit, or Failure Audit). By default, all event types are listed.
Event Source	Allows you to filter events based on the source of the event. The drop-down box lists the software that might generate events, such as Application Popup and DHCP. By default, events triggered by all sources are listed.
Category	Allows you to filter events based on the category that generated the event. The drop-down box lists the event categories. By default, events in all categories are listed.

TABLE 15.5 Filter Properties for Logs *(continued)*

Property	Description
Event ID	Allows you to filter events based on a specific event number.
User	Allows you to filter events based on the user who caused the event to be triggered.
Computer	Allows you to filter events based on the name of the computer that generated the event.
From-To	Allows you to filter events based on the date and time that the events were generated. By default, events are listed from the first event to the last event. To specify specific dates and times, select Events On from the drop-down list and select dates and times.

In Exercise 15.1, you will view events in Event Viewer and set log properties.

All of the exercises in this chapter can be done from either your Windows 2000 member server or domain controller.

EXERCISE 15.1

Using the Event Viewer Utility

1. Select Start ➤ Programs ➤ Administrative Tools ➤ Event Viewer.

2. Click System Log in the left pane of the Event Viewer window to display the System log events.

3. Double-click the first event in the right pane of the Event Viewer window to see its Event Properties dialog box. Click the Cancel button to close the dialog box.

4. Right-click System Log in the left pane of the Event Viewer window and select Properties.

5. Click the Filter tab. Clear all the check marks under Event Types except those in the Warning and Error check boxes, then click the OK button. You should see only Warning and Error events listed in the System log.

6. To remove the filter, return to the Filter tab of the log Properties dialog box, click the Restore Defaults button at the bottom of the dialog box, and click the OK button. You should see all of the event types listed again.

7. Right-click System Log and select Clear All Events.

8. You see a dialog box asking if you want to save the System log before clearing it. Click the Yes button. Specify the path and filename for the log file, then click the Save button. All the events should be cleared from the System log.

Understanding the Windows 2000 Boot Process

Some of the problems that cause system failure are related to the Windows 2000 boot process. The boot process starts when you turn on your computer and ends when you log on to Windows 2000.

To identify problems related to the boot process, you need to understand the steps involved in the process, as well as how the BOOT.INI file controls the process. Also, you should create a Windows 2000 Server boot disk that you can use to boot the operating system if your computer suffers a boot failure. These topics are covered in the following sections.

Reviewing the Normal Boot Process

The Windows 2000 boot process consists of five major stages: the preboot sequence, the boot sequence, kernel load, kernel initialization, and logon. Many files are used during these stages of the boot process. The following sections describe the steps in each boot process stage, the files used, and the errors that might occur.

Finding the Boot Process Files

Most of the boot process files reside in the root of the system partition. In the Windows 2000 Server documentation, you will see the terms *system partition* and *boot partition*. The system partition is the computer's active partition where the files needed to boot the operating system are stored. This is typically the C: drive. The boot partition refers to the partition where the system files are stored. You can place the system files anywhere. The default folder for the system files is WINNT and is referred to as the variable *Windir*. The system partition and boot partition can be on the same partition or on different partitions.

File attributes are used to specify the properties of a file. Examples of file attributes are System (S), Hidden (H), and Read-only (R). This is important to know because, by default, System and Hidden files are not listed in Windows Explorer or through a standard DIR command. If you look for these files but don't see them, they may just be hidden. You can turn on the display of System and Hidden files in Windows Explorer by selecting Tools ➢ Folder Options and clicking the View tab. In this dialog box, select the Show Hidden Files and Folders option, and uncheck the Hide File Extensions for Known File Types and Hide Protected Operating System Files options.

The Preboot Sequence

A normal boot process begins with the preboot sequence, in which your computer starts up and prepares for booting the operating system.

File Accessed in the Preboot Sequence

During the preboot sequence, your computer accesses the *NTLDR* file. This file is used to control the Windows 2000 boot process until control is passed to the NTOSKRNL file for the boot sequence. The NTLDR file is located in the root of the system partition. It has the file attributes of System, Hidden, and Read-only.

Steps in the Preboot Sequence

The preboot sequence consists of the following steps:

1. When the computer is powered on, it runs a *Power On Self Test* (*POST*) routine. The POST detects the processor you are using, how much memory is present, what hardware is recognized, and whether

the BIOS (Basic Input/Output System) is standard or has Plug-and-Play capabilities. The system also enumerates and configures hardware devices at this point.

2. The BIOS points to the boot device, and the *Master Boot Record* (*MBR*) is loaded.

3. The MBR points to the active partition. The active partition is used to specify the partition that should be used to boot the operating system. This is normally the C: drive. Once the MBR locates the active partition, the boot sector is loaded into memory and executed.

4. As part of the Windows 2000 installation process, the NTLDR file is copied to the active partition. The boot sector points to the NTLDR file, and this file executes. The NTLDR file is used to initialize and start the Windows 2000 boot process.

Possible Errors during the Preboot Sequence

If you see errors during the preboot sequence they are probably not related to Windows 2000 Server, since the operating system has not yet been loaded. The following are some common causes for errors during the preboot stage:

Symptom	Possible cause
Improperly configured hardware	If the POST cannot recognize your hard drive, the preboot stage will fail. This error is most likely to occur in a computer that is still being initially configured. If everything has been working properly and you have not made any changes to your configuration, a hardware error is unlikely.
Corrupt MBR	Viruses that are specifically designed to infect the MBR can corrupt it. You can protect your system from this type of error by using virus-scanning software. Also, most virus-scanning programs can correct an infected MBR.

No partition is marked as active	This can happen if you used the FDISK utility and did not create a partition from all of the free space. If the partition is FAT16 or FAT32 and on a basic disk, you can boot the computer to DOS or Windows 9*x* with a boot disk, run FDISK, and mark a partition as active. If you created your partitions as a part of the Windows 2000 installation and have dynamic disks, marking an active partition is done for you during installation.
Corrupt or missing NTLDR file	If the NTLDR file does not execute, it may have been corrupted or deleted (by a virus or malicious intent). You can restore this file through the ERD, which is covered later in this chapter.
SYS program run from DOS or Windows 9*x* after Windows 2000 installation	The NTLDR file may not execute because the SYS program was run from DOS or Windows 9*x* after Windows 2000 was installed. If you have done this, the only solution is to reinstall Windows 2000.

The Boot Sequence

When the preboot sequence is completed, the boot sequence begins. The phases in this stage include the initial boot loader phase, the operating system selection phase, and the hardware detection phase.

Files Accessed in the Boot Sequence

Along with the NTLDR file, which was described in the previous section, the following files are used during the boot sequence:

- *BOOT.INI* is used to build the operating system menu choices that are displayed during the boot process. It is also used to specify the location of the boot partition. This file is located in the root of the system partition. It has the file attributes of System and Hidden.

- *BOOTSECT.DOS* is an optional file that is loaded if you choose to load an operating system other than Windows 2000. It is only used in dual-boot or multi-boot computers. This file is located in the root of the system partition. It has the file attributes of System and Hidden.

- *NTDETECT.COM* is used to detect any hardware that is installed and add information about the hardware to the Registry. This file is located in the root of the system partition. It has the file attributes of System, Hidden, and Read-only.

- *NTBOOTDD.SYS* is an optional file that is used when you have a SCSI (Small Computer Standard Interface) adapter with the onboard BIOS disabled. (This option is not commonly implemented.) This file is located in the root of the system partition. It has the file attributes of System and Hidden.

- *NTOSKRNL.EXE* is used to load the Windows 2000 operating system. This file is located in *Windir*\System32 and has no file attributes.

Steps in the Boot Sequence

The boot sequence consists of the following steps:

1. For the initial boot loader phase, NTLDR switches the processor from real mode to 32-bit flat memory mode and starts the appropriate mini file system drivers. Mini file system drivers are used to support your computer's file systems and include FAT16, FAT32, and NTFS.

2. For the operating system selection phase, the computer reads the BOOT.INI file. If you have configured your computer to dual-boot or multi-boot and Windows 2000 recognizes that you have choices, a menu of operating systems that can be loaded is built. If you choose an operating system other than Windows 2000, the BOOTSECT.DOS file is used to load the alternate operating system, and the Windows 2000 boot process terminates. If you choose a Windows 2000 operating system, the Windows 2000 boot process continues.

3. If you choose a Windows 2000 operating system, the NTDETECT.COM file is used to perform hardware detection. Any hardware that is detected is added to the Registry, in the HKEY_LOCAL_MACHINE key. Some of the hardware that NTDETECT.COM will recognize includes communication and parallel ports, the keyboard, the floppy disk drive, the mouse, the SCSI adapter, and the video adapter.

4. Control is passed to NTOSKRNL.EXE to start the kernel load process.

Possible Errors during the Boot Sequence

The following are some common causes for errors during the boot stage:

Symptom	Possible Cause
Missing or corrupt boot files	If NTLDR, BOOT.INI, BOOTSECT.DOS, NTDETECT.COM, or NTOSKRNL.EXE is corrupt or missing (by a virus or malicious intent), the boot sequence will fail. You will see an error message that indicates which file is missing or corrupt. You can restore these files through the ERD, which is covered later in this chapter.
Improperly configured BOOT.INI file	If you have made any changes to your disk configuration and your computer will not restart, chances are your BOOT.INI file is configured incorrectly. The BOOT.INI file is covered after the next sections about the boot process stages.
Unrecognizable or improperly configured hardware	If you have serious errors that cause NTDETECT.COM to fail, you should resolve the hardware problems. If your computer has a lot of hardware, remove all of the hardware that is not required to boot the computer. Add each piece of hardware one at a time and boot the computer. This will help you identify which piece of hardware is bad or is conflicting for a resource with another device.

The Kernel Load Sequence

In the kernel load sequence, the Hardware Abstraction Layer (HAL), computer control set, and low-level device drivers are loaded.

The NTOSKRNL.EXE file, which was described in the previous section, is used during this stage.

The kernel load sequence consists of the following steps:

1. The NTOSKRNL.EXE file is loaded and initialized.

2. The HAL is loaded. The HAL is what makes Windows 2000 portable to support platforms such as Intel and Alpha.

3. The control set that the operating system will use is loaded. The control set is used to control system configuration information, such as a list of device drivers that should be loaded.

4. Low-level device drivers, such as disk drivers, are loaded.

If you have problems loading the Windows 2000 kernel, you will most likely need to reinstall the operating system.

The Kernel Initialization Sequence

In the kernel initialization sequence, the HKEY_LOCAL_MACHINE\HARDWARE Registry and Clone Control set are created, device drivers are initialized, and high-order subsystems and services are loaded.

The kernel initialization sequence consists of the following steps:

1. Once the kernel has been successfully loaded, the Registry key HKEY_ LOCAL_MACHINE\HARDWARE is created. This Registry key is used to specify the hardware configuration of hardware components when the computer is started.

2. The Clone Control set is created. The Clone Control set is an exact copy of the data that is used to configure the computer and does not include changes made by the startup process.

3. The device drivers that were loaded during the kernel load phase are initialized.

4. Higher-order subsystems and services are loaded.

If you have problems during the kernel initialization sequence, you might try to boot to the Last Known Good configuration, which is covered in the "Using Advanced Startup Options" section later in this chapter.

The Logon Sequence

In the logon sequence, the user logs on to Windows 2000 and any remaining services are loaded.

The logon sequence consists of the following steps:

1. After the kernel initialization is complete, the Log On to Windows dialog box appears. At this point, you type in a valid Windows 2000 username and password.

2. The service controller executes and performs a final scan of HKEY_LOCAL_MACHINE\SYSTEM\CurrentControlSet\Services to see if there are any remaining services that need to be loaded.

If logon errors occur, they are usually due to an incorrect username or password or to the unavailability of a domain controller to authenticate the request (if the computer is a part of a domain). See Chapter 4, "Managing Users and Groups," for more information about troubleshooting user authentication problems.

Errors can also occur if a service cannot be loaded. If a service fails to load, you will see a message in the System Log of Event Viewer. Using the Event Viewer utility is covered earlier in this chapter.

Editing the BOOT.INI File

The BOOT.INI file is located in the active partition and is used to build the boot loader menu and to specify the location of the Windows 2000 boot partition. It also specifies the default operating system that should be loaded if no selection is made within the default time allotment. You can open and edit this file to add switches or options that allow you to control how the operating system is loaded. Figure 15.5 shows a fairly common example of a BOOT.INI file, opened in Notepad.

FIGURE 15.5 A sample BOOT.INI file

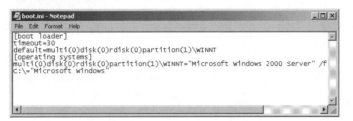

The following sections describe the BOOT.INI ARC (Advanced RISC Computing; RISC stands for Reduced Instruction Set Computing) naming conventions and how to edit the BOOT.INI file.

WARNING If you make changes to your disk configuration, you may see a message stating the number of the BOOT.INI file needs to be changed. This is the ARC number that points to the boot partition. If you try to restart your computer before you edit this file, you will find that the computer will not start.

ARC Naming Conventions

In the BOOT.INI file, the ARC path is used to specify the location of the boot partition within the disk channel. ARC names are made up of the information shown in Table 15.6.

TABLE 15.6 ARC Naming Conventions

ARC Path Option	Description
multi (*w*) or scsi (*w*)	Identifies the type of disk controller that is being used by the system. The multi option is used by IDE controllers and SCSI adapters that use the SCSI BIOS. The scsi option is used by SCSI adapters that do not use the SCSI BIOS. The number (w) represents the number of the hardware adapter you are booting from.
disk (*x*)	Indicates which SCSI adapter you are booting from if you use the scsi option. If you use multi, this setting is always 0.
rdisk (*y*)	Specifies the number of the physical disk to be used. In an IDE environment, it is the ordinal of the disk attached to the controller and will always be a 0 or a 1. On a SCSI system, this is the ordinal number of the SCSI drive.
partition (*z*)	Specifies the partition number that contains the operating system files. The first partition is always 1.

As an example, the BOOT.INI file shown in Figure 15.5 contains the following line:

```
multi(0)disk(0)rdisk(0)partition(1)\WINNT= "Microsoft
Windows 2000 Server"
```

This indicates that the boot partition is in the following location:

- `multi(0)` is an IDE controller or a SCSI controller with the BIOS enabled.

- `disk(0)` is 0 since the `multi` option was used.

- `rdisk(0)` specifies that the first disk on the controller is being used.

- `partition(1)` specifies that the system partition is on the first partition.

- `\WINNT` indicates the folder that is used to store the system files.

- `"Microsoft Windows 2000 Server"` is what the user sees in the boot menu.

BOOT.INI Switches

When you edit your `BOOT.INI` file, you can add switches or options that allow you to control how the operating system is loaded. Table 15.7 defines the `BOOT.INI` switches.

TABLE 15.7   BOOT.INI Switches

Switch	Description
/basevideo	Boots the computer using a standard VGA video driver. This option is used when you change your video driver and then cannot use the new driver.
/fastdetect=comx	Keeps the computer from auto-detecting a serial mouse attached to a serial port.
/maxmem:n	Specifies the maximum amount of RAM that is recognized. This option is sometimes used in test environments where you want to analyze performance using different amounts of memory.
/noguiboot	Boots Windows 2000 without loading the GUI. With this option, a command prompt appears after the boot process ends.

BOOT.INI File Access

Because the BOOT.INI file is marked with the System and Hidden attributes, it is not normally seen through Windows Explorer or the DOS DIR command. The following sections explain how to modify the attributes of the BOOT.INI through Windows Explorer and the DOS ATTRIB command.

Changing Attributes through Windows Explorer

To access and change the BOOT.INI attributes through Windows Explorer, take the following steps:

1. Select Start ➢ Programs ➢ Accessories ➢ Windows Explorer.

2. In Windows Explorer, expand My Computer and right-click Local Disk (C:).

3. Select Tools ➢ Folder Options and click the View tab.

4. In the View dialog box, click the Show Hidden Files and Folders radio button, and uncheck the Hide File Extensions for Known File Types and Hide Protected Operating System Files (Recommended) check boxes, as shown in Figure 15.6.

FIGURE 15.6 The View tab of the Folder Options dialog box

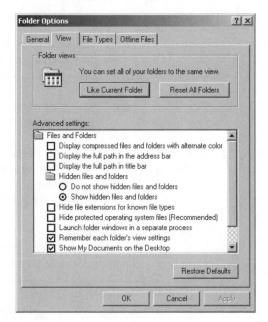

5. You see a dialog box with a warning about displaying protected operating system files. Click the Yes button to display these files. Then click the OK button.

6. You should now see the BOOT.INI file in the root of the C: drive. To change the file attributes, right-click the BOOT.INI file and select Properties.

7. The boot.ini Properties dialog box appears, as shown in Figure 15.7. Uncheck the Read-only attribute at the bottom of the dialog box and click the OK button.

FIGURE 15.7   The boot.ini Properties dialog box

8. Open the BOOT.INI file by double-clicking the file in Windows Explorer.

9. When you're finished editing the BOOT.INI file, you should reset its file attributes by selecting Tools ➤ Folder Options ➤ View ➤ Restore Defaults.

Changing Attributes through the *ATTRIB* Command

The DOS ATTRIB command provides a quick way to access the BOOT.INI file. To use the ATTRIB command, take the following steps:

1. Select Start ➤ Programs ➤ Accessories ➤ Command Prompt.

2. In the Command Prompt dialog box, type **ATTRIB** and press Enter. You should see all of the files that reside at the root of C: and their current file attributes.

3. Type **ATTRIB BOOT.INI −S −H** and press Enter to remove the System and Hidden file attributes.

4. Type **EDIT BOOT.INI** and press Enter to execute the EDIT program and open the BOOT.INI file for editing.

5. When you're finished editing the BOOT.INI file, choose File ➢ Save to save the file and File ➢ Exit to exit the EDIT program.

6. Reset the file attributes by typing **ATTRIB BOOT.INI +S +H** and pressing Enter.

Creating the Windows 2000 Boot Disk

After you create a *Windows 2000 boot disk*, you can use it to boot to the Windows 2000 Server operating system in the event of a Windows 2000 Server boot failure.

The BOOT.INI file on the Windows 2000 Server boot disk contains a specific configuration that points to the computer's boot partition. This might keep a Windows 2000 boot disk that was made on one computer from working on another computer.

In Exercise 15.2, you will create a Windows 2000 boot disk.

EXERCISE 15.2

Creating a Windows 2000 Boot Disk

1. Put a blank floppy diskette in your floppy drive.

2. Select Start ➢ Programs ➢ Accessories ➢ Windows Explorer.

3. In Windows Explorer, expand My Computer, right-click 3½ Floppy (A:), and select Format. Accept all of the default options and click the Start button.

4. You see a dialog box warning you that all the data will be lost. Click the OK button.

5. When you see the Format Complete dialog box, click the OK button, then click the Close button to close the Format dialog box.

6. Select Start ➢ Programs ➢ Accessories ➢ Command Prompt.

7. In the Command Prompt dialog box, type **ATTRIB** and press Enter. You see all of the files at the root of the C: drive. Note the file attributes of the NTLDR, NTDETECT.COM, and BOOT.INI files.

8. Type **ATTRIB NTLDR -S -H -R** and press Enter.

9. Type **COPY NTLDR A:** and press Enter.

10. Type **ATTRIB NTLDR +S +H +R** and press Enter.

11. Repeat steps 8 through 10 for the NTDETECT.COM and BOOT.INI files, to remove the file attributes, copy the file, and replace the file attributes. If you have a SCSI adapter with the BIOS disabled, you will also need to copy the NTBOOTDD.SYS file.

12. Verify that all of the files are on the boot disk by typing **DIR A:**.

13. Type **Exit** to close the Command Prompt dialog box.

14. To test your Windows 2000 boot disk, select Start ➢ Shut Down ➢ Restart and click the OK button.

15. Label your Windows 2000 boot disk and put it in a safe place.

If the BOOT.INI file for the computer has been edited, you will need to update the BOOT.INI file on your Windows 2000 boot disk.

Using Advanced Startup Options

The Windows 2000 advanced startup options can be used to troubleshoot errors that keep Windows 2000 Server from successfully booting.

To access the Windows 2000 advanced startup options, press the F8 key when prompted during the beginning of the Windows 2000 Server boot process. This will bring up the Windows 2000 Advanced Options menu, which allows you to boot Windows 2000 with the following options:

- Safe Mode

- Safe Mode with Networking

- Safe Mode with Command Prompt

- Enable Boot Logging

- Enable VGA Mode

- Last Known Good Configuration

- Directory Services Restore Mode

- Debugging Mode

- Boot Normally

Each of these advanced startup options is covered in the following sections.

Starting in Safe Mode

When your computer will not start, one of the basic troubleshooting techniques is to simplify the configuration as much as possible. This is especially important when you do not know the cause of your problem and you have a complex configuration. After you have simplified your configuration, you determine whether the problem is in the basic configuration or is a result of your more complex configuration. If the problem is in the basic configuration, you have a starting point for troubleshooting. If the problem is not in the basic configuration, you proceed to restore each configuration option you removed, one at a time. This helps you to identify what is causing your error.

If Windows 2000 Server will not load, you can attempt to load the operating system through Safe Mode. When you run Windows 2000 Server in *Safe Mode*, you are simplifying your Windows configuration as much as possible. Safe Mode loads only the drivers and services needed to get the computer up and running. The items loaded with Safe Mode include basic files and drivers for the mouse (unless you have a serial mouse), monitor, keyboard, hard drive, standard video driver, and default system services. Safe Mode is considered a diagnostic mode, so you do not have access to all of the features and devices in Windows 2000 Server that you have access to when you boot normally, including networking capabilities.

A computer booted to Safe Mode will show *Safe Mode* in the four corners of your Desktop, as shown in Figure 15.8.

FIGURE 15.8   A computer running in Safe Mode shows Safe Mode in each corner of the Desktop.

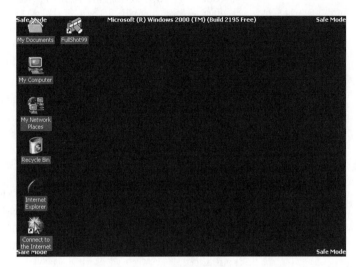

If you boot to Safe Mode, you should check all of your hardware and software settings in Control Panel to try to determine why Windows 2000 Server will not boot properly. After you take steps to fix the problem, attempt to boot to Windows 2000 Server normally.

In Exercise 15.3, you will boot your computer to Safe Mode.

EXERCISE 15.3

Booting Your Computer to Safe Mode

1. If your computer is currently running, select Start ➢ Shutdown ➢ Restart.

2. During the boot process, press the F8 key to access the Windows 2000 Advanced Options menu.

3. Highlight Safe Mode and press Enter. Then log on as Administrator.

4. When you see the Desktop dialog box letting you know that Windows 2000 is running in SafeMode, click the OK button.

5. Select My Network Places ➢ Entire Network. You should see an error message stating that you are unable to browse the network (because you are in Safe Mode). Click OK to close the error dialog box.

6. Select Start ➢ Settings ➢ Control Panel ➢ System ➢ Hardware ➢ Device Manager. Look in Device Manager to see if any devices are not working properly.

7. Don't restart your computer yet; you will do this as a part of the next exercise.

Enabling Boot Logging

Boot logging creates a log file that tracks the loading of drivers and services. When you choose the *Enable Boot Logging* option from the Advanced Options menu, Windows 2000 Server loads normally, not in Safe Mode. This allows you to log all of the processes that take place during a normal boot sequence.

This log file can be used to troubleshoot the boot process. When logging is enabled, the log file is written to *Windir*\ntbtlog.txt. A sample of the ntbtlog.txt file is shown in Figure 15.9.

FIGURE 15.9 The Windows 2000 boot log file

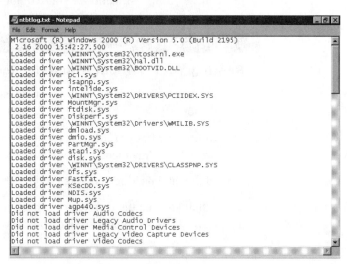

In Exercise 15.4, you will create and access a boot log file.

EXERCISE 15.4

Using Boot Logging

1. Start your computer. (If your computer is currently running, select Start ➢ Shutdown ➢ Restart.)

2. During the boot process, press the F8 key to access the Windows 2000 Advanced Options menu.

3. Highlight Enable Boot Logging and press Enter. Then log on as Administrator.

4. Select Start ➢ Programs ➢ Accessories ➢ Windows Explorer.

5. In Windows Explorer, expand My Computer, then C:. Open the WINNT folder and double-click ntbtlog.txt.

6. Examine the contents of your boot log file.

7. Shut down your computer and restart in normal mode.

The boot log file is cumulative. Each time you boot to any Advanced Options menu mode (except Last Known Good Configuration), you are writing to this file. This allows you to make changes, reboot, and see if you have fixed any problems. If you want to start from scratch, you should manually delete this file and reboot to an Advanced Options menu selection that supports logging.

Using Other Advanced Options Menu Modes

The other selections on the Advanced Options menu work as follows:

- The *Safe Mode with Networking* option is the same as the Safe Mode option, but it adds networking features. You might use this mode if you need networking capabilities in order to download drivers or service packs from a network location.

- The *Safe Mode with Command Prompt* option starts the computer in Safe Mode, but instead of loading the Windows 2000 graphical interface, it loads a command prompt. Experienced troubleshooters use this mode.

- The *Enable VGA Mode* option loads a standard VGA driver without starting the computer in Safe Mode. You might use this mode if you changed your video driver, did not test it, and tried to boot to Windows 2000 with a bad driver that would not allow you to access video. Enable VGA Mode bails you out by loading a default driver, providing access to video so that you can properly install (and test!) the correct driver for your computer.

When you boot to any Safe Mode, you automatically use VGA Mode.

- The *Last Known Good Configuration* option boots Windows 2000 using the Registry information that was saved the last time the computer was successfully booted. You would use this option to restore configuration information if you have improperly configured the computer and have not successfully rebooted the computer. When you use the Last Known Good Configuration option, you lose any system configuration changes that were made since the computer last successfully booted.

- The *Directory Services Restore Mode* option is used by Windows 2000 Server computers that are configured as domain controllers to restore the Active Directory. This option is not available on Windows 2000 Server computers that are installed as member servers.

- The *Debugging Mode* option runs the Kernel Debugger, if that utility is installed. The Kernel Debugger is an advanced troubleshooting utility.

- The *Boot Normally* option boots to Windows 2000 in the default manner. This option is on the Advanced Options menu in case you got trigger happy and hit F8 during the boot process, but really wanted to boot Windows 2000 normally.

Windows 2000 handles startup options in a slightly different way than Windows NT 4 does. In Windows NT 4, the boot loader menu shows an option to load VGA mode, which appears each time you restart the computer. In Windows 2000, this has been moved to the Advanced Options menu to present the user with a cleaner boot process. Also, in Windows NT 4, you need to press the spacebar as a part of the boot process to access the Last Known Good Configuration option.

Using Startup and Recovery Options

The Startup and Recovery options are used to specify the default operating system that is loaded and specify which action should be taken in the event of system failure. You can access the Startup and Recovery options from your Desktop by right-clicking My Computer, selecting Properties from the pop-up menu, clicking the Advanced tab, and then clicking the Startup and Recovery button. Alternatively, select Start ➤ Settings ➤ Control Panel ➤ System ➤ Advanced ➤ Startup and Recovery. You will see the dialog box shown in Figure 15.10.

FIGURE 15.10 The Startup and Recovery dialog box

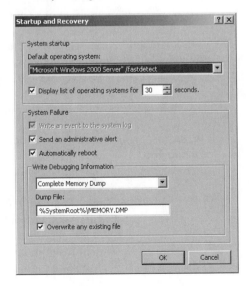

The options that can be specified through the Startup and Recovery dialog box are described in Table 15.8.

TABLE 15.8   Startup and Recovery Options

Option	Description
Default Operating System	Specifies the operating system that is loaded by default if no selection is made from the operating system selection menu (if your computer dual-boots or multi-boots and an operating system selection menu appears during bootup). By default, this option is set to Microsoft Windows 2000 Server.
Display List of Operating Systems for *x* Seconds	Specifies how long the operating system selection menu is available before the default selection is loaded (if your computer dual-boots or multi-boots and an operating system selection menu appears during bootup). By default, this option is set to 30 seconds.
Write an Event to the System Log	Specifies that an entry is made in the System log any time a system failure occurs. By default, this option is enabled, which allows you to track system failures.
Send an Administrative Alert	Specifies that a pop-up alert message will be sent to the Administrator any time a system failure occurs. By default, this option is enabled, so the Administrator is notified of system failures.
Automatically Reboot	Specifies that the computer will automatically reboot in the event of a system failure. By default, this option is enabled, so the system restarts after a failure without intervention. You would disable this option if you wanted to see the blue screen for analysis.
Write Debugging Information	Specifies that debugging information (a memory dump) is written to a file. You can choose not to create a dump file or to create a small memory dump (64KB) file, a kernel memory dump file, or a complete memory dump file. Complete memory dump files require free disk space equivalent to your memory and a page file that is at least as large as your memory with an extra 2MB. The default setting is to write debugging information to a complete memory dump.

TABLE 15.8 Startup and Recovery Options *(continued)*

Option	Description
Overwrite Any Existing File	If you create dump files, allows you to create a new dump file that overwrites the old dump file or to keep all dump files each time a system failure occurs. This option is selected by default.

In Exercise 15.5, you will access the Startup and Recovery options and make changes to the settings.

EXERCISE 15.5

Using Startup and Recovery Options

1. From your Desktop, right-click My Computer and choose Properties. Click the Advanced tab and then click the Startup and Recovery button.

2. Change the Display List of Operating Systems option from 30 seconds to 10 seconds.

3. In the Write Debugging Information section, choose (None) from the drop-down list.

4. Click the OK button to close the Startup and Recovery dialog box.

Creating Windows 2000 Server Setup Boot Disks

You can create floppy disks that can be used to boot to the Windows 2000 Server operating system in case your computer will not boot and will not read the CD-ROM drive. These disks are called the *Windows 2000 Server Setup Boot Disks*.

From these diskettes, you can perform the following tasks:

- Reinstall the Windows 2000 Server operating system if you do not have access to the CD-ROM drive.

- Use the Recovery Console.

- Use an Emergency Repair Disk (ERD)

Using the Windows 2000 Server Setup Boot Disks to install Windows 2000 is described in Chapter 1, "Getting Started with Windows 2000 Server." The Recovery Console and ERD are covered later in this chapter.

The Windows 2000 Server Setup Boot Disks are not specific to a computer. They are general Windows 2000 Server disks, which can be used by any computer running Windows 2000 Server.

To create the Windows 2000 Server Startup disks, you need four high-density floppy disks. Label them as follows:

- Windows 2000 Server Setup Boot Disk

- Windows 2000 Server Setup Disk #2

- Windows 2000 Server Setup Disk #3

- Windows 2000 Server Setup Disk #4

The command to create boot disks from Windows 2000 or Windows NT is *MAKEBT32.EXE*. The command to make boot disks from Windows 9x or 16-bit operating systems is MAKEBOOT.EXE.

Setup disks created for Windows 2000 Server will not work with Windows 2000 Professional. Setup disks created for Windows 2000 Professional will not work with Windows 2000 Server.

Once you have formatted and labeled your floppy disks, you are ready to create the Setup Boot Disks, in Exercise 15.6. This exercise requires four high-density floppy disks. You also need the Windows 2000 Server CD.

EXERCISE 15.6

Creating Windows 2000 Server Setup Boot Disks

1. Label each of your high-density floppy disks as follows.

   a. Windows 2000 Server Setup Boot Disk

   b. Windows 2000 Server Setup Disk #2

    c. Windows 2000 Server Setup Disk #3

    d. Windows 2000 Server Setup Disk #4

2. Insert the Windows 2000 Server CD into your CD-ROM drive.

3. Select Start ➢ Run ➢ Browse. Select your CD-ROM drive, then select BOOTDISK, and then select MAKEBT32. Click the OK button.

4. In the command-prompt dialog box, specify the floppy drive to copy the image to. This is normally your A: drive.

5. Insert the disk labeled Windows 2000 Server Setup Boot Disk. The files will be copied.

6. When prompted, insert Windows 2000 Server Setup Disks #2, #3, and #4, pressing Enter after you insert each one.

7. After the disks have been created, put them in an easily accessible place. You will use them in Exercise 15.8.

Using the Backup Utility

The *Windows 2000 Backup* utility allows you to create and restore backups, and create an *Emergency Repair Disk (ERD)*. Backups protect your data in the event of system failure by storing the data on another medium, such as another hard disk or a tape. If your original data is lost due to corruption, deletion, or media failure, you can restore the data using your backup. The ERD is a subset of a backup that you can use to restore configuration information quickly.

Microsoft ✔ *Exam Objective*

Recover System State and user data.

- Recover System State data and user data by using Windows Backup.

To access the Backup utility, select Start ➢ Programs ➢ Accessories ➢ System Tools ➢ Backup. This brings up the Backup window, as shown in Figure 15.11.

FIGURE 15.11 The Backup window

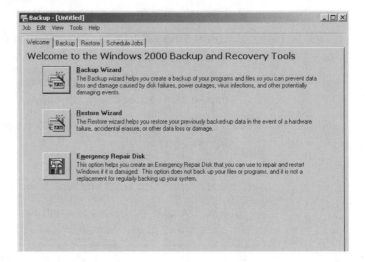

From this window, you can start the Backup Wizard, start the Restore Wizard, or create an ERD. These options are covered in the following sections.

Creating and Using an ERD

You can use the ERD to repair and restart Windows 2000 Server in the event that your computer will not start or if the system files have been damaged. You should create an ERD when the computer is installed and then update the ERD after making any changes to the configuration of your computer. This option does not back up any system data.

You can repair the following items with the ERD:

- The basic system
- System files
- The partition boot sector
- The startup environment
- The Registry (return the Registry to its original configuration)

In the next sections, you will learn how to create and use an ERD.

Preparing an ERD

To create an ERD, click the Emergency Repair Disk button in the opening Backup utility window. This brings up the Emergency Repair Disk dialog box, which asks you to insert a blank, formatted floppy disk into drive A:. At this point, you can also specify whether you want to back up the Registry to the ERD. If the Registry will fit onto your ERD, you should select this option. When you click OK, the system data will be copied to the ERD.

You should update your ERD after you make any major configuration changes to your computer.

You will create an ERD in Exercise 15.7. You will need a blank, formatted, high-density floppy disk for this exercise.

EXERCISE 15.7

Creating an Emergency Repair Disk

1. Select Start ➤ Programs ➤ Accessories ➤ System Tools ➤ Backup.

2. Click the Emergency Repair Disk button.

3. The Emergency Repair Disk dialog box appears. Insert a blank, formatted floppy disk into drive A:.

4. Select the Also Back Up the Registry to the Repair Directory option.

5. Click OK. The system data will be copied to the ERD.

6. A confirmation dialog box appears. Click the OK button to close this dialog box.

Using an ERD

The ERD is not a bootable disk and can be accessed only by using the Windows 2000 Server Setup CD or the Windows 2000 Server Setup diskettes that are created from the CD.

In Exercise 15.8, you will restore your system using the ERD. You will need the four Windows Server Setup Boot Disks you created in Exercise 15.6 and the ERD you created in Exercise 15.7. You will also need the Windows 2000 Server CD.

EXERCISE 15.8

Restoring Your System with an Emergency Repair Disk

1. Restart your computer using the Windows 2000 Server Setup Boot Disk.

2. When prompted, insert Windows 2000 Server Setup Disk #2, #3, and #4, pressing Enter after you insert each one.

3. From the Welcome to Setup dialog box, press the R key to choose to repair a Windows 2000 installation.

4. From the Windows 2000 Repair Options dialog box, press R to repair the Windows 2000 installation using the emergency repair process.

5. Press the F key to choose Fast Repair.

6. Insert your ERD and press Enter. Then press Enter again in the next dialog box.

7. Press Enter to indicate that you want the Setup program to examine your computer's drives.

8. Insert the Windows 2000 Server CD into your CD-ROM drive and press Enter. The emergency repair process will examine the files on your drive.

9. When prompted, remove any floppies from your floppy drives and the Windows 2000 Server CD from the CD-ROM drive. You computer will restart automatically.

In Windows NT, you create ERDs through the RDISK command. This command is not available in Windows 2000.

Using the Backup Wizard

The *Backup Wizard* takes you through all of the steps that are required for a successful backup. Before you start the Backup Wizard, you should be logged on as an Administrator or a member of the Backup Operators group.

To use the Backup Wizard, take the following steps:

1. Start the Backup program and click the Backup Wizard button.

2. The Welcome to the Windows 2000 Backup and Recovery Tools dialog box appears. Click the Next button.

3. The What to Back Up dialog box appears. This dialog box allows you to select what you will back up. You can choose to back up everything; back up just selected files, drives, or network data; or back up only the system state data. System state data includes system configuration information, as explained in the next section. For this example, select the Back Up Selected Files, Drives, or Network Data radio button, then click the Next button.

4. The Items to Back Up dialog box appears, as shown in Figure 15.12. Check the items that you want to back up and click the Next button.

FIGURE 15.12   The Items to Back Up dialog box

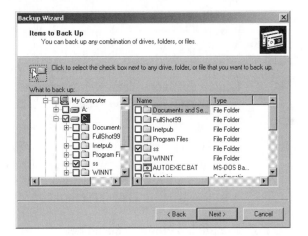

5. The Where to Store the Backup dialog box appears, as shown in Figure 15.13. You can either type in the backup media or filename, or click the Browse button to locate it. Clicking the Browse button brings up the Open dialog box. Select the drive, give your backup a filename (for example, you might use the date as the filename), and click the Open button. You return to the Where to Store the Backup dialog box. When your backup media or filename path is correct, click the Next button.

FIGURE 15.13 The Where to Store the Backup dialog box

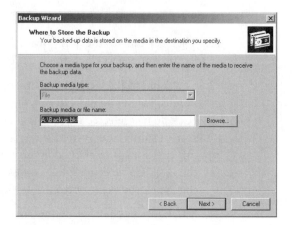

6. The Completing the Backup Wizard dialog box appears. If all of the information is correct, click the Finish button.

Clicking the Advanced button in the Completing the Backup Wizard dialog box brings up a dialog box that allows you to specify the type of backup: Normal, Copy, Incremental, Differential, or Daily. These backup types are discussed in the "Selecting a Backup Type" section later in this chapter.

7. During the backup process, the Wizard displays the Backup Progress dialog box, as shown in Figure 15.14. Once the backup process is complete, you can click the Report button in this dialog box to see details of the backup session. Figure 15.15 shows an example of a backup report.

FIGURE 15.14 The Backup Progress dialog box

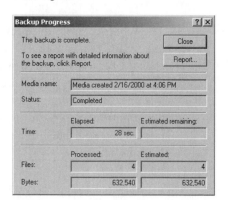

FIGURE 15.15   An example of a backup report

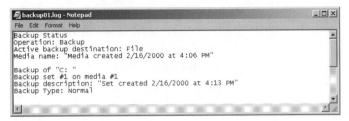

In Exercise 15.9, you will use the Backup Wizard. You will need a blank, formatted, high-density floppy disk for this exercise.

Using the Backup Wizard

1. Create a folder on your D: drive called **DATA**. Create some small text files in this folder. The size of all of the files combined should not exceed 1MB.

2. Select Start ➤ Programs ➤ Accessories ➤ System Tools ➤ Backup.

3. In the opening Backup window, click the Backup Wizard button.

4. In the Welcome to the Windows 2000 Backup and Recovery Tools dialog box, click the Next button.

5. In the What to Back Up dialog box, click the Back Up Selected Files, Drives, or Network Data radio button. Then click the Next button.

6. In the Items to Back Up dialog box, select My Computer, expand D:, and check the DATA folder. Click the Next button.

7. In the Where to Store the Backup dialog box, click the Browse button. In the Open dialog box, select Floppy (A:). For the filename, enter the date (in the *mmddyy* format). Then click the Open button.

8. In the Where to Store the Backup dialog box, click the Next button.

9. Verify your selections in the Completing the Backup Wizard dialog box. Then click the Finish button.

EXERCISE 15.9 *(continued)*

10. When the Backup Wizard completes, click the Report button in the Backup Progress dialog box. This will show the backup log in a Notepad window. Close this window when you are finished viewing the report.

11. Close all of the Backup Wizard dialog boxes.

Managing System State Data

System state data refers to a collection of system-specific configuration information. You can manage the availability of system state data by using the Backup utility to back up this information on a regular basis.

Microsoft
Exam
Objective

Manage and optimize availability of System State data and user data.

On any Windows 2000 computer, system state data consists of the Registry, the COM+ Class Registration database, and the system boot files. On Windows 2000 Server computers, system state data will also include the Certificate Services database (if the server is configured as a certificate server). On Windows 2000 Server computers that are domain controllers, system state data also includes the Active Directory services database and the SYSVOL directory, which is a shared directory that stores the server copy of the domain's public files.

If you need to restore system state data on a domain controller, you should restart your computer with the advanced startup option Directory Services Restore Mode. This allows the Active Directory directory service database and the SYSVOL directory to be restored. If the system state data is restored on a domain controller that is a part of a domain where data is replicated to other domain controllers, you must perform an authoritative restore. For an authoritative restore, you use the Ntdsutil.exe command, then restart the computer.

If you have a backup device attached to your computer, you can follow the steps in Exercise 15.10 to back up your system state data. This information will not fit on a single floppy disk.

EXERCISE 15.10

Backing Up System State Data

1. Select Start ➢ Programs ➢ Accessories ➢ System Tools ➢ Backup.

2. In the opening Backup window, click the Backup tab.

3. Under My Computer, click the System State check box and select the backup media or filename that will be used for the backup.

4. Click the Start Backup button.

5. When the Backup is complete, click the Report button in the Backup Progress dialog box.

6. The backup log appears in a Notepad window. Close this window when you are finished viewing the report.

7. Close all of the Backup dialog boxes.

Configuring Backup Options

You can configure more specific backup configurations by selecting backup options. To access the backup options, start the Backup program and select Tools ➢ Options. This brings up the Options dialog box. This dialog box has five tabs with options for controlling the backup and restore processes: General, Restore, Backup Type, Backup Log, and Exclude Files. The options of these tabs are covered in the following sections.

Configuring General Backup Options

The General tab, shown in Figure 15.16, contains options for configuring backup sessions. Table 15.9 describes these options.

FIGURE 15.16 The General tab of the Options dialog box

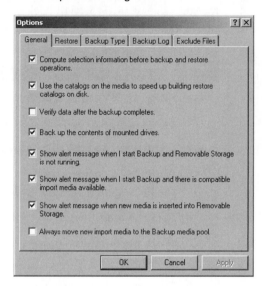

TABLE 15.9 General Backup Options

Option	Description
Compute Selection Information before Backup and Restore Operations	Estimates the number of files and bytes that will be backed up or restored during the current operation and displays this information prior to the backup or restore operation
Use the Catalogs on the Media to Speed Up Building Restore Catalogs on Disk	Specifies that you want to use an on-media catalog to build an on-disk catalog that can be used to select which folders and files will be restored during a restore operation
Verify Data after the Backup Completes	Makes sure that all data has been backed up properly

TABLE   15.9   General Backup Options *(continued)*

Option	Description
Back Up the Contents of Mounted Drives	Specifies that the data should be backed up on mounted drives; otherwise, only path information on mounted drives is backed up
Show Alert Message when I Start Backup and Removable Storage Is Not Running	Notifies you if Removable Storage is not running (when you are backing up to tape or other removable media)
Show Alert Message when I Start Backup and There Is Compatible Import Media Available	Notifies you when you start Backup if new media have been added to the Removable Storage import pool.
Show Alert Message when New Media Is Inserted into Removable Storage	Notifies you when new media are detected by Removable Storage.
Always Move New Import Media to the Backup Media Pool	Specifies that if new media are detected by Removable Storage, that media should be directed to the Backup media pool.

Configuring Restore Options

The Restore tab of the Options dialog box, shown in Figure 15.17, contains three options that relate to how files are restored when the file already exists on the computer:

- Do Not Replace the File on My Computer (Recommended)
- Replace the File on Disk Only If the File on the Disk is Older
- Always Replace the File on My Computer

FIGURE 15.17 The Restore tab of the Options dialog box

Selecting a Backup Type

The Backup Type tab, shown in Figure 15.18, allows you to specify the default backup type that will be used. You should select the type of backup based on the following:

- How much data you are backing up
- How quickly you want to be able to perform the backup
- The number of tapes you are willing to use in the event that you need to perform a restore operation

Table 15.10 describes the backup type options.

FIGURE 15.18   The Backup Type tab of the Options dialog box

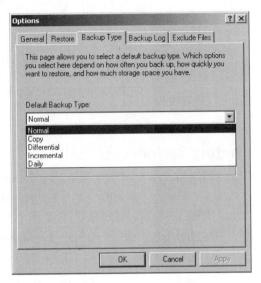

TABLE 15.10   Backup Type Options

Option	Description
Normal	Backs up all files and sets the archive bit as marked for each file that is backed up. Requires only one tape for the restore process.
Copy	Backs up all files and does not set the archive bit as marked for each file that is backed up. Requires only one tape for the restore process.
Differential	Backs up only the files that have not been marked as archived and does not set the archive bit for each file that is backed up. Requires the last normal backup and the last differential tape for the restore process.
Incremental	Backs up only the files that have not been marked as archived and sets the archive bit for each file that is backed up. Requires the last normal backup and all of the incremental tapes that have been created since the last normal backup for the restore process.

TABLE 15.10 Backup Type Options *(continued)*

Option	Description
Daily	Backs up only the files that have been changed today and does not set the archive bit for each file that is backed up. Requires each daily backup and the last normal backup for the restore process.

Setting Backup Log Options

The Backup Log tab, shown in Figure 15.19, allows you to specify the amount of information that is logged during the backup process. You can select from the following options:

Detailed   which logs all information, including the names of the folders and files that are backed up

Summary   which logs only key backup operations, such as starting the backup

None   which specifies that a log file will not be created

FIGURE 15.19   The Backup Log tab of the Options dialog box

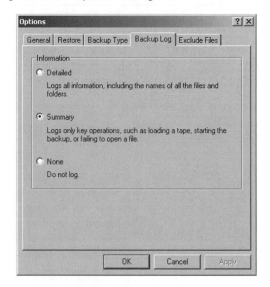

Excluding Files

The Exclude Files tab of the Options dialog box, shown in Figure 15.20, allows you to explicitly exclude specific files during the backup process. For example, you might choose to exclude the page file or application files.

FIGURE   15.20   The Exclude Files tab of the Options dialog box

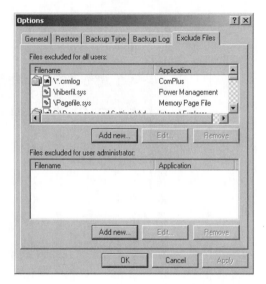

Using the Restore Wizard

Having a complete backup won't help you if your system fails unless you can successfully restore that backup. To be sure that you can restore your data, you should test the restoration process before anything goes wrong. You can use the *Restore Wizard* for testing purposes, as well as when you actually need to restore your backup.

To use the Restore Wizard, take the following steps:

1. Start the Backup program and click the Restore Wizard button.

2. The Welcome to the Restore Wizard dialog box appears. Click the Next button.

3. The What to Restore dialog box appears, as shown in Figure 15.21. Click the filename of the backup session that you want to restore and click the Next button. After you select the backup you want to restore, you can choose to restore the entire session, or you can selectively restore drives, folders, or files from the backup session.

FIGURE 15.21 The What to Restore dialog box

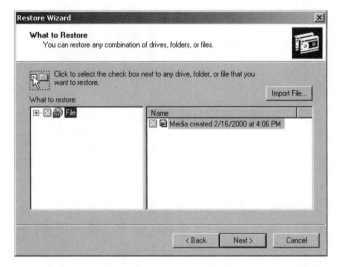

4. The Completing the Restore Wizard dialog box appears. If all of the configuration information is correct, click the Finish button.

Clicking the Advanced button in the Completing the Restore Wizard dialog box brings up a dialog box that allows you to select where files will be restored. You can choose from the original location, an alternate location, or a single folder.

5. The Enter Backup File Name dialog box appears, as shown in Figure 15.22. Verify that the correct filename is specified and click the OK button.

FIGURE 15.22   The Enter Backup File Name dialog box

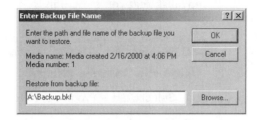

6. During the restoration process, the Wizard displays the Restore Progress dialog box, as shown in Figure 15.23. Once the restoration process is complete, you can click the Report button in this dialog box to see details of the restore session. Figure 15.24 shows an example of a restore report.

FIGURE 15.23   The Restore Progress dialog box

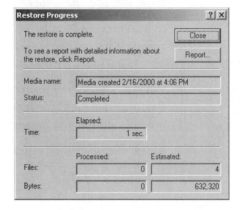

FIGURE 15.24   An example of a restore report

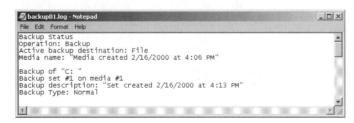

In Exercise 15.11, you will use the Restore Wizard. You will need the floppy disk that you created in Exercise 15.9 for this exercise.

EXERCISE 15.11

Using the Restore Wizard

1. Select Start ➢ Programs ➢ Accessories ➢ System Tools ➢ Backup.

2. In the opening Backup window, click the Restore Wizard button.

3. In the Welcome to the Restore Wizard dialog box, click the Next button.

4. In the What to Restore dialog box, click the filename of the backup session that you created in Exercise 15.9. Click the D: drive to put a check mark in the box. Click the Next button.

5. In the Completing the Restore Wizard dialog box, verify that everything is configured properly. Then click the Finish button.

6. In the Enter the Backup File Name dialog box, verify that the filename for the backup session is the same file you specified in Exercise 15.9. Then click the OK button.

7. When the Restore Wizard completes, click the Report button in the Restore Progress dialog box. Close the Notepad window when you are finished viewing the report.

8. Close all of the Restore and Backup dialog boxes.

Using the Recovery Console

If your computer will not start, and you have tried to boot to Safe Mode with no luck, there's one more option you can try. The *Recovery Console* is an option designed for administrators and advanced users. It allows you limited access to FAT16, FAT32, and NTFS volumes without starting the Windows 2000 Server graphical interface.

Microsoft ✓ ***Exam*** ***Objective***

Recover System State data and user data.

- Recover System State data and user data by using the Recovery Console.

Through the Recovery Console, you can perform the following tasks:

- Copy, replace, or rename operating system files and folders. You might do this if your boot failure was caused by missing or corrupt files.

- Enable or disable the loading of services when the computer is restarted. If a particular service may be keeping the operating system from booting, you could disable the service. If a particular service is required for successful booting, you want to make sure that service loading was enabled.

- Repair the file system boot sector or the MBR. You might use this option if a virus may have damaged the system boot sector or the MBR.

- Create and format partitions on the drives. You might use this option if your disk utilities will not delete or create Windows 2000 partitions. Normally, you use a disk-partitioning utility for these functions.

In the following sections, you will learn how to access and use the Recovery Console.

Starting the Recovery Console

If you have created the Windows 2000 Server Setup Disks, you can start the Recovery Console from them. Alternatively, you can add the Recovery Console to the Windows 2000 startup options, but you need to configure this prior to the failure. Each of these options is covered in the following sections.

Starting the Recovery Console with the Windows 2000 Server Setup Disks

To use the Recovery Console from the Windows 2000 Server Setup Disks, take the following steps:

1. Restart your computer using the Windows 2000 Server Setup Boot Disk.

2. Insert each of the other Windows Server Setup Disks in turn, as prompted.

3. In the Welcome to Setup dialog box, press the R key to repair a Windows 2000 installation.

4. From the Windows 2000 Repair Options menu, press the C key to repair Windows 2000 using the Recovery Console. The Windows 2000 Recovery Console will start.

See the section "Using the Recovery Console" after the next section for details on how to use the Recovery Console.

Adding the Recovery Console to Windows 2000 Startup

You can add the Recovery Console to the Windows 2000 Server startup options so it will be available in the event of a system failure. This configuration takes about 7MB of disk space to hold the CMDCONS folder and files. To set up this configuration, take the following steps:

1. Insert the Windows 2000 Server CD into your CD-ROM drive. You can disable auto-play by pressing the Shift key as the CD is read. From a command prompt on the \I386 folder, type **WINNT32 /CMDCONS**.

2. The Windows 2000 Setup dialog box appears, asking you to confirm that you want to install the Recovery Console, as shown in Figure 15.25. Click the Yes button.

FIGURE 15.25   The Windows 2000 Setup dialog box

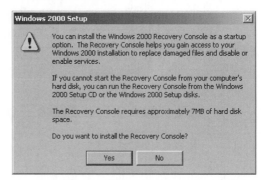

3. The installation files will be copied to your computer. Then you will see a dialog box letting you know that the Recovery Console has been successfully installed. Click the OK button to continue.

The next time you restart your computer, you will see an option for the Microsoft Windows 2000 Recovery Console. You will learn how to use the Recovery Console in the next section.

In Exercise 15.12, you will add the Recovery Console to the Windows 2000 startup options. You will need the Windows 2000 Server CD for this exercise.

EXERCISE 15.12

Adding the Recovery Console to the Windows 2000 Setup

1. Insert the Windows 2000 Server CD in your CD-ROM drive. Hold down the Shift key as the CD is read to prevent auto-play.

2. Select Start ➢ Programs ➢ Accessories ➢ Command Prompt.

3. Change the drive letter to your CD-ROM drive.

4. From the CD drive letter prompt (*x:\>*), type **CD I386** and press Enter.

5. From *x:\I386>*, type **WINNT32 /CMDCONS**.

6. In the Windows 2000 Setup dialog box, click the Yes button to confirm that you want to install the Recovery Console.

7. After the installation files are copied to your computer, a dialog box appears to let you know that the Recovery Console has been successfully installed. Click the OK button.

8. Shut down and restart your computer. In the startup selection screen, select the option for Microsoft Windows 2000 Recovery Console.

9. At the command prompt, type **EXIT** to close the Recovery Console. You return to the Windows Desktop.

Using the Recovery Console

After you add the Recovery Console, you can access it by restarting your computer. In the operating system selection menu, you will see an option for Microsoft Windows 2000 Recovery Console. Select this option to start the Recovery Console.

The Recovery Console presents you with a command prompt and very limited access to system resources. This keeps unauthorized users from using the Recovery Console to access sensitive data. The following are the only folders you can access through the Recovery Console:

- The root folder
- The *Windir* folder and the subfolders of the Windows 2000 Server installation
- The CMDCONS folder
- Removable media drives such as CD-ROM drives

If you try to access any other folders besides the ones listed above, you will receive an "access denied" error message.

In the Recovery Console, you cannot copy files from a local hard disk to a floppy disk. You can only copy files from a floppy disk or CD to a hard disk, or from one hard disk to another hard disk. This is for security purposes.

You should use the Recovery Console with extreme caution. Improper use may cause even more damage than the problems you are trying to fix.

If your computer dual-boots with other Windows 2000 operating systems, the first option you must specify is which Windows 2000 operating system you will log on to. Next, you must specify the Administrator password for the system you are logging on to.

When the Recovery Console starts, you can use the commands listed in Table 15.11.

TABLE 15.11 Commands Available with the Recovery Console

Command	Description
ATTRIB	Used to set file attributes. You can set file attributes for Read-only (R), System (S), Hidden (H), or Compressed (C).

TABLE 15.11   Commands Available with the Recovery Console *(continued)*

Command	Description
BATCH	Used to execute commands in a specified input file.
CHDIR (CD)	Used to navigate the directory structure. If executed without a directory name, the current directory is displayed. (CHDIR and CD work the same way.)
CLS	Used to clear any text that is currently displayed on the console.
CHKDSK	Used to check the disk and display a disk status report.
COPY	Used to copy a single file from one location to another. COPY does not support wildcards and does not copy files to removable media, (such as floppy disks).
DELETE (DEL)	Used to delete a single file. Wildcards are not supported. (DELETE and DEL work the same way.)
DIR	Used to display lists of files and subdirectories in the current directory.
DISABLE	Used to disable Windows 2000 system services and drivers.
DISKPART	Used to manage disk partitions. If executed without a command-line argument, a user interface is displayed.
ENABLE	Used to enable Windows 2000 system services and drivers.
EXIT	Used to quit the Recovery Console and restart the computer.
EXPAND	Used to expand compressed files.
FIXBOOT	Used to write a new boot sector onto the computer's system partition.
FIXMBR	Used to repair the MBR of the computer's boot partition.

TABLE 15.11 Commands Available with the Recovery Console *(continued)*

Command	Description
FORMAT	Used to prepare a disk for use with Windows 2000 by formatting the disk as FAT16, FAT32, or NTFS.
HELP	Used to display help information for Recovery Console commands.
LISTSVC	Used to list all available services and drivers on the computer, as well as the current status of each service and driver.
LOGON	If the computer is configured for dual-booting or multi-booting, used to log on to other installations as the local administrator.
MAP	Used to display the current drive letter mappings.
MKDIR (MD)	Used to create new directories. (MKDIR and MD work the same way.)
MORE	Used to display a text file on the console screen. (Same as TYPE.)
RENAME (REN)	Used to rename a single file. (RENAME and REN work the same way.)
RMDIR (RD)	Used to delete directories. (RMDIR and RD work the same way.)
SYSTEMROOT	Used to specify that the current directory is the system root.
TYPE	Used to display a text file on the console screen. (Same as MORE.)

In Exercise 15.13, you will use the Recovery Console. This exercise assumes that you completed Exercise 15.12 to add the Recovery Console to the Windows 2000 startup options.

EXERCISE 15.13

Using the Recovery Console

1. Restart the computer. In the operating system selection menu, select the Microsoft Windows 2000 Recovery Console option.

2. Select the Windows 2000 installation you want to manage and press Enter. (If the computer has been configured as specified in this book, this will be option 1.)

3. Enter the Administrator password and press Enter. You see the C:\WINNT> prompt.

4. Type **DIR** and press Enter to see a current listing of available files and folders. In the listing, you can press Enter to scroll down line by line or the spacebar to scroll continuously.

5. Type **CD ..** and press Enter to move to the root of the C: drive. You see the C:\> prompt.

6. Type **DIR BOOT.INI** and press Enter to see the file attributes of the BOOT.INI file.

7. Type **MORE BOOT.INI** and press Enter to see the contents of the BOOT.INI file.

8. Type **LISTSVC** and press Enter to see a list of all the services and drivers.

9. Type **EXIT** to exit the Recovery Console and restart your computer.

Real World Scenario

The Last-Ditch Effort

You have just installed a new CD-RW device to your server. As you are loading the driver, your server hangs. You restart the computer, and it still won't boot. You attempt to start your server in Safe Mode, but even Safe Mode will not load. Before you panic, you should attempt to fix the problem through the Recovery Console.

To use the Recovery Console to fix this problem you would take the following steps: First, restart the computer using the Recovery Console. Once in the Recovery Console, disable the new driver you loaded that is causing the computer to hang. Restart the computer; it should boot. Use Device Manager to remove the driver.

Summary

In this chapter, you learned about the Windows 2000 Server system recovery options and utilities. We covered the following topics:

- Basic techniques that you can use to safeguard your computer and plan for disaster recovery

- The Event Viewer utility, including how to view the details of an event and manage log files

- The Windows 2000 boot process, including the steps in a normal boot, the BOOT.INI file, and how to create a Windows 2000 boot disk

- Advanced startup options, including Safe Mode, Enable Boot Logging, Last Known Good Configuration, and other options for booting in special modes

- Startup and Recovery options, which are used to specify what action Windows 2000 should take in the event of system failure

- Windows 2000 Server Setup Boot Disks, which are used to start Windows 2000 in the event of system failure and to access the Recovery

Console, and the Emergency Repair Disk (ERD), which can be used to repair problems that prevent your computer from starting

- The Windows Backup utility, which includes a Backup Wizard, a Restore Wizard, and an option for creating an ERD

- The Recovery Console, which is a special boot process that allows you limited access to your file system for replacement of files or specifying which services should be started the next time the computer is booted

Exam Essentials

Be able to use the Event Viewer.   Know how to access the Event Viewer and understand which events are stored in each of the Event Viewer logs.

Manage the Windows 2000 boot process.   List the files required within the Windows 2000 boot process. Be able to troubleshoot the boot process in the event of failure. Know the options that are configured within BOOT.INI and how the BOOT.INI file is configured. Be able to recover the boot files in the event of corruption.

Use the Windows 2000 advanced startup options   List the Windows 2000 Advanced Startup Options and under what circumstances it is appropriate to use each one.

Create Windows 2000 Server Setup Boot Disks.   Know the commands that are used to create the Windows 2000 Server Setup Boot disks. Know when you would need to use these disks.

Use the Windows 2000 Backup utility.   Be able to use the Windows 2000 Backup utility to perform system backup and restores. Understand what information is backed up through the System State Data option of backup. Be able to restore System State Data on a Windows 2000 domain controller. Be able to create an Emergency Repair Disk through Windows 2000 Backup. Understand the backup schemes and the amount of data backed up by each scheme and the number of tape sets that are required to restore based on the backup scheme used.

Use the Recovery Console   Know when it is appropriate to use the Recovery Console. Be able to install and use the Recovery Console.

Key Terms

Before you take the exam, be sure you're familiar with the following key terms:

Application log	NTBOOTDD.SYS
Backup Wizard	NTDETECT.COM
Boot Normally	NTLDR
BOOT.INI	NTOSKRNL.EXE
BOOTSECT.DOS	POST (Power On Self Test)
Debugging Mode	Recovery Console
Directory Services Restore Mode	Restore Wizard
Emergency Repair Disk (ERD)	Safe Mode
Enable Boot Logging	Safe Mode with Command Prompt
Enable VGA Mode	Safe Mode with Networking
Error event	Security log
Event Viewer	Success Audit event
Failure Audit event	System log
Information event	Warning event
Last Known Good Configuration	Windows 2000 Backup
MAKEBT32.EXE	Windows 2000 boot disk
Master Boot Record (MBR)	Windows 2000 Server Setup Boot Disks

Review Questions

1. You are the administrator for a large Windows 2000 network using Active Directory. You have delegated administrative control on several of your domains and want to track the changes that are made to the Active Directory. You enable auditing for Active Directory events. When performing maintenance on the domain controllers, what log should you check in the Event Viewer to see the results of the auditing?

   A. Directory Service

   B. System

   C. Security

   D. Active Directory

2. You have a third-party utility that is used to manage the Active Directory. Before you install the application, you backup your domain controllers. After you install the third-party application, you realize that one of your domains is corrupt. You remove the application and want to restore the Active Directory database. Which of the following actions is not required?

   A. Restore the ERD.

   B. Restore the System State Data.

   C. Perform an authoritative restore with the Ntdsutil utility and restart the computer.

   D. Boot the computer to Recovery Console Mode and perform an authoritative restore of the Active Directory.

3. You are a consultant who has been called in to troubleshoot a Windows 2000 Server that is not functioning properly. You suspect that some of the services are not loading properly during the boot sequence. What option can you use to see a list of drivers and services that are loading on your computer during the boot sequence?

   A. Configure Startup and Recovery options to enable boot logging.

   B. Press F5 during the boot sequence to see each driver and service as it is loading.

   C. Configure the BOOT.INI file with the /enablelog switch and reboot the computer.

   D. Use the advanced startup option Enable Boot Logging during the boot process.

4. In a remote Sales office, the server periodically fails. You want to configure this server so that when it hangs, it will automatically reboot without user intervention. What do you do?

   A. Configure the BOOT.INI file with the /autoboot switch.

   B. Configure the BOOT.INI file with the /autostart switch.

   C. Configure the Startup and Recovery options to automatically reboot the server.

   D. Create an AUTOEXEC.BAT file that automatically restarts the server.

5. You use a custom application on your Windows 2000 Server. The application requires that you manually edit the Registry to add a key and edit another key. When you restart the server you see a blue screen prior to accessing the logon screen. Which recovery option should you try first?

   A. Boot the computer in Safe Mode and fix the Registry settings.

   B. Boot the computer with the Last Known Good option.

   C. Use the last full backup you made to restore the server.

   D. Use the ERD that was created when the server was installed to restore the registry.

6. You are the administrator of a large network. When you boot the Sales server, you see an error message pop up on the server console, but you accidentally clear the screen before you can read the entire message. What can you do?

   A. Check the log file *Windir\nterrors.txt*.

   B. Check the log file *Windir* \errors.txt.

   C. Check the Event Viewer log files.

   D. Check the Windows Diagnostics log files.

7. When you attempt to start your Windows 2000 Server, your computer hangs during the boot process. What troubleshooting step should you take first?

   A. Attempt to start Windows 2000 using Safe Mode.

   B. Attempt to start Windows 2000 using the ERD.

   C. Use the Windows 2000 Server Setup Boot Disks to start the computer.

   D. Restore your server using your latest system backup.

8. You've just updated one of your drivers, and now your computer won't restart. How can you access the Last Known Good Configuration option?

   A. Press the spacebar when prompted during the boot sequence.

   B. Access the Advanced Options menu by pressing F8 when prompted during the boot sequence.

   C. Access the Advanced Options menu by pressing F6 when prompted during the boot sequence.

   D. There is no Last Known Good Configuration option in Windows 2000.

9. You have configured your Windows 2000 Server computer with Certificate Server. Which option should be configured in Windows Backup to ensure that all of the Certificate Server files are properly backed up?

   A. Back up *Windir*\\Certificate

   B. Back up *Windir*\\System32

   C. Back up *Windir*\\CertServices

   D. Back up the system state data

10. You are using Windows 2000 backup. You configure the backup program to back up the system state data. Which of the following options is not considered system state data?

    A. Registry

    B. The boot partition

    C. COM+ Class Registration database

    D. System boot files

11. You recently added a new partition to your hard drive. When you restart Windows 2000, you get an error that NTOSKRNL.EXE is missing or corrupt. Which file is most likely the problem and needs to be updated?

    A. NTOSKRNL.EXE

    B. BOOT.INI

    C. NTBOOTDD.SYS

    D. BOOTSECT.DOS

12. You have a SCSI adapter with the BIOS enabled. It is the only adapter in your computer. The adapter has two physical drives attached. The second drive contains the system boot partition. It is located on the first partition on the drive. What is the ARC path to the boot partition?

A. `scsi(0)disk(1)rdisk(0)partition(1)`

B. `scsi(1)disk(0)rdisk(1)partition(1)`

C. `multi(0)disk(0)rdisk(1)partition(1)`

D. `multi(0)disk(1)rdisk(0)partition(1)`

13. You are installing Windows 2000 Server on a computer that does not have CD access. You want to create the Server Setup Boot disks from a Windows 95 computer. Which of the following commands would you use to create the disks?

A. `BOOTDISK`

B. `MAKEDISK`

C. `MAKEBOOT`

D. `DISKBOOT`

14. Which of the following backup options backs up only the files that have not been marked as archived and sets the archive bit for each file that is backed up?

A. Copy

B. Differential

C. Incremental

D. Normal

15. You have chosen to use the differential backup method. You perform a full backup on Friday. On Monday, Tuesday, and Wednesday you perform differential backups. Early Thursday morning, the server fails. Within the following exhibit, drag and drop the tapes on the server that will be used to restore the server backup.

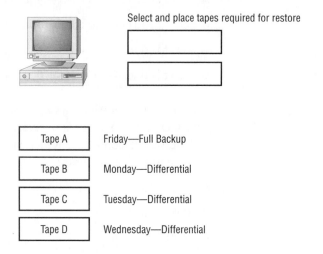

Select and place tapes required for restore

Tape A	Friday—Full Backup
Tape B	Monday—Differential
Tape C	Tuesday—Differential
Tape D	Wednesday—Differential

Answers to Review Questions

1. C. Within Event Viewer, the Security log is used to view all success and failure events for auditing. Directory Service logging would track Active Directory events that are not related to auditing.

2. D. If you need to restore system state data on a domain controller, you should restart your computer with the advanced startup option Directory Services Restore Mode. This allows the Active Directory service database and the SYSVOL directory to be restored. If the system state data is restored on a domain controller that is a part of a domain where data is replicated to other domain controllers, you must perform an authoritative restore. For an authoritative restore, you use the `Ntdsutil.exe` command, then restart the computer.

3. D. When the computer restarts, press F8 when prompted during the boot process. Select the Enable Boot Logging option. The log file will be written to *Windir\ntbtlog.txt* and will contain information about all of the drivers and services that were loaded during the boot process.

4. C. In order to have the computer automatically reboot when a system failure occurs, you select the Automatically Reboot setting in the Startup and Recovery dialog box. No `BOOT.INI` switches deal with automatic reboots. Windows 2000 does not boot through an `AUTOEXEC.BAT` file.

5. B. You use the Last Known Good configuration if you made changes to your computer and are now having problems. Last Known Good Configuration is an Advanced Options menu item that you can select during startup. It loads the configuration that was used the last time the computer booted successfully.

6. C. Whenever you see errors in Windows 2000, you should check Event Viewer. Event Viewer will show you important information about your computer (including detailed information about error messages).

7. A. When you troubleshoot your computer, you should try the more simple solutions first. In this case, try to boot your computer to Safe Mode. Safe Mode starts the server with the minimum number of services and drivers. If you can boot to Safe Mode, you can start troubleshooting. If this doesn't work, you can attempt more drastic measures.

8. B. In Windows NT 4, you access the Last Known Good Configuration option by pressing the spacebar when prompted during the boot sequence. In Windows 2000, the Last Known Good Configuration option is on the Advanced Options menu, which you access by pressing F8 during the boot sequence.

9. D. On Windows 2000 Server computers, system state data includes the Certificate Services database if the server is configured as a certificate server.

10. B. On any Window 2000 computer, system state data consists of the Registry, the COM+ Class Registration database, and the system boot files.

11. B. The BOOT.INI file is used to point to the location of the Windows 2000 boot partition. If you have recently modified your partitions, then it is likely that the ARC path to your boot partition needs to be updated.

12. C. In this case, you use multi, because the adapter is SCSI with the BIOS enabled. You only use scsi when you have a SCSI adapter with the BIOS disabled. With the multi option, disk is always 0. Rdisk refers to the number of the drive that you are using. The first drive is 0; the second drive is 1. Partition refers to the partition in the physical drive, and the first partition is 1.

13. C. The MAKEBOOT command is used to make Windows 2000 Server Setup Boot Disks from 16-bit operating systems. The MAKEBT32 command is used to make Windows 2000 Server Setup Boot Disks from 32-bit operating systems.

14. C. Incremental backups are used to back up only the files that have not been marked as archived and set the archive bit for each file that is backed up. This option requires the last normal backup and all of the incremental tapes that have been created since the last normal backup for the restore process.

15. With differential backups, you only need to restore the last full backup and the last differential tape.

Select and place tapes required for restore

Tape A

Tape D

Glossary

A

Accelerated Graphics Port (AGP) A type of expansion slot supported by Windows 2000. AGP is µused by video cards and supports high-quality video and graphics performance.

access control entry (ACE) An item used by the operating system to determine *resource* access. Each *access control list* (*ACL*) has an associated ACE that lists the permissions that have been granted or denied to the users and groups listed in the ACL.

access control list (ACL) An item used by the operating system to determine *resource* access. Each object (such as a folder, network share, or printer) in Windows 2000 has an ACL. The ACL lists the *security identifiers* (*SIDs*) contained by objects. Only those identified in the list as having the appropriate permission can activate the services of that object.

access token An object containing the *security identifier* (*SID*) of a running *process*. A process started by another process inherits the starting process's access token. The access token is checked against each object's *access control list* (*ACL*) to determine whether or not appropriate permissions are granted to perform any requested service.

account lockout policy A Windows 2000 policy used to specify how many invalid *logon* attempts should be tolerated before a user account is locked out. Account lockout policies are set through *account policies*.

account policies Windows 2000 policies used to determine password and *logon* requirements. Account policies are set through the *Microsoft*

Management Console (MMC) Local Computer Policy or *Domain Controllers Policy* snap-in.

ACE See *access control entry*.

ACL See *access control list*.

Active Desktop A Windows 2000 feature that makes the *Desktop* look and work like a Web page.

Active Directory (AD) A directory service available with the Windows 2000 Server platform. The Active Directory stores information in a central database and allows users to have a single user account (called a *domain user account* or *Active Directory user account*) for the network.

Active Directory user account A user account that is stored in the Windows 2000 Server *Active Directory's* central database. An Active Directory user account can provide a user with a single user account for a network. Also called a domain user account.

Active Directory Users and Computers On Windows 2000 Server *domain controllers*, the main tool used for managing the *Active Directory* users, groups, and computers.

AD See *Active Directory*.

adapter Any hardware device that allows communications to occur through physically dissimilar systems. This term usually refers to peripheral cards that are permanently mounted inside computers and provide an interface from the computer's bus to another medium such as a hard disk or a network.

Administrator account A Windows 2000 special account that has the ultimate set of security permissions and can assign any permission to any user or group.

Administrators group   A Windows 2000 built-in group that consists of *Administrator accounts*.

AGP   See *Accelerated Graphics Port*.

alert   A system-monitoring feature that is generated when a specific *counter* exceeds or falls below a specified value. Through the *Performance Logs and Alerts* utility, administrators can configure alerts so that a message is sent, a program is run, or a more detailed log file is generated.

anonymous access   A type of access for a Web site that allows public use of the site.

Anonymous Logon group   A Windows 2000 *special group* that includes users who access the computer through anonymous logons. Anonymous logons occur when users gain access through special accounts, such as the *IUSR_ computername* and *TsInternetUser* user accounts.

answer file   An automated installation script used to respond to configuration prompts that normally appear in a Windows 2000 Server installation. Administrators can create Windows 2000 answer files with the *Setup Manager* utility.

Application log   A log that tracks events that are related to applications that are running on the computer. The Application log can be viewed in the *Event Viewer* utility.

application server mode   A *Terminal Services* mode that gives users remote access to applications running on the server. Using this mode,

Terminal Services delivers the Windows 2000 *Desktop* environment to computers that might not otherwise be able to run Windows 2000 because of hardware or other limitations.

audit policy   A Windows 2000 policy that tracks the success or failure of specified security events. Audit policies are set through *Local Computer Policy* or *Domain Controllers Policy*.

Authenticated Users group   A Windows 2000 *special group* that includes users who access the Windows 2000 operating system through a valid username and password.

authentication   The process required to log on to a computer locally. Authentication requires a valid username and a password that exists in the local accounts database. An *access token* will be created if the information presented matches the account in the database.

automated installation   The process of installing Windows 2000 using an unattended setup method such as *Remote Installation Services (RIS)*, *unattended installation*, or *disk images*.

B

backup
The process of writing all the data contained in online mass-storage devices to offline mass-storage devices for the purpose of safekeeping. Backups are usually performed from hard disk drives to tape drives. Also referred to as archiving.

Backup Operators group   A Windows 2000 built-in group that includes users who can back up and restore the *file system*, even if the file system is

NTFS and they have not been assigned permissions to the file system. The members of the Backup Operators group can only access the file system through the *Windows 2000 Backup* utility. To be able to directly access the file system, the user must have explicit permissions assigned.

backup type   A *backup* choice that determines which files are backed up during a backup process. Backup types include *normal backup*, *copy backup*, *incremental backup*, *differential backup*, and *daily backup*.

Backup Wizard   A Wizard used to perform a *backup*. The Backup Wizard is accessed through the *Windows 2000 Backup* utility.

bandwidth   The total capacity of transmission media. Bandwidth is commonly expressed as bits per second (bps) or as Hertz (frequency).

Bandwidth Allocation Protocol (BAP)   A *PPP* option for *multilink* connections to control the amount of *bandwidth* used by connections to *RAS servers*.

bandwidth throttling   A method for limiting the maximum amount of *bandwidth* that can be used by a Web server.

baseline   A snapshot record of a computer's current performance statistics that can be used for performance analysis and planning purposes.

Basic Input/Output System (BIOS)   A set of routines in firmware that provides the most basic software interface drivers for hardware attached to the computer. The BIOS contains the *boot* routine.

basic storage   A disk-storage system supported by Windows 2000 that consists of *primary partitions* and *extended partitions*.

Batch group   A Windows 2000 *special group* that includes users who log on as a user account that is only used to run a batch job.

binding   The process of linking together software components, such as network *protocols* and *network adapters*.

BIOS   See *Basic Input/Output System*.

boot   The process of loading a computer's operating system, also called bootstrap. Booting usually occurs in multiple phases, each successively more complex until the entire operating system and all its services are running. The computer's *BIOS* must contain the first level of booting.

BOOT.INI   A file accessed during the Windows 2000 *boot* sequence. The `BOOT.INI` file is used to build the operating system menu choices that are displayed during the boot process. It is also used to specify the location of the *boot partition*.

Boot Normally   A Windows 2000 Advanced Options menu item used to boot Windows 2000 normally.

boot partition   The *partition* that contains the system files. The system files are located in C:\WINNT by default.

BOOTSECT.DOS   An optional file that is loaded if the user chooses to load an operating system other than Windows 2000. This file is only used in *dual-boot* or *multi-boot* computers.

bottleneck   A system *resource* that is inefficient compared with the rest of the computer system as a whole. The bottleneck can cause the rest of the system to run slowly.

C

caching   A speed-optimization technique that keeps a copy of the most recently used data in a fast, high-cost, low-capacity storage device rather than in the device on which the actual data resides. Caching assumes that recently used data is likely to be used again. Fetching data from the cache is faster than fetching data from the slower, larger storage device. Most caching algorithms also copy data that is most likely to be used next and perform *write-back caching* to further increase speed gains.

CAL   See *Client Access License.*

CD-based image   A type of image configured on a *Remote Installation Services (RIS)* server. A CD-based image contains only the Windows 2000 operating system.

CDFS   See *Compact Disk File System.*

central processing unit (CPU)   The main *processor* in a computer.

Check Disk   A Windows 2000 utility that checks a hard disk for errors. Check Disk (chkdsk) attempts to fix file-system errors and recover bad sectors.

CIPHER   A command-line utility that can be used to encrypt files on *NTFS volumes.*

cipher text   Encrypted data. Encryption is the process of translating data into code that is not easily accessible. Once data has been encrypted, a user must have a password or key to decrypt the data. Unencrypted data is known as plain text.

clean install   A method of Windows 2000 Server installation that puts the operating system into a new folder and uses its default settings the first time the operating system is loaded.

client   A computer on a network that subscribes to the services provided by a server.

Client Access License (CAL)   A license that allows a computer to legally access a Windows 2000 server or domain controller.

client license key packs   Sets of client licenses that a *Terminal Services license server* distributes to clients.

COM port   Communications port. A serial hardware interface conforming to the RS-232C standard for low-speed, serial communications.

Compact Disk File System (CDFS)   A *file system* used by Windows 2000 to read the file system on a CD-ROM.

compatibility script   A script that helps applications run on a *Terminal Services server.* Compatibility scripts should be run after the program is installed to achieve the best performance on a Terminal Services server.

compression   The process of storing data in a form that takes less space than the uncompressed data.

Computer Management   A consolidated tool for performing common Windows 2000 management tasks. The interface is organized into three main areas of management: System Tools, Storage, and Services and Applications.

computer name   A *NetBIOS* name used to uniquely identify a computer on the network. A computer name can be from 1 to 15 characters in length.

container   An *Active Directory* object that holds other Active Directory objects. *Domains* and *organizational units* are examples of container objects.

Control Panel   A Windows 2000 utility that allows users to change default settings for operating system services to match their preferences. The *Registry* contains the Control Panel settings.

CONVERT   A command-line utility used to convert a *partition* from *FAT16* or *FAT32* to the *NTFS* file system.

copy backup   A *backup type* that backs up selected folders and files but does not set the archive bit.

counter   A performance-measuring tool used to track specific information regarding a system resource, called a performance object. All Windows 2000 system resources are tracked as performance objects, such as Cache, Memory, Paging File, Process, and Processor. Each performance object has an associated set of counters. Counters are set through the *System Monitor* utility.

CPU   See *central processing unit.*

Creator Group   The Windows 2000 *special group* that created or took ownership of the object (rather than an individual user). When a regular user creates an object or takes ownership of an object, the username becomes the *Creator Owner*. When a member of the *Administrators group* creates or takes ownership of an object, the Administrators group becomes the Creator Group.

Creator Owner group   The Windows 2000 *special group* that includes the account that created or took ownership of an object. The account, usually a user account, has the right to modify the object, but cannot modify any other objects that were not created by the user account.

D

daily backup   A *backup type* that backs up all of the files that have been modified on the day that the daily backup is performed. The archive attribute is not set on the files that have been backed up.

data compression   The process of storing data in a form that takes less space than the uncompressed data.

data encryption   The process of translating data into code that is not easily accessible to increase security. Once data has been encrypted, a user must have a password or key to decrypt the data.

DCPROMO   A utility used to upgrade a server to a domain controller, after the server has been installed with the Windows 2000 Server operating system. The DCPROMO utility also can be used to downgrade a domain controller to a member server.

Debugging Mode   A *Windows 2000 Advanced Option menu item* that runs the Kernel Debugger, if that utility is installed. The Kernel Debugger is an advanced troubleshooting utility.

default gateway   A *TCP/IP* configuration option that specifies the gateway that will be used if the network contains routers.

demand-dial routing connections   Support for both *inbound connections* and *outbound connections* for an *RAS server*.

Desktop   A directory that the background of the Windows Explorer shell represents. By default, the Desktop includes objects that contain the local storage devices and available network *shares*. Also a key operating part of the Windows 2000 graphical interface.

device driver   Software that allows a specific piece of hardware to communicate with the Windows 2000 operating system.

Device Manager   A Windows 2000 utility used to provide information about the computer's configuration.

Dfs   See *Distributed file system*.

Dfs link   A component of the *Distributed file system (Dfs)* topology. A Dfs link points from the *Dfs root* to one or more *Dfs shared folders*.

Dfs replication   The replication of one or more *Dfs shared folders*. Dfs replication ensures that if the *host server* goes down, the files and folders that are part of the Dfs will be available.

Dfs root   A component of the *Distributed file system (Dfs)* topology. The Dfs root contains the *Dfs shared folders* and *Dfs links*. You can create a *domain-based Dfs root* or a *stand-alone Dfs root*.

Dfs shared folder   A component of the *Distributed file system (Dfs)* topology. *Dfs links* point to Dfs shared folders.

DHCP   See *Dynamic Host Configuration Protocol*.

DHCP server   A server configured to provide *DHCP* clients with all of their *IP* configuration information automatically.

dial-up networking   A service that allows remote users to dial into the network or the Internet (such as through a telephone or an *ISDN* connection).

Dialup group   A Windows 2000 *special group* that includes users who log on to the network from a dial-up connection.

differential backup   A *backup type* that copies only the files that have been changed since the last *normal backup* (full backup) or *incremental backup*. A differential backup backs up only those files that have changed since the last full backup, but does not reset the archive bit.

Digital Versatile Disc (DVD)   A disk standard that supports up to 4.7GB of data. One of DVD's strongest features is backward compatibility with CD-ROM technology, so that a DVD drive can play CD-ROMs. Formerly known as Digital Video Disk.

directory replication   The process of copying a directory structure from an export computer to an import computer(s). Any time changes are made to the export computer, the import computer(s) is automatically updated with the changes.

Directory Services Restore Mode A Windows 2000 Advanced Option menu item that is used by Windows 2000 Server computers that are configured as domain controllers to restore the *Active Directory*. This option is not available on Windows 2000 Server computers that are installed as member servers.

Disk Cleanup A Windows 2000 utility used to identify areas of disk space that can be deleted to free additional hard disk space. Disk Cleanup works by identifying temporary files, Internet cache files, and unnecessary program files.

disk defragmentation The process of rearranging the existing files on a disk so that they are stored contiguously, which optimizes access to those files.

Disk Defragmenter A Windows 2000 utility that performs *disk defragmentation*.

disk image An exact duplicate of a hard disk, used for *automated installation*. The disk image is copied from a reference computer that is configured in the same manner as the computers on which Windows 2000 will be installed.

Disk Management A Windows 2000 graphical tool for managing disks and *volumes*.

disk partitioning The process of creating logical *partitions* on the physical hard drive.

disk quota policies These policies are used to specify how much disk space can be allocated by users.

disk quotas A Windows 2000 feature used to specify how much disk space a user is allowed to use on specific *NTFS volumes*. Disk quotas can be applied for all users or for specific users.

distribution group A type of group that can be created on a Windows 2000 *domain controller* in the *Active Directory*. A distribution group is a logical group of users who have common characteristics. Distribution groups can be used by applications and e-mail programs.

Distributed file system (Dfs) A Windows 2000's Server feature that uses a central database of links that point to shares across the network. Dfs provides users with a central location to access files and folders that are physically distributed across a network. Files that are stored on several computers in a domain appear to the user to all reside in the same network share.

Distributed File System utility The Windows 2000 Server utility used to configure and manage the *Distributed file system (Dfs)*.

distribution server A network server that contains the Windows 2000 distribution files that have been copied from the distribution CD. Clients can connect to the distribution server and install Windows 2000 over the network.

DNS See *Domain Name System*.

DNS client policies These policies are used to configure DNS properties for Windows 2000 clients.

DNS server A server that uses *DNS* to resolve domain or host names to *IP addresses*.

domain In Microsoft networks, an arrangement of client and server computers referenced by a specific name that shares a single security permissions database. On the Internet, a domain is a named collection of hosts and subdomains, registered with a unique name by the InterNIC.

domain-based Dfs root   In the *Distributed file system (Dfs)*, a type of *Dfs root* that automatically publishes its Dfs topology to the *Active Directory*. A domain-based Dfs root has *Dfs replication* capabilities for fault tolerance.

domain controller   A Windows 2000 Server computer that stores the complete *domain* database.

Domain Controllers Policy   A *Microsoft Management Console (MMC) snap-in* used to implement domain account policies.

domain forest   A set of *domain trees* that does not form a contiguous namespace. For example, you might have a forest if your company merged with another company. With a forest, you could each maintain a separate corporate identity through your namespace, but share information across the *Active Directory*.

domain local group   A scope for a group on a Windows 2000 *domain controller*. A domain local group is used to assign *permissions* to *resources*. Local groups can contain user accounts, *universal groups*, and *global groups* from any domain in the *domain tree* or *domain forest*. A domain local group can also contain other domain local groups from its own local domain.

domain name   A name that identifies one or more *IP addresses*, such as sybex.com. Domain names are used in *URLs* to identify particular Web pages.

domain name server   An Internet host dedicated to the function of translating fully qualified domain names (host names) into *IP addresses*.

Domain Name System (DNS)   The *TCP/IP* network service that translates fully qualified domain names (host names) into *IP addresses*.

domain policies   Policies applied at the domain level that allow administrators to control what a user can do after logging on. Domain policies include *audit policies*, *security option policies*, and *user rights policies*. These policies are set through *Domain Controllers Policy*.

domain security   Security that governs a user's ability to access domain resources. Any *domain policies* you define override the *local policies* of a computer.

domain tree   A hierarchical organization of *domains* in a single, contiguous namespace. In the *Active Directory*, a tree is a hierarchy of domains that are connected to each other through a series of trust relationships (logical links that combine two or more domains into a single administrative unit).

domain user account   A user account that is stored in the Windows 2000 Server *Active Directory's* central database. A domain user account can provide a user with a single user account for a network. Also called an Active Directory user account.

drive letter   A single letter assigned as an abbreviation to a mass-storage *volume* available to a computer.

driver   A program that provides a software interface to a hardware device. Drivers are written for the specific devices they control, but they present a common software interface to the computer's operating system, allowing all devices of a similar type to be controlled as if they were the same.

driver signing   A digital imprint that is Microsoft's way of guaranteeing that a driver has been tested and will work with the computer.

dual-booting   The process of allowing a computer to *boot* more than one operating system.

dynamic disk   A Windows 2000 disk-storage technique. A dynamic disk is divided into dynamic *volumes*. Dynamic volumes cannot contain *partitions* or *logical drives*. You can size or resize a dynamic disk without restarting Windows 2000. Dynamic disks are accessible only to Windows 2000 systems.

Dynamic Host Configuration Protocol (DHCP)   A method of automatically assigning *IP addresses* to client computers on a network.

dynamic storage   A Windows 2000 disk-storage system that is configured as *volumes*. Windows 2000 Server dynamic storage supports *simple volumes, spanned volumes, striped volumes, mirrored volumes*, and *RAID-5 volumes*.

E

EB   See *exabyte*.

effective rights   The rights that a user actually has to a file or folder. To determine a user's effective rights, add all of the permissions that have been allowed through the user's assignments based on that user's username and group associations. Then subtract any permissions that have been denied the user through the username or group associations.

EFS   See *Encrypting File System*.

Emergency Repair Disk (ERD)   A disk that stores portions of the *Registry*, the system files, a copy of the partition boot sector, and information that relates to the startup environment. The ERD can be used to repair problems that prevent a computer from starting.

Enable Boot Logging   A Windows 2000 Advanced Options menu item that is used to create a log file that tracks the loading of *drivers* and *services*.

Enable VGA Mode   A Windows 2000 Advanced Options menu item that loads a standard VGA driver without starting the computer in *Safe Mode*.

Encrypting File System (EFS)   The Windows 2000 technology used to store encrypted files on *NTFS partitions*. Encrypted files add an extra layer of security to the *file system*.

encryption   The process of translating data into code that is not easily accessible to increase security. Once data has been encrypted, a user must have a password or key to decrypt the data.

ERD   See *Emergency Repair Disk*.

Error event   An *Event Viewer* event type that indicates the occurrence of an error, such as a driver failing to load.

Event Viewer   A Windows 2000 utility that tracks information about the computer's hardware and software, as well as security events. This information is stored in three log files: the *Application log*, the *Security log*, and the *System log*. On a domain controller, the Event Viewer also includes logs for Directory Service, DNS Server, and File Replication Service.

Everyone A Windows 2000 *special group* that includes anyone who could possibly access the computer. The Everyone group includes all of the users (including *Guests*) who have been defined on the computer.

exabyte A computer storage measurement equal to 1,024 *petabytes*.

extended partition In *basic storage*, a *logical drive* that allows you to allocate the logical partitions however you wish. Extended partitions are created after the *primary partition* has been created.

F

Failure Audit event An *Event Viewer* event that indicates the occurrence of an event that has been audited for failure, such a failed logon when someone presents an invalid username and/or password.

FAT16 The 16-bit version of the *File Allocation System (FAT)* system, which was widely used by DOS and Windows 3.*x*. The file system is used to track where files are stored on a disk. Most operating systems support FAT16.

FAT32 The 32-bit version of the *File Allocation System (FAT)* system, which is more efficient and provides more safeguards than *FAT16*. Windows 9*x* and Windows 2000 support FAT32. Windows NT does not support FAT32.

fault tolerance Any method that prevents system failure by tolerating single faults, usually through hardware redundancy.

File Allocation Table (FAT) The *file system* used by *MS-DOS* and available to other operating systems such as Windows (all versions), and OS/2. FAT, now known as *FAT16*, has become something of a mass-storage compatibility standard because of its simplicity and wide availability. FAT has fewer fault-tolerance features than the *NTFS* file system and can become corrupted through normal use over time.

file attributes Bits stored along with the name and location of a file in a directory entry. File attributes show the status of a file, such as archived, hidden, and read-only. Different operating systems use different file attributes to implement services such as *sharing*, *compression*, and *security*.

File Replication Service (FRS) The service used by the *Distributed file system (Dfs)* to automatically replicate *Dfs shared folders*. When changes are made to one shared folder, FRS updates the other shared folders to reflect the changes.

file system A software component that manages the storage of files on a mass-storage device by providing services that can create, read, write, and delete files. File systems impose an ordered database of files on the mass-storage device. Storage is arranged in *volumes*. File systems use hierarchies of directories to organize files.

File Transfer Protocol (FTP) A simple Internet protocol that transfers complete files from an FTP server to a client running the FTP client. FTP provides a simple, low-overhead method of transferring files between computers but cannot perform browsing functions. Users must know the *URL* of the FTP server to which they wish to attach.

frame A data structure that network hardware devices use to transmit data between computers. Frames consist of the addresses of the sending and receiving computers, size information, and a checksum. Frames are envelopes around packets of data that allow the packets to be addressed to specific computers on a shared media network.

frame type An option that specifies how data is packaged for transmission over the network. This option must be configured to run the *NWLink IPX/SPX/NetBIOS Compatible Transport* protocol on a Windows 2000 computer. By default, the frame type is set to Auto Detect, which will attempt to automatically choose a compatible frame type for the network.

FRS See *File Replication Service.*

FTP See *File Transfer Protocol.*

G

GB See *gigabyte.*

GDI See *Graphic Device Interface.*

gigabyte A computer storage measurement equal to 1,024 *megabytes.*

global group A scope for a group on a Windows 2000 *domain controller.* A global group is used to organize users who have similar network access requirements. Global groups can contain user and global groups from the local domain.

Graphics Device Interface (GDI) The programming interface and graphical services provided to *Win32* for programs to interact with graphical devices such as the screen and printer.

Group Policy policies These policies specify how Group Policies are applied to a computer.

groups Security entities to which users can be assigned membership for the purpose of applying the broad set of group permissions to the user. By managing permissions for groups and assigning users to groups, rather than assigning permissions to users, administrators can more easily manage security.

Guest account A Windows 2000 user account created to provide a mechanism to allow users to access the computer even if they do not have a unique username and password. This account normally has very limited privileges on the computer. This account is disabled by default.

Guests group A Windows 2000 built-in group that has limited access to the computer. This group can access only specific areas. Most administrators do not allow Guests group access because it poses a potential security risk.

H

HAL See *Hardware Abstraction Layer.*

Hardware Abstraction Layer (HAL) A Windows 2000 service that provides basic input/

output services such as timers, interrupts, and multiprocessor management for computer hardware. The HAL is a *device driver* for the motherboard circuitry that allows different families of computers to be treated the same by the Windows 2000 operating system.

Hardware Compatibility List (HCL)   A list of all of the hardware devices supported by Windows 2000. Hardware on the HCL has been tested and verified as being compatible with Windows 2000.

HCL   See *Hardware Compatibility List.*

home folder   A folder where users normally store their personal files and information. A home folder can be a local folder or a network folder.

host   An Internet server. A host is a node that is connected to the Internet.

host server   In the context of the *Distributed file system (Dfs)*, the domain server that contains the *Dfs root*. The host server automatically publishes the Dfs topology to the *Active Directory* and provides synchronization of the topology across the domain member servers.

HOSTS file   A file that is used to map *IP addresses* to *host* names. A HOSTS file can be used in place of a *DNS server*.

hot swapping   The ability of a device to be plugged into or removed from a computer while the computer's power is on.

HTML   See *Hypertext Markup Language.*

HTTP   See *Hypertext Transfer Protocol.*

Hypertext Markup Language (HTML)   A textual data format that identifies sections of a document such as headers, lists, hypertext links, and so on. HTML is the data format used on the World Wide Web for the publication of Web pages.

Hypertext Transfer Protocol (HTTP)   An Internet protocol that transfers HTML documents over the Internet and responds to context changes that happen when a user clicks a hyperlink.

I

IIS   See *Internet Information Services.*

inbound connections   Connections that allow incoming access to an *RAS server.*

incremental backup   A *backup type* that backs up only the files that have changed since the last normal or incremental backup. It sets the archive attribute on the files that are backed up.

Indexing Service   A Windows 2000 service that creates an index based on the contents and properties of files stored on the computer's local hard drive. A user can then use the Windows 2000 Search function to search or query through the index for specific keywords.

Industry Standard Architecture (ISA)   The design standard for 16-bit Intel-compatible motherboards and peripheral buses. The 32/64-bit *PCI* bus standard is replacing the ISA standard. Adapters and interface cards must conform to the bus standard(s) used by the motherboard in order to be used in a computer.

Information event   An *Event Viewer* event that informs you that a specific action has occurred, such as when a system shuts down or starts.

inherited permissions   Parent folder permissions that are applied to (or inherited by) files and subfolders of the parent folder. In Windows 2000, the default is for parent folder permissions to be applied to any files or subfolders in that folder.

initial user account   The account that uses the name of the registered user and is created only if the computer is installed as a member of a workgroup (not into the *Active Directory*). By default, the initial user is a member of the *Administrators group*.

Integrated Services Digital Network (ISDN)   A direct, digital, dial-up connection that operates at 64KB per channel over regular twisted-pair cable. Up to 24 channels can be multiplexed over two twisted pairs.

Interactive group   A Windows 2000 *special group* that includes all the users who use the computer's resources locally.

interactive logon   A *logon* when the user logs on from the computer where the user account is stored on the computer's local database. Also called a local logon.

interactive user   A user who physically logs on to the computer where the user account resides (rather than over the network).

internal network number   An identification for *NetWare* file servers. An internal network number is also used if the network is running File and Print Services for NetWare or is using IPX

routing. This option must be configured to run the *NWLink IPX/SPX/NetBIOS Compatible Transport* protocol on a Windows 2000 computer. Normally, the internal network number should be left at its default setting.

Internet Information Services (IIS)   Software that serves Internet higher-level protocols like *HTTP* and *FTP* to clients using Web browsers. The IIS software that is installed on a Windows 2000 Server computer is a fully functional Web server and is designed to support heavy Internet usage.

Internet Protocol (IP)   The Network layer protocol upon which the Internet is based. IP provides a simple connectionless packet exchange. Other protocols such as *TCP* use IP to perform their connection-oriented (or guaranteed delivery) services.

Internet Server Application Programming Interface (ISAPI) filter   A method for directing Web browser requests for specific *URLs* to specific ISAPI applications, which are then run. ISAPI filters are commonly used to manage customized logon authentication.

Internet service provider (ISP)   A company that provides dial-up connections to the Internet.

Internet Services Manager   A Windows 2000 utility used to configure the protocols that are used by *Internet Information Services (IIS)* and Personal Web Services (PWS).

internetwork   A network made up of multiple network segments that are connected with some device, such as a router. Each network segment is assigned a network address. Network layer protocols build routing tables that are used to route packets through the network in the most efficient manner.

InterNIC   The agency that is responsible for assigning *IP addresses.*

interprocess communications (IPC)   A generic term describing any manner of client/ server communication protocol, specifically those operating in the Application layer. IPC mechanisms provide a method for the client and server to trade information.

interrupt request (IRQ)   A hardware signal from a peripheral device to the microcomputer indicating that it has input/output (I/O) traffic to send. If the microprocessor is not running a more important service, it will interrupt its current activity and handle the interrupt request. IBM PCs have 16 levels of interrupt request lines. Under Windows 2000, each device must have a unique interrupt request line.

intranet   A privately owned network based on the *TCP/IP* protocol suite.

IP   See *Internet Protocol.*

IP address   A four-byte number that uniquely identifies a computer on an *IP internetwork.*

IPC   See *interprocess communications.*

IPCONFIG   A command used to display the computer's *IP* configuration.

IRQ   See *interrupt request.*

ISA   See *Industry Standard Architecture.*

ISAPI filter   See *Internet Server Application Programming Interface filter.*

ISDN   See *Integrated Services Digital Network.*

ISP   See *Internet service provider.*

K

KDC   See *key distribution center.*

Kerberos   A security protocol that is used in Windows 2000 Server to authenticate users and network services. This is called dual verification, or *mutual authentication.* Windows 2000 Server uses Kerberos version 5.

Kerberos policies   Policies that are used to configure computer security settings for *Kerberos* authentication. Kerberos policies are set through *account policies.*

kernel   The core process of a preemptive operating system, consisting of a multitasking scheduler and the basic security services. Depending on the operating system, other services such as virtual memory drivers may be built into the kernel. The kernel is responsible for managing the scheduling of *threads* and *processes.*

key distribution center (KDC)   A *domain controller* that is responsible for holding all of the client passwords and account information. When a Windows 2000 Server computer is installed as a domain controller, it automatically becomes a KDC.

L

Last Known Good Configuration   A Windows 2000 Advanced Options menu item used to load the control set that was used the last time the computer was successfully booted.

license server   A server that issues licenses to *Terminal Services clients*. This license is a digitally signed certificate that will remain with the client and cannot be used by any other client.

LMHOSTS file   A file used to map *NetBIOS names* to computers' *IP addresses*. An LMHOSTS file can be used in place of a *WINS server*.

Local Computer Policy   A *Microsoft Management Console (MMC) snap-in* used to implement local account policies.

local group   A group that is stored on the local computer's accounts database. Administrators can add users to local groups and manage them directly on a Windows 2000 computer.

local logon   A *logon* when the user logs on from the computer where the user account is stored on the computer's local database. Also called an interactive logon.

local policies   Policies that allow administrators to control what a user can do after logging on. Local policies include *audit policies*, *security option policies*, and *user rights policies*. These policies are set through *Local Computer Policy*.

local printer   A printer that uses a *physical port* and that has not been shared. If a printer is defined as local, the only users who can use the printer are the local users of the computer that the printer is attached to.

local security   Security that governs a local or interactive user's ability to access locally stored

files. Local security can be set through *NTFS permissions*.

local user account   A user account stored locally in the user accounts database of a computer that is running Windows 2000.

local user profile   A profile created the first time a user logs on, stored in the Documents and Settings folder. The default user profile folder's name matches the user's logon name. This folder contains a file called NTUSER.DAT and subfolders with directory links to the user's *Desktop* items.

Local Users and Groups   A utility that is used to create and manage local user and group accounts on Windows 2000 Professional computers and Windows 2000 member servers.

locale settings   Settings for regional items, including numbers, currency, time, date, and input locales.

logical drive   An allocation of disk space on a hard drive, using a *drive letter*. For example, a 5GB hard drive could be partitioned into two logical drives: a C: drive, which might be 2GB, and a D: drive, which might be 3GB.

Logical Drives   A Windows 2000 utility used to manage the logical drives on the computer.

logical port   A port that connects a device directly to the network. Logical ports are used with printers by installing a network card in the printers.

logical printer   The software interface between the *physical printer* (the *print device*) and the operating system. Also referred to as just a printer in Windows 2000 terminology.

logoff   The process of closing an open session with a Windows 2000 computer or network.

logon   The process of opening a session with a Windows 2000 computer or a network by providing a valid authentication consisting of a user account name and a password. After logon, network resources are available to the user according to the user's assigned *permissions*.

logon policies   These policies specify the restrictions that are associated with a user logging onto a Windows 2000 computer or domain.

logon script   A command file that automates the *logon* process by performing utility functions such as attaching to additional server resources or automatically running different programs based on the user account that established the logon.

M

MAC (media access control) address
The physical address that identifies a computer. Ethernet and Token Ring cards have the MAC address assigned through a chip on the network card.

MAKEBT32.EXE   The 32-bit command used to create *Windows 2000 Server Setup Boot Disks*.

mandatory profile   A *user profile* created by an administrator and saved with a special extension (.man) so that the user cannot modify the profile in any way. Mandatory profiles can be assigned to a single user or a group of users.

mapped drive   A shared network folder associated with a drive letter. Mapped drives appear to users as local connections on their computers and can be accessed through a drive letter using My Computer.

Master Boot Record (MBR)   A record used in the Windows 2000 *boot* sequence to point to the active partition, which is the partition that should be used to boot the operating system. This is normally the C: drive. Once the MBR locates the active partition, the boot sector is loaded into memory and executed.

MB   See *megabyte*.

MBR   See *Master Boot Record*.

megabyte   A computer storage measurement equal to 1,024 kilobytes.

member server   A Windows 2000 server that has been installed as a non-domain controller. This allows the server to operate as a file, print, and application server without the overhead of account administration.

memory   Any device capable of storing information. This term is usually used to indicate volatile *random-access memory (RAM)* capable of high-speed access to any portion of the memory space, but incapable of storing information without power.

Microsoft Management Console (MMC)
The Windows 2000 console framework for management applications. The MMC provides a common environment for *snap-ins*.

mirrored volume   A *volume* set that consists of copies of two simple volumes stored on two separate physical partitions. A mirrored volume set contains a primary drive and a secondary drive. The data written to the primary drive is mirrored to the secondary drive. Mirrored volumes provide fault tolerance, because if one drive in the mirrored volume fails, the other drive still works without any interruption in service or loss of data.

MMC   See *Microsoft Management Console*.

multi-booting   The process of allowing a computer to *boot* multiple operating systems.

multilink   A *PPP* option that allows several physical connections to an *RAS server* to be combined into a single logical connection.

mutual authentication   The type of authentication used with *Kerberos* version 5. With mutual authentication, the user is authenticated to the service and the service is authenticated to the user.

My Network Places   The folder that provides access to shared resources, such as local network resources and Web resources.

N

NetBEUI   See *NetBIOS Extended User Interface*.

NetBIOS   See *Network Basic Input/Output System*.

NetBIOS Extended User Interface (NetBEUI)   A simple Network layer transport protocol developed to support *NetBIOS* installations. NetBEUI is not routable, and so it is not appropriate for larger networks. NetBEUI is the fastest transport protocol available for Windows 2000.

NET USE   A command-line utility that provides a quick and easy way to map a network drive. This command has the following syntax: NET USE *x*: *computername\sharename*

NetWare   A popular network operating system developed by Novell in the early 1980s. NetWare is a cooperative, multitasking, highly optimized, dedicated-server network operating system that has client support for most major operating systems. Recent versions of NetWare include graphical client tools for management from client stations. At one time, NetWare accounted for more than 70 percent of the network operating system market.

network adapter   The hardware used to connect computers (or other devices) to the network. Network adapters function at the Physical layer and the Data Link layer of the *OSI model*.

Network Basic Input/Output System (NetBIOS)   A client/server *IPC* service developed by IBM in the early 1980s. NetBIOS presents a relatively primitive mechanism for communication in client/server applications, but its widespread acceptance and availability across most operating systems make it a logical choice for simple network applications. Many of the network *IPC* mechanisms in Windows 2000 are implemented over NetBIOS.

Network Basic Input/Output System (NetBIOS) name   A computer identification method used prior to Windows 2000 for Windows clients to communicate with other computers on the network. *WINS servers* are used to resolve Net-BIOS computer names to *IP addresses*.

Network group   A Windows 2000 *special group* that includes the users who access a computer's resources over a network connection.

Network News Transfer Protocol (NNTP)
An Internet protocol used to provide newsgroup services between NNTP servers and NNTP clients.

network printer   A *printer* that is available to local and network users. A network printer can use a *physical port* or a *logical port*.

New Technology File System (NTFS)   A secure, transaction-oriented file system developed for Windows NT and Windows 2000. NTFS offers features such as *local security* on files and folders, *data compression*, *disk quotas*, and *data encryption*.

NNTP   See *Network News Transfer Protocol*.

normal backup   A *backup type* that backs up all selected folders and files and then marks each file that has been backed up as archived.

NTBOOTDD.SYS   A file accessed in the Windows 2000 *boot* sequence. NTBOOTDD.SYS is an optional file (the *SCSI* driver) that is used when the computer has a SCSI adapter with the on-board *BIOS* disabled.

NTDETECT.COM   A file accessed in the Windows 2000 *boot* sequence. NTDETECT.COM is used to detect any hardware that is installed and add information about the hardware to the *Registry*.

NTFS   See *New Technology File System*.

NTFS permissions   Permissions used to control access to *NTFS* folders and files. Access is configured by allowing or denying NTFS permissions to users and groups.

NTLDR   A file used to control the Windows 2000 *boot* process until control is passed to the *NTOSKRNL.EXE* file.

NTOSKRNL.EXE   A file accessed in the Windows 2000 *boot* sequence. NTOSKRNL.EXE is used to load the *kernel*.

NTUSER.DAT   The file that is created for a *user profile*.

NTUSER.MAN   The file that is created for a *mandatory profile*.

NWLINK IPX/SPX/NetBIOS Compatible Transport   Microsoft's implementation of the Novell IPX/SPX protocol stack.

O

OEM branding   Configuring a logo or background to display original equipment manufacturer (OEM) information. OEM branding is an option offered by the *Setup Manager* during *answer file* creation.

Open Systems Interconnection (OSI) model   A reference model for network component interoperability developed by the International Standards Organization (ISO) to promote cross-vendor compatibility of hardware and software network systems. The OSI model splits the process of networking into seven distinct services, or layers. From top to bottom, the layers are Application, Presentation, Session, Transport, Network, Data Link, and Physical. Each layer uses the services of the layer below to provide its service to the layer above.

optimization   Any effort to reduce the workload on a hardware component by eliminating, obviating, or reducing the amount of work required of the hardware component through any means. For instance, file *caching* is an optimization that reduces the workload of a hard disk drive.

organizational unit (OU)   An *Active Directory* object that contains other objects. Each domain can consist of multiple OUs, logically organized in a hierarchical structure. OUs may contain users, groups, security policies, computers, printers, file shares, and other Active Directory objects.

OSI model   See *Open Systems Interconnection model*.

OU   See *organizational unit*.

outbound connections   Connections that allow users to dial out to external resources through an *RAS server*.

owner   The user associated with an *NTFS* file or folder who is able to control access and grant permissions to other users.

P

page file   Logical memory that exists on the hard drive. If a system is experiencing excessive paging (swapping between the page file and physical RAM), it needs more memory.

partition   A section of a hard disk that can contain an independent *file system volume*. Partitions can be used to keep multiple operating systems and file systems on the same hard disk.

password policies   Windows 2000 policies used to enforce security requirements on the computer. Password policies are set on a per-computer basis, and they cannot be configured for specific users. Password policies are set through *account policies*.

PB   See *petabyte*.

PCI   See *Peripheral Connection Interface*.

Per Seat licensing   A Windows 2000 Server licensing option that specifies that each client will be licensed separately and that each client can access as many servers as it needs to.

Per Server licensing   A Windows 2000 Server licensing option that specifies the concurrent number of network connections that can be made to a server.

Performance Logs and Alerts   A Windows 2000 utility used to log performance-related data and generate *alerts* based on performance-related data.

Peripheral Connection Interface (PCI)   A high-speed, 32/64-bit bus interface developed by Intel and widely accepted as the successor to the 16-bit *ISA* interface. PCI devices support input/output (I/O) throughput about 40 times faster than the ISA bus.

permissions   Security constructs used to regulate access to resources by username or group affiliation. Permissions can be assigned by administrators to allow any level of access, such as read-only, read/write, or delete, by controlling the ability of users to initiate object services. Security is implemented by checking the user's *security identifier (SID)* against each object's *access control list (ACL)*.

petabyte   A computer storage measurement that is equal to 1,024 *terabytes*.

physical port   A serial (COM) or parallel (LPT) port that connects a device such as a printer directly to a computer.

PING   A command used to send an Internet Control Message Protocol (ICMP) echo request and echo reply to verify that a remote computer is available.

Plug and Play   A technology that uses a combination of hardware and software to allow the operating system to automatically recognize and configure new hardware without any user intervention.

Point-to-Point Protocol (PPP)   A remote access protocol used with Windows 2000. PPP supports framing and authentication protocols. PPP is used to negotiate configuration parameters for local access protocols such as *TCP/IP*, IPX, and *NetBEUI*.

policies   General controls that enhance the *security* of an operating environment. In Windows 2000, policies affect restrictions on password use and rights assignments, and determine which events will be recorded in the *Security log*.

POST   See *Power On Self Test*.

Power On Self Test (POST)   A part of the Windows 2000 *boot* sequence. The POST detects the computer's *processor*, how much memory is present, what hardware is recognized, and whether or not the *BIOS* is standard or has *Plug-and-Play* capabilities.

Power Users group   A Windows 2000 built-in group that has fewer rights than the *Administrators group*, but more rights than the *Users group*. Members of the Power Users group can perform tasks such as creating local users and groups and modifying the users and groups that they have created.

PPP   See *Point-to-Point Protocol*.

Pre-Boot Execution Environment (PXE)   A technology that allows a client computer to remotely boot and connect to a *Remote Installation Service (RIS)* server.

primary partition   A part of *basic storage* on a disk. The primary partition is the first partition created on a hard drive. The primary partition uses all of the space that is allocated to the partition. This partition is usually marked as active and is the partition that is used to *boot* the computer.

print device   The actual physical printer or hardware device that generates printed output.

print driver   The specific software that understands a *print device*. Each print device has an associated print driver.

print processor   The process that determines whether or not a print job needs further processing once that job has been sent to the *print spooler*. The processing (also called *rendering*) is used to format the print job so that it can print correctly at the *print device*.

print queue   A directory or folder on the *print server* that stores the print jobs until they can be printed. Also called a *printer spooler*.

print server   The computer on which the printer has been defined. When a user sends a print job to a *network printer*, it goes to the print server first.

print spooler   A directory or folder on the *print server* that stores the print jobs until they can be printed. Also called a print queue.

printer   In Windows 2000 terminology, the software interface between the physical printer (called the *print device*) and the operating system.

printer pool   *A configuration that allows* one *printer* to be used for multiple *print devices*. A printer pool can be used when multiple printers use the same *print driver* (and are normally in the same location). With a printer pool, users can send their print jobs to the first available printer.

priority   A level of execution importance assigned to a *thread*. In combination with other factors, the priority level determines how often that thread will get computer time according to a scheduling algorithm.

process   A running program containing one or more *threads*. A process encapsulates the protected memory and environment for its threads.

process throttling   A method for limiting the percentage of *CPU* processing that can be used by a Web site.

processor   A circuit designed to automatically perform lists of logical and arithmetic operations. Unlike microprocessors, processors may be designed from discrete components rather than be a monolithic integrated circuit.

processor affinity   The association of a *processor* with specific *processes* that are running on the computer. Processor affinity is used to configure multiple processors.

protocol   An established rule of communication adhered to by the parties operating under it. Protocols provide a context in which to interpret communicated information. Computer protocols are rules used by communicating devices and software services to format data in a way that all participants understand.

PXE   See *Pre-Boot Execution Environment*.

R

RADIUS server   See *Remote Authentication Dial-In User Service server*.

RAID-5 volume   A *volume* set that stripes the data over multiple disk channels. RAID-5 volumes place a parity stripe across the volume. RAID-5 volumes are fault tolerant.

RAM   See *random-access memory*.

random-access memory (RAM)   Integrated circuits that store digital bits in massive arrays of logical gates or capacitors. RAM is the primary memory store for modern computers, storing all running software processes and contextual data.

RAS See *Remote Access Service.*

RDP See *Remote Desktop Protocol.*

real-time application A *process* that must respond to external events at least as fast as those events can occur. Real-time *threads* must run at very high *priorities* to ensure their ability to respond in real time.

Recovery Console A Windows 2000 option for recovering from a failed system. The Recovery Console starts Windows 2000 without the graphical interface and allows the administrator limited capabilities, such as adding or replacing files and enabling and disabling services.

REGEDIT A Windows program used to edit the *Registry*. It does not support full editing, as does the *REGEDT32* program, but it has better search capabilities than REGEDT32.

REGEDT32 The primary utility for editing the Windows 2000 *Registry*.

Regional Options A *Control Panel* utility used to enable and configure multilingual editing and viewing on a localized version of Windows 2000.

Registry A database of settings required and maintained by Windows 2000 and its components. The Registry contains all of the configuration information used by the computer. It is stored as a hierarchical structure and is made up of keys, hives, and value entries.

remote access policy A policy that specifies who is authorized to access an *RAS server.*

Remote Access Service (RAS) A service that allows network connections to be established over a modem connection, an *ISDN* connection, or a null-modem cable. The computer initiating the connection is called the RAS client; the answering computer is called the RAS server.

Remote Access Service (RAS) server A Windows 2000 Server computer that is running the *Routing and Remote Access service*. An RAS server authenticates and services requests from remote clients to connect to the network.

remote administration mode A *Terminal Services* mode that allows administrators to perform administrative tasks from virtually any client on the network.

Remote Authentication Dial-In User Service (RADIUS) server A server that stores a central authentication database and allows administrators to manage *RAS servers* from a single location.

remote control A feature used with *Terminal Services* to allow administrators to view or control a user's *session* from another session.

Remote Desktop Protocol (RDP) The protocol used with *Terminal Services* to allow *Terminal Services clients* to connect to the *Terminal Services server*. The Terminal Services server sends and receives commands to and from the client by using RDP.

remote installation Installation of Windows 2000 performed remotely through *Remote Installation Services* (*RIS*).

Remote Installation Preparation (RIPrep) image   A type of image configured on a *Remote Installation Services (RIS)* server. An RIPrep image can contain the Windows 2000 operating system and applications. This type of image is based on a preconfigured computer.

Remote Installation Services (RIS)   A Windows 2000 technology that allows the remote installation of Windows 2000. An RIS server installs Windows 2000 on RIS clients. The RIS server can be configured with a *CD-based image* or a *Remote Installation Preparation (RIPrep) image*.

Removable Storage   A Windows 2000 utility used to track information on removable storage media, which include CDs, DVDs, tapes, and jukeboxes containing optical discs.

rendering   The process that determines whether or not a print job needs further processing once that job has been sent to the spooler. The processing is used to format the print job so that it can print correctly at the *print device*.

replica   A folder within a replica set. Replica sets consist of one or more *shared folders* that participate in replication, for example through the *Distributed file system (Dfs)*.

Replicator group   A Windows 2000 built-in group that supports *directory replication*, which is a feature used by *domain controllers*. Only *domain user accounts* that will be used to start the replication service should be assigned to this group.

Requests for Comments (RFCs)   The set of standards defining the Internet protocols as determined by the Internet Engineering Task Force and available in the public domain on the Internet. RFCs define the functions and services provided by each of the many Internet protocols. Compliance with the RFCs guarantees cross-vendor compatibility.

resource   Any useful service, such as a *shared folder* or a *printer*.

Restore Wizard   A Wizard used to restore data. The Restore Wizard is accessed through the *Windows 2000 Backup* utility.

RFC   See *Request For Comments*.

RIPrep image   See *Remote Installation Preparation image*.

RIS   See *Remote Installation Services*.

roaming profile   A *user profile* that is stored and configured to be downloaded from a server. Roaming profiles allow users to access their profiles from any location on the network.

root share   In the context of the *Distributed file system (Dfs)*, a share used to replicate the *Dfs root*. Root shares are created on other member servers in a domain.

router   A Network layer device that moves packets between networks. Routers provide *internetwork* connectivity.

Routing and Remote Access service   A Windows 2000 Server service that allows an *RAS server* to connect mobile users to the network.

S

Safe Mode   A Windows 2000 Advanced Options menu item that loads the absolute minimum of *services* and *drivers* that are needed to start Windows 2000. The drivers that are loaded with Safe Mode include basic files and drivers for the mouse (unless a serial mouse is attached to the computer), monitor, keyboard, hard drive, standard video driver, and default system services. Safe Mode is considered a diagnostic mode. It does not include networking capabilities.

Safe Mode with Command Prompt   A Windows 2000 Advanced Options menu item that starts Windows 2000 in *Safe Mode*, but instead of loading the graphical interface, it loads a command prompt.

Safe Mode with Networking   A Windows 2000 Advanced Options menu item that starts Windows 2000 in *Safe Mode*, but it adds networking features.

SCSI   See *Small Computer Systems Interface*.

security   The measures taken to secure a system against accidental or intentional loss, usually in the form of accountability procedures and use restriction, for example through *NTFS permissions* and *share permissions*.

Security Configuration and Analysis tool   A Windows 2000 utility that is used to analyze and to help configure a computer's local security settings. Security Configuration and Analysis works by comparing the computer's actual security configuration to a security template configured with the desired settings.

security group   A type of group that can be created on a Windows 2000 *domain controller* in the *Active Directory*. A security group is a logical group of users who need to access specific resources. Security groups are used to assign permissions to resources.

security identifier (SID)   A unique code that identifies a specific user or group to the Windows 2000 security system. SIDs contain a complete set of *permissions* for that user or group.

Security log   A log that tracks events that are related to Windows 2000 auditing. The Security log can be viewed through the *Event Viewer* utility.

security option policies   Policies used to configure security for the computer. Security option policies apply to computers rather than to users or groups. These policies are set through *Local Computer Policy* or *Domain Controllers Policy*.

separator page   A page used at the beginning of each document to identify the user who submitted the print job. When users share a printer, separator pages can be useful for distributing print jobs.

serial   A method of communication that transfers data across a medium one bit at a time, usually adding stop, start, and check bits.

service   A *process* dedicated to implementing a specific function for another process. Most Windows 2000 components are services used by user-level applications.

Service group   A Windows 2000 *special group* that includes users who log on as a user account that is only used to run a *service*.

service pack   An update to the Windows 2000 operating system that includes bug fixes and enhancements.

session In the context of *Terminal Services*, a connection between a *Terminal Services client* and a *Terminal Services server*. Users log on through any client on the network and can see only their individual session.

Services A Windows 2000 utility used to manage the *services* installed on the computer.

Setup Manager (Setupmgr) A Windows 2000 utility used to create automated installation scripts or unattended *answer files*.

Setupmgr See *Setup Manager*.

share A *resource* such as a folder or printer shared over a network.

share permissions Permissions used to control access to shared folders. Share permissions can only be applied to folders, as opposed to *NTFS permissions*, which are more complex and can be applied to folders and files.

shared folder A folder on a Windows 2000 computer that network users can access.

Shared Folders A Windows 2000 utility for managing *shared folders* on the computer.

SID See *security identifier*.

Simple Mail Transfer Protocol (SMTP) An Internet protocol for transferring mail between Internet hosts. SMTP is often used to upload mail directly from the client to an intermediate host, but can only be used to receive mail by computers connected to the Internet.

simple volume A *dynamic disk* volume that contains space from a single disk. The space from the single drive can be contiguous or non-contiguous. Simple volumes are used when the computer has enough disk space on a single drive to hold an entire volume.

slipstream technology A Windows 2000 technology for *service packs*. With slipstream technology, service packs are applied once, and they are not overwritten as new services are added to the computer.

Small Computer Systems Interface (SCSI) A high-speed, parallel-bus interface that connects hard disk drives, CD-ROM drives, tape drives, and many other peripherals to a computer. SCSI is the mass-storage connection standard among all computers except IBM-compatible computers, which use SCSI or IDE.

SMTP See *Simple Mail Transfer Protocol*.

snap-in An administrative tool developed by Microsoft or a third-party vendor that can be added to the *Microsoft Management Console (MMC)* in Windows 2000.

spanned volume A *dynamic disk* volume that consists of disk space on 2 to 32 dynamic drives. Spanned volume sets are used to dynamically increase the size of a dynamic volume. With spanned volumes, the data is written sequentially, filling space on one physical drive before writing to space on the next physical drive in the spanned volume set.

special group A group used by the system, in which membership is automatic if certain criteria are met. Administrators cannot manage special groups.

spooler A service that buffers output to a low-speed device such as a printer, so the software outputting to the device is not tied up waiting for the device to be ready.

stand-alone Dfs root   In the *Distributed file system (Dfs)*, a type of *Dfs root* that does not use the *Active Directory* or support automatic replication.

stripe set   A single *volume* created across multiple hard disk drives and accessed in parallel for the purpose of optimizing disk-access time. *NTFS* can create stripe sets.

striped volume   A *dynamic disk* volume that stores data in equal stripes between 2 to 32 dynamic drives. Typically, administrators use striped volumes when they want to combine the space of several physical drives into a single logical volume and increase disk performance.

subnet mask   A number mathematically applied to *IP addresses* to determine which IP addresses are a part of the same subnetwork as the computer applying the subnet mask.

Success Audit event   An *Event Viewer* event that indicates the occurrence of an event that has been audited for success, such as a successful logon.

Sysprep   See *System Preparation Tool.*

System group   A Windows 2000 *special group* that contains system processes that access specific functions as a user.

System Information   A Windows 2000 utility used to collect and display information about the computer's current configuration.

System log   A log that tracks events that relate to the Windows 2000 operating system. The System log can be viewed through the *Event Viewer* utility.

System Monitor   A Windows 2000 utility used to monitor real-time system activity or view data from a log file.

system partition   The active *partition* on an Intel-based computer that contains the hardware-specific files used to load the Windows 2000 operating system.

system policies   Policies used to control what a user can do and the user's environment. System policies are mainly used for backward compatibility with Windows NT 4.

System Policy Editor   A Windows 2000 utility used to create *system policies.*

System Preparation Tool (Sysprep)   A Windows 2000 utility used to prepare a *disk image* for disk duplication.

System Tools   A Computer Management utility grouping that provides access to utilities for managing common system functions. The System Tools utility includes the *Event Viewer, System Information, Performance Logs and Alerts, Shared Folders, Device Manager,* and *Local Users and Groups* utilities.

T

Task Manager   A Windows 2000 utility that can be used to start, end, or prioritize applications. The Task Manager shows the applications and *processes* that are currently running on the computer, as well as *CPU* and *memory* usage information.

TB   See *terabyte.*

TCP   See *Transmission Control Protocol.*

TCP/IP   See *Transmission Control Protocol/ Internet Protocol.*

TCP/IP port   A *logical port*, used when a printer is attached to the network by installing a network card in the printer. Configuring a TCP/ IP port requires the IP address of the network printer to connect to.

terabyte (TB)   A computer storage measurement that equals 1,024 *gigabytes.*

Terminal Server User group   A Windows 2000 *special group* that includes users who log on through *Terminal Services.*

Terminal Services   A Windows 2000 Server service that allows *thin clients* to connect to a *Terminal Services server* and access many Windows 2000 features. In Terminal Services application server mode, clients can access the Windows 2000 *Desktop* environment and run applications. In Terminal Services remote administration mode, administrators can perform server administrative tasks remotely from a client.

Terminal Services client   A client that uses *thin-client* technology to deliver the Windows 2000 Server *Desktop* to the user. The client only needs to establish a connection with the server and display the graphical user interface information that the server sends. This

process requires very little overhead on the client's part, and it can be run on older machines that would not otherwise be able to use Windows 2000.

Terminal Services Client Creator   A Windows 2000 Server utility used to create 32-bit and 16-bit *Terminal Services client* software diskettes for use with client machines.

Terminal Services Configuration   A Windows Server utility used to change the properties of the *RDP-TCP* connection that is created when *Terminal Services* is installed and to add new connections.

Terminal Services Manager   A Windows 2000 Server utility used to manage and monitor users, *sessions*, and *processes* that are connected to or running on any *Terminal Services server* on the network.

Terminal Services server   A server that has *Terminal Services* installed. The Terminal Services server controls all of the *Terminal Services clients* that are connected to it. All Terminal Services operations take place on the Terminal Services server.

thin client   A client that has minimal requirements. With *Terminal Services*, a thin client can be run on a variety of machines, including older computers and terminals that would not otherwise be able to run Windows 2000.

thread   A list of instructions running in a computer to perform a certain task. Each thread runs in the context of a *process*, which embodies the protected memory space and the environment of the threads. Multithreaded processes can perform more than one task at the same time.

Transmission Control Protocol (TCP)   A Transport layer protocol that implements guaranteed packet delivery using the *IP* protocol.

Transmission Control Protocol/Internet Protocol (TCP/IP)   A suite of Internet protocols upon which the global Internet is based. TCP/IP is a general term that can refer either to the *TCP* and *IP* protocols used together or to the complete set of Internet protocols. TCP/IP is the default protocol for Windows 2000.

U

unattended installation   A method of installing Windows 2000 remotely with little or no user intervention. Unattended installation uses a *distribution server* to install Windows 2000 on a target computer.

UNC   See *Universal Naming Convention*.

Uniform Resource Locator (URL)   An Internet standard naming convention for identifying resources available via various *TCP/IP* application protocols. For example, `http://www.microsoft.com` is the URL for Microsoft's World Wide Web server site. A URL allows easy hypertext references to a particular resource from within a document or mail message.

universal group   A scope for a group on a Windows 2000 *domain controller*. A universal group is used to logically organize users and appear in the global catalog (a special listing that contains limited information about every object

in the *Active Directory*). Universal groups can contain users from anywhere in the *domain tree* or *domain forest*, other universal groups, and *global groups*.

Universal Naming Convention (UNC)   A multivendor, multiplatform convention for identifying shared resources on a network. UNC names follow the naming convention `\\computername\sharename`.

Universal Serial Bus (USB)   An external bus standard that allows USB devices to be connected through a USB port. USB supports transfer rates up to 12Mbps. A single USB port can support up to 127 devices.

upgrade   A method for installing Windows 2000 that preserves existing settings and preferences when converting to the newer operating system.

URL   See *Uniform Resource Locator*.

USB   See *Universal Serial Bus*.

user profile   A profile that stores a user's *Desktop* configuration and other preferences. A user profile can contain a user's Desktop arrangement, program items, personal program groups, network and printer connections, screen colors, mouse settings, and other personal preferences. Administrators can create mandatory profiles, which cannot be changed by the users, and roaming profiles, which users can access from any computer they log on to.

user rights policies   Policies that control the rights that users and groups have to accomplish network tasks. User rights policies are set through *Local Computer Policy* or *Domain Controllers Policy*.

username   A user's account name in a *logon-authenticated* system.

Users group   A Windows 2000 built-in group that includes end users who should have very limited system access. After a *clean install* of Windows 2000, the default settings for this group prohibit users from compromising the operating system or program files. By default, all users who have been created on the computer, except *Guest*, are members of the Users group.

V

video adapter   The hardware device that outputs the display to the monitor.

virtual memory   A *kernel* service that stores memory pages not currently in use on a mass-storage device to free the memory occupied for other uses. Virtual memory hides the memory-swapping process from applications and higher-level services.

virtual private network (VPN)   A private network that uses links across private or public networks (such as the Internet). When data is sent over the remote link, it is encapsulated, encrypted, and requires authentication services.

volume   A storage area on a Windows 2000 *dynamic disk*. Dynamic volumes cannot contain *partitions* or *logical drives*. Windows 2000 Server dynamic storage supports five dynamic volume types: *simple volumes*, *spanned volumes*,

striped volumes, *RAID-5 volumes*, and *mirrored volumes*. Dynamic volumes are accessible only to Windows 2000 systems.

VPN   See *virtual private network*.

W

Warning event   An *Event Viewer* event that indicates that you should be concerned with the event. The event may not be critical in nature, but it is significant and may be indicative of future errors.

Web browser   An application that makes *HTTP* requests and formats the resultant *HTML* documents for the users. Most Web browsers understand all standard Internet protocols.

Win16   The set of application services provided by the 16-bit versions of Microsoft Windows: Windows 3.1 and Windows for Workgroups 3.11.

Win32   The set of application services provided by the 32-bit versions of Microsoft Windows: Windows 95, Windows 98, Windows NT, and Windows 2000.

Windows 9*x*   The 32-bit Windows 95 and Windows 98 versions of Microsoft Windows for medium-range, Intel-based personal computers. This system includes peer networking services, Internet support, and strong support for older DOS applications and peripherals.

Windows 2000 Advanced Server   The current version of the Windows server software designed for medium-size to large networks. It includes all of the features of *Windows 2000 Server* plus network load balancing, cluster services for application fault tolerance, support for up to 8GB of memory, and support for up to eight processors.

Windows 2000 Backup The Windows 2000 utility used to run the *Backup Wizard*, run the *Restore Wizard*, and create an *Emergency Repair Disk (ERD)*.

Windows 2000 boot disk A disk that can be used to *boot* to the Windows 2000 Server operating system in the event of a Windows 2000 Server boot failure.

Windows 2000 Datacenter Server The most powerful server in the Microsoft server family. This operating system is designed for large-scale enterprise networks. Windows 2000 Datacenter Server includes all of the features of *Windows 2000 Advanced Server* and adds more advanced clustering services, support for up to 64GB of memory, and support for up to 16 processors (OEM versions can support up to 32-way SMP).

Windows 2000 Multilanguage Version The version of Windows 2000 that supports multiple-language user interfaces through a single copy of Windows 2000.

Windows 2000 Professional The current version of the Windows operating system for high-end desktop environments. Windows 2000 Professional integrates the best features of Windows 98 and Windows NT Workstation 4, supports a wide range of hardware, makes the operating system easier to use, and reduces the cost of ownership.

Windows 2000 Server The current version of the Windows server software designed for use in small to medium-sized networks. Windows 2000 Server can serve as a file and print server, an applications server, a Web server, and a communications server.

Windows 2000 Server Setup Boot Disks Floppy disks that can used to boot to the Windows 2000 operating system. With these disks, you can use the *Recovery Console* and the *Emergency Repair Disk (ERD)*.

Windows File Protection policies These policies are used to specify how Windows file protection policies will be applied.

Windows Internet Name Service (WINS) A network service for Microsoft networks that provides Windows computers with *IP addresses* for specified *NetBIOS names*, facilitating browsing and intercommunication over *TCP/IP* networks.

Windows NT The predecessor to Windows 2000 that is a 32-bit version of Microsoft Windows for powerful Intel, Alpha, PowerPC, or MIPS-based computers. This operating system includes peer networking services, server networking services, Internet client and server services, and a broad range of utilities.

Windows Update A utility that connects the computer to Microsoft's Web site and checks the files to make sure that they are the most up-to-date versions.

WINS See *Windows Internet Name Service.*

WINS server   The server that runs *WINS* and is used to resolve *NetBIOS names* to *IP addresses.*

WMI Control   A Windows 2000 utility that provides an interface for monitoring and controlling system resources. WMI stands for Windows Management Instrumentation.

workgroup   In Microsoft networks, a collection of related computers, such as those used in a department, that do not require the uniform security and coordination of a domain. Workgroups are characterized by decentralized management, as opposed to the centralized management that domains use.

write-back caching   A caching optimization wherein data written to the slow store is cached until the cache is full or until a subsequent write operation overwrites the cached data. Write-back caching can significantly reduce the write operations to a slow store because many write operations are subsequently obviated by new information. Data in the write-back cache is also available for subsequent reads. If something happens to prevent the cache from writing data to the slow store, the cache data will be lost.

write-through caching   A caching optimization wherein data written to a slow store is kept in a cache for subsequent rereading. Unlike *write-back caching*, write-through caching immediately writes the data to the slow store and is therefore less optimal but more secure.

Index

Note to the Reader: Throughout this index **boldfaced** page numbers indicate primary discussions of a topic. *Italicized* page numbers indicate illustrations.

H

M

N

O

Q

T

The Complete MCSE Solution

Microsoft's® exam track for the Windows 2000 MCSE requires four core and three elective exams. The core, design, and additional elective exams for the Windows 2000 MCSE are listed in the table below.

For more information, visit **www.microsoft.com/trainingandservices**.

Exam #	Exam Title	Product Title	ISBN
Required Core Exams			
70-210	Installing, Configuring, and Administering Microsoft Windows 2000 Professional	MCSE: Windows 2000 Professional Study Guide	ISBN: 0-7821-2751-7
		MCSE: Windows 2000 Professional Exam Notes	ISBN: 0-7821-2753-3
		MCSE: Windows 2000 Professional Virtual Trainer	ISBN: 0-7821-5008-X
		MCSE: Windows 2000 Professional Virtual Test Center	ISBN: 0-7821-3000-3
70-215	Installing, Configuring, and Administering Microsoft Windows 2000 Server	MCSE: Windows 2000 Server Study Guide	ISBN: 0-7821-2752-5
		MCSE: Windows 2000 Server Exam Notes	ISBN: 0-7821-2754-1
		MCSE: Windows 2000 Server Virtual Trainer	ISBN: 0-7821-5009-8
		MCSE: Windows 2000 Server Virtual Test Center	ISBN: 0-7821-3001-1
70-216	Implementing and Administering a Microsoft Windows 2000 Network Infrastructure	MCSE: Windows 2000 Network Infrastructure Administration Study Guide	ISBN: 0-7821-2755-X
		MCSE: Windows 2000 Network Infrastructure Administration Exam Notes	ISBN: 0-7821-2761-4
		MCSE: Windows 2000 Network Infrastructure Administration Virtual Trainer	ISBN: 0-7821-5007-1
		MCSE: Windows 2000 Network Infrastructure Administration Virtual Test Center	ISBN: 0-7821-3002-X
70-217	Implementing and Administering a Microsoft Windows 2000 Directory Services Infrastructure	MCSE: Windows 2000 Directory Services Administration Study Guide	ISBN: 0-7821-2756-8
		MCSE: Windows 2000 Directory Services Administration Exam Notes	ISBN: 0-7821-2762-2
		MCSE: Windows 2000 Directory Services Administration Virtual Trainer	ISBN: 0-7821-5010-1
		MCSE: Windows 2000 Directory Services Administration Virtual Test Center	ISBN: 0-7821-3003-8

(Already have your MCSE for NT 4 or taken the three core "NT" exams? If so, then you qualify to take the Accelerated Windows 2000 Exam in lieu of the four new core exams in the Windows 2000 MCSE track. The MCSE: Accelerated Windows 2000 Study Guide covers all objectives sets from the four core exams in a more concise manner on the assumption that you already have a pretty good sense of what the technology is about.)

Exam #	Exam Title	Product Title	ISBN
70-240	Microsoft Windows 2000 Accelerated Exam for MCPs Certified on Microsoft Windows NT 4.0.	MCSE: Accelerated Windows 2000 Study Guide	ISBN: 0-7821-2760-6
		MCSE: Accelerated Windows 2000 Exam Notes	ISBN: 0-7821-2770-3
Choose 1 More Core Exam			
70-219	Designing a Microsoft Windows 2000 Directory Services Infrastructure	MCSE: Windows 2000 Directory Services Design Study Guide	ISBN: 0-7821-2757-6
		MCSE: Windows 2000 Directory Services Design Exam Notes	ISBN: 0-7821-2765-7
or			
70-220	Designing Security for a Microsoft Windows 2000 Network	MCSE: Windows 2000 Network Security Design Study Guide	ISBN: 0-7821-2758-4
		MCSE: Windows 2000 Network Security Design Exam Notes	ISBN: 0-7821-2766-5
or			
70-221	Designing a Microsoft Windows 2000 Network Infrastructure	MCSE: Windows 2000 Network Infrastructure Design Study Guide	ISBN: 0-7821-2759-2
		MCSE: Windows 2000 Network Infrastructure Design Exam Notes	ISBN: 0-7821-2767-3
Choose 2 Electives			
70-222	Migrating from Microsoft Windows NT 4.0 to Microsoft Windows 2000	MCSE: Windows 2000 Migration Study Guide	ISBN: 0-7821-2768-1
		MCSE: Windows 2000 Migration Exam Notes	ISBN: 0-7821-2769-X
70-224	Installing, Configuring, and Administering Microsoft Exchange 2000 Server	MCSE: Exchange 2000 Server Administration Study Guide	ISBN: 0-7821-2898-X
		MCSE: Exchange 2000 Server Administration e-trainer	ISBN: 0-7821-5012-8
		MCSE: Exchange 2000 Server Aministration Virtual Test Center	ISBN: 0-7821-3017-8
70-225	Designing and Deploying a Messaging Infrastructure with Microsoft Exchange 2000 Server	MCSE: Exchange 2000 Design Study Guide	ISBN: 0-7821-2897-1
70-227	Installing, Configuring, and Administering Microsoft Internet Security and Acceleration (ISA) Server 2000	MCSE: ISA Server 2000 Administration Study Guide	ISBN: 0-7821-2933-1
70-228	Installing, Configuring, and Administering Microsoft SQL Server 2000 Enterprise Edition	MCSE: SQL Server 2000 Administration Study Guide	ISBN: 0-7821-2921-8
		MCSE: SQL Server 2000 Administration Virtual Test Center	ISBN: 0-7821-3016-X
70-229	Designing and Implementing Databases with Microsoft SQL Server™ 2000 Enterprise Edition	MCSE: SQL Server 2000 Design Study Guide	ISBN: 0-7821-2942-0
70-244	Supporting and Maintaining a Microsoft Windows NT Server 4.0 Network	MCSE: Windows NT Server 4.0 Support and Maintenance Study Guide	ISBN: 0-7821-2992-7